The VigilantCitizen

"Symbols Rule The World, Not Words Nor Laws"

Articles Compilation

3rd Edition - May 2014

For the lastest news, articles and updates,
visit the Vigiliant Citizen website at:

VigilantCitizen.com

Published by Omnia Veritas Ltd.

contact@omniaveritas.com

Copyright Notice

All materials contained in this book are protected by copyright laws, and may not be reproduced, republished, distributed, transmitted, displayed, broadcast or otherwise exploited in any manner without the express prior written permission of Vigilant Citizen.

Fair Use Disclaimer

This book contains copyrighted material the use of which has not always been specifically authorized by the copyright owner. We are making such material available in our efforts to advance understanding of environmental, political, human rights, economic, democracy, scientific, and social justice issues, etc.. We believe this constitutes a 'fair use' of any such copyrighted material as provided for in section 107 of the US Copyright Law. If you wish to use copyrighted material from this site for purposes of your own that go beyond 'fair use', you must obtain permission from the copyright owner.

CONTENTS

vigilantcitizen.com

Foreword — 7

Section 1 Vigilant Reports

Mind Control Theories and Techniques used by Mass Media — 11
Dumbing Down Society Part 1: Foods, Beverages and Meds — 23
Dumbing Down Society Part 2: Mercury in Foods and Vaccines — 31
Dumbing-Down Society Part 3: How to Reverse its Effects — 37
Irrational Consumerism (or The Few Companies Who Feed the World) — 43
The Hidden Hand that Shaped History — 53
Top 10 Most Sinister PSYOPS Mission Patches — 62
The World of Mind Control Through the Eyes of an Artist with 13 Alter Personas — 74
KONY 2012: State Propaganda for a New Generation — 86
Monster High: A Doll Line Introducing Children to the Illuminati Agenda — 92
The Hidden Life of Marilyn Monroe, the Original Hollywood Mind Control Slave (Part-I) — 100
The Hidden Life of Marilyn Monroe, the Original Hollywood Mind Control Slave (Part-II) — 110

Section 2 Music Business

The Transhumanist and Police State Agenda in Pop Music — 128
The Hidden Meaning of Lady Gaga's "Telephone" — 134
Jay-Z's "Run This Town" and the Occult Connections — 140
The Esoteric Interpretation of The Black Eyed Peas' "Meet Me Halfway" — 146
Kanye West's "Power": The Occult Meaning of its Symbols — 152
Britney Spears, Mind Control and "Hold it Against Me" — 159
Lady Gaga's "Born This Way" – The Illuminati Manifesto — 170
Natalia Kills' "Zombie" and "Wonderland": Dedicated to Illuminati Mind Control — 180
Lady Gaga's "Judas" and the Age of Horus — 186
Paramore's "Brick by Boring Brick": A Song about Mind Control — 194
The 2011 VMAs: A Celebration of Today's Illuminati Music Industry — 201
Brown Eyed Girls' Video "Sixth Sense" or How the Elite Controls Opposition — 209
The Esoteric Meaning of Florence + the Machine's "Shake it Out" and "No Light No Light" — 216
From Mind Control to Superstardom: The Meaning of Lady Gaga's "Marry the Night" — 224
Doda and Vintage: Bringing the Illuminati Agenda to Eastern Europe Pop — 230
Madonna's Superbowl Halftime Show: A Celebration of the Grand Priestess of the Music Industry — 239
Whitney Houston and the 2012 Grammy Awards Mega-Ritual — 244
Katy Perry's 'Part of Me': Using Music Videos to Recruit New Soldiers — 254
Katy Perry's "Wide Awake" : A Video About Monarch Mind Control — 259
B.O.B. and Nicki Minaj's "Out of My Mind" or How to Make Mind Control Entertaining — 265
The Illuminati Symbolism of Ke$ha's "Die Young" and How it Ridicules the Indoctrinated Masses — 270
"Scream and Shout": A Video About Britney Spears Being Under Mind Control — 275
Emeli Sandé's "Clown": A Song About Selling Out to the Music Industry? — 280
Lil Wayne's "Love Me": A Video Glamorizing Kitten Programming — 285
Azealia Banks' "Yung Rapunxel": New Artist, Same Illuminati Symbolism — 290
Fjögur Píanó, a Viral Video About Monarch Mind Control? — 294
MTV VMAs 2013: It Was About Miley Cyrus Taking the Fall — 300
A-JAX and Ladies' Code: Two Blatant Examples of Mind Control Culture in K-Pop — 305
Britney Spears' "Work B*tch" and Iggy Azalea's "Change Your Life" — 313
Katy Perry's "Dark Horse": One Big, Children-Friendly Tribute to the Illuminati — 318
The Occult Meaning of Lady Gaga's Video "G.U.Y." — 324

Section 3 Movies and TV

The Occult Roots of The Wizard of Oz	333
"The Imaginarium of Doctor Parnassus" and Heath Ledger's Sacrifice	341
The Esoteric Interpretation of "Pan's Labyrinth"	348
The Occult Symbolism of Movie "Metropolis" and its Importance in Pop Culture	356
How the Animated Series G.I. Joe Predicted Today's Illuminati Agenda	366
Josie and the Pussycats: Blueprint of the Mind Control Music Industry	374
The Occult Interpretation of the Movie "Black Swan" and Its Message on Show Business	381
Roman Polanski's "Rosemary's Baby" and the Dark Side of Hollywood	390
"Sucker Punch" or How to Make Monarch Mind Control Sexy	401
"Labyrinth" Starring David Bowie: A Blueprint to Mind Control	410
'Contagion' or How Disaster Movies "Educate" the Masses	422
"They Live", the Weird Movie With a Powerful Message	430
The Hidden Symbolic Meaning of the Movie "2012"	439
The Movie "Videodrome" and The Horror of Mass Media	448
"The Cabin in the Woods": A Movie Celebrating the Elite's Ritual Sacrifices	455
"Prometheus": A Movie About Alien Nephilim and Esoteric Enlightenment	463
"Hide and Seek": The Most Blatant Movie About Monarch Mind Control Ever?	471
The Hidden (And Not So Hidden) Messages in Stanley Kubrick's "Eyes Wide Shut" (pt. I)	479
The Hidden (And Not So Hidden) Messages in Stanley Kubrick's "Eyes Wide Shut" (pt. II)	485
The Hidden (And Not So Hidden) Messages in Stanley Kubrick's "Eyes Wide Shut" (pt. III)	493
"Now You See Me": A Movie About the Illuminati Entertainment Industry?	500
The Esoteric Interpretation of the Movie "9": Heralding the Age of Horus	508
The Hidden Meaning of the Movie "Coraline"	516
The Esoteric Meaning of the Movie "Prisoners"	524

Section 4 Sinister Sites

Sinister Sites: The Georgia Guidestones	533
Sinister Sites – Israel Supreme Court	544
Sinister Sites – The Denver International Airport	552
Sinister Sites – Illuminati Pyramid in Blagnac, France	561
Analysis of the Occult Symbols Found on the Bank of America Murals	568
The Occult Symbolism of the Los Angeles Central Library	576
Sinister Sites: IRS Headquarters, Maryland	589

Section 5 Secret Arcana

Aleister Crowley: His Elite Ties and His Legacy	596
The Mysterious Connection Between Sirius and Human History	607
Origins and Techniques of Monarch Mind Control	617
Who is Baphomet?	625
The Order of the Illuminati: Its Origins, Its Methods and Its Influence on the World Events	635

Foreword

"Signs and symbols rule the world, not words nor laws."
- Confucius

This timeless quote perfectly sums up the aims of Vigilant Citizen. To understand the world we live in, we must understand the symbols surrounding us. To understand these symbols, we must dig up their origin, which are often deeply hidden in occult mysteries. Vigilant Citizen aims to go beyond the face value of symbols found in pop culture to reveal their esoteric meaning.

My quest for knowledge led me to obtain a Bachelor's degree in Communications and Politics in 2002. I mainly studied the way power uses mass media to shape and mold attitudes and opinions. My education was perfect to hold a job in political marketing or public relations, but did not fully satisfy my thirst for truth.

My efforts to further understand the forces governing the world lead me to study secret societies, mystery religions, esoteric schools and ancient civilizations. I spent the last nine years researching Theosophy, Freemasonry, Rosicrucianism, the Bavarian Illuminati and Western Occultism. These schools of thoughts have many things in common: they are based on Hermetic teaching, they attach extreme importance to symbolism and they recruit within their ranks the most powerful people in society. The natural result of this phenomenon is the display of occult symbolism in all aspects of society, especially in music, movies and buildings. I try to bring out the meaning of these symbols in a clear, concise and entertaining way.

I am also a music producer and I composed music for some fairly known "urban" artists. Experience in the field provided me some of the insight necessary to understand the prevailing state of mind in this industry. I today produce at an independant level.

Most of us have been trained to be blind to an entire dimension of our world. I created Vigilant Citizen to share some of what I found.

Enjoy.

About the initial shock of learning the "Truth"

I remember when I first learned about the "Truth" and it wasn't pretty. I remember learning about how the mass media lie to our faces on a daily basis. About how the educational system only teaches the youth what they need to become obedient workers. About how politics are merely a puppet show and that, regardless of who is in office, the same Agenda will be going forward. About how our rights and freedoms are being revoked. About how the masses are purposely being dumbed-down. About how simple values are rejected from popular culture and replaced by shallow materialism and glorification of immediate fulfillment of impulses.

Learning about these things was overwhelming and, to be honest, it really pissed me off. I remember being depressed for days, repeating to myself "Everything I was ever told was a lie". I was disgusted by the world I grew up in and the people I used to look up to. That was an awful phase. But, looking back, I realized that it was just a phase – one that all seekers of truth eventually need to go through. It is shocking, disheartening, confusing and totally not cool. But necessary.

As I pursued my research and as I gained a little wisdom and experience, that nasty feeling eventually went away. Gloria Steinem famously wrote "The truth will set you free. But first, it will piss you off." That is certainly true. But after the "pissed off" phase, better understanding our world leads to an extremely valuable reward: Knowledge, wisdom and happiness.

Although I do not consider this site to contain all of the "Truth", simply a small part of it, I nevertheless hope its contents is insightful enough to prompt in some people a "thirst for more". I sometimes get e-mails from readers who are still under the initial shock of learning the Truth. They describe the same symptoms I felt when I was in the same situation and some are rather mad at me for causing this in them. Although I realize that this kind of information can engender fear and even paranoia in some people, I believe that the sooner one goes through that phase, the better. Because once the blizzard goes away, a new path appears … and it looks pretty darn nice. Converting the initial shock into useful knowledge

After learning about the true nature of the forces shaping our world, a natural response is to look for solutions. One might say "Now that I know all of this, what can I do to fix the problem?" I usually leave this part of the thought process open-ended in my articles because I believe that the thinking, the questioning and the research required at this stage is something that all of us should do. After having been told what we should do during our entire lives, it is time to get our own brains going. Only a healthy, well-educated mind can determine what should be done next. I believe that those who push ready-made, one-size-fits-all solutions do not help their fellow men (in fact, they might be trying to exploit them). Instead of encouraging independent thinking they are simply furthering the "sheep" mentality that is so prevalent today … just with a different shepherd. For this reason, I do not push a great big solution for all. I do, however, encourage readers to discuss and debate their views, because it is one the healthiest thing we can do.

The clash of ideas found in the discussions on this site is certainly one of its most important features. The insight provided by commentators is often enlightening (thanks to those who participate in discussions!). Some force us to consider unique ideas and perspectives. Some people believe non-violent protests are the ultimate solution, while others state that salvation must go through religious faith while others want to see an all-out revolution. Others do not believe that any of this is even happening. I honestly do not claim to know the exact path that would lead humanity to freedom. There is however one thing that I KNOW helps all the readers of the site: Understanding what is real and what is fake.

Differentiating the Real from the Fake: A Liberating Step

After a period of time of actively seeking the Truth through research and questioning, discerning what is real and what is illusion becomes an easy task. Instead of mindlessly absorbing everything that is communicated through mass media, a truth seeker will have the ability to say "Wait, this is BS. I do not believe it and I reject it." The erection of a gateway that controls the acceptance of messages in our minds, also known as "critical thinking", is one of the main benefits of truth seeking. This site focuses on mass media because its multiple outlets are used to sell illusion and delusion to the masses. They also define what is acceptable, what is desirable and what is not.

Watching a few hours of MTV programming is enough to understand that its contents promotes a specific set of values to the youth, notably the importance of materialism, the cult of celebrity and fame, the glorification of appearances and of the superficial, the sexualization and fetishization of everything and so forth. A young person that has not developed the ability to think critically will absorb this information, integrate it and, ultimately, live by it. However, an educated mind will realize that all of these values are artificial constructs and deceiving illusions. A great majority of spiritual currents in History have identified these very things as the "great deceptions", pitfalls for the soul. Today, mass media are so omnipresent and persuasive that billions willingly fall into that trap. It takes a lot of "deprogramming" to make the average person realize: "I am not super famous, I do not have paparazzi after me, I am not on the cover of magazines, I do not have a Gucci handbag nor a BMW with Louis Vuitton seats ... and so what? That is all garbage anyway!" Coming to this realization is one of the most liberating things one can experience, as a lot of unnecessary pressure magically disappears.

This realization also leads to a new appreciation for the simplest things in life that are, coincidentally, the most important things in life. Spending time with loved ones, appreciating the world's beauty and becoming a better person cost absolutely nothing, yet they are keys to true happiness. Our current System is looking to lead us away from these values because they create people who are not dependent of the System. The System needs us to crave and want, and to live for the crap that is sold to us. It needs us to spend our paychecks, to load our credit cards and to take on ridiculous mortgages in order for us to replicate what we see on TV. Our debts are the chains that link us to them and we willingly chain ourselves.

What is more profitable to them? A strong family based on morals, values and traditions or a shallow individual who looks to fill the gaping hole in his/her life with appearances and consumer products? Who is the easier to influence toward a specific idea or agendas? Our current System is a giant wheel that needs each one of us pushing in order for it to advance. Without us, the wheel goes nowhere.

The effects of rejecting what is fake and embracing what is real is the equivalent of eradicating a cancer that slowly eats away the spirit. But before curing an illness, one must identify it. The articles on this site attempt to locate and identify the cancerous message that is being communicated to the masses, especially to the youth. Once the cause is known and understood, it is a lot easier to cure the sickness.

So, despite the doom and gloom, knowing the ugly truth should not lead to unhappiness. Quite to the contrary, learning what we should avoid also leads to learning what we should embrace. These wonderful things are within our reach and always will be. Some would say that these things are the very reason why we are on earth ... and no power-hungry elite can ever take these things away from us.

Section 1
Vigilant Reports

In-depth articles on various topics - all necessary in order to be a true "vigilant citizen".

Mind Control Theories and Techniques used by Mass Media

Mass media is the most powerful tool used by the ruling class to manipulate the masses. It shapes and molds opinions and attitudes and defines what is normal and acceptable. This article looks at the workings of mass media through the theories of its major thinkers, its power structure and the techniques it uses, in order to understand its true role in society.

Most of the articles on this site discuss occult symbolism found in objects of popular culture. From these articles arise many legitimate questions relating to the purpose of those symbols and the motivations of those who place them there, but it is impossible for me to provide satisfactory answers to these questions without mentioning many other concepts and facts. I've therefore decided to write this article to supply the theoretical and methodological background of the analyzes presented on this site as well as introducing the main scholars of the field of mass communications. Some people read my articles and think I'm saying "Lady Gaga wants to control our minds". That is not the case. She is simply a small part of the huge system that is the mass media.

Programming Through Mass Media

Mass media are media forms designed to reach the largest audience possible. They include television, movies, radio, newspapers, magazines, books, records, video games and the internet. Many studies have been conducted in the past century to measure the effects of mass media on the population in order to discover the best techniques to influence it. From those studies emerged the science of Communications, which is used in marketing, public relations and politics. Mass communication is a necessary tool to insure the functionality of a large democracy; it is also a necessary tool for a dictatorship. It all depends on its usage.

In the 1958 preface for A Brave New World, Aldous Huxley paints a rather grim portrait of society. He believes it is controlled by an "impersonal force", a ruling elite, which manipulates the population using various methods.

> "Impersonal forces over which we have almost no control seem to be pushing us all in the direction of the Brave New Worldian nightmare; and this impersonal pushing is being consciously accelerated by representatives of commercial and political organizations who have developed a number of new techniques for manipulating, in the interest of some minority, the thoughts and feelings of the masses."
> - Aldous Huxley, Preface to A Brave New World

His bleak outlook is not a simple hypothesis or a paranoid delusion. It is a documented fact, present in the world's most important studies on mass media. Here are some of them:

Elite Thinkers

Walter Lippmann

Walter Lippmann, an American intellectual, writer and two-time Pulitzer Prize winner brought forth one of the first works concerning the usage of mass media in America. In Public Opinion (1922), Lippmann compared the masses to a "great beast" and a "bewildered herd" that needed to be guided by a governing class. He described the ruling elite as "a specialized class whose interests reach beyond the locality." This class is composed of experts, specialists and bureaucrats. According to Lippmann, the experts, who often are referred to as "elites," are to be a machinery of knowledge that circumvents the primary defect of democracy, the impossible ideal of the "omnicompetent citizen." The trampling and roaring "bewildered herd" has its function: to be "the interested spectators of action," i.e. not participants. Participation is the duty of "the responsible man", which is not the regular citizen. Mass media and propaganda are therefore tools that must be used by the elite to rule the public without physical coercion. One important concept presented by Lippmann is the "manufacture of consent", which is, in short, the manipulation of public opinion to accept the elite's agenda. It is Lippmann's opinion that the general public is not qualified to reason and to decide on important issues. It is therefore important for the elite to decide "for its own good" and then sell those decisions to the masses.

Walter Lippman

> "That the manufacture of consent is capable of great refinements no one, I think, denies. The process by which public opinions arise is certainly no less intricate than it has appeared in these pages, and the opportunities for manipulation open to anyone who understands the process are plain enough. . . . as a result of psychological research, coupled with the modern means of communication, the practice of democracy has turned a corner. A revolution is taking place, infinitely more significant than any shifting of economic power. . . . Under the impact of propaganda, not necessarily in the sinister meaning of the word alone, the old constants of our thinking have become variables. It is no longer possible, for example, to believe in the original dogma of democracy; that the knowledge needed for the management of human affairs comes up spontaneously from the human heart. Where we act on that theory we expose ourselves to self-deception, and to forms of persuasion that we cannot verify. It has been demonstrated that we cannot rely upon intuition, conscience, or the accidents of casual opinion if we are to deal with the world beyond our reach."
> – Walter Lippmann, Public Opinion

It might be interesting to note that Lippmann is one of the founding fathers of the Council on Foreign Relations (CFR), the most influential foreign policy think tank in the world. This fact should give you a small hint of the mind state of the elite concerning the usage of media.

> "Political and economic power in the United States is concentrated in the hands of a "ruling elite" that controls most of U.S.-based multinational corporations, major communication media, the most influential foundations, major private universities and most public utilities. Founded in 1921, the Council of Foreign Relations is the key link between the large corporations and the federal government. It has been called a "school for statesmen" and "comes close to being an organ of what C. Wright Mills has called the Power Elite – a group of men, similar in interest and outlook shaping events from invulnerable positions behind the scenes. The creation of the United Nations was

a Council project, as well as the International Monetary Fund and the World Bank."
- Steve Jacobson, Mind Control in the United States

Some current members of the CFR include David Rockefeller, Dick Cheney, Barack Obama, Hilary Clinton, megachurch pastor Rick Warren and the CEOs of major corporations such as CBS, Nike, Coca-Cola and Visa.

Carl Jung

Carl Jung is the founder of analytical psychology (also known an Jungian psychology), which emphasizes understanding the psyche by exploring dreams, art, mythology, religion, symbols and philosophy. The Swiss therapist is at the origin of many psychological concepts used today such as the Archetype, the Complex, the Persona, the Introvert/Extrovert and Synchronicity. He was highly influenced by the occult background of his family. Carl Gustav, his grandfather, was an avid Freemason (he was Grand Master) and Jung himself discovered that some of his ancestors were Rosicrucians. This might explain his great interest in Eastern and Western philosophy, alchemy, astrology and symbolism. One of his most important (and misunderstood) concept was the Collective Unconscious.

Carl Jung

"My thesis, then, is as follows: In addition to our immediate consciousness, which is of a thoroughly personal nature and which we believe to be the only empirical psyche (even if we tack on the personal unconscious as an appendix), there exists a second psychic system of a collective, universal, and impersonal nature which is identical in all individuals. This collective unconscious does not develop individually but is inherited. It consists of pre-existent forms, the archetypes, which can only become conscious secondarily and which give definite form to certain psychic contents."
- Carl Jung, The Concept of the Collective Unconscious

The collective unconscious transpires through the existence of similar symbols and mythological figures in different civilizations. Archetypal symbols seem to be embedded in our collective subconscious, and, when exposed to them, we demonstrate natural attraction and fascination. Occult symbols can therefore exert a great impact on people, even if many individuals were never personally introduced to the symbol's esoteric meaning. Mass media thinkers, such as Edward D. Bernays, found in this concept a great way to manipulate the public's personal and collective unconscious.

Edward Bernays

Edward Bernays is considered to be the "father of public relations" and used concepts discovered by his uncle Sigmund Freud to manipulate the public using the subconscious. He shared Walter Lippmann's view of the general population by considering it irrational and subject to the "herd instinct". In his opinion, the masses need to be manipulated by an invisible government to insure the survival of democracy.

Edward Bernays

> *"The conscious and intelligent manipulation of the organized habits and opinions of the masses is an important element in democratic society. Those who manipulate this unseen mechanism of society constitute an invisible government which is the true ruling power of our country.*
>
> *We are governed, our minds are molded, our tastes formed, our ideas suggested, largely by men we have never heard of. This is a logical result of the way in which our democratic society is organized. Vast numbers of human beings must cooperate in this manner if they are to live together as a smoothly functioning society.*
>
> *Our invisible governors are, in many cases, unaware of the identity of their fellow members in the inner cabinet."*
> - Edward Bernays, Propaganda

Bernay's trailblazing marketing campaigns profoundly changed the functioning of American society. He basically created "consumerism" by creating a culture wherein Americans bought for pleasure instead of buying for survival. For this reason, he was considered by Life Magazine to be in the Top 100 most influential Americans of the 20th century.

Harold Lasswell

In 1939-1940, the University of Chicago was the host of a series of secret seminars on communications. These think tanks were funded by the Rockefeller foundation and involved the most prominent researchers in the fields of communications and sociological studies. One of these scholars was Harold Lasswell, a leading American political scientist and communications theorist, specializing in the analysis of propaganda. He was also of the opinion that a democracy, a government ruled by the people, could not sustain itself without a specialized elite shaping and molding public opinion through propaganda.

Harold Lasswell

In his Encyclopaedia of the Social Sciences, Lasswell explained that when elites lack the requisite force to compel obedience, social managers must turn to "a whole new technique of control, largely through propaganda." He added the conventional justification: we must recognize the "ignorance and stupidity [of] … the masses and not succumb to democratic dogmatisms about men being the best judges of their own interests."

Lasswell extensively studied the field of content analysis in order to understand the effectiveness of different types of propaganda. In his essay Contents of Communication, Lasswell explained that, in order to understand the meaning of a message (i.e. a movie, a speech, a book, etc.), one should take into account the frequency with which certain symbols appear in the message, the direction in which the symbols try to persuade the audience's opinion, and the intensity of the symbols used.

Lasswell was famous for his media analysis model based on:

Who (says) What (to) Whom (in) What Channel (with) What Effect

By this model, Lasswell indicates that in order to properly analyze a media product, one must look at who produced the product (the people who ordered its creation), who was it aimed at (the target audience) and what were the desired effects of this product (to inform, to convince, to sell, etc.) on the audience.

Using a Rihanna video as an example, the analysis would be as follows: WHO PRODUCED: Vivendi Universal; WHAT: pop artist Rihanna; TO WHOM: consumers between the ages of 9 and 25; WHAT CHANNEL: music video; and WHAT EFFECT: selling the artist, her song, her image and her message.

The analyzes of videos and movies on The Vigilant Citizen place a great importance on the "who is behind" the messages communicated to the public. The term "Illuminati" is often used to describe this small elite group covertly ruling the masses. Although the term sounds quite caricatured and conspiratorial, it aptly describes the elite's affinities with secret societies and occult knowledge. However, I personally detest using the term "conspiracy theory" to describe what is happening in the mass media. If all the facts concerning the elitist nature of the industry are readily available to the public, can it still be considered a "conspiracy theory"?

There used to be a variety of viewpoints, ideas and opinions in popular culture. The consolidation of media corporations has, however, produced a standardization of the cultural industry. Ever wondered why all recent music sounds the same and all recent movies look the same? The following is part of the answer:

Media Ownership

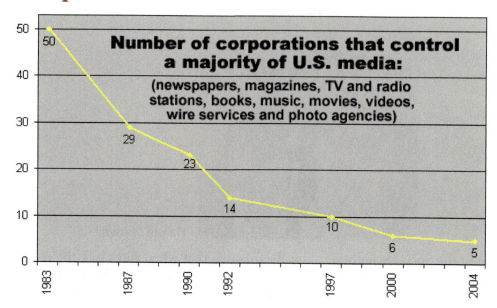

As depicted in the graph above, the number of corporations owning the majority of U.S. media outlets went from 50 to 5 in less than 20 years. Here are the top corporations evolving around the world and the assets they own.

AOL Time Warner

> "A list of the properties controlled by AOL Time Warner takes ten typed pages listing 292 separate companies and subsidiaries. Of these, twenty-two are joint ventures with other major corporations involved in varying degrees with media operations. These partners include 3Com, eBay, Hewlett-Packard, Citigroup, Ticketmaster, American Express, Homestore, Sony, Viva, Bertelsmann, Polygram, and Amazon.com. Some of the more familiar fully owned properties of Time Warner include Book-of-the-Month Club; Little, Brown publishers; HBO, with its seven channels; CNN; seven specialized and foreign-language channels; Road Runner; Warner Brothers Studios; Weight Watchers; Popular Science; and fifty-two different record labels."
> - Ben Bagdikan, The New Media Monopoly

AOL Time Warner owns:

- 64 magazines, including Time, Life, People, MAD Magazine and DC Comics
- Warner Bros, New Line and Fine Line Features in cinema
- More than 40 music labels including Warner Bros, Atlantic and Elektra
- Many television networks such as WB Networks, HBO, Cinemax, TNT, Cartoon Network and CNN
- Madonna, Sean Paul, The White Stripes

Viacom

Viacom owns:

- CBS, MTV, MTV2, UPN, VH1, Showtime, Nickelodeon, Comedy Central, TNN, CMT and BET
- Paramount Pictures, Nickelodeon Movies, MTV Films

- Blockbuster Videos
- 1800 screens in theaters through Famous Players

THE WALT DISNEY COMPANY

"Disney ownership of a hockey team called The Mighty Ducks of Anaheim does not begin to describe the vastness of the kingdom. Hollywood is still its symbolic heart, with eight movie production studios and distributors: Walt Disney Pictures, Touchstone Pictures, Miramax, Buena Vista Home Video, Buena Vista Home Entertainment, Buena Vista International, Hollywood Pictures, and Caravan Pictures.

The Walt Disney Company controls eight book house imprints under Walt Disney Company Book Publishing and ABC Publishing Group; seventeen magazines; the ABC Television Network, with ten owned and operated stations of its own including in the five top markets; thirty radio stations, including all the major markets; eleven cable channels, including Disney, ESPN (jointly), A&E, and the History Channel; thirteen international broadcast channels stretching from Australia to Brazil; seven production and sports units around the world; and seventeen Internet sites, including the ABC group, ESPN.sportszone, NFL.com, NBAZ.com, and NASCAR.com. Its five music groups include the Buena Vista, Lyric Street, and Walt Disney labels, and live theater productions growing out of the movies The Lion King, Beauty and the Beast, and King David."
- Ibid

The Walt Disney Company owns:

- ABC, Disney Channel, ESPN, A&E, History Channel
- Walt Disney Pictures, Touchstone Pictures, Hollywood Pictures, Miramax Film Corp., Dimension and Buena Vista International
- Miley Cyrus/ Hannah Montana, Selena Gomez, Jonas Brothers

VIVENDI UNIVERSAL

Vivendi Universal owns:

- 27% of US music sales, labels include: Interscope, Geffen, A&M, Island, Def Jam, MCA, Mercury, Motown and Universal
- Universal Studios, Studio Canal, Polygram Films, Canal +
- Numerous internet and cell phone companies
- Lady Gaga, The Black Eyed Peas, Lil Wayne, Rihanna, Mariah Carey, Jay-Z

SONY

Sony owns:
- Columbia Pictures, Screen Gems, Sony Pictures Classics
- 15% of US Music sales, labels include Columbia, Epic, Sony, Arista, Jive and RCA Records
- Beyonce, Shakira, Michael Jackson, Alicia Keys, Christina Aguilera

A limited number of actors in the cultural industry means a limited amount of viewpoints and ideas making their way to the general public. It also means that a single message can easily saturate all forms of media to generate consent (i.e. "there are weapons of mass destruction in Iraq").

The Standardization of Human Thought

The merger of media companies in the last decades generated a small oligarchy of media conglomerates. The TV shows we follow, the music we listen to, the movies we watch and the newspapers we read are all produced by FIVE corporations. The owners of those conglomerates have close ties with the world's elite and, in many ways, they ARE the elite. By owning all of the possible outlets having the potential to reach the masses, these conglomerates have the power to create in the minds of the people a single and cohesive world view, engendering a "standardization of human thought".

Even movements or styles that are considered marginal are, in fact, extensions of mainstream thinking. Mass medias produce their own rebels who definitely look the part but are still part of the establishment and do not question any of it. Artists, creations and ideas that do not fit the mainstream way of thinking are mercilessly rejected and forgotten by the conglomerates, which in turn makes them virtually disappear from society itself. However, ideas that are deemed to be valid and desirable to be accepted by society are skillfully marketed to the masses in order to make them become self-evident norm.

In 1928, Edward Bernays already saw the immense potential of motion pictures to standardize thought:

> "The American motion picture is the greatest unconscious carrier of propaganda in the world today. It is a great distributor for ideas and opinions. The motion picture can standardize the ideas and habits of a nation. Because pictures are made to meet market demands, they reflect, emphasize and even exaggerate broad popular tendencies, rather than stimulate new ideas and opinions. The motion picture avails itself only of ideas and facts which are in vogue. As the newspaper seeks to purvey news, it seeks to purvey entertainment."
> – Edward Bernays, Propaganda

These facts were flagged as dangers to human freedom in the 1930's by thinkers of the school of Frankfurt such as Theodor Adorno and Herbert Marcuse. They identified three main problems with the cultural industry. The industry can:

1- reduce human beings to the state of mass by hindering the development of emancipated individuals, who arcapable of making rational decisions;
2- replace the legitimate drive for autonomy and self-awareness by the safe laziness of conformism and passivity;
3- validate the idea that men actually seek to escape the absurd and cruel world in which they live by losing themselves in a hypnotic state self-satisfaction.

The notion of escapism is even more relevant today with advent of online video games, 3D movies and home theaters. The masses, constantly seeking state-of-the-art entertainment, will resort to high-budget products that can only be produced by the biggest media corporations of the world. These products contain carefully calculated messages and symbols which are nothing more and nothing less than entertaining propaganda. The public have been trained to LOVE its propaganda to the extent that it spends its hard-earned money to be exposed to it. Propaganda (used in both political, cultural and commercial sense) is no longer the coercive or authoritative communication form found in dictatorships: it has become the synonym of entertainment and pleasure.

> "In regard to propaganda the early advocates of universal literacy and a free press envisaged only two possibilities: the propaganda might be true, or it might be false. They did not foresee what in fact has happened, above all in our Western capitalist democracies — the development of a vast mass communications industry, concerned in the main neither with the true nor the false, but with the unreal,

the more or less totally irrelevant. In a word, they failed to take into account man's almost infinite appetite for distractions."
– Aldous Huxley, Preface to A Brave New World

A single piece of media often does not have a lasting effect on the human psyche. Mass media, however, by its omnipresent nature, creates a living environment we evolve in on a daily basis. It defines the norm and excludes the undesirable. The same way carriage horses wear blinders so they can only see what is right in front of them, the masses can only see where they are supposed to go.

> *"It is the emergence of mass media which makes possible the use of propaganda techniques on a societal scale. The orchestration of press, radio and television to create a continuous, lasting and total environment renders the influence of propaganda virtually unnoticed precisely because it creates a constant environment. Mass media provides the essential link between the individual and the demands of the technological society."*
> – Jacques Ellul

One of the reasons mass media successfully influences society is due to the extensive amount of research on cognitive sciences and human nature that has been applied to it.

Manipulation Techniques

> *"Publicity is the deliberate attempt to manage the public's perception of a subject. The subjects of publicity include people (for example, politicians and performing artists), goods and services, organizations of all kinds, and works of art or entertainment."*

The drive to sell products and ideas to the masses has lead to an unprecedented amount of research on human behavior and on the human psyche. Cognitive sciences, psychology, sociology, semiotics, linguistics and other related fields were and still are extensively researched through well-funded studies.

> *"No group of sociologists can approximate the ad teams in the gathering and processing of exploitable social data. The ad teams have billions to spend annually on research and testing of reactions, and their products are magnificent accumulations of material about the shared experience and feelings of the entire community."*
> - Marshal McLuhan, The Extensions of Man

The results of those studies are applied to advertisements, movies, music videos and other media in order to make them as influential as possible. The art of marketing is highly calculated and scientific because it must reach both the individual and the collective consciousness. In high-budget cultural products, a video is never "just a video," Images, symbols and meanings are strategically placed in order to generate a desired effect.

> *"It is with knowledge of the human being, his tendencies, his desires, his needs, his psychic mechanisms, his automatisms as well as knowledge of social psychology and analytical psychology that propaganda refines its techniques."*
> – Propagandes, Jacques Ellul (free translation)

Today's propaganda almost never uses rational or logical arguments. It directly taps into a human's most primal needs and instincts in order to generate an emotional and irrational response. If we always thought rationally, we probably wouldn't buy 50% of what we own. Babies and children are constantly found in advertisements targeting women for a specific reason: studies have shown that images of children trigger in women an instinctual need to nurture, to care and to protect, ultimately leading to a sympathetic bias towards the advertisement.

Strange 7Up ad exploiting the cuteness of babies.

Sex is ubiquitous in mass media, as it draws and keeps the viewer's attention. It directly connects to our animal need to breed and to reproduce, and, when triggered, this instinct can instantly overshadow any other rational thoughts in our brain.

Subliminal Perception

What if the messages described above were able to reach directly the viewers' subconscious mind, without the viewers even realizing what is happening? That is the goal of subliminal perception. The phrase subliminal advertising was coined in 1957 by the US market researcher James Vicary, who said he could get moviegoers to "drink Coca-Cola" and "eat popcorn" by flashing those messages onscreen for such a short time that viewers were unaware.

> *"Subliminal perception is a deliberate process created by communications technicians, by which you receive and respond to information and instructions without being consciously aware of the instructions"*
> – Steve Jacobson, Mind Control in the United States

Although some sources claim that subliminal advertising is ineffective or even an urban myth, the documented usage of this technique in mass media proves that creators believe in its powers. Recent studies have also proven its effectiveness, especially when the message is negative.

> *"A team from University College London, funded by the Wellcome Trust, found that it [subliminal perception] was particularly good at instilling negative thoughts. There has been much speculation about whether people can process emotional information unconsciously, for example pictures, faces and words," said Professor Nilli Lavie, who led the research. We have shown that people can perceive the emotional value of subliminal messages and have demonstrated conclusively that people are much more attuned to negative words."*
> - Key to subliminal messaging is to keep it negative, study shows, Wellcome Trust

A famous example of subliminal messaging in political communications is in George Bush's advertisement against Al Gore in 2000. Right after the name of Gore is mentioned, the ending of the word "bureaucrats" – "rats" – flashes on the screen for a split second. The discovery of this trickery caused quite a stir and, even if there are no laws against subliminal messaging in the U.S., the advertisement was taken off the air.

As seen in many articles on The Vigilant Citizen, subliminal and semi-subliminal messages are often used in movies and music videos to communicate messages and ideas to the viewers.

Desensitization

In the past, when changes were imposed on populations, they would take to the streets, protest and even riot. The main reason for this clash was due to the fact that the change was clearly announced by the rulers and understood by the population. It was sudden and its effects could clearly be analyzed and evaluated. Today, when the elite needs a part of its agenda to be accepted by the public, it is done through desensitization. The agenda, which might go against the public best interests, is slowly, gradually and repetitively introduced to the world through movies (by involving it within the plot), music videos (who make it cool and sexy) or the news (who present it as a solution to today's problems). After several years of exposing the masses to a particular agenda, the elite openly presents the concept the world and, due to mental programming, it is greeted with general indifference and is passively accepted. This technique originates from psychotherapy.

> *"The techniques of psychotherapy, widely practiced and accepted as a means of curing psychological disorders, are also methods of controlling people. They can be used systematically to influence attitudes and behavior. Systematic desensitization is a method used to dissolve anxiety so the the patient (public) is no longer troubled by a specific fear, a fear of violence for example. [...] People adapt to frightening situations if they are exposed to them enough".*
> – Steven Jacobson, Mind Control in the United States

Predictive programming is often found in the science fiction genre. It presents a specific image of the future – the one that is desired by the elite – and ultimately becomes in the minds of men an inevitability. A decade ago, the public was being desensitized to war against the Arab world. Today, the population is gradually being exposed to the existence of mind control, of transhumanism and of an Illuminati elite. Emerging from the shadows, those concepts are now everywhere in popular culture. This is what Alice Bailey describes as the "externalization of the hierarchy": the hidden rulers slowly revealing themselves.

Occult Symbolism in Pop Culture

Contrarily to the information presented above, documentation on occult symbolism is rather hard to find. This should not come as a surprise as the term "occult", literally means "hidden". It also means "reserved to those in the know" as it is only communicated to those who are deemed worthy of the knowledge. It is not taught in schools nor is it discussed in the media. It is thus considered marginal or even ridiculous by the general population.

Occult knowledge is NOT, however, considered ridiculous in occult circles. It is considered timeless and sacred. There is a long tradition of hermetic and occult knowledge being taught through secret societies originating from ancient Egyptians, to Eastern Mystics, to the Knights Templar to modern day Freemasons. Even if the nature and the depth of this knowledge was most probably modified and altered throughout the centuries, mystery schools kept their main features, which are highly symbolic, ritualistic and metaphysical. Those characteristics, which were an intricate part of ancient civilizations, have totally been evacuated from modern society to be replaced by pragmatic materialism. For this reason, there lies an important gap of understanding between the pragmatic average person and the ritualistic establishment.

> "If this inner doctrine were always concealed from the masses, for whom a simpler code had been devised, is it not highly probable that the exponents of every aspect of modern civilization – philosophic, ethical, religious, and scientific-are ignorant of the true meaning of the very theories and tenets on which their beliefs are founded? Do the arts and sciences that the race has inherited from older nations conceal beneath their fair exterior a mystery so great that only the most illumined intellect can grasp its import? Such is undoubtedly the case."
> - Manly P. Hall, Secret Teachings of All Ages

The "simpler code" devised for the masses used to be organized religions. It is now becoming the Temple of the Mass Media and it preaches on a daily basis extreme materialism, spiritual vacuosity and a self-centered, individualistic existence. This is exactly the opposite of the attributes required to become a truly free individual, as taught by all great philosophical schools of thought. Is a dumbed-down population easier to deceive and to manipulate?

> "These blind slaves are told they are "free" and "highly educated" even as they march behind signs that would cause any medieval peasant to run screaming away from them in panic-stricken terror. The symbols that modern man embraces with the naive trust of an infant would be tantamount to billboards reading, 'This way to your death and enslavement,' to the understanding of the traditional peasant of antiquity"
> - Michael A. Hoffman II, Secret Societies and Psychological Warfare

In Conclusion

This article examined the major thinkers in the field of mass media, the media power structure and the techniques used to manipulate the masses. I believe this information is vital to the understanding of the "why" in the topics discussed on The Vigilant Citizen. The "mass population" versus "ruling class" dichotomy described in many articles is not a "conspiracy theory" (again, I hate that term), but a reality that has been clearly stated in the works of some of the 20th century's most influential men.

Lippmann, Bernays and Lasswell have all declared that the public are not fit to decide their own fate, which is the inherent goal of democracy. Instead, they called for a cryptocracy, a hidden government, a ruling class in charge of the "bewildered herd." As their ideas continue to be applied to society, it is increasingly apparent that an ignorant population is not an obstacle that the rulers must deal with: It is something that is DESIRABLE and, indeed, necessary, to insure total leadership. An ignorant population does not know its rights, does not seek a greater understanding of issues and does not question authorities. It simply follows trends. Popular culture caters to and nurtures ignorance by continually serving up brain-numbing entertainment and spotlighting degenerate celebrities to be idolized. Many people ask me: "Is there a way to stop this?" Yes, there is. Stop buying it.

> "If a nation expects to be ignorant and free, it expects what never was and never will be."
> - Thomas Jefferson

Dumbing Down Society Part I: Foods, Beverages and Meds

Is there a deliberate effort by the government to dumb down the masses? The statement is hard to prove but there exists a great amount of data proving that the ruling elite not only tolerates, but effectively introduces policies that have a detrimental effect on the physical and mental health of the population. This series of articles looks at the many ways the modern man is being dumbed down. Part I looks at the poisons found in everyday foods, beverages and medications.

The theme of dumbing-down and dehumanizing the masses are often discussed in articles on The Vigilant Citizen. The presence of those concepts in popular culture are, however, only the outward and symbolic expression of the profound transformation happening in our society. Scientific data has been proving for years that governments around the world are tolerating the selling of many products which have a direct and negative effect on cognitive and physical health. As we will see in this article many everyday products cause brain damage, impaired judgment and even a lower IQ.

Is a dumber population something that is desired by the elite? Hitler once said "How fortunate for the leaders that men do not think." An educated population knows its rights, understands the issues and takes action when it does not approve of what is going on. Judging by the incredible amount of data available on the subject, it seems that the elite want the exact opposite: an unhealthy, frightened, confused and sedated population. We will look at the effects of medication, pesticides, fluoride and aspartame on the human body and how those products are being pushed by people from inside the power structure.

Prescription Drug Abuse

America has witnessed during the last decades a staggering rise of drugs being prescribed to treat all kinds of problems. Children are particularly affected by this phenomenon. Since the 1990s, an ever-rising proportion of American children are being diagnosed with "illnesses" such as Attention Deficit Disorder (ADD) and are prescribed mind-altering drugs, such as Ritalin.

> "The DEA has become alarmed by the tremendous increase in the prescribing of these drugs in recent years. Since 1990, prescriptions for methylphenidate have increased by 500 percent, while prescriptions for amphetamine for the same purpose have increased 400 percent. Now we see a situation in which from seven to ten percent of the nation's boys are on these drugs at some point as well as a rising percentage of girls."
> - DEA Report, add-adhd.org

Today, children who show too much energy, character or strength are being willfully sedated with powerful drugs which directly affect the way their brains function. Are we going in the right direction here?

Even if ADD is not a clearly defined and documented disorder – it causes NO observable biological effects whatsoever – children are still being diagnosed with the illness in great numbers. This raises important ethical questions.

> "Pediatricians as well as ethicists have also voiced their concerns in usage of these stimulants. In an article published in the New York Times, they have questioned the appropriateness of medicating

children without a clear diagnosis in hopes that they do better in school. They also asked whether the drugs should be given to adults failing in their careers or are procrastinators. They question the worthy of this method.

This concern have also been voiced out in the January 2005 issue of Pediatrics in which the large discrepancies between pediatricians' practice patterns and the American Academy of Pediatrics (AAP) guidelines for the assessment and treatment of children with attention-deficit/hyperactivity disorder (ADHD) was bought forth. The article also stated that because the medical community didn't come to a consensus on how to diagnose ADD/ADHD, they should not be making extensive decisions as to how to treat individuals who have been diagnosed with the disorder."
- Ibid.

The usage of Ritalin at a young age breaks the psychological threshold people maintain towards the usage of prescription pills, which makes those children more likely to consume psychotropic drugs later in their lives. We should not be surprised to witness a dramatic increase of consumption of antidepressants in the years to come. The trend is already beginning:

"In its study, the U.S. Centers for Disease Control and Prevention looked at 2.4 billion drugs prescribed in visits to doctors and hospitals in 2005. Of those, 118 million were for antidepressants.

The use of antidepressants and other psychotropic drugs — those that affect brain chemistry — has skyrocketed over the last decade. Adult use of antidepressants almost tripled between the periods 1988-1994 and 1999-2000. Between 1995 and 2002, the most recent year for which statistics are available, the use of these drugs rose 48 percent, the CDC reported."
- Elizabeth Cohen, CNN

The use of prescription pills might be of a great help for specific and properly diagnosed cases. The pharmaceutical industry however, which has many "friends" in the highest levels of government, is pushing for the widespread use of psychiatric drugs within the public. Since 2002, a great number of pills claiming to fix all kinds of mental conditions have been marketed to the public, but many of those pills were approved for sale without proper research for side effects. Even worse: the side effects might have been known but hidden to the public. Below is a list of warnings issued on commonly sold psychiatric drugs. Some of those side effects are actually frightening as a pill should not be able to have that much power over the human brain. Think about it: Some drugs are subject to warnings because they can cause you to … commit suicide?

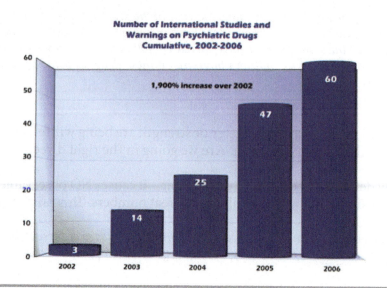

2004

March 22: The Food and Drug Administration (FDA) warned that Prozac-like antidepressants (called Selective Serotonin Reuptake Inhibitors or SSRIs) could cause "anxiety, agitation, panic attacks, insomnia, irritability, hostility, impulsivity, akathisia [severe restlessness], hypomania [abnormal excitement] and mania [psychosis characterized by exalted feelings, delusions of grandeur]."

June: The Therapeutic Goods Administration, the Australian equivalent of the FDA, reported that the latest antipsychotic drugs could increase the risk of diabetes.

June: The FDA ordered that the packaging for the stimulant Adderall include a warning about sudden cardiovascular deaths, especially in children with underlying heart disease.

October 15: The FDA ordered its strongest "black box" label for antidepressants warning they could cause suicidal thoughts and actions in under those under 18 years old.

October 21: The New Zealand Medicines Adverse Reactions Committee recommended that older and newer antidepressants not be administered to patients less than 18 years of age because of the risk of suicide.

December 17: The FDA required packaging for the "ADHD" drug, Strattera, to advise that "Severe liver damage may progress to liver failure resulting in death or the need for a liver transplant in a small percentage of patients."

2005

February 9: Health Canada, the Canadian counterpart of the FDA, suspended marketing of Adderall XR (Extended Release, given once a day) due to reports of 20 sudden unexplained deaths (14 in children) and 12 strokes (2 in children).

April 11: The FDA warned that antipsychotic drug use in elderly patients could increase the risk of death.

June 28: The FDA announced its intention to make labeling changes to Concerta and other Ritalin products to include the side effects: "visual hallucinations, suicidal ideation [ideas], psychotic behavior, as well as aggression or violent behavior."

June 30: The FDA warned that the antidepressant Cymbalta could increase suicidal thinking or behavior in pediatric patients taking it. It also warned about the potential increased risk of suicidal behavior in adults taking antidepressants.

August: The Australian Therapeutic Goods Administration found a relationship between antidepressants and suicidality, akathisia (severe restlessness), agitation, nervousness and anxiety in adults. Similar symptoms could occur during withdrawal from the drugs, it determined.

August 19: The European Medicines Agency's Committee for Medicinal Products warned against child antidepressant use, stating that the drugs caused suicide attempts and thoughts, aggression, hostility, aggression, oppositional behavior and anger.

September 26: The Agenzia Italiana del Farmaco (Italian Drug Agency, equivalent to the FDA) warned against use of older (tricyclic) antidepressants in people under 18 years old. It also determined the drugs were associated with heart attacks in people of any age.

September 29: The FDA ordered that labeling for the "ADHD" drug Strattera include a boxed warning about the increased risk of suicidal thinking in children and adolescents taking it.

October 17: The FDA warned that the antidepressant Cymbalta could cause liver damage.

October 24: The FDA withdrew the stimulant Cylert from the market because of the risk of liver toxicity and failure.

November: The FDA warned that the antidepressant Effexor could cause homicidal thoughts.

2006

February 9: The FDA's Drug Safety and Risk Management Advisory Committee urged that the strongest "black box" warning be issued for stimulants, because they may cause heart attacks, strokes and sudden death.

February 20: British authorities warned that Strattera was associated with seizures and potentially lengthening period of the time between heartbeats.

March 22: An FDA advisory panel heard evidence of almost 1,000 reports of kids experiencing psychosis or mania while taking stimulants.

May 3: FDA adverse drug reaction reports linked antipsychotic drugs to 45 child deaths and 1,300 serious adverse reactions, such as convulsions and low white blood cell count.

May 12: The manufacturer of Paxil warned that the antidepressant increases the risk of suicide in adults.

May 26: Health Canada issued new warnings of rare heart risks for all drugs prescribed for "ADHD," including the risk of sudden death.

June 2: An FDA study determined that the antipsychotic drug, Risperdal, might cause pituitary tumors. The pituitary gland, at the base of the brain, secretes hormones that promote growth, and regulates body functions. Antipsychotics may increase prolactin, a hormone in the pituitary gland, and this increase has been linked to cancer. Risperdal was found to increase prolactin levels more frequently than in other antipsychotics.

July 19: The FDA said antidepressant packaging should carry warnings that they may cause a fatal lung condition in newborns whose mothers took SSRI antidepressants during pregnancy. Migraine sufferers also need to be warned that combining migraine drugs with SSRIs could result in a life-threatening condition called serotonin syndrome.

Food Poisoning

The modern man ingests in his lifetime an incredible amount of chemicals, artificial flavors and additives. Although there is growing awareness regarding healthy eating, there is also a lot of misinformation and disinformation.

At the present time, a single company – Monsanto – produces roughly 95% of all soybeans and 80% of all corn in the US. Considering this, the corn flakes you had for breakfast, soda you drank at lunch and beefstew you ate for dinner likely were produced from crops grown with Monsanto's patented genes. There are numerous documents and films exposing Monsanto's strong-arming of the agricultural industry, so I won't expand on that issue. It is however important to note that a virtual monopoly currently exists in the food industry and there's a unhealthy link between Monsanto and the American government: Many people who have passed laws in the fields of food, drugs and agriculture were also, at some point on the payroll of Monsanto. In other words, the elite decides which foods are sold to you.

Public officials formerly employed by Monsanto:

Justice Clarence Thomas worked as an attorney for Monsanto in the 1970s. Thomas wrote the majority opinion in the 2001 Supreme Court decision J. E. M. Ag Supply, Inc. v. Pioneer Hi-Bred International, Inc.|J. E. M. AG SUPPLY, INC. V. PIONEER HI-BREDINTERNATIONAL, INC. which found that "newly developed plant breeds are patentable under the general utility patent laws of the United States." This case benefited all companies which profit from genetically modified crops, of which Monsanto is one of the largest.

Michael R. Taylor was an assistant to the Food and Drug Administration (FDA) commissioner before he left to work for a law firm on gaining FDA approval of Monsanto's artificial growth hormone in the 1980s. Taylor then became deputy commissioner of the FDA from 1991 to 1994. Taylor was later re-appointed to the FDA in August 2009 by President Barack Obama.

Dr. Michael A. Friedman was a deputy commissioner of the FDA before he was hired as a senior vice president of Monsanto.

Linda J. Fisher was an assistant administrator at the United States Environmental Protection Agency (EPA) before she was a vice president at Monsanto from 1995 – 2000. In 2001, Fisher became the deputy administrator of the EPA.

Former Secretary of Defense Donald Rumsfeld was chairman and chief executive officer of G. D. Searle & Co., which Monsanto purchased in 1985. Rumsfeld personally made at least $12 million USD from the transaction.

Many laws (approved by ex-Monsanto employees) have facilitated the introduction and the consumption of genetically engineered foods by the public.

> *"According to current statistics, 45% of corn and 85% of soybeans in the United States is genetically engineered (GE). Estimates of 70-75% of processed foods found at our local supermarkets are believed to contain GE ingredients.*
>
> *Other GE foods are canola, papayas, radicchio, potatoes, rice, squash or zucchini, cantaloupe, sugar beets, flax, tomatoes, and oilseed rape. One non-food crop that is commonly GE is cotton. The GE hormone recombinant bovine growth hormone (rBGH or Prosilac) was one of the first GE products allowed to enter the nation's food supply. The U.S. Food and Drug Administration (FDA) approved Monsanto's rBGH in 1993."*
> - Anna M. Salanti, Genetically Engineered Foods

Although it is yet impossible to determine the long-term effects of genetically engineered foods on the human body, some facts have already been established. GE foods contain less nutrients and, most importantly, they are "chemical-friendly".

> "One of the features of GE foods is their ability to withstand unlimited application of chemicals, including pesticides. Bromoxynil and glyphosate have been associated with developmental disorders in fetuses, tumors, carcinomas, and non-Hodgkin's lymphoma. Studies indicate that Monsanto's recombinant Bovine Growth Hormone (rBGH) causes treated cows to produce milk with an increased second hormone, IGF-1. This hormone is associated with human cancers. Recommendations by the Congressional watchdog agency, Government Accounting Office (GAO), recommended that rBGH not be approved. The European Union, Canada, and others have banned it. The UN has also refused to certify that using rBGH is safe."
> – Ibid

Genetic modifications engineered by Monsanto makes their products bigger and more aesthetically pleasing. Another, less discussed "improvement" is the plants' ability to withstand nearly unlimited amounts of Roundup brand pesticides. This encourages farmers to use that brand of pesticides which is produced by … Monsanto.

Studies on Roundup link the powerful pesticide and herbicide to many health problems such as:

- Increased risks of the cancer non-Hodgkin's lymphoma
- Miscarriages
- Attention Deficit Disorder (the real one)

Fluoride

Another source of harmful chemicals is found in the modern man's water supplies and soft drinks. As of 2002, the CDC statistics show that almost 60% of the U.S. population receives fluoridated water through the taps in their homes. The official reason for the presence of fluoride in our tap water? It prevents tooth decay. Ok … really? Is this mildly important benefit worth the consuming of great amounts of this substance by the population? Some studies even denied the dental benefits of fluorided water.

> "Scientists now believe that the main protective action from fluoride does not come from ingesting the chemical, with the teeth absorbing it from inside the body, but from direct absorption through topical application to teeth. This means swallowing water is a far less effective way to fight cavities than brushing with fluoridated toothpaste."
> - Critics raise red flag over fluoride in tap water, The Globe and Mail

So why is fluoride still found in tap water? Here are some quick facts about fluoridation chemicals:

- they were once used as pesticides
- they are registered as "poisonous" under the 1972 Poisons Act, in the same group of toxins as arsenic, mercury and paraquat
- fluoride is scientifically classed as more toxic than lead, but there is about 20 times more fluoride than lead in tap water

Many studies have been conducted on the effects of fluoride on the human body and some notable adverse effects have been noted: it changes bone structure and strength, impairs the immune system and it was linked to some cancers. Another alarming consequence of fluoridation is its effects on brain functions:

> "In 1995, neurotoxicologist and former Director of toxicology at Forsyth Dental Center in Boston, Dr. Phyllis Mullenix published research showing that fluoride built up in the brains of animals when exposed to moderate levels. Damage to the brain occured and the behavior patterns of the animals was adversely effected. Offspring of pregnant animals receiving relatively low doses of fluoride showed permanent effects to the brain which were seen as hyperactivity (ADD-like symptoms). Young animals and adult animals given fluoride experienced the opposite effect — hypoactivity or sluggishness. The toxic effects of fluoride on the central nervous system was subsequently confirmed by previously-classified government research. Two new epidemiological studies which tend to confirm fluoride's neurotoxic effects on the brain have shown that children exposed to higher levels of fluoride had lower IQs."
> - Fluoridation / Fluoride Toxic Chemicals In Your Water, Holistic Healing

A lesser known, but extremely important side effect of fluoride is the calcification of the pineal gland.

> "Up until the 1990s, no research had ever been conducted to determine the impact of fluoride on the pineal gland – a small gland located between the two hemispheres of the brain that regulates the production of the hormone melatonin. Melatonin is a hormone that helps regulate the onset of puberty and helps protect the body from cell damage caused by free radicals.
>
> It is now known – thanks to the meticulous research of Dr. Jennifer Luke from the University of Surrey in England – that the pineal gland is the primary target of fluoride accumulation within the body.
>
> The soft tissue of the adult pineal gland contains more fluoride than any other soft tissue in the body – a level of fluoride (~300 ppm) capable of inhibiting enzymes.
>
> The pineal gland also contains hard tissue (hyroxyapatite crystals), and this hard tissue accumulate more fluoride (up to 21,000 ppm) than any other hard tissue in the body (e.g. teeth and bone)."
> - Fluoride Deposition in the Aged Human Pineal Gland, Jennifer Luke School of Biological Sciences, University of Surrey

Other than regulating vital hormones, the pineal gland is known to serve an esoteric function. It is known by mystic groups as the "third eye" and has been considered by many cultures to be part of the brain responsible for spiritual enlightenment and the "link to the divine". Is enlightenment out of bounds for the modern man?

> "In the human brain there is a tiny gland called the pineal body, which is the sacred eye of the ancients, and corresponds to the third eye of the Cyclops. Little is known concerning the function of the pineal body, which Descartes suggested (more wisely than he knew) might be the abode of the spirit of man."
> – Manly P. Hall, The Secret Teachings of All Ages

Aspartame

Aspartame is an artificial sweetner used in "sugar-free" products such as diet sodas and chewing gum. Since its discovery in 1965, Aspartame caused great controversy regarding its health risks – primarily causing brain tumors – and was denied its application to be sold to the public by the FDA. Searle, the company attempting to market Aspartame then appointed Donald Rumsfeld as CEO in 1977 … and things changed drastically. In a short period of time, Aspartame could be found in over 5,000 products.

> "Donald Rumsfeld was on President Reagan's transition team and the day after he took office he

> *appointed an FDA Commissioner who would approve aspartame. The FDA set up a Board of Inquiry of the best scientists they had to offer who said aspartame is not safe and causes brain tumors, and the petition for approval is hereby revoked. The new FDA Commissioner, Arthur Hull Hayes, overruled that Board of Inquiry and then went to work for the PR Agency of the manufacturer, Burson-Marstellar, rumored at $1000.00 a day, and has refused to talk to the press ever since."*
> - Donald Rumsfeld and Aspartame, NWV

Years after its approval by the FDA, leading scientists still urge the organization to ban this product.

> *"Dr. John Olney, who founded the field of neuoscience called excitotoxicity, attempted to stop the approval of aspartame with Attorney James Turner back in 1996. The FDA's own toxicologist, Dr. Adrian Gross told Congress that without a shadow of a doubt, aspartame can cause brain tumors and brain cancer and violated the Delaney Amendment which forbids putting anything in food that is known to cause Cancer. Detailed information on this can be found in the Bressler Report (FDA report on Searle)."*
> - Ibid

These symptoms are however only the tip of the iceberg. Aspartame has been linked to severe illnesses and long term health issues.

> *"According to the top doctors and researchers on this issue, aspartame causes headache, memory loss, seizures, vision loss, coma and cancer. It worsens or mimics the symptoms of such diseases and conditions as fibromyalgia, MS, lupus, ADD, diabetes, Alzheimer's, chronic fatigue and depression. Further dangers highlighted is that aspartame liberates free methyl alcohol. The resulting chronic methanol poisoning affects the dopamine system of the brain causing addiction. Methanol, or wood alcohol, constitutes one third of the aspartame molecule and is classified as a severe metabolic poison and narcotic."*
> - Ibid

In Conclusion

If the main message of this website has been to this point "watch what enters your mind", the main message of this article is "watch what enters your body." The consumption of the products stated above will probably not cause an immediate and noticeable effect. But, after many years of ingesting those substances, one's thoughts become increasingly clouded and foggy, the ability to concentrate becomes hindered and judgment becomes impaired. In other words, the once sharp mind becomes dull. What happens when a population is heavily sedated and poisoned on a daily basis? It becomes numb, zombie-like and docile. Instead of asking important questions and seeking a higher truth, the dumbed-down mass simply accomplishes its daily tasks and absorbs whatever the media tells them. Is this what the elite is looking to create?

There is, however, a silver lining here. Many of the negative effects of the substances described above are reversible. And YOU are the one who decides what enters your body. This article provides a brief overview of dangers lurking for the unaware consumer, but tons of information is available on which to base enlightened decisions. Your body is a temple. Will you allow it to be desecrated?

Dumbing Down Society Part 2: Mercury in Foods and Vaccines

Even though mercury is known to degenerate brain neurons and disrupt the central nervous system, it is still found in processed foods and mandatory vaccines. In this second part of the series examining the intentional dumbing-down of society, this article will discuss the presence of mercury in common foods and vaccines.

The first article in this series – Dumbing Down Society Pt 1: Foods, Beverages and Meds – looked at the effects of aspartame, fluoride and prescription pills on the human brain. These substances all cause a decrease of cognitive power which, on a large scale, leads to a dumbing down of the population that is ingesting them. This second article focuses on another toxic product found in everyday foods and mandatory vaccines: mercury.

Mercury is a heavy metal naturally found in the environment. However, it is not suitable for human consumption, as it is extremely harmful to the human body, especially the brain. While some people say that anything can be consumed in moderation, many experts agree that no amount of mercury is safe for the human body. Despite this and the many studies concerning the negative effects of mercury, the heavy metal is continually added to mandatory vaccines and processed foods.

Mercury is known to cause brain neuron degeneration and to disturb the central nervous system. Direct exposure to the metal causes immediate and violent effects:

> *"Exposure to high levels of metallic, inorganic, or organic mercury can permanently damage the brain, kidneys, and developing fetus. Effects on brain functioning may result in irritability, shyness, tremors, changes in vision or hearing, and memory problems."*
> -Agency for Toxic Substances and Disease Registry, "Mercury"

Most people do not come in direct contact with mercury, but are exposed to small doses at a time, resulting in a slow but steady poisoning of the brain. As the years go by, the effects of the substance impairs judgment and rational thinking, decreases memory and disrupts emotional stability. In other words: It makes you dumber.

Mercury has also the unfortunate ability to transfer from pregnant woman to their unborn babies. According to the Environmental Protection Agency, mercury passed on to the fetus during pregnancy may have lasting consequences, including memory impairment, diminished language skills and other cognitive complications.

It has been highly publicized that mercury is found in dangerous quantities in seafood, such as tuna, swordfish and tilefish. This creates a rather ironic situation: Instead of making you smarter because of all the Omega-3 they contain, the fish produce exactly the opposite effect on the brain due to mercury poisonning.

Unfortunately, mercury is also found in other products: vaccines and high-fructose corn syrup.

Vaccines

> *"I think it's absolutely criminal to give mercury to an infant."*
> – Boyd Haley, Ph.D., Chemistry Department Chair, University of Kentucky

Mercury is found in great quantities in mandatory vaccines. Before we get into the details of it, here are some facts about vaccines in America as noted by Dr. Sherri Tenpenny:

- The U.S. government is the largest purchaser of vaccines in the country. In fact, nearly 30 percent of the Centers for Disease Control's (CDC) annual budget is composed of purchasing vaccines and ensuring vaccination is completed for every child in the country.

- Private insurance companies, which do the best liability studies, have completely abandoned coverage for damage to life and property due to: Acts of God, nuclear war, nuclear power plant accidents and … vaccination.

- Laws have been passed to protect vaccine manufactures from liability, while at the same time, state laws require parents to inject their children with up to 100 vaccination antigens prior to entering school. If a vaccine injury–or death–occurs after a vaccine, parents cannot sue the doctor, the drug company or the government; they are required to petition the Vaccine Court for damages, a process that can take years and often ends with a dismissal of the case.

- Each state has school vaccination laws that require children of appropriate age to be vaccinated for several communicable diseases. State vaccination laws mandate that children be vaccinated prior to being allowed to attend public or private schools. Failure to vaccinate children can not only result in children being prohibited from attending school, but their parents or guardians can receive civil fines and criminal penalties. Schools don't usually tell parents is that in every state, an exemption exists allowing parents to legally refuse vaccines while still allowing their children to attend school.

- The medical industry advocates vaccines, often demanding that parents vaccinate their children in order to remain under their doctor's care. A sizable portion of a pediatrician's income is derived from insurance reimbursement for vaccinations. The ever-expanding vaccination schedule that includes increasingly more expensive vaccines has been a source of increased revenues for vaccinating doctors.

Thimerosal

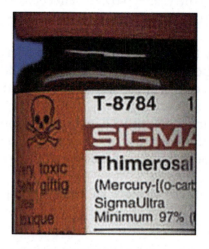

A child receives approximately 21 vaccines before the age of six and 6 more before the age of 18, for a total of 27 shots during childhood. Many of these injections contain Thimerosal, a preservative added to the shots, made of 49% mercury. The unprecedented use of mercury on children has created a generation of cognitively impaired children.

The symptoms experienced by children exposed to mercury are real and can be directly linked to the vaccines they were given as infants. It's ironic that the vaccines given to these young people are meant to protect them, when in fact they are adversely affecting their neurological development.

On top of causing an entire generation of babies to have their brains damaged, the use of Thimerosal in vaccines has been linked by many scientists to the staggering rise of autism in the past two decades. Did the dumbing-down campaign go too far?

> *"In children who are fully vaccinated, by the sixth month of life they have received more mercury from vaccines than recommended by the EPA. There are many similarities in symptoms between mercury toxicity and autism, including social deficits, language deficits, repetitive behaviors, sensory abnormalities, cognition deficits, movement disorders, and behavioral problems. There are also similarities in physical symptoms, including biochemical, gastrointestinal, muscle tone, eurochemistry, neurophysiology, EEG measurements, and immune system/autoimmunity."*
> - Vaccination Risk Awareness Network, "General Vaccine Issues - Mercury in Vaccines"

Due to the suspected link between vaccines and autism, more than 5,000 U.S. families have filed claims in a federal vaccine court against the companies producing the vaccines. In most cases, the plaintiffs received no compensation and all correlation between the illness and vaccines was denied by the defendants. A public relations war has been going on for years, as studies and counter-studies have appeared, proving or denying the links between vaccines and autism, depending where they originate from. The studies claiming that vaccines are safe have often been funded by the very companies that produce them.

Despite the denials, Thimerosal is slowly–and silently–being phased out of vaccines for babies. Not too long after the phasing out began, cases of autism have sharply dropped in the country.

> *"Published in the March 10 issue of the Journal of American Physicians and Surgeons, the data show since mercury was removed from childhood vaccines, the reported rates of autism and other neurological disorders in children not only stopped increasing but actually dropped sharply – by as much as 35 percent. Using the government's own databases, independent researchers analyzed reports of childhood neurological disorders, including autism, before and after removal of mercury-based preservatives.*
>
> *According to a statement from the Association of American Physicians & Surgeons, or AAPS, the numbers from California show that reported autism rates hit a high of 800 in May 2003. If that trend had continued, the reports would have risen to more than 1,000 by the beginning of 2006. But the number actually went down to 620, a real decrease of 22 percent, and a decrease from the projection of 35 percent."*
> - Ibid.

The phasing out of Thimerosal from vaccines intended for children is all well and good, but the preservative is still found in many vaccines intended for adults. Did someone realize that mercury in vaccines is too strong for children, making them sick and ultimately unproductive, but perfect to dumb-down fully developed adults? The ruling class is not looking to create a generation of autistic people who would need constant care, but a mass of "useful idiots" that can accomplish repetitive and mind-numbing tasks, while accepting without questioning what they are being told.

As of today, Thimerosal is still found in Influenza vaccines, commonly known as the flu shot. Those shots are seasonal, meaning that patients are encouraged to come back every winter to get their yearly vaccine/dose of mercury.

Makers of the Influenza vaccine say it boasts a "solid health record," meaning the shot does not seem cause observable illnesses. What is NEVER discussed, however, is the slow and gradual brain neuron degeneration most individuals go through, year after year, due constant mercury poisoning. This process of slowing down brain functions is not easily observable nor quantifiable but it is still happening on a world-wide scale. If mercury can completely disrupt the fragile minds of children enough to possibly cause autism, it will, at the very least, impair fully developed minds.

Almost as if created to generate demands for vaccines, new diseases appear periodically around the world that, with the help of mass media scare campaigns, cause people to beg their officials for the miracle shot that they are told will cure everybody.

H1N1, also known as the Swine Flu, was the latest of those scary diseases that terrified millions of people for several months. When the shot became available, heavily promoted and massive vaccination campaigns sprung around the world. One fact that was not promoted: Swine flu was often easily curable, and not very different than the "regular" flu. Another fact that was not promoted: Most of the flu shots contained Thimerosal.

Depopulation?

Other than simply dumbing down the population, vaccines might be aiding in depopulation efforts. In a speech in April 2010, Bill Gates mentioned the use of vaccines in the effort to reduce world population.

> "Gates made his remarks to the invitation-only Long Beach, California TED2010 Conference, in a speech titled, 'Innovating to Zero!.' Along with the scientifically absurd proposition of reducing man-made CO_2 emissions worldwide to zero by 2050, approximately four and a half minutes into the talk, Gates declares, 'First we got population. The world today has 6.8 billion people. That's headed up to about 9 billion. Now if we do a really great job on new vaccines, health care, reproductive health services, we lower that by perhaps 10 or 15 percent.'
>
> In plain English, one of the most powerful men in the world states clearly that he expects vaccines to be used to reduce population growth. When Bill Gates speaks about vaccines, he speaks with authority. In January 2010 at the elite Davos World Economic Forum, Gates announced his foundation would give $10 billion (circa ¤7.5 billion) over the next decade to develop and deliver new vaccines to children in the developing world."
> - F. William Engdahl, Bill Gates On 'Vaccines To Reduce Population'

High-Fructose Corn Syrup (HFCS)

A poison is a "substance that causes injury, illness, or death, especially by chemical means." Going by this definition, high-fructose corn syrup (HFCS) is truly a poison. HFCS is a highly processed sweetner made from corn that has been used since 1970. It continues to replace white sugar and sucrose in processed foods and is currently found in the majority of processed foods found in supermarkets. Studies have determined that Americans consume an average of 12 teaspoons a day of the sweetner.

Due to its sweetening propreties, HFCS is obviously found in sugary products like jams, soft drinks and pre-packaged baked goods. However, many people do not realize that it is also found in numerous other products, including soups, breads, pasta sauces, cereals, frozen entrees, meat products, salad dressings and condiments. HFCS is also found in so-called health products, including protein-bars, "low-fat" foods and energy drinks.

How can something that taste so good be so bad? Here are some facts about HFCS:

- Research links HFCS to increasing rates of obesity and diabetes in North America, especially among children. Fructose converts to fat more than any other sugar. And being a liquid, it passes much more quickly into the blood stream.

- Beverages containing HFCS have higher levels of reactive compounds (carbonyls), which are linked with cell and tissue damage leading to diabetes.

- There is some evidence that corn fructose is processed differently in the body than cane sugar, leading to reduced feelings of satiation and a greater potential for over-consumption.
- Studies by researchers at UC Davis and the University of Michigan have shown that consuming fructose, which is more readily converted to fat by the liver, increases the levels of fat in the bloodstream in the form of triglycerides.

- Unlike other types of carbohydrate made up of glucose, fructose does not stimulate the pancreas to produce insulin. Peter Havel, a nutrition researcher at UC Davis who studies the metabolic effects of fructose, has also shown that fructose fails to increase the production of leptin, a hormone produced by the body's fat cells. Both insulin and leptin act as signals to the brain to turn down the appetite and control body weight. Havel's research also shows that fructose does not appear to suppress the production of ghrelin, a hormone that increases hunger and appetite.

- Because the body processes the fructose in HFCS differently than it does cane or beet sugar, it alters the way metabolic-regulating hormones function. It also forces the liver to kick more fat out into the bloodstream. The end result is that our bodies are essentially tricked into wanting to eat more, while at the same time, storing more fat.

- A study in The Journal of the National Cancer Institute suggested that women whose diet was high in total carbohydrate and fructose intake had an increased risk of colorectal cancer.

- HFCS interferes with the heart's use of key minerals like magnesium, copper and chromium.

- HFCS has been found to deplete the immune system by inhibiting the action of white blood cells. The body is then unable to defend against harmful foreign invaders.

- Research suggests that fructose actually promotes disease more readily than glucose. Glucose is metabolized in every cell in the body, but all fructose must be metabolized in the liver. The livers of test animals fed large amounts of fructose develop fatty deposits and cirrhosis, similar to problems that develop in the livers of alcoholics.

- HFCS is highly refined–even more so than white sugar.

- The corn from which HFCS is derived is almost always genetically modified, as are the enzymes used in the refining process.

- There are increasing concerns about the politics surrounding the economics of corn production (subsidies, tariffs, and regulations), as well as the effects of intensive corn agriculture on the environment.

Several studies have observed a strong correlation between the rise HFCS in the past years and the rise of obesity during the same period of time.

Obesity, on top of being unhealthy for the body, directly affects brain functions. Some researchers have even questionned the role of obesity in brain degeneration.

> "Research scientists have long suspected that a relationship existed between obesity and a decline in brain power. New studies now confirm the contention that being overweight is detrimental to the brain. Researchers at the University of California in an article published in the Archives of Neurology demonstrated a strong correlation between central obesity (that is, being fat around the middle) and shrinkage of a part of the brain (the hippocampus) fundamental for memory (as measured on MRI scans)."
> - David Perlmutter, MD , "Obesity and Brain Function"

This does not mean that obese people are dumb. It does however mean that their brain is probably not processing as effectively as it could be.

But even if HFCS does not make you fat, it will still affect your brain. Recent studies have shown that the sweetener contains … you've guessed it … mercury!

> "One study – published in the journal, Environmental Health – shows mercury in nine out of 20 samples of commercial high-fructose corn syrup. The second study – by the Institute for Agriculture and Trade Policy (IATP) – finds nearly one in three of 55 brand-name foods contained mercury, especially dairy products, dressings and condiments. The brands included big names like Quaker, Hershey's, Kraft and Smucker's."
> - Sahar Aker , "Want some mercury with your favorite (HFCS) foods?"

In Conclusion

Despite the existence of many studies describing the negative effects of mercury on the human brain, governments still push for the increased vaccination of the population with shots containing Thimerosal. Furthermore, governing bodies have protected the pharmaceutical companies who produce the vaccines and foods containing HFCS against any type of lawsuits. The fact that many high executives of these companies also hold key positions within the government, might provide an explanation. There are indeed a restricted amount of persons holding positions of high power in both the private and public sector. These people, in what are clear cases of conflict of interest, collide at the top to form what this site refers to as "the elite" or "the ruling class." Most of these people have never been elected to governmental positions, yet they create public policies that further their agenda, regardless of the political party in power. Look at the membership of the Bilderberg Group, the Committee of 300 or the Council of Foreign Relations and you will find the CEOs of companies producing your food and medication … and the same people who pass laws governing your food and medication.

Since no public official is likely to betray his peers and fund-raisers to become a whistleblower, it is up to each one of us to learn about what we consume. The cliché saying "read the labels" is quite true, but if you have no idea what "monosodium glutamate" means, reading the label will not help you. This series of articles aims to raise basic awareness of the most harmful substances found in everyday products. I personally cannot claim to have a perfect diet … I grew up in the 80s and love the taste of processed foods like candy, sodas … even Hamburger Helper. But as you find more information and as you begin to realize that every step in the right direction really does make you feel better, each subsequent step becomes easier. No one can do it for you: It's up to you to take that next step … whether it is toward your detoxification or to Burger King.

Dumbing-Down Society Part 3: How to Reverse its Effects

The first two parts of this series describes the negative effects that some commonly consumed chemicals have on the body and brain. This third and final part looks at some natural ways to keep the brain healthy and provides tips to rid the body of dangerous substances. In other words, how to fight back against the dumbing down of society.

Parts I and II of this series of articles identified some toxic substances found in common foods and medicines and described some of their effects on the human brain. The main culprits discussed were aspartame, mercury, fluoride and high fructose corn syrup (HFCS). Whether these substances disturb the nervous system, decrease cognitive function, impair judgment, or affect the memory, the net result is the general dumbing down of society.

All is not doom and gloom, however. Nature, with its wonderful tendency to restore equilibrium, provides us humans the cure to almost any affliction we might develop. Ancient healers even believed that nature helped humans discover the cure to their illnesses in subtle and mysterious ways:

> "The plant might also be considered worthy of veneration because from its crushed leaves, petals, stalks, or roots could be extracted healing unctions, essences, or drugs affecting the nature and intelligence of human beings – such as the poppy and the ancient herbs of prophecy. The plant might also be regarded as efficacious in the cure of many diseases because its fruit, leaves, petals, or roots bore a resemblance in shape or color to parts or organs of the human body. For example, the distilled juices of certain species of ferns, also the hairy moss growing upon oaks, and the thistledown were said to have the power of growing hair; the dentaria, which resembles a tooth in shape, was said to cure the toothache; and the palma Christi plant, because of its shape, cured all afflictions of the hands."
> - Manly P. Hall, The Secret Teachings of All Ages

So, after dwelling in the awful world of poisonous chemicals and corrupted officials, the only fitting way to conclude this series of articles is to explore the all-natural ways to restore health.

Stop the Toxification

Warning: This article provides tips to naturally detoxify the body. If you are in need of a serious detox program, please consult a professional.

The first step in ridding your body from poisons is, quite logically, to stop ingesting poisons. It sounds simple enough, but this step is probably the most difficult, as many toxins are found in everyday foods and even tap water. An increased vigilance is necessary in everyday life and, sometimes, some annoying actions must be taken to keep the toxins out of your body. Nevertheless, once you actually feel your body and mind healing, you'll be proud of your efforts.

Before we look at the ways to avoid specific toxins, here are some general guidelines any health-conscious person should apply at all times: Avoid processed foods and artificial drinks. Instead, look for organic and locally grown produce or, even better, grow your own fruits, vegetables and herbs. By doing so, you automatically avoid many harmful substances, including MSG, HFCS, pesticides, sodium fluoride and mercury. You also save money, which is always nice. When buying groceries, always read the labels and, as they say, if you can't read it, don't eat it.

Here are specific ways to avoid particular toxins:

AVOIDING FLUORIDE

There are two types of fluoride: calcium fluoride and sodium fluoride. Calcium fluoride is naturally found in water sources, while sodium fluoride is a synthetic waste product of the nuclear, aluminum, and phosphate fertilizer industries. Guess which type is found in our water? Right, the nasty one. Regular water filters such as Brita do a good job in reducing the taste of metals and chemicals in the water but they do not filter out the fluoride. Purifying the water through reverse osmosis is the most effective way to remove sodium fluoride from water.

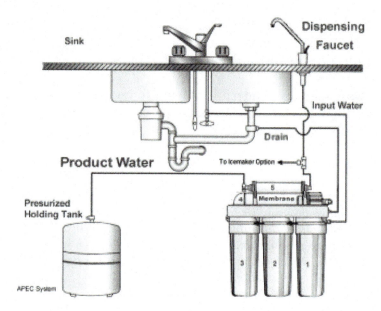

Standard reverse osmosis system

Some processed foods also contain high concentrations of sodium fluoride, including instant tea, grape juice products, and soy milk for babies, so once again, avoid processed foods. Also, switch to a fluoride-free toothpaste (or at least try not to swallow the $0.93 Colgate you bought at Walmart).

Consuming foods rich in calcium and magnesium help prevent fluoride intoxication, as they prevent the poison from attaching to the body.

> "Magnesium is a very important mineral that many are lacking. Besides being so important in the metabolism and synthesis of nutrients within your cells, it also inhibits the absorption of fluoride into your cells! Along with magnesium, calcium seems to help attract the fluorides away from your bones and teeth, allowing your body to eliminate those toxins. So during any detox efforts with fluoride, it is essential that you include a healthy supplemental dose of absorbable calcium/magnesium as part of the protocol."
> - Paul Fassa, How to Detox Fluoride from Your Body

AVOIDING MERCURY

First, if you or your children are being vaccinated, always request a Thimerosal-free shot. Second, avoid fish and seafood with high mercury levels; fish with the highest levels of mercury are marlin, orange roughy, shark, swordfish, tilefish and tuna (ahi, albacore and Yellowfin). Some seafood has low mercury levels, making them safer to consume, including anchovies, catfish, clam, crab, shrimp, flounder, salmon, sardine, tilapia and trout. As rule of thumb, bigger fish contain more mercury since they eat smaller fish and absorb all their mercury, and live longer, allowing mercury to build up.

Avoiding Aspartame

Always read labels and avoid "sugar-free" products. Aspartame is found in soft drinks, over-the-counter drugs & prescription drugs (very common, listed under "inactive ingredients"), vitamin & herb supplements, yogurt, candy, breath mints, cereals, sugar-free chewing gum, cocoa mixes, coffee beverages, instant breakfasts, gelatin desserts, frozen desserts, juice beverages, laxatives, milk drinks, shake mixes, tabletop sweeteners, tea beverages, instant teas and coffees, topping mixes and wine coolers.

Avoiding HFCS

Read the labels and if you find high fructose corn syrup at the top the list of ingredients, tell the product "oh no you didn't!", snap your fingers with attitude and put it back on the shelf. Ignore the confused looks of other shoppers.

We will now look at some all-natural ways to detox the body from harmful substances.

Cilantro

The standard procedure for removing heavy metals from the body is called "chelation." It is accomplished by administering a chelating agent – usually dimercaptosuccinic acid (DMSA) – that binds to the heavy metals in the body and cause them to be naturally flushed out. This type of treatment is quite strenuous, has many side-effects and should be undertaken only with medical supervision.

If, however, you believe that ridding the body of a harsh substance with another harsh substance might be self-defeating, I tend to agree with you. Fortunately there are herbs and spices that naturally act as chelating agents: Cilantro does a great job at it.

The most widely used and loved herbs and spices worldwide are derived from the same plant, Coriandrum sativum. The leaves of this plant are frequently referred to as cilantro, while the seeds are most commonly called coriander. Other than making any dish spectacular, the herb has the unique power of neutralizing mercury.

> *"This kitchen herb is capable of mobilizing mercury, cadmium, lead and aluminum in both bones and the central nervous system. It is probably the only effective agent in mobilizing mercury stored in the intracellular space (attached to mitochondria, tubulin, liposomes etc) and in the nucleus of the cell (reversing DNA damage of mercury)."*
> - Dietrich Klinghardt, MD, PhD, Chelation: How to remove Mercury, Lead, & other Metals

Studies have however suggested that cilantro only moves the problem to other parts of the body and thus must be used with another agent to complete the detoxification process.

Chlorella: Cilantro's Side-Kick

In addition to repairing and activating the body's detoxification functions, chlorella is known to bind to all known toxic metals and environmental toxins and facilitate their evacuation. This makes chlorella cilantro's perfect side-kick.

> *"Because cilantro mobilizes more toxins then it can carry out of the body, it may flood the connective*

tissue (where the nerves reside) with metals, that were previously stored in safer hiding places.

This process is called re-toxification. It can easily be avoided by simultaneously giving an intestinal-toxin-absorbing agent. Our definite choice is the algal organism chlorella. A recent animal study demonstrated rapid removal of aluminum from the skeleton superior to any known other detox agent.

Cilantro causes the gallbladder to dump bile — containing the excreted neurotoxins — into the small intestine. The bile-release occurs naturally as we are eating and is much enhanced by cilantro. If no chlorella is taken, most neurotoxins are reabsorbed on the way down the small intestine by the abundant nerve endings of the enteric nervous system"
- Ibid

Garlic

We may not be sure if garlic actually repels vampires, but we can be certain it repels toxins from the body.

"Garlic contains numerous sulphur components, including the most valuable sulph-hydryl groups, which oxidize mercury, cadmium and lead and make these metals water-soluble. (…) Garlic also contains the most important mineral, which protects from mercury toxicity, bioactive selenium."
- Ibid

So, garlic zaps mercury and lead and helps the body evacuate the metals from the body. Perhaps bad breath is the way to good health.

Turmeric (Curcuma)

This plant from the ginger family is widely used in Southeast Asia as a spice and its cleaning powers have been renowned for centuries. Turmeric is enshrined in Ayurvedic medicine as the king of spices. The bitter spice helps cleanse the liver, purify the blood, and promotes good digestion and elimination. It possesses powerful anti-inflammatory properties, but none of the unpleasant side effects of anti-inflammatory drugs. It has been used for skin cleansing, color enhancement and food preservation.

"Turmeric steps up the production of three enzymes–aryl-hydrocarbon-hydroxylase, glutathione-S-transferase, and UDP-glucuronyl-transferase. These are chemical "knives" that break down potentially harmful substances in the liver. Turmeric offers similar protection for people who are taking medications such as methotrexate and other forms of chemotherapy, which are metabolized by, or shuttled through, the liver."
- James A. Dukes, Ph D., Dr. Duke's Essential Herbs

Scientific studies have recently discovered that mixing black pepper with tumeric exponentially increases its healing properties on the body. No wonder traditional South Asian recipes often combine the two spices. So don't hold back … grind some black pepper into that tumeric!

Omega-3

It is not a secret that consuming the fatty acids found in fish brings many healthy benefits. The acids do wonders for our brains. In fact, Omega-3 is literally our brain's fuel, helping to maintain its core functions. Our most important organ heavily relies on Eicosapentaenoic acid (EPA) and Docosahexaenoic acid (DHA), two long-chain

Omega-3 fatty acids that our bodies cannot create. The only way to obtain those acids is through diet.

> "Most health professionals believe that DHA is the fatty acid that is most important for healthy structure and development of the brain and for vision so it is vital that there is enough DHA in the diet during pregnancy and in the first few years of a child's life. EPA on the other hand, is essential for healthy functioning of the brain on a day to day basis, which means that throughout your life you need a constant supply of EPA."
> - David McEnvoy, Why Fish Oil is Brain Fuel

Here are some facts about Omega-3 that are of particular interest in the context of those articles:

- Research by the University of Western Australia found that women who took fish oil supplements during the latter part of their pregnancy had babies with better hand-to-eye coordination, were better speakers and could understand more at the age of two and a half than babies whose mothers who were given olive oil instead.

- A study by Aberdeen University, led by professor Lawrence Whalley, found that fish oil helps the brain to work faster, increases IQ scores and slows down the aging process.

- The Durham trials led by Dr. Madeleine Portwood have consistently found that fish oil improves behaviour, concentration and learning in the classroom.

- Researcher Natalie Sinn in Australia found fish oil to be more effective than Ritalin for ADHD.

- Hibbeln et al. looked at diet in 22 countries and found an significant association between low fish consumption and post-natal depression.

- Dr. Malcolm Peet found that ethyl-EPA, a highly concentrated form of Omega 3, dramatically reduces depression.

Fish oil also plays an important role in ridding the brain of unwanted substances:

> "The fatty acid complexes EPA and DHA in fish oil make the red and white blood cells more flexible thus improving the microcirculation of the brain, heart and other tissues. All detoxification functions depend on optimal oxygen delivery and blood flow. EPA and DHA protect the brain from viral infections and are needed for the development of intelligence and eyesight. The most vital cell organelle for detoxification is the peroxisome. These small structures are also responsible for the specific job each cell has.
>
> In the pineal gland the melatonin is produced in the peroxisome, in the neurons dopamine and norepinephrine, etc. It is here, where mercury and other toxic metal attach and disable the cell from doing its work."
> - Dietrich Klinghardt, MD, PhD, Chelation: How to remove Mercury, Lead, & other Metals

That is all well and good, but what are the best sources of fish oil? Consuming large quantities of fish would be the logical choice, but knowing that many species contain high levels of mercury, doing so might actually cause further damage to the brain. For this reason, Omega-3 supplements are probably the best way to keep the body well-stocked with EPA and DHA.

When selecting an Omega-3 supplement, you need to make sure it is molecularly distilled and is high in both

DHA and EPA, especially DHA. Molecular distillation is a special process that removes all the toxins from the oil (including mercury), ensuring it is safe for human consumption. Avoid low-grade products. They often contain low levels of fatty acids and are filled with other oils and preservatives.

Final Advice: Sleep, Sweat and Stimulate

- Sufficient sleep is vital to keeping the body and the brain in good condition. Conversely, sleep deprivation impairs one's ability to think handle stress, maintain a healthy immune system and moderate one's emotions.

- Regular exercise is critically important for detoxification. It allows the evacuation of toxins through skin while improving the entire metabolism.

- Stimulate your brain: read, think, meditate and challenge it constantly.

In Conclusion

This article examines the ways to avoid harmful substances in everyday products and looks at a handful of all-natural ways to free the body from their poisonous grasp. In addition to providing us the necessary nutrients used by the body to evacuate toxins, the natural substances described in this article also help maintain general heath. Regularly consuming cilantro, garlic, turmeric and Omega-3 boosts the immune system, improves rational thinking and increases memory. The amazing properties of those simple ingredients are only now being (slowly) documented by science, but they have been used by cultures worldwide for centuries.

We are conditioned to treat ailments caused by artificial products with other artificial products, that, in turn, can cause other ailments. It is only by breaking this vicious circle that we can reclaim ownership of our brains and reach our fullest potential. So, today's a new day: Put down the cheeseburger-flavored Doritos … and change your life.

Irrational Consumerism (or The Few Companies Who Feed the World)

Not many people realize that most of the processed foods available on the market, whether they be in groceries or fast-food chains, all come from the same few companies. Even less people realize that these companies are major actors in elite organizations who decide health, social and economic policies around the world. We'll look at the big three companies who feed the world, their many brands and the tactics they undertake to make people crave their products.

If one were to carefully study the labels on packaged products in an average grocery store, one would probably notice that the same company names appear repeatedly: Nestlé, Kraft, General Mills and a few others. Many brands offering good ol' fashioned homemade or all-natural/organic foods are nothing more than subsidiaries of these few world-wide mega-companies. The major difference between the main brand and the subsidiaries is packaging and advertising, which are targeted to reach different markets. In order to preserve the carefully crafted image surrounding a product, connections to the mother company are often conveniently hidden. Imagine an advertisement for bottled water going like this: "Drink pure, clear, refreshing Aquafina water, bottled with care from remote natural sources in the Himalayas … BROUGHT TO YOU BY PEPSICO, THE MAKER OF TACO BELL AND CHEETOS MIGHTY ZINGERS!" That would probably spoil the healthy, natural image they are trying to create for the product.

That is the reason marketing and branding are the most vital part of the food industry. Each product must live in its own "world", separate from its mother company and similar products. Advertising is so powerful that two similar brands of cereal, made from the same basic ingredients, can be targeted to entirely different markets. For example, are Special K and Rice Krispies so different? From a strictly rational viewpoint, these products are nearly identical in shape, taste and ingredients. From an irrational (marketing) viewpoint however, they are in two different worlds. Advertisements for Rice Krispies revolve around colorful cartoon characters and played during Saturday morning kids' shows while Special K tends to show fit women doing yoga (or on their way to or from yoga). Rice Krispies boxes have games and toy giveaways, while Special K's box gives access to a "weight loss challenge" website. All of this is smoke and mirrors, however, because at the end of the line, whether you choose one, the other or pretty much any other cereal in the grocery store, you're eating the same thing and your money ends up at the same place.

The processed-food industry can be considered a true oligopoly. Together, the three leading food companies, Nestle, Kraft Foods and PepsiCo, achieve a dominant proportion of global processed-food sales. In fact, these three companies are often used as an example of "Rule of Three" in business schools, since they are a real-life example of a market being dominated by three gigantic actors. Their position as worldwide food providers has made these conglomerates extremely powerful, and they are represented in most elite organizations such as the Council of Foreign Relations. This not only allows them to provide their preferred policies on nutrition and health issues across the globe, but on economic, political and social issues as well. Such prominence also allows these companies to ensure their continued market dominance, through policy-making, access to insider information and the intimidation of potential competitors. If considered objectively, the oligopoly of major companies like these are a direct threat to free market theories.

Today, if a small food company were to create a new revolutionary product, it would find it difficult to obtain distribution without giving up its rights to one these conglomerates. In addition to dominating the shelves, the Big Three control most of the worldwide channels of distribution, to the point that up-and-coming companies cannot reach the consumers without dealing with them. The only way small business owners can avoid years of struggle and rejection to obtain shelf-space in supermarkets is to strike a licensing deal with one of the giants, where the owner cedes the ownership and the rights to the product in exchange for royalty checks (which are usually a small percentage of the sales). Each licensing deal consolidates these companies' position and eliminates threats from any potential competitor who creates game-changing products.

Here are the top three companies and a summary list of their multiple brands:

1- Nestlé

Nestlé is the world's largest food company. It has 6,000 brands, with a wide range of products across a number of markets including coffee, bottled water and other beverages, chocolate, ice cream, infant foods, performance and healthcare nutrition, seasonings, frozen and refrigerated foods, confectioneries and pet food. In 2009, consolidated sales were close to $120 billion USD and investments in research and development were $2.24 billion USD. The chairman of the company, Mr. Brabeck-Letmathe, is on the Board of Directors of Credit Suisse Group, L'Oréal and ExxonMobil. He is also a member of ERT (European Round Table of Industrialists) and a member of the Foundation Board of the World Economic Forum (an important actor in the push for a world government). Products sold by Nestlé include:

Cereals

Cinnamon Toast Crunch
Cheerios (outside US, Canada and Australia)
Cini Minis
Honey Nut Cheerios (outside US, Canada and Australia)
Oat Cheerios
Cookie Crisp
Golden Grahams
Honey Stars
Koko Krunch
Milo Cereals
Nestlé Corn Flakes
Nesquik
Shreddies
Shredded Wheat
Clusters
Trix

YOGURT

Munch Bunch
Ski

COFFEE

Bonka
Nescafé
Nespresso
Partner's Blend
Ricoffy
Ristretto
Ricoré
Sical
Tofa
Taster's Choice
Zoégas
Shrameet

WATER

Aberfoyle
Aqua D'Or
Aqua Pod
Acqua Panna
Al Manhal
Aquapod
Arrowhead
Buxton
Contrex
Deer Park
Hépar
Ice Mountain
Henniez
Korpi
Levissima
Nestlé Aquarel
Nestlé Vera
Ozarka
Perrier
Poland Spring
Powwow
Minere
Pure Life/Pureza Vital
Quézac
San Pellegrino
San Bernardo
Viladrau
Vittel
Zephyrhills

OTHER DRINKS

Nestea (Joint venture with Coca-Cola, Beverage Partners Worldwide)
Enviga (Joint venture with Coca-Cola, Beverage Partners Worldwide)
Milo
Carnation
Caro
Nesquik
Libby's
Growers Direct Organic Fruit Juices
Good Host
Juicy Juice
Ski up and go

SHELF-STABLE PRODUCTS

Bear Brand
Carnation
Christie
Coffee-Mate
Dancow
Gloria
Klim
La Lechera
Milkmaid
Nespray
Nestlé
Nesvita
Nestlé Omega Plus
Nido
Ninho
Svelty
Emswiss
Milo

ICE CREAM

Camy
Dreyer's
Edy's
Frisco
Häagen-Dazs (North America and the United Kingdom)
Mivvi

Nestlé
Nestlé Drumstick
Oreo (Canada)
Peters (Australia)
Push-Up
Schöller
Skinny Cow

INFANT FOODS

Alete
Alfare
Beba
Cérélac
FM 85
Gerber (the world's largest baby food company)
Good Start
Guigoz
Lactogen
Nan
NAN HA
NanSoy
Neslac
Nestlé
Nestogen
Nido
PreNan

PERFORMANCE NUTRITION

Musashi
Neston
Nesvita
PowerBar
Pria
Supligen

HEALTHCARE/NUTRITION

Boost
Carnation Instant Breakfast
Nutren
Peptamen
Glytrol
Crucial
Impact
Isosource
Fibersource

Diabetisource
Compleat
Optifast
Resource

SEASONINGS

Buitoni
Maggi
Carpathia
CHEF
Thomy
Winiary

FROZEN FOODS

Stouffer's
Lean Cuisine
Buitoni
Hot Pockets
Lean Pockets
Papa Guiseppi
Tombstone Pizza
Jack's Pizza
DiGiorno Pizza
California Pizza Kitchen Frozen

CHOCOLATE, CONFECTIONERIES AND BAKED GOODS

100 Grand Bar
Aero
After Eight
Allens
Animal Bar
Baby Ruth
Bertie Beetle (Australia)
Big Turk (Canada)
Black Magic
Boci (Hungary)
Blue Riband
Bono(Brazil)
Breakaway
Butterfinger
Butterfinger BB's
Butterfinger Crisp
Bon Pari (Czech Republic, Poland and Hungary)
Cailler
Caramac
Carlos V

Chips Ahoy! (Canada)
Coffee Crisp
Chunky
Drifter
Frigor
Galak/Milkybar
Goobers
Heaven
Hercules Bars (with Disney)
Icebreakers
Kit Kat (Hershey's in the US)
Lion
Matchmakers
Milky Bar
Mirage
Joff
Munchies
Nestlé Alpine White
Nestlé with Almonds
Nestlé Crunch
Nestlé Crunch Crisp
Nestlé Crunch with Caramel
Nestlé Crunch with Peanuts
Nestlé Crunch Pieces
Nestlé Crunch White
Nestlé Milk Chocolate
Nestlé Princessa
Nestlé Wonder Ball
Nips
Nuts (Europe)
Oh Henry (except US)
Peppermint Crisp
Perugina Baci
Polo
Quality Street
Raisinets
Rolo (Hershey's in the US)
Rowntrees

Fruit Pastilles
Jelly Tots
Pick & Mix
Randoms
Fruit Gums
Tooty Frooties
Juicy Jellies
Snowcaps

Smarties
Texan Bar
Toffee Crisp
Toll House cookies
Turtles
Walnut Whip
Violet Crumble
Yorkie
XXX mints
Petcare

Alpo
Beneful
Cat Chow
Dog Chow
Fancy Feast
Felix
Friskies
Go Cat
Butchers
Bakers
Winalot
Gourmet
Mighty Dog
Mon Petit
ONE
Pro Plan
Purina
Tidy Cats
Controversy

Nestlé has faced ongoing resistance around the world for its promotion of breast milk substitutes (infant formula), especially in third world countries. According to campaigners, Nestlé contributes to the unnecessary suffering and even deaths of babies, largely among the poor.

> *"Advocacy groups and charities have accused Nestlé of unethical methods of promoting infant formula over breast milk to poor mothers in developing countries. For example, IBFAN claim that Nestlé distributes free formula samples to hospitals and maternity wards; after leaving the hospital, the formula is no longer free, but because the supplementation has interfered with lactation, the family must continue to buy the formula. IBFAN also allege that Nestlé uses "humanitarian aid" to create markets, does not label its products in a language appropriate to the countries where they are sold, and offers gifts and sponsorship to influence health workers to promote its products. Nestlé denies these allegations."*
> - Wikipedia, "Nestlé Boycott"

2- Kraft Foods

A subsidiary of Philip Morris (the maker of Marlboro cigarettes). Kraft Foods is the largest confectionery, food, and beverage corporation headquartered in the United States. It markets many brands in more than 155 countries; eleven of its worldwide brands each earn more than $1 billion annually. Like Nestle, Kraft has consolidated its status in the food oligarchy by buying gigantic brands such as Nabisco (Oreos, Chips Ahoy, Fig Newtons, Ritz, etc.) and Cadbury (Ferrero Rocher, Dairy Milk, Caramilk, etc.).

Kraft's CEO Irene Blecker Rosenfeld was rated the "2nd most powerful woman in the world" by Forbes. Not surprising since most of the world consumes Kraft foods. Before joining Kraft, Rosenfeld was Chairman and Chief Executive Officer of Frito-Lay, a division of PepsiCo (another of the "Big Three"). Kraft's brands include:

Toblerone chocolate bars
A1 Steak Sauce
Ali Coffee
Arrowroot biscuits
Back to Nature
Baker's (chocolate)
Balance Bar
Better Cheddars
Boca Burger
Bonox
Breakstone's
BullsEye Barbecue Sauce

Café HAG
California Pizza Kitchen (grocery store items)
Calumet Baking Powder
Cameo (biscuits)
Capri Sun (juice drink)
Carte Noire
Cheesybite
Cheese Nips
Cheez Whiz

PepsiCo
Chips Ahoy! (cookies)
Christie (Canadian division of Nabisco)
Claussen (pickles)
Clight
Club Social (crackers)
Cool Whip (non-dairy whipped cream)
CornNuts (snack food)
Côte d'Or (Belgium)
Country Time (powdered drink mix)
Cracker Barrel
Crystal Light
Dairylea (Europe)
Delissio (Canada)
DiGiorno (pizza)
Easy Cheese
Fig Newtons
Fudgee-O (Canada)
General Foods International
Grape-Nuts (breakfast cereal)
Grey Poupon (mustard)
Handi-Snacks
Honey Maid
In-A-Biskit (Australia)
Jack's Pizza
Jacobs (Europe)
Jell-O (gelatin dessert)
Jet-Puffed Marshmallows
Kenco (United Kingdom)
Knox (gelatin)
Knudsen (dairy products)
Kool-Aid (flavored drink mix)
Kraft BBQ Sauce
Kraft Caramels
Kraft Macaroni and Cheese
Kraft Dinner (Canada)
Kraft Easymac
Kraft Mayo
Kraft Bagelfuls
Kraft Peanut Butter (Canada)
Kraft Singles (pasteurized prepared cheese product)
Kraft Sandwich Spread
Lefèvre-Utile
Lunchables
Maxwell House (coffee)
Miracle Whip (salad dressing spread)
Nabisco
Nabob (coffee) (Canada)
Naked Drinks
Nilla
Nutter Butter
Onko (coffee)
Oreo (cookie)
Oscar Mayer
Grated Parmesan cheese
Philadelphia cream cheese
Pigrolac
Planters
Polly-O (cheese)
Premium (a Nabisco brand of saltine crackers)
Pretzels
P'tit Québec
Prince Polo
Pure Kraft Salad Dressings
Ritz
Royal baking powder
Seven Seas (salad dressings)
Sanka (decaffeinated coffee)
Shake 'n Bake
Simmenthal (canned meat)
Snackabouts
SnackWells
South Beach Living
Starbucks (grocery store items)
Stove Top stuffing
Suchard
Taco Bell (grocery store items)
Tang
Tassimo (single-serve coffee machines using pods branded as T-Discs)

PepsiCo

PepsiCo Incorporated is a global Fortune 500 corporation headquartered in Purchase, Harrison, New York, with interests in the manufacturing, marketing and distribution of beverages, grain-based snack foods and other products. If you hadn't guessed it, its main product is Pepsi Cola, but soda pop is not the company's only product. In fact, a teenager with the munchies could easily leave a convenience store with three or four PepsiCo products without realizing it (or caring).

PepsiCo is a "Premium" member of the Council of Foreign Relation and of the Brookings institute, two of the most important organizations for the world's elite. The chairman and CEO of PepsiCo, Indra Nooyi, is part of the World Economic Forum. Within these organizations, executives from PepsiCo and other mega-corporations like Sony (the largest label in the music industry), Nike (the largest shoe seller in the world), Rockefeller Group International, and Lockheed Martin (the largest defense company in the world), work alongside various heads of state (including past US presidents), policy-makers (such as current US Secretary of State Hilary Rodham Clinton) and image makers (like Tom Brokaw and George Clooney), to develop political, social and economic opinions and recommendations affecting entire countries. The policies favored by these organizations are collectively steering the world towards a unified world government and a single world currency, in what is often referred as a "New World Order".

PepsiCo brands include:

Drinks:

AMP
Brisk
Mountain Dew
Ocean Spray
Mist
Aquafina
Lipton Ice Tea
MUG
Pepsi
Sobe
Gatorade
Tropicana
No Fear Energy Drink
Propel Enhanced Water
Starbucks (retail products)

Foods:

Lay's
Doritos
Tostitos
Cheetos
Fritos
Sun Chips
Baked!
Frito Lay Dips
Baken-Ets
Chester's Puffcorn
Cracker Jack
El Isleno Plantain Chips
Frti-Lay Peanuts
Funyuns
Gamesa

Grandma's
Matador
Maui Style Potato Chips
Miss Vickie's
Munchies
Munchos
Natural
Nut Harvest
Quaker
Rold Gold
Ruffles
Sabritones
Santitas
Smartfood
Spitz
Stacy's

Yep, even the good ol' trustworthy Quaker guy is part of PepsiCo.

THE SPIN-OFF COMPANY

PepsiCo also feeds millions daily through its spin-off company, Yum!, which owns restaurant chains including Pizza Hut, Taco Bell, KFC, Hot 'n Now, East Side Mario's, D'Angelo Sandwich Shops, Chevys Fresh Mex, California Pizza Kitchen and Stolichnaya.

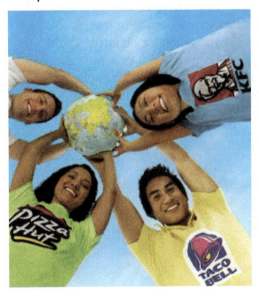

An odd picture from Yum!'s official website.

Many of the products listed above have existed for decades, some for over a century. What is the secret of such enduring success? First, the recipe has to be just right. As mentioned above, Nestlé spent more than $2 billion dollars in 2009 alone for research and development, which is mostly used to pay people in lab coats to create the most appealing, taste-bud satisfying, addicting and, of course, cost-effective products possible. The addictive properties of salt, fat, sugar and other chemicals are well known to the $2 billion-per-year researchers. Processed foods contain a carefully calculated mix of chemicals and additives that send "satisfying" signals to the brain, which the brain then continues to seek out in the form of cravings.

However, there are countless companies selling similar products. So in order to keep consumers coming back to their specific brand, corporations invest billions of dollars in the second secret of success: "brand loyalty" achieved through marketing and advertising.

In Conclusion

Why should one care about which company sells which product? Primarily, it is a question of health. Almost all of the hundreds of products cited in this article contain toxic ingredients, from excessive amounts of saturated fat to additives like MSG, High Fructose Corn Syrup (HFCS), mercury and/or aspartame. These substances, and many more like them, are poisonous to the body, the nervous system and the brain (as discussed in the article Dumbing Down Society: Food, Beverages and Meds). Processed foods are making the entire world fatter, sicker and dumber, even though only a few companies produce them. It is vital to know and recognize them … so you can avoid them. It is also important to recognize the basic marketing tactics that are being used to push consumers to buy processed foods.

The issue is much larger than individual health, however. To be aware of the companies selling your food is to be aware of important actors of the world elite. As the saying goes "control the food and you control the people". If you believe it is important to know the truth about the world's power structure, it is fundamental to know about these companies and understand their extensive reach throughout all areas of our global society. They might "only" sell food, but their power and position gives these conglomerates an active role in world governance, including economy, politics, law-making and even the military (who do you think supplies military mess halls?). The Big Three and globally dominant corporations like them are part of policy-setting "think tank" organizations such as the Council on Foreign Relations and the Bilderberg Group, which serve as the true motors behind global change. Should PepsiCo have a say in the invasion of a country such as Iran? Well, it does. And every time you buy a Pepsi or a bag of Doritos or jug of Tropicana, you are helping them become richer and more powerful. Luckily, however, there is an easy way to stop supporting these companies: Simply replace the processed products you buy from these companies with fresh foods bought from local businesses. You'll improve your health and your local economy, but most importantly, you'll also become the elite's worst nightmare: a rational consumer.

The Hidden Hand that Shaped History

Has the course of History been directed by a small group of people with common interests? The paintings and pictures of the great men of the past centuries reveal a common thread which links them together. Is it a coincidence that many of them hid one of their hands when posing for a portrait? It seems unlikely. We'll look at the Masonic origin of the "hidden hand" and the powerful men who used the sign in famous portraits.

> "Today's thinking toward a democratic world state is neither a new trend nor an accidental circumstance; the work of setting up the background of knowledge necessary to the establishing of enlightened democracy among all nations has been carried on for many hundreds of years by secret societies."
> - Manly P. Hall, Secret Destiny of America

Is there a hidden force behind the world events of the past centuries? Are the fall of European monarchies, the bringing forth of the Age of Enlightenment and our path towards a world democracy part of a great plan lead by a "hidden hand"? Before the advent of mass media, portraits depicting their leaders in majestic poses were the only artifacts people had. Do these portraits have an occult meaning?

One of those poses is the "hiding of the hand". I remember my history teacher trying to explain why Napoleon was often shown with a hand inside his shirt. The common explanation went along these lines:

> "Many theories have been presented as to why Napoleon is traditionally depicted with his hand in his waistcoat. Some of these theories include: he had a stomach ulcer, he was winding his watch, he had an itchy skin disease, in his era it was impolite to put your hands in your pockets, he had breast cancer, he had a deformed hand, he kept a perfumed sachet in his vest that he'd sniff surreptitiously, and that painters don't like to paint hands."
> - Tom Holmberg

Unless all the individuals discussed in this article had stomach ulcer or deformed hands, the gesture of hiding one's hand simply has to have a specific meaning. It does. Most of the people using this sign are proven (and often enthusiastic) members of the Freemasons. Considering the great importance of this gesture in Masonic rituals and the fact that all of the elite were either part of Freemasonry or knew of it, it is simply impossible that the recurrence of this sign could be the result of a coincidence. The "hidden hand" can, in fact, be found in the rituals of the Royal Arch Degree of Freemasonry and the world leaders that use this sign are subtly saying to other initiates of the order: "This is what I'm part of, this is what I believe in and this is what I'm working for".

The Royal Arch Degree

The Royal Arch Degree (the 13th degree of the Scottish Rite or the 7th degree of the York Rite) is also known as the Mason of the Secret. During this Degree, initiates are said to receive great Masonic truths.

> "The members of this Degree are denominated companions, and are "entitled to a full explanation of the mysteries of the Order"; whereas in the former Degrees they are recognized by the common, familiar appellation of brothers, and kept in a state of profound ignorance of the sublime secret which is disclosed in this Chapter. This accords with the custom of Pythagoras, who thus distinguished his pupils. After a probation of five years, as stated before, they were admitted into the presence of the

preceptor, called his companions, and permitted to converse with him freely. Previous to the expiration of that term he delivered his instructions to them from behind a screen"
- John Fellows, Fellows's Inquiry into the Origin, History, and Purport of Freemasonry

The Triple Tau.

"If we pass on to the Royal Arch, we receive a wonderful accession of knowledge, and find every thing made perfect; for this is the nec plus ultra of Masonry, and can never be exceeded by any human institution."
- George Oliver, Lectures on Freemasonry

It is during this degree that the initiate learns the sacred name of God.

"A Degree indescribably more august, sublime, and important than any which precede it, and is, in fact, the summit and perfection of ancient Masonry. It impresses upon our minds a belief in the being of a God, without beginning of days or end of years, the great and incomprehensible Alpha and Omega, and reminds us of the reverence which is due to His Holy NAME."
- George Oliver, Historical Landmarks

This holy name is Jahbulon, a combination of words meaning "god" in Syriac, Chaldaic and Egyptian.

"JEHOVAH. Of the varieties of this sacred name in use among the different nations of the earth, three particularly merit the attention of Royal Arch Masons:

1. JAH. This name of God is found in the 68th Psalm, v. 4.

2. BAAL OR BEL. This word signifies a lord, master, or possessor, and hence it was applied by many of the nations of the East to denote the Lord of all things, and the Master of the world.

3. ON. This was the name by which JEHOVAH was worshiped among the Egyptians."
- Malcolm C. Duncan, Duncan's Masonic Ritual and Monitor

The initiation ritual to this degree re-enacts the return to Jerusalem of three Most Excellent Masons who were held captive in Babylon. I won't go through the whole ceremony and symbolism but at one point, the initiate is asked to learn a secret password and a hand sign in order to go through a series of veils. The following image depicts the hand sign required to go through the second veil, as documented in Duncan's Masonic Ritual and Monitor:

"Master of Second Veil: "Three Most Excellent Masters you must have been, or thus far you could not have come; but farther you cannot go without my words, sign, and word of exhortation. My words are Shem, Japhet, and Adoniram; my sign is this: (thrusting his hand in his bosom); it is in imitation of one given by God to Moses, when He commanded him to thrust his hand into his bosom, and, taking it out, it became as leprous as snow. My word of exhortation is explanatory of this sign, and is found in the writings of Moses, viz., fourth chapter of Exodus":

"And the Lord said unto Moses, Put now thine hand into thy bosom. And he put his hand into his bosom; and when he took it out, behold, his hand was leprous as snow"
- Malcolm C. Duncan, Duncan's Masonic Ritual and Monitor

SIGN OF THE MASTER OF THE SECOND VEIL.

As stated above, this hand gesture is said to be inspired by Exodus 4:6. In this biblical verse, the heart ("bosom") stands for what we are, the hand for what we do. It can thus be interpreted as : What we are is what we ultimately do. The symbolic significance of this gesture might explain the reason why it is so widely used by famous Masons. The hidden hand lets the other initiates know that the individual depicted is part of this secret Brotherhood and that his actions were inspired by the Masonic philosophy and beliefs. Furthermore, the hand that executes the actions is hidden behind cloth, which can symbolically refer to covert nature of the Mason's actions. Here are some of the famous men who used this hand signal.

Napoleon Bonaparte

Napoleon Bonaparte (1769-1821) was a military and political leader of France whose actions shaped European politics in the early 19th century. He was initiated into Army Philadelphe Lodge in 1798. His brothers, Joseph, Lucian, Louis and Jerome, were also Freemasons. Five of the six members of Napoleon's Grand Council of the Empire were Freemasons, as were six of the nine Imperial Officers and 22 of the 30 Marshals of France. Bonaparte's association with Masonry has always been played down in historical records. Masonic researcher J.E.S. Tuckett addresses the situation:

"It is strange that evidence in favor of the Great Napoleon's membership of the Masonic Brotherhood has never been examined in detail, for the matter is surely one of interest, and – seeing the

remarkable part that remarkable men played in the affairs of Europe, at a time when Continental Freemasonry was struggling out of chaos into regular order – it cannot be without an important bearing upon Masonic history"

Napoleon in his study at the Tuileries, 1812

In his essay on Napoleon and Masonry, Tuckett claims:

"There is incontestable evidence that Napoleon was acquainted with the nature, aims and organization of Freemasonry: that he approved of and made use of it to further his own ends"
- J.E.S. Tuckett, Napoleon I and Freemasonry

Napoleon was also said to be aided by occult powers. In 1813 he was defeated at Leipzip and behind him was a "Cabinet of Curiosities" in which a Prussian officer discovered his Book of Fate and Oraculum. Originally this Oraculum was discovered in one of the Royal tombs of Egypt during a French military expedition of 1801. The emperor ordered the manuscript to be translated by a famous German scholar and antiquarian. From that time onward, the Oraculum was one of Napoleon's most treasured possessions. He consulted it on many occasions and it is said to have "formed a stimulus to his most speculative and most successful enterprises."

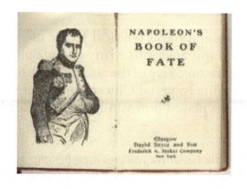

Karl Marx

Karl Marx is known today to be the founder of modern Communism. Despite being denied by some Masons, Marx is said to have been a 32nd degree Grand Orient Freemason. Marx became the spokesman of the atheist and socialist movement of Europe. He planned the replacement of monarchies with socialist republics, with the next step conversion to communist republics.

George Washington

George Washington was one of the Founding Fathers of the United States and is considered to be the "most important American Mason". Charles Willson Pealed produced this painting when Washington was 52 years old. Notice the position of Washington's feet: they form an oblong square. The position of the feet are of utmost importance in Masonic symbolism.

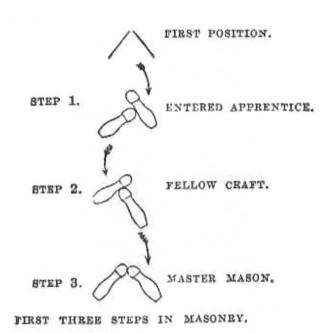

FIRST THREE STEPS IN MASONRY.

Wolfgang Amadeus Mozart

Wolfgang Amadeus Mozart is considered to be one of the most prolific and influential composers of music ever. He also was a Freemason and was initiated in the Austrian lodge Zur Zur Wohltatigkeit on Dec. 14th 1784. Mozart's creations often incorporated important Masonic elements. The Magic Flute opera was mainly based on Masonic principles.

> *"The music of the Freemasons contained musical phrases and forms that held specific semiotic meanings. For example, the Masonic initiation ceremony began with the candidate knocking three times at the door to ask admittance. This is expressed musically as a dotted figure. This figure appears in*

Mozart's opera The Magic Flute in the overture, suggesting the opening of the Masonic initiation."
- Katherine Thompson, The Masonic Thread in Mozart

The musical progression of The Magic Flute was based on the Golden Ratio (1,6180…), the proportion of everything that is considered divine by Mystery Schools.

Here are compositions created by Mozart for use in Masonic lodges:

- Lied (song) "Gesellenreise, for use at installation of new journeymen"
- Cantata for tenor and male chorus Die Maurerfreude ("The Mason's Joy")
- The Masonic Funeral Music (Maurerische Trauermusik)
- Two songs to celebrate the opening of "Zur Neugekrönten Hoffnung"
- Cantata for tenor and piano, Die ihr die unermesslichen Weltalls Schöpfer ehrt
- The Little Masonic Cantata (Kleine Freimaurer-Kantate) entitled Laut verkünde unsre Freude, for soloists, male chorus, and orchestra

Marquis de Lafayette

Marquis de Lafayette was a 33rd degree Freemason. According to Willam R. Denslow's 10,000 Famous Freemasons, Lafayette was a French military officer who was a general in the American Revolutionary War and a leader of the Garde Nationale during the bloody French Revolution. Lafayette was also made an honorary Grand Commander of the Supreme Council of New York. More than 75 Masonic bodies in the U.S. have been named after him, including 39 lodges, 18 chapters, 4 councils, 4 commanderies, and 7 Scottish rite bodies.

Salomon Rothschild

Salomon Rothschild was the founder of the Viennese branch of the prominent Mayer Amschel Rothschild family. The most powerful family in the world has greatly influenced the policies of Germany, France, Italy and Austria. The Rothschilds are also the main players behind the creation of Zionism and the state of Israel.

The power of the Rothschilds went way beyond the confines of the Masonic lodge. They are said to be part of the 13 "Illuminati Bloodlines". An analysis of the recently built Supreme Court of Israel (see article here) confirms the Rothschild's embrace of Masonic symbolism.

Simon Bolivar

Known as "El Libertador" (the Liberator), Bolivar is considered to be the "George Washington of South America". He joined Freemasonry in Cadiz, Spain, received the Scottish Rite degrees in Paris and was knighted in a Commandery of Knights Templar in France in 1807. Bolivar founded and served as master of Protectora de las Vertudes Lodge No. 1 in Venezuela. The country of Bolivia is named after him. Bolivar also served as the president of Colombia, Peru and Bolivia in the 1820's. He belonged to the Order and Liberty Lodge No. 2 in Peru.

Notice in the image above the position of his feet (oblong square) and the checkerboard pattern of the floor, also Masonic. His stance might have been inspired by the Knights of Christian Mark Degree as depicted in Richardson's Monitor of Freemasonry.

In Conclusion

As seen above, thee leaders using the "hidden hand" gesture had a great influence on world history and many were confirmed Masons. This gesture is an obvious yet widely overlooked detail which hints at the leader's embrace of occult philosophy. By understanding this fact and by recognizing the IMMENSE influence these leaders had on the course of History, we can begin to realize the hidden force which is currently steering the world toward international democracy.

Members of these brotherhoods might have maintained different opinions and even adhered to different factions (communism vs. capitalism), but the fundamental philosophy, beliefs and ultimate goals are still the same: the coming of an "Age of Reason and Enlightenment". Of course, any serious researcher is already aware of the role of Masonry in the unfolding of world history. The "hidden hand" gesture, so often used by historical figures is simply the outward expression of this little known fact. As Confucius said, "Signs and symbols rule the world, not words nor laws." These people's words and policies will eventually be twisted and forgotten, but their image will remain for the ages.

Top 10 Most Sinister PSYOPS Mission Patches

Mission patches are used by military and space organizations to identify, symbolize and describe a mission's objectives and its crew. This tradition is also observed in the shady world of PSYOPS where each secret mission of the Pentagon gets its patch. These patches offer a rare glimpse into the Pentagon's secret operations and the symbolism on them is rather striking: ominous and cryptic phrases, dark occult symbolism, references to secret societies, and sometimes even a rather dark sense of humor. Here's the top 10 most sinister PSYOPS patches.

In 1965, NASA began using cloth patches to identify each of its missions and to symbolize the missions' objectives and their crew. Each rocket launch has therefore a patch designed by crew members and in collaboration with the official design team. The patches are then proudly displayed on equipment and worn by NASA astronauts and other personnel affiliated with a particular manned or unmanned space mission.

Various NASA mission patches

Since then, other organizations involved in space travel and secret operations began using mission patches, including those that specialize in PSYOPS (psychological warfare): the CIA, the Department of Defense and the National Reconnaissance Office (NRO). What does space travel have to do with psychological warfare? Spy satellites. Since 1960, the NRO (whose existence was only declassified in 1992) has launched dozens of secret spy satellites into space, collecting an incredible amount of information on the United States' friends, enemies and citizens.

As it is nearly impossible to obtain information regarding these highly classified endeavours, mission patches offer a rare glimpse into the world of PSYOPS. Even if one is not well-versed in symbolism, it is easy to perceive a sinister "vibe" emanating from the patch designs. Laced with strange symbols, ominous creatures, obscure Latin phrases and even dark humor, these patches reflect the mindstate of those wearing the patches.

The trailblazer in this area of research is Trevor Paglen, who, in 2008, published the book "I Could Tell You But Then You Would Have to be Destroyed by Me: Emblems from the Pentagon's Black World". By the means of hundreds of Freedom of Information requests, he obtained and analyzed forty mission patches. From the book reviews:

> "The iconography of the United States military. Not the mainstream military, with its bars and rib-

bons and medals, but the secret or 'black projects' world, which may or may not involve contacting aliens, building undetectable spy aircraft, and experimenting with explosives that could make atomic bombs look like firecrackers. Here, mysterious characters and cryptic symbols hint at intrigue much deeper than rank, company, and unit."
—UTNE Reader

"Of course, issuing patches for a covert operation sounds like a joke ... but truth be told, these days everything is branded. Military symbols are frequently replete with heraldic imagery—some rooted in history, others based on contemporary popular arts that feature comic characters—but these enigmatic dark-op images, in some cases probably designed by the participants themselves, are more personal, and also more disturbing, than most."
—Steven Heller, The New York Times Book Review

Since the release of this book, new mission patches have been released that are as strange and cryptic as their predecessors. If these patches are meant to symbolize "the values of the crew and the objectives of the mission", perhaps we should be a little concerned. Here are the top 10 most sinister mission patches:

#10 – Alien Face

TENCAP is an acronym for "Tactical Exploitation of National Capabilities" and is a collection of programs involving the cutting edge of warfare.

"The purpose of the AF TENCAP program is to exploit the current and future potential of existing national, commercial, and civil space systems and national air-breathing systems, and to provide these capabilities to the warfighter as rapidly as possible."
- Federation of American Scientists, Air Force Tactical Exploitation of National Capabilities

In PSYOPS, "Special" almost invariably means "black" or highly classified. Does the "highly classified part" of the mission have something to do with the fact that the badge bears the face of an alien? The saying at the bottom does not help: The phrase "Oderint Dum Metuant" is usually associated with Caligula, the first-century Roman emperor whose name became synonymous with depravity, madness, and tyranny. It translates as "Let them hate so long as they fear." Right.

#9 All Your Base Are Belong to Us

A giant angry dragon clutching the planet, bringing destruction from space. That's a nice way to symbolize space missions. In PSYOPS symbolism, dragons typically represent signals-intelligence satellite launches; the dragons' wing patterns symbolize the satellites' massive gold-foil dish antennae meant to collect all types of information from earth. The phrase "Omnis Vestri Substructio Es Servus Ad Nobis" can loosely be translated to "All your base are servant to us". This phrase does not make much sense, except that it vaguely states that the world is owned by those who made that patch. But this phrase is also reminiscent of a geeky 2002 Internet meme based on a poor translation in an old-school Sega game.

The biggest internet meme of 2002, a badly translated Sega game.

This allusion to popular culture is quite funny yet disturbing … I'm pretty sure they truly believe that all our base are belong to them.

#8 Hymn to Pan.

The PAN satellite was launched in September 2009 and is so top-secret that no military or governmental organization claimed to have built it.

> "A United Launch Alliance Atlas V rocket has launched with PAN, a classified satellite which will be operated by the US Government. The launch was on time, at the start of a two hour, nine minute launch window which opened at 21:35 GMT (17:35 local time). Unusually for an American government satellite, the agency responsible for operating the spacecraft has not been disclosed."
> - Nasa Space Flight

According to the patch, PAN stands for "Palladium at Night", Palladium being a silvery-white metallic element that is probably present in the satellite. The mission is so secret, however, that it is jokingly said that the name PAN actually stands for "Pick a Name" (notice the subtle question mark underneath the rocket on the patch).

PAN is also the name of an ancient horned god important in occultism and that has a strange link with the history of rocket science in the United States.

The ancient god Pan, a nature deity with phallic attributes. Is it me or is the PAN mission patch also rather phallic?

Jack Parsons, a pioneer in American space propulsion who is often credited for having "propelled" the United States into the space age (a crater of the moon is named in his honor), was also a notorious occultist. He was a prominent member of the Ordo Templi Orienti (the O.T.O.), an occult secret society popularized by Aleister Crowley. Seeing no separation between his professional and his occult work, Parsons was known to chant Crowley's poem entitled Hymn to Pan before each test rocket launch.

> "Parsons would dance and chant poetry—most notably Crowley's "Hymn to Pan"—before rocket tests."
> - Goeffrey Landis, The Three Rocketeers

Is Pan still invoked during rocket launches?

#7 Supra Summus

This is a patch for a NRO spy-satellite launch. Those familiar with this site will probably recognize this Illuminati 101 symbolism: An unfinished pyramid topped by the All-Seeing Eye. This All-Seeing Eye requires help: it needs spy satellites to be even more all-seeing.

"LMA" at the bottom right most likely refers to Lockheed Martin Aerospace, which is the ultimate Big Brother mega-company working with the CIA, NRO, NSA and IRS.

Above the All-Seeing Eye is written "Supra Summus", which can be translated to "Most Superior and Highest", which, if nothing else, indicates a healthy level of self-esteem.

Other NRO spy-satellite launches have also used similar designs.

#6 Two Faced Shadow Guy

The 23rd Space Operations Squadron (23 SOPS) is a United States Air Force unit located at New Boston Air Force Station in New Hampshire. The patch of this mission features a creepy-looking figure in a creepy hood looking over the earth with creepy eyes, staring creepily at the American continent. However, that is not the creepiest thing in this patch. If you look closely at the contour of the black face, you'll see another face, with pointy nose and pointy ears, looking left. Who is this creepier dude within an already creepy dude? And what's up with all the layers of creepy?

The saying "Semper Vigilans" means "Always Vigilant". At least I can relate to that. But in the context of this patch, it is definitely creepy.

#5 The Grid

Are you thinking of selling your condo and your Prius in order to leave everything and "go off the grid"? Try it and this knight might slash your head off. It would probably be useless anyhow. Look closely at this patch: there is no "off the grid". This patch actually depicts the "information grid" those crazy conspiracy theorists keep rambling about, complete with nodes at the intersections.

Defenders of the Domain is a subgroup of the NSA Information Assurance group and is comprised of individuals "who are on the front lines in developing the strategy, the concepts, the planning and the technical implementation in the Information Assurance domain. They are the true leaders in the world of Cybersecurity." In other words, they monitor the cyberspace using the latest technologies.

The man with the sword is in the distinct dress of a Knight Templar, this ancient group of Crusaders that became an occult secret society. The Knight represents the descendants of the Templars, the modern Illuminatus.

#4 NRO Snakes

This is another mysterious patch of the NRO. The program associated with this patch is totally unknown. All we know is that it is represented by three menacing vipers wrapped around the the earth, making us all warm and fuzzy inside. The Latin inscription "Nunquam Ante Numquam Iterum" translates to "Never before, never again." What never happened before and will never happen again? We may never know.

#3 I Could Tell You…

You know that a mission is top-secret when not even an obscure symbol can be used to represent it. This patch was designed as a generic insignia for "black" projects conducted by the Navy's Air Test and Evaluation Squadron Four. The Latin phrase "Si Ego Certiorem Faciam … Mihi Tu Delendus Eris" is roughly translated to "I could tell you … but then I'd have to kill you". That is cliché phrase, but considering these are the people who actually created it, they probably don't think it is corny. In fact, they're probably dead serious about it.

Furthermore, there is a twist on the phrase. According to Paglen, the Latin phrase is worded in a peculiar way in order to refer to Greek and Roman texts.

> "The Latin phrase Si Ego Certiorem Faciam … Mihi Tu Delendus Eris roughly translates into a cliché commonly heard in the vicinity of "black" programs: "I could tell you, but then I'd have to kill you."
>
> But the phrasing here is unusual because it is written in the passive voice: a more accurate translation of the Latin would be "I could tell you, but then you would have to be destroyed by me." By employing the passive voice, the patch's designer makes two references that would not exist in other phrasings. The first reference is to the Greek god of Chaos, Eris, about whom Homer wrote in Book Four of the Iliad: "[Eris] whose wrath is relentless … is the sister and companion of murderous Ares, she who is only a little thing at the first, but thereafter grows until she strides on the earth with her head striking heaven. She then hurled down bitterness equally between both sides as she walked through the onslaught making men's pain heavier."
>
> The passive phrasing of the Latin also echoes the words of the second-century BCE Roman senator Cato the Elder, who roamed the Senate repeating the words Carthago delenda est—"Carthage must be destroyed." In 149 BCE, Cato got his way and Rome attacked the North African city, located near present-day Tunis. Three years after beginning their assault, the Roman army overran Carthage, tore down its walls, and sold its inhabitants into slavery. After the Roman Senate declared that no one would ever again live where the city had stood, legend holds that Rome salted the earth around the city in order to ensure that Carthage would remain a wasteland."
> - Trevor Paglen, Shades of Black

So the badge does not contain a simple death threat: it also alludes to a "wrath from above" of mythological proportions, turning your city into a wasteland for generations to come. Now that's a threat.

#2 Get Your Kicks on 66

The Minotaur program is composed of top-secret NRO spy-satellite launching missions. Minotaurs are bull-headed creatures from Greek mythology that are always angry, violent and merciless. Minotaurs bear many resemblances to the Middle-Eastern deity Molech, a bull-headed god with the body of a man to whom child sacrifices were made.

Molech

n this patch for NROL-66, the red Minotaur (as if hailing directly from hell) is holding a street sign of the mythical route 66. It is rather difficult not to see an allusion to the devil (who is often portrayed in red) and the number 666.

Furthermore, according to some occult researchers, route 66 was originally laid out to become a sort of "occult pilgrimage".

> *"The famous old American highway "Route 66" was laid out by Freemasons with the apparent intention of sending masses of automobile riders into a self-processing occult "trip."*
>
> *Route 66 began at the Buckingham Fountain in Chicago, near the site of the University of Chicago's collection of Aztec ritual incunabula. It ended in Barstow, California in the Mohave desert, which is for the Freemasons, the cosmic graveyard of the West, the final destiny of Anubis, the celestial jackal, otherwise known as Sirius (see Giorgio de Santillana and Hertha Von Dechend, Hamlet's Mill: An Essay on Myth and th Frame of Time, p. 358).*
>
> *If this version of Route 66 smacks of some medieval pilgrimage made more appropriately on a camel than by car, it is for good reason. Most of Route 66 was based on a road forged in 1857 by Lt. Edward Beale and his caravan of the U.S. Camel Corps."*
> - Michael A. Hoffman II, Secret Societies and Psychological Warfare

So who is really getting their kicks on Route 66?

#1 The Devil You Know

This patch for NROL-49 depicts a phoenix rising from the flames with the flag of the United States in the background. The Latin words "Melior Diabolus Quem Scies" roughly translates to mean "The Devil You Know," as in the phrase "Better the devil you know than the devil you don't know". Cryptic. According to NASA, this saying refers to the return of the use of an old system after attempting to use a new one, which had resulted in failure.

> "The mission patch for NRO L-49 shows a phoenix rising out of a fire, with the words "melior diabolus quem scies", which translate into English as "better the devil you know", indicating the return to the older system following the failure of the attempt to replace it."
> - www.nasaspaceflight.com, Delta IV Heavy launches on debut West Coast launch with NRO L-49

It is a rather odd choice of words for a governmental agency, but definitely on-par with this whole sinister, hellish theme going on with PSYOPS patches.

Another patch related to NRO-49 depicts the satellite as a winged fiery being (referred to by NASA as a devil named Betty) who is holding a trident and a wrench.

"An image of a devil features on the launch patch. The old tradition of giving rockets personal names

also appears to have been revived; Delta 352 seems to have been named "Betty", and the Atlas V that launched from Vandenberg last year was named 'Gladys'."
- Ibid.

The patch shows the moon (or a comet?) partially covering the earth. If you look closely, there are letters in the detail of the grey astral body. What do they refer to? At the bottom of the patch, the Latin phrase is also enigmatic: "Primoris Gravis Ex Occasus". Primoris means "First", Gravis stands for "important, heavy or serious" and Occasus means "setting of the sun, the West, or fall". In other words, I don't know what it means. "First heavy setting of the sun"? "The most important thing after the sunset"? "First serious fall"? Regardless of the exact meaning, there seems to be an emphasis on the concept of darkness. Betty is pure darkness wrapped in flames and is partially covering the sun. There is a grey celestial body moving towards the earth ... and we're still talking about a spy-satellite. Okay.

Honorable Mentions

There are many other patches giving a glimpse in the somehow twisted world of PSYOPS:

Wizards controlling the earth through magic is a recurring theme in PSYOPS patches. Is magick still a part of rocket launching like in the times of Jack Parsons and the O.T.O.?

 What do the letters at the bottom mean? None of your f***ing business. No, I'm not being rude...that's what the letters stand for.

 Another NRO patch, one that pretty much sums up the meaning of all of the above. The spy-satellite is symbolized by an angry dragon clutching the entire planet with its four claws holding a diamond in its tail. It does not seem to preoccupied with our privacy and other petty things like that.

In Conclusion

Although it isn't possible to know exact meaning of the symbols found in these mission patches, they still provide a rare insider's look at the philosophy, the mind state and the background of the organizations creating them. Sorcerers controlling the earth, vipers surrounding the earth, angry dragons clutching the earth … this is how they perceive themselves and their work. My question is: Should we maybe be a little concerned? One could argue that these patches are meant to be menacing to America's enemies. This could be true, but most satellites launched by the NRO are meant to spy on North America, hence the emphasis on the continent in many of these patches.

One thing is certain, mission patches are the most honest descriptions we have of these secret missions. Since most of the patches were not intended for mass exposure, they are devoid of public relations sugar-coating. The patches do not talk about "bringing democracy and the light of freedom to the world"… they show the world in chains and in flames, controlled by dragons and sorcerers, and their words threaten death and destruction.

The occult symbolism illustrated in these patches is also reminder that these organizations have relations to secret societies and are "in the know". And those who are not in the know, the uninitiated masses, the profane, are not welcome.

 "Procul Este Profani": "Keep your distance, you who are uninitiated."

Vigilant Reports

The World of Mind Control Through the Eyes of an Artist with 13 Alter Personas

Kim Noble is a rare occurrence: a trauma-based mind control survivor with over 13 alter personas who don't know each other but who all paint. She has suffered DID and MPD (dissociative identity disorder and multiple personality disorder) for most of her life, as a result of an extremely traumatic childhood. Each one of her alters paints with a personal and distinctive style but they all have one thing in common: they reveal the dark world of mind control programming, from its horrific techniques to its symbolism. We'll look at the works of this unique artist who reveals a world that is totally hidden from the masses.

Many articles on this site point out the presence of mind control symbolism in popular culture. Photo shoots, music videos and movies often glamorize and trivialize mind control and its symbolism by associating it with famous stars and trendy happenings. The fact however remains that these references celebrate one of the most abominable practices known to man: trauma based mind control, also called Monarch programming. Originating from the secret CIA project called MK-Ultra, Monarch programming subjects its victims to some of the most sadistic tortures conceivable.

The works of Kim Noble vividly document the life of a mind control slave through the eyes of 13 alter personas. While a few of these alters paint peaceful landscapes and nature scenes, most of them depict horrific aspects of mind control such as physical torture, electroshock, violent sexual abuse, dehumanization and dark occult rituals. The stories told by these paintings are almost too much to bear, yet they likely actually happened to Kim Noble as they precisely reflect accounts of other Monarch survivors. Looking at the works of Kim Noble not only reveals gritty details of an abominable practice carried on by "elite" organizations, it reveals the symbolism that is also thrown in our faces on a daily basis through corporate-owned mass media. Let's look at the life and works of Kim Noble.

Who Is Kim Noble?

I have the feeling that Kim Noble herself would have trouble answering this question. Here's the biography found on her official website.

> "Kim Noble is a woman who, from the age of 14 years, spent 20 years in and out of hospital until she made contact with Dr Valerie Sinason and Dr Rob Hale at the Tavistock and Portman Clinics. In 1995 she began therapy and was diagnosed with Dissociative Identity Disorder (originally named multiple personality disorder). D.I.D is a creative way to cope with unbearable pain. The main personality splits into several parts with dissociative or amnesic barriers between them. It is a controversial disorder but Kim has had extensive tests over 2 years by leading psychology professor at UCL, John Morton, who has established there is no memory between the personalities and that she has the misfortune of representing the British gold standard over genuine dissociation.
>
> Having no formal art training, Kim and 13 of her personalities (alters) became interested in painting in 2004 after spending a short time with an art therapist. These 12 artists each have their own distinctive style, colours and themes, ranging from solitary desert scenes to sea scenes to abstracts, collages, and paintings with traumatic content. Many alters are unaware that they share a body with other artists.
>
> What is remarkable to all is both the quality of their work and the speed of their progress. Within five years of starting to paint they have already had seventeen successful solo exhibitions and participated in an equal number of group exhibitions. Kim was also the first Artist in Residence at Springfield University Hospital in Tooting, South West London."
> - Kim Noble's Official Website (kimnoble.com)

Despite the fact that she has to live with 13 alter personas – who randomly take control of her body – Kim Noble is fortunate enough to be living a relatively normal life. The fact that the programming stopped at a young age have helped her become "well-adjusted". She has a teenage daughter named Aimee, who was mostly raised by the motherly alter named Bonny.

In the past few years, Kim Noble enjoyed some mainstream exposure and was featured in national newspapers such as The Telegraph, The Guardian, The Independent and several others. She even appeared at the Oprah Show, where she was interviewed and was shown switching personas. As you might expect from mainstream media, the coverage of Noble's condition was extremely superficial and focused on exploiting the "freak" aspect of her condition for shock value. The true cause of her condition, trauma-based mind control, which is extensively described in her works, is almost never mentioned.

Although most articles and interviews about Noble "applauded" her courage and whatnot, none of them dared discussing the core message of her work and the system that it describes. Many of Noble's paintings depict terrible scenes of organized, institutionalized and systematic violence, torture, and child abuse combined with elaborate occult symbolism. It is obvious that the trauma Noble went through was not caused by a single sadistic father but by an organized entity that held many children. The only article I found delving into the mind control aspect of Noble's work was The Art of Dissociation from the excellent website Pseudo-Occult Media. However, to most newspapers, Noble's work is nothing more than an example of "outsider art" (a term popularized by trendy art-world douches to identify art created by people with mental problems). Most observers are fascinated by the fact that each one of Noble's alters paint with a distinctive style, but it's as easy to recognize that her collective works describe her past as a Monarch programming victim.

The "real" Kim Noble does not recall any of the abuse she suffered – her several of her alters do, however, and they express all of it in their paintings.

> "To all intents and purposes, each of Kim's personalities is an artist in their own right: Patricia paints the solitary desert landscapes, Bonny's pictures often feature robotic dancing figures or "frieze people", Suzy repeatedly paints a kneeling mother, Judy's canvasses are large, conceptual pieces while

Ria's work reveals deeply traumatic events involving children.

These disturbing images are at the root of Kim's extraordinary condition; DID is a creative mental survival strategy whereby the personality splits at a young age due to severe and chronic trauma. The number of personalities that exist often depends on how long the trauma lasts. But Kim herself has no memory of being abused as a child; she has been protected over the years by her alters.

"I've been told I was abused and to me at this moment in time, it's too much. It goes in one ear and out the other. It's no good retraumatising me and telling me something I don't want to know – in any case, there would be a switch."

Kim has good reason to fear learning about her past as it's possible that if she acquires too much information, she won't be able to cope and will "disappear". It's happened twice before. (omega)

This is where it gets really weird – for Kim isn't Kim at all. The personality I am interviewing is Patricia and it is she who manages her and Aimee's lives, but Patricia wasn't always the dominant personality. Before Patricia took over, Bonny held the fort and two years previous to Bonny, it was Hayley.

Kim watches me closely as she explains: "You see Kim is just the 'house', the body. There isn't a 'Kim' at all – she has completely split. So we answer to the name Kim but really I am Patricia. When people call us 'Kim' I suppose many of us just assume it's a nickname, but once people know you they don't use your name very often in conversation."

Of the 20 or so personalities who share "Kim", some are easily identifiable: there is 15-year-old Judy who is anorexic and bulimic, maternal Bonny, religious Salome, depressed Ken, sensible Hayley, Dawn, Patricia and elective mute MJ. There are also a handful of children "frozen" in time. A few of the alters know about the DID but many are unaware – or refuse to accept it.

"Judy doesn't believe in the DID," explains Kim. "She's only a teenager and she calls our therapist a nutter when she tries to explain it to her. She's so young, she doesn't even think Aimee is her daughter. She knows about me and she thinks that I'm a terrible mother because I'm always leaving Aimee. To her, it's totally normal to keep coming and going. She probably thinks that you come and go too."

There are certain "triggers" that can force a change and gradually Kim has learnt what they are in order to avoid them – but it doesn't stop her switching up to three or four times a day."
- The Independent, "Kim Noble, a Woman Divided"

Let's look at some of the works created by some of Kim Noble's alters as they each provide a different look at the shady world of Monarch programming. Regular readers of the Vigilant Citizen might realize that a lot of the symbolism found in Noble's paintings are also found in popular culture.

Warning: Several of these paintings depict disturbing scenes which might not be suitable for young or sensitive readers.

Bonny

Bonny, who was Kim's "dominant" alter for a few years, is a warm and motherly figure. Most of her paintings portray humans as mechanical robots – which is one of the ways one could describe a mind control slave. Other pieces are more directly related to Monarch programming such as this one, aptly titled "I'm Just Another Personality".

"I'm Just Another Personality" visually represents the splitting of the subject in several alters. The central figure, or the core personality has become simply "another personality". It is blindfolded, representing the victims total blindness to its condition.

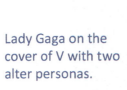

Lady Gaga on the cover of V with two alter personas.

Another piece made by Bonny, ironically named I-Test, symbolically depicts the reality of a mind control slave.

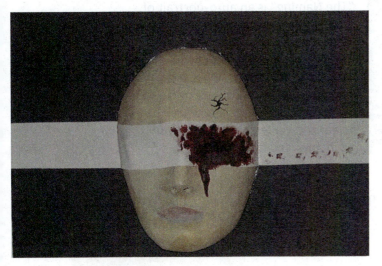

"I-Test" portrays a blank, emotionless face with blindfolded eyes. The skull is cracked, representing the fracturing of the psyche. One of the eyes is bloody and we can assume that it has been poked out. The symbol of the missing/hidden eye is extremely important in the world of Monarch mind control. It symbolically represents the loss of half of victim's vision of the world - the other half being "taken out" and controlled by the handlers. In occult symbolism, the emphasis on one eye can refer to the Eye of Horus, the All-Seeing Eye, a symbol of the occult elite.

A promotional t-shirt of the movie Sucker Punch (which was all about Monarch Programming - see "Sucker Punch" or How to Make Monarch Mind Control Sexy) featuring a bloodied eye.

A cracked face on a promotional poster of Black Swan - another movie with heavy mind control elements.

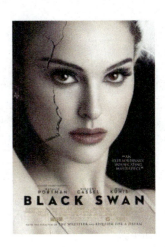

Golden Dawn

Golden Dawn is the alter that saw the birth her daughter Aimee. However, Dawn believes that Aimee is still a baby and does not recognize the teenage girl that lives with her. The name "Golden Dawn" has a heavy occult connotation as it is the name of an important and powerful secret society that taught Hermetic Kabbalah, astrology, occult tarot, geomancy, and alchemy to its initiates. It held within its ranks prominent occultists such as Arthur Edward Waite and Aleister Crowley. The process of Monarch mind control combines state-of-the-art "science" (if you can call torture "science") with ancient occultism, whether it be in hermetic theories, kabbalistic symbolism or invocation rituals. It is therefore no surprise that she was given this occult-inspired name.

Her piece entitled "The Naming" visually depicts the process of creating and naming a new alter.

"The Naming" is an auto-portrait of Kim with one eye that was removed from the face and placed above her, bloody, which conveys the violent nature of the process. Once again, mind control is symbolized by the loss of an eye which appears to have been replaced by a text/poem that was probably used to program her.

Most of Dawn's other paintings feature a limbless, mannequin-like figures who are subjected to various methods of torture.

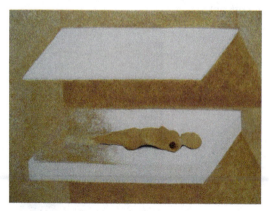

"Armless Goddess" portrays a hopelessly powerless figure, ironically referred to as goddess.

"Armed Goddess" depicts another traumatic torture scene.

Key

The alter "Key" appears to have a profound understanding of the process of mind control and its underlying occult aspect. The name "Key" might refer to terms such as the "Key of the Mysteries" or "Solomon's Key" as she seemed to have been programmed to understand some of the occult concepts utilized in mind control. Most this alter's works describe the programming process as a kabbalistic "Great Work", with the Tree of Life (the main symbol of the Kaballah) as the main object of focus.

"It Happens" is an extremely detailed work describing the several layers of programming required to traumatize and program a mind control victim. The title "It Happens" is a disabused way of saying that … all of this really happened.

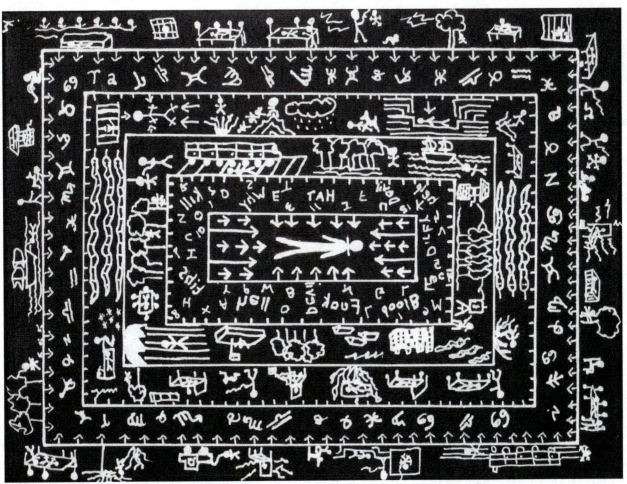

"It Happens" is comprised of overlapping layers surrounding a central figure: a helpless person strapped to a bed. The head is symbolically "decapitated" from the body using a line, representing the concept of dissociation. Each one of the overlapping layers contains a set of pictographs representing either traumatic events or occult symbolism. The outer layer depicts scenes of victims being electrocked, hung from a tree, being caged, raped (sometimes with animals), caged, buried alive and more. From this outside layer, arrows point towards the second layer, which contains zodiac signs. According to F. Springmeier, zodiac signs are used as a code to assign and file body programs. The center layer surrounding the victim contains words such as "Hell", "Devil", "Blood" and "Kill" which are shock words used to further traumatize the victim.

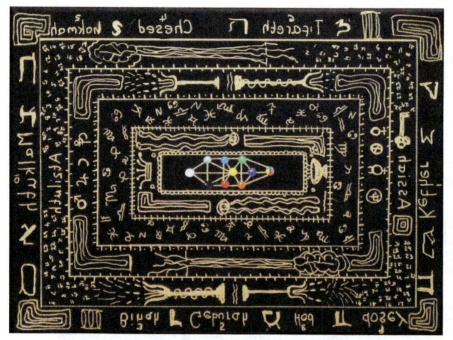

This one, entitled "Golden Kaballa", uses the same basic layout as the previous image but replaces scenes of trauma with occult symbols and the central figure with the kabbalistic Tree of Life. Each one of the Tree of Life's colourful spheres, named Sephirots, are used in Monarch mind control as "compartments" to store alter personas. The outer layer of the work contains the name of each of the ten spheres of the Tree of Life with its associated Hebrew letter.

By overlapping the trauma depicted in "It Happens" with occult aspects of "Golden Kabballah", we get a rather complete idea of the process of mind control. They schematize, with near mathematical precision, a process that is described by authors on mind control such as Fritz Springmeier.

> *"The Cabala is synonymous with Hermeticism or Hermetic magic. The Cabala was jewish-babylonian magic. The jewish black magicians brought it to Europe. It began to get widespread notice in Europe after Enlightenment period. The great pyramid according to the occult is a symbol of the Cabalistic Tree of Life–the branches of the tree form the four streams or lines to the base of the pyramid. Because the Cabala is the basis of their hermetic magic, Illuminati systems will be fairly consistent in the make of a slave's internal Tree of Life and Tree of Evil. (...)*
>
> *The rooms of the tree of life have names. Essentially, every Illuminati hierarchy victim, has the Cabalistic tree of life placed in them. This tree lies below the other trees. The circles that make up the internal Cabalistic Tree of Life are called rooms or quads by the various survivors. Alters can use the internal Tree of Life to work magic internally. It also reminds deeper alters of cult control. The circles of the tree are rooms that can be entered into. Mt. Qabbalah is a figurative mountain in the Cabala."*
> - Fritz Springmeier, The Illuminati Formula to Create a Mind Control Slave

Another piece, entitled "Seven Levels" is another highly detailed account of the process of dissociation. Comprised of several layers, this works depicts, from bottom to top, the "evolution" of a slave from the hell of trauma to the "heavenly" feeling of dissociation. The bottom two layers depict several horrific scenes of trauma. For example, we see in the bottom left corner a pregnant women giving birth to a dead child in a pool of blood under disturbing phrases such as "No Life", "Death" and "Blood Death All Around". There are also several caged children, others being electroshocked and others hung upside down. Inverted crosses are found all around these two bottom layers, reminding us that these traumatic events are Satanic Ritual Abuse (SRA).

All of this trauma, pain and suffering seems to be "channelled" towards the layers above, consisting of a plethora of occult symbols such as the Tree of Life, the signs of the zodiac and All-Seeing eyes. It is during this occult level that the transformation occurs.

The top layer layer represents the (only) escape to all this trauma: dissociation. It is represented by an angelic figure rising to the sky. Looking closely however, we see an All-Seeing Eye in the sky, which reminds us that this escape is not true freedom, but a controlled state that has been induced by the handlers.

Judy

This alter is a teenage girl who is anorexic. Most of her paintings place a heavy emphasis on the concept of duality – one of the most basic occult concepts exploited by mind control rituals. Duality is an ancient hermetic concept which is traditionally represented with the juxtaposition of the colors black and white, as with the Masonic checkerboard pattern or the symbol of the Ying Yang.

Judy's works often give a prominent place to the Masonic checkerboard floor, the surface on which occult rituals and ceremonies take place in secret societies. She was probably heavily exposed to the concept of duality (good girl vs evil girl – something that is also found in popular culture) and the symbol of the checkered floor was probably physically used during programming.

"Crying Rose" fully exploits the theme of duality used on mind control victims to create a "split of personality". The crying girl, who is dressed in a checkered dress, reflects the checkerboard pattern floor, therefore insinuating that duality is occurring within her.

This piece, titled "Symbolic or What", is indeed ... symbolic. Two girls (or two personas of the same girl) avoid stepping on the checkerboard floor due to the presence of a snake. The appear to be covering their genitals, implying that the snake is phallic symbol. The painting also attests to the great psychic power of the checkerboard pattern on victims, a trait that was probably part of the programming.

This painting portrays Monarch slaves as literal pawns on a chessboard, who are "played with" to then be disposed by their handlers.

This self-portrait depicts Judy as a person divided into opposite entities. The concept of duality is therefore very present and represented by the juxtaposition of the colors black and white. The shock words and insults on the image recall the violent and abusive process that leads to the fragmentation of the personality.

Ria Pratt

The paintings made by Ria Pratt are the most graphic and disturbing but also the most revealing. The alter believes she is a 12 year old girl and has vivid recollections of the trauma she has been subjected to, whether it be sexual, physical or dehumanizing. Simply watching these paintings is a difficult experience – it is further disheartening to realize that she actually lived these situations.

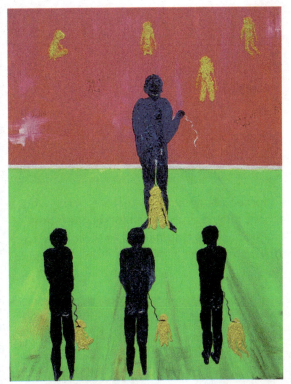

This self-portrait depicts Judy as a person divided into opposite entities. The concept of duality is therefore very present and represented by the juxtaposition of the colors black and white. The shock words and insults on the image recall the violent and abusive process that leads to the fragmentation of the personality.

Entitled "Too Much", the painting depicts a victim being electro-shocked by a handler with a sick smile. The pain is "Too Much" to handle, resulting in the victim's dissociation.

"What Ted Saw" depicts the abuse of a small child by its handlers. "Ted" is the small Teddy Bear sitting on the floor. Young mind control victims are often given Teddy Bears by their handlers to make them develop an emotional attachment to them. This attachment is then exploited by the handlers to create emotional trauma.

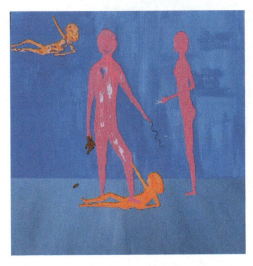

In "Ted's Legless", Ria's handler rips off one of her best friend's legs while forcibly holding her on the ground. The trauma causes dissociation, which is represented by the transparent version of the girl. Haunting words are inscribed on the wall: "Help Me Please" and "Pratt was Here".

Vigilant Reports

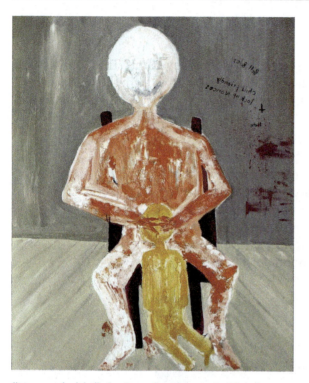

"Unspeakable" depicts the unspeakable: the abuse of small children by their handlers. Strange phrases a written on the wall along with an inverted cross, a symbol that appears to be hardwired into the brains of Monarch slaves.

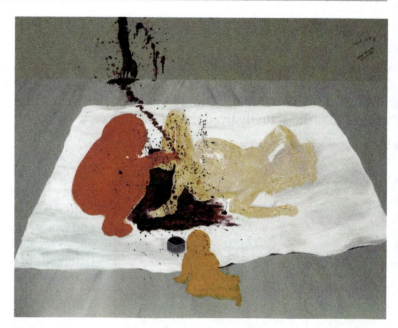

"No No!" depicts a forced abortion or premature birth - who was probably pregnant due to abuse. The bloody operation is witnessed by Ria, probably to traumatize her. According to Ellen P. Lacter, fetuses are either sacrificed in rituals or used as slaves.

Children caged up like animals about to be tortured by a dissociated handler.

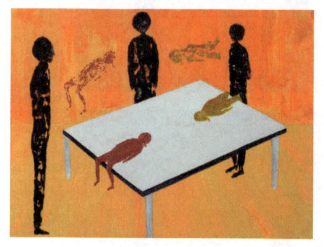

Another of abuse involving children, who have dissociated (transparent bodies floating).

In Conclusion

Although Kim Noble enjoyed some mainstream exposure, the true source of the artist's condition – Monarch programming – is nowhere to be found in mass media. Analyzed in its entirety, Noble's body of work describes a highly organized and complex system that appears to hold great amounts of knowledge- occult and scientific – as well as material resources. This system also appears to literally own humans, mostly children, who are abused and traumatized to create within them programmable alter personas. The fact that no newspapers dared to investigate (or even mention) anything related to MK-Ultra, a program that was proved to use the exact techniques described in the paintings, tells volumes about the power of those operating it. The soulless handlers depicted in Noble's paintings are not lone psychopaths, but high level officials of the Illuminati system who enjoy media immunity. In fact, they are sometimes part of the media as the worlds of the entertainment business and Monarch programming often collude.

Partly for this reason, the symbolism used during Monarch programming has spilled over to the mainstream entertainment business. Some of the world's biggest stars are products of mind control. The same symbols used in the programming of Monarch slaves is sent to the world through mass media. High level mind control handlers and slaves (those who have "succeeded" at the various levels of programming) end up operating in show business. Some of our favorite entertainers are nothing more than puppets whose strings are pulled by unseen handlers. Well, these handlers are "unseen" to most, but they certainly make themselves "seen" through the symbolism placed in the media.

Many of the symbols described on this site directly originate from the shady world of Monarch programming, which uses a complex system of occult images and powerful triggers. Although most of us are fortunate enough not to live through the hell endured by these MK slaves, we are still subject to a form of programming using movies, television, music and other forms of mass media. Those who operate behind the scenes attempt to slowly normalize their existence and their depraved behaviour. Why are children being so aggressively sexualized in mass media? Is it because people in the entertainment business are connected with the people who commit the horrific acts portrayed above? Sadly, the reality is sicker than the fiction.

KONY 2012: STATE PROPAGANDA FOR A NEW GENERATION

The overnight viral sensation KONY 2012 brought worldwide awareness to the African war criminal Joseph Kony. Beneath this commendable cause, lies however an elaborate agenda that is presented in the video in a very manipulative way. We'll look at the agenda behind KONY 2012 and how it uses reverse psychology to not only justify a military operation in Africa, but to actually have people demand it.

KONY 2012 is a viral sensation that swept the entire world in less than 24 hours. Its main subject is the African rebel leader Joseph Kony, his war crimes and the clearly defined "movement" to stop him. Countless celebrities have endorsed the movement, news sources have reported it and social media is buzzing with it. While the problem of guerrilla warfare and child soldiers has plagued Africa for decades, and several documentaries have already been produced regarding the issue, this particular 29-minute video made managed to obtain mass exposure and support.

KONY 2012 is less of a documentary than it is a highly efficient infomercial that is tailor-made for the Facebook generation, using state-of-the-art marketing techniques to make its point. Young people like "underground movements" and want to feel like they are changing the world. KONY 2012 taps into these needs to bring about something that is not "hip" or "underground" at all: A military operation in Uganda. Not only that, it urges the participants of the movement to order stuff, to wear bracelets that are associated with an online profile and to record their actions in social media. This makes KONY 2012 the first artificially created movement that is fully track-able, monitor-able and quantifiable by those who engendered it. In other words, what appears to be a movement "from the people" is actually a new way for the elite to advance its agenda.

A Propaganda Experiment

The video begins with an interesting statement: "The next 27 minutes are an experiment. But in order for it to work, you have to pay attention". It is an experiment as it tests a new, groundbreaking way to get an agenda accepted by the Facebook generation. In the past, when the government needed to justify the invasion of a country, the President would sit in front of the camera and tell the public why war should be declared in this area of the world. In the case of KONY, the military agenda is disguised as grassroots activism, where the US army entering Uganda would be perceived as a "victory of the people", effectively reversing the communications model.

Towards the end of the video, an image is displayed explaining how decisions (and messages) start from the top of the pyramid (the elite) and are communicated to the masses through mass media and such.

Due to the advent of social media, the above diagram has become a lot less effective to get a message across to the young generation. It is not CNN reports and the President addressing the nation anymore, it is about "liking" Facebook pages and viral YouTube videos. This is where messages now come across. Always studying, analyzing and exploiting the most effective ways to persuade public opinion, KONY 2012 appears to be an attempt to test out the effectiveness of a "viral" propaganda campaign. By creating this "movement" and making young people actually DEMAND the U.S. government intervene in Africa, the masterminds behind this campaign would manage the impossible: Reversing the propaganda model in order to make it emanate from the people. By doing so, the elite's agenda is not only accepted by the masses, it is perceived as a victory by them.

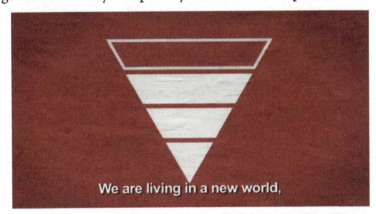

"We are living in a new world" indeed. The KONY 2012 logo aptly represents how a viral video and social media can reverse the propaganda model. Don't be fooled however. Power is still not in the hands of the base of the pyramid … far from it. It is all about appearances.

When the war on Iraq was declared, a great portion of young Americans opposed the war. How is it they are now begging the government to send troops to Africa? A simple video, specifically conceived for the Facebook generation did the trick. As it is the case in most campaigns to justify a war, the first goal was to identify a bad guy.

Identifying the Bad Guy

By associating Kony with Bin Laden and Hitler in this poster, KONY 2012 is promoting war.

I have absolutely no intention of defending Joseph Kony or to say "he's not that bad". He, along with many other guerrilla factions across Africa, has committed despicable atrocities. However, the problem of child soldiers has existed for decades and there are literally hundreds of Joseph Konys across the African continent. In some cases, some of the armies are actually funded by Western countries. If we would truly go to the root of the issue, we'd discover that Africa has been plagued with the problem of warring factions and rebel guerrillas ever since Western forces "liberated" their colonies and divided the continent of Africa according to Western interests. Indeed, instead of setting the boundaries of each country according to the geographic location of the ethnic groups and tribes that live there, countries were created according to the economic needs of colonizing forces such as Great Britain, France and others. The net result is: A bunch of artificial countries that each contain several tribes, ethnic groups, languages and religions. When one group takes power, the others are repressed, which leads to violence and rebellion. Add to the mix extreme poverty due to resources being siphoned out of Africa by Western countries and you've got a breeding ground for merciless warlords. As long as this problem exists, Joseph Konys will continue to emerge in Africa.

But the video mentions none of this. All it says is that arresting Kony would "make the world better". KONY 2012 is all about identifying a bad guy, "making him famous" and have people demand his death by U.S. forces. Fixing the true cause of problems in the third world has never been on the Agenda. But picking out a "bad guy" to justify military action has always been part of it. If in the case of Saddam Hussein, "facts" (that ultimately proved false) were given to justify the invasion of Iraq. A different technique is being used with Kony, one that originates from advertising.

Any marketing specialist will tell you: "Facts don't sell, emotions do". The first part of KONY 2012 solely addresses emotions. It is about making the filmmaker likeable, showing gut-wrenching images of African kids in pain, in misery and in despair. Then, the turning point: Joseph Kony is the cause of all of this. Not centuries of exploitation and devastation by Western forces in Africa that lead to chaos, lawlessness and poverty. No, it's Kony. That bastard. George Clooney is really mad at him right now. He even tweeted about it.

Another marketing strategy is to appeal to the lowest common denominator. In other words, to get a message across, one must address the audience as if it was made of kids. KONY 2012 does exactly this by ridiculously oversimplifying the problem and explaining it to an actual child – who represents the viewers. This is not surprising though, as this is how the masses are perceived by the higher ups.

Here's what this scene implies: "Look, dumb-ass, even this little kid gets it. So you better get it."

Once the viewers had their emotions stirred, got infantilized and had the problem spelled out to them as if they were in kindergarten, the table is set for the true goal of the video: Defining the agenda.

Defining the Agenda

KONY 2012 is a movement backed by some of the world's most powerful entities and has precise goals. As the movie's intro states, it is an experiment. It is an opportunity to create a movement that can be fully trackable, quantifiable and manageable through social media whose culmination is a U.S. military intervention in Uganda. The carrying out of this mission will not only be perceived as a victory, it will restore young people's faith in democracy. What the members of this movement might not realize is that they are helping the advancement of the elite's agenda towards a New World Order.

This poster aptly summarizes how the Illuminati works. Political parties are irrelevant as both work towards the same Agenda.

he second part of the movie let's go of emotions and describes to the viewers what the elite expects from them. U.S. troops are already in Uganda, but, according to the movie, Kony "changed his tactics"… Damnit Kony, you and your sneaky tactics. Apparently, high tech satellites, unmanned drones and all kinds of radars are not enough to catch this guy. Nope, in order to catch him, a complicated plan, involving the purchase of an "Action Kit" and the registering an ID bracelet on a website is required. Makes sense.

Those who want to "Stop Kony" are required to wear a bracelet bearing a unique code which needs to be registered at a website. Of course, personal information is requested.

Once the bracelet is registered, members can associate it with their Facebook account, which will keep track of all KONY-related actions. The end result is: every single member of KONY 2012 will be known, identified and easily tracked – with constantly updated information. All of this data will of course be collected, scrutinized and stored by those in charge.

Furthermore, members are asked to contribute a "few dollars a month" to TRI, an organization whose ultimate goal is American military intervention in Uganda.

TRI's logo is an inverted "Peace" sign. In symbolism, an inverted sign means that it stands for the opposite of the regular sign. In other words, TRI is about war. Peace does not involve "equipping" and "training" government forces to fight rebel factions. As the novel 1984 states, WAR IS PEACE, FREEDOM IS SLAVERY, and IGNORANCE IS STRENGTH.

To support the cause and to make it popular, a bunch of elite-sponsored artists and politicians have been enlisted, including Lady Gaga, Jay-Z, Rihanna, Oprah, George Clooney, Bono, etc. While some of them might be genuinely

Am I seeing warmongering George W. Bush in here? The dude that lied to the whole country in order to attack Iraq for its oil and stuff? Hmm. Weird.

concerned about problems in Africa, most of them are pawns of the elite that are used to promote its agenda. After going past the celebrities and the emotions, the end result of this campaign is simple and steeped in real politik: Since the fall of rival superpower USSR, Western forces have sought to bring down and to control regional powers around the world, mostly in third countries. Uganda is part of that plan. The same way the spectre of Bin

The video clearly shows what is the goal of this "movement": U.S. troops taking charge of the Ugandan army, the same way it took charge of the Iraqi, Libyan and other armies in the past few years.

Laden was used to invade Afghanistan, Kony is being used to enter Uganda.

In Conclusion

KONY 2012 is a cleverly orchestrated campaign specifically aimed at today's youth, the future citizens of the world. Using state-of-the-art techniques and new technologies, the campaign is a first attempt at "reverse propaganda", where the agenda APPEARS to emanate from the people. By using emotions, irrational thoughts and superficial explanations, KONY 2012 attempts to trick well-meaning people, who desire to make a positive change in the world, to instead fuel a gigantic war machine that is controlled by the world's elite.

Is KONY 2012 trying to eradicate child-soldiers or is it attempting to create a new kind of child-soldiers?

...Right.

Monster High: A Doll Line Introducing Children to the Illuminati Agenda

Monster High is a highly successful toy franchise that is somewhat similar to the Bratz doll line, as both are comprised of edgy, fashionable characters with attitude. Like many other toy franchises, Monster High is much more than a doll line: It is a multi-platform franchise comprised of toys, DVDs, a web series, music videos, video games, books, clothing accessories, and much more.

The brand distinguishes itself with its unique, twisted universe inspired by monster movies and sci-fi horror. All of the characters are either offspring of known movie monsters or some kind of undead zombies. While Monster High's slogan is "Be yourself, be unique, be a monster!", this franchise also communicates deeper messages to its young audience. In fact, a closer look at the stories in Monster High reveals that it is perfectly in sync with the Illuminati's Agenda as it promotes themes such as hypersexualization, superficiality, a culture of death and even Monarch Mind Control. As seen in previous articles on this site, these themes are abundant in mass media and, the fact that they are present in a doll line for kids further proves that there's a continuous effort to expose impressionable minds to a specific set of symbols and values.

This should not come as a surprise, as Monster High was created by the world's largest toy company, Mattel, with revenues of over $6.2 billion per year. The chairman of the board of directors, Robert A. Eckert, is a long-time member of the Trilateral Commission and the Bilderbergs, the two most powerful elite circles shaping the world today. As you might know, company representatives who attend these elite meetings are there because their brands can help push the elite's long-term Agenda. Powerful, world-reaching companies such as Mattel do not simply sell products, they sell a culture associated with them. Considering how children get attached and even obsessed with their dolls and the universe that surrounds them, what better way to reach young minds and to teach them the values of a New World Order future? Let's look at Monster High and the universe it introduces to young children.

The Monster High Universe

The world of Monster High is basically a high school populated with the offspring of famous monstrous figures like Dracula and Frankenstein. The characters wear outfits that lean strongly to the sexy side, making one wonder what kind of message this is delivering to Monster High's target audience: girls under the age of 10. Even more disturbing, the back story and symbolism associated with many of the characters strongly refer to dark concepts, such as Monarch Mind Control. Indeed, most Monster High characters are either artificially created or a product of some kind of experiment and many of them do not really have a mind of their own. They are all literally dead and animated by some kind of unholy force. When one adds this fact to the symbolism and persona associated with each character, one starts to realize that Monster High is about a bunch of MK slaves.

The characters of Monster High are dressed in outfits that are rather inappropriate for high school. Also, their lockers are shaped like coffins with skull heads for locks. In short, it is all about pushing a culture of sex and death on young, impressionable children.

Frankie Stein

Frankie Stein is the daughter of Frankenstein. Her entire body is stitched up together and, sometimes, she loses some of her body parts. In MK symbolism, this represents the powerlessness of slaves and their fragmented nature. Also, notice her "logo" at the top right: fractured and stitched up skull – representing a fragmented mind.

Frankie Stein is an artificial creation put together by a mad scientist (a MK handler?). Her story states that she 15 days old (yes, days, not years). In other words, her alter persona was created by her handler 15 days ago. Her head is held together by two screws, symbolizing her not having a mind of her own. The screws are of different color because they are of different polarity, negative and positive. This refers to the concept of duality that is always inculcated to MK Slaves. To further emphasize the concept of duality, her eyes are different colors, her hair is striped black and white and her bio page states that her favorite color is "black and white stripes".

Frankie Stein can eletroshock herself and others – a reference to electroshock torture used in Monarch Mind Control to program slaves.

Frankie Stein electroshocked.

Here's Frankie Stein on a bedding set giving the One-Eye sign. Yes, little girls can now sleep draped in Illuminati symbolism.

Speaking of which, here's a "Happy New Year" message from Monster High with another prominent One-Eye sign

OPERETTA

As if to highlight her connection to Illuminati music industry, all of the symbolism relating to Operatta (even her logo) revolves around the One-Eye sign. Like the Lady Gaga and the Rihannas of this world, she is almost always emphasizing one eye. Also, I'm not sure how she can walk with these shoes – but that's another story.

You'll notice that her guitar is shaped like a coffin as well, because, apparently, death is so cool.

Operetta practices her music in a place called the Catacombs. The symbolism of her hideout is quite blatant.

Operatta's stage is "overseen" by a prominent All-Seeing Eye.

In short, Operatta appears to be telling young girls: "If you want to be part of the music business, you have to embrace this Illuminati imagery".

Werecats

As we've seen in previous articles on this site, Sex Kitten programming is represented in popular culture with feline prints and cat-like attributes on attractive girls. The Werecat sisters are all about that.

The Werecat sisters' symbolism is all about Kitten Programming. The twins (on the right) truly do not have a mind of their own.

The back story regarding the Werecat sisters is quite dark and similar to the story of many actual MK Slaves. The webisode named The Nine Lives of Toralei, describes how Werecat sister Toralei is an orphan roaming the streets who gets picked up, and locked up, by "the System".

The Werecat sisters "behind bars" ... or re-educated by the System.

> "Some children live in foster homes, or with adopted parents, or in orphanages, or with caretakers and guardians. Because these children are at the mercy of the non-related adults, these types of children frequently are sold to become mind-controlled slaves of the intelligence agencies. In review, remember that because many of these organizations are controlled by the Illuminati; an Illuminati slave may often work for one of these front groups, while the Illuminati maintain control over the base-program."
> - Fritz Springmeier, The Illuminati Formula to Create a Mind Control Slave

The sisters are then "recruited" by the "headmistress" of Monster High. You'll notice that she is holding her head in her hand, a way of showing that MK Handlers are also often mind controlled.

Is Monster High actually an MK programming site? Hmmm.

Relevant fact: Marilyn Monroe, the prototype of Kitten Programing was also declared a "Ward of the State" and lived in foster homes during her youth. Another relevant fact: The father of MK-Ultra, Josef Mengele, experimented on thousands of twins to perfect mind-control techniques.

Videos

The Monster High website contains numerous animated webisodes that are extremely popular (each one of them has racked up several million YouTube views). While the main goal of these video shorts is to sell dolls, there is nevertheless a lot of symbolism in them. Also, some videos refer to mind-control concepts in a rather blatant way. Let's look at some of these videos.

Dueling Personality

This video deals with the core of Monarch Programming: The creation of completely separate alter personas. Frankie Stein's boyfriend, named Jackson, discovers that he has an alter personality that acts completely separately from him. At the beginning of the video he says:

> "So every time I wake up in some dark alley alone and confused, its all because of him! I've got so much to say to that guy. But I can't even confront him about it … because he's me."

Holt, Jackson's "cool" alter persona has a tattoo around one eye, as if to emphasize the Illuminati Mind Control stuff underlying this story.

In the end Frankie Stein breaks up with Jackson and his alter until they can "settle their differences". Why are children exposed to this? What's the point? I don't think many young girls relate to this story.

Anyways, Jackson's problems with his alter persona pop up in several other webisodes.

In the episode entitled "I Know What You Did Last Frightday", the headmistress triggers Jackson's alter persona using music – an actual MK technique – because she needs the creative Holt to paint a mural.

Undo the Voodoo

Another webisode focuses on Hoodude, a voodoo doll that is having a bad day and, because he's a voodoo doll, everyone at school is having a bad day.

Hoodude is yet another character that is artificially created and that doesn't really have a mind of his own. Also, there's a one-eye thing is going on with his different-colored buttons.

Voodoo magic is yet another very important aspect of Monarch Mind Control that is represented in Monster High.

> "In discussing how trauma-based mind-control is done, voodoo must be included as a component. Many of the Mind-controlled slaves have had voodoo as part of their trauma, and many had voodoo dolls placed into their Systems. When vows and oaths are made, an object is given to the satanic cult or the Illuminati for the Keeper of the Seals to guard. If the vow is broken voodoo magic can be used against the offender by using the object given in the sealing."
> - Ibid.

To solve Hoodude's problem, the girls at school ask for the help of Scarah the mind reader.

Scarah reads Hoodude's mind.

It is interesting to note that many actual MK Slaves receive ESP (extra-sensory perception) training – which include telepathy, mind reading and remote viewing.

Scarah then tells her friends that they need to literally enter Hoodude's head to fix his self-esteem issues.

The girls in some kind Mind Control lab to enter Hoodude's head.

Inside Hoodude's brain, the girls find the part of the brain relating to self-esteem and "reprogram" him to love himself.

Scarah reconnects two loose wires inside Hoodude's brain so he loves himself again.

Hoodude can now look at himself in the mirror and love himself again.

In short, this video is about an artificially created "doll" that doesn't act as expected. He is then literally mind controlled and reprogrammed to have more self esteem. Hoodude did not work at bettering himself or at accepting his flaws, some mind reader entered his brain to reprogram him. I don't think that's great lesson for kids.

There are many other Monster High videos that are filled with this kind of symbolism. However, I believe we've all suffered enough going through just these three.

In Conclusion

I can imagine some people reading this article and thinking: "He's talking dolls and cartoons now? How about talking about the real issues like politics, grumble, grumble". Yes, on a superficial level, talking about dolls and cartoons may not come off as "serious" analysis. However, we must remember that, for the powers that be, there is nothing more serious than capturing the minds of children at a young age in order to mold them for the future. For propagandists, there is no age limit for pushing a message. They realize that the younger the audience, the more effective their message will be. Marketing specialists know that brand loyalty is taught at very early age (i.e. Heinz Ketchup, Kellogs cereal, etc.) and propaganda messages simply another product to market.

So what kind of message does a franchise like Monster High communicate to children? There are several levels.

On a basic level, the characters of Monster High are obviously hypersexualized as they are dressed in outfits that can only be found in sex shops. Considering the doll's target market (girls under 10 years old), we can imagine how this trains girls to believe that, in order to be cool, they have to be very sexy, very early. Then, there's this whole death-worship thing going on, with coffin-shaped lockers and coffin-shaped cellphones and coffin-shaped guitars and skulls everywhere. Mix these two very visible aspects together and you've got the sex-and-death mass media cocktail that is constantly pushed to all audiences, but particularly young people. Furthermore, the characters in Monster High evolve in a context that is completely obsessed with superficiality, appearances and materialism – all values that are actively promoted to today's youth. When Monster High fans grow out of their doll-playing phase, they will most likely start watching music videos and TV shows that promote the exact same set of values. Sadly, they will question none of it because they have been exposed to this Agenda since their tender youth.

On secondary level, almost everything in Monster High relates in one way or another to the dark, disturbing world of Illuminati Mind Control. The school can be likened to a MK-programming center, led by a "headmistress" whose own head pops off in a literal symbol of dissociation. All of the students are either artificial creations or zombies who do not have a mind of their own (funny how the line's theme song ends with the words "Don't you want to be a Monster too?" Concepts associated with trauma-based mind control such as alter-personas, duality, dissociation, kitten programming and even electroshock torture are represented in Monster High. As if that wasn't enough, the whole Monster High franchise is laced with the Illuminati symbolism I've described time and time again on this site, proving that, not only is this symbolism not accidental, but that this Agenda is being promoted everywhere ... even to young children who just want to play with dolls.

So why do they do this? Because, as Hitler stated: "He alone, who owns the youth, gains the future."

The Hidden Life of Marilyn Monroe, the Original Hollywood Mind Control Slave (Part-I)

Marilyn Monroe is possibly the most iconic figure in American culture and the most recognizable sex symbol of all times. However, behind Monroe's photogenic smile was a fragile individual who was exploited and subjected to mind control by powerful handlers. The first part of this two-part series will look at the hidden life of Marilyn, a Hollywood Monarch slave.

Marilyn Monroe is the ultimate sex symbol, embodying everything that Hollywood represents: glamor, glitz and sex-appeal. Her iconic sensual blonde persona forever revolutionized the movie industry and, to this day, is greatly influential in popular culture. While Marilyn represents everything that is glamorous about Hollywood, the disturbing story of her private life equally represents everything that is dark in Hollywood. Marilyn was indeed manipulated by high level "mind doctors" who controlled every aspect of her life and caused her to basically lose her mind. Her death, at the young age of 36 is one of the first "mysterious celebrity deaths" in popular culture. While many facts point to a murder, it is still classified as a "probable suicide".

While many biographers explain away Marilyn's hardships with "psychological issues", piecing together facts about her life combined with knowledge of the dark side of Hollywood reveals something a lot darker: Marilyn Monroe was one of the first celebrities subjected to Monarch mind control, a branch of the CIA's MK Ultra program Through trauma and psychological programming, Monroe a became high level puppet of the shadow elite, even became JFK's Presidential Model.

When Monroe's programming lost its effect and she started to break down, some argue that she was "thrown off the freedom train", an MK ULTRA term for designating slaves that are killed when they are not useful (and potentially dangerous) to their handlers.

The first part of this series of articles will look at the real life and career of Monroe, an isolated girl whose great beauty became a true curse.

Her Early Years

Norma Jeane as a teenager

Norma Jeane Mortenson had a difficult and unstable youth. She never knew her father and her mother was mentally unstable and incapable of taking care of her. In My Story, Monroe wrote that she recalled seeing her mother "screaming and laughing" as she was forcibly taken to a State Hospital.

At age 11, Norma Jeane was declared a ward of the state. She lived in a total of 11 foster homes throughout her youth; when there was no foster home available, she sometimes ended up at the Hollygrove Orphanage in Los Angeles. As if moving from one foster home to another wasn't difficult enough, Norma Jeane recalled being treated harshly in several of them. Even worse, she was abused in at least three of them.

For instance, at age 11, Norma Jeane was adopted by her mother's best friend Grace McKee and her new husband, Ervin Silliman "Doc" Goddard. There, "Doc" repeatedly sexually assaulted her, which forced Norma Jeane to move out. In another case, when she was in middle-school, Norma Jean was sent to her great-aunt's house in Compton, California. There, one of her great-aunt's sons abused her, forcing her, again, to move out. Here is another account of abuse:

> "She told of being whipped by one foster mother for having touched 'the bad part' of her body. Another more serious incident occurred when she was eight. One evening a lodger she called Mr. Kimmel (Marilyn said later that this was not his real name) asked her to come into his room and locked the door behind her. He put his arms around her. She kicked and struggled. He did what he wanted, telling her to be a good girl. (In a later interview Marilyn stated that the abuse involved fondling).
>
> When he let her out, he handed her a coin and told her to buy herself an ice cream. She threw the coin in his face and ran to tell her foster mother what happened, but the woman wouldn't listen.
>
> 'Shame on you,' her foster mother said. 'Mr. Kimmel's my star boarder.'
>
> Norma Jean went to her room and cried all night.
>
> Marilyn said she felt dirty and took baths days after it happened to feel clean. Such repeated attempts to feel clean through showers or baths are typical behavior for victims of assault.
>
> Marilyn said she began to stutter after the incident and reverted to it at times of stress. When she told one interviewer about the abuse, she began stuttering.
>
> The evidence points to the fact that she was an abused child whose early sexualization led to her inap-

propriate behavior as an adult.
- Daily Mail, "The magic red sweater that turned 'Norma Jeane, string bean' into Marilyn Monroe"

Norma Jeane's unstable and sometimes traumatic youth made her a perfect candidate for Monarch mind control. Being a ward of the state, she had no stable family.

> *"Some children live in foster homes, or with adopted parents, or in orphanages, or with caretakers and guardians. Because these children are at the mercy of the non-related adults, these types of children frequently are sold to become mind-controlled slaves of the intelligence agencies."*
> - Fritz Springmeier, The Illuminati Formula to Create a Mind Control Slave

Norma Jeane's background made her a prime target for Beta Programming (also known as Kitten programming). Being an attractive and charismatic woman looking to be part of show business, she also had the perfect profile for it.

> *"Beta is the second Greek letter, and it represents the sexual models and alters that the Programmers are creating. The primitive part of the brain is involved in this type of programming. An early abuse event will be used to anchor this programming."*
> - Ibid.

Contact with Occult Hollywood

Before becoming famous, Norma Jeane went by the name of Mona and worked as a stripper at a Burlesque house in Los Angeles. There, she came in contact with Anton LaVey, the man who would later found the highly influential Church of Satan. According to Springmeier, LaVey was an MK handler and Monroe became one of his "Kitten" slaves.

> *"Marilyn Monroe was an orphan, and during her infancy the Illuminati/CIA programmed her to be a Monarch slave. Before becoming an actress, while she was still a stripper, she spent time with the founder of the Church of Satan Anton LaVey. Victims of LaVey have pointed him out as a mind-control programmer."*
> - Ibid.

LaVey's biography also mentions an "affair" with Monroe, which was probably more than that.

> *"When the carnival season ended, LaVey would earn money by playing organ in Los Angeles area burlesque houses, and he relates that it was during this time period that he had a brief affair with a then-unknown Marilyn Monroe."*
> - Magus Peter H. Gilmore, Anton Szandor LaVey: A Biographical Sketch

Anton LaVey visiting Monroe's grave, 1967.

Around the same time period, LaVey was involved with another actress, one that was known for being the "working man's Marilyn Monroe": Jayne Mansfield. The relationship between the two was also described as an "affair", but the reality was a lot darker.

> "Anton LaVey has been the mind-control handler/programmer of a number of Hollywood actors & actresses, including Jayne Mansfield and Marilyn Monroe, who both serviced him as sexual slaves".
> - Anton Szandor LaVey, Whale.to

Pictures of Jayne Mansfield with Anton LaVey

Marilyn Monroe and Jayne Mansfield had a lot in common. Both were "blond bombshells" (neither were natural blondes) and are credited for "sexualizing" Hollywood. Both were Playboy playmates, both had an "affair" with Anton LaVey and both had an "affair" with Robert F. Kennedy and John F. Kennedy (the "affair" was actually them being Presidential Models). Finally, both died in their 30s.

A Star Living Like an Inmate

Another common point between Monroe and Mansfield is that they were both part of the Blue Book Model Agency. It is there that Norma Jean metamorphosed into the iconic Marilyn Monroe.

When Norma Jeane was recruited as a model, she had curly red hair. This "girl next door" will soon get a Hollywood makeover and embody a new persona named Marilyn Monroe.

Industry insiders convinced Norma Jeane to undergo aesthetic surgery, to change her name to Marilyn Monroe and to change her hair color to platinum blonde. Monroe's sensual, "dumb blond" persona allowed her to land roles in several movies which began a clear culture shift in Hollywood.

In the movie "Gentlemen Prefer Blondes", Marilyn adorns her trademark platinum blonde "Hollywood" hairdo. In this movie, she plays the role of a sensual yet materialistic woman that is not afraid of using her charm to obtain what she wants. This type of character will be repeated time and time again in popular culture.

Norma Jeane used Marilyn Monroe as a stage name for several years, but in 1956, she accomplished a strange but symbolic move: She legally changed her name to Marilyn Monroe. The change reflected many sad truths about her personal life: In mind-control terms, the changing of her name to Marilyn Monroe represents the suppression of her "core persona" in order to only allow her programmed alter persona to exist. Marilyn was only what "they" wanted her to be.

As several biographies have revealed, Marilyn had little to no personal freedom. She had no contact with her family, and her handlers isolated her in order to further control her and to avoid "real" people from helping her to realize that she was being manipulated. The only people that she was in contact with were her "psychologists" and her handlers.

> "Marilyn's existence was not of a rich person, but more like of an inmate. Marilyn was allowed to have no personal life, outside of the dictates of the programmers and her masters. The programmers and users bore down so hard on controlling Marilyn that they repeatedly came close to driving her insane."
> - Springmeier, Op. Cit.

Marilyn was also constantly under high surveillance. Years after her death, an incredible amount of surveillance equipment was found in one of her homes.

> "In 1972, actress Veronica Hamel and her husband became the new owners of Marilyn's Brentwood home. They hired a contractor to replace the roof and remodel the house, and the contractor discovered a sophisticated eavesdropping and telephone tapping system that covered every room in the house. The components were not commercially available in 1962, but were in the words of a retired Justice Department official, "standard FBI issue." This discovery lent further support to claims of conspiracy theorists that Marilyn had been under surveillance by the Kennedys and the Mafia. The new owners spent $100,000 to remove the bugging devices from the house."
> - Source: IMDB

Under the Spell of Mind Doctors

In 1956, Marilyn converted to Judaism and married her third husband, screenwriter Arthur Miller. At this point, the only people in Monroe's life were her husband and her acting teacher Lee Strasberg and her psychiatrists Margaret Hohenberg, Marianne Kris and Ralph Greenson.

> "Marilyn's life was incredibly monotonous for her. Her doctor's appointments (I later learned these were appointments with psychiatrists) and her acting lessons were virtually all she had to to look

forward to."
- Lena Pepitone, Marilyn Monroe Confidential: An Intimate Account"

Lee Strasberg, Monroe's acting coach. According to Elia Kazan: "He carried with him the aura of a prophet, a magician, a witch doctor, a psychoanalyst and a feared father of a Jewish home."

The ultimate proof that these individuals were the ONLY people in Marilyn's life is that they inherited most of her fortune. Lee Strasberg alone inherited 75% of her estate while Dr. Kris obtained 25%.

"Marilyn began associating with Lee and his wife Paula Strasberg from around 1955, very quickly they became a colossal influence in Marilyn's life, taking over almost every aspect of her very being.

Many of Marilyn's friends and colleagues watched this happen and felt very uncomfortable about it but were powerless to do anything about it. Whilst she was married to Arthur Miller, Miller had begun to voice these concerns to Marilyn.

During the final year of her life there were signs that her faith in the Strasbergs' was weakening and that she no longer wanted them to have the control. It has been said that she was in the process of dispensing with their services – this was seen as another indicator that Marilyn was intending to change her Will."
- Loving Marilyn, Who Owns Marilyn's Things?

After her death, Marilyn's Will was contested due to her being under "undue influence" of her handlers.

"On 25th October 1962, the Los Angeles Times reported that Marilyn Monroe's Will was being contested by her long time business manager Inez Melson. Miss Melson, who was not a beneficiary of the Will claimed that Marilyn was under undue influence of either Lee Strasberg or Dr Marianne Kris at the time the Will was made."
- Ibid.

Another proof of the excessive control of "mind doctors" on Marilyn's life is the fact that her psychiatrist Ralph Greenson was the one who found Monroe dead. Why was he at her house late at night? As we'll see in the next part of this series of articles, the circumstances of her death are incredibly suspicious.

In short, as it is the case for most Monarch slaves, Marylin's handlers were in charge of every aspect of her life. Contact with family members was totally forbidden.

"Although Marilyn Monroe had family, her doctors, psychologists, and acting coaches isolated her from them. (…) Members of the Hogan family, who lived in the Los Angeles area, had attempted to

make contact with Marilyn Monroe after she was famous, and their efforts to connect with her were blocked."
- Jennifer Jean Miller, "Was Phenergan Marilyn Monroe's Silent Killer, and Was She a Victim of Psychological Abuse, Medical Malpractice and Wrongful Death?"

Disconnected from her family and with virtually no friends, Monroe was visiting therapists almost daily. Were these visits actually programming sessions? One thing is for sure, as the visits augmented in frequency, Monroe became worse. One particularly hunting account is the "Surgeon Story", a text written by Monroe herself.

The Surgeon Story

The Surgeon Story is a text written in poem form by Monroe where she describes being cut open by Lee Strasberg and her psychiatrist Margaret Hohenberg. While some describe this story as Marilyn's recollection of a nightmare, other researchers claim that it is actually a description of a mind control session.

> *Best finest surgeon—Strasberg*
> *to cut me open which I don't mind since Dr. H*
> *has prepared me—given me anaesthetic*
> *and has also diagnosed the case and*
> *agrees with what has to be done—*
> *an operation—to bring myself back to*
> *life and to cure me of this terrible dis-ease*
> *whatever the hell it is—(...)*
>
> *Strasberg cuts me open after Dr. H gives me*
> *anesthesia and tries in a medical way to comfort me –*
> *everything in the room is WHITE in fact I can't even see anyone just white objects -*
>
> *they cut me open – Strasberg with Hohenberg's ass.*
> *and there is absolutely nothing there—*
> *Strasberg is*
> *deeply disappointed but more even—*
> *academically amazed*
> *that he had made such a mistake. He*
> *thought there was going*
> *to be so much—more than he had ever*
> *dreamed possible ...*
> *instead there was absolutely nothing—*
> *devoid of*
> *every human living feeling thing—*
> *the only thing*
> *that came out was so finely cut sawdust—like out of a raggedy ann doll—and the sawdust*
> *spills*
> *all over the floor & table and Dr. H is*
> *puzzled*
> *because suddenly she realizes that this is a*
> *new type case. The patient ... existing*
> *of complete emptiness*
> *Strasberg's dreams & hopes for theater*
> *are fallen.*
> *Dr. H's dreams and hopes for a permanent*

*psychiatric cure
is given up—Arthur is disappointed—
let down.*

In this odd and disturbing story, Monroe describes being drugged and cut open by her psychiatrists. She writes that she "didn't mind the operation" because she was "prepared". Was she dissociating? There is also mention of her seeing "only white" which might refer to sensory deprivation – a method used in MK Ultra programming.

Once cut open, the doctors only found "finely cut sawdust" inside of her "like out of a raggedy ann doll". These are the typical words of an MK slave who have completely lost touch with their true core personality. Marilyn perceives herself as an "empty" doll.

According to Jason Kennedy, a member of Marilyn's family, the Surgeon's Story describes Mind Control techniques such as sensory deprivation and the administration of dissociative anesthetic drugs.

> *"Online publications have referred to the "Surgeon Story" as a dream or nightmare. Even a musician, Annie Clark, was inspired to write a song with the lyrics, "Best, finest surgeon/Come cut me open", because she believed Marilyn wrote the words due to her reverence of Lee Strasberg during her studies with him.*
>
> *Jason, on the other hand, likened it to a very real time in the life of Marilyn Monroe, and her narrative of the experience, after being subject to mind-control techniques and drugs at the hands of Lee Strasberg and Dr. Margaret Hohenberg, when she underwent private sessions with the duo in 1955 to help release blocks in her acting techniques.*
>
> *Their methodology consisted of having Marilyn Monroe delve into painful childhood memories, they told her, to make her into a great actress.*
>
> *According to Jason's research, the pair convinced Marilyn this was all a part of "helping" her. He said she was confused from the start as she documented the "Surgeon Story" details, correcting her own details of the story from "pupil" or "student", to coining herself the "patient".*
>
> *"It was a mental operation," Jason said. "She wasn't physically cut, but mentally cut open."*
>
> *He said it was used to break her down and change her behavior.*
>
> *"This had nothing to do with acting," Jason continued. "It was pure and simple extortion using mind control techniques. Also, 'mind-control drugs' were only one aspect of the process of mind-control. Sensory deprivation, dissociative anesthetic drugs, and psychic driving are part of an overall process of mind-control."*
>
> *Lee Strasberg often referred to himself as doctor, including in his 1965 book, "Strasberg At The Actor's Studio: Tape Recorded Sessions".*
> *- Ibid.*

Whether or not this story actually happened, it nevertheless conveys the inner-thoughts of a mind control slave who is powerless against her handlers and their clinical attempts to program and modify her. Sadly, other traumatic events caused by her handlers were all too real.

Traumatized by Her Handlers

In 1961, Dr. Kris convinced Marilyn to check in at Payne Withney psychiatric ward. The events that ensued are shocking considering the fact that Marilyn was a world-renowned movie star – but not surprising considering the fact that she was a mind control slave. Here's what happened at the psychiatric ward:

> *"Kris had driven Marilyn to the sprawling, white-brick New York Hospital—Weill Cornell Medical Center, overlooking the East River at 68th Street. Swathed in a fur coat and using the name Faye Miller, she signed the papers to admit herself, but she quickly found she was being escorted not to a place where she could rest but to a padded room in a locked psychiatric ward. The more she sobbed and begged to be let out, banging on the steel doors, the more the psychiatric staff believed she was indeed psychotic. She was threatened with a straitjacket, and her clothes and purse were taken from her. She was given a forced bath and put into a hospital gown.*
>
> *On March 1 and 2, 1961, Marilyn wrote an extraordinary, six-page letter to Dr. Greenson vividly describing her ordeal: "There was no empathy at Payne-Whitney—it had a very bad effect—they asked me after putting me in a 'cell' (I mean cement blocks and all) for very disturbed depressed patients (except I felt I was in some kind of prison for a crime I hadn't committed. The inhumanity there I found archaic ... everything was under lock and key ... the doors have windows so patients can be visible all the time, also, the violence and markings still remain on the walls from former patients.)"*
>
> *(...)*
>
> *A psychiatrist came in and gave her a physical exam, "including examining the breast for lumps." She objected, telling him that she'd had a complete physical less than a month before, but that didn't deter him.*
>
> *When she refused to cooperate with the staff, "two hefty men and two hefty women" picked her up by all fours and carried her in the elevator to the seventh floor of the hospital. ("I must say that at least they had the decency to carry me face down.... I just wept quietly all the way there," she wrote.)*
>
> *She was ordered to take another bath—her second since arriving—and then the head administrator came in to question her. "He told me I was a very, very sick girl and had been a very, very sick girl for many years."*
>
> *Dr. Kris, who had promised to see her the day after her confinement, failed to show up, and neither Lee Strasberg nor his wife, Paula, to whom she finally managed to write, could get her released, as they were not family."*
> - Marilyn and Her Monsters, Vanity Fair

Another less publicized aspect of Monroe's life is her two failed pregnancies. While most biographies state that she suffered miscarriages, some accounts hint that, in reality, the miscarriages were provoked. Provoking miscarriages is a common practice in MK Ultra and, reading Marilyn's own words, it appears that her baby was taken away by her handlers. In Pepitone's book, Marilyn reportedly said about her pregnancy:

> *"Don't take my baby. So they took my baby from me... and I never saw it again."*
> - Pepitone, Op. Cit.

The book basically states that Marilyn did not suffer a miscarriage. "They" took her baby away.

> "After Marilyn had a healthy baby it was taken away from her and she was never allowed to see it. It was very likely sacrificed. Marilyn was too afraid to ask what they were going to do with it."
> - Springmeier, Op. Cit.

According to her biographies, Marilyn lost both her babies at Polyclinic Hospital, the place where, according to Springmeier, she was being programmed.

> "The operation took place at Polyclinic Hospital where Marilyn had lost her baby the year before... Marilyn said: "Going back to that hospital's a nightmare... Pain? What 'pain?". For her, the only pain was in not having her own child"
> - Pepitone, Op. Cit.

> "Notice she always goes back to the Polyclinic Hospital. Monarch victims have had to endure vast amounts of horrible torture. They learn to survive by disassociation. When Marilyn says "What is pain?" she is being accurate in reflecting her response to pain. She could not have pain–because she would disassociate it. Certain alters are created to take the pain, and the other alters don't have to experience it."
> - Springmeier, Op. Cit.

In Conclusion

In the first part of this series of articles, we looked at the hidden life of Marilyn Monroe – one that reveals the dark side of Hollywood. Marilyn was not only thoroughly manipulated by her handlers, but actually mistreated and traumatized in order to "keep her down" and reinforce programming. The chilling facts mentioned above originate from different sources but, when they are put together, they paint a sad, yet crystal clear picture of the life of a Hollywood MK slave. Trauma, abuse, isolation, mind control and constant surveillance were part of Monroe's daily life.

This kind of abuse however takes a severe toll on the victims and, after a while, a total breakdown almost inevitably ensues. At that point, MK slaves are usually "thrown off the freedom train". Was this Marilyn's ultimate fate?

The Hidden Life of Marilyn Monroe, the Original Hollywood Mind Control Slave (Part-II)

In the second part of this two part series, we'll look at the end of Marilyn Monroe's career and the circumstances around her death – all of which were typical for a victim of mind control. We will also examine her legacy in the shady MK Ultra underworld and how she became a symbol for Monarch Programming in Hollywood.

The first part of this series of articles described the hidden side of Marilyn Monroe's childhood and her beginnings in the entertainment industry. While Monroe projected the image of a glamorous sex symbol, the reality of her day-to-day life was pretty much the opposite: She was controlled, abused, exploited and even traumatized by various handlers while living in prison-like conditions. Her difficult situation slowly lead to a total mental breakdown and, when she apparently lost her usefulness to those controlling her, she lost her life in very strange circumstances.

Monroe's legacy lives on, however, and in some ways she is more relevant today than ever in the entertainment industry ... but for the wrong reasons. There are now a great number of mind control slaves in Hollywood and those behind the scenes have made Marilyn Monroe the ultimate symbol of Beta Programming. There are several Marilyn Monroes in Hollywood, these days, all projecting an attractive image while being subjected to the same control and hardship as Monroe was. And all of them get associated with Monroe at one time or another in their career. Is it a coincidence? If you read my series of articles Symbolic Pics of the Month, you probably know that the use of Monroe's image is often repeated on a specific type of celebrity ... too often to be simply a coincidence.

Let's look at the end of Monroe's career, the circumstances of her death and how her image is exploited by today's Illuminati industry.

Presidential Model

At the height of her career, Marilyn got involved with the highest power figure in the world: The President of the United States, John F. Kennedy. While some historians classify their relationship as an "affair", researchers in Monarch mind control claim that she was actually a presidential model – the highest "level" of Beta Programming slaves who are used to "service" Presidents.

If true, the existence of presidential models is quite a troubling concept, one that proves the power and the importance of Monarch Mind Control in elite circles.

> "Presidential models" were/are allegedly used by big time entertainers and politicians as playthings; mind controlled puppets programmed to perform assorted acts at the bidding of their manipulative "handlers". Supposedly Marilyn Monroe was the first Monarch slave who achieved "celebrity" status. For those unfamiliar with the term "Presidential model", I'll refer them to The Control of Candy Jones by Donald Bain and Long John Nebel. As the story goes, Long John Nebel–a New York radio personality in the 50s-70s–discovered via hypnosis that his wife, Candy Jones, was a victim of just this sort of mind control project, one of the many MK-ULTRA mind slaves, programmed by CIA "spychiatrists" and used by high mucky muck dignitaries to perform their whims, among other assorted duties such as being used as drug mules and message couriers for this vast network of morally deficient power brokers. More has come to light in this regard in recent years by way of similar allegations disbursed widely across the Internet, as well as such highly controversial books as Trance Formation In America by Mark Phillips and Kathy O'Brien, wherein Ms. O'Brien relates her own troubling tales of MK-ULTRA and Monarch abuse."
> - Adam Gorightly, "An Interpretation of Kubrick's Eyes Wide Shut"

According to mind-control researchers, Marilyn was the first "high profile" presidential model, a situation that required her handlers to exercise extreme control on what she said and did in public.

> "They stripped Marilyn of any contact with the outside world to insure that their mind control would work. They were afraid that something might go wrong with the first Presidential slave that was allowed to be highly visible to the public"
> - Fritz Springmeier, The Illuminati Formula to Create a Mind Control Slave

Marilyn singing "Happy Birthday Mr. President" to JFK on May 19th 1962. In this iconic moment of U.S. History, Monroe sings to the President in a sultry voice while wearing a skin-tight dress with nothing under it. When one knows the "hidden side of history" this event was actually about a Beta Programming slave singing to the President she is servicing - for the whole world to see.

"High level" Monarch slaves are often identified with gems and stones to identify their status. Presidential models are reportedly identified with diamonds.

> "For bona-fides & recognition signals, the Monarch slaves wear diamonds to signify they are presidential models. (...) Emeralds mean drugs, rubies mean prostitution, diamonds (rhinestones) Presidential Model work."
> - Ibid.

In the movie "Gentlemen Prefer Blondes", Monroe famously performs the song "Diamonds are a Girl's Best Friend". Was there a double meaning to that song?

Relevant fact: The dress worn by Monroe while singing "Happy Birthday Mr. President" contained more than 2500 rhinestones. Was it a way to identify her as a Presidential Model? One thing is for sure, behind the smiles and the diamonds, things were extremely sour for Marilyn during that time period. In fact, that Presidential performance was actually one of her last public appearances, as she was found dead less than three months later.

Slowly Breaking Down

The last months of Marilyn's life were characterized with erratic behavior, strange anecdotes and several "intimate" relationships with high-powered individuals. As she was increasingly showing signs of serious mental distress, she also had affairs with several men (JFK, his brother Bobby Kennedy, Marlon Brando, etc.) and according to a biography Marilyn Monroe: My Little Secret by Tony Jerris, with some women as well.

As a Beta Slave, she was also used by industry people. In June DiMaggio's book Marilyn, Joe and Me the author describes how she was forced to service old men and that she had to completely dissociate from reality (an important aspect of MK programming) to be able to go through the disgusting acts.

> "Marilyn couldn't afford emotions when she had to sleep with wrinkled old men to survive in the business. She had to protect herself by virtually turning them (emotions) off during those times – as if she were playing a part in order to remove herself from the horror of the situation. When these highly placed, high-priced moguls owned her body and soul, she couldn't afford a life of her own. There were times, she told me, when she came home exhausted from a day's shoot and some powerful old geezer would telephone her and her skin would crawl. After some of the horrors she would come over and stay in our shower for an hour or more. She wanted to wash away the terrible experience she'd had to endure".
> - June DiMaggio, Marilyn, Joe and Me

In the last months of her life, Marilyn was reportedly very difficult to work with and her behavior caused observers to worry about her situation. During the shooting of her last completed movie, The Misfits, Monroe had a "serious illness" that was never disclosed but was reportedly treated by a ... psychiatrist. In other words, mind control.

> "Monroe was frequently ill and unable to perform, and away from the influence of Dr. Greenson, she had resumed her consumption of sleeping pills and alcohol. A visitor to the set, Susan Strasberg, later described Monroe as "mortally injured in some way," and in August, Monroe was rushed to Los Angeles where she was hospitalized for ten days. Newspapers reported that she had been near death, although the nature of her illness was not disclosed. Louella Parsons wrote in her newspaper column that Monroe was "a very sick girl, much sicker than at first believed", and disclosed that she was being treated by a psychiatrist."
> - Wikipedia, "Marilyn Monroe"

In 1962, Marilyn began filming Something's Got to Give, but she was so ill and unreliable that she ultimately got fired and sued by the studio 20th Century Fox for half a million dollars. The movie's producer Henry Weinstein stated that Marilyn's behavior during the filming was horrifying:

> "Very few people experience terror. We all experience anxiety, unhappiness, heartbreaks, but that was sheer primal terror."
> - Anthony Summers, "Goddess"

Weinstein observed that Marilyn's was not having regular "bad days" or mood swings. She was feeling "sheer primal terror" – something that products of trauma-based Mind Control often end up experiencing.

The Last Sitting

In late June 1962, Marilyn modeled for a photoshoot with photographer Bert Stern for Vogue magazine. Six weeks later, she was found dead. There is something troubling about those images as they show a sensual yet aging Monroe, drunk and with a eyes that somewhat lost of their spark. Whether it was intentional or not, this photoshoot is symbolic for several reasons.

In Stern's book The Last Sitting, the photographer chose to include pictures that were crossed out by Marilyn because they were deemed unsatisfactory. Now knowing that she would be "crossed out" a few weeks later, probably because she was deemed unsatisfactory by her handlers, there is something prophetic about these images.In Stern's book The Last Sitting, the photographer chose to include pictures that were crossed out by Marilyn because they were deemed unsatisfactory. Now knowing that she would be "crossed out" a few weeks later, probably because she was deemed unsatisfactory by her handlers, there is something prophetic about these images.

Knowing what would happen to her a few weeks after this shoot, this red veil on her face and these closed eyes can symbolically portray Marilyn's sacrifice by the industry.

This photoshoot, taken at the most difficult time of her life – after a "miscarriage", a divorce, a forced trip to a psychiatric ward, and all kinds of abuse, will also be remembered as her most revealing and intimate one. As Marilyn's life got more difficult, she also became increasingly sensual – which is what Beta Programming slaves are programmed to do. However, like other MK slaves, she did not live past the age of 40.

Her Death

Marilyn Monroe was found dead by her psychiatrist Ralph Greenson in her bedroom on August 5, 1962. While her death was classified as a "probable suicide" due to "acute barbiturate poisoning", it is still one of the most debated conspiracy theories of all time. There are indeed a great number of facts pointing toward murder, yet the truth about her death has never been official acknowledged. Since Marilyn's demise, a great number of other celebrities have lost their lives in similar circumstances. To those who are aware of the dark side of the entertainment industry, the modus operandi of the occult elite has become quite clear.

In Marilyn's case, the evidence is quite startling. In fact, so much evidence has been destroyed that it is difficult not to believe in a cover-up. Jack Clemmons, the first LAPD officer who investigated the death scene, has gone on record to state that he believes that she was murdered. Many other detectives have said the same, but no murder charges were ever filed.

Three people were present in Marilyn's house at the time of her death: Her housekeeper Eunice Murray, her psychiatrist Dr. Ralph Greenson, and her internist Dr. Hyman Engelberg. The investigation around Marilyn's death revealed that Dr. Greenson called the police over an hour after Dr. Engelberg pronounced her dead. The behavior of the three present at the scene was described as "erratic". Here are parts of the official timeline of events of that fateful night.

> *7–7:15 p.m.: Joe DiMaggio Jr., son of baseball player Joe DiMaggio (and thus Monroe's former stepson) phones her about his broken engagement to a girl in San Diego. DiMaggio Jr. said when interviewed that Monroe sounded cheerful and upbeat. On duty with the Marines in California, DiMaggio was able to place the time of the call because he was watching the seventh inning of a Baltimore Orioles-Los Angeles Angels game being played in Baltimore. According to the game's records the seventh inning took place between 10 and 10:15 p.m. Eastern Daylight Time; thus, Monroe received the call around 7 p.m. California time.*
>
> *7:30–7:45 p.m.: Peter Lawford (President Kennedy's brother-in-law) telephones Monroe to invite her to dinner at his house, an invitation she had declined earlier that day. According to Lawford, Monroe's speech was slurred and was becoming increasingly indecipherable. After telling him goodbye the conversation abruptly ends. Lawford tries to call her back again, but receives a busy signal. Telephone records show that this is the last phone call Monroe's main line received that night.*
>
> *8 p.m.: Lawford telephones Eunice Murray, who is spending the night in Monroe's guest house, on a different line asking if the maid would check in on her. After a few seconds, Murray returns to the phone telling Lawford that she is fine. Unconvinced, Lawford will try all night long to get in touch with Monroe. Lawford telephones his friend and lawyer Milton A. "Mickey" Rudin, but is advised to keep away from Monroe's house to avoid any public embarrassment that could result from Monroe possibly being under the influence.*
>
> *10 p.m.: Housekeeper Eunice Murray walks past Monroe's bedroom door and later testifies that she saw a light on under the door, but decided not to disturb Monroe.*
>
> *3:00 a.m.: Eunice Murray calls Marilyn's personal psychiatrist, Dr. Greenson, on the second telephone line, she cannot wake Monroe. She is sure something is very wrong after peeking into her barred bedroom window.*
>
> *3:40 a.m.: Dr. Greenson arrives and tries to break open the door but fails. He looks through the*

French windows outside and sees Monroe lying on the bed holding the telephone and apparently dead. He breaks the glass to open the locked door and checks her. He calls Dr. Hyman Engelberg. There is some speculation that an ambulance might have been summoned to Monroe's house at this point and was later dismissed

4:30 a.m.: Police are called and arrive shortly after. The two doctors and Murray are questioned and indicate a time of death of around 12:30 a.m. Police note the room is extremely tidy and the bed appears to have fresh linen on it. They claim Murray was washing sheets when they arrived. Police note that the bedside table has several pill bottles, but the room contains no means to wash pills down as there is no glass and the water is turned off. Monroe was known to gag on pills even when drinking to wash them down. Later a glass is found lying on the floor by the bed, but police claim it was not there when the room was searched.

5:40 a.m.: Undertaker Guy Hockett arrives and notes that the state of rigor mortis indicates a time of death between 9:30 and 11:30 p.m. The time is later altered to match the witness statements.

6 a.m.: Murray changes her story and now says she went back to bed at midnight and only called Dr. Greenson when she awoke at 3 a.m. and noticed the light still on. Both doctors also change their stories and now claim Monroe died around 3:50 a.m. Police note Murray appears quite evasive and extremely vague and she would eventually change her story several times. Despite being a key witness, Murray travels to Europe and is not questioned again.
- Wikipedia, "Death of Marilyn Monroe"

To sum up some strange events that happened that night: The police were called more than an hour after Monroe was found dead; the room was cleaned up by the maid and linen were changed AFTER she was found dead; there were multiple pill bottles in her room, but no water; a glass was later found on the floor, but was not there when the room was first searched; the time of death given by the witnesses changed several times. Finally, prime witness (and a possible suspect), Eunice Murray leaves the country and is never questioned again.

Pill bottles found next to Monroe's body.

Circumstances surrounding Monroe's autopsy are also extremely suspicious, as the conclusion of the most important reports clearly show that swallowing pills was not the cause of her death. Furthermore, there appears to be a clear effort to suppress all evidence that might lead to the true cause of Monroe's death.

"The pathologist, Dr. Thomas Noguchi, could find no trace of capsules, powder or the typical discoloration caused by Nembutal in Monroe's stomach or intestines, indicating that the drugs that killed her had not been swallowed. If Monroe had taken them over a period of time (which might account

> *for the lack of residue), she would have died before ingesting the amount found in her bloodstream. Monroe was found lying face down. There was also evidence of cyanosis, an indication that death had been very quick. Noguchi asked the toxicologist for examinations of the blood, liver, kidneys, stomach, urine and intestines, which would have revealed exactly how the drugs got into Monroe's system. However, the toxicologist, after examining the blood, did not believe he needed to check other organs, so many of the organs were destroyed without being examined. Noguchi later asked for the samples, but the medical photographs, the slides of those organs that were examined and the examination form showing bruises on the body had disappeared, making it impossible to investigate the cause of death.*
>
> *The toxicology report shows high levels of Nembutal (38–66 capsules) and chloral hydrate (14–23 tablets) in Monroe's blood. The level found was enough to kill more than 10 people. An examination of the body ruled out intravenous injection as the source of the drugs. Coroner Dr. Theodore Curphey oversaw the full autopsy. Apart from the cause of death as listed on the death certificate, the results were never made public and no record of the findings was kept."*
> - Ibid.

In 1985, British journalist Anthony Summers investigated the circumstances surrounding Monroe's death. He managed to obtain an interview with the maid Eunice Murray for a BBC report. She inadvertently admitted some damning facts.

> *"For the BBC program Eunice Murray initially repeated the same story she had told Robert Slatzer in 1973 and the police in 1962. She apparently noticed the camera crew starting to pack up and then said, "Why, at my age, do I still have to cover this thing?" Unknown to her, the microphone was still on. Murray went on to admit that Monroe had known the Kennedys. She volunteered that on the night of the actress' death, "When the doctor arrived, she was not dead." Murray died in 1994 without revealing further details."*
> - Ibid.

Despite all of these facts, the truth about Marilyn's death is still not out in the open. As is the case for many other celebrity deaths, there is an aura of mystery surrounding it and a whole lot of answered questions. In other words, it fits the profile of a typical occult elite assassination that has the power to keep law enforcement from revealing the truth.

Some researchers have attempted to pin-point who instigated the murder. Some cite the Kennedys, the CIA, her psychologists or other individuals. It is perhaps wiser to take a step back and to look at the wider picture: Most of the people around Monroe were part of the same system. It was not a single person who decided to kill her, she was a MK slave who was "thrown off the freedom train". Like many others after her, she was a celebrity who was exploited when she was useful and eliminated when her programming started to break down.

> *"The deeper meaning here is that all Monarch slaves are expendable if they cross the line, and many of these victims reportedly have been "discarded" in just such a manner after they become a certain age and are no longer desirable as prostitute/slaves, or if they in someway break free of their programming and are considered a "risk"."*
> - Op. Cit. Gorightly.

Symbol of Beta Programming in Today's Entertainment Industry

While Marilyn Monroe quickly became a larger-than-life icon representing all that is hot and glamorous in Hollywood, she also became, in the shady world of MK-Ultra, a symbol of Beta Programming in Hollywood. Today, more than ever, many young starlets raised in the entertainment industry follow in Marilyn's footsteps – as if it was all planned out for them. Manipulated by handlers, they are lead to fame and fortune, but also go through trauma-based mind control, abuse, exploitation, break downs and, sometimes, early death. In all cases, these celebrities are made to embody Marilyn Monroe at one stage of their career, as if it was a sick requirement by the MK puppeteers, who make it a point to identify their slaves to the clueless masses. How many videos or photoshoots featuring major stars are said to "channel" Marilyn Monroe? Too many to be a coincidence. In some cases, the resemblance is not only aesthetic. Here are some examples.

BRITNEY SPEARS

One of the most obvious cases of mind control in today's entertainment industry is Britney Spears. From her childhood as a Mouseketeer to her adulthood living under the conservatorship of her father and fiancée (aka her handlers), Britney has always been closely monitored by powerful figures. Like so many other slaves, she has gone through breakdowns, substance abuse, and is often described as a "drugged zombie" by those closest to her.

In this stage performance, Britney recreates the iconic flowing dress Monroe moment.

Britney is reportedly "obsessed" with Monroe. According to Wonderwall, Britney demands that a collection of Marilyn Monroe DVDs be on-hand in all her hotel rooms. She also visits Marilyn's grave regularly and wants to be buried in the same cemetery. Are Beta slaves programmed to adulate Marilyn?

ANNA-NICOLE SMITH

Anna-Nicole Smith's life was very similar to Monroe's, right down to the tragic end. Famous for her curves and her "dumb blonde" persona popularized by Monroe, her life in the spotlight was typical of a Beta slave. In the final years of her life, she was in a relationship with her attorney Howard K. Stern – who acted more as a MK handler than a husband.

Anna-Nicole also had to live through some incredibly traumatic events. For instance, in 2006, right after giving birth to her daughter, her 20 year-old son came to visit her ... and mysteriously died right in her hospital room. The cause of his death was never clear but, as usual, the reason given by mass media is "drugs". Was this a sacrifice by the occult elite to traumatize Anna-Nicole Smith the Beta slave? One thing is for sure, the event completely changed for the rest of her life. (Note that Monroe lost two unborn babies and claims they were "taken from her" by unidentified people).

Less than three weeks after the death of her son, Anna-Nicole "committed" to handler Howard. K. Stern in an unofficial ceremony. Five months later, Smith was found dead in a hotel room in Florida. She lost her life at age 39 due to a "combination of drugs". In short, Smith's resemblance to Monroe was not only physical, she was programmed to relive Monroe's life.

One of the numerous occasions Smith was made to look exactly like Monroe.

In Conclusion

In this two-part series of articles, we looked at Marilyn Monroe's youth, career, death and legacy. In all of these stages, Monroe's life was imprinted with trauma, abuse and mind control. As a victim of Beta Programming, when she was not working on a project, she was literally passed around for her " intimate services". Towards the end of her life, Marilyn was JFK's Presidential Model, a situation that could have been explosive if revealed to the public. Both of them would die shortly afterwards in circumstances that remain extremely shady and suspicious.

Even after Monroe's death, her image continues to be used ad-nauseam to identify those who are following in her footsteps by the same system that controlled her entire life. Why do the most iconic figures in our pop culture often end up living tragic lives? Is it because there is something terribly wrong in the entertainment industry? I'll let Marilyn Monroe sum up the situation.

> *"Hollywood is a place where they pay you 50,000 dollars for a kiss and 50 cents for your soul"*
> - Marilyn Monroe

Section 2
Music Business

Music is connected to the soul in ways too profound to fully comprehend. Combined with the symbolic imagery of music videos, a simple song can become a powerful communicational tool.

Music Business

The 2009 VMAs: The Occult Mega-Ritual

From unexpected drama to shocking performances, MTV's 2009 Video Music Awards managed once again to raise eyebrows and get people talking. What most people missed, however, were the occult meanings encoded in the VMAs. The TV event was in fact a large scale occult ceremony, complete with an initiation, a prayer and even a blood sacrifice. We'll look at the symbolism that appeared during the show.

MTV's Video Music Awards have often incorporated dark and strange acts, containing some occult symbolism. This year's version, however, outdid itself. The show left most people wondering what was wrong with Kanye West or trying compute the madness of Lady Gaga's performance. The only way to understand the full meaning behind those performances is to look into esoteric teachings. The fact is that the whole awards show took the most common rituals of occult orders and re-enacted them in a show witnessed by the entire world.

This year's VMA's were very different from other awards shows. They focused on a very limited number of artists (Beyonce, Taylor Swift, Lady Gaga), while ignoring many others who were equally successful. The "chosen" artists became characters in the VMA's ceremony and acted out different ritual dramas. This might sound totally crazy to the average MTV viewer but those acquainted with the practices of occult orders (such as Freemasonry) can decode the references to sacred rituals. There are numerous types of fraternities and rituals, from the most noble to the most infernal, and they have existed throughout History. The VMAs were decisively inspired by dark, sinister and even Satanic ceremonies. Let's look at those rituals.

The High Priestess' Words of Wisdom

Madonna's sermon at the 2009 VMAs.

Madonna, the music industry's High Priestess, the revered "elder" of MTV, opens the show with a very solemn eulogy for Michael Jackson. She admitted never really knowing or "connecting" with him, but she was still chosen to pay him tribute. Madonna is a well known and publicized adept of the Kaballah, the esoteric school of Judaism which is studied in most occult orders. Rabbi Ariel Bar Tzadok explained how she uses (or abuses) Kaballah symbolism in her music:

"I discovered that Madonna's famous dabbling with sacred Jewish mysticism has taken an interesting *turn. In her latest music video for the theme song of a new James Bond movie, the "material girl" of old is transforming herself into a "Kabbalah girl." Aside from the traditional Madonna blend of music and sensuality, in this video we see Madonna has a Holy Name of G-d tattooed onto her right shoulder. Tattooing, mind you, is a practice forbidden under Torah Law, all the more so abhorred by the Kabbalah. Granted the tattoo may not be real or only temporary but nonetheless, any expression of performing a forbidden act is itself forbidden and inexcusable. Unfortunately, Madonna's abuse of Kabbalah and traditional Torah Judaism does not stop here.*

Later in the video we see Madonna winding leather straps around her left arm in the exact same format and style as holy tefillin are worn by religious Jewish men. Tefillin consist of a small leather box containing scared parchments. These are then strapped to one's left biceps, and the strap is wound down the left arm and around the hand. Granted Madonna did not go so far as to defame the tefillin boxes themselves. Yet, it is quite clear that the wrapping of the straps around her arm is done in orthodox Torah style. This act of hers is pure sacrilege."
- Rabbi Ariel Bar Tzadok, Madonna's Kabbalah – Not Kosher

Madonna's tribute focused on the fact that MJ was "otherworldly" and "a king" but she insisted on the fact that he was also a human being. It was wisdom that could only be imparted by the High Priestess. Members of the audience bowed their heads and meditated on her words. They had a deep Kabbalisitic resonance. The speech was followed by a video tribute to Jackson, beginning oddly with 'Thriller' and displaying the face of MJ as a decaying zombie, risen from the dead, on a huge screen. We then hear Price's verse in the song saying:

> *"Darkness falls across the land*
> *The midnite hour is close at hand*
> *Creatures crawl in search of blood*
> *To terrorize yawls neighbourhood*
> *And whosoever shall be found*
> *Without the soul for getting down*
> *Must stand and face the hounds of hell*
> *And rot inside a corpses shell*
> *The foulest stench is in the air*
> *The funk of forty thousand years*
> *And grizzy ghouls from every tomb*
> *Are closing in to seal your doom*
> *And though you fight to stay alive*
> *Your body starts to shiver*
> *For no mere mortal can resist*
> *The evil of the thriller"*

It is only fitting that MJ's greatest was included in his tribute, but this did seem a rather gruesome way to start a posthumous tribute. Someone, somewhere made some odd choices, but this somehow fitted the "vibe" of the rest of the show.

Taylor Swift's Initiation

Taylor Swift wins the "Best Female Video" award and goes up on stage to give her thank yous. Kanye West pops out of nowhere, taking the mic from her hand, and informs her that Beyonce has "one of the best videos of all time". This scene has caused much controversy and has earned Kanye the title of "Douchebag of the year" plus a the honor of being called a "jackass" by the President of the United States. I might shock some people by saying this… but this "unexpected" event was… STAGED! There I said it. Did you ever watch a crappy reality show and had the gut feeling that the whole thing was scripted? Well, I've got an overload of that feeling while watching this scene. None of the people involved (not even Beyonce making her "I can't believe this is happening" face) are good actors. Furthermore, I've been following Kanye's career since his beginnings and I've retained one important fact about him: the only thing Kanye West cares about, is Kanye West. So if he had to throw a hissy fit about something, it would had been about him not winning. Not Beyonce. Him.

"Imma let you finish!"

This scene is in fact Taylor Swift's initiation into what I call "The Circle of Chosen Artists". The pupil is humiliated in front of her peers and told that she is not worthy to be on the same stage as Beyonce, the queen of the ceremony. Almost all groups, fraternities and gangs carry out an initiation process to test the recruit's character, strength and worth. Swift's ordeal was to have Kanye ruin her first award ever and to be told that she didn't deserve this recognition. The rapper is known for bitching during award shows so he was the perfect candidate to make it all seem "unexpected".

The Prayer

"Who wants to pray to the Devil with me?"

Jack Black comes out dressed as a heavy metal guy on steroids to promote a video game. At one point he asks the audience to put their devil horns in the air and the proceeds to pray to the "darklord Satan". The whole thing is light-hearted and comical but I don't see any other way a prayer to Satan can be inserted into a primetime show without getting a truckload of complaints from "concerned parents". The scene starts off semi-funny but Jack Black finishes off on a more serious note by saying: "I ask you to grant tonight's nominees with continued success in the music industry". This last phrase actually reveals a dark truth about the entertainment business.

So the net result of this scene is this: everybody threw up their "devil horns" hand sign, then took each other's hands and prayed to Satan. This piece of pre-rehearsed comedy might have been an insignificant skit in another show. But in the context of this one, with its many recreations of occult rituals, the skit takes on a whole other, sinister meaning.

The Blood Sacrifice

Lady Gaga's performance was hailed as "brilliant" by many music fans. If you however ask them what it symbolizes, their expression becomes questioning. Here's what Gaga said about her performance during an interview at gagadaily.com

> **"Do you think it will be one of those defining moments people will remember at the VMAs?"**
> *"I know it will. I sort of have this philosophy about things: there's never a reason to do something unless it's going to be memorable, unless it's going to change things, unless it's going to inspire a movement. With the song and with the performance, I hope to say something very grave about fame and the price of it."*
>
> **"Something grave? What?"**
> *"You'll have to see."*
>
> **"What are you going to wear?"**
> *"I would say that the fashion for the performance is a representation of the most stoic and memorable martyrs of fame in history. It's intended to be an iconic image that represents people. I think after watching the performance and maybe studying it after you watch it on YouTube, you'll see the references and the symbols come through."*

The setting for the performance is very symbolic. Gaga performs in a temple or maybe an aristocratic mansion, complete with columns, chandeliers and paintings. Occult rituals, mind control experiments and even human sacrifices have constantly been rumored to take place in those kinds of settings. One feature I cannot ignore is the presence of two massive pillars beneath an arch.

The decor of Gaga's performance. Notice the two pillars and the arch above

Masonic lithograph

This obvious reference to Freemasonry hints to the occult and ritualistic aspect of Gaga's performance. Masons are known to carry out ritual dramas in their lodges; live re-enactments of allegorical stories. Gaga's performance symbolizes her rise to fame and the sacrifice she had to make in order to succeed.

When the bloody Gaga is lifted into the air, an eerie light comes out from between the pillars and the dancers lift their arms in the air in praise. Many ancient religions carried out ritual sacrifices to please the gods. Blood sacrifices have also been viewed by black magicians as the ultimate way to collect spiritual energy. The final scene of the performance conveys the presence of this mysterious "force" after a sacrifice.

Rising star.

Right after her performance, Gaga appears dressed all in red, with her face completely covered in red. She is basically a walking, talking blood sacrifice. It represents the aftermath of fame, the hellish life that follows the sacrifice, the selling of the soul for success in the music industry.

Pink's Masonic Initiation

The initiate is blindfolded and attached to a cord with the left breast and left leg exposed

There is no way a Mason could watch this performance without recalling his initiation into the First Degree. Here's a description by Mark Stavish:

> "The candidate for initiation is stripped of all material possessions and dressed in a strange and peculiar garb (...). This includes a blindfold and a length of rope called a cable tow."

Music Business

He continues

> "The blindfold used represents secrecy, darkness and ignorance as well as trust. The candidate is led into the lodge room for initiation but is not able to see what is happening. He is bound about the waist and arm with the cable tow."
> - Mark Stavish, Freemasonry: Rituals, Symbols and History of the Secret Society

Pink is blindfolded and bound with ropes. Her costume exposes her left breast, as is the case with Masonic initiates. Instead of having her left leg exposed, Pink's costume bears a diamond pattern which is very reminiscent of the floors in Masonic lodges.

Inside an Eastern Star Lodge.

Pink's performance was a dizzying display of acrobatics which undoubtedly left her (and the viewers) totally disoriented. This is also a feature of Freemasonry's First Degree initiation:

> "He is then blindfolded and a cord in the form of a noose is passed round his neck. At this point the novice is entering the marginal stage, associated with ordeals; he cannot see, his sense of direction has been confused and he has been dressed like a victim for execution."
> - J.S. La Fontaine, Initiation – Ritual Drama and secret knowledge across the world

Pink's performance was yet another blatant reference to ritual dramas in occult orders.

Taylor Swift's Acceptance into the Order

"Can we try this again now?"

After Swift's public humiliation, Beyonce, the queen of the ceremony, calls her up on stage to let her "have her moment". She appears from backstage (as if awaiting her cue) in a red dress which is strikingly similar to Beyonce's.

Taylor Swift being called on stage represents the fact that she has now been accepted as an equal to Beyonce and has become one of the "chosen ones". The matching dresses also convey this sense of belonging to a new group. She has "passed the test" – the ordeal of being humiliated – and she can now reap the rewards of being an insider.

In Conclusion

Award ceremonies like the VMAs define and crystallize the pop culture of an era. They consecrate the chosen artists while leaving the others dwelling in the shadows of anonymity. As shown above, the whole show was heavily permeated with occult symbolism, primarily focusing on the "initiation" aspect of it. Why is MTV exposing young people (who know nothing about occultism) to such rituals? Is there a subliminal effect on the viewers? Are we educating the new generation to accept these symbols as part of popular culture? There is definitely a second layer of interpretation in many of MTV's products. To decode the symbols is to understand the inner-workings of the entertainment industry.

The Transhumanist and Police State Agenda in Pop Music

Today's pop music is filled with symbols and messages aimed to shape and mold today's youth. Apart from the occult symbolism discussed in other articles, other parts of the elite's agenda are communicated through music videos. Two of those parts are transhumanism and the introduction of a police state. We'll look at the way those agendas are part of the acts of Rihanna, Beyonce, Daddy Yankee and the Black Eyed Peas.

As seen in previous articles on this site, the world's biggest stars exploit common themes in their work, permeating popular culture with a set of symbols and values. The cohesiveness of the message that is communicated to the masses, regardless of the artists' musical genre, attests to the influence of a "higher power" over the industry. Other articles on this site have explored the way Illuminati symbolism, based on secret society occultism, has been reflected in popular videos. Exposing and desensitizing the world to the elite's sacred symbols is, however, only one aspect of their agenda. Other aspects of Illuminati control are reflected in today's popular music as well, including: mass mind control, transhumanism (the "robotization" of the human body) and the gradual introduction of a virtual police state. Through the news, movies and the music industry, this agenda is being insidiously presented to the masses, using various techniques. If the news scares people into accepting measures diminishing their personal freedoms and ushering in a "new era", the music business accomplishes the same job by making it seem sexy, cool and trendy. This angle is mainly aimed at the younger crowd, which is much more susceptible to "take in" the industry's message.

Transhumanism

"Transhumanism is an international intellectual and cultural movement supporting the use of science and technology to improve human mental and physical characteristics and capacities. The movement regards aspects of the human condition, such as disability, suffering, disease, aging, and involuntary death as unnecessary and undesirable. Transhumanists look to biotechnologies and other emerging technologies for these purposes. Dangers, as well as benefits, are also of concern to the transhumanist movement.

The term "transhumanism" is symbolized by H+ or h+ and is often used as a synonym for "human enhancement". Although the first known use of the term dates from 1957, the contemporary meaning is a product of the 1980s when futurists in the United States began to organize what has since grown into the transhumanist movement. Transhumanist thinkers predict that human beings may eventually be able to transform themselves into beings with such greatly expanded abilities as to merit the label "posthuman". Transhumanism is therefore sometimes referred to as "posthumanism" or a form of transformational activism influenced by posthumanist ideals.

The transhumanist vision of a transformed future humanity has attracted many supporters and de-

tractors from a wide range of perspectives. Transhumanism has been described by one critic, Francis Fukuyama, as the world's most dangerous idea, while one proponent, Ronald Bailey, counters that it is the "movement that epitomizes the most daring, courageous, imaginative, and idealistic aspirations of humanity".
- Wikipedia

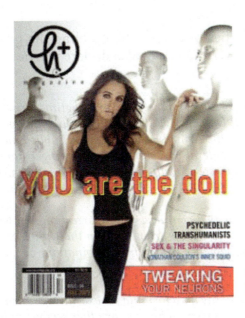

Cover of H+, a transhumanist magazine. The headline says it all.

What is almost never mentioned is the fact that those technological "improvements" will be out of reach for the average man. The huge price tags of those scientific discoveries will render them only accessible to a select elite. While the common man is forced to seek nourishment in genetically modified, chemically altered and even poisonous foods, the elite is trying to achieve immortality through science. Even if the masses cannot have access to those discoveries, mass media makes transhumanism cool, desirable and, ultimately, acceptable.

POLICE STATE

George W. Bush's Patriot Act has enabled the American government to expand surveillance of its citizens, whether it be phone calls, e-mails and physical movements. It also gave the government almost unlimited powers of arrest, detention, search and seizure. Donald E. Wilkes, Professor of Law at the University of Georgia School of Law describes this last concept:

> "I want to examine here a single section of the USA Patriot Act–section 213, definitely one of the most sinister provisions of this monstrous statute.
>
> In euphemistic language that conceals the provision's momentous significance, section 213 states that with regard to federal search warrants "any notice required … to be given may be delayed if … [1]the court finds reasonable cause to believe that providing immediate notification of the execution of the warrant may have an adverse result …; [2] the warrant prohibits the seizure of any tangible property … except where the court finds reasonable necessity for the seizure; and [3] the warrant provides for the giving of such notice within a reasonable period of its execution, which period may thereafter be extended by the court for good cause shown."
>
> Section 213 may be couched in Orwellian terminology, but there is no doubt about what it does. Section 213 is the first statute ever enacted in the history of American criminal procedure to specifically authorize an entirely new form of search warrant-what legal scholars call the sneak and peek

warrant (also dubbed the covert entry warrant or the surreptitious entry warrant). A sneak and peek search warrant authorizes police to effect physical entry into private premises without the owner's or the occupant's permission or knowledge to conduct a search; generally, such entry requires a breaking and entering."
- Donald E. Wilkes, Flagpole Magazine Sept 2002.

Subsequent acts have further diminished civil liberties of citizens by enabling the government to declare any American a "terrorist" with little to no proof. The government can also declare martial law with little or no valid reason.

"The John W. Warner Defense Authorization Act of 2006, "named for the longtime Armed Services Committee chairman from Virginia," was signed October 17, 2006, by President George W. Bush. The Act "has a provocative provision called 'Use of the Armed Forces in Major Public Emergencies'," the thrust of which "seems to be about giving the federal government a far stronger hand in coordinating responses to [Hurricane] Katrina-like disasters," Jeff Stein, CQ National Security Editor wrote December 1, 2006.

"But on closer inspection, its language also alters the two-centuries-old Insurrection Act, which Congress passed in 1807 to limit the president's power to deploy troops within the United States ... 'to suppress, in a State, any insurrection, domestic violence, unlawful combination, or conspiracy'," Stein wrote.

"But the amended law takes the cuffs off" and "critics say it's a formula for executive branch mischief," Stein wrote, as "the new language adds 'natural disaster, epidemic, or other serious public health emergency, terrorist attack or incident' to the list of conditions permitting the President to take over local authority — particularly 'if domestic violence has occurred to such an extent that the constituted authorities of the State or possession are incapable of maintaining public order.'"

"One of the few to complain, Sen. Patrick J. Leahy, D-Vt., warned that the measure virtually invites the White House to declare federal martial law. ... It 'subverts solid, longstanding posse comitatus statutes that limit the military's involvement in law enforcement, thereby making it easier for the President to declare martial law,' he said in remarks submitted to the Congressional Record on Sept. 29."
- sourcewatch.org, Establishing martial law in the United States

We'll see how those concepts are cleverly inserted into pop music in order to create specific climate in the collective consciousness.

Rihanna's Hard and AMA Performance

In hip-hop slang, the term "hard" usually refers to someone who is street-savvy, gritty, rebellious and who is decisively "not down with police". Hard transposes this term to a military context. Her militaristic video features a gang of uniformed men dancing under the orders of "General Rihanna". We've come a long way from Public Enemy's Fight the Power…it is now Submit to the Power. All of this military/dictatorial imagery is mixed with Rihanna's sexy moves and outfits, appealing to the masses' basest instinct: sex. This generates in the viewer an unconscious positive response to this otherwise terrible backdrop. I mean, who likes to be in a war zone? Not people who have experienced it, that's for damn sure.

How come guns were always censored from music videos (especially rap) until very recently? Is it only acceptable when they are used to promote war and a police state?

Ummm, I don't really relate to all of this.

In this symbolic image, Rihanna's Mickey Mouse hat represents Mind Control. She is sitting on the phallic symbol that is the tank's cannon. In other words, she is a pawn of the Illuminati agenda.

Her performance in the 2009 American Music Awards also contains a great deal of noteworthy elements. The intro video is a disturbing display of dehumanization and Mind Control lead by a "shadow government". Rihanna is a cyborg being programmed by the insertion of a microchip inside of her (RFID anyone?). Notice the shadowy appearance of those performing the surgery.

A semi-robotic Rihanna on an operation table. A computer chip is being inserted in her by shadowy figures.

Rihanna strapped to a turning device with mannequin parts in the background relate to mind control. The dancers in riot gear point guns everywhere relate to police state. All and all, one big Illuminati extravaganza.

Beyonce's Grammy Performance

Beyonce walks on stage with a bunch of men dressed in riot gear... the type of unit a police state would use to repress opposition during popular turmoil. What are they doing in Beyonce's performance? Contributing to permeate popular culture with police-state imagery.

Is the American public being mentally prepared for martial law?

Daddy Yankee's Performance at Premio Lo Nuestro 2010

Reggaeton superstar Daddy Yankee has likely been chosen to promote the Agenda to the Latino community. His performance at the Premio Lo Nuestro awards in Miami is simply a perfect Illuminati fit. At the beginning the performance, a picture of Daddy Yankee standing under a Masonic compass is displayed.

Daddy Yankee under a Masonic compass

Daddy Yankee's is surrounded by dancers looking like robotic cyber-police/soldiers. The name of his new single is Descontrol, which means "lose control". Interesting.

The Black Eyed Peas' Imma Be Rocking that Body

This long video is all about the merger of humans and robots, which is, as seen above, the ultimate goal of transhumanism. It starts with Fergie saying "we are not robots!" … only to see her become a half-robot shooting a gun that causes an irresistible need to breakdance.

Will.I.Am starts his verse by saying "Imma be the upgraded new negro", which pretty much sums up the transhumanist philosophy.

At the end of the video, Fergie wakes up from her "dream". It sure was cool when she was a robot, wasn't it?

The upgraded new Will.I.Am and friends?

In Conclusion

Articles on this site have mainly focused on the occult symbols found in music videos. There are, however, other aspects of the Illuminati agenda that are present in popular culture. Transhumanism and the establishment of a virtual police state are two objectives that are slowly but surely being implemented with little to no public debate. Movies, video games and the music industry are doing the job of leading the masses' collective consciousness towards a new era by saturating the airwaves with those concepts. The "robot agenda", as some observers call it, has been an intricate part of the music industry for years now and examples of it are way too many to enumerate. The theme of the "upgraded human" due to his robotization has been exploited by most of today's international stars. There is a difference between a trend and an agenda.

The "police state" element found in video and performances is relatively new but equally, if not more, disturbing. Music has always been a healing, liberating and emancipating medium. Looking at the music industry's products of the last years, is there a possibility of it being hijacked by an ever-intrusive elite? Think about who owns the record companies.

The Hidden Meaning of Lady Gaga's "Telephone"

Lady Gaga's 9-minute video featuring Beyoncé is steeped in weirdness and shock value. Behind the strange aesthetic, however, lies a deeper meaning, another level of interpretation. The video refers to mind control and, more specifically, Monarch Programming, a covert technique profusely used in the entertainment industry. We'll look at the occult meaning of the video "Telephone".

Just when I thought I'd written everything I had to write about Lady Gaga, Telephone comes out. An inevitable deluge of e-mails instantly followed, demanding an article about it. So I watched the video and, gosh darnit, the people who wrote those e-mails were right. There are, yet again, a whole bunch of Illuminati/mind control symbols in Lady Gaga's latest video. I can't say I was surprised, however, knowing that Jonas Akerlund co-wrote and directed the video. In the article Lady Gaga, the Illuminati puppet (which I suggest you read before this one), I dissected the Akerlund-directed video Paparazzi and its references to mind-control programming. Telephone acts as a sequel to Paparazzi, where Gaga still plays the role of a mind-controlled drone who kills people. This concept is never openly discussed by the artists when they are asked to explain their videos because it is not meant to be understood for the masses. The hidden meaning of the video actually depicts the elite's contempt for the general population, hence the scene of ritual murder of average Americans in a diner by mind-controlled slaves. Don't know what the hell I'm talking about? Keep reading.

The Hidden Meaning of the Song

When I first heard Telephone on the radio, I thought the song was about Lady Gaga receiving phone calls from an annoying dude while she's out in a club. I could already picture a video of Gaga on a dance floor not answering her cellphone. I've imagined this video because I was interpreting the song at its face value and going by its literal meaning, like most people do. Akerlund's video has however infused a second, deeper meaning to the song, giving it an entirely new dimension. In an interview with E! Online, Gaga herself explained this fact:

> "There was this really amazing quality in 'Paparazzi,' where it kind of had this pure pop music quality but at the same time it was a commentary on fame culture. In its own way, even at certain points working with Jonas Åkerlund, the director of both videos really achieved this high art quality in the way that it was shot. I wanted to do the same thing with this video—take a decidedly pop song, which on the surface has a quite shallow meaning, and turn it into something deeper."

What is never stated, however, is that this "deeper meaning" found in Gaga's video relates to mind control, a covert practice used by the military, the CIA, religious cults and the Illuminati elite. It is used to program human beings to become mental slaves and to execute specific tasks. In Paparazzi, Gaga plays the role of a mind-controlled slave who was "programmed" to poison and kill her boyfriend. Telephone is a continuation of this story, where Gaga goes to jail for her crime.

In the video, the "telephone" is a metaphor for Gaga's brain and the fact that she is not answering that phone (her brain) means that she has "dissociated" from reality. Dissociation is the ultimate goal of Monarch mind control. It is induced by traumatizing events, such as electroshock therapy or torture, to force the victim to dissociate from reality. This enables the handlers to create in the victim an alter personality that can be programmed to perform various tasks, such as carrying out an assassination.

> "Trauma-based mind control programming can be defined as systematic torture that blocks the victim's capacity for conscious processing (through pain, terror, drugs, illusion, sensory deprivation, sensory over-stimulation, oxygen deprivation, cold, heat, spinning, brain stimulation, and often, near-death), and then employs suggestion and/or classical and operant conditioning (consistent with well-established behavioral modification principles) to implant thoughts, directives, and perceptions in the unconscious mind, often in newly-formed trauma-induced dissociated identities, that force the victim to do, feel, think, or perceive things for the purposes of the programmer. The objective is for the victim to follow directives with no conscious awareness, including execution of acts in clear violation of the victim's moral principles, spiritual convictions, and volition.
>
> Installation of mind control programming relies on the victim's capacity to dissociate, which permits the creation of new walled-off personalities to "hold" and "hide" programming. Already dissociative children are prime "candidates" for programming".
> - Ellen P. Lacter, Ph.D., The Relationship Between Mind Control Programming and Ritual Abuse

Gaga's brain as a non-answering telephone is represented in two separate occasions during the video:

Gaga's head is the telephone. She is not answering that phone, which is symbolic of her dissociative mind state.

The telephone receiver is made out of hair and covers her left eye, representing Illuminati mind control.

So in the context of the video, the telephone is Gaga's mind and the dance club is representative of her dissociative state, the "magical place" mind-controlled slaves are trained to escape to during traumatic events.

> "Hello, hello, baby
> You called, I can't hear a thing.
> I have got no service
> in the club, you say, say

Wha-Wha-What did you say, huh?
You're breaking up on me
Sorry, I cannot hear you,
I'm kinda busy.

K-kinda busy
K-kinda busy
Sorry, I cannot hear you, I'm kinda busy."

By "kinda busy", Gaga means she has dissociated from reality. Real life is calling her brain but she "has no service", she's not there. The chorus pretty much epitomizes this concept.

"Stop callin', stop callin',
I don't wanna think anymore!
I left my head and my heart on the dance floor.
Stop callin', stop callin,
I don't wanna talk anymore!
I left my head and my heart on the dance floor."

Gaga is not thinking or talking for herself anymore, her head and her heart have been dissociated from her core personality due to Monarch programming.

Video Analysis

The video is a Quentin Tarentino-esque short film which is heavily inspired by Thelma and Louise and peppered with tons of product placements and transvestites. That surely wasn't the video I was picturing when I first heard that song. From the comments I've read, the video left many fans confused about its meaning. This is quite understandable, knowing that most viewers have no idea what the song is really about. When the hidden "mind control" meaning is brought to light, the symbolism of the video becomes evident and the storyline becomes more coherent. I will now attempt to go through the many symbolic scenes of the video and explain their occult meaning.

Do the cigarettes covering her eyes represent her blindness to her highly toxic life as a mind controlled drone?

Gaga then sits down and "gets busy" with an inmate, but is interrupted by a phone call. She seems to be enjoying a special status in the jail … maybe due to the fact that she is a slave only obeying orders … and that she is needed again.

Gaga is then bailed out by Beyoncé and leaves prison. Inside the car, Gaga and Beyoncé engage into a highly dissociative conversation. It basically sounds like dialogue between two mind-controlled slaves. The phrase "Trust is like a mirror. You can fix it if it's broke but you can still see the crack in the motherfucker's reflection" can refer to a cheating boyfriend and can also refer to the permanent damage caused by the fragmenting of one's personality in mind control.

The dynamic duo then enters an all-American, good ol'-fashioned diner. Beyoncé meets with probably the biggest douche in the universe (played by Tyrese Gibson) and proceeds to poison him. At this point, Gaga comes out of the kitchen with poisoned honey and serves it to the customers.

Gaga stares blankly (the way a dissociated mind-controlled assassin would stare) while Tyrese eats the poison.

The mass murder begins … people eat up Gaga's poisoned honey and die. Does this represent the Illuminati elite poisoning the masses with toxic media?

Lady Gaga turns the a-ok hand in front of her eye (representing the Illuminati's "All-Seeing Eye") into a gun pointed towards the viewer … the masses eating all of the poison served to them.

The entire clientele of the all-American diner gets poisoned and dies. You might have noticed the emphasis on "bees" and "honey" during the entire video. Gaga calls Beyoncé "Honey Bee". She also serves poisoned honey to the diner's customers. What does this signify? Beyoncé and Gaga's poisonous honey is actually their music and videos, which are served to the general public through mass media. You can figure out the rest.

While the customers are agonizing and dying, Beyoncé puts on the Mickey Mouse sunglasses, the same glasses worn by Gaga in Paparazzi while killing her boyfriend.

Beyoncé wearing Mickey Mouse sunglasses

Gaga with Mickey Mouse sunglasses in Paparazzi

In both videos, the singers wore the glasses during the killings, hinting to the fact that they are programmed to execute the poisonings. As stated in previous articles, Mickey Mouse ears or designs often occultly refer to mind control , probably because Disney films were known to be used on MK slaves during their programming.

Gaga and Beyoncé then start dancing in "patriotic" outfits surrounded by the lifeless bodies of dead Americans ... pretty disturbing. In her interview with E! Online about Telephone, Gaga stated she wanted to take

> "(...) the idea that America is full of young people that are inundated with information and technology and turn it into something that was more of a commentary on the kind of country that we are."

Is that what she meant?

To sum up the situation in the diner, we have Lady Gaga and Beyoncé dancing around dead people and singing about the fact they are dissociative, mind-controlled drones.

> "Can call all you want,
> but there's no one home,
> and you're not gonna reach my telephone!"

Gaga and Beyoncé finally flee the crime scene. Gaga is then shown in front of the Pussy Wagon wearing a leopard-print suit, a reference to "sex kitten" programming.

Beta (aka Kitten) Programming

> "BETA. Referred to as "sexual" programming. This programming eliminates all learned moral convictions and stimulates the primitive sexual instinct, devoid of inhibitions. "Cat" alters may come out at this level."
> - Ron Patton, Project Monarch

In the final scene, Gaga and Beyoncé prance around wearing dresses by Emilie Pirlot. Beyoncé's black dress and the veils hint to the ritualistic nature of the murders.

Illuminati Signs

As stated in previous articles, the hiding of one eye and the "a-ok" sign (which seemingly means 666 in the music industry) are flashed by all Illuminati artists, apparently to show their allegiance. There are a truckload of them in this video.

Gaga dressed in police tape, covering one eye. Knowing the trauma mind control victims must go through, her body is truly a crime scene.

In Conclusion

Telephone is yet another Lady Gaga product permeated with references to mind control and Illuminati symbolism. Gaga's "commentary" on today's youth is certainly not a positive one. The video basically says: America is ready to eat any poisonous crap the elite serves them, and that is accomplished through controlled puppets. I will now pre-address comments I'm bound to receive:

"How is Lady Gaga mind controlling me? I'm not feeling controlled to do anything"
I am not saying that Gaga is controlling your mind. I'm saying her video is ABOUT mind control. This disturbing theme keeps reoccurring in pop music. What you should ask yourself is this: does mass media shape and mold our society's values and beliefs? Billions of dollars invested yearly in marketing say yes.

"Your articles are a form of mind control."
Someone voicing an opinion on a website is not a form of mind control. Quite to the contrary, it is a freedom guaranteed by the first amendment. To compare this article to the ritual abuse mind control victims have to go through is a total aberration. If you were forced to read out loud this article numerous times while being deprived of food and sleep, then maybe it could qualify as mind control.

"She is doing it on purpose to piss you off"
I heard this comment when Bad Romance came out and after her Grammy performance, where her hype man alluded to her "mind-controlling music". As much as I would like to believe that I've got that much influence on today's biggest star, I highly doubt that Gaga, her staff, her video directors and her record label with its millions of dollars would concentrate all of their creative efforts to piss off one blogger. The truth is: She was doing this before this site was even online and she keeps doing it now. Her works, like the works of many other pop stars, are part of a greater agenda. It used to focus on exposing the youth to materialism and sexual promiscuity, but it has now expanded to occult symbolism, mind control and transhumanism.

Am I reaching you or is your telephone busy?

Jay-Z's "Run This Town" and the Occult Connections

Jay-Z's video called "Run This Town" (featuring Rihanna and Kanye West) contains occult symbolism relating to secret societies. It has been long rumored that Jay-Z is part of some sort of occult order (probably Freemasonry) due to the hints slipped in his songs and his imagery. "Run This Town" certainly adds fuel to the fire. We'll look at the symbolism in this song and in his clothing line, Rocawear.

I'm pretty sure Jay-Z does it on purpose and that he appreciates the attention it gets him. He has been steadily displaying occult symbolism in his songs, videos and in the designs of his Rocawear clothing line. The Brooklyn rapper has lately been associating himself through telling hints to Freemasonry, Illuminati and other orders. Is he now initiated in one of those Brotherhoods and eager to show it off? Why does he appear in other videos containing occult meanings (see Rihanna's "Umbrella" or Beyonce's "Crazy in Love")?

The video to "Run This Town" was directed by Anthony Mandler. The least we can say is that Mandler certainly knows how to insert dark symbolism into a video.

"Do What Thou Wilt"

The O.T.O's motto on Jay-Z hoodie.

Before we get into the video, a couple of things need to be explained in order to understand Jay-Z's mindset and where he gets his ideas from. The symbols that will be discussed in this article can't be coincidences or a collection of random items. Jay-Z draws his inspiration from specific sources and associates with like-minded people (director Anthony Mandler) to integrate those ideas. A telling example can be found in the second trailer video for "Run This Town". We see Jay-Z explaining the concept of the video while wearing a black hoodie bearing the saying "Do What Thou Wilt".

Aleister Crowley: Reformer of the O.T.O. whose motto was "Do what Thou Wilt". He also enjoyed being called "The wickedest man in the world".

"Do What Thou Wilt" is the official dictum of the Ordo Templi Orientis (O.T.O.) and of its reformer, occultist Aleister Crowley. The O.T.O. is a hermetic order modeled after Freemasonry and German Illuminism and teaches its initiates the secrets of the Mysteries, gnosticism, sex magick, Kaballah and other occult sciences. Contrarily to Freemasonry, the O.T.O. is however based on the "Law of Thelema" which main precept is "Do What Thou Wilt be the whole of the Law". Although this saying was interpreted in different ways, most agree that it refers to the dismissal of conventional moral and ethical rules in order to find one's "True Will". In other words, the usual guidelines by which good and evil are determined have to be blurred and forgotten to obtain the true path to illumination. (For more information on Crowley, read the full article entitled Aleister Crowley: His Elite Ties and His Legacy at our sister site). Crowley explains this notion rather clearly here:

> "There are no "standards of Right". Ethics is balderdash. Each Star must go on its own orbit. To hell with "moral principle"; there is no such thing"
> - Crowley, Aleister. The Old and New Commentaries to Liber AL, II,28.

Although not officially considered "satanic", the O.T.O. does fully embrace the Luciferian doctrine (see Crowley's poem "Hymn to Lucifer) and its high level members are referred to as "Most Illuminated and Most Puissant Baphomet". Baphomet is of course the horned androgynous idol of Western Occultism.

Is Jay-Z part of the O.T.O. or does he just like that shirt? Don't know. We will however see that he is very educated in the field of occult symbolism and that he enjoys hinting people that he associates with the Brotherhood.

"Run This Town" Analysis

This is the video at face value: Jay-Z, Rihanna and Kanye West are performing in front of an angry mob, which is apparently out to overthrow the current order of things and thus "Run This Town". The aesthetics of the video are reminiscent of movements led by rebel factions in third world African or Latino countries . When one listens closely to the lyrics however, something seems to be "off". Jay-Z and Kanye are mainly rapping about how rich and famous they are and are describing bourgeoisie luxuries such as Maison Martin Margiela clothes, bottles of Riesling and Maybach cars. This isn't exactly the type of speech Che Guevara would give. Despite the looks, the artists aren't quite revolutionary, they can even be considered pro-establishment. Is this a political rebellion or could it be philosophical/spiritual? The visuals of the video hint a second, occult meaning to the song. At the beginning of the video, a man hands a lit torch to Rihanna who holds it up in the air. This symbolic gesture sums up perfectly

Rihanna handed a lit torch

the concept of the video.

Anybody vaguely familiar with occultism can easily associate the symbol of the lit torch held high to Lucifer a.k.a. the Light Bearer. Most occult orders secretly acknowledge Lucifer as being the savior of humanity, the fallen angel who liberated men from the oppression of the biblical God (Jehovah, Yahweh). These orders (the main one being Freemasonry) have been working for centuries towards the overthrow of the rule of organized religions to usher in a new age or a "New Order". At the philosophical center of this order: the Luciferian Doctrine, where men are free to become gods by their own means. The Torch of Illumination is the ultimate symbol of this philosophy and can be found in many instances (see Statue of Liberty, a gift from French Freemasons). The goal of the Illuminist has been put in plain in simple words: they are dedicated to the "coming forth of the conquering light". "Run This Town" visually represents this aim in a clear way for the initiates yet concealed for the profane. Consequently, the video contains a second level of interpretation: "Run This Town" is an announcement of the coming of a New World Order, lead by secret (Luciferian) societies. Rihanna's ominous intro explains how it is going down.

> *Feeling it coming in the air, hear the screams from everywhere, I'm addicted to thrill, Its a dangerous love affair, can't be scared when it goes down, got a problem tell me now, Only thing that's on my mind is who gon run this town tonight, who gon run this town tonite*

Rihanna's lyrics are announcing an imminent change that might terrify or enrage some people ("hear the screams from everywhere"). The torches hint to a new spiritual and philosophical era where Lucifer is king. She is "addicted to the thrill" of being on the dark side and she knows that dealing with it is a "dangerous love affair". But regardless of all of this, it all comes down to control, hence "Only thing that's on my mind is who gon run this town tonight". Then Jay-Z comes along and announces the coming of "Roc Nation" (Roc being a diminutive of Rocafella, the name of his record label, which is based on the elite family Rockefeller).

> *We are, yeah, I said it, we are This is Roc Nation, pledge your allegiance Get y'all fatigues on, all black everything Black cards, black cars, all black everything And our girls are blackbirds, riding with they Dillingers I get more in-depth if you boys really real enough This is La Familia, I'll explain later But*

for now, let me get back to this paper I'm a couple bands down and I'm tryna get back I gave Doug a grip, I lost a flip for five stacks Yeah, I'm talking five comma six zeroes dot zero ? Back to running circles 'round niggas, now we squared up

Jay-Z is asking you to "Pledge your allegiance" to the new ruler and to wear black everything to honor him. Jay's lyrics contain hints to Freemasonry who are hidden in the double meaning of some lines. "I gave Doug a grip" means he gave Doug a stack of money but the double meaning to that line would refer to the Masons' secret handshakes which are called "grips". And who is Doug? Might be Doug Morris. The last line of his first verse is "Back to running circles' round niggas, now we squared up". Aside from its obvious meaning, it also refers to the important Masonic concept of "squaring the circle", which is way too deep to explain here ("I get more in-depth if you boys really real enough"). In the second verse, Jay-Z says "It's the return of thee god", which refers to the Luciferian belief of men being gods. This term is often used in NY slang and originates from the fact that many rappers were Five-Percenters, a philosophy based on the belief that all men are gods. Further in the song Jay-Z says: "I'm in Maison, ugh, Martin Margiela" which is a upper-end fashion store. English speaking people usually pronounce the french word "maison" to sound like "mayzaun". Jay-Z however says it to sound like "mason" as in "Freemason". There is an obvious double-meaning here meant to catch the ear of the listener. He basically says "I'm in Mason" to make people say "huh did he really say that?" as "I'm a Freemason" but he then continues by saying "ugh, Martin Margiela". The little pause after he says those words accentuate the effect. Then Rihanna comes back with the chorus.

Life's a game but it's not fair I break the rules so I don't care So I keep doing my own thing Walking tall against the rain Victory's within the mile Almost there, don't give up now Only thing that's on my mind Is who gon' run this town tonight

She says that the game of life is corrupted but she still succeeds because she "breaks the rules". In other words, she ignores the boundaries between good and evil to achieve her goals. This might remind you of the saying "Do What Thou Wilt" of the Ordo Templi Orientis described above. Those lines refer to her as a person and also to the Order as a whole, who is prepared to commit the most horrible acts to reach its goals. "Victory's within the mile" means that the realization of the New World Order is at its final stages and that the Illuminati-sponsored revolution is

Rihanna throwing Rocafella sign which is the left eye inside a triangle

about to happen.

So "Run This Town" contains obvious hints leading towards Luciferian philosophy and occult orders. The fire of Lucifer's torch esoterically represents divine knowledge and wisdom brought to men. Fire in this video is however a destructive force. What type of knowledge are we giving these rebellious people, who represent the masses of fans?

Jay-Z and Occult Symbolism

Jay-Z's clothing line "Rocawear" has incorporated obvious occult symbols in its designs. Some are so blatantly Masonic that he probably couldn't get away with it if he wasn't effectively implicated with them. In interviews, Jay-Z has said to be actively involved in the choices of designs of his clothing line. Here are some examples:

All-Seeing Eye in Triangle

"Masters of the Craft" is a 100% Masonic saying and the All-Seeing Eye of the Great Architect depicted here is directly taken from Masonic works. Notice also the secret handshake depicted in a circle.

The logo above is designed to look like the Eye of Horus

Kanye wearing a shirt with the head of Baphomet

Prodigy's Crusade

Prodigy's ain't down with that crap

Rapper Prodigy from the mythical group Mobb Deep has occasionally denounced Jay-Z's affiliation with the Illuminati in the last years. Here's an URB article on the subject.

> Like he does in his monthly blog on Vibe.com, the incarcerated Prodigy recently spewed more of his conspiracy theories via a handwritten letter to URB. This time, he reveals the moment his eyes were opened to the sham he calls "the government, religions, politics, the Federal Reserve, and I.R.S." According to P, in 1996, after reading a book by Dr. Malichi Z. York titled Leviathan 666, he was moved so much, he cried, and that was his "moment of clarity." "I was crying for all of humanity, but mostly for my black people 'cause I then realized it was all a sham," Prodigy writes in his letter to URB. "The government, religions, politics, the Federal Reserve, the I.R.S., and everything that we believe and live by is a joke." Even worse, the rapper says that many popular rappers are aware of these society secrets, but choose not to speak on it for fear of not being accepted by corporate America. One, in particular, is Jay-Z.
>
> Occult Secrets of Jay Z, Kanye & Nas "J.Z. knows the truth, but he chose sides with evil in order to be accepted in the corporate world. J.Z. conceals the truth from the black community and the world, and promotes the lifestyle of the beast instead," he wrote. Prodigy says that Jay grew up grew up in Dr. York's "Nuwabian" community in Brooklyn as a kid, and is "aware" of these evils — rogue government, elitists running the country, etc. Because of Jay'z refusal to speak on the topics Prodigy has been doing so since his incarceration, he will make it a point to wage war against him. "J.Z is a God damn lie. I have so much fire in my heart that I will relentlessly attack J.Z, Illuminati, and any-every other evil that exists until my lights are put out," P writes. "This negativity I speak of is an actual living entity that uses us as food. We must sever ties with it in order to see things for what they really are. This negative energy is created and harnessed by the Illuminati secret government and they will make you spread this energy without you even knowing it. But people like J.Z. are very well aware. He was schooled by Dr. York," he continued.
> - URB Magazine

In Conclusion

The least we can say is that Jay-Z has "affinities" with occultism and secret societies. "Run This Town" only adds to the suspicions surrounding him due to the symbolism and philosophy displayed in the video. In light of those facts, some questions arise: has Jay-Z sided with the elite to succeed in the corporate world? Is he used to promote NWO agenda? Or is this an act to fuel rumors and to add a little "mystique" around his persona? Maybe it's all of the above. Maybe he's doing this to get people like me writing and to generate buzz around his latest album. If this article has promoted Jay-Z, so be it. At least people will know what the the hell they're saluting when they're throwing up that Roc sign.

The Esoteric Interpretation of The Black Eyed Peas' "Meet Me Halfway"

The Black Eyed Peas' "Meet Me Halfway" is a catchy song with deceptively simple lyrics. A viewing of the video, however, reveals the song's true meaning: a quest for spiritual enlightenment, based on esoteric teachings. This article looks at the occult symbolism of the song and the video and explains its spiritual meaning.

The path to illumination

I've known of The Black Eyed Peas since they were an underground rap group struggling for recognition. Apparently tired of anonymity, the group recruited Fergie, a sultry R&B singer, and set their focus on the pop market. Their desire to appeal to the lowest common denominator produced pop gems such as the ode to idiocy Let's Get Retarded (which later had to be changed to Let's Get it Started due to complaints) and eventually launched them to super-stardom. My lack of tolerance for corniness caused me avoid the group for years, but some readers sent me the group's latest video, "Meet Me Halfway". I was stunned by the incredible depth of the video. Its symbolism reaches deep into Mystery religions of antiquity and reveals tenets of esoteric schools such as the Kaballah. Pretty unexpected from the group also known for singing "My hump, my hump, my hump, my hump, my lovely lady lumps".

After viewing the video, it is fairly obvious that the director did not want to convey a simple love song. It is about the union of the physical and the astral planes, of the male and female principles and between humanity and divinity. It is about the yearning of a being of the mundane world to seek a higher truth. The video is drenched with occult symbolism used in esoteric schools such as the Kaballah, Freemasonry, Theosophy, Gnostic Christianity and more.

Fergie, the Human Soul

The video starts with Fergie lying down in a lush, green jungle. She is on the physical plane, on planet earth which is abundant with terrestrial life and life-giving humidity. She is the archetypal Eve in the Garden of Eden. Despite all the beauty surrounding her, Fergie is looking to the sky and yearning for "something more", which is currently unattainable to her. She feels that there is something missing.

I can't go any further than this
I want you so badly, it's my biggest wish

Fergie is singing to her divine nature, to her higher self which seems infinitely far from her, yet it can still hear her. She went as far as humanly possible in her spiritual quest and she is asking her spiritual self to make a move towards her. She is heard.

Apl.de.ap, the Divine Soul

Rapper apl.de.ap (yes, that's his name) plays the role of Fergie's higher consciousness, the missing piece needed to obtain spiritual enlightenment. He is dressed in garments reminiscent of eastern sages or mystics and is meditating. The fact that he is levitating, surrounded by an aura, rotating and multiplying himself further conveys this sense of ethereal, non-human presence. He is not a physical human, but Fergie's spiritual counterpart. Apl.de.ap's lyrics communicate that as much as Fergie wants to connect with her higher-self, the higher-self longs to reunite with Fergie as well. They were forming a single unit before she "fell" into material existence and they want to "become one" again.

Cool, I spent my time just thinkin thinkin thinkin bout you
Every single day yes, I'm really missin missin you
And all those things we use to use to use to do
Hey girl, what's up, it used to used to be just me and you
I spent my time just thinkin thinkin thinkin bout you
Every single day, yes I'm really missin missin you
And all those things we use to use to use to do
Hey girl what's up, yo what's up, what's up, what's up

Apl.de.ap's character completes Fergie in every way. She is physical, he is spiritual; she is lives in terrestrial life, he is lives in nothingness; she is female, he is male. In alchemical terms, she is the Mercury and he is the Sulfur. This concept of "two souls" is all-important Kabbalistic teachings.

Apl.de.ap uses a Torah Pointer to consult his map. In this esoteric context it is used for Kabbalistic studies. Does the Kabbalah provide the road map to enlightenment?

A Torah Pointer

Here's an explanation of Kabbalistic philosophy using the Zohar's (the most important work of Kabbalah) interpretation of the Genesis:

> "The Zohar holds the concept of two Adams: the first a divine being who, stepping forth from the highest original darkness, created the second, or earthly, Adam in His own image. The higher, or celestial, man was the Causal sphere With its divine potencies and potentialities considered as a gigantic personality; its members, according to the Gnostics, being the basic elements of existence. This Adam may have been symbolized as facing both ways to signify that with one face it looked upon the proximate Cause of itself and with the other face looked upon the vast sea of Cosmos into which it was to be immersed. Philosophically, Adam may be regarded as representative of the full spiritual nature of man – androgynous and nor subject to decay. Of this fuller nature the mortal man has little comprehension. Just as spirit contains matter within itself and is both the source and ultimate of the state denominated matter, so Eve represents the lower, or mortal, portion that is taken out of, or has temporal existence in the greater and fuller spiritual creation."
> - Manly P. Hall, Secret Teachings Of All Ages

Will.I.Am, the Vehicle

Exploring the universe on the back of his elephant, Will.I.Am is the liaison between the spiritual and the terrestrial world. He could be called a "cosmic travel agent". He is seeking the gateway that would allow Fergie and Apl.de.ap to unite again. This sense of travel is well reflected in his lyrics:

Girl, I travel round the world and even sail the seven seas
Across the universe I go to other galaxies
Just tell me where you want, just tell me where you wanna to meet
I navigate myself myself to take me where you be
Cause girl I want, I, I, I want you right now
I travel uptown (town) I travel downtown
I wanna to have you around (round) like every single day
I love you alway .. way

Notice on the elephant the symbol of a double-headed eagle, which is very similar to the symbol of the Scottish Rite of Freemasonry.

Is Freemasonry the "gateway" to Kabbalistic enlightenment?

The Pine Cone Staff

Apl.de.ap gets up and starts his search for Fergie, his lost counterpart. He is the active principle searching, while Fergie is the passive principle, laying down on earth and waiting. Together they will become complete. In his walk through the cosmic desert, we can see that he is holding a very symbolic staff:

Pine cone staff

Pine cones have always been occultly associated with spiritual enlightenment. Whether we look at ancient Babylonians, Egyptians, Greeks or Christians, the pine cone has represented the mysterious link between the physical and the spiritual worlds, which can be found in the human brain. The pineal gland, also known as the third eye, is represented by the pine cone in occult symbolism. It is taught by Mystery schools to open the doors to spiritual perception once the seven Chakras are properly activated.

Pine Cone Staff of Osiris surrounded by the two serpents of the Kundalini. The staff represents the spine and the pine cone represents the pineal gland.

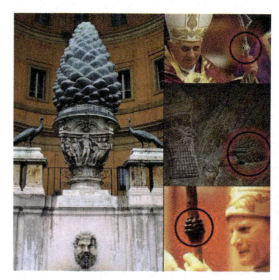
Giant pine cone at the Vatican

Manly P. Hall explains the importance of the pine cone in Freemasonry and ancient civilizations:

> *"Sufficient similarity exists between the Masonic CHiram and the Kundalini of Hindu mysticism to warrant the assumption that CHiram may be considered a symbol also of the Spirit Fire moving through the sixth ventricle of the spinal column. The exact science of human regeneration is the Lost Key of Masonry, for when the Spirit Fire is lifted up through the thirty-three degrees, or segments of the spinal column, and enters into the domed chamber of the human skull, it finally passes into the pituitary body (Isis), where it invokes Ra (the pineal gland) and demands the Sacred Name. Operative Masonry, in the fullest meaning of that term, signifies the process by which the Eye of Horus is opened. E. A. Wallis Budge has noted that in some of the papyri illustrating the entrance of the souls of the dead into the judgment hall of Osiris the deceased person has a pine cone attached to the crown of his head. The Greek mystics also carried a symbolic staff, the upper end being in the form of a pine cone, which was called the thyrsus of Bacchus. In the human brain there is a tiny gland called the pineal body, which is the sacred eye of the ancients, and corresponds to the third eye of the Cyclops. Little is known concerning the function of the pineal body, which Descartes suggested (more wisely than he knew) might be the abode of the spirit of man. As its name signifies, the pineal gland is the sacred pine cone in man – the eye single, which cannot be opened until CHiram (the Spirit Fire) is raised through the sacred seals which are called the Seven Churches in Asia."*
> - Manly P. Hall, Secret Teachings of All Ages

The Enlightenment

Taboo stares in awe at the sun, the metaphorical representation of divinity. The process of enlightenment has started. He is the bridge "to the other side".

> *Let's walk the bridge, to the other side*
> *Just you and I (just you and I)*
> *I will fly, I'll fly the skies, for you and I (for you and I)*
> *I will try, until I die, for you and I, for you and I, for for you and I,*
> *For for you and I, for for you and I, for you and I*

Taboo literally "sees the light"

The Opening of the Gateways

After searching, Will.I.Am opens the portal which will allow Fergie and Apl.de.ap, the two souls, to finally unite. All that is left to do is simply to walk through.

The higher-self enters a pyramid-shaped gateway, representing the spiritual world and the triune nature of divinity

The lower-self enters a cube-shaped gateway, representing the material plane and planet Earth

In Conclusion

The video to the Black Eyed Peas' Meet Me Halfway features many symbolic elements of esoteric spirituality. Many schools of thought have been mentioned here, such as the Kaballah, Buddhism, Alchemy and Freemasonry. This might be confusing for readers who are not acquainted with those concepts but you only need to keep one thing in mind: all of these schools teach different paths leading the same goal, which is spiritual enlightenment. It is the "Inner-Christ" of the Gnostic Christians, the "Great Work" of Alchemy and the "Lost Key" of Freemasonry.

In the context of this website, where many videos analyzed present sinister messages, many people will want to ask me: Is this video good or bad? My answer is: It is what you want it to be … and what you want it to be will probably be a result of your religious background and your personal beliefs. The message of this video is pure occultism, as in "the representation of spiritual truths through symbolism", and it represents the beliefs of the true "Illuminatus", those who genuinely seek spiritual enlightenment. The satanic, mind-control symbols seen in previous articles are corrupted, negatively charged, occult by-products. The same way male and female principles, positive and negative energies and light and darkness exist, so exists "good" and "evil" occultism, often typified by white and black magic. The good will inspire people to reach to the sky and ask a higher truth to "meet them halfway", while the evil will leave them confused and tormented, obsessed by materiality and screaming to nobody in particular "Let's get retarded".

Kanye West's "Power": The Occult Meaning of its Symbols

Kanye West's "Power" is a short, almost stationary video that manages to tell a profound story in symbolic language. By decoding the occult meaning of the symbols present in this moving tableau, the viewer discovers who really holds the "power" in the world and understands the story of Kanye West's initiation. We will look at the meaning of those symbols as they appear in the video.

Rapper and producer Kanye West has always found a way to stand out from the crowd. His video Power is no exception. It differs from the MTV norm in many regards, whether you look at the content or the form. The duration of the video, the filming style and the subject matter are quite distinct from today's typical rap videos as it is short (1:43), filmed in a single shot (compared to the one-shot-per-second standard of music videos) and is very rich in archetypal symbolism.

Director Marco Brambilla sought to depict the concept of power in the form of a "video tableau", a moving painting that slowly reveals itself to the viewer with a continuous camera movement. The director seem to have perfected this technique in his previous creation, Civilization, a video mural created for the new Standard Hotel in New-York city. The symbolism present there is simply overwhelming.

For Power, Brambilla went for a neo-classic aesthetic, but still created a piece full of symbolic and cultural references. As it was the case for paintings of the neo-classic era, each object, each symbol and each detail in the video conveys an important meaning, a meaning that is needed to understand the entire story. As we will see later, many symbols in the video have a deep occult meaning and many of them point to Freemasonry and Mystery schools. By doing so, the director clearly states what type of power is being presented in the video. We will therefore look at the meaning of the symbols displayed in the video as they appear in the shot.

Symbols of the Video

The video starts off with a close-up of Kanye West with glow-in-the-dark eyes, as if he was "illuminated" from within. He stands between an infinite row of Ionic columns, which represent "wisdom" in Masonic symbolism.

Kanye with illuminated eyes between rows of twin pillars

Two Pillars

As regular readers of this site already know, the occult meaning of the twin pillars is ancient, profound and present in the symbolism of almost all mystery schools of History. There are many layers of interpretation attributed to the two columns, but one constant is always present: The pillars represent the entrance – the gateway – to the world of the initiate. Behind the columns can be found the key to the Mysteries and, consequently, the source of true power. This concept has been used for in many cultures and schools of thought.

The two columns called the "Pillars of Hercules" in Ancient Greece stood at the gateway to the sphere of the enlightened

"The city of the philosophic elect rises from the highest mountain peak of the earth, and here the gods of the wise dwell together in everlasting felicity. In the foreground are the symbolic pillars of Hercules which appear on the title page of Bacon's Novum Organum, and between them runs the path which leads upward from the uncertainties of earth to that perfect order which is established in the sphere of the enlightened."
- Manly P. Hall

Pillars of Hercules in Francis Bacon's "New Atlantis" as a gateway to the New World

Masonic initiate standing between the twin pillars as the third pillar, in the same fashion as Kanye West in the video.

Two pillars leading to Jacob's Ladder in this Masonic tracing board

In Power, Kanye is standing at the mouth of the gateway to the "sphere of the enlightened," right at the border of the corrupt and decadent material world. So, right from the start of the video, the director reveals the true nature of power in this world: It is not your democratically elected officials, but those who consider themselves to be behind those pillars. One of the most significant lines of the song is

"In this white man's world, we the ones chosen"

Does Kanye's "white man's world" refer to the hidden rulers, the Illuminati, who are hidden behind those pillars? Did they choose Kanye West and give him Power by permitting him to become an influential figure in the entertainment industry? Was he chosen to become one of them? The next symbol might shed some light into this.

Horus

Horus pendant on Kanye's chain

The next thing that catches the viewer's eye is most probably that gigantic chain with Horus' head as a pendant. Horus is an ancient Egyptian deity that has an extreme importance in occult mysteries. Considered to be the Sky god, he is more often represented with the symbol of a single eye. The Eye of Horus is an ancient Egyptian symbol of protection and royal power from deities, in this case from Horus or Ra.

> "Horus, the son of Osiris and Isis, was called "Horus who rules with two eyes." His right eye was white representing the sun while his left eye was black representing the moon. According to Egyptian legend Horus lost his left eye during a fight with his murderous uncle, Seth, to revenged his father's death. Seth tore out his nephew's eye but lost the fight because the assembly of the gods declared Horus the victor. The eye was reassembled by the magic of Thoth. Then Horus gave the eye to Osiris who experienced rebirth in the underworld."
> - Jordan Michael, Encyclopedia of Gods

The importance of the "one-eye" in occult symbolism has been highlighted in many articles on The Vigilant Citizen. The All-Seeing Eye found on the Great Seal of the United States and many other occult symbols originate from the Eye of Horus.

The Eye of Horus as depicted by the Golden Dawn Mystery School

The symbolism of Horus is especially of great importance in Freemasonry, as the path of an initiate through the Masonic degrees is described as the process by which the Eye of Horus is opened.

So Kanye stands at the gateway between the corrupt world of the profane and the exclusive world of the illuminated, wearing a Horus pendant, an unmistakable symbol of the Mysteries. One might say: "Well maybe Kanye just likes Egyptian things." Maybe so, but in the context of this video, where all details are important and extremely meaningful, Horus becomes another piece of this symbolic puzzle.

Horned Girls

The entrance of the gateway of pillars is guarded by two horned albino girls holding a staff. Their features are very reminiscent of depictions of Isis and Hathor, goddesses of ancient Egypt. Another allusion to Egyptian magic.

Kanye standing between two horned female figures

Isis and Hathor crowning Queen Nefertari. Both goddesses were depicted with bovine horns on their heads.

Isis was the mother of Horus (discussed above) and was the goddess of motherhood, nature and magic. Hathor was also considered as a maternal deity while also being the goddess of music, dance and fertility. Both Isis and Hathor were known to welcome and protect the dead during their journey to the afterlife, a concept that is particularly interesting in the context of the video.

> "The goddess (Hathor) [...] manifests two aspects of her divine power: first of all, she participates in the afterlife rite of passage, by means of which the deceased attains eternal life, and, second, she demonstrates her special connection to the Egyptian king. Hathor is rightly called a royal goddess, and in this role she is linked in various ways to the life of the pharaoh. Often the pharaoh would call himself the oldest son of Hathor."
> - Archive for Research in Archetypal Symbolism

Kanye, perhaps symbolizing the Pharaoh, is standing at the gateway to eternal wisdom, about to be executed/assassinated/sacrificed under the watchful eyes of Hathor, the "royal goddess." Are the goddesses welcoming Kanye "behind the veil," protecting him in this rite of passage to immortality? In occult circles, new candidates must symbolically die and be reborn to complete their initiation process. Is Kanye being killed an allegory for his initiation?

Sword of Damocles

Sword hanging above Kanye West's head

Wenceslas Hollar's depiction of the Sword of Damocles

While doing some preliminary research on this video, I came across an article on MTV.com titled Kanye West's 'Power' Video: A Cultural Cheat Sheet. Here's what it says about the sword hanging above his head:

> *"Dragonlance: An image of a sword descending into a crown hovers over Kanye's head, bringing to mind Volume Two of Douglas Niles' series "The Crown and the Sword: The Rise of Solamnia," in which Sir Jaymes Markham commands the orders of the Rose, Sword and Crown."*
> - Kanye West's 'Power' Video: A Cultural Cheat Sheet, MTV.com

Really? The director of this neo-classical themed video, was inspired by an obscure fantasy novel released in, like, 2006? Seriously? Good job, MTV, in keeping our youth clueless. The descending sword is more probably a reference to the Sword of Damocles, a pretty widely known legend.

> *"The Damocles of the anecdote was an obsequious courtier in the court of Dionysius II of Syracuse, a fourth century BC tyrant of Syracuse. Damocles exclaimed that, as a great man of power and authority, Dionysius was truly fortunate. Dionysius offered to switch places with him for a day, so he could taste first hand that fortune. In the evening a banquet was held where Damocles very much enjoyed being waited upon like a king. Only at the end of the meal did he look up and notice a sharpened sword hanging directly above his head by a single horse-hair. Immediately, he lost all taste for the fine foods and beautiful girls and asked leave of the tyrant, saying he no longer wanted to be so fortunate.*
>
> *Dionysius had successfully conveyed a sense of the constant fear in which the great man lives. Cicero uses this story as the last in a series of contrasting examples for reaching the conclusion he had been moving towards in this fifth Disputation, in which the theme is that virtue is sufficient for living a happy life. Cicero asks "Does not Dionysius seem to have made it sufficiently clear that there can be nothing happy for the person over whom some fear always looms?"*
> - Wikipedia, Damocles

The tale of the Sword epitomizes the constant danger faced by those in positions of power. Kanye stands there, in a state of impending doom, knowing he can be executed at any time. Right after we see the sword of Damocles, a figure appears holding a dagger and attempting to stab him. The assassination will not happen by dagger, however, as two other figures leap out of nowhere holding swords to accomplish the "Killing of the King."

Killing of the King – The Initiation

Ritual initiation represented in a display of geometry and symmetry

At the ending of the video, the decadent women and the dagger-holding assassins all disappear as two swords are about to hit him. Are we sacrificing the King?

The concept of regicide is reflected in the single's cover art. It depicts Kanye's severed, crowned head with a sword firmly jammed into it. Apparently Kanye was king and he got killed. Is this a symbol for a Masonic ritual? Note the stone on which Kanye's head is placed. Is it the "perfect ashlar" of the Masons that represents the state of a perfected initiate?

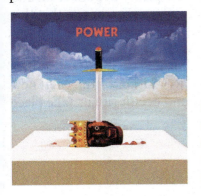

Covert art of Power portraying the killing of Kanye West as a king.

A perfect ashlar in a Masonic lodge. In Masonic symbolism, the candidates start their journeys as allegorical "rough ashlars" and, through knowledge and wisdom, smooth out their edges in order to become a perfect ashlar.

Some occult researchers have stated that the "Killing of the King" is the name of a Masonic rite of passage to obtain the 33rd degree (see "King Kill 33" by James Shelby Downard & Michael A. Hoffman II). Semi-interesting sidenote: King Kill 33 is also the name of a Marilyn Mason song, with rather interesting lyrics. Another sidenote: Researchers have reported that Killing of the King rites often happens in public, as more witnesses give more power to the ritual, hence … JFK. A completely crazy theory?… DYR (Do your research).

Back to Kanye and his standing … the two swords flying towards him never actually touch him but instead form a triangular shape above his head, possibly hinting to a "symbolic" killing and not an actual one. Notice the position of the crown above Kanye's head. The combination of those elements form an interesting image.

Masonic Square and Compass

In Conclusion

To sum up the the video, Kanye stands at the border between Masonic knowledge and the decadence of the mundane life, represented by lustful and gluttonous women, lounging around eating grapes. Kanye says "goodbye cruel world / I see you in the morning", as he has been "chosen" to take part in an initiation process that is often metaphorically described as a "long night," followed by a glorious awakening as a new being. In order to accomplish this, Kanye needs to kill his old self and be ritualistically reborn. Once this is done, true power is within his grasp.

This "moving painting" is definitely a multi-layered artwork, with many levels of interpretation: the first level is a commentary on power by using timeless symbols taken from ancient art; the second level describes a Masonic initiation with a ritual murder and an imminent rebirth.

This video lasts a mere minute and forty-three seconds but it manages to give the viewers plenty to ponder on and many symbols to decode. Looking at its meaning from a pop culture point of view, it is interesting to note that this short-film, intended to be viewed by the general public (especially young people), describes the concept of power with overt Masonic symbolism and occult references. This causes the uninformed viewers to unconsciously associate those symbols with the concept of Power, while "those in the know" get the "insider's wink" sent by this video. Power ultimately becomes another piece in the on-going process called the "Revelation of the Method," where the true source of power gradually and subliminally reveals itself to the world and occult rituals take place right in front of the public's eyes.

How long before the complete revelation?

> "The clock's tickin' / I just count the hours"

Britney Spears, Mind Control and "Hold it Against Me"

Britney Spears is a pop icon who simultaneously embodies the glamour of stardom and the destructive side of fame. She has reached the heights of super-stardom and the lows of tabloid humiliation. Her erratic behavior lead to numerous questions regarding her mental stability, but most are unaware of the most important fact: She is a product of Illuminati mind control. In fact, the video for "Hold it Against Me" symbolically portrays the manipulation and mind control she goes through. This article will look at significant events in Britney Spears' life and at the hidden meaning of the video "Hold it Against Me".

Britney Spears is the prototype of the modern pop star: young, sexy, controversial and completely manipulated by the entertainment industry. She has been literally groomed since childhood by industry execs to become a pop star. From working in Broadway at 8 years old and the Mickey Mouse Club at 12 to becoming a world-renowned pop star at 17, Britney is a true "showbiz child". Today, most agree that she has reached the status of pop icon. Rolling Stone magazine wrote that Britney is "one of the most controversial and successful female vocalists of the 21st century," and "spearheaded the rise of post-millennial teen pop".

Despite her seven hit albums and her iconic status, most will remember Britney Spears not for her music, but for the drama surrounding her personal life. She was indeed involved in a long list of controversies and rumors regarding her love life, her past, her virginity, her drug use, her mental stability and even her parenting skills. While some believe that Britney deserves this public ridicule due to the fact she's a "talentless hack" or "trailer trash" living a decadent lifestyle, others see in Britney the classic symptoms of a young performer who went through the devastating mind control machine of the entertainment industry. Britney indeed bears many classic symptoms of a Monarch programming victim. Further, the video of Hold it Against Me contains many visual clues that hint at Britney's mental prison. We will first look at some significant events in Britney's life and how they are related to trauma-based mind control, then we'll look at the occult meaning of the video Hold it Against Me.

Raised in the Illuminati Entertainment Industry

Although it is difficult to determine which celebrities have actually undergone trauma-based mind control programming, Britney Spears displays the most obvious symptoms. She grew up in rural Louisiana in a family plagued with substance abuse and violence, making her an ideal candidate to be handed over to the industry. At age eight, Britney and her mother Lynne travelled to Atlanta for an audition in the 1990'ss revival of The Mickey

Mouse Club. Casting director Matt Cassella rejected her due to her young age, but still referred her to their talent agent Nancy Carson. Britney was then introduced to what Springmeier calls "The Network". She then moved with her mother to New York and attended the Professional Performing Arts School. Soon after, she landed a job as an understudy in the Broadway musical Ruthless! with other industry child Natalie Portman.

At the age of 13, Britney was finally cast in the Mickey Mouse Club and entered Disney's Illuminati mind-control system.

Britney Spears in the Mickey Mouse Club. Other stars in this picture: Christina Aguilera, Justin Timberlake and Ryan Gosling.

The Mickey Mouse Club is one of Disney's many projects aimed to recruit and mold child stars. The corporation obviously means to make money off these young talents, but there is also a more sinister side to its operations. Disney has been used by the occult elite since its beginnings in the 1930s and has closely worked with the government on numerous occasions. Disney was hired by the government to produce numerous propaganda films and Walt Disney himself even participated in secret CIA secret projects. According to several researchers, Disney was part of the CIA's MK-ULTRA program: Its properties were used for mind-control experiments and many of its productions deliberately contained mind-control triggers and symbolism.

> "This author theorizes that the reason the FBI and CIA are so touchy about letting people know that Walt worked for the government is that the Network knows how the FBI and CIA worked together to procure children for mind-control programming purposes. Because Disney and Disneyland played such as an enormous role in Mind Control, Disney's connection to them, although on the surface a seemingly minor fact, is in reality a minor fact sitting on top of an enormous ghastly secret."
> - Fritz Springmeier, Deeper Insights Into the Illuminati Formula

> "CA–Disneyland has been an off hour site for Illuminati and satanic rituals for years. Programming has gone on using Disneyland as one big prop for programming. Many of the Disney movies are used for programming, and some Disney scripts are especially tailored for Monarch slave programming. The Peter Pan programming can use the ship. The space programming can use the space props. The satanic programming can use the castles. Lots of mirror programming is done at Disneyland, and Disneyworld. There is also Magic Mountain programming, and programming using the Around the World Dolls, and its theme song. Some of Wizard of Oz and the Cinderella programming was also done at Disneyland using costumes. Preverbal children are taken to Disneyland to get them ready for the scripts."
> - Fritz Springmeier, The Illuminati Formula to Create a Mind Control Slave

Disney's involvement in mind control also reflected on the The Mickey Mouse Club and its trademark mouse ears became a symbol of mind control.

> "In 1955, Walt Disney made his cartoon character Mickey Mouse real by creating a fan club–the Mickey Mouse Club, which aired five days a week usually just as children came home from school. Twenty-four children called Mouseketeers would help Mickey, and they would dance and sing and do skits. The Mickey Mouse Club adored the unique, cute little beanie Mickey Mouse caps with their big ears mounted to each side of the beanie. In the 1950's, most kid viewers of the show wanted their own "Mouse Ears" and to become a Mouseketeer, especially children who were receiving Mickey Mouse scripts in their total mind-control programming."
> - Springmeier, Op. Cit.

Once a Mouseketeer, always a Mouseketeer

According to ex-Illuminati programmer Svali, many pop singers are used by the Illuminati to promote their messages and perpetuate the idea of mind control. In one interview, Britney Spears and the Mickey Mouse Club are specifically mentioned:

> "I believe that Brittany Spears, and others are being used by them to sing lyrics they like. (…) In fact, many of the top pop singers come from an internship with the "Mickey Mouse club" (yep, good old Walt the Illuminist's Empire) and I believe they are offered stardom in exchange for allegiance or mind control."
> - Svali, "Exclusive Interview with an Ex-Illuminati Programmer/Trainer"

Sex Kitten Programming

In 1998, Spears signed with Jive records and released her first solo album …Baby One More Time. As it is the case for almost all teenage Disney stars, Britney's image was focused on a blend of childhood innocence and sexuality – the sexualization of childhood is now a recurring theme in pop culture. It is also the bid of Illuminati Sex Kittens (those who underwent beta programming) to be portrayed in the media as teenage sex-symbols. In her first video, Britney is dressed as a Catholic school girl while singing the sexually charged lyrics "hit me baby one more time". Some of her early photoshoots exploited the same theme, causing controversy.

About the above picture, Britney (who was 16 at the time) claimed that Lachapelle tricked her into a sexy shoot:

> "Sexy superstar BRITNEY SPEARS is fond of the sexy photos taken of her by DAVID LaCHAPELLE for ROLLING STONE magazine – but insists the legendary snapper tricked her into it. The BOYS beauty was just 16 when LaChapelle snapped her in her bedroom surrounded by dolls, and the finished product shocked readers around the world.
>
> But Britney – who is now proud of the images – insists she had no idea they would turn out to be so

saucy. She says, "He came in and did the photos and totally tricked me. They were really cool but I didn't really know what the hell I was doing. And, to be totally honest with you, at the time I was 16, so I really didn't.

"I was back in my bedroom, and I had my little sweater on and he was like, 'Undo your sweater a little bit more.' The whole thing was about me being into dolls and in my naive mind I was like, 'Here are my dolls!'

"And now I look back and I'm like, 'Oh my gosh, what the hell?' But he did a very good job of portraying me in that way. It certainly wasn't peaches and cream."
- Contact Music, "Britney: David Lachapelle Tricked Me Into Sexy Photos"

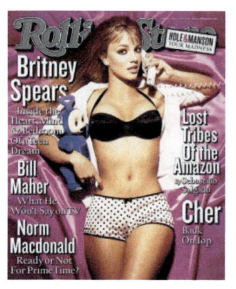

1999 Rolling Stone cover. In her first magazine cover, Britney is in a sexy outfit and holding a Teletubbies doll. The AFA said it is "a disturbing mix of childhood innocence and adult sexuality".

A Dave Lachapelle (no stranger to mind control symbolism) photo mixing innocence and sexuality. The multiple dolls are also a Monarch programming references to multiple alter personalities.

Tattoos are often significant in Monarch programming. One of Britney Spear's first tattoos – a butterfly (a Monarch is a type of butterfly) leaving a vine – symbolizes the slave emerging from the elite's bloodline system. Tattoos are the preferred way of the Illuminati to identify Monarch slaves (see former Disney child star Vanessa Hudgens first tattoo).

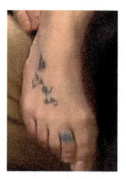

Butterfly leaving a vine, Spear's first tattoo.

"A note should be made that the American intelligence agencies tattooed some of their slaves with blue Monarch butterflies, bluebirds, or roses for identification purposes. (…)."
- Op Cit. Springmeier.

After a couple of albums, where she went from singing "I'm not that innocent" to "I'm a slave 4 U" (can we be less subtle?), Britney became a fully grown woman and an industry veteran. Her "consecration" into the Illuminati industry was celebrated by Madonna in a symbolic performance during the 2003 VMAs, alongside fellow Mouseketeer Christina Aguilera.

Dressed in wedding gowns, Britney and Christina were wed to "Hollywood" by the Kabbalistic High Priestess Madonna. Both stars have Kabbalah-inspired tattoos.

Breakdown

It has been observed that years of Monarch programming often result in the subject breaking down around the age of 30. The unbearable abuse these slaves have to live through cannot be sustained for decades, especially when one is under constant public scrutiny. Celebrities who go through this kind of life almost inevitably succumb to drug abuse and self-destructive behavior. When their programming starts to fail, they often die in mysterious circumstances. Look at the lives of Monarch slaves such as Marilyn Monroe, Judy Garland and Anna Nicole Smith and see if you detect any similarities. Hopefully, this won't happen to Britney.

Britney as Marilyn Monroe (the original entertainment industry sex kitten). Her hands are bound, symbolizing restraint and lack of control. You will probably notice that most industry Sex Kittens will pose as, or refer to, Marilyn Monroe at one point or another during their career.

In the past years, numerous events surrounding Britney Spears led to the questioning of her mental stability. Many strange episodes, documented by various sources, show that Britney often exhibits telling symptoms of a Monarch slave. One of them is having multiple personalities.

Monarch slaves are trained to dissociate and to take on alter personas, each of them having their own characteristics and even different accents. People close to Britney have described these precise symptoms:

> "Sources are now painting a very disturbing picture of Britney Spears, or whoever she happens to be at any given moment.

> *We're told the whole British accent thing — well, it's more than an accent. Britney has multiple personalities, including, as people in her life call it, "the British girl." We're told when Spears loses the British personality, she has absolutely no idea what she did during the time she assumed that personality.*
>
> *Sources say Brit has a number of other identities, where she becomes "the weepy girl, the diva, the incoherent girl," and on and on.*
>
> *Sources say Britney had become the British girl the day she didn't show for her deposition and has no recollection of it."*
> - TMZ, Britney's Multiple Personality Disorder

> *"Britney Spears' recent bizarre behaviour may be down to multiple personality disorder, it has been revealed. The troubled singer's 'favourite' identity appears to involve talking with a British accent, inspired by her latest boyfriend, Birmingham-born paparazzo boyfriend Adnan Ghalib. Sources claim the singer, 26, is suffering from dissociative identity disorder, which leads the sufferers to take on various personalities to dissociate them from reality."*
> - Daily Mail, "The many faces of Britney: Singer has 'multiple personality disorder' - and thinks she's British"

During her turbulent period with Kevin Federline, many accounts surfaced regarding her suicidal tendencies and her alleged bisexuality – other characteristics of a Monarch Sex Kitten.

Probably the most infamous moment of Britney's public life is her head-shaving incident. The event occurred the day after she was admitted to rehab – "rehab" often being a code word for "programming". At closer look at the details of this bizarre incident bear all of the signs of a mind-control slave attempting to break free from their handler's control.

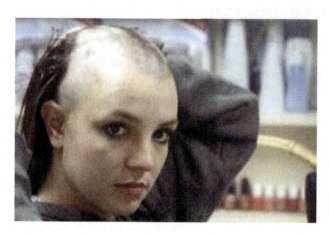

Britney shaving her head

Witnesses of the event claimed that Britney said that "she was tired of having things plugged into it (her head) and did not want anybody touching her". Is she referring to the abuse given by her mind-control handlers? Britney's radical act of shaving her head might be a desperate attempt to "shed her old self" and restart anew. What did Britney refer to when mentioning "things plugged into her head"? One of the only instances in which something is plugged into someone's head is during electroshock therapy- one of Monarch programming's basic techniques (though it should be called electroshock torture).

> *"Electroshock is used to create the dissociation from trauma during the programming, and later it is used to remove memories after the slave has carried out a mission, or to instill fear and obedience*

in a reluctant slave. Slaves generally carry horrible body memories of excruciating electro-shock tortures to their entire bodies. As the slaves begin a therapeutic deprogramming process they will recover these horrible memories, not to mention many other painful memories."
- Springmeier, Op. Cit

Despite Britney's multiple attempts to break free, she is still under the Illuminati's control. Proof of a celebrity's allegiance can often be found in the slave's body of work. Celebrities are indeed used to propagate the symbolism relating to mind control and to hide in plain sight the Illuminati's modus operandi. Hold it Against Me is another blatant example of this Agenda as the video symbolically portrays Britney's mind control by the industry.

Hold it Against Me

Hold it Against Me was directed by Jonas Akerlund, today's go-to director for mind-control/occult imagery (see this previous Vigilant Citizen article on Lady Gaga's Telephone). Not unlike Telephone, the video has absolutely nothing to do with the song's lyrics. While the song is apparently about having sex with a stranger met in a club (promoting promiscuity to teens is always part of the Agenda), in the video there is no guy, no club and no sex. We only see Britney, trapped in a giant cylindrical modernist nightmare, attached to intravenous lines and wearing a wedding gown. The video gives the song another meaning: It becomes about Britney's mind control and her alter personas. It is the classic Illuminati industry story of the "good girl gone bad" and all of the ritualistic symbols and color codes described in previous articles are thoroughly apparent.

At the beginning of the video, Britney is shown in a huge cylinder composed of television monitors and video cameras. This space symbolizes Britney's "media prison". Like mind control slaves, she is constantly monitored by her handlers using cameras. She is also being "programmed" as monitors continually display footage of Britney's past videos. She is closed to the outside world and can only see the images that are fed to her, which are of herself as portrayed by handlers.

High tech devices monitor and program Britney in her mind control prison.

Britney is wearing a white wedding gown that hints at the ritualistic aspect of the video. The white dress symbolizes Britney's purity and innocence at the beginning of the process. This will, of course, change.

To further emphasize Britney's mind control, she is shown attached to intravenous (IV) lines.

IV therapy is the giving of substances directly into a vein. It is used in hospitals to deliver medication, blood transfusions and lethal injections. It is also used in Monarch programming.

"The following is a partial list of these forms of (trauma-based mind control) torture: (...)

16. Drugs to create illusion, confusion, and amnesia, often given by injection or intravenously.
17. Ingestion or intravenous toxic chemicals to create pain or illness, including chemotherapy agents."
- Ellen P. Lacter, Ph.D, Kinds of Torture Endured in Ritual Abuse and Trauma-Based Mind Control

"If an alter is not being cooperative when they are accessed, they can be locked in place mentally and given a quick shot of a fast-acting hypnotic-inducing drug. One drug which was popular for programming was demerol, which would be administered intravenously (an IV). It takes about 5-7 minutes to take full effect after administration via an I.V. The dosage can be administered so that the effect remains until the programming session is over."
- Springmeier, Op. Cit.

Britney connected to intravenous lines.

During the chorus of the song, Britney magically levitates.

Notice the semi-hidden Baphomet head in the cylinder, emphasizing the occult nature of Britney's mind control.

In the video, the chorus is the moment where Britney dissociates and therefore symbolically levitates. In actual mind control, the dissociative slave gets a feeling of light-headedness, as if one is floating. The lyrics of the chorus emphasize the concept of escaping reality, in other words, dissociating:

If I said my heart was beating loud
If we could escape the crowd somehow
If I said I want your body now
Would you hold it against me

Cause you feel like paradise
I need a vacation tonight
So if I said I want your body now

Would you hold it against me

Due to the pain and torment lived by the mind-control victim, dissociating actually "feels like paradise" as the slave stops feeling physical pain. They are encouraged by their handlers to escape to their "happy place". In other words, they "need a vacation".

While Britney is levitated, strange eyeless dancers emerge from under her gown.

Beings with no eyes appear while Britney is levitated

The lack of eyes of these dancers gives them a non-human quality. Do they represent the spirits/demons assigned to mind-control slaves during the occult rituals conducted by their handlers?

After the dissociation scene, the next step of Monarch programming is symbolically depicted: the creation of the alter persona. This happens in a big, messy ritual where the virginal Britney dressed in white gets soiled and consumed.

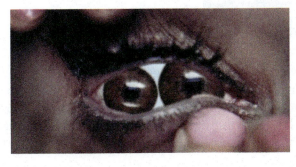

This shot of one eye with two pupils is shown for about a half of a second. It is however very significant: it represents the existence of two personalities within the same person.

During the breakdown of the song, Britney's IV lines start spilling out colored paint (instead of blood?) all over her white dress and the monitors showing images of her youth. It is the blood sacrifice, the soiling of her innocence, the ritual abuse she must take from her handlers.

A soiled and consumed Britney.

While this happens, another scene depicts two Britneys fighting – a visual representation of what happens in the slave's psyche: the battle between two personalities.

Two Britney's fighting, sporting different colors, representing the distinct nature of each persona.

At the end of the battle, a new Britney emerges from the process. From the pure and innocent Britney dressed in a white wedding gown is created a bad, Sex-Kitten version of Britney, who is dressed in black BDSM-style leather and surrounded with men wearing masks.

The new Britney

Britney's transformation is complete in yet another video exploiting the "good girl gone bad through mind control" theme – a theme that all female pop stars seemingly have to go through. The ritualistic metamorphosis from pure to promiscuous as portrayed by other stars including Rihanna (Umbrella), Lady Gaga (Bad Romance), Christina Aguilera (Not Myself Tonight), Mariah Carey (It's Like That) and many others has taken place once more. Young viewers witness yet another ritual that is subliminally concealed in symbols and color codes.

In Conclusion

Britney is, without a doubt, a modern pop icon embodying both the inspiring and repulsive side of fame. She has achieved her life-long dream of becoming a successful singer, yet this success has required her to become part of a dark, manipulative, abusive system. Of the many pop stars promoting the Illuminati mind control agenda, Britney is one of the most obvious cases of an actual Monarch slave. We have looked at some events where Britney exhibited typical symptoms of a mind-control slave but many other instances could have been added. While it is easy ridicule the behavior and the work of pop stars, most people have absolutely no idea of the pain and the trauma these people have to suffer in order to be in the spotlight. The reason why some stars are able to remain popular and obtain airplay is because they are part of the System. Britney is part of it and, at this point, I don't think she has much of a choice. Like other industry puppets, she is even forced to portray her own mind control in her works.

The Akerlund-directed video Hold it Against Me symbolically depicts the process of mind control and occult transformation in a semi-subliminal fashion. The constant usage of this concept in pop culture has many goals, including: numbing the viewers to the system's symbolism and motive, forcing the performers to go through mega-rituals witnessed by millions of viewers, and hiding in plain sight the true nature of the industry. According to the Illuminati's occult philosophy, it is their karmic duty to reveal their actions (whether in a subliminal, coded matter or not): Concealing and revealing is the game they play.

Critics of Hold it Against Me video said that "Britney didn't seemed involved in the video and was not appearing to be having fun". Would you have fun if you were forced to reenact a trauma you've been experiencing for your entire life?

Lady Gaga's "Born This Way" – The Illuminati Manifesto

Lady Gaga's single "Born This Way" introduces the viewers to the birth of a "new race" and to a new world, using intricate imagery and a precise narrative. It is a psychedelic trip filled with occult and archetypal symbols, telling the story of a cosmic birth and new ideals. However, behind its outward message of acceptance, a more sinister message lies embedded in the symbolism of the video. We will look at the underlying meaning of "Born This Way" and analyze the meaning of the occult symbolism in the video.

Lady Gaga is back, y'all. And she's got horns on her forehead. And she's in space. And she's making 90's dance music. And my head just exploded. But seriously, Born this Way seems to provoke in people two opposite reactions, depending on their knowledge of occult symbolism. It is either "What the heck just happened here?" or "This is really blatant". The reason is simple. The video contains new strange elements that might confuse viewers but it also contains symbolism that is extremely ancient. Although the video is set in a futuristic, intergalactic world, it deals with the most primal concept of humanity: motherhood. It plays on human's archetypal fascination and/or repulsion towards the act of giving birth.

Although the lyrics of Born This Way are about unconditional acceptance, with a special focus on homosexuality, the video's scope goes way beyond the subject of sexual orientation. It narrates the birth of a new race within humanity. Laurieann Gibson, the creative director of the video describes this concept:

> "At first, when I thought about birthing a new race and adding the prosthetics, I thought that maybe they should have a certain way they should walk or maybe they move a certain way, but then I realized it is actually a race within our race; it's a mindset."
> - MTV.com, "Lady Gaga Wanted 'Born This Way' To Be 'A Viral Message'"

Gaga is not giving birth to a human but to a "new race" within humanity. The symbolism of the video makes it clear that this birth is not natural, but artificially provoked. A twisted immaculate conception. As is the case for most Lady Gaga videos, the theme of mind control is important in the video. It is the process through which the metamorphosis will take place. In Monarch programming terms, we are witnessing the birth of a new persona within the "core personality" of humanity. The birth is happening within the minds of people and is visually represented by creepy facial horns.

(If you have not read previous articles on this site, mind control programming is the process through which a handler causes within a subject the "birth" of a new persona that can be programmed at will, through trauma and abuse. It is an actual process used by the CIA – MK-Ultra – and symbolism pertaining to this practice is widely present in popular culture. In the context of the video, the programming does not happen on a single person, but on a mass scale – a new race).

Furthermore, the esoteric imagery in the video describes a world change that is occurring as an alchemical process: The creation of magic through the unification of opposing forces portrayed through the use of archetypal symbols and messages. Yup, we're still talking about a Lady Gaga video.

The Director

Although Born This Way is considered new and innovative, it is a perfect continuation of the themes exploited by previous Lady Gaga videos. Nick Knight, the director of the video, brings a different look and feel to Gaga's message, but it remains very "elite friendly". The fashion photographer is known for his visually dazzling photos and has worked with Alexander McQueen, Calvin Klein, Christian Dior, Kylie Minogue, Gwen Stefani and many others. His past work has also contained allusions to Monarch mind control.
Knight's distinctive style in Born This Way was inspired by surrealist painters such as Salvador Dali and Francis Bacon. Let's look at the video's symbolism.

One of director Nick Knight's most famous images for Alexander McQueen. The scar on the mannequin's forehead implies "playing with her head". The blank stare and the missing eye (symbolic of Illuminati control) further accentuate the theme of mind control in this image.

The Immaculate Conception

The video begins with the superposition of two evocative symbols:

A unicorn inside an inverted pink triangle.

Pink triangles pointing downwards were used in Nazi concentration camps to denote homosexual men. The same pink triangle pointing upwards has become a symbol of gay pride and gay rights. On an esoteric level, triangles pointing down are archetypal symbols representing the sacred feminine (in opposition to the upwards pointing triangle representing the phallic masculine). The inverted triangle is emblematic of the womb, the vessel and the uterus. It is the passive principle awaiting the active principle.

Inside the triangle is a unicorn, an ancient mythological creature emblematic of purity, spiritual enlightenment and fierceness – the horn is often viewed as symbolic of the union of with God. In esoteric terms it refers to the third eye or the pineal gland.

In Christian symbolism, the Unicorn is a symbol of Christ. It is also often associated with the Virgin Mary.

> "Symbolically, the unicorn is a representation of Jesus, the horn represents the unity of Jesus and God, its fierceness and defiance were said to be a reminder that nothing can control Jesus against his will, and the small size of the animal represented Jesus' humility."
> - Heather Changeri, The Virgin and the Unicorn

The link between the unicorn and the concept of virginity was popularized by a medieval myth describing how to hunt the creature. In order to catch a unicorn, a virgin is put in the field; the animal then comes to her and is caught, because it lies down in her lap.

Virgin and Unicorn by Domenichino (1602), a tale which has probably been inspired by Christian symbolism (or the other way around). According to Honorius of Autun in his Speculum de Mysteriis Ecclesiae: "Christ is represented by this animal, and his invincible strength by its horn. He, who lay down in the womb of the Virgin, has been caught by the hunters; that is to say, he was found in human shape by those who loved him".

This unicorn is inside a womb symbolically represented by the inverted triangle and therefore symbolically awaiting birth. The concept of purity associated with unicorn implies an "immaculate conception" as no sexual relation was needed to provoke this cosmic pregnancy (yes, I just said "cosmic pregnancy"). Gaga herself referred to this song in similar terms.

> "I wrote ['Born This Way'] in 10 f—ing minutes. And it is a completely magical message song. And after I wrote it, the gates just opened, and the songs kept coming. It was like an immaculate conception."
> - Lady Gaga, Our Lady of Pop, Vogue Magazine

According to Carl Jung, whether we look at the religious or occult meaning of the unicorn, it ends up portraying the same concept: the union of seemingly opposite forces (i.e. purity and strength).

> "The unicorn's most vital function has been as a symbol, whether of power or virility, or purity, or the combination of opposites, of the male horn and the female body. Many modern interpreters regard this last role as the crucial one and relate it to the symbolism of the soul as the spark of divine light in the darkness of matter and evil, the body, and to the concept of the hermaphrodite as the perfect union of opposites."
> - Carl Jung, Man, Myth and Magic

That's a lot of text to explain a single frame of the video. It is, however, an important frame because it sums up the entire concept of the video in a single image: the birth of a spiritual/galactic/metaphorical entity from an immaculate conception.

But what exactly is being born? In her narrative, Gaga says it is a new race, but the video, and the video's director, suggests that it is a race born within the existing race, from people's own minds. In the video, a symbolic image replaces the unicorn.

Mask at the back of Gaga's head

Gaga has two faces, not unlike Janus, the god of gateways and beginnings. In mind-control terms, the mask implies the existence of a programmed alter-personality. Porcelain masks are used in the actual (and horrific) Monarch programming process on slaves and handlers (in the video, Gaga seems to embody both roles).

> "Fire torture and melted wax is used to make the child victim believe their face has been burned. Then the programmer generously gives the traumatized alters a porcelain mask. The alter getting the Porcelain face may be given a "gem" hypnotically like Jade and that becomes their secret name. There are several different methods that are available to lay in the porcelain face programming. There has been a great deal of porcelain casts made of people's faces and then masks made of them. In fact, when a handler dies, at least in one case the replacement handler wore a mask to look like the previous handler."
> - Fritz Springmeier, The Illuminati Formula Used to Create an Undetectable Total Mind Controlled Slave

The mask inside the triangle implies the birth of a synthetic being, a human construct: a pre-established mindset for humanity. After this, Gaga begins her "Manifesto of Mother Monster", describing the mindset.

Manifesto of Mother Monster and Birth

Gaga announces the birth of a new race in a speech with heavy occult undertones that contains references to ancient hermetic principles.

> "This is the manifesto of Mother Monster: On G.O.A.T., a Government-Owned Alien Territory in space, a birth of magnificent and magical proportions took place."

The magical birth took place on a "Government-Owned Alien Territory" – which is alluding to the fact that the birth is taking place under the supervision and approval of the powers that be: the elite, the Illuminati. It is also a great way to form the acronym G.O.A.T. and a great way to bring up Baphomet.

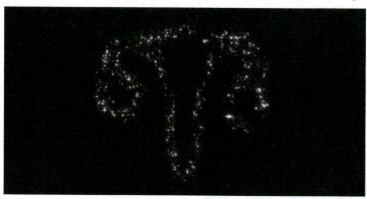

As Gaga says "GOAT", a star formation shaped as a goat head is shown, an allusion to the Goat of Mendez and/or Baphomet. It is also shaped like a uterus. The movie Pan's Labyrinth also draws a link between the faun's horned head and the shape of the uterus – a symbolic gateway to another realm.

Gaga, playing the role of the Virgin about to give birth is symbolically shown inside the goat head, which emphasizes the occult and ritualistic nature of the birth taking place. Baphomet, represented by a goat's head, is symbolic of magic created by the union of opposite forces, hence its androgyny (see the erect phallic symbol and the female breasts).

The goat-headed Baphomet, as depicted by Eliphas Levi. Baphomet's androgyny and its "As Above, So Below" hand gesture illustrate the all-important concept of union of opposite forces and are all visually represented in Born This Way.

Baphomet is of great importance in Aleister Crowley's Thelema – a modern occult philosophy that seems to be a source of inspiration for Gaga's Manifesto. According to Crowley, Baphomet is a representative of the spiritual nature of the spermatozoa, while also being symbolic of the "magical child" produced as a result of sex magic. As such, Baphomet represents the Union of Opposites, especially as mystically personified in Chaos and Babalon, combined and biologically manifested with the sperm and egg united in the zygote.

> "He is 'The Devil' of the Book of Thoth, and His emblem is Baphomet the Androgyne who is the hiero glyph of arcane perfection ... He is therefore Life, and Love. But moreover his letter is ayin, the Eye, so that he is Light; and his Zodiacal image is Capricornus, that leaping goat whose attribute is Liberty."
> - Aleister Crowley, Magick Book 4

Concepts similar to those expressed by Crowley are incorporated to the Manifesto:

> "But the birth was not finite. It was infinite. As the wombs numbered and the mitosis of the future began, it was perceived that this infamous moment in life is not temporal, it is eternal. And thus began the beginning of the new race, a race within the race of humanity, a race which bears no prejudice, no judgment, but boundless freedom."

Is the "mitosis of the future" equivalent to Crowley's "new eon"? The emphasis on the term "liberty" and "freedom" might be a reference to Crowley's "Do What Thou Wilt" ethos, a concept calling for the seeking of one's "True Will" without regard for the boundaries of ethics, moral principles or the concept of good and evil. The embrace of both good and evil is further portrayed in the video.

As Gaga says these words, she is shown giving birth to … something. As this something gets pushed out, butterflies appear.

Butterflies emerging from Gaga's womb.

Butterflies (especially Monarch butterflies) are symbolic of Monarch programming. Mind-control slaves who successfully create an alter-persona are compared to butterflies emerging from their cocoon. This implies that Gaga's "new race" or "new philosophy" is not something that occurs naturally in society. It is rather something that will be forced on humanity using mind-control techniques.

Soulless, Gaga-clone newborns and a bunch of butterflies flying around them.

The creation of this "beautiful" race leads to the birth of an evil entity, which seemingly exists to protect its interests and force its will upon the world.

"But on that same day, as the eternal mother hovered in the mulitverse, another more terrifying birth took place: the birth of evil. And as she herself split into two, rotating in agony between two ultimate forces, the pendulum of choice began its dance. It seems easy, you imagine, to gravitate instantly and unwaveringly towards good. But she wondered, how can I protect something so perfect without evil?"

As those words are being said, the camera slides upwards towards Gaga, forming a semi-hidden skull head made of human bodies, symbols of sacrifice representing the evil that resulted from birthing the "pure" creation. This concept is illustrated by the symbol of ying and yang and the Masonic checkered floor, where black and white coexist in an infinite pattern.

Semi-hidden human skull above a pyramidal structure made of red human bodies.

The evil force is represented by human skulls, which symbolically represent the elite's death-culture, which celebrates sacrifices in order to generate "new life". To illustrate the "political and governmental" aspect of this concept Gaga is shown firing a military rifle while church bells ring (announcing death of the masses).

Gaga firing a rifle, a celebration of depopulation and human sacrifices. She waves her blond hair as she is shooting, a continuation of the Agenda to make government oppression and violence "sexy".

Evil is therefore depicted as a necessary force to balance the existence of good (or what is portrayed as good in the video, as mind control is never "good").

Thought this song was about gay pride? Apparently not. Oh, and then the song starts.

Him or H-I-M

The song starts with an odd statement:

> "It doesn't matter if you love him, or capital H-I-M"

Who is "Him" and, more importantly who is capital H-I-M? At first glance, "Him" can be interpreted as a masculine lover, in accordance with the "gay pride" aspect of the song. In that case, who or what is "capital H-I-M"? Is it God? In that is she referring to the distance between homosexuality and traditional religions? HIM is also the name of a popular Finnish rock band whose acronym stands for "His Infernal Majesty". In this context, is Gaga saying "It doesn't matter if you love him (God), or capital H-I-M (Satan)"? If that is the case, it would certainly fit with the dualistic, good versus evil, message of the video and the Thelemic theme of her manifesto.

Further in the song, another line states:

> "A different lover is not a sin
> Believe capital H-I-M (hey, hey, hey)"

In this spiritual context, is the "regular lover" God and the "different lover" His Infernal Majesty?

Dualism continues to be visually represented throughout the video with scenes celebrating life and love juxtaposed with scenes of celebrating death.

Lots of ewey-gooey love

Brain-dead zombies – the fate of who do not become part of the new "horned" race.

The rest of the video is a lot less symbol-intensive, as the focus shifts on choreography and female crotch-grabbing.

The video ends with a symbolic image, one to be expected when understanding the dualistic theme portrayed throughout the video. The last frame of the video is the opposite of the first, as the pink triangle is pointing upwards. This alludes to the appropriation of this Nazi symbol by the gay rights movement and its reversal.

Zombie Gaga inside an upright pink triangle

On an esoteric level, the upright triangle is the response to the inverted triangle and signals the end of the alchemical process. It represents the union of the opposites, in order to accomplish the Great Work: the occult transformation of men. When combined, the upright and the inverted triangle become a six-pointed star, a symbol known as the Philospher's Stone or the Seal of Solomon.

The Hermetic Seal of Solomon composed with two interlaced triangles pointing in opposite directions.

"The interlacing triangles or deltas symbolize the union of the two principles or forces, the active and passive, male and female, pervading the universe ... The two triangles, one white and the other black, interlacing, typify the mingling of apparent opposites in nature, darkness and light, error and truth, ignorance and wisdom, evil and good, throughout human life."
- Albert G. Mackey, Encyclopedia of Freemasonry

If the video started with the unicorn inside the inverted triangle, symbolizing the impending birth of a pure spiritual being, the video ends with the opposite energy, death and corruption. Zombie-gaga, the evil by-product of the change imposed by G.O.A.T. In order for magic to happen, both of these triangles are necessary and they need to be united.

Meaning of the Video

The song by itself has an uplifting message: to love and accept oneself unconditionally, the way God made us. However (there's always a "however" with Gaga), the video takes things to another level. The "Manifesto of Mother Monster" and its related symbolism give the song a cosmic-battle-between-good-and-evil quality, interlaced with the heralding of a new race and, to use Crowley's terminology, a new eon.

In the context of the video, Born This Way is actually a tail of REbirth and of transformation. As Gaga's choreographer stated, it is a race within our race; it's a mindset. This change of mindset is not portrayed as the result of a natural evolution, but rather as a forced change symbolized by the Monarch programming imagery. All of this is happening in the Government-Owned-Alien-Territory, a clever way of stating that this new race is something that the occult elite wants to see happening. In the video, Gaga (and hundreds of clones) are created in a high-tech, government-owned lab. Are we truly preaching no prejudice, no judgment, but boundless freedom? The Manifesto's ideals therefore only apply to the new, forcefully created race, which is distinguishable from "normal" people by the horn thingies. Is this a sign of superiority? Are the horns any different than the pink triangle used to distinguish gays during the Nazi regime?

Those who do not adhere to this mind-controlled race will apparently feel the wrath of "evil Gaga" and be killed because, as she says, How can I protect something so perfect without evil? The video contradicts and twists the liberating meaning of the song and turns it into something rather oppressive and disturbing. The "new race" is the masses of the New World Order, under the influence of mass mind control and pushed into a precise kind of spirituality, resembling a dumbed-down version of Crowley's Thelema. This world metamorphosis is perceived by the occult elite as an alchemical transformation, a Great Work. It is visually represented by the opposing forces illustrated throughout the video. The process is meant to create something "pure and perfect", a new world that is purged from its non-desired elements (portraying a New World Order as the end result of an alchemical process is often referred to in elitist art – see the article Analysis of the Occult Symbols Found on the Bank of America Murals). From the viewpoint of the masses, who must go through this forced rebirth, the process is ugly, terrifying and pure evil. The video however, – as most offerings of pop culture – portrays the view of the elite.

In Conclusion

In order to keep the youth interested and attracted to the elite's agenda, creators of pop videos cleverly combines fresh visuals with mind-numbing repetition. Each new video attempts to bring an exciting or shocking element to generate some interest but, at the end of the line, the core message remains stubbornly on-par with the Illuminati Agenda. Born This way uses the classic technique of duplicity, which can be defined as "contradictory doubleness of thought, speech, or action; especially, the concealment of one's true intentions by deceptive words or actions". The song's lyrics say one thing, but the powerful symbols within the video go in the opposite direction. This leads to a contradiction our minds attempt to resolve: Is "boundless freedom" equivalent to the coercive new world portrayed by Gaga?

Despite the superficial eccentricity of the song, Born This Way is about conforming and adhering to a pre-defined mindset, a philosophy that is compatible with a New World Order. It is not Gaga's vision, it is their vision. It is the mind state they want you to adopt in order for them to carry on with their Agenda unopposed. This is what they want you to think: There are no important values or moral codes; good and evil are a big blur and being a mindless zombie is cool. If you think this way, "you're on the right track baby". I'm not. Guess I wasn't born that way.

Natalia Kills' "Zombie" and "Wonderland": Dedicated to Illuminati Mind Control

In the last few years, the pop music scene has incorporated gradually increasing doses of Illuminati mind control symbolism in its music videos. Newcomer pop singer Natalia Kills is definitely another step in this direction. While other pop stars blend subversive symbolism with other themes and subjects matters, Natalia's videos appear to solely focus on mind control imagery. We'll look at Natalia Kills' career videos "Zombie" and "Wonderland".

Natalia Kills is an English singer-song writer who signed with will.i.am and Interscope Records. Not unlike other female pop stars, Natalia began working in the entertainment industry at a young age (7). In 2005, Natalia Kills was a rapper known as Verbalicious and released a single entitled Don't Play Nice, a playful party-rap song with Natalia sporting a radically different style and image.

After being taken under the wing of Cherrytree Records, an Interscope imprint, her name changed to Natalia Kills, her musical style switched to electro-pop and her overall image became a lot darker, fashion-conscious and twisted. In other words, she morphed into an Illuminati pop star.

Although not at the same level of worldwide popularity, Natalia Kills is often compared to Lady Gaga. Though her fans probably don't appreciate the comparison, there are indeed several similarities between the singers: They both began singing at a young age; they both signed with Interscope's Cherry Tree Records; they both underwent an extreme metamorphosis after being signed becoming edgy and hyper-sexualized; both changed their artist names after signing with Cherry Tree; both worked with the same producers (count the shout outs to Cherry Cherry Boom Boom in their songs); and most significantly, both incorporate heavy occult and mind control imagery in their videos.

There is a slight difference in Natalia Kills' world, however: believe it or not, the mind control imagery and symbolism is even more blatant. Her songs and videos can actually be read as a diary of a Monarch programming victim. Natalia's world is dominated by the concepts of torture, oppression, sadistic handlers, violence, sexual abuse and drugs. In all three of her videos, Natalia is degraded and abused, always combining sex and violence (our two most primal instincts).

Natalia's first single, Mirrors, flaunts all of the seemingly obligatory references to mind control through symbolism (fractured mirrors, caged heart, etc.) and BDSM (Bondage/Domination/Sadism/Masochism). However, it is her two subsequent singles, Zombie and Wonderland, that clearly associate Natalia with Monarch mind control Let's look at the symbolism of these two videos.

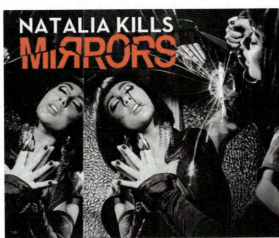

Reflections and fractured mirrors – symbolic of the fractured and fragmented personalities of mind control victims.

Zombie

Without the video, Zombie appears to be a song about being in love with a cold-hearted guy who does not return phone calls. Aw. The setting of the video, however, definitely does not match this interpretation: Natalia is strapped to a table in what looks like a cold laboratory (mind-control facility?), and is controlled by an unseen person who is sadistically torturing her … and with whom Natalia is in love.

Reflections and fractured mirrors – symbolic of the fractured and fragmented personalities of mind control victims.

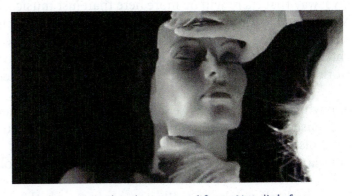

A mask is meticulously removed from Natalia's face. Masks are actually used on Monarch slaves to program and confuse them. They symbolically represent the slaves' artificially created personas that can be put on and removed at the will of the handler. The handler's rubber gloves only prove that Zombie is not about a relationship between lovers but between a slave and her programmer.

In the context of the video, it becomes clear that the lyrics are actually about the sick, twisted, forcibly generated infatuation felt by a slave towards her handler. The beginning of the song describe the relationship:

> *I'm in love with a zombie*
> *Can't keep his hands off me*

> *I think he's looking at me*
> *But he's looking right through me*
>
> *You think you're so cool boy*
> *Blood rushing through my veins now*
> *Do you want me for my body*
> *Do you want me for my brain, brain, brain, brain*

Can't keep his hands off me is one of the references to the abusive nature of the sexual "relationship" between Natalia and her handler. The last two lines of this verse are actually the most chilling: *Do you want me for my body/ Do you want me for my brain, brain, brain, brain*. The handler, aka the zombie, actually wants her brain, meaning the ultimate goal is mind control. He is abusing her to cause trauma and dissociation, which psychologically creates alter personas, the ultimate goal of Monarch programming. The video makes it clear: We are definitely not talking about a pretty-boy player who does not return calls, but a sadistic, Josef Mengele-type figure. So the Zombie is a mind control handler and the song's chorus is "I'm in love with a Zombie" ... disturbingly wrong yet most listeners will never get the song's true meaning (zombies are so cool, right?).

After witnessing this cold, robotic single, I had the feeling that Natalia's subsequent videos would be nothing less than symbolism-fests, since new singers always push the blatantness a step further ... guess I was right.

Wonderland

To those who know are familiar with mind control symbolism, the name of this single, Wonderland, is a dead giveaway that there will be more here than just music. Alice in Wonderland is the primary movie associated with Monarch programming, as it is an actual programming tool. Using associations in the movie, slaves are indeed encouraged to "Walk through the looking glass" – meaning they dissociate from reality. In the fairy tale, Alice enters a fantasy world where everything is magical, inverted and unstable, a world similar to the slave's internal world, where everything can be modified by the handler.

Knowing this, the otherwise seemingly random and incomprehensible story of the video Wonderland starts making sense. If you have read other articles on this site, you can probably recognize and identify the meaning of these symbols, since they are found in countless other music videos. The constant use of the same set of symbols across popular culture is not a coincidence: A story is being told in veiled terms for those who have "eyes to see".

The song itself speaks of disillusionment towards the magical world of fairy tales. This feeling is particularly true for mind-control victims, who are programmed using fairy tales by their handlers. The enchanting world of these stories is of course in sharp contrast to the horrid day-to-day reality of these victims, but they are programmed to recognize parallels between the stories and their disassociated inner-psyche. This is reflected in the first verse of Wonderland:

> *I'm not Snow White, but I'm lost inside this forest*
> *I'm not Red Riding Hood, but I think the wolves have got me*
> *Don't want those stilettos, I'm not, not Cinderella*
> *I don't need a knight, so baby, take off all your armor*

This verse describes the mental confusion (lost inside this forest), the control by handlers (I think the wolves have got me) and even the sexual abuse (Don't want those stilettos) inflicted on MK victims by the very same people who tell them the fairy tales. Despite these references, one could argue that the song itself can be interpreted as wanting "true love" and not "make believe". Well, as always we can turn to the video for clarification… and in this video is is pretty clear, there is no love involved.

Filled with semi-subliminal flashes of powerful words and gruesome images, the video makes no allusions to a love interest, but plenty of references to mind control. Some of the phrases flashed on screen are actual mantras hammered into the heads of mind-control victims to confuse and traumatize them.

"Love is pain" is cited in Fritz Springmeier's book "The Illuminati Formula To Create a Mind Controlled Slave" as one of the actual inversions used by mind control handlers on their victims. The slaves are actually programmed to perceive torture as a form of love. From the book: "The Programmer also takes into consideration what are called 'power words'. Those are words which have specific meaning for the person. The programmers also love to use reversals and puns, for instance (…) 'Life is death, and death is life', 'Pain is love, and love is pain.'"

The video begins with a kind of ritualistic procession, where Natalia – dressed in red, the occult color of sacrifice – is forcibly lead somewhere by men in riot gear. The scene is peppered with short flashes showing the police beating people during a riot – placing the video in the context of an oppressive police state.

Natalia as Red Riding Hood … being lead to the wolves.

Natalia is followed by women dressed in black and holding a red flag, alluding to the ritualistic nature of this procession. She is taken to a secured building where she is forced to attend a highly symbolic dinner.

Under the supervision of the police in riot gear, the dinner takes place on a checkerboard pattern floor – the Masonic ritualistic floor featured in countless other videos.

The dinner table itself is replete with symbols alluding to mind control. Some examples:

A cupcake laced with pills – mixing things children love with the cause of their abuse.

Limbless dolls on the dinner table. Like the arm-less mannequins seen in Zombie, these dolls represent the powerlessness of mind control slaves.

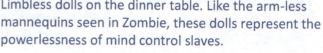

Dinner guests wearing white rabbit masks. In Alice in Wonderland, Alice followed the white rabbit down the rabbit hole, leading her to Wonderland. In Monarch programming the slave is told to "follow the white rabbit" to reach Wonderland – a code word for total dissociation. In the video, the white rabbit is swallowing a pill, telling Natalia to do the same.

In another scene, Natalia is shown being blinded by the hands of several unseen people. This symbolic image is also used in other mind-control themed videos to represent the handlers blinding and controlling the slave.

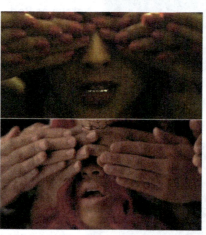

Top: Natalia Kills in Wonderland; Bottom: Rihanna in the short video advertising her perfume (see article on this advertisement here). Both videos contain heavy Monarch symbolism and both feature this disturbing scene.

The dinner is held under the supervision of police in riot gear. As seen in previous articles, there is a conscious effort to "normalize" the presence of these symbols of a police state in popular culture, hence their presence in numerous music videos and musical performances.

After "popping her pills", Natalia becomes a little rowdy, prompting the cops to raid the place and savagely beat her up. She is then taken outside, where her sacrifice will take place.

A medieval-style executioner about the chop off Natalia's head.

In the beginning of the video, Natalia was shown dressed in red (the color of sacrifice) and followed by women dressed in black (death and morning). Her ritual sacrifice was planned from the start. In mind -ontrol terms, the process caused Natalia to dissociate, go to Wonderland and "lose her head". The transformation, which occurred on the checkerboard patterned floor, caused Natalia to lose control of her mind and of her actions. Through the trauma of oppression, drugs and physical abuse, Natalia has dissociated and gone to Wonderland, the only refuge to her trauma.

As the axe goes down, the screen rips and the word "Wonderland" appears in red, associating the head chopping with the true meaning of the word "Wonderland" in this song. The video ends with an inspiring image, meant to uplift a generation of young minds:

Natalia's head chopped off with a bunch of flies around it. An adequate symbol of our pop culture.

In Conclusion

As pop star veterans lose their edge and their "magic", newcomers sweep onto the scene to enchant pop fans all over again. Record labels and the Illuminati record industry as a whole are aware of the nature of the business, which is fueled by young people constantly seeking the next cheap thrill and the hottest trend. In a matter of months, fans can go from "OMG she's the best I'll luv her forevz" to "Yawn, lame". So, in case people ever get tired of Lady Gaga, her record label is already grooming the next generation to serve up the Illuminati symbolism.

As the public becomes increasingly desensitized to the Agenda, videos keep marching towards more graphic and uncensored portrayals of mind control, which is arguably the most sadistic and evil practice in the world. Natalia's videos can be read as a diary of a Monarch victim, where she describes a world dominated by oppression, torture, violence, sexual abuse and drugs. The horrific world of Monarch slaves is exposed as Natalia is abused and degraded by unseen forces, but the whole thing is presented as cool and fashionable.

Natalia does not currently enjoy the level of exposure of Rihanna or Lady Gaga. She however has everything it takes to become an industry favorite – a perfect candidate to lead a nation of Zombies to Wonderland.

Lady Gaga's "Judas" and the Age of Horus

Lady Gaga's "Judas" video is a modern retelling of biblical stories, where Jesus and his disciples are portrayed as a biker gang. But don't mistake the video for a Bible lesson as it twists and turns important scenes to give them a very different meaning. In fact, it can be argued that the video symbolically describes an important aspect of Gaga's work and of society in general: a rejection of Christianity in order to make way to what has been called the Age of Horus. This article will look at the origins and the symbols found in Lady Gaga's "Judas".

When I first watched Judas, I immediately told myself: "There is no use to write about this, it is simply too obvious". I mean Gaga is in love with Judas … and Judas betrayed Jesus. It is a direct continuation of Gaga's anti-Christian and pro-Illuminati theme through symbols, as described in previous articles. What can I add to it that hasn't been said? So I ignored the video … until I began receiving e-mails. Tons of them. Many people did not understand the message of the video, some did not get the Biblical references and the way they were twisted to communicate a new message; other simply did not know who Judas was. As it is symbolic on many levels, I realized that decoding this video could help many readers — who I call my "Little Vigis" (No.). The video doesn't only summarize the underlying spiritual message found in Gaga's work, but it describes an important phenomenon happening in society in general – a phenomenon that is part of the Illuminati agenda: the "de-holyfication" of traditional religions.

In her recent interviews, Gaga has given several interpretations of the song. In an interview with E! Online she said that it was not meant as an attack of Christianity:

> "I don't view the video as a religious statement, I view it as social statement. I view it as a cultural statement."

On Amp Radio Gaga explained that:

> "It's about falling in love with the wrong man over and over again."

In another interview with Google, Gaga went deeper into the philosophical theme of the song, which is in accordance with the teachings of some occult schools we'll describe later.

> "The song is about honoring your darkness in order to bring yourself into the light. You have to look into what's haunting you and need to learn to forgive yourself in order to move on."

The videos for Gaga's songs Alejandro (analyzed here) and Born This Way (analyzed here) communicated specific spiritual messages through meanings and symbols. Traditional religious symbols are stripped of their "holy aura" while other symbols, inspired by those of the Illuminati, are introduced and glorified to her young viewers. Of course, this phenomenon does not happen only in Gaga's works, but is a trend in mass media in general. Aleister Crowley, an occultist who remains an incredibly influential figure in the entertainment industry, claimed the Age of Horus, a new stage in human history, would be defined by the abandonment of traditional religions in order to embrace a new kind of spirituality (read the full article on Crowley here). The same vision for a "new Aeon" is shared by the world elite, where its plans for a New World Order heavily rely on the existence of a single world religion, based on a specific set of values that are compatible with is Agenda. Mass media plays an important role in this paradigm shift – and the results are astonishing. In less than a century, the Western World has witnessed a drastic decline in religious faith, especially Christian. Never such a profound societal change happened in such a short period of time. Of course, Gaga herself is not responsible for this drastic shift, but Judas, in its meaning and symbolism, perfectly describes the transitional period we are going through, as society is taken to, in Crowley's words, the Age of Horus.

It is therefore in this social and religious context that Judas was released. First seen riding with Jesus, Gaga goes into a transition and falls for Judas, the man who ultimately caused the death of Jesus. Gaga's conversion is symbolic of society in general, where the altruistic tenets of Christianity have been replaced by a more "self-celebrating" philosophy – embodied in the video by the character of Judas. In short, the story symbolizes the passage towards Crowley's Age of Horus, and Gaga's "Eye of Horus" makeup effectively seems to emphasize this point. As seen in previous articles, Gaga is no stranger to Crowley' philosophy (her Manifesto at the beginning of Born This Way is heavily inspired by his Thelema). This philosophy is, in turn, the basis of the new kind of spirituality that is sold to the masses through media.

To explain Judas, I need to "get Biblical" because the song and the video are heavily inspired by Biblical verses. So, before we get into it, let's start by understanding the main character: Judas.

Who was Judas?

Judas giving Jesus the kiss of death.

Judas Iscariot was one of Jesus' twelve disciples. Due to his money-management skills, he was put in charge of the group's money box. Despite having chosen him to become his follower, Jesus knew from the start that Judas would eventually betray him. At one point he even refers to him as "the devil".

> *Jesus replied, "Didn't I choose you, the twelve, and yet one of you is the devil?" (Now he said this about Judas son of Simon Iscariot, for Judas, one of the twelve, was going to betray him.)*
> - John 6:70-71

During his time as a disciple, Judas had some "issues" with Jesus, causing him to stir up trouble within the group.

An important event involving Judas happened during the washing of Jesus' feet by Mary Magdalene using expensive ointments. Offended by what he called a waste of money, Judas protested and even caused other disciples complain. This is one of the Biblical passages that was recreated (with a significant twist) in Gaga's video:

> *Then, six days before the Passover, Jesus came to Bethany, where Lazarus lived, whom he had raised from the dead. So they prepared a dinner for Jesus there. Martha was serving, and Lazarus was among those present at the table with him. Then Mary took three quarters of a pound of expensive aromatic oil from pure nard and anointed the feet of Jesus. She then wiped his feet dry with her hair. (Now the house was filled with the fragrance of the perfumed oil.) But Judas Iscariot, one of his disciples (the one who was going to betray him) said, "Why wasn't this oil sold for three hundred silver coins and the money given to the poor?" (Now Judas said this not because he was concerned about the poor, but because he was a thief. As keeper of the money box, he used to steal what was put into it.) So Jesus said, "Leave her alone. She has kept it for the day of my burial. For you will always have the poor with you, but you will not always have me!"*
> - John 12:1-8

Shortly after this incident, Judas meets with the chief priests of Israel – the ones who were trying to "bring down" Jesus – and strikes a deal. He would betray and hand over Jesus to the Pharisees and the police force in exchange for thirty silver coins:

> *Then one of the twelve, the one named Judas Iscariot, went to the chief priests and said, "What will you give me to betray him into your hands?" So they set out thirty silver coins for him.*
> - Matthew 26:14-15

During the Last Supper, Jesus tells his disciples that one of them would betray him and reveals it would be Judas:

> *When he had said these things, Jesus was greatly distressed in spirit, and testified, "I tell you the solemn truth, one of you will betray me." The disciples began to look at one another, worried and perplexed to know which of them he was talking about. One of his disciples, the one Jesus loved, was at the table to the right of Jesus in a place of honor. So Simon Peter gestured to this disciple to ask Jesus who it was he was referring to. Then the disciple whom Jesus loved leaned back against Jesus' chest and asked him, "Lord, who is it?" Jesus replied, "It is the one to whom I will give this piece of bread after I have dipped it in the dish." Then he dipped the piece of bread in the dish and gave it to Judas Iscariot, Simon's son.*
> - John 13:21-26

At this moment, it is said that Satan possessed Judas:

> *And after Judas took the piece of bread, Satan entered into him. Jesus said to him, "What you are about to do, do quickly."*
> - John 13:27

Judas then leads the chief priests and the police to Jesus, identifying him with a kiss:

> *Right away, while Jesus was still speaking, Judas, one of the twelve, arrived. With him came a crowd armed with swords and clubs, sent by the chief priests and experts in the law and elders. (Now the betrayer had given them a sign, saying, "The one I kiss is the man. Arrest him and lead him away under guard.") When Judas arrived, he went up to Jesus immediately and said, "Rabbi!" and kissed him. Then they took hold of him and arrested him.*
> - Mark 14:43-46

After Jesus' condemnation, Judas regretted his betrayal and sought to reverse his actions by returning the money, but it was too late and he commits suicide:

> *Now when Judas, who had betrayed him, saw that Jesus had been condemned, he regretted what he had done and returned the thirty silver coins to the chief priests and the elders, saying, "I have sinned by betraying innocent blood!" But they said, "What is that to us? You take care of it yourself!" So Judas threw the silver coins into the temple and left. Then he went out and hanged himself.*
> - Matthew 27:3-5

Most of the passages described above are recreated in the video, but they are given a twist, where roles and symbols are reversed, effectively changing the fundamental meaning of the Biblical stories. As a result, the video ends with a very different "moral of the story".

Gaga as Mary Magdalene

The video portrays Jesus and his disciples as a biker gang riding around with skull-and-bone insignias on their backs (nice touch). Gaga is riding with Jesus, playing the role of Mary Magdalene.

Although it is not clearly specified in the Bible, Mary Magdalene is said to be the prostitute who was about to get stoned to death by an angry mob until Jesus came along and said: "Y'all country-ass, donkey-riding peasants better drop them rocks and go on home before things get REAL ugly up in here". Wait, that's what Samuel L. Jackson would have said. Jesus actually said: "Let he who is without sin cast the first stone".

At the very end of Judas, Gaga is seen stoned to death, insinuating that Jesus was not there to save her.

Gaga as Mary Magdalene stoned to death. In Judas, Jesus has failed to save Gaga. Also, does this scene portray Gaga being persecuted by people who are offended by her music?

So Gaga plays the role of Mary Magdalene where Magdalene is not only the friend and disciple of Jesus, but his lover. This portrayal of Mary Magdalene as Jesus' mate became popular in the past few decades with books such as The Jesus Scroll (1972), Holy Blood, Holy Grail (1982), The Gospel According to Jesus Christ (1991), The Da Vinci Code (2003), The Two Marys: The Hidden History of the Mother and Wife of Jesus (2007); and by films like Bloodline (2008). These alternative accounts on Jesus Christ's life originate from modern interpretations of Gnostic and apocryphal texts (mainly the Nag Hammadi) where Magdalene is described as Jesus' "favorite disciple" and "companion". An interpretation of the apocryphal Gospel of Philip even alludes to Jesus "often kissing Mary Magdalene on the lips".

Some occult circles believe that Jesus lived well beyond the age of 33 (a number they believed was selected for symbolic reasons). Some claim that Jesus married Mary Magdalene with whom he had a daughter named Sarah. Some even claimed that they moved to Southern France, where they started the fabled Merovingian Bloodline.

Judas therefore portrays Mary Magdalene from this angle, where Gaga is the wife of Jesus. However, she only has eyes for Judas.

The Video

The video begins with Gaga riding with Jesus, yelling in his ear "Judas Juda-ah-as", almost as if it was an incantation. Usually, when your girl yells the name of some other dude right in your ear, it means something's up.

From a spiritual point of view, Gaga was "riding with Jesus" – representing the embrace of Christianity – until she fell in love with Judas – a force that is opposed to it. But what kind of force are we referring to? Is it the elite's peculiar brand of occultism, mainly represented by the symbol of the Eye of Horus?

Yes, as stated in previous articles, hiding one eye refers to the Eye of Horus. I don't see how Gaga can make this clearer for you.

In the video, Jesus is shown doing good deeds and healing people while Judas is pretty much a douche bag, getting drunk and grabbing women all over the place. Yet Gaga is in love with him. The character of Judas is an embodiment of Crowley's saying "Do What Thou Wilt" – or Lavey's Church of Satan concept of hyper-egoism, where the fulfillment of one's desires is seen as a basic requirement to true enlightenment. Gaga is seduced by and identifies with the values embodied by Judas' and is therefore in love with him. By doing so, she turns her back on Jesus' altruism and selflessness.

The recreation of Mary Magdalene washing of Jesus feet...with the addition of Judas drinking a beer with a non-approving look.

One scene recreates Mary Magdalene's washing of Jesus feet which, as seen above, made Judas angry and jealous. In the video's version of the story, Judas is however right there with Jesus, his naked feet next to his, apparently also ready to get this treatment reserved for great people. Judas is therefore not simply a disciple of Jesus, but his equal. Afterwards, Judas, being the self-centered jerk that he is, spills his beer on Gaga ... but Gaga loves him that way. The first lyrics of the song describe this reversal from the Biblical story, where Judas is the one getting washed by Gaga.

> *When he calls to me, I am ready*
> *I'll wash his feet with my hair if he needs*
> *Forgive him when his tongue lies through his brain*
> *Even after three times, he betrays me*

"I'm on your side Judas, you're the best".

Later in the video, there appears to be some kind of showdown between Jesus and Judas. Gaga – who is still Jesus' lover – goes to Judas holding a golden gun, apparently to kill the one who would betray her spouse. Instead of a bullet, the gun "shoots out" lipstick. Gaga puts it on Judas' mouth as if saying "go ahead and kiss Jesus, you have my blessing".

Gaga does not simply reject Jesus, she is an active agent in his bringing down. One of her eye is hidden, confirming that this is part of the Illuminati agenda (bringing down religions).

Judas giving Jesus the kiss of death.

The song also describes Gaga's participation in "bringing Jesus down":

> *I'll bring him down, bring him down, down*
> *A king with no crown, king with no crown*

The "king with no crown" is more than likely Jesus, who is wearing during the entire video the Crown of Thorns. In Biblical accounts, that painful crown was put on his head by soldiers before his crucifixion in order to humiliate the one who claimed to be the "King of the Jews".

Is this a reference to the great whore of Babylon who is said to "sit on many waters"? There is another reference to the Great Whore in the video.

So, despite Jesus' virtuous deeds, Gaga is attracted to Judas. The Betrayer is portrayed as a rowdy, egoistical and devious being, which is not surprising since it is stated that Judas was possessed by Satan at the time he betrayed Jesus. Judas personifies the antithesis of Jesus' selfless ways and represents the self-centered philosophy described by modern occultists such as Aleister Crowley whose philosophical tenets, describes the self as "the center of the universe". Anton Lavey's Satanic Bible describes the need for a "new religion" based on man's earthly needs.

> *Past religions have always represented the spiritual nature of man, with little or no concern for his carnal or mundane needs. They have considered this life but transitory, and the flesh merely a shell; physical pleasure trivial, and pain a worthwhile preparation for the "Kingdom of God". How well the utter hypocrisy comes forth when the "righteous" make a change in their religion to keep up with man's natural change! The only way that Christianity can ever completely serve the needs of man is to become as Satanism is NOW.*
>
> *It has become necessary for a NEW religion, based on man's natural instincts, to come forth. THEY have named it. It is called Satanism.*
> - Anton Lavey, The Satanic Bible

Gaga, playing Mary Magdalene, is attracted to Judas' ways. She not only "converts" to his side but also effectively brings Jesus down. This attraction to the "dark side" is summed up in these simple words:

> *I wanna love you,*
> *But something's pulling me away from you*
> *Jesus is my virtue,*
> *Judas is the demon I cling to*

In Conclusion

Going beyond simple shots at Christianity for pure shock value, Judas summarizes the underlying spiritual messages found in Lady Gaga's works which are, in turn, a reflection of the elite's philosophy that needs to be taught to the masses. Whether it is intentional or not, Judas symbolizes the spiritual shift of humanity as it enters what is "the Age of Horus". Crowley considered the last two thousand years to be the Age of Osiris, ruled by Christianity's "emphasis on death, suffering, sorrow and the denial of the body". He however considered this era to be necessary to give birth to the Age of Horus, whose Aeon would lead humanity to a new kind of spirituality. Other esoteric schools describe this shift in different words. Some describe it as the Age of Aquarius taking the place of the Age of Pisces, which was dominated by Christianity (they say Jesus was associated with the symbol of the fish because he ruled the Age of Pisces). Is this the reason Gaga's words refer to the "future of culture"?

In the most Biblical sense,
I am beyond repentance
Fame, hooker, prostitute wench vomits her mind
But in the cultural sense
I just speak in future tense

Whether the general population subscribes to these esoteric predictions or not, it certainly is "following the script" that was laid out. The same way Lady Gaga was eyeing Judas while riding with Jesus, society as a whole has let go of the core tenets of Christianity to embrace a philosophy that is compatible with Crowley's Thelema. Even if most people do not even know what is the Thelema, they live by it on a daily basis. That being said, organized religions and the elite are not necessarily opposite forces. Religions and religious sects have often been used as tools of the political elite to divide-and-conquer countries and to oppress and to manipulate the masses. Times have however changed and, today, the Illuminati is looking to unite the world under a single world government and a single world religion. This religion's values are based on egoism, materialism and the sexualization of pretty much everything. Most music videos, movies and TV shows subtly celebrate these values. In other words, they want you to be in love with Judas.

Paramore's "Brick by Boring Brick": A Song about Mind Control

"Brick by Boring Brick" by the band Paramore describes the adventures of a girl in a fantasy land. The wonder quickly turns into a nightmare and the friendly creatures turn against her. What is the meaning of this video? The answer is concealed in the symbolism of the video and alludes to a disturbing practice: mind control.

I've been often asked if the symbolism described in my previous articles are found in music videos outside of the R&B genre I usually analyze. The answer is sadly 'yes' and Paramore's Brick by Boring Brick is a stunning example. This pop-punk band, described as "emo without being whiny or bratty" primarily appeals to kids and teenagers.

They have obtained worldwide success and numerous awards for their singles crushcrushcrush and Decode. The band has been featured in numerous movies (Twilight) and video games. The newest album of the band, named Brand New Eyes, introduces to the fans symbolism they are probably not familiar with. Looking at the promotional material, readers of this site will probably recognize signs and symbols used by other pop stars as well. To make it simple: Paramore seems to have been influenced by the Illuminati. Brick by Boring Brick steers away from the usual high school themes of the band to tackle a subject that is totally oblivious to most teenagers: mind control and, more precisely, Monarch Programming.

That Darned One Eye Sign

As seen with Lady Gaga, Rihanna and other artists using mind control symbolism in their videos, Paramore has adopted the "One-Eye" symbol in their promotional pictures:

Monarch Programming

As discussed in previous articles, Monarch Programming is a mind-control technique used mostly on children to make them dissociate from reality.

> *"One of the primary reasons that the Monarch mind-control programming was named Monarch programming was because of the Monarch butterfly. The Monarch butterfly learns where it was born (its roots) and it passes this knowledge via genetics on to its offspring (from generation to generation). This was one of the key animals that tipped scientists off, that knowledge can be passed genetically. (...)*
>
> *The primary important factor for the trauma-based mind-control is the ability to disassociate. It was discovered that this ability is passed genetically from generation to generation. American Indian tribes (who had traumatic ritual dances and who would wait motionless for hours when hunting), children of Fakirs in India (who would sleep on a bed of nails or walk on hot coals), children of Yogis (those skilled in Yoga, who would have total control over their body while in a trance), Tibetan Buddhists, children of Vodoun, Bizango and other groups have a good ability to disassociate.*
>
> *The children of multigenerational abuse are also good at dissociation. The Illuminati families and European occultists went to India and Tibet to study occultism and eastern philosophy. These Europeans learned yoga, tantric yoga, meditations, and trances and other methods to disassociate. These skills are passed on to their children via genetics. A test is run when the children are about 18 months old to determine if they can dissociate enough to be selected for programming or not."*

\- The Illuminati Formula Used to Create an Undetectable Total Mind Controlled Slave

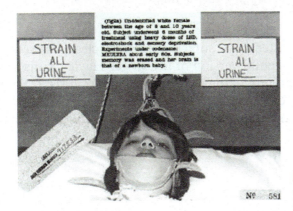

Mind Control Victim, 1961

During sexual abuse, electroshock therapy and all kinds of sadistic tortures, mind control slaves are encouraged to dissociate from reality and to go to "a happy place". The use of fairy tale imagery is used to reinforce programming and to create an alternate reality. The victim's brain, in self-preservation mode, creates a new persona (an "alter") as a defense mechanism to the abuse. The blurring of the lines between reality and fantasy makes the slave totally oblivious of his/her true state.

Paramore's latest album is called "Brand New Eyes", which has obvious mind control/Illuminati connotations. The cover features a pinned butterfly with its wings separated from its body ... symbolic indeed.

Brick by Boring Brick

Paramore's song is, at face value, about a girl escaping her problems and acting childish only to realize that it makes things worse. Behind this first degree meaning, lies a second layer of interpretation: the song describes, in chilling detail, the reality of a mind-control slave. The video manages to assemble all of the symbolism usually associated with Monarch Programming in about three minutes, leaving no doubt concerning this secondary meaning of the song.

Right from the start of the video, the subject matter of the song is made very clear. The setting is totally unreal and synthetically created. A little girl, apparently a child version of the singer Hayley, runs towards a strange world, bearing monarch butterfly wings on her back, symbolizing that she is a Monarch slave. She almost reluctantly enters a symbolic gateway, representing the start of her dissociative state. The door violently shuts down behind her, which hints the viewers to the fact that this wonderland is forcibly induced on the child. The lyrics of the first verse describe the reality of the slave.

> *Well she lives in the fairy tale*
> *Somewhere too far for us to find*

Forgotten the taste and smell
Of a world that she's left behind
It's all about the exposure the lens I told her
The angles are all wrong now
She's ripping wings off of butterflies

The girl lives in a "fairy tale", which is her dissociative mind state. It is "too far for us to find" due to the fact that this world can only be found in the confines of her consciousness. The slave has been removed from her family and the real world to live in a confined environment. She has "forgotten the taste and smell" of the the "real world" she has left behind. She lives in a prison for kids, a human rat laboratory and she is constantly manipulated by her handlers. All of her senses are subject to constant pressure and pain and her perception of reality is completely distorted: "The angles are all wrong now". She is a Monarch slave and is thus "ripping wings off of butterflies".

Keep your feet on the ground
When your head's in the clouds

The dissociative state experienced by Monarch slaves is often described as a sensation of weightlessness. While her feet are on the ground, her consciousness is in an alternate reality or "in the clouds".

The girl in the video walks around this strange world filled with fairy tale characters which are reminiscent of those found in Alice in Wonderland or the Wizard of Oz, the stories most commonly associated with mind control. The blurriness of the scenes and the presence of mushrooms in the background refer to the use of hallucinogenic drugs during Monarch Programming.

The girl enters a castle, representing her inner consciousness. Mirrors, reflections and the girl's multiplication symbolize the girl's fragmented/compartmentalized mind state.

The girl stands still while an independent, alternate personality, looking back at her through the mirror brushes her hair. Mirrors and castles are triggers that are often used in Monarch Programming.

> "The premise of trauma-based mind control (a version of which was known as the MK Ultra program) is to compartmentalize the brain, and then use techniques to access the different sections of the brain while the subject is hypnotized. Entire systems can be embedded into a person's mind, each with its own theme, access codes and trigger words. Some of the most common and popular symbolisms and themes in use are Alice in Wonderland, Peter Pan and The Wizard of Oz, mirrors, porcelain/harlequin masks, the phoenix/phoenix rising, rainbows, butterflies, owls, keys, carousels, puppets/marionettes and dolls, willow trees, tornadoes, spirals/helixes, castles, rings, hallways and doors, elevators and stairs."
> - Carissa Conti, Mind Control Themes and Programming Triggers in Movies

The second verse of the song describes a disturbing reality of Monarch slaves.

> *So one day he found her crying*
> *Coiled up on the dirty ground*
> *Her prince finally came to save her*
> *And the rest you can figure out*
> *But it was a trick*
> *And the clock struck 12*

This is the picture painted by this verse: the slave's handler enters her "cell", where she is coiled up and deeply traumatized. The floor is dirty. It has been documented that victims of mind control are forced to live rooms littered with feces (I can't make this stuff up). Her "prince", who is in fact her handler, comes in to "save her from her pain". Handlers are often portrayed as the slave's savior, who will guide them through traumatic events. The line "And the rest you can figure out" alludes to the worst: the "prince" came to rape her. It was a trick, he was not a prince, only a sadistic handler furthering the girl's trauma with sexual abuse. During those repeated assaults, the slaves are forced to dissociate from reality. The lyrics of the song's bridge aptly define this concept.

> *Well you built up a world of magic*
> *Because your real life is tragic*
> *Yeah you built up a world of magic*

She has built, brick by brick, a wall in her consciousness that dissociates her from reality. She escapes into a world of magic due to the extreme trauma she has to live through on a daily basis.

The Awakening

Probably because the girl's curiosity concerning her own mind has lead her too far, the world of wonders quickly becomes nightmarish. Creepy puppets make their way out of the mirrors. The characters of her fairy tale world suddenly become terrifying. An evil-looking character, dressed as a thief holding an ax, approaches her. Is she being reprimanded by her handlers for "not following the script" of her programming? The girl is understandably freaked out and runs away. The lyrics explain this difference between reality and fiction.

> *If it's not real*
> *You can't hold it in your hand*
> *You can't feel it with your heart*
> *And I won't believe it*
>
> *But if it's true*
> *You can see it with your eyes*
> *Or even in the dark*
> *And that's where I want to be, yeah*

The girl runs out of the castle and falls into the grave dug by … Paramore? That is not really cool of them. Hayley gets up, throws the girl's doll into the grave and they start burying her. At face value, this can interpreted as the burial of the "young irresponsible girl" living in a fairy tale. On a second level, this can be seen as the burial of the innocence of a child after experiencing traumatic events.

If you have keen eyes, you can notice a white rabbit inside the hole. Is it the white rabbit of Alice in Wonderland?

As Morpheus says in the Matrix:

> *"You take the red pill – you stay in Wonderland and I show you how deep the rabbit hole goes. "*

Whatever the meaning one attributes to the burial, the message of the video is not to sympathetic to the girl's quest of self-knowledge and emancipation. Seems like they're saying "This is what you get for trying to know your real self".

In Conclusion

After viewing the video a couple of times, I asked myself if the song was actually a denunciation of mind-control practices ... maybe it was trying to inform and warn people on the subject. So I visited some Paramore-related sites and forums to see if the song had sparked discussions concerning its deeper meaning. I quickly came back to the reality of things: Young people listen to this music and they have absolutely NO IDEA what's going on. About 97% of educated adults are totally unaware of the existence of mind control (let alone its symbolism), so to expect high schoolers know about this is totally absurd. Here are some actual comments from fans about this song: "I luv the Badabada part!", "Hayley looks great in blonde!" or "I don't like the burying part!".

So with that in mind I keep asking myself: Why do we use symbolism and triggers associated with mind control in videos aimed at the young people? They are totally oblivious to the reality of Monarch programming, so why do we expose them to it? After realizing that the group has adopted some of the Illuminati symbolism discussed in previous articles, the answer became very clear: They are part of the System, with a capital "S". This System hypnotically conditions people to accept mind control as part of their daily lives and the trend is becoming increasingly apparent. I can already hear the naysayers saying "nay" to everything and finding ways to rationalize everything that has been discussed here. Maybe they should ponder on those words:

> *"Even as he dances to the tune of the elite managers of human behavior, the modern man scoffs with a great derision at the idea of the existence and operation of a technology of mass mind control emanating from media and government. Modern man is much too smart to believe anything as superstitious as that!*
>
> *Modern man is the ideal hypnotic subject: puffed up on the idea that he is the crown of creation, he vehemently denies the power of the hypnotist's control over him as his head bobs up and down on a string."*
> - Michael A. Hoffman II, Secret Societies and Psychological Warfare

The 2011 VMAs: A Celebration of Today's Illuminati Music Industry

MTV's Video Music Awards give out "Moon Man" trophies to music artists who have had success during the previous year. But there is much more to it than shiny trophies. The VMAs are a celebration of the Illuminati industry, of those who push its agenda and a promotional tool to put the next generation of "initiates" into the spotlight. We'll look at the 2011 VMAs, the stars that were celebrated and the material that leads them there.

The MTV Video Music Awards are considered to be a few hours of performances and award acceptance speeches mixed with a few shocking moments to generate publicity. But there is more to the award ceremony than meets the eye. This mega-media-event, broadcast around the world, serves several important purposes: First, it is a major promotional tool that allows a select group of artists to gain exposure and recognition while ignoring others; second, it is an almost ritualistic celebration of the Illuminati industry, spotlighting the artists who have pushed its agenda over the previous year. My article on the 2009 VMAs described the ritualistic and symbolic elements that were found throughout the show - there was a definite occult element underlying the show which reflected the mind state of the industry.

The 2011 VMAs arguably contained less occult ritualistic elements, but was still a tightly choreographed show featuring a very select number of artists. These few actors took turns, performing, presenting and awarding each other Moon Men. In other words, the VMAs can be compared to a burlesque play where a few actors take turns appearing on stage to interact with each others. Sometimes, new characters are introduced while others are "killed off".

Almost all of the artists who were recognized at the VMAs have been featured in some way on this site (Vigilant Citizen, in case you forgot), which is not surprising as most or all of their work pushes some part of the Illuminati agenda. The main actors of this show were: Lady Gaga (of course), Katy Perry, Jessie-J, Jay-Z, Kanye West, Nicki Minaj, Beyonce and Odd Future. Wearing crazy, outlandish costumes and taking on theatrical personas, many of the artists featured in the award were not themselves, but playing characters. In fact, the show began with a long speech by Lady Gaga playing the role of a greasy Italian dude from the 1950s.

Let's look at the several "acts" of the 2011 VMA's and their meaning in the context of the Illuminati industry.

Artists and presenters emerged from a womb-like stage. They were literally coming out of the "belly of the beast".

Lady Gaga's Alter Persona

Gaga's alter-ego opening the VMAs

The show opens with Gaga's latest stunt: An male alter-ego that is a greasy annoying New York dude. Many of Gaga's singles are accompanied with a complicated setup, including characters and theatrical props (remember the horns on her heads?) – all of which get exposure in several media outlets, including TV and magazines.

For her single Yoü And I, Gaga introduced Joe Calderone, a male alter-ego. Like most of Gaga's other stunts, most people have absolutely no idea why Gaga did what she did. Why was she dressed as an Italian dude to sing a country-rock song? What's the point? Like most of Gaga's other stunts, the occult meaning of this whole charade can be found in the music video.

While the video could be the subject of an entire article, I can sum it up in two words: mind control. More specifically, it is about Monarch programming and the creation of alter-egos through the use of trauma-inducing techniques. In the video, Gaga is shown bound and tortured by a cruel handler who subjects her to the most common methods of mind control: Electroshock therapy, sexual abuse, the injection of drugs and physical torture. Yes, all of these things were portrayed in the video, along with the presence the several alter-egos created by the process.

So Lady Gaga, who is already an alter-persona of Stefanie Germanotta (the real person) has another level of alter-ego that is pretty much the exact opposite of Lady Gaga: Male, dressed in drab clothes, not glamorous, not famous, etc. In Calderone's long speech at the beginning of the VMAs, he says that Gaga left him and that he wants to be reunited with her. In occult terms, the union of opposites is called the "Alchemical Wedding" and is often represented by the figure of Baphomet – an androgynous, goat-headed deity. The title Yoü And I represents the union of the two opposite personas, Gaga and Joe Calderone, and, since they are basically same person, this ultimately creates an androgynous entity, not unlike Baphomet. In Kabbalistic lore, androgyny is perceived as the highest level of occult achievement and the concept of duality is strongly instilled in mind control victims. In other words, the presence of Joe Calderone at the VMAs is a big tribute to mind control. Good way to start a show. But Gaga did not stop there. She committed to her persona and played the role of Calderone during the entire show.

Other Alter Personas

Lady Gaga's alter-persona was heavily featured at the VMAs, but most of the artists that participated in the awards also incorporate alter personas in their acts.

NICKI MINAJ

Nicki Minaj is already a created alter persona, very different from the real person that is Onika Tanya Maraj. The odd, fashion-crazy, surgically-enhanced persona that is Minaj is a made-for-the-music-industry character created to become a star. On top of that alter, there is Roman Zolanski, a male alter-ego that appeared on some songs and that will probably be appearing a lot more in the future. Roman Zolanski is based on Roman Polanski, the movie producer who was charged for rape by use of drugs and lascivious act upon a child under 14 a few years ago.

During the 2011 VMAs, Nicki wore a Harajuku-inspired dress featuring mirror fragments (a Monarch symbol representing the fragmenting of personality). The combination of "kiddie" accessories with the sexiness of the dress' cut (it's "revealing" at the right places) is a little questionable.

KATY PERRY

Katy Perry was also all over the VMAs this year as one of the "main characters". Her latest single titled Last Friday Night introduced Katy's fans to her odd alter-ego: a nerdy 13 year old girl.

Katy Perry's young alter-ego waking up next to some unknown perv.

To sum up the Last Friday Night video, the awkward teenager gets a make-over from Rebecca Black in order to look like a slut, then gets drunk and has a menage à trois. Great message to girls between ages 10-14!

Odd Tributes

Every award show presents tributes to artists who had an outstanding career and to the greats who left this world. The VMAs are no exception but these tributes are becoming increasingly odd, insincere and dedicated to victims of the industry. In the article on the 2009 VMAs, I described the tribute to Michael Jackson, which was given by Madonna – someone who did not particularly "click" with MJ. The tribute also featured a weird video montage featuring him as zombie – which is a strange way to honor a dead person.

The 2011 VMAs presented two tributes that were just as weird as they were almost mocking the artist in question.

BRITNEY SPEARS

Britney was the recipient of the Michael Jackson Video Vanguard Award for her "influence in music video and dance"… although she did not direct any of her videos nor devise any of her choreography … but let's forget this detail. To emphasize the non-sincerity of the tribute and to make sure to point out that "this is all an act", the award is presented by an imaginary character…Lady Gaga's Joe Calderone. Britney, who is a true mind control victim of the industry and who has often shown the desire to leave it all, is given an award by an alter-ego that is basically a tribute to mind control.

The tribute then proceeds to show a mix of Britney's most popular videos whose costumes and choreography were reproduced by young girls.

The tribute to Britney's career was performed by young girls in skimpy outfits, reminding us of Britney's "contribution" to the sexualization of children agenda.

When Britney finally gets on stage to accept her award, an awkward Joe Calderone pretty much steals the show. Upon receiving her award, instead of giving acceptance speech and "having her moment", Britney proceeds to … present Beyonce and goes on with Joe Calderone about how great she is. I am pretty sure that was scripted and forced on her, making this probably the most insincere tribute of all time. Or was it?

AMY WINEHOUSE

Having lost her life a few weeks prior to the awards, it was only fair that Amy Winehouse got a tribute for her great talent. However, her death might have been the result of a ritual sacrifice and the tribute was at least as odd as the one for Michael Jackson, another great who died in strange circumstances.

Russell Brand was selected to honor Amy Winehouse. He alluded to her great voice but mostly talked about how she was a "crazy person, stinking of booze and wondering around London". He then went on to say that she was afflicted with a "disease" that affect a lot of people, alcoholism and drug addiction, although no traces of drugs were found in Winehouse nor at her home at the time of the death. Why not focus on the human being and her accomplishments?

The tribute performance that followed featured several images of Amy Winehouse with one eye hidden, which, as readers of this site know, is a symbol of Illuminati control.

In the short video compilation before Bruno Mars' performance, we see Winehouse hiding one eye, then another.

Image of Amy with one eye hidden during the performance

The First Couple and the Big Announcement

Like the last few VMA awards, Jay-Z and Beyonce were pretty much the King and Queen of the 2011 ceremonies. First, Jay-Z and Kanye West performed the first single from their album Watch the Throne. This album opens with a revealing song entitled No Church in the Wild (featuring Odd Future's Frank Ocean). The song describes a philosophy that is akin to Aleister Crowley's "Thelema". Kanye West's verse goes as follows:

> *Coke on her black skin made a stripe like a zebra*
> *I call that jungle fever*
> *You will not control the threesome*
> *Just roll the weed up until I get me some*
> *We formed a new religion*
> *No sins as long as there's permission*
> *And deception is the only felony*
> *So never f-ck nobody wit'out tellin' me*

Aleister Crowley's motto was "Do What Thou Wilt" which seems to be echoed in Kanye saying "We formed a new religions/No sins as long as there's permission". Crowley was also known to have extensively experimented with drugs and sexuality in a spiritual context – another concept reflected by his verse. Later in the song, Kanye appears to be referring to relations with a Monarch sex kitten:

Thinkin' 'bout the girl in all-leopard
Who was rubbin' the wood like Kiki Shepard
Two tattooes, one read "No Apologies"
The other said "Love is cursed by monogamy"

The song therefore echoes similar themes to those communicated by other pop stars (such as Gaga) – which is the philosophy that is promoted by the entertainment industry.

Going back to the show, MTV's first couple had an important announcement to its loyal subjects: the first lady is with child and will be giving birth to the successor of the king.

Beyonce in front of the womb-like stage, holding her own womb.

Proving the importance of the couple, this silent pregnancy announcement shattered all previous Twitter records with more than 8,000 tweets a second. This kind of attention reminded me of Jay-Z's almost prophetic verse in the song New Day, from the album that was released about two weeks prior to the VMAs:

Sorry junior, I already ruined ya
'Cause you ain't even alive, paparazzi pursuin' ya
Sins of a father make yo' life ten times harder
I just wanna take ya to a barber
Bondin' on charters, all the shit that I never did
Teach ya good values, so you cherish it
Took me 26 years to find my path
My only job is cuttin' the time in half
So at 13 we'll have our first drink together

I would never speak ill of an unborn child. I will just hope that he/she won't become another Willow Smith.

Presenting the New Generation

The VMAs do not only celebrate current Illuminati artists, it "initiates" a new generation of artists who will carry the Illuminati torch into the future. A couple of new acts stood out in the 2011 VMAs.

Jessie J, who already released a few symbolic music videos (see the article entitled Jessie J's "Price Tag": It's Not About Money, It's About Mind Control), enjoyed great exposure during that night by occupying the Throne, where she performed about a dozen times.
The artist who obtained the most publicity was however Tyler the Creator from the alternate-rap, shock-rap, lo-fi

rap, horrorcore rap, whatever-you-wanna-call-it-rap group Odd Future. Considered to be (by people who know nothing about rap) the "new Wu-Tang Clan", Odd Future obtained great praise from artists like Kanye West, who

Jessie J sat on the Throne during the VMAs as a "new initiate".

deemed Yonkers to be the song of the year, while getting criticized by others, such as Chris Brown, who tweeted: "All this demonic music is wack as shi*! I never claim to be no saint but by no means am I trying to promote death, violence,and destruction with my music!".

Whatever your opinion is on Tyler the Creator, it is obvious that his theatrical talent, his "anything to shock" attitude, his promotion of self-destruction and his love for inverted crosses will make him a perfect fit in the Illuminati industry. Expect to see a lot more of him in the future.

The video Yonkers has pretty everything needed to shock viewers: Tyler the Creator eats a cockroach, throws up, says things like "Jesus called, he said he's sick of the disses I told him to quit bitching, this isn't a f*cking hotline For a f*cking shrink, sheesh, I already got mine" and ultimately hangs himself. Not unlike other artists at the VMA's, Tyler has an alter-ego named Wolf Haley.

In Conclusion

The VMAs are not simply a show designed to give out awards. They define who's hot and who's not. They celebrate in a ritualistic matter the type of "creativity" that is appreciated by the industry – superficial shock value. As we have seen in this article, almost all of the artists who obtained exposure during the VMAs have released albums and videos that were directly in line with the Illuminati agenda which includes: the promotion of mind control, self-destruction, materialism, superficiality, the sexualization of children and the demeaning of religions. Pushing these kinds of messages through lyrics and symbols is a requirement to be in the "good graces" of the industry – which is a giant, controlling machine, that works with codes and rituals and that heavily calculates and filters the messages sent to the masses.

Although many of the artists featured on the show are "eccentric" and "original", the core message remains the same and is remarkably consistent, regardless of the musical genre. Aspiring artists who dream to obtain this level of celebrity, understand that this is the "mold to fit" in order to obtain success. The VMAs are an artificial creation that artificially promotes artists to create artificial hype. It is a fake show, filled with fake personas who sing with fake voices, wearing fake wigs and cracking fake smiles, giving fake tributes to other fakes who have been fake longer than them. Are there still real, authentic artists who sing from the heart and do not push "industry-approved" messages? Yes, but you won't find them watching the VMAs. So turn off that TV and see what the real world has to offer.

Brown Eyed Girls' Video "Sixth Sense" or How the Elite Controls Opposition

Backed by big money and millions of fans, the Korean pop music industry (K-Pop) has taken over the airwaves of Asia and the world. Although groups such as Brown Eyed Girls do not sing in English, they definitely bring to the masses the same Illuminati symbolism pushed by pop stars in the Western world. The video of "Sixth Sense" is a true manifesto of the elite, describing how it controls entertainers and uses them to indoctrinate the masses. This article analyzes the meaning of the symbolism in Brown Eyed Girls' music video "Sixth Sense".

In last year's article "Narsha and SHINee: Illuminati Infiltration of K-Pop", I looked into the symbolism of two popular K-Pop videos and how they fit in the global Illuminati agenda. Since then, Korean pop has only gotten bigger as record labels like NegaNetwork and SM Entertainment churn out new boy and girl bands at a hectic pace. These labels are almost "pop music sweatshops" as scandals have arisen regarding the mistreatment of K-Pop stars and the signing of "slave contracts". These labels are, in turn, owned and controlled by the same elite global media corporation who own American and British labels and pop stars. In this context, is it surprising that K-Pop videos show its stars tied down and submitting to a totalitarian power?

The video of Sixth Sense from the very popular girl band Brown Eyed Girls, could not better portray the elite's control on media and entertainment. More than simply displaying Illuminati symbolism, the video presents the blueprint of how popular figures can be used to communicate a specific message using sex and music as an incentive. Each one of the group's members are shown in a different position of submission, each representing the different ways the elite controls entertainers to serve its interests. While Myrio, Narsha, Ga-In and Jea appear to be rebelling against an authoritative police state, they are, at the end of the day, controlled opposition, serving in the elite's Hegelian dialectic. Yes, all of these complex concepts are found in a K-Pop video intended for children and teenagers. Are they being warned or indoctrinated by the message of the video? Let's look at the symbolism of the video and the messages it communicates to the viewers.

The Premise of Sixth Sense

The video takes place in the context of a totalitarian police state, where media is tightly controlled and people are tightly monitored.

The video begins showing police in riot gear and video cameras, setting it in a Big-Brotherish police state.

The regime is controlled by a masked figured named "the Absolute" (according to an interview with the lyricist of the group), who could easily be associated with the "masked" occult elite.

The Absolute looking over its army of riot police. Yet another music video getting young people used to the idea of an oppressive police state.

There appears to be some resistance to the Absolute's regime, namely Brown Eyed Girls. They are shown standing in defiance of the riot police and appear to be taking a stance against the oppression of the Absolute. As an ultimate gesture of defiance, the group starts singing. Do they sing about freedom and liberation? Are they singing out what is on everyone's mind? No, not really. The listeners are treated to the same pseudo-sexual drivel all pop songs numbs our brains with. Here's a translation of the first verse:

> *Your thirsty face starts sweating*
> *And your flesh is on the tip of my sharp fingers*
>
> *The bubble in champagne*
> *Explodes, good pain*
> *No need to worry, love is just a game*

What does this have to do with resistance? Not much. In fact, the song is about the exact opposite: Not resisting but giving in to the "Sixth Sense". Are B.E.G. truly in opposition to the riot police or are they in fact on their side? The six-pointed star on the police uniforms represent the "Sixth Sense" so it would seem both sides are about the same thing.

The riot police wears a star with its lowest point red, symbolizing the sixth sense. In occult symbolism, upside down triangles represents the vulva, the feminine energy and reproduction.

What exactly is the "Sixth Sense"? Judging by the lyrics of the song and the symbolism of the video, it is sexual energy – the most basic and primal of human instincts. It is the easiest way to capture and keep the attention of an audience and is used ad-nauseam in pop music to generate interest in otherwise insipid songs. Pretty girls can make things such as a fascist police-state cool. On an esoteric level, reproductive organs are part of the base chakra, which can explain why it is associated in the video with the lowest point of the sixth-pointed star. While the five other senses send information to the brain to be processed and analyzed, the carnal impulse in humans bypasses all of that and directly taps into our primal urges. For this reason, sexuality can be (successfully) used to sell anything, including music videos.

At the start of the song, Ga-In immediately points towards her "upside down triangle", singing "Touch Touch". I guess that's all there need to be known about the Sixth Sense.

B.E.G. is therefore singing about how great the Sixth Sense is, in front of riot police wearing a symbol representing the Sixth Sense. Are they really on the same side? It is still early to say, however the video goes on to show the backstory of each of the group's members. In the video's narrative, they each have been used by the Absolute in a different way, each of them representing a facet of Illuminati control in the entertainment business.

Facets of Illuminati Control

During the video, each member of B.E.G. is shown in a different setting, yet in a similar situation: They are all controlled and monitored by the Absolute and forced to play a role in the advancement of its Agenda. The character played by each member represents a facet of Illuminati control in the entertainment business.

Miryo, the rapper of the group as the "messenger".

Miryo is shown standing in front of the luxurious palace of the Absolute. She is therefore "owned" by him and speaks for him (the double "S" on the palace stands for Sixth Sense). Miryo appears to be strong and confident but, upon closer look, we realized that she is actually tied down. She is forced to speak into microphones (representing the media) to transmit the message of the Absolute. This image represents the fact that artists are used as mouthpieces by the elite, who utilize their popularity and charisma to deliver messages. When Miryo signed that record contract to become a professional singer, she indeed became the property of the elite.

Narsha's character is very animalistic, sensually crawling around on four legs like a cat. She is wearing leopard-print shorts, which, as readers of this site know, represents Kitten/beta programming in mind control symbolism (see the article entitled Origins and Techniques of Monarch Mind Control for more information regarding Mind Control). She is also surrounded by animal cages, which represent the dehumanization and captivity of mind control slaves at the hands of their handlers. Actual MK slaves are said to be often held in animal cages to cause trauma. Despite her forced state, Narsha appears to enjoy being watched, which is how Beta Kittens are programmed to act.

Narsha representing mind control and Kitten Programming.

Narsha is shown in juxtaposition with a cat walking around the elite's palace, furthering the association with Kitten programming.

In an interview, the lyricist of the group Kim Eana explains Narsha's role:

> "Narsha represents the 'sixth sense' in itself, and embodies the animalistic lyrics in the song (such as "The tips of my sharp nails become embedded into your skin"). Since there is a recurring 'jungle cat' theme, Narsha was directed to act as wildly as possibly for the video. The lights inside the cages are flashlights, a symbol of constantly being watched and observed. What's interesting about her character is that although she looks afraid of it, she also seems to enjoy being observed."

Jea, representing sacrifice.

At first glance, the scene featuring Jea appears to be somewhat poetic, with her floating in water and whatnot. On closer look, we realize that she is tied up to the piece of wood and is left there to die, in a matter vaguely similar to Christ tied up to the cross. We also realize that this is taking place in the pool of the elite's palace. In other words, they placed her there to sacrifice her.

Jea therefore represents the ritual sacrifices of the occult elite. More than being simple employees, public figures that are part of the Illuminati industry sometimes become unwilling parts of Illuminati rituals. The lyricist of the group confirms that

> "Jea represents the image of sacrifice. She's tied to tree branches, an idea derived from religion. Although the scene looks beautiful from afar, the viewer is able to see that Jea is being pressed down and chained."
> - Kim Eana

Ga-in, the traitor.

Ga-In's character appears to have been beaten and humiliated by the Absolute's regime as a result of being a traitor. She is now tied to a chair, between Masonic pillars and is being filmed by a camera. She is the "example", showing to others what happens to those who attempt to go against the Absolute.

The Uprising

At one point, all of this singing and dancing apparently gets everyone riled up and ready to start a revolution. The members of B.E.G., who were shown above to be restrained and monitored, become aggressive and rebellious (although they never truly free themselves). The riot police feeds from this energy and become rebellious too. They are shown questioning themselves as they remove their helmets to reveal their faces. These soldiers are not simple pawns, they are young men with emotions and stuff. They turn against their ruler and rush towards him as water cannons protect the palace.

At that point, the mask of the Absolute is shown thrown on the ground. The scene then reverts to reality and shows again the riot police about to rush B.E.G.

The golden mask, representing the hidden, faceless elite is shown on the ground, leading the viewers to think that the revolt was a success.

There is no uprising. The riot police is right where is was.

The rebellion incited by the girls was one big fantasy dreamt up by B.E.G. and the army. They are now back to the cold, hard reality: You cannot fight the Absolute.

Meaning of the Video

Under the guise of entertainment, the video of Sixth Sense gives its viewers a rather harsh lesson in power and politics. A basic analysis of the story, answering simple questions such as "who won the battle?" and "what's the moral of the story?", reveals that the elite won and that resistance is useless. In fact, there never was any actual resistance as B.E.G. were manipulated by the Absolute all along. The uprising was nothing but a mere illusion, proving to the viewers that they can be lead to believe anything they see.

Presented as heroes of the people, B.E.G. is shown to be inciting a riot and being agents of liberation. The only thing they however truly accomplished is a mere distraction, a temporary escape to a world filled with brave and determined people, ready to fight for freedom. This is what mass media accomplishes on a daily basis: Putting in the spotlight artists who are, in appearance, rebellious and uncompromising, yet following their messages is exactly what the elite wants the masses to do. In communication-theory terms, the viewers are subjected to a Hegelian dialectic, where a thesis and anti-thesis are proposed, but engaging in either one of them ultimately advances the agenda of the elite. In other words, it is one big circular mind-screw. Here's a little description of how it works:

> "For the elite of his day, and for the monetary elite today, the Hegelian dialectic provides tools for the manipulation of society.
>
> To move the public from point A to point B, one need only find a spokesperson for a certain argument and position him or her as an authority. That person represents Goalpost One. Another spokesperson is positioned on the other side of the argument, to represent Goalpost Two.
>
> Argument A and B can then be used to manipulate a given social discussion. If one wishes, for in stance, to promote Idea C, one merely needs to promote the arguments of Goalpost One (that tend to promote Idea C) more effectively than the arguments of Goalpost Two. This forces a slippage of Goalpost Two's position. Thus both Goalpost One and Goalpost Two advance downfield toward Idea C. Eventually, Goalpost Two occupies Goalpost One's original position. The "anti-C" argument now occupies the pro-C position. In this manner whole social conversations are shifted from, say, a debate over market freedom vs. socialism to a debate about the degree of socialism that is desirable.
>
> The Hegelian dialectic is a powerful technique for influencing the conversations of cultures and nations, especially if one already controls (owns) much of the important media in which the arguments take place. One can then, as the monetary elite characteristically do, emphasize one argument at the expense of the other, effectively shifting the positions of Goalposts One and Two."
> - Daily Bell, Hegelian Dialectic

Pop stars often play the role of "Goalpost Two" in entertainment videos, but the blatant symbolism of these videos show that they are truly working for the hidden rulers.

The final scene from Beyonce's "Run the World (Girls)", saluting the riot police. While, at first, Beyonce appears to be leading a resistance or a liberation movement, this final scene tells the viewers that, regardless what they just saw, she still obeys the orders of the powers that be. Like Sixth Sense, this video also emphasizes the power of sexuality to control the masses with lyrics such as "My persuasion can build a nation/ Endless power, the love we can devour/ You'll do anything for me."

Although the four members of B.E.G. were shown to be somewhat rebellious, the core of their message was, at the end, exactly what the elite wanted to communicate. The concept of Sixth Sense appeals to the shutting down of intellectual and cognitive functions to "surrender" to the mesmerizing effect of lust in mass media. It is during this somewhat hypnotized and slightly aroused state that messages can effectively reach the viewer's brains with maximum effectiveness.

In Conclusion

By analyzing the political message of Sixth Sense, one forgets that this video is primarily aimed at children and teenagers. While listening to the music and admiring their idols' dancing, the viewers are exposed to a powerful lesson that sticks in the subconscious mind: Resistance is futile. Even worse, resistance does not even exist as those who appear to be resisting are just leading you towards the elite's goal. These kinds of propaganda videos existed under dictatorships, but today they are passed around as "entertainment". They get massive airplay on MTV and millions of hits on YouTube. In reality, nobody is forced to watch these videos, but they are nevertheless quite popular. Is there a reason why people willingly subject themselves to this kind of elite propaganda? Yes. These videos appeal to their Sixth Sense … and people like that.

The Esoteric Meaning of Florence + the Machine's "Shake it Out" and "No Light No Light"

Florence + the Machine obtained commercial and critical success by releasing music with a distinct sound and feel. Although her works are often covered by mass media, one aspect of her act is rarely mentioned: the esoteric symbolism of her songs and videos. We will look at the meaning of the videos "Shake it Out" and "No Light No Light", two enigmatic videos from the album Ceremonials.

Florence + the Machine is different from most of the singers mentioned on the Vigilant Citizen for several reasons. First, there is obvious talent and artistry involved in her works, making them more profound than most pop songs out there. Second, there is a definite occult influence in her music but it is not hidden or concealed, but rather all out in the open. In an interview with Nylon magazine, Florence stated:

> "I wanted to be a witch when I was a kid. I was obsessed with witchcraft. At school, me and my two friends had these spell books; I always wanted a more magical reality. I had a little shrine at home and I did a spell to try and make the boy in the other class fall in love with me."

Despite this known fact, I never found any review or analysis of Florence + the Machine's work from an occult point of view, a field Florence Welch is obviously well versed in. The videos of her first album Lungs had some occult concepts infused into them. For example, her hit Dog Days are Over alludes to the dog star Sirius, an all-important celestial body in esoteric teachings (for more information, read the article entitled The Mysterious Connection Between Sirius and Human History). Her second album, Ceremonials, is slightly darker and more focused on profound esoteric concepts that deserve some analyzing.

The videos of Shake it Out and No Light No Light both contain enigmatic imagery (see the confused comments on YouTube) that relate to ancient occult concepts. Analyzed from an esoteric point of view, both videos can indeed by seen as "ceremonies" where symbols and colors describe a story of profound transformation. The imagery of Shake it Out tell the story of an initiation ritual in a strange secret society while No Light No Light describes a profound spiritual change in the context of duality. We'll look at the esoteric meaning of both videos.

Shake it Out

Taking place in a strange masquerade ball with masked guests – reminiscent of the secret society orgy in the movie "Eyes Wide Shut" - Shake it Out follows Florence's evolution. From being shy and reserved, she becomes ecstatic and almost demented. In an interview, Welch described the video's setting this way:

> "Think of a psychedelic 1920s dress party with a demonic twist. Possession meets The Great Gatsby. (...) We were kind of going for a sort of 'Gatsby at West Egg'-style house party but with maybe slightly ritualistic and sort of satanic undertones and séances."

In this strange setting, there are several Florences, with different personalities and wearing dresses with symbolic colors. Each of them tell a different part of the story of Florence's initiation and its results. As we have seen in previous articles on this site, the theme of initiation is often found in modern pop videos and there is one thing they all have in common: a focus on the colors white, red and black. This video is no exception as the color of Florence's dresses tell alot about the meaning of the character she is embodying.

At the beginning of the video, Florence wears a pearl/gold colored dress and looks shy and almost reticent as she enters the ball. She is obviously the "guest of honor" but she is unsure of what she is walking into.

Florence shyly descending the stairs to the ball.

As she enters the ball, she is greeted with strange cloaked and mask figures. Some of them are quite weird but interesting.

A mask representing Hypnos, the Greek god of sleep - from which the term "hypnosis" comes from. He is the twin of Thanatos, the god of death and His palace was a dark cave where the sun never shines. At the entrance were a number of poppies and other hypnogogic plants.

This mask with multiple faces appears to be a favorite in elite "Illuminati balls"..

Baron Alexis de Redé (right) wearing a similar multi-face mask at an actual Rothschild ball in 1972.

The ceremony is centered around her and with good reason: it is her initiation ritual. One of the figures blindfolds Florence.

Florence is blindfolded by a man in a red cape.

The blindfolding of new initiates is an intricate part of Masonic-like rituals and bear a very symbolic meaning: they represent the candidate's prior blindness and ignorance.

Image taken from Duncan's Ritual of Freemasonry describing the initiation of a new Mason. He is blindfolded and walked around the Lodge.

The lyrics of the song sustain the overall theme of these kinds of initiations as they pertain to the abandoning of a dark past and the embracing of a new life. Some parts of the song are particularly interesting as they appear to allude to specific aspects to Masonic initiations. This following passage refers to candidates being "in the dark" before the completion of the initiation.

> It's always darkest before the dawn (…)
> And I've been a fool and I've been blind

Other passages of the song are oddly reminiscent of the oaths that are recited during Masonic initiations. For example, these lines:

> I am done with my graceless heart
> So tonight I'm gonna cut it out and then restart

can be related to this part of the Masonic initiatory ceremony:

> "Oh! that my breast had been torn open, my heart plucked out, and placed upon the highest pinnacle of the Temple, there to be devoured by the vultures of the air …"

Another part of the song refers to several aspects of an initiation, whether it being the "end of a road", the concept of darkness (most secret society initiations place candidate in dark rooms for a period of time to represent death and rebirth) and preparedness to suffer (during the initiation ritual)

> And I'm damned if I do and I'm damned if I don't
> So here's to drinks in the dark at the end of my road
> And I'm ready to suffer and I'm ready to hope
> It's a shot in the dark and right at my throat

This last line is also similar to a portion of the Masonic oath.

> "I arose, and on my passage around the Lodge was accosted by three Fellow Crafts, who thrice demanded of me the secrets of a Master Mason; and, on being refused, the first gave me a blow with the twenty-four-inch gauge, across my throat"

Whether or not these allusions to secret societies were intentional, they definitely give a sense of "spiritual rebirth" to the song.

In another scene where Florence plays the role of "new initiate", she is shown taking part of a séance to communicate with spirits, confirming the occult nature of the gathering.

Florence at a séance table with other members.

Is this what engendered Florence in red?

The Florence that is dressed in a red dress is drastically different, as if she was possessed by a spirit.

In another part of the video, Florence is dressed in red – the color of sacrifice and initiation – and has a completely different demeanour. She is unrestrained, dances frantically and appears to be slightly possessed. While she seems to be having the time of her life, she also appears to be consumed and disturbed by whatever is effecting her.

Another Florence appears to be a result of the initiation: a pure and angelic Florence dressed in white, symbol of purity and innocence. She runs out of the party and climbs on a tree, looking godly and at peace.

Florence in a pure and virginal white dress.

Florence in red is therefore the opposite of the shy and innocent Florence dressed in white. These two personas reflect the occult concept of duality that takes place within her, a concept that is also reflected in the lyrics with passages such as:

> *Cause looking for heaven, for the devil in me*
> *Looking for heaven, for the devil in me*
> *Well what the hell I'm gonna let it happen to me*

A forth persona is shown in the video: a cool, calm and powerful Florence dressed in black formal wear – symbolizing the full-fledged society member.

Florence dressed in black in a private setting - dancing with two masked men.

No Light No Light

No Light No Light has none of the subtlety of Shake it Out. It rather violently clashes two diametrically opposing forces battling for nothing less than Florence's soul. The imagery of the video is based on contrasts and opposites, using concepts such as light and darkness, good and evil, black and white, civilization and tribalism, church and sorcery and so forth. The two main scenes of the video that are pitted against each other are so clichéd that they border on caricature: an entranced voodoo doctor practicing black magic versus innocent church choir boys. The opposition is vivid, yet both worlds appear to be part of Florence's experience (she was in choir during her youth, while also dabbling in occultism). The two scenes bring up an almost archetypal sense of good and evil, thus symbolically representing the eternal struggle that is happening within Florence's soul.

The first scene shows a masked man, sitting in the dark, in front of lit candles and a voodoo doll. The shaman is inside a Masonic Lodge. Although it is dark, we can notice the Masonic throne, the Blazing Star above it and the all-important checkerboard-patterned floor.

The shaman sticking a needle inside a voodoo doll. The Masonic checkerboard floor is the space on which occult rituals and ceremonies take place. The black and white pattern represents the coexistence of good and evil repeated in an infinite pattern and is therefore a visual representation of the concept of duality.

Like the checkerboard pattern, the video visually depicts the eternal fight between two opposing forces in the spiritual realm, but it uses human figures instead. Opposed to the voodoo shaman is another evocative image: young choir boys inside a church.

Church choir boys represent the force opposite to the shaman.

So Florence is standing atop of a skyscraper, looking somewhat confused, knowing that she must make a choice, trying to hang on. This sense of uncertainty is reflected in the lyrics:

> "I was disappearing in plain sight
> Heaven help me, I need to make it right
> You want a revelation, You want to get it right
> But it's a conversation, I just can't have tonight"

Florence appears to be under the spell of the shaman as he hurts her by sticking needles inside the voodoo doll. At one point, Florence lets go and embarks into a gigantic free-fall from the top of a tall building. She crashes through the church's stained glass ceiling and floats in a burst of light.

Florence enters the church, but not from the front door, by crashing from the ceiling.

Florence enters the church from above, floats in mid-air and takes a position that makes her appear to be Christ-like. This symbolic image refers to the Gnostic concept of "inner-Christ", where salvation and godhood is obtained from within by illumination. Florence is then caught by the choir boys and carried somewhere. Her embrace of "good" apparently kills the voodoo doctor who begins convulsing. By banishing the evil that had control of her, Florence attained Gnosis and therefore became "like Christ".

This video has caused controversy because it was deemed racist. These observers claim that the "bad guy" is a stereotypical tribal-voodoo shaman and is, in fact, a "black face", a non-black person painted black, like they used to do back when media was openly racist. At one point during the video, we see Florence, a red-headed white woman running away from evil that is represented by a black guy. It is also noted that she is saved by a European choir that is exclusively composed of white boys. With that being said, can we truly say that the video is purposely racist? I honestly cannot say and that is not the point of the article. I can, however, say that race is indeed used in a symbolic way to emphasize the occult concept of duality and to further develop the sense of opposition between the two scenes.

As said above, humans are used in this video to depict abstract the concept of struggle between opposing forces, as depicted by the symbol of Ying and Yang. The struggle is happening inside of Florence, on a spiritual level, hence the spiritual imagery of the video. Everything about these forces is opposed, including their skin color – white and black – as they become an embodiment of the checkerboard pattern floor. White is traditionally associated with good and black with evil. This unfortunately translates very badly when it comes to skin color but the direction of the video appears to have taken this bold step anyways.

The lyrics of the song further accentuate the concept of struggle between good and evil. While it can be interpreted as a song to a lover, the vocabulary that is used, along with the video's imagery, alludes to a spiritual struggle. The entity she is speaking to appears to have an ethereal quality as she mentions she is witnessing A revelation in the light of day. With that being said, who or what is she talking to? To God (who brings revelation)? The Devil (who is said to have blue eyes)?

> *"No light, no light in your bright blue eyes*
> *I never knew daylight could be so violent*
> *A revelation in the light of day*
> *You can't chose what stays and what fades away*
> *And I'd do anything to make you stay"*

There is a definite sense of ambiguity which only emphasizes on the concept of duality, where opposing forces are part of a greater whole. In other words, good and evil, God and Satan are considered to be "two sides of the same coin".

In Conclusion

Florence + the Machine's videos for Ceremonials indeed include a great deal of ceremony and ritual. Through the symbolism and color codes found in the videos, Shake it Out and No Light No Light both tell stories that take place on the esoteric plane, mainly involving the all-important concept of duality. The first video is centered around the concept of initiation in the context of a high-society masquerade ball (sometimes referred to as an Illuminati ball). The second video opposes spiritual figures representing good and evil that border on caricature, where Florence, a soul in peril, frees herself from the spell of a voodoo shaman to be saved by a church choir, which represent her own good and dark side. That being said, one can argue that it was the shaman (her dark side) who pushed Florence towards her own enlightenment. Is he therefore truly evil or simply part of a greater scheme? That is the mystery of duality and these are the esoteric concepts that transpire from Florence + the Machine's works. Does that make her message good or evil? To quote her words: "Looking for heaven, for the devil in me".

From Mind Control to Superstardom: The Meaning of Lady Gaga's "Marry the Night"

The music video "Marry the Night" tells the story of Lady Gaga's rise to fame in the entertainment industry. Oddly enough, her "journey" begins with her describing the symptoms of a trauma-based mind control victim. Is there a deeper meaning to this video? We'll look at the symbolism of "Marry the Night" and its underlying occult meaning.

Lady Gaga generated a great buzz among her fans when she announced that the video to Marry the Night would reveal a part of her past. Did her fans expect the video to begin with a traumatized Gaga inside a psychiatric ward with a bunch of lobotomized girls? Probably not. But from that strange starting point, the video proceeds to depict Gaga's rise to super-stardom. How does all of that tie in together? To most, this doesn't really make any sense. However, to those who understand the relation between trauma-based mind control and the entertainment industry, it makes perfect sense. While many of her previous videos referred to mind control in subtle and symbolic ways (see previous articles on Vigilant Citizen), Marry the Night takes it a step further, pretty much spelling it out. At the very start of the video, Gaga's monologue defines in unequivocal terms the plight of a mind control victim. Despite her hardships, she says, she is determined to make it in the music business and is ready to do whatever it takes to reach her goal. She therefore "marries the night", an expression that has a profound meaning.

The video is Lady Gaga's directorial debut and, according MTV.com it is basically a "big thank you" to Interscope Records – the record label that signed her. This is definitely true but the video also says thanks to those behind her record label: the "Night" that she married. Let's look at the video's most important scenes.
In the Psychiatric Ward

The intro of the video shows Gaga as the patient of some kind of psychiatric ward. While laying on a stretcher that is pushed by two nurses, Gaga describes the way she perceives reality. Affected by a violent trauma, Gaga escapes into her own world to be able to go on. The mental dissociation that is described by Gaga is in direct accordance with the purpose of trauma-based mind control, the basis of Monarch Programming (see the article Origins and Techniques of Monarch Mind Control for more information). Monarch programming uses various methods, including violence, drugs and abuse to induce violent trauma and cause the victim to dissociate – a natural defense mechanism of the brain. The fracture of the personality that results from the process is then exploited by the mind-control handlers to program within the subject's mind new "alter" personalities. This is also described in Marry the Night, as Gaga creates a new persona to obtain superstardom.

The process also causes the victims to have huge memory gaps when recollecting the past. In during the intro of the video, Gaga describes how a victim of Monarch programming would perceive reality:

> *"When I look back on my life, it's not that I don't want to see things exactly as they happen, it's just that I prefer to remember them in an artistic way. And truthfully, the lie of it all is much more honest, because I invented it. Clinical psychology arguably tells us that trauma is the ultimate killer. Memories are not recycled like atoms and particles in quantum physics. They can be lost forever. It sort of like my past is an unfinished painting and, as the artist of that painting, I must fill in all the ugly holes and make it beautiful again. Its not that I've been dishonest, it's just that I loathe reality."*

Gaga basically says that she went through trauma that was so horrific that it caused her to dissociate from reality. Since she cannot cope with the true nature of her existence, her psyche has "filled in all the ugly holes" and created an inner-world where she can escape and survive mentally. This is exactly what happens with MK slaves, who, while dissociated into their fantasy world, get programmed by their handlers. Gaga then proceeds to describe how her dissociated mind perceives her surroundings.

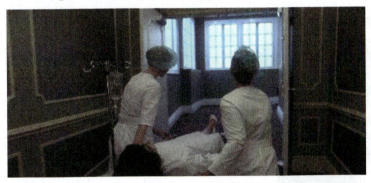

The nurses wear their caps in a "stylish" way because we are seeing Gaga's dissociated perception of reality

In Gaga's reality, the nurses are wearing "next season Calvin Klein" and she is wearing Giuseppe Zanotti shoes. Also, the nurses' caps are tilted to the side like Parisian berets because she thinks "it's romantic". So what we are seeing is not reality, but Gaga's perception of reality that has been distorted by trauma. Since she loves fashion, the fashion world is integrated in her mental escape to make reality bearable. The premise of this scene is very similar to the movie Sucker Punch (analyzed in the article entitled "Sucker Punch" or How to Make Monarch Mind Control Sexy), where a young patient of a psychiatric hospital dissociates from reality before getting a lobotomy.

Lobotomies also appear to be happening in Gaga's ward. As she arrives in her room, we notice that it is filled with brain-dead girls with bandages around their heads. This hints that Gaga's "institution" deals with mind control-related stuff.

On her bed, Gaga speaks with a nurse – who also happened to have delivered her when she was born. This is rather odd (for many reasons) but confirms that Gaga's existence has been under tight control since her youth. Is this bit part "autobiographical" or fiction? Hard to say.

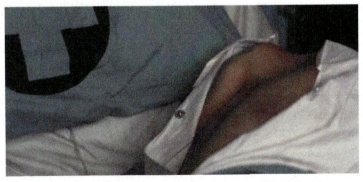

Something happened to her back

When Gaga turns around, her back reveals that something awful happened to her. The nurse tells her "No intimacy for two weeks", which hints to the fact that the trauma might of been of a sexual origin. She nevertheless tells the nurse that "she'll make it" and that "she'll be a star" because she has "nothing left to lose". In other words, the trauma she suffered left her lost and empty but that hole can be filled by her two obsessions: fame and success.

The Metamorphosis

After the depressing hospital scene, Gaga is in her apartment when she gets a phone call from her manager announcing that she's been dropped by her label. She replies "But I'm an artist!", as if artistic integrity is the top priority of record labels. She then loses it and goes into a topless frenzy involving Cheerios and smudged makeup. The messy scene is juxtaposed with images of Gaga gracefully dancing ballet – as a "true artist". The two scenes are diametrically opposed yet have noticeable similarities. The ballet scene ends with Gaga topless and crying, indicating that both scenes happen at the same time: One in real life and one in her head.

Gaga topless and crying, like in the apartment scene. This represents how Gaga perceives herself, yet she is rejected by her label.

In the next scene, Gaga is in the the tub, accomplishing a significant task: Dying her hair blonde. Her new alter-persona is being created, the one that will become a pop star.

The transformation from Stefani Germanotta to the alter Lady Gaga symbolized by the dying of her hair blonde. She is beginning to do what is needed to make it in the entertainment industry - A shallow alter-ego that will do what is required by record labels. While she's doing this, she's humming "Marry the Night", something she is actually beginning to accomplish here.

Once the transformation is complete, Gaga says goodbye to her ballet company (were they the ones that were lobotomized earlier?). The "true artist" is gone and the superficial diva is born. The camera stays on the art of the room for several seconds, probably due to its symbolic meaning. (the scene was shot at Snug Harbor Cultural Center in NY).

The camera then pans to the room's oculus (a circular window at the apex of a dome) with a sun as the pupil of the "eye". The oculus transitions into a full moon. As the scene turns from day to night, Stefani disappears and Lady Gaga emerges.

As the camera pans, we see several interesting things. At the top of this shot is Poseidon, the king of Atlantis with his trademark pitchfork. Although he was probably painted there because the shooting location is a harbor (a nautical place), the god takes another meaning in the context of the video: Poseidon is an important figure in the occult elite's mythology as he is the king of Atlantis, the place where the Mysteries have originated from. Under Poseidon is a lighted star similar to the Blazing star found in Masonic lodges. Underneath the star is written "The Cross is My Anchor" - a Christian saying - but in reverse. I am pretty that the phrase is not actually written in reverse in Snug Harbor. Why was the image flipped? Does this represent Gaga's spiritual shift as she "Marries the Night"?

The camera then pans to the room's oculus (a circular window at the apex of a dome) with a sun as the pupil of the "eye". The oculus transitions into a full moon. As the scene turns from day to night, Stefani disappears and Lady Gaga emerges.

Marrying the Night

Most music sites say that Marry the Night is about going out, partying and having fun in New York city. But, as it is often the case with Gaga's works, the symbolism and the imagery of the video hints at a deeper, more ritualistic meaning. As we have seen above, Gaga is passionately fueled by her drive for success and she appears to realize that the key to make it in the industry is: Initiation. Or, in more sinister terms, selling one's soul.

In the context of the video, the expression "marry the night" takes an almost metaphysical connotation. Marriage is a religious ritual, a binding association between two people. What does it mean when one marries the night? It can mean associating with people who deal in the dark: the occult elite (those we call the Illuminati). It can also signify embracing one's own flaws and "dark side". In all cases, there is a definite sense of "rebirth" in the process. And, that's what we see: A blond Lady Gaga (the alter of Stefani Germanotta) emerges from a Trans-Am dressed in black.

Gaga then goes to "Pop Star Training". No more ballet, it's all about doing cool, hip, music video choreography now. Once her training is complete, Gaga is ready for the "big time". She becomes a glamorous diva and dances what is almost a parody of MTV music videos.

With her cool shades and fashionable backup dancers, Gaga now has what it takes to be a product of the music industry.

We are then treated to a video montage of Gaga living the highs and lows of stardom, complete with gigantic hats, bathroom stall door slamming action and emotionally instability. However, all of this crap pays off: Gaga gets signed to record label.

When you "Marry the Night" (or sell your soul), the doors of the music business magically open. Gaga gets an appointment with Interscope Records.

The video ends with an odd and ominous scene:

In this fiery scene Gaga is dressed in red - the color symbolic of sacrifice and initiation. She is wearing a Paco Rabane hat that is fashionable and symbolic: it completely hides her head. It is owned by the Night now.

Gaga's live performance on X Factor also exploited the theme of headless-ness in a rather graphic way.

The setting of Gaga's performance on X Factor emphasizes on the underlying occult meaning of the song. The full moon, the torches and the religious imagery play on the spiritual significance of "marrying the night". Gaga began the song with her head literally chopped off, a perfect way to describe what figuratively happens to industry pawns.

In Conclusion

Although many describe Marry the Night as a "new direction" for Lady Gaga, the video still exploits her favorite theme: The price of fame. The intro of the video is basically a introductory course in trauma-based mind control, where she describes how dissociating allows her to cope with reality. As the artistic brunette turns into a blonde diva, the Lady Gaga alter-ego is created, one that will do what is required to make it in the music business. The most important requirement is "marrying the night", which is a poetic way of saying "selling one's soul" and associating with the dark side. Gaga had to deny everything she previously was to become a brand new person. Therefore, beneath the fashion and the dancing, the video hides an underlying ritualistic theme, as the death of a ballet dancer gives birth to an MTV pop star. From the broken girl who had nothing to lose to international superstar, it took a marriage with the dark side to turn things around. But at what cost? The final scene of the video, complete with hellish fire and a sacrificial red dress tells volumes.

In the grand scheme of things, despite her apparent originality, Gaga brings to the youth a message that is very similar to other pop stars: "Mind control is cool, everyone is doing it" and "Submit to the dark side and you'll get what you want". But when things get scary and the night becomes an abusive husband, asking for divorce won't be an option. Ask Princess Diana.

Doda and Vintage: Bringing the Illuminati Agenda to Eastern Europe Pop

The Illuminati Agenda in popular culture has become a worldwide phenomenon and it hasn't spared Eastern Europe. Doda's "Bad Girls" and Vintage's "Trees" are two examples of very symbolic music videos that are extremely popular in Russia and Poland. We'll look at these two video and see how their symbolic content is completely on-par with the world elite's agenda.

What is called "the Illuminati" functions on a global scale, so it is only natural that its propaganda machine is also deployed on a global scale. While the American and British artists reach most of the world, "regional" stars are also used to propagate the elite's Agenda to specific ethnic groups. Previous articles on Vigilant Citizen have described the Illuminati symbolism found in music from Korea, Japan, Latin America and Russia. Despite the difference in culture and language between these countries, today's globalized mass media machine manages to expose the entire world to a specific Agenda and to a precise set of symbols.

Eastern Europe is obviously not exempt from the media machine. Not unlike the rest of the world, pop stars are often handpicked, signed to international record labels and put in the spotlight using videos that are in line with the Illuminati Agenda. In this article, we will look at Doda's "Bad Girls" and Vintage's "Trees", two videos that, despite their limited market, have managed to get a lot of airplay and millions of YouTube views. Although not in the same language, both videos are a direct reflection of the philosophy and the goals of the Illuminati and act as a kind of "local distributors" of the elite's Agenda. Let's look at the message of these videos.

Doda's "Bad Girls"

At first glance, one would be tempted to qualify Doda as a "bimbo". And her first album cover would probably agree with you.

However, Doda is an extremely popular and influential figure in Poland. In fact, CNN ranked her as as the tenth most famous Pole in history. Yes, in HISTORY. That list includes Pope Jean-Paul II, Copernicus and Marie Curie. Furthermore, the Polish magazine Viva! placed her among the ten most influential women in Poland. Not bad for a bimbo. She also has a knack for creating controversy. In 2010, she caused quite a stir when she stated that the Bible was written "by people who drank too much wine and smoked herbal cigarettes".

Doda's popularity and sex appeal made her a perfect choice for Illuminati propaganda. After a few albums with the rock band Virgin, Doda began a solo career as a pop singer and her album, the Seven Temptations, appear to have all of the hallmarks of a true Illuminati piece.

The video, "Bad Girls", reads like an Illuminati for Dummies: Polish Edition book, cramming into its few minutes of musical horror a complete array of messages. Some might say: "The Illuminati Agenda exists in the U.S., but not in Poland" and so forth. Well, Doda is signed with Universal Music, one of the five media conglomerates that distribute mass media across the world. It owns labels like Interscope, Geffen, A&M, Defjam, Island and Motown. She is therefore part of the elite's system and was apparently chosen to be the Illuminati's representative in Poland.

Bad Girls

The video takes place in a setting that the Illuminati loves: A futuristic dystopian police state. Cameras and "telescreens" everywhere, police in riot gear and a faceless ruler: This imagery is present in pop videos around the world.

The "hero" of the story is Doda, a half-human half-robot, who emerges from some kind of transhumanist scientific lab. The promotion of the merger of humans and robots is a staple of the agenda, as seen in the article "The Transhumanist and Police State Agenda in Pop Music".

The elite's preferred way of depicting their pop stars: Half-robots kept alive by a gigantic machine. The other "Bad Girls" are also attached to the machine.

There's an English version of the song but the lyrics are kind of ... nonsensical. However, they still manage to convey the fact that she's "down with the dark side".

"I know my way of my Babylon
All demons know, my booty show
Girl dress to kill I'm hell on heels
So come with me, we'll go oh"

After blasting their way out of the lab, Doda and her girls then meet up in a restaurant that apparently serves humans: Another example of making dehumanization "cool" in music videos.

This restaurant is decorated with humans the same way steakhouses are decorated with cows. How engrossing.

In this restaurant for cannibals, Doda and her "bad girls" plan their attack on the big boss of the city.

The girl on the left has one eye hidden. Yes, Polish people also need to be exposed to this Illuminati One-Eye crap.

However, the meeting is interrupted by police in riot gear – a common sight in elite-supported videos (see the article entitled The Transhumanist and Police State Agenda in Pop Music).

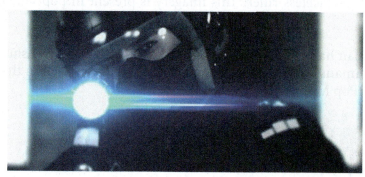

The girl on the left has one eye hidden. Yes, Polish people also need to be exposed to this Illuminati One-Eye crap.

When Doda sees the guards, she basically loses it and kills them with an animal-like scream (or something of the sors). Most people would be satisfied with such a result, but not Doda. She goes to the morgue where the dead guards are found and … gets sexy with one of them.

After she's done with the dead guy, a strange phrase appears on his chest, one that appears to sum up the culture of death mass media keeps pushing on the world: "No Death, No Fun".

"No Death, No Fun" … is this the slogan of the occult elite that has plans for massive depopulation and enjoys ritual sacrifices?

Doda's desecration of a dead body is not over. She accomplishes a symbolic gesture that confirms who is behind the message of the video.

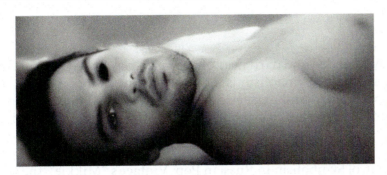

Doda takes out one of the guy's eyes. Again, we have a reference to the "one-eye" symbol.

Doda uses the guard's eye go past the security system that protects the access that leads to the King of the City. After a corny fight scene, Doda "overthrows" the King of the City and sits at his throne. A pill then emerges from her hand and, looking at the camera, Doda says "Try Me".

Doda shows the viewers the pill they must "swallow" - symbolizing the doctrine they must accept - while urging them to "try her".

The sign on the pill has a heavy meaning. It is the symbol of Mercury, who is also known as Hermes - the "chief god" of the occult elite. Usually, the bottom part of the symbol resembles a plus (+) sign however, in this case, one extremity has been elongated, making the sign look like an inverted cross - a symbol used in Satanism. We therefore have a devil head sitting atop an inverted cross. Can't get more blatantly symbolic than that.

Doda's overthrow of the King of the City can also be interpreted on a personal level. Since the video is very "anatomical", the action of the video could happen inside a person's body and mind. In this context, Doda and her girls, who were conceived in government labs, represent the Illuminati agenda that was conceived and calculated in elite think tanks. The message is inherently poisonous (hence "Bad Girls") but is disguised as something sexy and attractive.

Doda (representing the propaganda) goes through the viewer's eye (represented by the poking out of the guard's eye) in order to access the brain – represented by the King of the City. She overthrows him and sits at his place, which represents a successful fight against the mind. Doda then asks the viewers to try her "Bad Girls" pill.

Therefore, in short, the same way Doda emerges from a lab and takes over the city, Illuminati propaganda emerges from think tanks and seeks to take over the masses' brains through mass media. Popular culture promotes corrupt and debasing values, degrades human life and pushes transhumanism because this is where the elite want to take the world. Will you be swallowing the pill?

Vintage's "Trees"

If Doda's "Bad Girls" is a big, loud, heavy-handed and darn near offensive display of symbolism, Vintage's "Trees" is a much more soothing experience. The subtle symbolism is, however, all the more powerful. While the video appears to be just another other semi-spiritual, pseudo-esoteric and vaguely sensual music video (see Madonna's "Frozen"), this one, when carefully decoded, has a heavy symbolic meaning: It describes the coming of a "new era" … but not before heavy tribulations.

As seen in the article entitled Mind Control Symbolism in Russian Pop: Vintage's "Mikkie", the group has already produced Illuminati-heavy music videos. That being known, is it surprising that the group's latest video depicts the ultimate goal of the occult elite, namely the creation of a New World Order? Let's look at the video's most symbolic scenes.

Anna in a red dress - the ritualistic color of initiation and sacrifice.

The video begins in a dry and windy desert. Everything in the scene is in monochrome except for Anna's dress, which is bright red. As we've seen in several previous articles, red clothing represents initiation and sacrifice. Anna walks towards a pyramid made of half-naked people who appear to be mesmerized by a mysterious source of light.

The people that make up the pyramid seem to be revering a light at the apex of the pyramid. The source of that light is unknown … for now.

This pyramidal shape and its glowing capstone are very similar to a symbol many of you might be familiar with: The pyramid and All-Seeing Eye of the Great Seal of the United States – the main symbol associated with the occult elite, the Illuminati.

Does the pyramid and lighted capstone in Vintage's video refer to the Great Seal of the USA - which represents the unfinished "Great Work" of the occult elite?

While the pyramid in Vintage's video is very similar to the one on the Great Seal, there is a notable difference between the two: The one in the video is made of people. These people blending together to form the base of the pyramid represent the masses, which is the true source of power of the elite. Without the compliance (and ignorance) of the general population, the "Great Work" of the elite – a New World Order – would never happen. The people in the pyramid are very cattle-like, acting like lascivious zombies who are subject to their basest instincts.

Inside the pyramid is basically one big orgy - which goes in line with the elite's view of the masses: A big herd of animals that need to be kept distracted and under control.

A recurrent scene in the video appears to refer to the occult powers of sexuality, whether it be for illumination or manipulation.

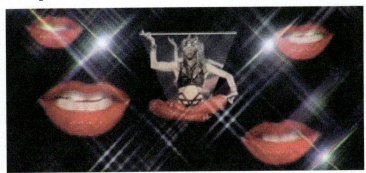

Anna is sitting in a "chakra activation" position and performing a gesture reminiscent to Baphomet's "As Above so Below" hand sign. Behind Anna is an inverted triangle, a symbol that occultly represents the feminine. The combination of all of these images, and, of course, the lips, point towards Sex Magick - a tool used by occultists for enlightenment, but that can also be used to control and manipulate.

Eliphas Levi's depiction of Baphomet in the same "chakra activation" position and performing a similar handsign.

The video then goes "underground", where an important process occurs: The impregnation of Anna.

Below the ground, Anna is dressed in black (color of death and rebirth) and is tied up. She is surrounded by a bunch of nasty looking guys who are about to do nasty things to her.

In the following scene, we see the result of this simulated gang bang: A pregnant Anna posing in a way similar to the classic painting "Birth of Venus". We then see a countdown from the year 2012 to the year zero, which is associated with the birth year of Jesus Christ.

Anna is shown pregnant and on top of the world while the years countdown to the year zero. Who will she give birth to?

When the countdown is over, a figure appears at the top of the illuminated pyramid:

Anna appears with a crown of thorns, dressed in white

Is this the second coming of Christ … or the coming of the anti-Christ? This new figure is definitely not the result of an "immaculate conception" as her conception happened while she was tied up and raped in a hellish, underground setting. The Christ figure is nevertheless revered by the masses. Anna-Christ then raises her hand and causes a great deal of death and destruction.

As the Christ figure raises her arm, civilization in its entirety appears to collapse.

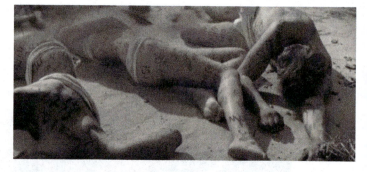

Many people from the masses die from the tribulations - a fact that Anna-Christ doesn't seem to care about and that Anna in red almost celebrates.

After the period of "tribulations" is, a New World (Order) can start to grow.

After the death and destruction caused by Anna-Christ, the video ends with new life emerging from the ground.

This video is symbolic on several levels. It combines history, civilization and spirituality in a tale of initiation, death and rebirth. Atop an illuminated pyramid, a spiritual leader appears at the year zero – which denotes the beginning of a new Age, a new era or a new aeon – shakes up the entire world. While this figure appears to be the second coming of Christ, those who are acquainted with the Book of Revelation might notice that this new leader, which was conceived in an underground pit, bears many similarities to the Bible's description of the Antichrist (also referred to as "the Beast").

> "The beast, which you saw, once was, now is not, and will come up out of the Abyss and go to his destruction. The inhabitants of the earth whose names have not been written in the book of life from the creation of the world will be astonished when they see the beast, because he once was, now is not, and yet will come."
> - Revelation 17:8 (NIV)

As we have seen in previous articles (i.e. the article on the movie Metropolis), the Illuminati places a great importance on the Book of Revelation and its telling of the Apocalypse. The esoteric interpretation of this Biblical enigma associates it with the end of the Age of Pisces and the beginning of the Age of Aquarius.

On an occult level, the process shown in the video can be compared to the steps of the Great Work of Alchemy: Nigredo, Albedo and Rubedo (translated to Blackening, Whitening and Reddening). These are the three alchemical steps to turn a crude metal into gold and, on a spiritual level, to turn a profane person to an illuminated person. These steps are represented by Anna's clothing. In alchemy, the step of Blackening involves the putrefaction and decomposition of a body into its primal matter in order to create new life and is associated with "the difficulties man has to overcome on his journey through the underworld". Anna was dressed in black in the scene where she was in an underground pit and "being consumed" by men. The process of Blackening leads to the birth of a new life, which is the step of Whitening – represented by Anna-Christ dressed in white. The final step, the Reddening, is manifested when man is master over both the physical as the spiritual world and is represented by Anna in red, the initiate who is the center focus of the video.

The world elite often represents its plans towards a New World Order as an alchemical "Great Work". An example of this can be found on the Murals in headquarters of Bank of America (see the article Analysis of the Occult Symbols Found on the Bank of America Murals). According to their philosophy, the entire world can be subject to the same alchemical transformation that is applied to a single individual. The process would undoubtedly involve a lot of death and destruction but that appears to be "part of the plan" (as portrayed by the dead bodies found in the video). Is this why the coming of an Antichrist is portrayed in a positive way in the video?
In Conclusion

Doda's "Bad Girls" and Vintage's "Trees" are two very different videos, yet they have an important thing in common: they both portray critical parts of the Illuminati Agenda in mass media. While the first video is a perfect example of how popular culture aims to debase the masses with self-destructive values, the second describes the "grand scheme of things", according to the elite's philosophy.

These two videos are just two examples of the Illuminati's efforts to expose the entire world to its Agenda and symbolism. Through veiled tales of initiation and transformation, the masses unconsciously witness, via "entertainment", celebrations of their own demise. In the same way that the people in Vintage's pyramid revere an unknown source of light, the masses idolize stars that work for an unseen elite. Will the masses be one day indoctrinated enough to welcome a "saviour" that will appear at the top of the Illuminati's pyramid? Only time will tell.

Madonna's Superbowl Halftime Show: A Celebration of the Grand Priestess of the Music Industry

When I learned that Madonna – aka the Grand Priestess of the music industry – would be performing at the Superbowl halftime show, I thought: "This should be interesting". And it was. While most were amazed by a woman in her fifties dancing around with LMFAO and others were annoyed at her lip-syncing, I was interested with something else: the flurry of symbolism flashed to billions of viewers worldwide. While most considered Madonna's performance as an entertaining interlude to the most important football game of the year, those blessed with symbol-literacy will probably agree with the following statement: Madonna's halftime show was a big celebration of the Illuminati industry and of its Grand Priestess, Madonna.

A week before the Superbowl, Madonna described on Anderson Cooper the spiritual importance she attributed to her halftime show:

> "The Superbowl is kind of like the Holy of Holies in America. I'll come at halfway of the "church experience" and I'm gonna have to deliver a sermon. It'll have to be very impactful."

It is rather appropriate that this Kaballah-intiate referred to the Superbowl as the "Holy of Holies" as it was the name of the most sacred place in Solomon's Temple. No one was ever permitted to enter the Holy of Holies but the High Priest. This privilege was only granted on the Day of Atonement, to offer the blood of sacrifice and incense before the mercy seat. Madonna's analogy was therefore telling of the mindset behind her performance. Let's look at the main parts of her show.

Vogue or Entrance of the Priestess

Madonna entrance is an elaborate procession fit for a High Priestess or even a goddess.

Pushed by hundreds of Roman soldiers and welcomed by hundreds of women, Madonna's glorious entrance is a reflection of her status in the entertainment world.

Her first performance was highly influenced by ancient Egypt-Sumeria-Babylon and Madonna's costume recalls an ancient Babylonian goddess.

The decor of Madonna's first performance combines elements from ancient Egypt, Sumeria and Babylon. Madonna herself is dressed in a way that highly resembles an Ancient Sumerian/Babylonian goddess, Inanna-Ishtar.

Ishtar with her foot on a roaring lion and wearing a distinctive headdress resembling Madonna's horned crown. Ishtar is often depicted with wings, a feature that is recalled on Madonna's "carriage".

Ishtar was a powerful and assertive goddess whose areas of control and influence included warfare, love, sexuality, prosperity, fertility and prostitution. She sought the same existence as men, enjoying the glory of battle and seeking sexual experiences. Madonna's portrayal as Ishtar is therefore quite interesting as one can argue that the pop singer has embodied, throughout her career, the same assertive yet highly sexual qualities of Ishtar, even achieving a state of power in the music industry that is usually reserved to men. On an esoteric level, Ishtar is associated with the planet Venus, known as the Morning Star or the Evening Star.

The presence of two Sphinxes in front of Madonna greatly resembles the tarot card The Chariot. According to Manly P. Hall: "This card signifies the Exalted One who rides in the chariot of creation. The sphinxes drawing the chariot resent the secret and unknown power by which the victorious ruler is moved continuously through the various parts of his universe."

So, in this mythologically-charged setting, Madonna performed Vogue. During the performance, covers of Vogue Magazine were displayed, a publication that is at the forefront of Illuminati symbolism in fashion (as seen in the series of articles Symbolic Pics of the Month).

Vogue ends with a symbol that is consistent with the Egyptian-Babylonian theme of the performance, one that is also of highest importance in occult Secret Societies such as Freemasons, the Rosicrucians and the Illuminati: the

Winged Sun-Disk.

The song ends with the displaying of a Winged Sun-Disk.

The symbol of the winged-sun inside a Masonic lodge.

Egyptian mystics used the winged sun for ritualistic magic and invocations:

> "Emblematic of the element of air, this consists of a circle or solar-type disk enclosed by a pair of wings. In ritual magic it is suspended over the alter in an easterly direction and used when invoking the protection and co-operation of the sylphs."
> -Hope, Murry, "Practical Egyptian Magic"

The winged sun is still being used today by groups like the Freemasons, the Theosophists and the Rosicrucians.

> "The Winged Globe is pre-eminently a Rosicrucian symbol, although the Illuminati may lay claim to it, and it may be admitted that it is of Egyptian origin. The Winged Globe is the symbol of the perfected soul making its flight back to the source of its creation in the Elysian fields beyond."
> -Swinburne, Clymer, "The Rosicrucians, Their Teachings"

The display of this symbol, although apparently trivial and aesthetic, emphasizes on the occult spiritual dimension underlying Madonna's entire performance.

Give Me All Your Luvin' or Madonna's Sex Kittens

Later in the show, Madonna performed her new single Give Me All Your Luvin'. The song features two new industry favorites: Nikki Minaj and M.I.A. In the song's music video and during the Superbowl performance, these two female rappers are portrayed in a specific way: Instead of being presented as full-fledged artists contributing to Madonna's song, they are portrayed as her "minions" who are cheering for the industry's High Priestess. This "relationship" where Madonna is in power – and therefore the handler – is drenched in Mind Control symbolism, specifically Beta Programming, also know Sex Kitten Programming.

In the video for Give me Your Luvin', Madonna, Nikki Minaj and M.I.A. are dressed as Marilyn Monroe, the ultimate prototype of Sex Kitten Programming.

Another symbol associated with Sex Kitten programming is feline prints clothing and textiles. The entire halftime show was an animal-print extravaganza.

Like a Prayer or the Final Sermon

Madonna closed the halftime show with one of her biggest hits: Like a Prayer. The video of this song was always controversial due to its mixing of religious themes with sexuality. As the song starts, the show takes on a very solemn and spiritual vibe as Madonna and Cee-Lo Green enter the stage to give the final sermon. Religious figures are usually dressed in white to represent purity and godliness. The two singers where dressed in black robes and black robes are usually used in…black masses.

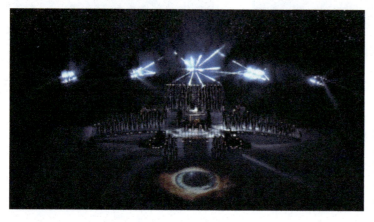

As the song begins, a huge eye pupil is displayed before the stage, hinting to the Illuminati-influence of this spiritual performance.

Madonna's halftime show ends in a dramatic yet very significant matter:

At the end of her performance, the floor opens underneath Madonna's feet and she falls into oblivion.

As Madonna is swept in what appears to be the "Underworld", Madonna sings "I hear you call my name, And it feels like home". This is another inversion of conventional religious symbolism as "home" should be in the heavens. In Madonna's case, she obviously didn't go in that direction. The show ends with a message no one can disagree with.

The words "World Peace" appear on the stage, a PR-friendly slogan used by those pushing for a New World Order lead by a one world government.

In Conclusion

When taken individually, the symbols described above can be simply considered as "cool-looking" and most Superbowl viewers did not give them much attention. The packing all of these signs and symbols in one comprehensive 13 minute performance cannot however be dismissed as "random images". Quite to the contrary, the combination of all of these symbols form a whole and define with great depth the underlying philosophy and Agenda of those in power – the Illuminati. Madonna's embrace of the Illuminati symbolism discussed on this site coincides with her signing with Interscope Records, one of the main purveyors of Illuminati symbolism in the music industry. Her halftime show performance can therefore be considered as the "launching" of her three-album (and 40 million dollars) relationship with the prominent label. Madonna's Superbowl performance has shown that, despite the fact that she is an industry icon and that she pioneered most of the themes modern pop stars still exploit, she still needs to fit the mold and to embrace the same symbolism rookie pop stars.

Laced with profound imagery, Madonna's halftime performance was a massive Illuminati ritual, one that was witnessed by billions of viewers. On this Superbowl "Day of Atonement", Madonna, the High Priestess of the Illuminati industry, entered the Holy of Holies of America and delivered a 13 minutes sermon that was heard by all…but understood by few.

Whitney Houston and the 2012 Grammy Awards Mega-Ritual

The 2012 Grammy Awards took place in a horrible context: the wake of the sudden, mysterious death of Whitney Houston. The show went on nevertheless ... but not without a great deal of strange symbols and events that made one thing very clear: There is a definite dark side to the entertainment business. We will look at the facts surrounding Whitney Houston's death, the symbolic elements of the 2012 Grammy Awards (including Nikki Minaj's ritualistic performance) and see how the ceremony turned into another mega-ritual.

I had a feeling that in 2012 the occult agenda of the entertainment industry would be kicked in high gear. I was right: In the span of a week, the most important night in sports (the Superbowl – see the article about it here) and music (the Grammys) were infused with ritualistic elements witnessed by millions of viewers. While the Superbowl half-time show lasted only 13 minutes, the ritual surrounding the Grammys lasted for days and its aftermath is still going on as odd facts and accounts regarding Whitney Houston continue to surface in the media.

This article will list several facts and events that took place before, during and after the Grammy Awards that have a symbolic significance in the grand scheme of things. While some of the facts mentioned here might have been the result of coincidence or poor timing, they still came together in one big, classic case of synchronicity. In other words, apparent coincidences sometimes reveal an underlying pattern behind events.

> "Carl Jung described synchronicity as " the experience of two or more events that are apparently causally unrelated or unlikely to occur together by chance and that are observed to occur together in a meaningful manner. Synchronistic events reveal an underlying pattern, a conceptual framework that encompasses, but is larger than, any of the systems that display the synchronicity. Concurrent events that first appear to be coincidental but later turn out to be causally related are termed inco-incident."

When we look at the facts and the occurrences surrounding Whitney Houston's death coupled with the symbolic elements of the 2012 Grammy awards, the entire "event" has the looks of an occult ritual, complete with a blood sacrifice, a celebration and even a "re-birth". Some of the things described below were pre-planned, while others were possibly just odd coincidences. However, the overwhelming and almost palpable energy emanating from the 2012 Grammys definitely made some things align in a synchronistic fashion. Let's look at the most significant events that happened during that fateful weekend.

Strange Facts Surrounding Whitney Houston's Death

If you read other articles on this site, you probably noticed that everything surrounding Whitney Houston's is astonishingly on-par with other celebrity "sacrifices". Accounts of strange events before the death, bizarre behavior of the authorities when the death was discovered, conflicting reports, vagueness surrounding the cause of the death and, to top it off, a worrying "response" from the music industry through the Grammys. Her case followed the same pattern as several other celebrity deaths that were blamed on drugs despite many conflicting reports. As it was the case for these other celebrities, the media almost automatically launched a campaign depicting Whitney as a hopeless drug addict. Maybe she was a drug addict, but that might only be the tip of the iceberg … a symptom of the true illness that killed Whitney: the music business.
Strange Events

As in the cases of Michael Jackson, Amy Winehouse, Heath Ledger, Brittany Murphy and many others, bizarre events preceded and followed the death of Whitney Houston. After reviewing all of those accounts, one cannot help but wonder: Was Whitney's death truly an accident or was it a deliberate sacrifice planned by "unseen forces"? While most media reports drum into people's heads that "Whitney Houston = Drugs", some sources reveal other details that might lead to other paths of thinking. Here's Roger Friedman's account of things that happened at the Beverly Hilton on February 11th:

> **Whitney's Death: An Earlier Incident?**
>
> *Whitney Houston's death made for a long day's journey into night at the Beverly Hilton. While the Clive Davis Grammy dinner had to proceed downstairs in the ballroom–with 800 guests already filing in as the news was breaking–Whitney remained in state, so to speak, in her fourth floor suite. She was not removed until just moments before the party ended–a little after midnight. She'd been in the suite, discovered in her bathtub. But there were many people in the suite when this happened at 3:50pm including her daughter Bobbi Kristina, her brother Gary, sister in law Pat Houston, and another player in this story — a nightlife friend who'd been guiding her around town the last few days as she was photographed in states of duress.*
>
> *What you don't know is that around 11pm, paramedics were called back to the fourth floor. Security and police raced back to the 4th floor. A medical wheelchair with restraints was brought in through the back entrance to the hotel. Bobbi Kristina "freaked out"–well, she'd been upstairs for hours with her mother's dead body in the next room. It was understandable. The paramedics thought they were going to to have to take her to the hospital. But calm was restored. For ten minutes, though, security cleared the entire lobby of the hotel while the concert was going on inside the ballroom. I was out there at that moment, and it was one of the strangest scenes ever.*
>
> *Then there's the mysterious story of a leak that occurred the night before from Whitney's group of suites. A man on the third floor right underneath Houston's suite suddenly experienced water cascading into his bathroom from above at 2:30am. It wasn't just a trickle. The man called security, then went upstairs to the fourth floor to see what was going on. He swears to me that it was Whitney's bathtub that was overflowing. He also says that a flat screen television had been been broken–the screen was smashed. My sources at the hotel say there was a "leak" but that it wasn't from Whitney's room. "They [her group] have a lot of rooms up there," says the hotel source. My source, this man, insists that he was told it was Whitney Houston's room. It does seem to have been part of her group of rooms.*
>
> *There are many mysteries here. None of them have been reported or solved by TMZ or one of the other muckraking tabloids. I know the man who had to pull Whitney out of the bathtub yesterday and*

attempt to give her CPR. He told me, "She was already dead. There was nothing I could do."

More on Whitney's death and the Grammy party follows in the next post. And believe me, dear readers, this isn't easy. I've known Whitney Houston and her family for over 25 years. She was a beautiful girl with a big heart. She was full of optimism. Her mother is one of the finest people. The people who worked for and with her were devoted to her. When the shock turns to anger there will be a lot of finger pointing. But in the end, Whitney ruled her own world.
- Source: Forbes

I am not a criminal investigator and I cannot solve all of the mysteries surrounding Whitney's death but the fact that her body was there for hours, while a pre-Grammy party was happening just below is a little off-putting. Why wasn't it simply cancelled? Isn't the presence of the dead body of a legendary singer in the same exact location as the party reason enough to cancel it? Was there some type of twisted thrill of partying right below Houston's body?

In another article, Roger Friedman noted the presence of a strange "Hollywood insider" lurking around Whitney Houston that was also around Michael Jackson during his "difficult periods". Who is that guy?

Whitney Houston's Mystery Friend Was Also Michael Jackson's Pal

Here's the one person in the Whitney Houston story whose name you have not heard, and who has remained a mystery: a Dutch man from Amsterdam who goes by the name of Raffles van Exel. He is also known – in court records—as Raffles Dawson and Raffles Benson. He was on the fourth floor of the Beverly Hilton Hotel in one of Houston's suites when she died. He appeared downstairs in the lobby shortly thereafter, wearing aviator sunglasses, sobbing.

As usual, he had an entourage in tow, including Quinton Aaron, the actor who played the football player in "The Blind Side." Raffles, in one of his many PR Newswire releases, recently announced that he's producing movies with Aaron. It's just one of many ventures he announces regularly. For someone who has no obvious means of support, he is a regular on PR Newswire and You Tube. On the latter, you can find him interviewing friends of Michael Jackson. It is assumed that he sells stories to tabloids. He regularly includes names of tabloid reporters like Kevin Frazier of "The Insider" on his Tweets.

Despite the shock of Whitney's death, Raffles still made it downstairs to Clive Davis's party. He was dressed in formal wear, had Whitney's tickets in his hand, and intended to sit at her table. Just inside the ballroom he was comforted by celebrities to whom he related his story—"I found Whitney." Gayle King hugged him. Quincy Jones listened patiently to his story. A security guard told me later, "Well, he was up there." He was also hanging around with Houston all week prior to her death. On Tuesday when she emerged from a nightclub, looking disheveled, Raffles appears in a photograph on TMZ like a deer in headlights. He is standing right behind her in a powder blue suit. On Twitter, he wrote: "STOP reading the stupid blogs.. Whitney had a great time, she looked amazing. Nothing was wrong, it was just DAMN hot in that club."

But who is Raffles van Exel? He's one of Hollywood's mysteries. I first met him in 2005 hanging around the Jackson family during Michael Jackson's child molestation trial. After Michael went abroad, Raffles was often seen with Michael's father, Joseph Jackson. He trades on being an "insider" when there's a scandal. No one really knows him, but he's always where there's action and celebrities. On the internet he claims to own a number of companies including Raffles Entertainment. He's also been sued a couple of times, once by a partner in something called Max Records, Inc., and once by a private aviation company in Los Angeles. I spoke to the plane company and they said they can't com-

ment because the situation is ongoing. On Twitter he claims to be managing "my girl," Chaka Khan. There are plenty of pictures of Raffles on the internet with celebrities. You can see him with everyone from Magic Johnson to Sandra Bullock. If ever there was a real life Zelig, he is it.

It's not a surprise that Raffles has turned up in Whitney Houston's story. Last October, he and Whitney and others traveled to North Carolina with Whitney's sister in law Patricia Houston for something called a Teen Summit. It was billed as part of The Patricia Houston Foundation, an organization for which there is no official 501 c3 registration. Pat Houston, married to Whitney's brother Gary, has been Whitney's manager for years. (Whitney's own foundation for children ceased functioning years ago.) She also owns a consignment shop in North Carolina, and a candle company called Marion P. Candles, with Whitney.

Look for Raffles at Whitney's funeral tomorrow. In the old days he used to wear a yellow jacket full of black question marks—like The Riddler. On Saturday night, as he pulled in various guests to Clive Davis's party past the velvet ropes, he was wearing a Michael Jackson-like tuxedo. He lives in West Hollywood now, but his official domicile—and where he's been sued—is Chicago. He has not responded to countless emails and phone messages.
- Source: Forbes

Was this man instrumental in Whitney's sacrifice? Did Whitney fall out of the good graces of the music industry elite? Was she becoming difficult to manipulate? Was she sacrificed to introduce her successor? Difficult to say, but Whitney appeared to have premonitions about her death. Some reports described her as "manic" and agitated while others state that Whitney felt that "her days were numbered". Shortly before her death, Whitney was spotted handing singer Brandy a message whose contents remained a mystery.

What was in Whitney's secret note to Brandy?

Singer Brandy has one of the last messages ever delivered by Whitney Houston — but she's not telling anyone what it says.

On Feb. 9 in Los Angeles, Houston approached the younger singer as she and fellow singer Monica and mentor Clive Davis were conducting an interview with E!

A post on RyanSeacrest.com says Houston "crashed" the interview, then goes on to say "Whitney seemed a bit manic as she told Monica about swimming 'two hours a day,' and conspicuously handed a note to Brandy before hugging Davis."

When E! later asked Brandy directly what the note said, she replied "I'm going to just not say what it was and just keep it to myself for my own personal reasons." She also told the network "Whitney meant everything to me … She's the reason that I sing."

Brandy and Houston starred in the 1997 remake of Rodgers and Hammerstein's "Cinderella." Brandy also is the elder sister of singer Ray J, who had reportedly dated Houston on and off over the last two years of her life. Ray J gained notoriety in 2003 when a sex tape of him with Kim Kardashian was leaked to the public.

E! has video of Houston handing the note to Brandy, and Brandy's comments about not revealing its contents.
- Source: MSNBC

The Number 11

When dealing with occult rituals, numerology takes on a primordial importance. In the case of Whitney Houston, the number 11 is definitely a factor. In elite occult circles, the number 11 is a "master number" (it cannot be reduced) and, because it exceeds the number 10 (the number of perfection) by 1, it is usually associated with bad foreboding and black magic. Qabbalists associate the number 11 with transgression of the law, rebellion, war, sin, sorcery and martyrdom.

For this reason, the occult elite often associates mega-rituals involving sacrifice with the number 11. What was the massive mega-ritual of the modern times? September 11th – involving the Twin Towers. At what exact time do we "remember" WWI soldiers who sacrificed their lives for their rulers? At the eleventh hour of the eleventh day of the eleventh month – Veterans Day, aka Remembrance Day.

Going further than the date of her death, another link associates Whitney and her death with Lady Gaga and previous Grammy awards. As some know, Lady Gaga had close ties with fashion designer Alexander McQueen, who was no stranger to occult and mind control symbolism in his work. McQueen died on February 11th, 2010.

During the 2011 Grammy Awards, Gaga stated about her song "Born This Way":

> "I need to thank Whitney Houston. I wanted to thank Whitney, because when I wrote 'Born this Way,' I imagined she was singing it – because I wasn't secure enough in myself to imagine I was a superstar. So, Whitney, I imagined you were singing 'Born This Way' when I wrote it."

"Born This Way" was released on February 11th, 2011. Exactly one year later, Whitney Houston dies on February 11th, 2012. Did Gaga (or her handlers) know something that the rest of us didn't? Her outfit evidently shows that death was on her mind.

Artists usually have their award ceremony wardrobes selected well in advance. Apparently, death was on Gaga's (or her handler's) mind.

Another little fact: Whitney's room number was 434 – which in Qabbalistic numerology equals 11 (4+3+4).

Statements from Industry Veterans

Who is better placed than artists who have worked in the music industry for years to provide insightful takes on the death of Whitney Houston? They obviously do not hold the ultimate truth and they might just be trying to make sense of things like the rest of us, but they have first -and experience when it comes to the workings of the music industry.

During an interview on Good Morning America, industry giant Celine Dion bluntly blamed the "bad influence" of show business for Whitney's death. She even stated that you "have to be afraid" of show business.

> "It's just really unfortunate that drugs, bad people or bad influence took over. It took over her dreams. It took over her love and motherhood. When you think about Elvis Presley and Marilyn Monroe and Michael Jackson and Amy Winehouse, to get into drugs like that, for whatever reason. Is it because of the stress and bad influence? What happens when you have everything? What happens when you have love, support, the family, motherhood? You have responsibilities of a mother and then something happens and it destroys everything. That's why I don't do parties and I don't hang out. That's why I'm not part of show business. We have to be afraid. I've always said you have to have fun and do music and you can never be part of show business because you don't what it's going to get yourself into. You have to do your work and get out of there."
> - Source: Vancouver Sun

Is Celine Dion's avoidance of show business the reason she manages to be relatively scandal-free?

Another legendary diva, Chaka Khan, was even more direct when explaining the true cause of Whitney's death. During an interview with Piers Morgan, she stated:

> "I think we all, as artists, because we're highly sensitive people, and this machine around us, this so-called 'music industry,' is such a demonic thing. It's sacrifices people's lives and their essences at the drop of a dime … I had a manager once say to me, ' You know you're worth more money dead than alive.'
>
> I mean, I've cried for her, a lot over the years, so many times. In a way I've mourned her, because I felt something was gonna happen because she was so close to the wire."
> - Source: Eonline

Was Chaka Khan exaggerating when using the terms "demonic" and "sacrifice" when describing the music industry? Judging by the symbolism found at the Grammy awards, she was probably right on the dot.

The Mega-Ritual that Was the 2012 Grammy Awards

The Grammy Awards has been dubbed "music's biggest night" and, since the music industry is ruled by an occult elite, "music's biggest night" reflects this elite's code. Because of Whitney Houston's death, the 2012 edition of the Grammy Awards had a peculiar feel that was almost palpable through the television screen. Intentionally or not, Whitney's death was tied-in with the awards ceremony and the symbolism that transpired from it.

The ceremony began in a very peculiar fashion, especially given the context of the Whitney's death. Bruce Springsteen yelled to the crowd "Are you alive out there?", then sang the song We Take Care of Our Own, a mantra that was repeated throughout the evening. Well, I know someone who was definitely not alive out there – the very person that was on everyone's mind when the show began. And, in the last years of her life, she wasn't particularly well taken care of, either. In fact, as I stated in the article, What Happened to Whitney Houston, I believe that something terrible happened to Whitney Houston that went way beyond using drugs. She was mentally, psychologically and even spiritually disturbed. Was she under mind control or the subject of some kind of dark rituals? Difficult to say. But, as Springsteen chanted We Take Care of Our Own as if it was the anthem of the industry, I couldn't help but think that Whitney was probably not "one of them". Her "industry-approved" replacement, however, is "one of them".

Out With the Old, In With the New?

Industry mogul Clive Davis with Whitney Houston and Jennifer Hudson.

A day before Whitney's death, Clive Davis told Piers Morgan that Jennifer Hudson was "the next Whitney". While Whitney was being reduced to the state of has-been, constantly humiliated by tabloid stories, Hudson was being groomed to become the next industry diva. After being discovered on American Idol, Hudson's career took off … right after the violent murders of her mother and brother in 2008. Her first public appearance after the traumatic event was singing the Star-Spangled Banner during Superbowl XLIII.

At the 2012 Grammy Awards, who do you think was chosen to pay tribute to the fallen artist by singing her greatest hit I Will Always Love You?

In her tribute to Houston, Hudson was literally placed "in the spotlight" while a picture of Houston floated above her.

Another artist of Whitney's calibre re-emerged triumphant, almost like a re-birth after a period of silence: Adele. However, the symbolic ceremony of the 2012 Grammy Awards could not be completed without a true ritual dealing with the spiritual realm. Nikki Minaj took care of that.

The Black Mass

The Grammy Awards ceremony may have begun with a heart-felt prayer for Whitney Houston, but it ended with an all-out Satanic Black Mass. From her "red carpet" entrance to her musical performance, Nikki Minaj played the role of a woman possessed by a demon named "Roman Zolanski". The 2012 Grammy Awards were apparently chosen to "exorcise" this demon from Nikki and to present it to the world as her new alter-ego. In last year's Grammy Awards, Lady Gaga also presented a new persona for Born This Way: a Gaga with horns on her forehead.

Nicki Minaj enters the Grammys in a ritualistic red robe, color of sacrifice and initiation. Was it a reference to Whitney's blood sacrifice?

In a music industry permeated with the concept of mind control, alter-personas that are completely separate from the artists are now the norm. As discussed in the article Origins and Techniques of Monarch Mind Control, the goal of Monarch programming is to create new personalities within a mind-control victim using violent trauma and frightening rituals. The personas that are created are fully programmable by their handlers and can even speak with a different accent, as is the case with Minaj's alter persona. The chorus of Minaj's song Roman Holiday appears to refer to the process of mind control:

> *Take your medication, Roman*
> *Take a short vacation, Roman*
> *You'll be okay*
> *You need to know your station, Roman*
> *Some alterations on your clothes and your brain*
> *Take a little break, little break*
> *From your silencing*
> *There is so much you can take, you can take*
> *I know how bad you need a Roman holiday*

Mind-control slaves are highly medicated and have their clothes (outward style) and brain "altered" by their handlers. This is accomplished by forcing the victim to dissociate from reality through intense trauma and pain: "There is so much you can take" before the mind dissociates from reality or goes on a "Roman Holiday".

Minaj's alter-persona is named Roman Zolanski. He has his own strange accent and is evidently the product of evil rituals. The name of this alter is inspired by movie director Roman Polanski, who produced Rosemary's Baby, a movie about the birth of the Anti-Christ (see the article about it here). Polanski is even more famous for being charged with rape by use of drugs, perversion, sodomy, lewd and lascivious act upon a child under 14, and furnishing a controlled substance to a minor in 1977. Strange fellow to be inspired by. He is however an intricate piece in the history of the occult entertainment industry so this "tribute" to him by an industry pawn such as Minaj is not surprising.

Actual Monarch programming is accomplished using a strong undercurrent of Satanic imagery to disturb and traumatize the victim. In the case of Minaj's performance, her alter ego was exorcised in a Satanic Black Mass – which is, in essence, a mockery and a desecration of a conventional Christian mass.

Minaj begins her performance tied up in what appears to be Catholic church. The force that possesses her is apparently too strong to hold her down though, and as the church windows explode, she is unbound. Minaj then descends into a church gone wild, complete with strippers rubbing on young priests who are attempting to pray to God (was that really necessary?).

Then, as the choir make a mockery of the classic Christian hymn O Come All Ye Faithful, a pope figure enters and makes Minaj levitate.

In short, Minaj's performance presented the world her new alter-ego who will be rapping on her next album. Her performance made it clear that Roman Zolanski is nothing less than a demon that was created with Minaj and exorcised from her through a Black Mass ritual. If the performance alone was enough to trouble some viewers, when it is put in the context of Whitney Houston's death that happened about 24 hours beforehand (a singer that was never shy about her Christian faith), the whole thing takes on an even more troubling dimension. Ancient magicians drew on the power of blood sacrifices to carry on Black Magic rituals. With Whitney's death still fresh in everyone's mind, the Black Mass that was proudly presented by the 2012 Grammy Awards had all the more potency on its worldwide viewers.

In Conclusion

This article presented a great number of facts and symbols that point towards the conclusion that Whitney Houston's death may have been a blood sacrifice and that the 2012 Grammy Awards had occult ritualistic elements within it. Even if all of these events were not deliberately planned by industry handlers, they all contribute to a clear and disturbing picture of the music industry.

While Whitney Houston's life was ending under bizarre circumstances and she was portrayed in the media as a hopeless drug addict, a new generation of Illuminati-approved artists were being placed in the spotlight. They willingly participated in the occult ritual that was the Grammy Awards and played their role in the tragic-comedy of the music industry, even if it meant losing their essence and their soul. What happens to those who don't play along with the system or rebel against it? They disappear from the spotlight, and sometimes they disappear from this earth in less than dignified circumstances. Because, as the mantra of the 2012 Grammy Awards indicates: The elite take care of their own. And no one else.

Katy Perry's 'Part of Me': Using Music Videos to Recruit New Soldiers

In her music video 'Part of Me', Katy Perry ditches her wigs and latex dresses to put on a Marines uniform. While some might find this style change "refreshing", the video for 'Part of Me' has a very specific agenda: To entice young people to enlist in the military. We'll look at how 'Part of Me' is a three-minute long advertisement to recruit new soldiers for the U.S. military.

Katy Perry is usually known for wearing blue wigs and sexy dresses, but she gives it all up in Part of Me. Yup, watch out terrorists, Katy Perry is an army girl now. While "pop culture observers" welcomed Katy Perry's image change, qualifying it as "refreshing", most missed an important fact: In Part of Me, Katy Perry is used to push yet another agenda of the elite – the recruitment of young people into the military. If we look at it objectively, Part of Me is, in fact, a three-and-half-minute long "Join the Military" advertisement disguised as a music video. It contains all of the components found in regular TV ads for the Marines and any other army-related ads: cool high-tech war machines, excitement and action, being "All You Can Be" and so forth. But most importantly, it presents the military and, by extension, war, as the perfect escape from the bummers of regular life.

The video was shot at an actual U.S. Marine base, using actual Marines, which means that the video is truly a "sponsored message" from the Marines. By appealing to young people using singers they look up to and themes they can relate to, the U.S. military is looking to address an important issue: Getting more young people to enlist. There is indeed a growing need for fresh blood in the military as the U.S. government and other Western countries are putting intense pressure on so-called "Axis of Evil" regional powers such as Iran and Syria. The numerous military expeditions of the past few years (Iraq, Afghanistan, Libya), and increasing calls to bring home enlisted soldiers who have done multiple tours of duty means that as the U.S. prepares for upcoming conflicts, new soldiers are needed to enlist and be shipped abroad. Instead of paying for a 30-second TV commercial, military marketing specialists probably realized that they could get better results by investing in the music video of a star that is popular with teenagers. While regular "Be All You can Be" TV commercials were effective in the past, today's young generation watches less TV and more YouTube. So why not use pop stars who getting hundreds of millions of YouTube views and who are already used to push other aspects of the elite's agenda?

Not a New Concept

Governments have always used the most advanced forms of mass media advertising to entice citizens to enlist in the armed forces. During World War I, the face of Uncle Sam was plastered all over the United States in order to recruit new soldiers. However, as the years went by, and television made its appearance, posters of the bearded fellow pointing at you with a stern look somewhat lost its effectiveness.

During the 1950s, although mandatory drafts were in full force, the military still looked for opportunities for good PR. When Elvis Presley, the hottest and most controversial artist of the time, joined the army as a regular soldier, the press was given "full access", and were even allowed take pictures of him in his drawers while getting weighed in.

Elvis' career as a soldier was highly publicized, as countless pictures of him flooded mass media.

Elvis' immense charm, charisma and popularity gave the army great visibility, successfully enticing young people of the rebellious "Rock'n'Roll" generation to be interested in the military.

Since the 1950s, marketing techniques have improved in both efficiency and sophistication. In fact, today, the best advertisement often parades itself as no advertisement – in the advertising industry, messages are known to be received more effectively when indirectly reaching an audience that believes it is being entertained. To achieve this, celebrities and pop stars are often used as vehicles to reach the minds of young people with specific messages without them even realizing it. Katy Perry's Part of Me is an example of this technique, as nowhere in the video does it state that it is an advertisement for the U.S. military. Perry's video was simply used by the military to reach its target audience–teenagers approaching the age of enlistmen–but the whole thing appears as if it was a "creative" decision of Katy Perry the Artist.

Watching Part of Me immediately reminded me of the Simpsons episode were Bart and his friends were chosen by a producer to form a boy band. The group's hit single was Yvan Eht Nioj, which was "Join the Navy" in reverse. It was later discovered that Bart Simpson's group was used by the Navy to push subliminal messages to young people

Party Posse's music video featured the group doing cool army things in Iraq such as driving dunebuggeys and flying jet fighters.

in order to get them to become soldiers.
While Perry's video relies on overt imagery rather than subliminal messages (as far as I know), Part of Me is based on the same agenda as portrayed in the Simpsons: To reach teenagers using the great appeal of pop stars. Let's look

at the most important scenes of the video.

Part of Me

Katy walks away from her douchebag boyfriend. Although the video is basically a commercial for the United States military, it begins with a relationship-related scene in order to make the video relatable and to give it an emotional element.

The video begins with a concept most teenagers can relate to: Heartbreak. Katy catches her boyfriend kissing another woman. so she barges in and breaks up with him.

When Katy reads this actual US Marines sticker, she is immediately sold.

Katy then drives to a gas station. She is very mad, confused and impulsive, so she obeys to the first advertisement she encounters. I bet marketers would love to have more people like Katy.

When facing heartbreak, some people might try to feel better with a chocolate fudge sundae or maybe a nice walk around the block. But in Katy's case, she joins the US industrial-military complex and gets trained to fight guerrilla warfare abroad. Don't get me wrong, I have respect for soldiers in the military, but I think a life-changing decision like joining the Marines should not be made in a moment of emotional frenzy.

Katy is now the property of the U.S. military complex.

Nevertheless, Katy makes this decision, cutting her hair in a boyish fashion and trading her Blackberry for a Marines uniform.

The rest of the video is very similar to armed forces commercials seen on TV where big guns, big machines and scenes of hardcore combat training are presented in a dynamic matter to appeal to young people who are bored

Katy burns a letter from her boyfriend (representing her old life) while hanging out with her Marines buddy. He's REALLY there for her. Camaraderie between soldiers is an important selling point to help recruit personnel and is heavily promoted in this video.

with their lives. The lyrics of the song are cleverly mixed with the images of the video to make the advertisement even more effective. For instance, when Perry sings "I just wanna throw my phone away, Find out who is really

Katy is now in a military base, shooting a rifle and will most likely be shipped to a warzone in the near future. Take THAT cheating boyfriend, that'll show you!

there for me", she is seen with her fellow soldiers, implying that her Marines buddies will never let her down. When Katy sings: "I fell deep and you let me drown, But that was then and this is now ... Now look at me", she is shown firing a rifle as if it was a great accomplishment. Yep, look at her:

Katy, you say you're "sparkling" but you're being trained to fight guerrilla warfare in the Middle East, which is known to be extremely bloody, violent and often involve civilian casualties. So, yeah, I'm not sure that "sparkling" is the best word to describe your situation.

During the bridge of the song, Katy sings "Now look at me, I'm sparkling, A firework, a dancing flame, You won't ever put me out again, I'm glowing, oh woah oh". During that time she is shown patrolling a mock Middle-Eastern village, used for real-life military training for guerrilla warfare simulations. This is another clever association between the song's lyrics and the images in the video, provoking a positive association between the two.
Later in the video, the positive and uplifting words of the chorus are mixed with all-out war scenes involving soldiers running, tanks rolling and helicopters flying. There's definitely some cognitive dissonance here because, in case some people don't know, war is NEVER positive nor uplifting. It is ALWAYS terrible, violent and horrifying. However, in order to recruit new soldiers, advertisers need to make the whole "military experience" appear wonderful.

So, in short, discovering that her boyfriend is cheating on her has Katy Perry enlist in the Marines, to be trained for combat, and, ultimately, be used as cannon fodder in conflicts she likely doesn't fully understand. The elite seems to be looking for lost youth to fight their wars. Was Part of Me an Illuminati-sponsored message to find new recruits for its armed branch, the U.S. military-industrial complex?

Katy is now caught up in the business of war, where death, mutilation, horror and trauma can get in the way of conquering Third World countries for resources and power. But hey, at least Katy's douchebag boyfriend isn't there!

A single eye above the trigger of a gun indicates that this military-themed video is a product of the elite's agenda ... who happen to have a bunch of wars planned in the coming years.

In Conclusion

Watching a bit of "international news" is enough to make one realize that there is currently a lot of pressure on "bad" countries such as Syria, Iran and Uganda, and that public opinion is being prepped for new military conflicts. The prospect of future wars, along with the countless existing warzones around the world, are generating a great need for new soldiers military in the U.S. and other Western countries. Since military drafts are no longer an option, new and innovative ways are being used to reach the army's target audience (teenagers) and to get them interested in enlisting in armed forces. Katy Perry's Part of Me is an obvious Marines recruitment advertisement disguised as a music video, with the Marine's "cool" weaponry, intensive training and soldier camaraderie all presented in a dynamic and appealing matter. The military and war are presented as ideal escapes from life's bummers, like a cheating boyfriend, and geared to appeal to a generation of bored teenagers. But is war really the perfect way to forget about a bad relationship? Go ask a war veteran.

Katy Perry's "Wide Awake" : A Video About Monarch Mind Control

Katy Perry's music video "Wide Awake" is another offering from the pop music industry that conceals references to Monarch programming within its symbolism. References to this practice occur often in mass media but are often coded using specific symbols and imagery. We'll look at the hidden meaning of Katy Perry's "Wide Awake".

Many articles on this site described how many items of popular culture conceal within their symbolism references to an unknown, horrendous practice: Monarch programming. This technique of mind control seeks to create fully "programmable" individuals and is used by the shadowy elite in fields such as the military, politics and the murky underworld. Another area in which mind control (especially Monarch programming) is used is the entertainment business – not only because some celebrities are actual victims of mind control, but because entertainment is used to subtly normalize and glamorize this awful practice through symbolism.

Katy Perry's video Wide Awake is yet another music video that alludes to the concept of Monarch programming through its storyline and its imagery. While this might not be obvious to most people, those who have some knowledge of the subject of mind control find it extremely blatant.

In many ways, the video resembles works that have been previously analyzed on this site, such as the movies Labyrinth and Sucker Punch and music videos like Paramore's Brick by Boring Brick. All of these productions visually represent the inner-world of Monarch slaves through a specific set of symbols: mirrors, butterflies (especially Monarch butterflies), mazes and so forth. Not only do these objects aptly portray psychological concepts, they are actual "trigger images" used in mind control on Monarch slaves. Wide Awake fully utilizes this set of symbols, which gives the storyline a deeper, and more disturbing, meaning.

Most mainstream media articles on Wide Awake say that it is about Katy Perry "navigating the maze of fame". While this might be true, the video cannot be completely explained without considering the element of Monarch programming. For instance, why is Perry shown at sitting on a wheelchair, completely "out of it" inside a health institution? Probably because there is more to the video than meets the eye. Let's look at the deeper meaning of its scenes.

Wide Awake

At the beginning of the video, we see Katy completing the filming of her popular video California Gurls. She is wearing her now famous pink wig. She is fully into her "sexy pop star" persona.

Katy is doing what is expected of her in front of the cameras.

When she enters her dressing room, Katy removes her wig, which symbolically represents her switching to another alter (this gesture was also an important part of Lady Gaga's video Marry the Night). Katy then stares at herself in the mirror for a while – until she dissociates from reality (dissociation is an important part of mind control) and enters a fantasy world. This world is, in fact, the inner-world of Katy Perry's psyche.

Katy stands at a gateway flanked by two pillars. In esoteric symbolism, pillars guard the entrance of sacred and mystical places. In this case, it is Katy's own mind.

Katy soon realizes that her inner-world is a dark labyrinth that if full of traps and dangers. She doesn't appear to know the way inside her own mind. She even gets caught in traps that were placed by her handlers.

During mind control, handlers literally take control of the slave's mind and can program everything within it. This causes the slave to become a stranger inside his/her own mind as their thoughts are meticulously controlled and programmed.

Katy realizes that she won't make it through the maze without an important element – one that has been stripped from her during the her programming: Her core persona. Through fireworks emerging from her breasts (of course), she calls for help and her core persona appears before her in the form of a young Katy.

Katy's core persona is the "real her" (Katheryn Elizabeth Hudson), complete with her values and convictions. It is the personality she had before being subjected to programming. Mind control seeks to strip individuals from their core persona in order to program a new one that will easily comply with orders. Here, Katy has the opportunity of reconnecting with her core persona. It will indeed become her guide.

Katy and her core persona then enter a room full that truly screams out "Monarch programming".

Katy and little Katheryn find themselves in a room full of mirrors. The dark-and-light floor represents duality, a concept extremely important in mind control programming. The fact that little Katheryn's reflection does not appear in the mirror emphasizes the fact that the girl is not real, but a part of Katy's psychology. Katy's dress is full of butterflies, a rather strong reminder that she is under Monarch Programming.

Looking through the mirror, Katy sees nasty-looking paparazzi. While she is mesmerized by the sight, her core persona realizes that the world around Katy is shattering (inner-worlds of Monarch slaves are programmed by handlers and can be modified or destroyed at will). Desperate, Katy breaks the mirror in front of her and leaves the room, a symbolic act representing her attempting to break out of her programming.

As Katy breaks the mirror, we see butterflies flying off her dress – an image that emphasizes the fact that she is breaking out of Monarch programming.

Music Business

Breaking Out?

Then next scene is in sharp contrast to the rest of the video. While before it was all about fantasy and mystery, we are now in a cold, sterile health institution. In other words, we appear to be out of Katy's head and back to reality. Katy appears to be completely "shut down", sitting on a wheel chair in what appears to be a mental institution. Is this her MK programming site?

Katy looks like what MK victims must look like after enduring the trauma of Mind control . She is totally "out of it" and probably drugged by the strawberry she is holding.

Mind control slaves are subjected to all kinds of torture by their handlers. At some point during the "treatment", the pain, whether physical or emotional, becomes too much to bear and their brain's natural response is to dissociate from reality. Handlers actually want their subjects to dissociate as it facilitates programming. They use movies such as Alice in Wonderland and Wizard of Oz to program victims to dissociate "through the looking glass" or "over the rainbow". Up until now, the video took place in Katy's dissociative inner-world.

While Katy is somewhat of a zombie, her core persona, little Katheryn, is "Wide Awake" and is determined to get out of there. Some people, however, do not want to see that happen.

Two men with horned heads (see Baphomet) block Katheryn's way to freedom. Do these non-human, evil-looking men represent Katy's handlers?

However, Katheryn's will-power blasts the horned guys away and even brings Katy back to life.

The lyrics of the song convey this sense of liberation from a deceitful and oppressive state of mind. Here's the first chorus:

> *I'm wide awake*
> *Yeah, I was in the dark*
> *I was falling hard*
> *With an open heart*
> *I'm wide awake*

How did I read the stars so wrong?
I'm wide awake
And now it's clear to me
That everything you see
Ain't always what it seems
I'm wide awake
Yeah, I was dreaming for so long

So, at this point, one might ask: Is this video about Katy actually breaking out of mind control? The rest of the video might answer the question.

Upon leaving the institution, Katy and her core persona find themselves back in the fantasy land.

Katy and her core persona are back in the dissociative fantasy land - at the other side of the Labyrinth where things seem nicer.

This cat with hypnotic eyes is a reminder that Katy might still be tightly monitored and under the control of her handlers. The butterflies on Katy's head are also a good indicator of this fact.

At this point, Katheryn hopes on her bike and leaves Katy. Before leaving, Katheryn leaves Katy a gift ... a symbolic gift.

Katheryn, the core, authentic persona of Katy says goodbye. Why is she leaving? Isn't our core personality something we should ALWAYS have?

Back in her dressing room, realizes that she's been given a butterfly. Did her Katheryn give Katy the poisonous gift of being back under mind control?

The butterfly leads us from the dressing room to a stage, before a performance of the song Teenage Dreamss. In other words, Katy (and viewers of the video) have gone full circle and are back at the starting point. Although a quest appears to have been completed and foes appear to have been defeated, Katy is back in her "sexy pop star" persona, complete with lollipop bras. This is who she is now, a product of the music industry. Her core persona is gone.

Did she learn from something from Katheryn and is now better equipped to face the pitfalls of celebrity? Maybe. However, the orgy of butterflies in the video reminds us that, in the end, she is still under the control of the music industry and the MK symbolism it promotes.

In Conclusion

Katy Perry's Wide Awake is a prime example of Monarch programming symbolism being promoted in mass media products. While it may be deemed "original" and "imaginative" by many, it is strikingly similar to other MK-themed video analyzed on this site. For instance, Paramore's Brick by Boring Brick also features a younger (purer) version of the singer, a flurry of butterflies, rooms full of mirrors and so forth. Why are all of these symbols found in these unrelated videos (any countless others)? It is because these symbols are, in fact, related: They are symbols of Monarch Programming mind control. This is the common thread uniting these symbols. It also explains the otherwise puzzling plots of the videos.

Although it is probably the most disgusting and vicious concept known to man, Monarch programming is often referenced in popular culture. And, since Monarch programming is one of the ways the occult elite keeps a stranglehold on many areas, including the entertainment industry, it is often subtly glamorized in mass media. Most people let all of this imagery go straight to their minds without even understanding its true meaning. However, there is one way to not allow these unwanted messages to reach our brains: Be TRULY wide awake.

B.O.B. and Nicki Minaj's "Out of My Mind" or How to Make Mind Control Entertaining

"Out of My Mind" is considered to be an upbeat and funny song about B.O.B. being completely crazy. A closer look at the song's lyrics and video however reveal that it is yet another attempt to glamorize one of the elite's most despicable practices: Mind Control Programming. We'll look at B.O.B. and Nicki Minaj's "Out of My Mind" and how it refers to Monarch Mind Control.

B.O.B.'s Out of My Mind is about him being a crazy so, fittingly enough, the video takes place in a mental institution. While most would stop their analysis there, a closer look at the song and video reveal that B.O.B. is getting a specific type of "treatment". Some people are "out of their minds" due to mental health problems, but others are there by force. Those that have mental health problems usually get treated by competent people while those who "lost it" by force get treated extremely badly. They are violently abused and traumatized by sadistic handlers until they completely dissociate from reality – literally going "out of their minds". This is what we call ritual abuse, the basis of Monarch Mind Control. Out of My Mind is a caricaturized, yet blatant, illustration of the process of Mind Control.

As we've seen in previous articles on Vigilant Citizen, making Monarch programming cool, fashionable and, ultimately, acceptable is an important part of the elite's Agenda. On a regular basis, we see popular artists releasing material that is rife with Mind Control and Illuminati symbolism, in order to keep the elite's Agenda fresh and new – making sure it stays on TV, radio and getting plenty of hits on YouTube. Performed by two of rap's hottest artists, Out of My Mind gives Mind Control imagery yet another go at the airwaves. Despite its disturbing nature, the video is presented in a lighthearted, sexy way, which comes across as positive and attractive to young viewers. Let's look at the video's main scenes.

B.O.B. is Not Receiving Proper Treatment

The video begins with B.O.B. and Nicki Minaj locked inside a cell and acting all crazy. On the wall behind them are carvings that appear to be made by someone that is crazy and paranoid, but, on closer look, one can decipher words and symbols directly referring to Illuminati mind control. There are several All-Seeing Eyes, a symbol that not only represents the occult elite, but is central in actual mind control programming. This ancient occult symbol is at the center of systems used to program MK slaves and was even used by the father of mind control, Josef Mengele.

> "The All-Seeing Eye is placed in the center of Star's systems, just like Mengele would put in an All-Seeing Eye."
> - Fritz Springmeier, The Illuminati Formula to Create a Mind Control Slave

Behind B.O.B. are weird carvings such as the All-Seeing Eye inside a spaceship. There are also unsettling phrases such as "They are us" and "We are them". Who are "They"? Is this a reference to the elite controlling these artists and making them their pawns? Hence ..."We are them"?

Not only does the All-Seeing Eye represent the occult elite, it also represents constant surveillance and monitoring, that there is no escaping the handler's grasp. For this reason, many MK slaves become obsessed with the symbol and find themselves drawing it everywhere.

> "Because the slave is monitored from so many different unseen methods, it does begin to seem hopeless to some to ever be free of Big Brother. If you add to all this, that the slave has been programmed repeatedly that there is no escaping their All-seeing eyes, then it is easy to see why so many slaves acquiesce & just comply."
> - Fritz Springmeier, Deeper Insights into the Illuminati Formula

At the bottom left, we see a carving saying "They see" with a creepy eye in between. Who are "They"? Maybe the symbol right next to it bears the answer: An eye inside a triangle, symbol of the Illuminati.

While B.O.B. is jumping around in his cell, some unfriendly looking fellows, who do not appear to be caregivers, march toward his cell. At the center of them, an evil-looking, Josef Mengele-type appears ready to program the rapper.

Looking like a sadistic mad scientist, the man in the middle brings B.O.B. a straitjacket. He is accompanied by four agents dressed in riot gear.

At this point, it should be clear that B.O.B. is not at a typical mental health institution. He is at programming site, run by high level "scientists" and heavily armed governmental agents. As seen in previous articles, normalizing police state agents is also part of the Agenda.

B.O.B. is taken by force somewhere to probably be abused and tortured by the creepy scientist who is coldly looking over in the back.

Of course, the video sugarcoats the dark reality behind it, by making every appear fun! and sexy! Therefore, the tools used to torture B.O.B. are brought in by nurses in outfits that are ... non-regulatory.

While Monarch programming is atrociously cruel, videos like this one make the concept trivial and even unconsciously positive to young, unaware viewers.

B.O.B.'s lyrics in the first verse refer to him being evaluated by "they" and even names classic mind control techniques. Here's part of it:

> "My brain is on vacation, they telling me
> And I'm bi-polar to the severity
> And I need medication, apparently
> And some electrocompulsive therapy"

The main goal of mind control is to traumatize victims severely enough to cause them to completely dissociate from reality. Once this is accomplished, handlers can program new alter personas into the blank slate that their brain has become. While dissociated, MK slaves are literally "out of their minds". In B.O.B.'s verse, the phrase "My brain is on vacation, they telling me" aptly describes an MK slave that has dissociated from reality. The lines "And I need medication, apparently/ And some electrocompulsive therapy" refer to two important techniques of Mind Control: The usage of drugs ("medication") and electroshock torture.

> "Another basic component of the Monarch program is lots of electroshock. Stun guns, staffs with hidden electric cattle prods, and cattle prods are frequently used on the slaves. Electroshock is used to create the dissociation from trauma during the programming, and later it is used to remove memories after the slave has carried out a mission, or to instill fear and obedience in a reluctant slave. Slaves generally carry horrible body memories of excruciating electro-shock tortures to their entire bodies. As the slaves begin a therapeutic deprogramming process they will recover these horrible

memories, not to mention many other painful memories."
- Ibid.

As if to emphasize the importance of this technique in the song, we hear an electroshock sound effect during B.O.B's verse – a sound that probably terrifies actual MK victims.

Dr. Minaj

The next part of the video is B.O.B.'s "Psych Evaluation", performed by "Dr." Minaj. We soon realize that she is not there to hear about B.O.B's feelings, but rather to practice a technique that is extensively employed by mind control handlers: To humiliate, insult and demean victims to further their trauma. Minaj proceeds to diss the hell out of B.O.B. and his career, making the rapper come close to tears. In this excerpt, she ridicules one of B.O.B's hits:

*"Now can we pretend them airplanes in the night skies
Are like shooting stars?
Well, you gon' really need a wish right now
When my goons come through and start shooting stars"*

Of course, in actual programming, handlers are a lot more cruel, sadistic and hurtful but the basic concept is nevertheless present.

Minaj then goes into stripper mode and hints to the fact that she might be under mind control herself.

Dr. Minaj removes her white coat to reveal a sexy outfit with a prominent leopard print pattern. In mind control, feline prints are used to identify Sex Kittens – products of Beta programming. Minaj's stripper-like demeanor confirms her being a Sex Kitten.

It has been reported that MK handlers are often under mind control themselves and this scene appears to describe this fact.

Towards the end of her verse, Minaj says:

*"You know, I graduated Summa Cum Laude
That's why they thinking I'm Illuminati"*

It is rather odd to refer to these "crazy Illuminati rumors" while playing the role of a MK slave/handler in a video promoting Monarch mind control. Also, nobody with even a little knowledge believes that Nicki is "part of the Illuminati". Rather, she is one of the several pawns used by the industry to promote an Agenda … and she will probably be dropped as soon as her "cool factor" is gone, like hundreds of other pop stars before her.

In what appears to be a moment of lucidity, Minaj offers to free B.O.B. from his shackles. Her handler alter however appears to kick back in and she leaves the room somewhat confused and embarrassed.

Parole Board

After his weird encounter with Dr. Minaj, B.O.B. is taken to the parole board.

B.O.B. enters the room pushed by an over-armed police guy and with his head covered so he doesn't know where he is. I'm pretty sure they don't do that in regular mental institution. However, keeping victims confused and in the dark is a common tactic used Monarch programming.

While B.O.B. raps before the parole board, one of the judges gets all hot for B.O.B., asking him to call her. Yes kids, being a MK slave is very attractive.

The video ends with B.O.B. and Minaj looking lost and confused, asking repeatedly "If I'm here ... and you're there ... and I'm here ... and you're there". Hmm, are they confused about who they are? About their core and alter personalities? That's how MK slaves feel. B.O.B. then whispers to Minaj: "Shhh ... they might be listening".

In Conclusion

At first glance, Out of My Mind appears to be a fun song about being wild and crazy, but a closer look at the lyrics and the video reveals that it actually refers to extremely specific aspects of Monarch Mind Control. Once this fact is known, the song suddenly stops being fun and turns into a disturbing case of normalizing and glamorizing of the cruel practice that is Mind Control. We see and hear references to trauma, dissociation, being drugged, electrocuted, roughed up by government agents and even manipulated by handlers. While all of this sounds horrible written out, catchy rhymes and sexy nurses make the pill easy to swallow for young viewers who will probably jump around screaming "I'm out of my f*cking mind!".

In the end, Out of My Mind is yet another example of the elite's Agenda being marketed to young music fans. Mind control is heavily used by the elite to keep a stronghold on various areas of power, particularly the entertainment industry. While not all pop artists are victims of Mind Control, most have signed contracts that make them pawns of the occult elite, and force them to give up control of their creative creations. While rappers used to be about "fighting the power" and "representing the streets", they are now seen in cells, confused, and abused by cops and mad scientists, talking about being electroshocked. The music industry has been hijacked, folks ... and while videos like this may make it obvious to some, most will just laugh and say "You're out of your mind".

The Illuminati Symbolism of Ke$ha's "Die Young" and How it Ridicules the Indoctrinated Masses

Ke$ha's "Die Young" is probably one of the most blatant Illuminati videos ever released. While the symbolism is so overt that it is almost ridiculous, there's an underlying message to the video: Even if you're dumb enough to embrace all of that Illuminati brainwash, you're still not part of the elite and therefore, still subject to "Die Young".

Ke-dollarsign-ha has never been the most inspirational singer around. She started her career as an alcoholic party girl that's not too strict about personal hygiene (see the Tik Tok line "Before I leave brush ma teeth with a bottle of Jack") and, for her new album, she turned into some kind of Illuminati witch-type deal. She is far from the only pop star that has gone through this kind of metamorphosis and it was probably pre-planned by her record label. How many singers have gone from an "around-the-way" girl to an Illuminati figurehead? That's what the industry does.

To the untrained eye this kind of transformation is usually somewhat subtle ... Ke$ha's Die Young is anything but. In fact, it is one giant clusterfreak of Illuminati symbols. It is so obvious and in-your-face that it forced mainstream music sources such as Billboard.com to "admit" that the video was all about Illuminati symbols. Interestingly enough, not too long ago, these same sites were calling sites like Vigilant Citizen "batshit crazy" for even alluding to the existence of these symbols and describing their meaning. Now these sites say "Yeah, there are Illuminati symbols" in a matter-of-fact way. What happened to the batshit crazy part? However, the mainstream sites still only refer to this concept in an extremely superficial way, not giving any insight on their true meaning and the real Agenda behind it all.

Some might rationalize what is happening by saying: "Ke$ha did it for the LOLs and to make fun of the conspiracies". This is plausible, but this argument is now surfacing every time a video contains Illuminati symbolism. Are all videos now making fun of conspiracies? In reality, Ke$ha didn't do anything for any LOLs. She did not direct the video. She is just performing what she is told to perform, like most pop stars. The fact of the matter is: Illuminati symbols are becoming more prevalent because that was the plan all along: To gradually make them part of popular culture. The occult elite is revealing itself and the masses are dancing to their tunes.

The real issue at stake is however not the symbols that are flashed on screen, but the underlying messages that are communicated to the viewers. It is about the Agenda – about making specific values and attitudes cool and desirable to young people. It is about promoting the culture of death (i.e. Die Young), about sexualizing everything, about materialism, about a corrupted and debased brand of spirituality and so forth.

As I watch Ke$ha and her gang fondling themselves, I can't help but wonder: Is the video making fun of the masses that have been brainwashed by the lifestyle promoted by the elite? Let's look at the video.

An Orgy ... Of Symbols

The video takes place in Mexico, where Ke$ha and a bunch of cult followers arrive at a cabin. We quickly realize that the group arriving literally worships death.

As the car door opens, a Skull and Bones symbols flashes, representing the cult of death emanating from this car.

Skull and Bones is also the name of Yale's elite secret society, which includes members such as George Bush Sr., George Dubya and John Kerry.

Is "Evil" written on the side of the car?

The car is, in fact, a hearse – these big black cars used to carry dead people. So, yeah, there's definitely some death-worshiping going on here.

When the hearse is opens, we see Ke$ha in a black veil, posing as if she was some sort of sexual religious statue. She is then carried on the shoulders of her gang of mimbos, as in cultures where people carry statues of the Virgin Mary on the streets.

While this is happening, a bunch of symbols are flashed on the screen. Vigilant Citizen readers probably instantly recognized them.

Ke$ha wearing an All-Seeing Eye ring while hiding one eye. Just making sure you understand who she is working for.

Inverted crosses (a symbol of the Church of Satan) flash about five thousand times during the video. They're working very hard to make that Satanic crap trendy.

In another scene, Ke$ha and her gang play at pulling tarot cards (to determine who's the sacrificial lamb of the night?). Ke$ha pulls the "Devil" card and everybody bursts into laughter. So much fun is to be had with Satanic symbols!

Looking at the way Ke$ha's gang acts, the only word that comes to mind to describe them is "not too bright". What is the first thing they do when they enter the cabin they drove so far to reach? They trash it. I realize that trashing things is a cool, rock star thing to do, but even drunk rock stars know to trash a place when they LEAVE, not when arrive and actually NEED a facility.

"This place is too nice. Let's destroy it and then have sex on broken furniture. Yeah, we're idiots".

After mindlessly wrecking the place, there is one thing left to do: Mindlessly dance to a generic pop song. Of course, the dancing quickly turns into an orgy, all of which happens with a bunch of occult symbols all around.

Ke$ha sits a the throne of the "orgy", under a pentacle. While this symbol is not associated with Satanism, it is used in occult rituals, hinting that there's a Sex-Magick aspect behind all of this.

While this is happening, Ke$ha does the one-eye sign, a way of saying that this sex and death worshiping cult that is full of suggestible idiots (representing the masses) is sponsored by the Illuminati industry.

While this is happening, Ke$ha does the one-eye sign, a way of saying that this sex and death worshiping cult that is full of suggestible idiots (representing the masses) is sponsored by the Illuminati industry.

Throughout the video, symbols are flashed on screen, mainly triangles that are either upright or reversed. In esoteric symbolism, upright triangles represent the masculine principle while reverse triangles represent the feminine principle. The combination of both represents the union of opposites and, in more "human" terms, sexual intercourse. So, while people are frolicking in the video, symbols convey the concept of Sex Magick on an almost subconscious level.

In case all of the stuff happening on screen is not enough to make you understand young viewers that sex is happening there, shots of wolves doing it might light a bulb above their heads. Also, is that a way to give a "shout-out" to bestiality – one of the "guilty pleasures" of the sick Illuminati elite?

The orgy goes on until cops arrive and start shooting. When this happens, Ke$ha walks decidedly towards the armed cops.

Since the song is called Die Young, we are lead to think that Ke$ha is shot and killed by the police. Die Young is therefore yet another video that depicts police state oppression and violence as normal, even cool. The moral of the story? Even if you have been thoroughly brainwashed by Illuminati propaganda and have lived your life according to the debased culture promoted by mass media, you are still a disposable pawn according to the elite. You might believe you are a "rebel" going against "The Man" but you're actually playing right in their hands. Far from being "enlightened", these symbols and this way of life are conceived and manufactured by the elite to dumb-down the masses, in order to make them suggestible and manipulable.

Even if you're dumb enough to be brainwashed by Illuminati propaganda (to the point of having an Illuminati symbol right on your ass), you are not exempt from police state oppression. You might be doing what the elite wants you to do, but that doesn't mean you're part of it.

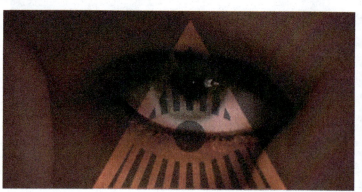

Just making sure you understand who's sponsoring this video.

The culture of death that is now prevalent in mass media is extremely present in this song. The phrase "We're gonna die young" is repeated countless times (in a upbeat matter) as if to drill in teenager's skulls that human life is not valuable. This is right on par with the elite's depopulation Agenda.

In Conclusion

Readers of this site might be realizing that the symbolism that has been pointed out for years is becoming increasingly prevalent and obvious in mass media. The process is gradual yet very noticeable and the concept of Revelation of the Hierarchy is in full force in the entertainment business. It has been said that the best way of hiding something is in plain sight. The Illuminati symbolism we see in popular culture is becoming so prevalent that it is BECOMING popular culture. While some might claim that "it's a trend" or that "Ke$ha is making fun of it", they don't see the important reversal is happening here: Trends used to come from the streets to then be picked up and reflected by mass media; Nowadays, trends are CREATED by mass media and forced on the world through repetition and omnipresence.

There is however more at stake here than simply the presence of symbols in music videos. There are tons of videos with the same message and symbolism as Die Young – all promoting the same Agenda. Brainwashed by thousands of hours of music videos, young people become like the cult followers in Ke$ha's video, pushed to live pointless, self-destructive lives based on the gratification of their lowest impulses. Indulging in one's animalistic instincts has always been considered to be the opposite of reaching spiritual enlightenment – and that's exactly what the elite wants. If the masses were to gain enough awareness to avoid the traps and pitfalls set up by the system, the virtual enslavement caused by debt and mass-media mind control would crumble.

The way of life "glamorized" by the elite causes people to be lost, devoid of strong values and suggestible to mass-media propaganda. However, in the end, even if they do exactly what is expected from them, the masses are still perceived by the elite as a brainless cattle that needs to be put in its place by a strong police force. As Ke$ha and her fans mindless yell "we're gonna die young", thinking they are cool and edgy, they actually unknowingly celebrate their own servitude to a tune created by their rulers. Go Animals!

"Scream and Shout": A Video About Britney Spears Being Under Mind Control

will.i.am and Britney Spears' video "Scream and Shout" features Britney "singing" in a British accent. But that's not the only mind-control related part of this video. In this article, we'll look at the Monarch programming symbolism in "Scream and Shout".

Britney Spears is probably the most obvious victim of mind control in the music industry. If the strange facts regarding her personal life are not enough to convince an educated observer, the symbolism surrounding her act tells it all. Almost as if her handlers were mocking her sad mental state while bragging about it to the public, Britney is made to perform in videos such as Hold it Against Me and Scream and Shout – which symbolically refer to her own mental slavery.

Like all things related to the occult elite, the message is conveyed in veiled symbolic ways that require some prior knowledge to be understood. Viewed in this way, Scream and Shout is yet another example of a pop video laced with mind control symbolism hidden under the guise of "style" and aesthetics.

While will.i.am appears to be playing the role of the handler (he "selects" a Monarch programming alter persona at the beginning of the video), Britney plays the role of the slave, even singing with a weird British accent – as if an alter persona had been triggered. Monarch slaves can indeed be programmed to embody a totally different identity, complete with a back story and an accent.

The disturbing fact about Britney singing with a British accent is that, during the time she made tabloid news for "mental problems", she was caught speaking with a British accent in real life. Here's an article from 2008 that describes Britney's strange behavior. It even states that her odd behavior is symptomatic of "dissociative identity disorder" – a medical term that pretty much describes what Monarch programming is all about.

> *Britney Spears Lapses Into a British Accent*
>
> *Britney Spears has a new accessory to go with her pink wig: a British accent.*
>
> *In the last several weeks, Spears, 26, has been videotaped numerous times trading her Louisiana twang for U.K. inflections.*
>
> *"She had the English accent thing going the whole time" while shopping at Kitson last Thursday, ac-*

cording to a source. "It didn't stop."

Even when angry, the accent appears. On an L.A. shopping trip to Macy's on Jan. 13, she screamed at the paparazzi, "Get out of my G—— face!" – in a British accent.

So is it all in fun or has she flipped her pink wig?

"When someone has dissociative identity disorder" – formerly known as multiple personality disorder – "each identity is split off from the other," says L.A. psychologist Renee A. Cohen, who is not treating Spears. "Each identity would have its own name, memories, behavioral traits and emotional characteristics."

Cohen says the critical question is: "When Britney uses the British accent, or appears to take on another identity, does she know she's Britney Spears?"

"Otherwise, she could simply be behaving this way for attention, for sympathy, or any other reason," adds Cohen. "It's foolish to attempt to diagnose her without a formal evaluation."

One possible influence could be Spears's maternal grandmother, Lilian Bridges, who was originally from England.

Also, Spears's new beau, photographer Adnan Ghalib, grew up in Birmingham, England.

According to paparazzi who trail the singer around the clock, one thing is for sure: the pink wig means something's changing.

"When she puts on the pink wig, you just know something crazy is about to happen," said one paparazzo.
- Source: People.com

So Britney, who has been diagnosed with severe psychological issues, sings with a British accent, a symptom of dissociative identity disorder, one of her reported conditions. Isn't this a little twisted? Using a symptom of mental illness in a pop song? Especially considering the fact that she most probably was told to do this? But the actual truth behind all of this is even more twisted: Britney does not simply have "psychological issues" … she is a victim of mind control. She most likely has several personas programmed into her – one which may have a British accent. In Scream and Shout this alter appears to be switched on. This might sound a little outlandish, but the symbolism in the video makes everything clear.

Scream and Shout … That It's About Mind Control

According to the video director Ben More, the theme of the video is multiplicity. More says the idea behind it "was essentially trying to reduce what the song is about to symbols". Britney multiplying herself and extensive MK-related imagery indeed give the video a dark symbolic meaning.

The video does not have an intricate storyline, instead it is comprised of a series shots with aesthetic appeal. And, of course, MK symbolism. Rather than babble for days about this video, I'll just highlight some of its symbolic shots – all of which follow themes promoted by the elite such as mind control and dehumanization.

Multiplying Personas

Is Will.I.Am selecting Britney's alter persona?

The video begins with will.i.am browsing through filters (à la Instagram) to apply on a picture of a butterfly. This scene can represent will.i.am as a Monarch Programming Handler who switches and triggers alter personas of an MK slave. This slave is represented here by a Monarch butterfly having alters applied to it the same way filters are applied to pictures. But who is the MK butterfly? Britney Spears with her fake British accent, of course.

On several occasions, Britney is shown "multiplying herself". Is it a way of symbolically representing her multiple personas? will.i.am gets the same treatment – handlers are often MK victims themselves.

In this apparently random scene, an unknown hooded person smashes into a wall and breaks in multiple pieces. Does this represent a MK slave fragmenting into multiple personalities?

Dehumanization

The theme of transhumanism, robotization and dehumanization is always prevalent in MK-themed videos, and this one is no exception. On top of the heavily auto-tuned and robotic singing in the video, viewers are treated to visuals that mirror the constant trend of dehumanization in mass media. Hidden under the guise of being futuristic, these images tells viewers what the elite thinks the future SHOULD look like.

Music Business

This artificial limb company probably paid a good chunk of change to have its product featured in the video. It is also featured in the video because it perfectly syncs with the robotic-dehumanized theme of the video.

The image from the video is reminiscent of this popular image representing transhumanism – which pushes the merging of humans with robots.

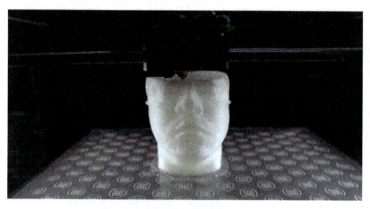

Here we see a 3D model of will.i.am being conceived ... a synthetic will.i.am created by a machine.

Portrayed as mounted trophies? The same way hunters proudly display the animals they shot? Not very engrossing.

One of this guy's eyes is apparently a camera lens – a creepy, futuristic way of placing the inevitable one-eye sign into the video.

One-Eye

will.i.am fires a net that catches a golden statue of naked woman. Did the handler find a new victim to program?

Of course, in this MK-Ultra themed video, there's some one-eye imagery going on.

Finding Another Victim?
In Conclusion

When one understands the true living conditions of Britney Spears as a Monarch slave under the control of MK handlers – the underlying meaning of her video Scream and Shout is somewhat unsettling. There is something seriously twisted in having her sing and perform about her own enslavement, going as far as having her adopt a British accent, like when she was completely "broken down" in 2008. There is something even more twisted in having young people from all over the world watching this imagery, not knowing that it symbolically refers to Monarch Programming, a practice that as sadistic as it is horrifying.

Regular readers of Vigilant Citizen might notice that there is redundancy in the messages and imagery found in recent pop videos. While this also causes some of my music business articles to be somewhat redundant, my goal is to highlight the pattern that emerges, to prove that there is a conscious and sustained effort to push a specific agenda to the masses. Each repetition is further proof that there is no coincidence or "reaching" here, just the execution of a clear and defined agenda focused on the propagation and normalization of a specific set of messages and symbols.

Given the way Britney is mocked in her own video, it is easy to understand that not only do those in control not have positive intentions … but that they relish the fact that they own this virtual slave. Considering that state of mind, wouldn't you think that they'd love to see the whole world, to certain extent, under this type of mind control?

Emeli Sandé's "Clown": A Song About Selling Out to the Music Industry?

Emeli Sandé's video "Clown" is simple, subtle and artistic but nevertheless conveys a very clear and disturbing message about the music industry and those that rule it. Is "Clown" about Emeli Sandé "selling her soul" to the elite? We'll look at the meaning of the song and music video.

Emeli Sandé is an English-born Scottish singer whose album Our Version of Events became the best selling album of 2012 in the UK. With three number one singles and widespread critical acclaim, Sandé is set to win a slurry of awards in 2013 and possibly more recognition "across the pond". Did her recent success come with a hefty price tag? Judging by the message conveyed in her single Clown, yes, yes it did.

It certainly doesn't take much analytical effort to understand that Clown portrays the music industry as a monolithic, coercive and even dangerous entity, lead by powerful people who demand nothing less than total submission from their chosen artists. In exchange for success, a damning contract (akin to an oath) must be signed that not only leads to relinquishing creative control, but, on a higher level, relinquishing an artist's very soul. Is this why Sandé became an important part of the London Olympics' Ceremonies (a seemingly blatant elitist occult ritual), where she sang in a disturbing segment entitled "Abide With Me", which told the story of a young child giving away his soul to a malevolent entity? Maybe. Let's look at the video.

Clowns Get No Respect

Clown is pretty much the opposite of most of the videos I describe on this site. There is no migraine-inducing fashion, no super-futuristic dance moves and no symbols being flashed every 3 seconds. Yet, in the end, the same dark reality is conveyed and the same elitist group is being acknowledged and referred to.

The video is shot in black and white, in the style of silent films of the 1920s. All of the action takes place in a single setting, a kind of meeting room where it seems important issues are being discussed. On one of the walls we read the words "Anywhere in the world and solar system". These words often appear on music industry contracts as a way of defining the true reach of it in case of legal issues. Also these words give this meeting room an ethereal dimension, one that transcends time and place.

The decisions being made seem to have a weight that supercedes any regular political or national entity. There are men in military uniforms resembling those worn during the reign of Hitler or Mussolini, though the racial diversity of this panel indicates that we are not looking at a traditional fascist government, but at something of a "higher level", hence the words "Anywhere in the world and solar system". Put another way, the video appears to refer to a dictatorship evolving on a supra-national level, such as maybe … the Illuminati and the NWO?

Emeli taken in by two soldiers

The video begins with a strange scene: Emeli enters this room escorted by two soldiers as if she were a prisoner, yet she is greeted with warm applause from around the room. Right from the start, the video describes the contradiction of being a star in this day and age: influential and revered by the masses, while still completely in submission to higher powers. The applause Emeli receives is almost sarcastic, as if saying "We are applauding you like your fans do — but we still own you".

Emeli is then presented with something that represents the dilemma of anyone who wants to make it big in the music industry.

Emeli is given a pen in order to sign a contract.

Before any words are even exchanged between the men and Emeli, the singer is expected to sign a contract. As we see by her reaction, this is not an ordinary business contract, but a document that will heavily impact the rest of her life. Signing this document equals relinquishing some of her rights, freedoms, creative control and … her soul?

Emeli refuses and says "No". Immediately, the men in the room show signs of impatience and become more forceful. One of the men steps up to her, tells her "Please, you must reconsider" and makes her sit down.

We then see other gestures indicating that Emeli's physical integrity is being violated. While these actions are somewhat subtle in the video, they are a symbolic way of referring to the physical and psychological violence stars can be subjected if they do not fully comply to the elite's will.

As a man steps up to Emeli, she gives a look saying "Why you touching me for?"

Emeli is given the paternal "look at me when I'm talking to you" move by a man in uniform.

Emeli is treated with the typical speech that is given to artists to convince them to sign a contract. She is told to take advantage of this rare opportunity to be rich and famous. We quickly get a sense that, if she refuses to sign with these people (the elite), she will never "make it" because they are basically the only path to celebrity, that there is apparently no way of making it big in the music industry but signing with this monolithic entity that is controlled by a closed group of individuals.

The men tell Emeli:

> "You have great talent, and the brightest of futures. All we require is your consent".

To which she replies:

> "You mean my surrender."

This implies that the contract is indeed one that forces Emeli to submit to the powers that be and to become a virtual puppet, or a clown. One man then replies:

> "We mean your co-operation"

This means that they want Emeli to willfully accomplish what is expected of her, even if she realizes that it goes against what she believes in … which is the meaning of "selling out".

When Emeli says

> "I want freedom, to be myself",

a man promptly replies:

> "What use is freedom … if you live in the gutter"

flaunting the prospect of material gain, and loss, in order to get her to sign the contract.

As she continues to hesitate, the men get angrier and start yelling at her. At one point, a man says "We need a decision" and a vote gets taken, although Emeli does not get a vote. By show of hands, the men decide what to do with

Emeli. With a single gesture, one man sums up her fate if she doesn't sign the contract.

By running his hand across his throat, this man is saying that Emeli's career is over. Also, since these men are in uniforms and that Emeli is a prisoner, she will probably be killed ... Maybe in "strange circumstances", not unlike many other uncompromising artists.

In short, if she does not accept the terms of the contract, these men will kill her. She is then reminded of the opportunity she is passing up:

"Success is impatient. You audience is waiting."

When presented again with the pen and paper, Emeli grabs the pen and begins singing the chorus of the song, confirming that she accepts the terms of the contract.

*"I'll be your clown
Behind the glass
Go 'head and laugh 'cause it's funny
I would too if I saw me
I'll be your clown
On your favorite channel
My life's a circus-circus
rounding circles
I'm selling out tonight"*

The song's lyrics describe the sadness of an artist who has been reduced to the status of a clown, a puppet that is told what to do in order to obtain material gain. As depicted in the video, the song's lyrics also convey the fact that she was forced into this contract, which is, when all is said and done, nothing more than glorified exploitation.

*"I'd be less angry if it was my decision
And the money was just rolling in
If I had more than my ambition
I'll have time to please
I'll have time to thank you as soon as I win"*

At the end of the video, Sandé signs the contract (although we don't actually see her do it) and is taken away by the soldiers. It would seem therefore, that this is yet another story of free will, freedom and integrity being forcefully taken away through coercion and power. It is another story depicting the victory of evil against good, of darkness against light. It is another "victory speech" of the Illuminati industry, blatantly showing off how it controls the industry, to the point that it makes its "clowns" sing about their own sad state of puppetry. While Emeli Sandé is arguably more talented and mature than most pop stars, Clown does not convey a message that is very different from what we have seen on this site. The only difference is that this song is aimed for the adult contemporary market, rather than the tween market.

In Conclusion

In this era where an increasingly monolithic music industry is revealing itself to a public that is still clueless, the messages reaching to airwaves are becoming increasingly filtered, similar and upsetting. The themes of rebellion, of the victory of the human spirit over a soul crushing system, of transcending boundaries through art are silenced and virtually banned from the music industry. Where are these groups that had a message? That stood for something? Who would prefer death to selling out? They do still exist – but they are not in the elite-controlled mass media anymore. Today, stars are either "chosen" from a young age and built from the ground up by the industry, or are talented individuals like Emeli Sandé who are "recruited" and forced to become a "clown".

Clown is about submission, about giving up, about the victory of oppression over the human spirit, about giving in to pressure, about accepting temporary material gain for success, about signing over one's soul over to a powerful, oppressive group. For some reason, these messages must be communicated to the public, as if to subliminally demoralize the masses, to make sure that no real role models or icons – those who uphold certain values above anything else – are there to inspire and give hope to the world.

While the song is full of regret and melancholy, it is still a "victory speech" from the Illuminati to the masses. In a very simple and theatrical matter, Clown describes how the industry functions, how it treats its stars and how it forces them to sell their soul. Some might interpret Clown as Sandé "speaking out" against the industry. But the "moral of the story" being told is that she gave in. And now she's on TV. And she sang during the Olympics in front of a billion people in a ceremony that was tainted with the symbolism of the elite, the same group depicted as forcing her to sign that contract in her video. Before her Olympic performance, perhaps Sandé sang to herself "I'm selling out tonight".

Lil Wayne's "Love Me": A Video Glamorizing Kitten Programming

Lil Wayne single "Love Me" (featuring Drake and Future) appears to be another rap song about easy girls and so forth. The symbolism of the video however adds a more sinister dimension to the song: It directly refers to Monarch Mind Control, specifically Kitten Programming, and even refers to its techniques. We'll look at the symbolism of Lil Wayne's "Love Me".

At first glance, Love Me appears to be yet another song where rappers brag about how many "hos" they got. While some might shake their heads at the unoriginality of the subject matter, others might shake their heads at the way women are portrayed in the video. However, I'll add another reason to shake your head: Love Me refers to the most terrible practice on earth, Monarch Mind Control. In short, Beta Programming (also known as Kitten Programming) is used to create brainwashed sex slaves.

> This programming eliminates learned moral convictions and stimulates the primitive instincts devoid of inhibitions. This training Program (usually for women) is for developing the "ultimate prostitute". This is the most used (by the abusers knowledgeable of the Project Monarch) program.
> - Mark Phillips, Operation Monarch

As we'll see in this article, the video contains ALL of the possible symbolism relating to Kitten Programming and it also emphasizes the slave status of the women in the video. Lil Wayne's girls are literally locked in cages and depicted as animals. They are also shown in situations that subtly allude to actual MK torture techniques that used to traumatize slaves and cause them to dissociate from reality. Of course, everything is portrayed in a cool and fashionable matter, to make sure young people embrace all of this with even realizing it. Let's look at the meaning of the video.

Women as MK Slaves, Rappers as Handlers

The song is about how women apparently love Lil Wayne. In the video, they however don't seem to have much of a choice because they are TRAPPED IN CAGES, inside a very dodgy-looking compound. In the very first seconds of the video, we see a semi-subliminal image that announces what the video is all about.

Music Business

The song is about how women apparently love Lil Wayne. In the video, they however don't seem to have much of a choice because they are TRAPPED IN CAGES, inside a very dodgy-looking compound.

Future sings about how "b*tches love him"... but he's not about to free them from their cages. This contradictory scene somewhat relates to how MK slaves are programmed to identify with and even "love" their handler through confusing mind games.

Locking slaves in cages an actual Monarch Programming technique to discipline, traumatize and dehumanize the victims.

A painting made by trauma-based mind control survivor Kim Noble (from the article The World of Mind Control Through the Eyes of an Artist with 13 Alter Personas) depicting children locked in cages and observed by a handler.

The many close-up shots of girls during the video all somehow allude to an aspect of Kitten Programming. Here are some of them:

This model has a feline prints on her face (which is used in mass media to refer to Kitten programming). To make sure you get the message, she also has cat eyes and is licking her "paw". At this point, the video is basically screaming out KITTEN PROGRAMMING.

Licking a blade is maybe sexily dangerous, but also refers to the mix of inhibiting lust and physical abuse involved in Kitten Programming.

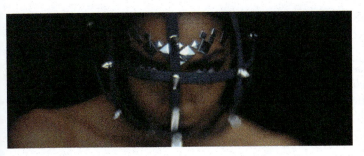
This headgear is reminiscent of BDSM stuff but is also a way to represent a slave's mind being trapped and controlled by a handler.

This model has a huge butterfly covering one of her eyes, which is probably the most blatant reference to Monarch mind control in the video.

In the video, Lil Wayne somewhat plays the role of the handler, where he's basically in control of these mesmerized women.

Here, Lil Wayne is in a bedroom that is full of water with women swimming in it. Aside from the fact that this water will probably cause a lot of water damage in that room, it is also a way to show that these slaves are literally "out of their element". Also, notice the frame on the left with butterflies in it. Yes, this is all about Monarch programming.

One of Lil Wayne's first rhymes is:

"These hos love me like Satan, man!"

We then see a quick flash of this image:

Lil Wayne as Satan, man.

This line is perplexing for a few reasons. Why do these "hos" love him like Satan? Is he implying that they were loving Satan to begin with? Whether it was intentional or not, this line has profound implications in the realm of Monarch Programming, as slaves are often victims of SRA (Satanic Ritual Abuse), are made to participate in traumatic rituals (where female slaves become "brides of Satan") and so forth. Sometimes MK handlers tell their slave they are Satan himself while they are abusing them to further trauma.

> *"Alters within a Monarch slave are conditioned by their servitude to believe that their life is controlled by Satan, who is stronger than God. Where was God when they needed him?"*
> - Fritz Springmeier, The Illuminati Formula to Create a Mind Control Slave

Another one of Wayne's rhymes is strangely reminiscent to the kind of dialogue a Kitten slave would have with a handler.

> *She say "I never wanna you make you mad,*
> *I just wanna make you proud"*
> *I say "baby, just make me c*m,*
> *Then don't make a sound"*

Soulless ... like a MK handler.

The last part of the video is also somewhat disturbing. It begins with "kittens" entering a white room. They then reach a bathtub full of red liquid (blood) and, for no apparent reason, make a big mess.

They move like cats. You know, like in Kitten programming.

The girls are all covered in blood, rolling around in it and everything. Is that supposed to be hot or something? Who in their right mind would do that? Nobody. But these women are NOT in their right mind.

Once again, this scene subtly refers to an actual Monarch practice that is used to traumatize slaves and engender dissociation.

> *"In searching for traumas to apply to little children, the Programmers found that these natural phobias which occur in most people from birth will work "wonderful" to split the mind. Along this line, the following are samples of traumas done to program slaves:*
> *(...) Immersion into feces, urine and containers of blood. Then being made to eat these things. These are standard traumas."*
> - Ibid.

While the real life implication of this scene is horrible, everything is nevertheless portrayed in a cool and stylized matter, where the models keep doing sensual faces to the camera (in real life, these faces would be completely distorted with pain).

In Conclusion

Like many other pop songs, Lil Wayne's Love Me has a simple surface meaning–him not caring about haters as long as his "hos" love him–but the music video adds a very sinister underlying meaning. Regular readers of this site understand that there's an undeniable pattern of reoccurring symbolism in popular culture and Love Me definitely adds to it. Indeed, in this video, ALL of the symbolism that is associated with Kitten Programming (one eye, butterflies, animal prints, etc.) is represented in the video, along with various references to real life Monarch Programming practices. While each individual element could have been present in the video to symbolize something else than MK-Ultra, tell me … what are the odds that ALL of these symbols being "randomly" inserted in one, four-minute video? As is the case for other videos reviewed on this site, it is not about pointing out single instances of random symbols, but understanding each piece as a whole and the hidden realities it refers to. One these hidden realities is Monarch programming, one of the occult elite's favorite practices, one that can be traced back to what Springmeier calls "generational satanic families".

While rap has always had a healthy dose of macho bravado, Love Me is a deformation of this "tradition", as it adds a sick, perverted twist to it, including allusions to violence, abuse and even torture. As years go by, this "pushing of the envelope" becomes more apparent as the original culture around hip-hop is slowly but surely becoming "Illuminati-friendly". Like many other movements in society, hip-hop has been co-opted by the elite to be used as a tool to indoctrinate young people. Are there still real rappers out there? Yes, tons of them. But you'll probably never seen them on the Grammys.

Azealia Banks' "Yung Rapunxel": New Artist, Same Illuminati Symbolism

Azealia Banks is a new rap artist garnering a lot of media attention. Unsurprisingly, her first major single is dedicated 100% to Illuminati symbolism and the Elite Agenda. We'll look at the occult symbolism of the video "Yung Rapunxel", more proof that the Illuminati Agenda is becoming increasingly prevalent with each new artist going "pop".

Azealia Banks signed with Interscope Records (home of countless "industry puppets") in 2011 and since then, she's basically been all about Illuminati symbolism ... and a strange Internet controversy. I first heard of Azealia Banks in 2012 when the music producer Munchi got mad at her and tweeted: "Go be a puppet bitch to someone else". Azealia then replied "@originalmunchi thinks I'm in the illuminati... I'm being very serious right now."

Munchi then posted more details on Facebook. Regarding the "Illuminati" reference, he wrote.

> "I think she is in the Illuminati (thirsty for fame and success by portraying occult references in every step you take is not something i want to affiliate with. Even less because it is a hype nowadays, it's fucking music yo)."

One year later, watching her first single Yung Rapunxel, we can conclude that Munchi was right. Of course, she is not IN the Illuminati. She is just another face used to push the same Agenda that is being pushed by countless other artists. Yung Rapunxel is indeed a rehashing of a lot of the Illuminati symbolism described on this site, mixed with some disturbing images for extra shock value. There is no deep storyline going on, just some strong visuals that blatantly communicate that she is completely on board with the Elite Agenda. Let's look at the symbolism of the video.

In Your Face Illuminati

Yung Rapunxel recalls the name "Rapunzel", the fairy tale princess who was trapped in a tower and who used her long hair to allow her Prince Charming to climb up to her. However, the video has absolutely nothing to do with any of that: It's all disturbing images and Illuminati symbolism. Nothing more, nothing less. As usual, the artist is portrayed as a person with little to no control over her own mind, surrounded with the elite's symbolism and, to top it off, some police state promotion.

The video begins with an image that sums up the whole situation at hand.

An owl with an eye of a different color flies out of Azealia's head, who also has one eye of a different color. Yes, another one-eye signal by a pop artist, very original. The owl is the most ancient symbol representing the Illuminati. Does the fact that it flies out of her head represent the fact that her mind is owned by Illuminati people?

The first level of the Bavarian Illuminati was called "Minerval" and was represented by Minerva's Owl. This pendant was worn by actual Bavarian Illuminati initiates. The logo of the Bohemian Grove, the elite's yearly gathering in California, is also an owl.

Inside Azealia's head, there's some hypnotic stuff going on, all related to Duality. MK Slaves are programmed to have a dualistic mind, with one personality mirroring and opposing the other. The above symbols closely resemble an important symbol in Wicca: the Triple Goddess.

Inside Azeala's head, there are multiple symbols representing the concept of duality such as the opposition of the colors black and white, the waning and waxing moon and the circular Yin Yang symbol. Also, the Hamsa symbol (the hand with an All-Seeing Eye) is there – probably to add an All-Seeing Eye to the mix.

A Triple Goddess pendant. In Wiccan mythology, the opposite of the Triple Goddess is the horned god, which represents masculine energy.

In this scene, Azealia is riding a bull – an ancient symbol representing the masculine principle. Above her is an upright moon crescent, an esoteric symbol representing the female principle. The combination of the two with the sexual connotation of the scene make it a representation of "sex magick" through the union of opposites.

While not inherently "evil", the symbols described above are definitely not there to communicate profound messages about the meaning of life. They're there because they represent the occult elite, ruled by secret societies like the O.T.O who revel in that symbolism. In short, it is about indoctrinating people with symbols they know nothing about because they represent those who rule the world. One scene appears to be reflecting this idea.

Azealia swallowing a pill that's actually mini "Beats by Dre" audio speaker. A great way of representing "swallowing" the Illuminati Agenda through entertainment acts.

Here, Azealia raps in front of a giant triangle topped by an All-Seeing Eye while owls fly around her. Could this be more blatantly Illuminati?

As if all of the above imagery wasn't enough to make this video an Illuminati manifesto, there is yet another crucial part of the Agenda that is in this video: Police State imagery. In the 2010 article "The Transhumanist and Police State Agenda in Pop Music", I described how videos are used to normalize the concept of a repressive police state. More than three years later, the trend is more prevalent than ever. Yung Rapunxel is yet another pop video featuring, for no apparent reason, police in riot gear.

Go away, nobody wants to see that in a music video.

At first, Azealia "rebels" against the police by doing something that is beyond useless: She breaks a glass bottle on the police's protective gear. Of course, this "rebellion" causes no damage the police squad at all. What's the point of that scene? Is it a way of saying that it is useless to fight against the police state?

Well, Azealia apparently thinks so because she gives up and she even literally bends over backwards in front of the police.

Azealia is probably not the best person to lead a revolution. Breaking a bottle on a helmet and bending over backwards is not a winning strategy.

With this, I pretty much described every single scene in the video – all of them having some sort of relation with the Elite Agenda. Oh wait, I forgot about one scene:

What is this? Kill it with fire!

In Conclusion

It is rather difficult to watch Yung Rapunxel without being slightly annoyed and disturbed by it. Many "edgy" Illuminati videos indeed leave viewers with a "wrong" and "uneasy" gut feeling because they tend to tap into negative energy. Judging by Yung Rapunxel's YouTube "likes" and "dislikes", this video is definitely not a fan favorite – and I'm guessing that those in charge were kind of expecting that response. But yet, it's there, as if to say that the Agenda is more important than the artist. Her Interscope Records label-mate Lady Gaga also released disturbing Illuminati-fueled videos and in doing so alienated a lot of her fan base who didn't relate to that crap. But, once again, the Agenda is more important than the artist. If people get tired of an artist, another one will get signed and push the same thing.

Some might say: "LOL Azealia be trollin yall conspararcy peeps with that Illumanaty shyt!". That's what I've been told countless times about Gaga, Ke$ha, Rihanna and many others. Those attempting to rationalizing this strong current maintain that these artists are doing it on purpose to get sites like Vigilant Citizen riled up. Does it make sense that all of the biggest stars in the world, with the million dollar machine backing them, are gearing their entire product towards "trolling" a few Internet websites in order to MAYBE get mentioned by them? That doesn't make sense. The fact is: The music industry is used by the powers that be to indoctrinate young people and push a specific Agenda. And if a rapper jumping around in front of a pyramid, All-Seeing Eyes and owls and submitting to an oppressive police force is not enough to convince you, then I guess nothing will.

Fjögur Píanó, a Viral Video About Monarch Mind Control?

The viral video Fjögur Píanó has been viewed several million times, but not many understand what it is truly about. While there is a great deal of mystery about the video, one thing is certain: There is a lot of mind control symbolism in the video. We'll look at the hidden meaning behind Fjögur Píanó.

Watching Fjögur Píanó is a strange experience. There's Shia Leboeuf and some girl naked, there's weird piano playing in the background, and a whole lot of butterflies. There's some dancing, some fighting and lollipops with little scorpions inside. What the hell is going on? And why? I won't claim that this article will fully decode this head-scratcher, but a lot of its symbolism strongly hints towards a specific concept: Monarch Mind Control. While this video is very unique and original (unlike many of the videos analyzed on this site), it nevertheless contains many classic elements of Monarch mind-control symbolism. When these symbols are decoded, the story starts to make a little more sense and an underlying message begins to surface

Fjögur Píanó is part of the series of videos accompanying the new album from the Icelandic band Sigur Rós. The band asked a dozen filmmakers to each choose a song from its album, Valtari, and shoot a video inspired by the music. All the directors received the same $10,000 budget and "zero instructions from the band". Probably due to its high profile cast and unexpected nudity, Fjögur Píanó quickly became a viral sensation, garnering media attention and millions of views across the web.

The video was directed by Alma Har'el, an Israeli filmmaker, who is known for directing music videos for several bands, as well as TV spots for Obama's first presidential campaign in 2008. Contrarily to her TV commercials, Har'el's work for Fjögur Píanó is strange, disturbing and difficult to comprehend. While it is somewhat impossible to extract a coherent narrative from the video, understanding some of its symbolism helps make sense of it. While some might interpret the video as being about difficult relationships, there are elements that seem to allude to something deeper and more disturbing. For example, why are there "outside people" controlling the main characters' environment? Let's look at the scenes of the short video.

Dazed and Confused

Right from the start, it is evident that the couple featured in this video is very confused, not in control of their destiny and trapped in a very restrained world.

The couple wakes up dazed and confused in a room that used to have frames hanged on the wall.

Shia and his girlfriend (played by Denna Thomsen) wake up with all kinds of bruises and marks on their bodies, but they do not seem to remember why. Obviously, a lot of abuse and violence happened to them the day before.

After waking up, Shia sees tally marks on Denna's back, similar to those used by prisoners to count days behind bars. This suggests both individuals are in a state of forced confinement, and the "prison" is apparently their own bodies.

The couple then engages in a choreographed dance that alludes to sexuality mixed with dominance and violence.

While dancing, Shia and Denna are wearing each others clothes. In Mind Control, the occult concept of the union of opposites is extremely important and used during programming. Are Shia and Denna actually two sides of the same person?

At the end of the dance, Shia and Denna perform a symbolic gesture: They "remove" their faces with their hand and then "let them go". The concept of removing faces or masks is used in actual mind-control programming to represent to removal and subsequent replacement of the core persona with alter personas. In the context of the video, there is a definite sense of the loss and confusion of identity between the two. They might even be two opposite sides of the same person.

The Handlers

After the dance, two strange dudes enter the room and give the couple suspicious-looking lollipops with scorpions inside. Since scorpions are known to be venomous insects, there is reason to believe that these lollipops aren't simply pieces of candy but most probably mind-altering drugs, such as those used in mind-control programming. The couple eagerly sucks on these lollipops, indicating that they are helplessly addicted to them.

Distracted by the candy given by his handlers, Shia doesn't seem to realize that he is being blindfolded and taken for a ride.

Simply by blowing on them, the handlers are able to get the couple to go where they want it to go. The fact that no physical contact is necessary to control the couple implies that it is all about … mind control.

While the handlers are taking the couple to another location, the camera focuses on an image featuring the one-eye sign along with a hole in heart – symbols associated with and used in Monarch programming.

The couple is ushered into a car where they take a "virtual" ride, with one of the handler in the driver's seat.

The car is not moving but images projected on a screen give the impression they are going to exotic places. This is reminiscent of the concept of dissociation in mind control, the process of causing the mind control subject to disconnect from reality, mentally transporting somewhere without ever actually moving.

In another scene, there isn't even a car. In other words, it is all about illusion. The "ride" is actually happening in the minds of the victims and the handlers (in MK, handlers are often under mind control as well).

Inside the car, the couple is completely obsessed with the lollipops, licking them in a lascivious and sexual way. The animal prints on Shia's clothing and inside the car hint to Beta (also known as Sex Kitten) Programming. In this type of programming, MK slaves are often given libido-inducing drugs.

Back in the Room

After the psychedelic ride, the couple is taken back to their room. The empty walls are now filled with frames containing dead butterflies, a sight that visibly disturbs the couple. After the buzz of the drugs, harsh reality settles in and the couple appears to have a rare moment of lucidity.

Shia is extremely concerned about the butterflies on the wall. These are not there simply for mere decoration – they represent something dark in profound. Perhaps they remind them of their state of mind control?

The couple then gets sexy and sensual, but Shia appears to be obsessed with a specific face, which he draws on Denna's body. He then draws the face on cardboard.

Unmistakable with his shiny third eye, Shia drew the face of his handler on Denna. Is she a creation of his handler?

As if to confirm the fact that Denna is a split from Shia's personality created by his handlers, Denna immediately shows what she truly is.

Denna takes a butterfly frame from the wall and shows it to Shia, as if saying "Look, this is what is happening to us. We are under mind control!".

Shia then appears extremely confused, going from tears, to laughter to anger. Obviously not happy about whatever Denna has told him, he breaks the butterfly frame. At this point, Denna apparently disappears and Shia is alone with himself – another hint pointing to the fact that she's part of his split personality. He then does something that is found in almost every single mind-control themed video:

Shia breaks a mirror, a symbolic image that represents his attempt to break from his programming. If you've read other articles on this site, you know that this gesture is almost inevitably found in fiction relating to mind control.

After destroying his room, Shia turns finds his girlfriend again (or the opposite side of himself) and starts hitting her.

As the couple fight, a scene shows a porcelain doll being broken with blood coming out of it. In mind-control programming, slaves are often depicted as dolls or puppets, which represent their powerlessness against their handlers.

After the fight, Shia adds a tally mark on Denna's back – another day as a mind control slave. Exhausted, they fall asleep.

Shia sleeps next to the same butterfly he woke up with. Despite all of his efforts, he is still under Monarch Programming.

The handlers then come in the room to clean it up and to remove the frames from the wall, leaving it in the same state it was the morning before. The couple then wakes up in the same way they did before, with the same bruises and scars. They start another day in the never-ending, mind-numbing loop that is the life of a mind-controlled slave.

In Conclusion

Fjögur Píanó is a cryptic and strange video that has been described as a "dream sequence without a narrative" by some critics. However, by decoding some of the video's symbolism, we discover that there is a story being told, one that is told in a very figurative fashion. The "official" explanation of the video states that it is about a difficult relationship and the many butterflies represent "beautiful things that die fast". While this might explain some of the video, there are other elements that cannot be ignored. The couple is obviously living in a state of virtual imprisonment, where every aspect of their lives are manipulated by outside forces: Shia and Denna's living environment is controlled and modified by the handlers; they are drugged, blindfolded and forcibly taken on weird, dissociative trips; and their attempts to break free are useless. In short, the couple is utterly powerless versus the world around them – the only thing they can do is add another tally mark on Denna's back.

In a somewhat hip, artistic and fashionable matter, Fjögur Píanó tells the story of mind-control slaves. While many have applauded the video's "genius", most have not understood its underlying meaning. In the end, viewers watching the video are like the couple in Fjögur Píanó: Taken for a ride, without any idea where they are being taken.

MTV VMAs 2013: It Was About Miley Cyrus Taking the Fall

The 2013 edition of the VMAs was not about music. It wasn't even about the symbolism I've described in past years. It was basically MTV saying: "There is nothing to celebrate in pop music this year, here's an awkward, cringe-worthy display of everything that is wrong in the entertainment industry".

I've written extensive articles about past VMA awards because they were filled with occult symbolism and messages. This year, not so much. It was about promoting major artists and their newest albums. But mostly, it was about providing a "shocking" moment that would get mass media talking for days. Miley Cyrus provided it.

Miley Cyrus: The Industry Slave Chosen to Take the Fall

Miley Cyrus' display at the VMAs was qualified by many as "trashy" and "embarrassing". It was indeed a strange sight to see. It was as if she was doing it on purpose to embarrass herself. Well, here's a moment of clarity: It WAS done on purpose and, moreseo, it was ALL staged. People commenting on Miley Cyrus appear to forget one, massive detail: There is an enormous marketing machine behind Miley Cyrus and there always was.

Miley's image has been heavily marketed by Disney since the days she took on the role of Hannah Montana – a girl who (appropriately enough) had a stage alter persona, with a different wig. Hannah Montana products often had butterflies on them, a slick reminder of how she was a Disney programming slave.

Until 2013, Miley was signed with Hollywood Records, a record label that was founded by Michael Eisner, the CEO of Disney. Hollywood Records also owns other child stars such as Demi Lovato, Selena Gomez and the Jonas

Brothers. Every artist in the record label's stable has a carefully crafted image to be marketed to its target public. Miley is now working with Britney Spears' ex-manager Larry Rudolph and signed with RCA records – one of the biggest music labels in the world that owns the likes of Justin Timberlake, Britney Spears and Ke$ha.

As a product of Mickey Mouse programming, Miley underwent a classic "good girl gone bad" treatment. Once a good, wholesome daddy's girl, Miley has turned into a bratty, sex freak who keeps sticking out her tongue and twerking for no reason. While most people are probably tsking at Miley, they do not realize that this whole thing coincided with the release of her new album – and that it was all ordered by her handlers. In other words, she was selected and programmed to be this year's main example of a "good girl gone bad", a process the occult elite wants the public to constantly witness. They want the masses to see innocence and wholesomeness turn into sleaze and trash. They want pop culture and the youth in general follow the same process. While alchemy is about turning stone into gold, the masses are made to witness the opposite process.

Miley's VMA performance is about a child star who was beloved by millions of young people showing what the industry has done to her. It is about shattering the innocence of her fans by having them witness her metamorphosis into one giant sex-obsessed caricature. I'm using the word caricature because it is safe to say that Miley was not 100% herself during the VMA's. Her oversexualized demeanor was characteristic of a Beta programming slave who had the switch turned "on". It was, however, not only about being overtly sexual. It was also (and mostly) about being annoying and embarrassing herself – as if it was a sick, humiliating ritual. Dressed and styled to look like a bratty child, jumping around with giant teddy bears, Miley's performance was all about getting a negative reaction from the public while continuing the ongoing agenda of sexualizing everything that is related to childhood.

Things got even stranger when Robin Thicke came out to perform Blurred Lines. As its name somewhat stipulates, that song blurs the line between being a flirty and all-out creepy. Its video has a strange handler-slave vibe, where Robin, Pharell and T.I. are all sharply dressed while the women dancing around them are completely naked … and being sung lines such as "You're an animal".

While "Blurred Lines" appears to be nothing more than a "fun and sexy video", the fact that the singers are fully dressed while the models are completely naked denotes a strong relationship of dominance. Forcing slaves to be naked while the masters are dressed is a classic psychological ploy to make slaves feel powerless, vulnerable and inferior.

It is therefore not a coincidence that Miley sang this particular song during the VMAs. Her whole act goes with the spirit of the song and, like in the video, there's a handler/slave relationship going on in during the performance.

As Miley was going crazy on stage, shots of the audience revealed how it was not amused. Facial expressions were ranging from shock, to despair to "WTF". One could almost feel the hate emanating from the room – and the entire nation – while she was performing. And that is what "they" (Miley's handlers) were gunning for. Miley was primed and set up to take that fall. Miley was even ridiculed during the intro of her own performance. The MTV awards needed its trademark "shock" moment and the industry needed its "sacrificial lamb" to keep its sick, occult, MK-Ultra system going.

During "Blurred Lines" Miley acted like a true Beta programming slave – while Robin acted like a handler. His strange suit featured a dualistic pattern that is used during the programming actual MK slaves. There was also something strange about seeing 20-year-old girl (dressed to look younger) rubbing herself on this 36-year-old (married) man.

While the "controversy" around Miley might help her sell more records for a while, the ongoing public humiliation that is forced on her by her handlers will most likely lead to some kind of meltdown in the future. In an article published in 2011, Miley's father Billy Ray Cyrus stated that her handlers (that's the word he used) cut him out of the loop and told him to "mind his business". Like other industry slaves, Miley has no contact with her family. In the interview, Billy Ray added that "Satan was attacking his family" that he was afraid to see her go down the same tragic path as Anna Nicole Smith (a Beta Kitten slave) and Michael Jackson (killed by the industry).

This performance and the public backlash that followed is proof of the tight control the industry has on its slaves. I am pretty sure that, deep down inside, Miley knew that this is all ridiculous and embarrassing. But there's nothing she can do about it.

Lady Gaga

Other than Miley Cyrus, Lady Gaga also got a little attention. Her new single Applause is basically a continuation of her "Fame Monster" theme where she's a performer that desperately seeks attention and fame. Gaga is ready to do anything to get it, even if that means doing the elite's bidding and throwing around its symbols.

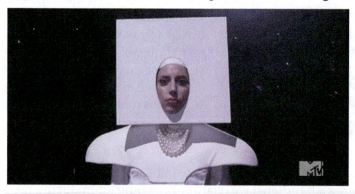

Gaga began her performance with her head inside a white square – as if saying that she's a "blank canvas". She is ready to be painted in any way possible to get applause.

We quickly see who "paints" Gaga.

During her first verse, Gaga wears the wig she had in the videos from her first album such as Paparazzi. She does the one-eye thing to make sure you know that her blank canvas was filled by the Illuminati Agenda.

During the second verse, she wears the wig she had in the video "Telephone" – the video was about MK programming and killing civilians ... remember? She does the one-eye thing again so you know that was also part of the Illuminati Agenda.

In the last part of her performance, Gaga unveils her last "persona" – an embodiment of the goddess Venus as depicted in "The Birth of Venus" by Botticelli.

Why did Gaga embody Venus? The association between the planet Venus and lust goes back thousands of years – since the times of Ishtar, the Babylonian goddess of sex and lust who was associated with Venus.

Gaga spent the rest of the VMAs as Venus, basically sitting there in a thong, letting people know that she is now Venus, goddess of sex. There is also a second, occult level to the importance of Venus in occult mysteries.

> "As the morning star, Venus is visible before sunrise, and as the evening star it shines forth immediately after sunset. Because of these qualities, a number of names have been given to it by the ancients. Being visible in the sky at sunset, it was called vesper, and as it arose before the sun, it was called the false light, the star of the morning, or Lucifer, which means the light-bearer. Because of this relation to the sun, the planet was also referred to as Venus, Astarte, Aphrodite, Isis, and The Mother of the

Gods."
- Manly P. Hall, The Secret Teachings of All Ages

The "Mother Monster" is apparently now the "Mother Goddess". Gaga's performance was, in short, a tribute to her past personas, and the "birth" of a new one – one that fits with the mythology and symbolism of the occult elite.

In Conclusion

While mass media backlash against Miley Cyrus is solely directed at Miley Cyrus, the big picture is completely being missed (or ignored). If "observers" and "critics" took their faces out of her bony behind and took a step back, they would maybe see what is truly happening: Miley Cyrus is, more than ever, owned and controlled by an enormous machine. Her image, her music and her performance is fully determined by her handlers. For some sick reason, she was chosen this year to embarrass herself and to traumatize all of the young people who grew up watching her. Miley was offered as a "sacrifice" to the public while adding to the complete breakdown of popular culture. Her performance was choreographed and staged to be as annoying and distasteful as possible. From the bratty hair, to the unflattering outfit, to the constant sticking out of the tongue, to the obsession with "twerking" without having the physical attributes to pull it off ... it was all planned to piss the world off.

While the masses are laughing and pointing at Miley Cyrus, those who handle her are laughing and pointing at the masses ... because they're falling right into this sick humiliation process. While I am not looking to add to the Miley Cyrus noise, someone needs to say it: She's a puppet and we need to look at those who are pulling the strings. We also need to look at what they are doing to people such as Miley Cyrus and, more importantly, to our youth in general. This is not about a single girl who lost her way, it is about a system making the world lose its way.

A-JAX and Ladies' Code: Two Blatant Examples of Mind Control Culture in K-Pop

Illuminati mind control symbolism does not only exist in the Western world. In Asia, the widely popular K-Pop scene is also replete with the same imagery. We'll look at the symbolism of A-JAX's "Insane" and Ladies' Code "Hate You", two blatant examples that prove the elite's symbolism is truly international.

K-Pop (pop music from South Korea) has garnered an incredible following across the world as its machine keeps creating new boy and girl bands and music videos that become instant YouTube hits. The "Korean wave" has hit not only Asia, but also Latin America, Northeast India, the Middle East, and North Africa. However, while K-Pop appears to have become somewhat of an alternative to Western pop culture, it is not exempt from the Illuminati symbolism and the Agenda found in Western pop. In fact, the symbolism is often more blatant and in-your-face with K-Pop videos, causing me to ask: Is K-Pop truly an alternative to Western pop or just an effective way for the elite to get its message across in Asia?

A quick look at K-Pop videos such as A-JAX's "Insane" and Ladies' Code "Hate You" is all it takes to realize that mind control symbolism is as heavily pushed in K-Pop than it is in the West. In fact, both of these videos basically read like a MK-101 manual, using all of the symbols associated with it and portraying the stars as slaves. K-Pop has effectively become another outlet for the elite to promote its "mind control culture", even alluding to its sadistic practices in stylish videos aimed at young (and unaware) people. Let's look at the videos and see how they fit right in with the MK Agenda that is also pushed in the Western world.

A-JAX's "Insane"

A-JAX is one of these K-Pop "idol" boy bands that were completely created by a record label and reality TV. Their video "Insane" contains all of the hallmarks of MK symbolism. Furthermore, it clearly depicts the singers as mind-controlled slaves who are hypnotized in a mental institution and dissociate to a world full of MK symbolism. How much clearer can it get?

The video takes place in a mental institution room, where the band members held there are constantly hypnotized by creepy doctors. Throughout the video, the members dissociate to an alternate world while physically staying in the room. Causing a slave to dissociate is the basic premise of Monarch mind control and the video clearly refers to this. Why expose children to this sick practice? Because it is part of the elite's Agenda.

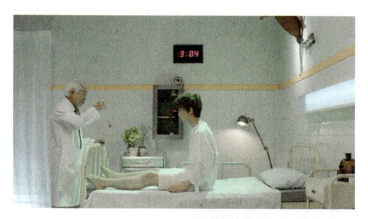 

The singer is in a room and hypnotized by a handler. Throughout the video, the clock displays random times, probably emphasize the fact that MK slaves lose all sense of time. Above the singer is a Baphomet head (we do not fully see it in this shot). This symbolic figure is an anchor point for the slave's alternate worlds.

The video completely conforms to the "codes" of MK culture: Here, the slave's dissociation is represented by "going through the looking glass".

As seen in previous articles, "going through the looking glass" is the classic symbol for dissociating from reality. It was taken from Alice in Wonderland, a story that is used as a tool to program slaves.

When the slave goes through the mirror, he enters his "internal world" as programmed by his handler.

In one scene, the "inner psyche" is represented by a room full of mirrors.

Those behind the making of the video appear to have a good knowledge of Monarch programming, because this is exactly how the internal world of Monarch slaves is made to be.

> "In programming Monarch slaves, mirrors are used a great deal. Within the Monarch slave's mind, countless mirror images are made. The slave sees thousands of mirrors everywhere in their mind."
> - Fritz Springmeier, The Illuminati Formula to Create a Mind Control Slave

The slaves then goes through another mirror and ends in another VERY symbolic scene: A room that solely consists of dualistic black and white patterns.

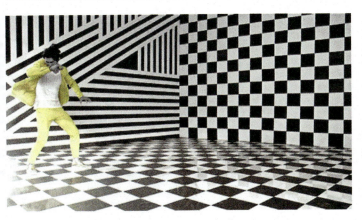
The pattern of this room was not randomly chosen: Dualistic patterns are used to program/hypnotize MK slaves.

This painting by Monarch slave survivor Kim Noble (read the article about her here) clearly shows the importance of the pattern in MK programming. The similarities between the music video and this painting is too striking to ignore.

The video clearly shows that the scenes of dissociation are happening in the slave's mind.

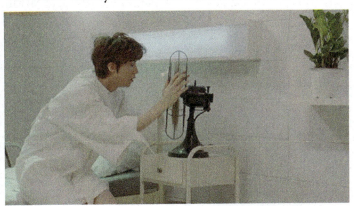
After seeing this guy in the checkerboard room with wind blowing at him, we see him in the hospital room facing a fan, implying that he is physically in the institution but that his mind has completely dissociated.

This singer has dissociated to another room. There are pentagrams all over his clothes. Combined with the Baphomet head behind him, this scene refers to the black magic rituals that happen during the slaves' programming.

At one point, the Baphomet-head's eyeballs creepily turn towards the viewers, emphasizing its importance and letting you know that "it is watching you".

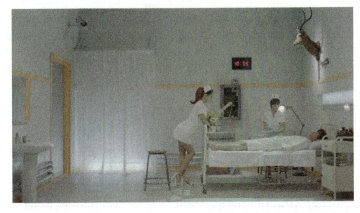
What kind of institution room has a Baphomet head right above the patient's bed while he's being hypnotized? A mind control programming site ... nowhere else.

Close-ups of the video camera tell the viewers that these A-JAX guys are not simply "Insane", they are being monitored and controlled by their handlers.

The slave holds the "key to his psyche" but, as we can see here, it consists of two rear ends with no key, hinting to the fact that slaves do not own the key to their own mind.

All of this leads to the ultimate goal of Monarch programming: The fracturing of the core persona and the creation of new ones.

The multiplication of the slave into new personas.

Almost every single frame of "Insane" is filled with imagery associated with and used in MK programming. While the song is about them being "insane", we clearly see that there is a lot more going on there. The singers are actively being hypnotized, monitored and controlled to dissociate from reality. Combined with occult symbolism, the video gives a complete picture of what MK culture is all about.

Ladies' Code "Hate You"

Reading the title of the song and a translation of the lyrics, most people would believe that "Hate You" is about a girl that hates her boyfriend but cannot leave him. However, the imagery of the video communicates something a lot more disturbing. There are absolutely no references to a love relationship in the video but plenty of references to another kind of relationship: One between an MK slave and her handler. Not only is the video replete with the basic symbolism we've seen in previous articles, it symbolically portrays the sick relationship between a programmed slaves and a sadistic handler.

The girl is sitting in a room full of dolls (which represent the slave's alter personas). On the wall are tally marks used by prisoners to count days behind bars. We therefore understand that the girl is "confined" and held there against here will. For a split second, the image of a caterpillar appears on screen.

Immediately after, the image of a butterfly appears on screen – the symbol of Monarch (a type of butterfly) programming.

When we combine the dolls, the tally marks and the butterfly, we obtain a clear reference to Monarch programming.

> "The name MONARCH is not necessarily defined within the context of royal nobility, but rather refers to the monarch butterfly.
>
> When a person is undergoing trauma induced by electroshock, a feeling of light-headedness is evidenced; as if one is floating or fluttering like a butterfly. There is also a symbolic representation pertaining to the transformation or metamorphosis of this beautiful insect: from a caterpillar to a cocoon (dormancy, inactivity), to a butterfly (new creation) which will return to its point of origin. Such is the migratory pattern that makes this species unique."
> - Ron Patton, Project Monarch

While the two above frames are pure mind control imagery, the rest of the video makes everything clearer regarding its true meaning.

Here the singer innocently (yet creepily) plays with a marionette.

She then becomes the marionette, controlled by unseen hands – a classic way of depicting an MK slave.

The other singers appear in similar scenes. They first play the role of the handler, then the slave.

The singer holds the doll in a forceful, restrictive way.

She is then held herself by unseen handlers.

This singer gives the doll a cruel and unusual punishment: she burns one of its eyes using a magnifying glass.

We then see her with an eye patch, implying that she got the same treatment and that she is a slave herself. Also, this is a slick way of flashing the unavoidable one-eye sign.

Speaking of the unavoidable one-eye sign, here it is again.

In this scene, the two singers are sitting behind a plate full of dolls that were torn apart. This is a symbol used to represent powerless and fragmented MK slaves. Like in A-JAX's video, there's a horned figure "presiding" over the scene.

This singer is strategically placed in front of the horns, making them appear as if they were sticking out of her head. This indicates that she is playing an MK handler. Here, she is holding a doll's head while brushing its hair.

For a split second, the image of a Baphomet-like skull flashes on her face, emphasizing the fact that these horns are not there for random reasons.

She then holds the doll's hair, confirming that she was a handler basically torturing (scalping) a slave represented by the doll.

A slave literally bound to her handler.

As the large number of screenshots taken from this video suggest, "Hate You" is pretty much a non-stop compilation of Monarch programming imagery. The members of Ladies' Code are made to play the role of handlers and slaves, symbolically recreating some of the horrendous torture actual slaves have to live through. The chorus, which repeats "I hate you" three times to end with "but I love you", can be interpreted as MK who despise their sadistic handlers, but that are nevertheless programmed into feeling something resembling love towards them. Sick? Yes.

In Conclusion

If you're a regular reader of this site, you can by now easily recognize the specific set of symbols that is used by the occult elite its promote MK culture. Those who are part of the Monarch programming system have created a disturbing culture surrounding it, complete with esthetics and symbols that are now omnipresent in mass media. All of this is packaged with catchy tunes and good-looking performers, which causes young people to subliminally associate this culture with positive feelings, even making it fashionable. As the above videos prove, this is all becoming increasingly blatant and interpreting these videos through the mind-control lens is almost impossible.

While the mind-control culture appears to have originated in the United States, the exact same set of symbols and meanings are also present in the booming South Korean pop scene. The fact that this is happening proves two things: First, the set of symbols I describe in videos is NOT a result of coincidence. It is cohesive imagery that originates from Monarch mind control. Second, it is obvious that at the top of all music industries, whether it be in America, Europe or Asia, the same occult elite are promoting the same Agenda. Why does Baphomet have to be in all of these videos across the world? Because the horned head represents those in power, and those in power are not your locally elected politicians, but a global elite. Through these videos, you are being told what the elite believes in and the sick practices it engages in. Are people rebelling against this? No, quite to contrary, they are dancing to it and paying money to purchase it. I guess A-JAX aren't the only ones who are Insane.

Britney Spears' "Work B*tch" and Iggy Azalea's "Change Your Life": Two Videos Celebrating Kitten Programming

*Britney Spears and Iggy Azalea were born on opposite sides of the world, but their videos "Work B*tch" and "Change Your Life" contain the same exact hidden meaning. Indeed, the symbolism of these videos are both celebrations of the mind control culture of the Illuminati entertainment industry, especially Kitten Programming.*

There are plenty of differences between Britney Spears and Iggy Azalea: Britney is from the U.S. while Iggy is from Australia; Britney is a veteran in the music business while Iggy is a newcomer; Britney sings pop while Iggy raps. Despite these surface differences, they both ultimately work for the same bosses who use their sex appeal to push the Illuminati Agenda. Work B*tch and Change Your Life were both released around the same time, they both take place in a "Las Vegas showgirl" context and they both convey the same exact twisted message: Being an industry Kitten is great because it will make you rich, famous and even powerful. Both videos are all about glamorizing the Mind-Control culture the occult elite revels in – although it is all about violent, disgusting and sadistic exploitation.

While on the surface, these videos appear to be about "empowerment" (I hate that word), they are actually celebrating the entertainment industry's exploitation of victims of Kitten programming. Let's look at the insidious symbolism of these videos.

Work B*tch

When one knows about Britney Spears' actual living conditions and mental state in the past few years, watching Work B*tch becomes somewhat difficult, as its message is ironic in the saddest way possible. In my several articles on Britney, I have described how, since her meltdown, she has become a literal slave, heavily medicated and with absolutely no power over her career, finances or personal life. Britney has been living under the conservatorship of various handlers since 2008, meaning that, during all of these years, she has never gained back control of her life.

Considering these facts, the lyrics of Work B*tch become somewhat disturbing, as they appear to be words a pimp who say to his "employee". Or what a Beta Kitten handler would tell an MK slave (like Britney) …

You wanna hot body
You want a Bugatti
You wanna Maserati
You better work b*tch
You want a Lamborghini
Sip martinis
Look hot in a bikini
You better work b*tch
You wanna live fancy
Live in a big mansion
Party in France

You better work b*tch

In the song and video, Britney plays the role of the handler who is yelling stuff at her slaves … the same kind of stuff she is probably told on a daily basis. Like most of Britney's recent releases, the song is almost ridiculing her condition, as if her handlers are saying: "Look at what we're doing with her. We're making her sing about her own captivity". To make things worse, Britney sings the song with a British accent. While, at first glance, this fact might be trivial, remember that in 2008, when Britney went through a gigantic meltdown, she was caught speaking with a British accent – a symptom of Multiple Personality Disorder, which is itself a symptom of Monarch Programming.

Knowing this fact, making Britney sing in a British accent is almost a code for showing that she's embodying another persona. She's a MK handler.

In the video, Britney bosses around Beta Kitten slaves around (they even have kitten ears), whipping them into submission and calling them bitches. Knowing Britney's condition, this is all rather twisted

This scene defines the entire video. Britney is holding Beta Kittens on a leash, controlling them. She stands on an inverted pyramid, perhaps to highlight the fact that Britney is actually NOT at the top of the pyramid. She is actually at the bottom of it, not unlike these leashed kittens.

Some might say: "That's an empowering video! Britney is being empowered! She empowers her fans by seeing her being so empowered!" Did I mention that I hate the word "empowered"? To empower means "to give power". Watching a video does not give you power. It actually accomplishes the exact opposite. Those who use the word "empowering" to describe a music video remind me of a Simpsons line about the word "proactive": "Excuse me, but "proactive" and "paradigm"? Aren't these just buzzwords that dumb people use to sound important?".

Britney herself admitted that she was not "empowered" by the video. Shortly after the release of the video, Britney called a radio station and stated that she was pressured into its highly sexualized concept, something she wants to stop doing ever since she became a mother. However, as stated above, she has no power over her own life or work.

Britney Spears implies she's being pressured to keep sexed-up image

Is Britney Spears being pressured to be overly sexual? That's what the pop star implied during a radio interview.

Spears told a Boston radio show that she wants to be more modest but she's pressured to maintain her sexy image. When discussing her latest music video for "Work Bitch," Spears said she made editors cut out a lot of the sexed-up scenes.

"Oh my God we showed way more skin and did way more stuff for the video than what is actually there," she said. "I cut, like, out half the video because I am a mother and because, you know, I have children and it's hard to play sexy mom while you're, you know, being a pop star as well."

The radio host then asked Spears straight out if she had people pushing her to shoot sexy scenes. She laughed and replied "Yes."

She said in her ideal world, her image would be different.

A lot of sex goes in to what I do... But sometimes I would just like to bring it back to the old days when it was like one outfit through the whole video, and you're just dancing through the whole video, and there's not that much sex stuff going on and it's just about the dance." (...)
- FOX News, Britney Spears implies she's being pressured to keep sexed-up image

Towards the end of the video, we see blindfolded mannequins being brought into the desert. They then explode.

Blindfolded mannequins represent the state of mind controlled slaves. Blowing them up into body parts represent the fragmenting of a slave's psyche into several personas. This image is used in several videos including Beyonce's "Crazy".

Work B*tch is therefore another tribute to Britney's own mind control status. While her situation is sad and disturbing, however, it doesn't stop new artists from following in her footsteps.

Change Your Life

A butterfly hiding one eye: That's Illuminati symbolism 101.

Iggy Azalea is a rapper from Australia who moved to the United States at the age of 16. She soon got signed by Interscope Records and almost immediately embraced that sweet, sweet Illuminati symbolism.

Iggy is now signed with Island Def Jam (also home to Rihanna, Kanye West and many others) and her single Change Your Life confirms that she's there to push the Agenda.

Inspired by the movie Showgirls, Change Your Life depicts Iggy as a Vegas dancer and T.I. as a club owner. While this premise is simple, when ones understand the symbolism of the video, it becomes the story of a Beta Kitten being initiated in the Illuminati industry.

The glass of this picture frame is shown broken at the beginning of the video for no apparent reason. This can represent the fractured personality of an MK slave. While not ALL broken glass represents fractured personalities, this image fits with the context of the rest of the video.

Iggy lays in bed with a baby tiger – a reference to Kitten Programming.

As its title states, the song is about Iggy apparently being able to "change your life" – going from rags to riches and so forth. Here are the lyrics of the chorus:

> *Imma change your life, Imma change it*
> *Imma change your life (life)*
>
> *Once you go great, you never go good*
> *You never go back, even if you could*
> *I'll show you my way, I got that good-good*
> *You never go back, even if you could*
>
> *Have you ever wished your life would change?*
> *Woke up and you lived your dreams*
> *Baby I could help you make that change*
> *I could show you how to do this thing*

While these lyrics are as "empowering" as Britney's Work B*tch, the video depicts Iggy as dancer who doesn't like her boss/pimp. In other words, she doesn't have power. Like Britney's song, it appears that the Illuminati is talking THROUGH Iggy, subtly letting young people know that "changing their lives" implies being exploited by the Illuminati industry. We once again see a twisted association between "making it big" and being an industry Beta kitten and, through symbolism, the video shows Iggy's initiation into the Illuminati industry.

Although Iggy does not appear to like the club owner played by T.I., she nevertheless gets intimate with him on the hood of a car. Why? Because that's what Beta Kittens do. On a more esoteric level, she wears a red dress, the symbolic color of initiation. After the encounter, we see a new Iggy in town.

Is copulating with her boss/handler a requirement in order for her to "change her life"? Does this represent the ritual initiation into the Illuminati industry?

As if to denote her initiation, she is wearing a top featuring a big All-Seeing Eye. She stands in front of a club named Cheetah, which is another clear reference to Kitten Programming. She sets fire to a car (is it her boss'?) to represent the "burning" of her old life.

In a scene that is shown in parallel to the one above, Iggy is dressed in white and is arrested by the police. Did she get arrested because she lit that car on fire? If that's the case, why is she dressed differently and why is this scene playing at the same time as the one above (and not after)? In actuality, this scene can represent what happens after initiation in the industry: the "good girl" dressed in white "is taken away for good" while the Illuminati-girl dressed in black (with an All-Seeing eye) remains.

Is that what Iggy means by "Once you go great, you never go good"? In the words of Iggy, once you're initiated: "You never go back, even if you could".

In Conclusion

Released around the same time, Britney's Work B*tch and Iggy's Change Your Life are similar in several ways: They both depict the artists as Vegas dancers, they are both drenched in Kitten Programming imagery, the lyrics are both written from the point of view of those controlling them and, more importantly, both have an psuedo-empowering message that revolves around the glorifying being an industry Beta Kitten.

Sadly, to "make it" in the Illuminati industry, stars must sell their bodies and give up their soul. This process is celebrated in these videos and sold to young girls around the world. Furthermore, as the MK symbolism of the videos subtly imply, these artists who "made it" are not in control of what's happening – they're actually slaves to their owners. Britney Spears' life is probably the most transparent case of a pop star under heavy mind control. In a rare moment of clarity, Britney went on record and stated that Work B*tch went too far and was too sexual. However, she did it anyway ... because Beta slaves do not call the shots in their own lives. What did Britney's handlers tell her when she was opposed working on that video? "You better work b*tch".

Katy Perry's "Dark Horse": One Big, Children-Friendly Tribute to the Illuminati

Katy Perry's "Dark Horse" is a fun and colorful video taking place in Ancient Egypt. However, behind the cartoonish style of the video, viewers are exposed to a great deal of symbolism of the occult elite and messages regarding its power. We'll look at the symbolism of "Dark Horse".

Katy Perry is a gigantic pop star, mainly because her songs and videos appeal to teens and pre-teens while her sex-appeal captures the attention of the older crowd. This makes her a perfect tool to be used by the elite to communicate its messages and, as seen in previous articles about her, her songs and videos are fully used for that purpose. Dark Horse, however, is on a whole other level. It is pure, relentless, in-your-face Illuminati symbolism, interlaced with references to the elite's brand of black magic and mind control. Playing the role of "Katy-Patra", a Egyptian pharaoh reminiscent of ancient sex symbol Cleopatra, Katy Perry rules over her subjects the same way the occult elite rules over the world.

In my article on the 2014 Grammy Awards, I described Katy Perry's performance of Dark Horse as a black magick ritual disguised as a music performance. The video goes straight to the roots of this sorcery: Egyptian Black Magick, the original source that is tapped into by today's dark secret societies.

Before we look at the actual video, let's look at its trailer, which contains a few interesting elements.

The Trailer

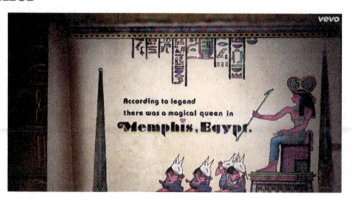

The trailer mentions a "magical Queen" in Egypt. We see the Queen sitting in front of her subjects, which are mind-controlled sex kittens.

Then the trailer states that Kings would travel from "Brooklyn to Babylon" to meet her. Babylon, which was a real ancient metropolis located where Iraq is today, was ruled by various ancient empires and has long been an epicenter of the elite's black magic.

The Eye of Horus, aka the All Seeing Eye, inside a pyramid, the elite's favorite symbol. Prepare to see a WHOLE LOT of it in the music video.

Let's look at the video.

Dark Horse

Dark Horse takes place in a colorful, child-friendly version of Ancient Egypt that's been "hip-hop-ized" about 15% to appeal to its target audience. Katy Perry plays the role of an evil, greedy, egoistical, despotic pharaoh named Katy-Patra who destroys men for their belongings. What a great lesson for girls under the age of 14. In a wider sense, Katy-Patra's rule represents the occult elite taking resources and power from nations (represented by the kings). What a great lesson for the rest of the world.

Illuminati Pharaoh

Throughout the video, it is firmly established that Katy-Patra is an evil tyrant using black magic to control and destroy people while having a bunch of kitten slaves at her feet. Kind of like what the occult elite does. And of course there are all kinds of blatant symbols that show her to be a representative of the Illuminati.

The Eye of Horus stamped on her wig. Very classy.

Doing the One-Eye sign so it is clear what this all about.

The next scenes tell plenty about the occult-elite influenced mythology of the video. Katy-Patra is looked upon by Anubis, the jackal-headed god of death, probably because she likes to kill people. Behind her is the falcon-headed god Horus wearing gold chains (to make him look "cool" to young, impressionable viewers). Notice that he only has one eye – a reference, once again, to the All-Seeing Eye of Horus. More importantly, Katy-Patra is surrounded by a golden snake, which probably refers to the evil Egyptian god Apep.

Katy-Patra naked and surrounded by Egyptian gods.

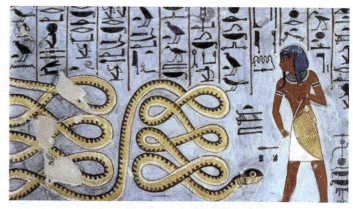

Apep is an evil god in ancient Egyptian religion depicted as a snake/serpent and a dragon. He is the deification of darkness and chaos. He is the enemy of light, order and truth (Ma'at). In the context of Katy-Patra's rule of general evil, her being surrounded by Apep is more than fitting. It also fits the Illuminati rule of power.

Three 6 Mafia rapper Juicy J makes an appearance in the video and his entrance is pretty darn symbolic too. He literally emerges from some kind sarcophagus, which features the occult-elite's favorite symbol in lieu of eyes: The Eye of Horus inside a triangle. On top of all of that symbolism, we must never forget another part of the Agenda: Exposing young people to hyper-sexualization.

The symbol on the eyes is not even Egyptian, it is purely Masonic. The symbolism in the entire video is not exclusively "Egyptian", but is the specific symbolism of the occult elite.

Although she's a powerful pharaoh, Katy-Patra always finds the time to do some pole-dancing on a stage marked with a Eye of Horus. She is also backed by her Kitten slaves – much like her young fans who imitate her, who she refers to as "Katycats"

Katy-Patra's Suitors

The video is essentially about kings from other nations trying to wow Katy-Patra with amazing gifts. The first suitor offers her a gigantic diamond. Katy-Patra immediately orders her kitten slaves to snatch that diamond from the suitor.

The guys is all like "you want that diamond don't you". He is wearing an eye-patch, hiding one eye, indicating that he's another idiot that's trying to be down with the elite.

Katy-Patra's examines the diamond through a big Eye of Horus thingie. There is however a problem: That Eye of Horus is NOT TRANSPARENT.

The above image is symbolic for a few reasons: First, it tells the viewers that Katy-Patra plays the role of the occult elite in the video. Second, she CANNOT see through the Eye (it is opaque). She instead sees the diamond through the elite's "eyes", which are focused on greed, power and material possessions. Finally, children who watch music videos need to be exposed to that one-eye sign all the time.

I could stop the video analysis here. What else do you truly need to know about the video? Katy Perry is looking at a big diamond using an Eye of Horus to hide one eye. This scene is a 100% continuation of about everything I've ever talked about on this site. And there it is again, right in our faces, in one of the world's most popular videos. Really, how can anyone think that all this symbolism is "just a coincidence"? Anyhow, back to the video.

The eye-patched sap gets zapped by magic emerging from the eyes of Katy-Patra's throne. That's what you get for trying to suck up to Illuminati.

She then takes the guy's jewels and stuffs them in her mouth, giving herself the classic "greedy moron" look.

The next suitor tries to entice Katy-Patra's gluttony by offering her food. He offers Katy-Patra food the same way poor nations give up their resources to the global elite. Of course, things do not turn out great for that guy, either.

The last suitor brings what Katy-Patra really wants: Power.

This guy has a big Illuminati symbol (i.e. not Egyptian) right between his nipples. He must have something extra good for Katy-Patra.

Katy-Patra receives a gigantic floating pyramid which hides, under a golden layer, an illuminated structure.

Seeing this pyramid, Katy-Patra gets very excited because that's what she, and the elite, truly wants: Unlimited occult power over the world. The illuminated pyramid essentially represents the Illuminati's high-tech control over the world.

When Katy-Patra steps on top of the unfinished pyramid, she becomes imbued with crazy magical powers. She even grows wings.

Standing on top of the Illuminati pyramid, Katy-Patra turns into a super-powerful tyrant. That's probably not a good thing. More importantly, she becomes a personification of the goddess Isis.

The video ends with Katy-Patra becoming a super-Illuminati pharaoh ... and everyone bows down to her ... and the suitor turns into a chihuahua. The moral of the video? Illuminati.

In Conclusion

It is rather hard to believe that all of this Illuminati symbolism was packed into a video that only lasts 3 minutes and 40 seconds. It is even harder to believe that some people still cannot see the obvious pattern of symbols found

in mass media that transcends artists, music genres and even media outlets. Far from being random, these symbols have been used for centuries to represent the occult elite and they are now all over the place.
More than just flashing symbols, the video Dark Horse tells a darker story: the occult elite's insatiable greed for ultimate power while dismissing the petty rulers operating underneath it. Katy-Patra indeed takes resources from various kings of the world and then destroys them. In the end, she climbs on an Illuminati pyramid and turns into an unstoppable pharaoh imbued with magical powers. Could the brainwashing be more obvious?

In short, Dark Horse is Illuminati propaganda aimed at children, using bright colors and catchy hooks to subliminally teach them who rules the world and who controls the idols that they love and emulate. Of course, none of this is clearly spelled out. Instead, it comes at you through symbolism … like a dark horse.

The Occult Meaning of Lady Gaga's Video "G.U.Y."

Lady Gaga's video for her song "G.U.Y." has a lot of viewers asking "What the heck did I just watch?" While at first the video may appear to be a bunch of nonsensical and random imagery, as usual, there is meaning behind the images. And, as usual, it is in line with the occult elite's philosophy and mythology. In this article, we'll look at the esoteric meaning of Gaga's video "G.U.Y.".

Lady Gaga has been around for while now (my first article about her was almost five years ago) and, although many have tired of her attention-seeking stunts, she still maintains a solid, and dedicated, fan base. Her video entitled G.U.Y. got her fans excited, but reading comments on YouTube, most of them openly don't get what is happening in the seven-minute production. And who can blame them? There are men in suits fighting with bows and arrows, there are the Real Housewives of Hollywood playing instruments, there's Michael Jackson being resuscitated, and there are Legos. This headache-inducing video that spans several songs nevertheless contains a linear and (somewhat) logical storyline and meaning. To truly understand it, however, one must be aware of the mythology invoked in Gaga's video (and her entire album) and the occult meaning behind it. Once these important connections are made, the rest begins to make a little more sense.

As is the case with most Lady Gaga videos, there are a few obvious pop culture references – which are profusely commented on by music reviewers – but the underlying, fundamental story goes unnoticed, or at least unmentioned. Nonetheless, this story is steeped in the mythology that is upheld by the occult elite.

The sexually charged video premiered on NBC's show Dateline on March 22, right before a report about two teenage girls who were abducted and abused. Why did the video premier on Dateline, of all shows – and why right before this kind of report? Maybe for the same reason Gaga had a "vomit artist" vomit on her during her live performances at the recent SXSW: Her work often ends up promoting what she appears to be denouncing. In the case of the "vomit artist", under the guise of "being yourself" or whatever, she's actually glamorizing bulimia and all-around self-destruction.

Fallen Angel

The first scene of the video is quite enigmatic, clearly announcing that it is a Gaga flick, where the line between profound artistry and random nonsense is always difficult to define. It begins with a bunch of men in suits fighting in a field, grabbing at dollar bills. Then we see Lady Gaga on the ground with wings on her back.

A fallen angel.

The fall of Lucifer as depicted in John Milton's "Paradise Lost".

Gaga is pierced by an arrow that was apparently shot by one of the suit guys who is holding a bow. Why was Gaga shot down? Do the men represent music industry scumbags? Maybe. One thing is for sure: Gaga was an angel flying in the sky, minding her own business, then was shot down, becoming a fallen angel. And who is the most important fallen angel in History? Lucifer, of course.

While one could argue that Gaga playing the role of a fallen angel might not inherently imply that she's referring to Lucifer, a look at the symbolism later in the video strongly points towards it. Indeed, much of the video plays on the esoteric associations between Lucifer, Venus and Ishtar, which I will cover a little further down.

Back in the video, a wounded Lucifer-Gaga gets up and walks towards civilization, ending up in front of the Hearst Castle. The location of the video is significant for several reasons. The castle was built by newspaper tycoon William Randolph Hearst, one of the most powerful and richest men in American history and the inspiration behind the film Citizen Kane. The mansion used to be a popular meeting point for Hollywood stars and the political elite. Like Gaga's work, the Hearst Castle combined entertainment and the occult elite.

Unsurprisingly, William Randolph Hearst was himself an important figure of the occult elite.

> "William Randolph Hearst was part of the Illuminati, he was part of the branch Illuminati — at what could be termed the 6th degree. William Randolph Hearst was totally into paganism. That is very obvious by a tour of his mansion in California which has been turned into a museum."
> - Fritz Springmeier, The Illuminati Formula to Create a Mind Control Slave

> "Illuminatus William Randolph Hearst gave Anton LaVey some big help. His Avon Publishing published his Satanic Bible in 1969 (it was first released in Dec. '69). Since then it has reportedly gone through over 30 printings. LaVey's next book The Satanic Rituals also was published by Hearst Avon in 1972. It talks about the power that blood sacrifices give the magician. Hearst's papers also gave him publicity."
> - Ibid.

> "William Randolph Hearst Jr., was a 33 degree mason and a very powerful man in the media world."
> - B.Huldah, The JFK Files

> "The newspaper tycoon William Randolph Hearst, a high-degree Illuminati initiate, funded his early

> *"crusades". The Hearst mansion in California is furnished with hundreds of ancient Egyptian and other Near and Middle Eastern artefacts. Most of them are original and were shipped to the United States by Hearst at enormous expense.*
>
> *It was Hearst's support for Franklin Delano Roosevelt that won "FDR" the Democratic nomination and the presidency in 1933. Roosevelt, the wartime president, was one of the great Illuminati frontmen of the 20th century (see ...And The Truth Shall Set You Free). The Rockefellers, Witneys, and Vanderbilts, all Illuminati bloodline families, have funded other Graham "crusades".*
> - David Icke, The Biggest Secret

Given Hearst's connection to the elite, it is of course not surprising that the Hearst castle was built with the occult elite's mythology in mind – which is, in turn, the mythology Lady Gaga is always attempting to sell to the youth.

Lucifer-Gaga arrives in front of the Hearst Castle and is greeted by hooded men.

Of course, the two guardians of this Castle of the Occult Elite won't let Lucifer die like this. They get her inside the castle so she can get a ritual fit for a fallen angel.
Venus

When Gaga enters the castle, the song Venus begins. Gaga's entire album is centered around multiple representations of Venus (in the video for Applause, she is dressed as Venus as depicted in Botticelli's painting The Birth of Venus). In G.U.Y, the theme of Venus is still central in numerous symbolic ways, including its esoteric association with Lucifer.

Since ancient times, the planet Venus has been known as the Morning Star and the Evening Star. The Romans designated the morning aspect of Venus as Lucifer, meaning "light bringer". In the Bible, Lucifer, the angel cast out of the heavens, is also referred to as the morning star.

> *"How you have fallen from heaven, morning star, son of the dawn! You have been cast down to the earth, you who once laid low the nations"*
> - Isaiah 14:12, NIV

The association between Lucifer and Venus remains of the utmost importance in modern occultism.

> *"In the modern occultism of Madeline Montalban, Lucifer's identification as the Morning Star (Venus) equates him with Lumiel, whom she regarded as the Archangel of Light, and among Satanists he is seen as the "Torch of Baphomet" and Azazel. However, in lesser-known Kabbalah lore, Lumiel was also described as an angel of the earth, though usually Sandalphon and Uriel are the only Archangels associated with the element of earth. In any case, Lumiel's precise identity has always been controversial and many people, who tried to discover his true nature, eventually came to refer Lumiel*

as a "dark angel".
- Wikipedia entry for Lucifer

Therefore, Gaga playing the role of a fallen angel while a song named Venus plays in the background is far from being random. While the word Venus is repeated throughout the song, another important symbol appears on screen.

While a dying Lucifer-Gaga is being carried by hooded men, the path to her "burial site" is paved with the symbol of the star of Ishtar.

The eight-pointed Star of Ishtar has been mentioned several times on this site as it is an important symbol in occult Mysteries. Ishtar is the Babylonian goddess of fertility, love, war, and sexuality and is considered to be the "divine personification of the planet Venus". This ancient Semitic symbol therefore completes the esoteric representation of the concept of Lucifer-Venus-Ishtar, a profound, mysterious and extremely important concept in the Mysteries of occult secret societies.

Why was the symbol of the star of Ishtar embedded on the floor of the Hearst Castle? As stated above, William Randolph Hearst was a 33rd degree Freemason and an Illuminatus who was highly knowledgeable in occult symbolism. The symbol of the star of Ishtar often appears on the floor of "occult-themed" buildings (see my articles on the Los Angeles Central Library and the Manitoba Legislative Building).

In this symbolically-charged setting, Gaga is taken to the castle's Neptune pool where a death ritual takes place.

On Gaga is placed an arrangement of flowers and ... Monarch butterflies. Is this a way of saying that Gaga's death and rebirth is done through Monarch Programming?

Rebirth

After the death ritual, Gaga is reborn and greets Himeros, the god of sexual desire. Her hair is now platinum blonde and, from being an angel, Gaga is now all about sexuality. Does this represent the creation of the persona of Lady Gaga by the occult elite music business?

After the rebirth, everything in the video turns to white and things become highly sexual.

While Gaga's rebirth is happening the Real Housewives of Beverly Hills make an appearance playing the role of the muses, daughters of Zeus. The fact that they clearly do not know how to play these instruments and that there's obviously no harp or cello in the actual song add to the fact that this is all about being fake, phony and plastic.

In this scene, Gaga has her head on a work created by the "lego artist" Nathan Sawaya. What a great way to show how Gaga's persona is artificially built and completely empty inside.

Here Gaga holds a lego apple with a bite taken from it which is a reference to the apple of the Garden of Eden. The apple was given by Lucifer and gave humans knowledge of good and evil. In occult Mysteries, Lucifer is viewed as a "savior" who gave humans the knowledge to become gods themselves.

Revenge

While Gaga's rebirth seems to be all about love, she is also brewing a revenge master plan … a very strange and disturbing master plan that involves a rather unholy science.

Gaga enters a room containing four tombs connected to a computer. From them emerge Jesus Christ, Gandhi, and Michael Jackson.

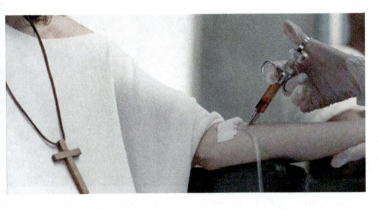

Nurses then proceed to draw blood from each zombie, including Jesus, which is kind of not respectful.

There are several things that do not make sense in this scene. One of them is: Why is Jesus even there? Isn't the whole point of his story is that he resurrected and ascended to heaven? Why is he even in a tomb? And why does Lady Gaga have access to it? I mean, according to Christianity, Jesus was not some "guy".

Anyhow, each one of these three figures are meant to represent a trait that should be present in Gaga's vision of the ultimate "guy". Interesting fact: All of these figures were killed by the "powers that be" in their time, after which their message and "aura" was used for all kinds of foul agendas. Also, you might have noticed that there are four tombs, but only three men are shown. According to the director (and the credits), the missing figure was John Lennon, but Gaga decided to remove him from the video. Interesting fact: Lennon was also assassinated (and most likely by an MK stooge).

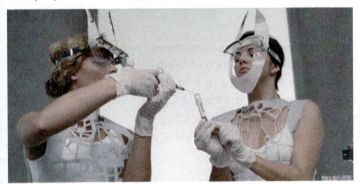

The blood is collected by nurses wearing stylized horns.

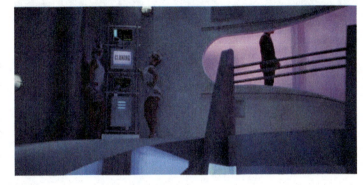

Horns equals playing God and that's exactly what the horned nurses do. The horned nurses begin cloning a bunch of dudes wearing black suits.

While the cloning is happening in the background, Gaga and friends dance very sexily. Playing God and cloning people using the blood of dead people is indeed very hot. If I saw Jesus-cloning going on, I'd also want to take off my shirt and dance feverishly.

Once Gaga's army of clones (strange way to represent her fans) is complete, she goes to the offices of the suited men who shot her down in the beginning of the video.

Gaga and her clone army storm the office building and Gaga force-feeds some execs the blood of Jesus, Ghandi and Michael Jackson. I'm pretty sure that anyone of these three figures would approve of Gaga's plan. Or maybe they'd be like "Hey Gaga, give me back my blood. What the hell is wrong with you?"

From white, everything now switches to black. Gaga wears crow wings on her head. In Ancient Greece and other civilizations, crows were considered to be omens of death.

"Look at me, I'm a clone AND a douchebag." This what Lady Gaga-sponsored science produces.

Gaga and her clone army storm the office building and Gaga force-feeds some execs the blood of Jesus, Ghandi and Michael Jackson. I'm pretty sure that anyone of these three figures would approve of Gaga's plan. Or maybe they'd be like "Hey Gaga, give me back my blood. What the hell is wrong with you?"

The video ends with an upsetting scene: Thousands of cloned "guys" mindlessly leaving the Hearst Castle to annoy the world.

This is how the elite sees consumers of popular culture: a bunch of brainless clones doing as they're told. The clones emerge from the Hearst Castle (an occult elite hotspot), indicating that these clones are made the occult elite's way.

To sum up this video, Gaga begins as a fallen angel who got shot down from the heavens by greedy business men. She is then "initiated" inside a Hollywood-occult-elite castle where she is reborn as a lustful blonde goddess. She then quickly uses her powers to create an army of clones using blood from Jesus Christ, Gandhi and Michael Jackson. Yup.

In Conclusion

G.U.Y. is profoundly steeped in the elite's symbolism and mythology. Shot at the Hearst Castle, a mansion built by a high-level Illuminatus, G.U.Y. tells viewers where the messages communicated in popular culture emerge from. The same way William Randolph Hearst manipulated public opinion with his brand of "yellow journalism", today's culture affects public opinion through pop stars.

The video starts with symbolism that is strongly Luciferian – and Luciferianism is all about becoming gods. Then Gaga actually becomes a god and starts giving life to a new race of clones. Of course, all of those messages are coated with a large amount of "love" and sexiness to make them easy to digest for today's average viewer.

In short, G.U.Y. is a typical Lady Gaga video. And like all typical Lady Gaga videos, while the story appears to be uplifting and "empowering" (man, I hate that word), its factory-created, mindless clones and occult Illuminati symbolism actually glorify elite repression and mass mind control.

… Kind of like having someone vomit on you to denounce bulimia.

Section 3
Movies and TV

Ever since their creation, motion pictures are not only used to entertain, but to influence and condition the masses.

The Occult Roots of The Wizard of Oz

With its memorable story and its cast of colorful characters, the Wizard of Oz quickly became an American classic. More than a hundred years after the release of this book, kids everywhere are still enchanted by Oz's world of wonder. Few, however, recognize that, under its deceptive simplicity, the story of the Wizard of Oz conceals deep esoteric truths inspired by Theosophy. Here we'll look at the Wizard of Oz's occult meaning and its author's background.

Although the Wizard of Oz is widely perceived as an innocent children's fairy tale, it is almost impossible not to attribute a symbolic meaning to Dorothy's quest. As in all great stories, the characters and the symbols of the Wizard of Oz can be given a second layer of interpretation, which may vary depending on the reader's perception. Many analyses appeared throughout the years describing the story as an "atheist manifesto" while others saw it as a promotion of populism. It is through an understanding of the author's philosophical bckground and beliefs, however, that the story's true meaning can be grasped.

L. Frank Baum, the author of the Wizard of Oz was a member of the Theosophical Society, which is an organization based on occult research and the comparative study of religions. Baum had a deep understanding of Theosophy and, consciously or not, created an allegory of Theosophic teachings when he wrote the Wizard of Oz.

What is Theosophy?

The Theosophical Society is an occult organization, mainly based on the teachings of Helena P. Blavatsky, which seeks to extract the common roots of all religions in order to form a universal doctrine.

> "But it is perhaps desirable to state unequivocally that the teachings, however fragmentary and incomplete, contained in these volumes, belong neither to the Hindu, the Zoroastrian, the Chaldean, nor the Egyptian religion,.neither to Buddhism, Islam, Judaism nor Christianity exclusively. The Secret Doctrine is the essence of all these. Sprung from it in their origins, the various religious schemes are now made to merge back into their original element, out of which every mystery and dogma has grown, developed, and become materialized."
> - H.P. Blavatsky, The Secret Doctrine

The seal of Theosophy

The three declared objects of the original Theosophical Society as established by Blavatsky, Judge and Olcott (its founders) were as follows:

> "First — To form a nucleus of the Universal Brotherhood of Humanity, without distinction of race, creed, sex, caste, or color.
> Second — To encourage the study of Comparative Religion, Philosophy, and Science.
> Third — To investigate the unexplained laws of Nature and the powers latent in man."
> - The Theosophist, vol 75, No 6

The main tenets of Theosophy are thoroughly described in Blavatsky works Isis Unveiled and The Secret Doctrine. At the core of Theosophical teachings are the same tenets found in many other occult schools: the belief of the presence of a "divine spark" within every person which, with the proper discipline and training, can lead to spiritual illumination and a state of virtual godliness.

Another important principle found in Theosophy is reincarnation. It is believed that the human soul, like all other things in the universe, go through seven stages of development.

> "Theosophical writings propose that human civilizations, like all other parts of the universe, develop cyclically through seven stages. Blavatsky posited that the whole humanity, and indeed every reincarnating human monad, evolves through a series of seven "Root Races". Thus in the first age, humans were pure spirit; in the second age, they were sexless beings inhabiting the now lost continent of Hyperborea; in the third age the giant Lemurians were informed by spiritual impulses endowing them with human consciousness and sexual reproduction. Modern humans finally developed on the continent of Atlantis. Since Atlantis was the nadir of the cycle, the present fifth age is a time of reawakening humanity's psychic gifts. The term psychic here really means the realization of the permeability of consciousness as it had not been known earlier in evolution, although sensed by some more sensitive individuals of our species."

The ultimate goal is of course to return to the state of divinity from which we've emerged. The same tenets (with subtle variations) can be found in other schools such as Rosicrucianism, Freemasonry and other orders teachings the Mysteries.

L.Frank Baum, a Notable Theosophist

Before writing the Wizard of Oz (or even contemplating becoming a children's story author), Baum held many jobs – one of which was editor of the Aberdeen Saturday Pioneer. In 1890, Baum wrote a series of articles introducing his readers to Theosophy, including his views on Buddha, Mohammed, Confucius and Christ. At that time, he wasn't a member of the Theosophical Society but he already showed a deep understanding of its philosophy. Here's an excerpt of his "Editor's Musings":

> "Amongst various sects so numerous in America today who find their fundamental basis in occultism, the Theosophist stands pre-eminent both in intelligence and point of numbers. Theosophy is not a religion. Its followers are simply "searchers after Truth". The Theosophists, in fact, are the dissatisfied with the world, dissenters from all creeds. They owe their origin to the wise men of India, and are numerous, not only in the far famed mystic East, but in England, France, Germany and Russia. They admit the existence of a God – not necessarily of a personal God. To them God is Nature and Nature is God…But despite this, if Christianity is Truth, as our education has taught us to believe, there can be no menace to it in Theosophy."
> - L. Frank Baum, Aberdeen Saturday Pioneer, January 25th 1890

L. Frank Baum

In another of his "Editor's Musings", Baum discusses the use of mystic symbolism in fiction, something he accomplished ten years later with the Wizard of Oz:

> "There is a strong tendency in modern novelists towards introducing some vein of mysticism or occultism into their writings. Books of this character are eagerly bought and read by the people, both in Europe and America. It shows the innate longing in our natures to unravel the mysterious: to seek some explanation, however fictitious, of the unexplainable in nature and in our daily existence. For, as we advance in education, our desire for knowledge increases, and we are less satisfied to remain in ignorance of that mysterious fountain-head from which emanates all that is sublime and grand and incomprehensible in nature."

At the end of this article, Baum goes into an all-out plead for more occultism in literature:

> "The appetite of our age for occultism demands to be satisfied, and while with the mediocrity of people will result in mere sensationalism, it will lead in many to higher and nobler and bolder thought;and who can tell what mysteries these braver and abler intellects may unravel in future ages?"
> - L. Frank Baum, Aberdeen Saturday Pioneer, February 22nd 1890

Two years after writing those articles, L. Frank Baum and his wife Maud Gage joined the Theosophical Society in Chicago. The archives of the Theosophical Society in Pasadena, California recorded the start of their membership as September 4th, 1892. In 1890, the Wizard of Oz was published. When asked about how Baum got his inspiration for the story, he replied:

> "It was pure inspiration…It came to me right out of the blue. I think that sometimes the Great Author

has a message to get across and He has to use the instrument at hand. I happened to be that medium, and I believe the magic key was given me to open the doors to sympathy and understanding, joy, peace and happiness."
- L. Frank Baum, cited by Hearn 73

The Wizard of Oz is much appreciated within the Theosophical Society. In 1986, The American Theosophist magazine recognized Baum as a "notable Theosophist" who thoroughly represented the organization's philosophy.

"Although readers have not looked at his fairy tales for their Theosophical content, it is significant that Baum became a famous writer of children's books after he came into contact with Theosophy. Theosophical ideas permeate his work and provided inspiration for it. Indeed, The Wizard can be regarded as Theosophical allegory, pervaded by Theosophical ideas from beginning to end. The story came to Baum as an inspiration, and he accepted it with a certain awe as a gift from outside, or perhaps from deep within, himself."
- American Theosophist no 74, 1986

So what is the esoteric meaning of this children's story, which came to Baum as a "divine inspiration"?

The Occult Meaning of The Wizard of Oz

The path to illumination

Here's a quick sum-up of the movie:

The film follows 12-year-old farmgirl Dorothy Gale (Judy Garland) who lives on a Kansas farm with her Aunt Em and Uncle Henry, but dreams of a better place "somewhere over the rainbow." After being struck unconscious during a tornado by a window which has come loose from its frame, Dorothy dreams that she, her dog Toto and the farmhouse are transported to the magical Land of Oz. There, the Good Witch of the North, Glinda (Billie Burke), advises Dorothy to follow the yellow brick road to the Emerald City and meet the Wizard of Oz, who can return her to Kansas. During her journey, she meets a Scarecrow (Ray Bolger), a Tin Man (Jack Haley) and a Cowardly Lion (Bert Lahr), who join her, hoping to receive what they lack themselves (a brain, a heart and courage, respectively). All of this is done while also trying to avoid the Wicked Witch of the West (Margaret Hamilton) and her attempt to get her sister's ruby slippers from Dorothy, who received them from Glinda.

The entire story of the Wizard of Oz is an allegorical tale of the soul's path to illumination – the Yellow Brick Road. In Buddhism (an important part of Theosophical teachings) the same concept is referred to as the "Golden Path".

The story starts with Dorothy Gale living in Kansas, which symbolizes the material world, the physical plane where each one of us starts our spiritual journey. Dorothy feels an urge to "go over the rainbow", to reach the ethereal realm and follow the path to illumination. She has basically "passed the Nadir" by demonstrating the urge to seek a higher truth.

Dorothy is then brought to Oz by a giant cyclone spiraling upward, representing the cycles of karma, the cycle of errors and lessons learned. It also represents the theosophical belief in reincarnation, the round of physical births and deaths of a soul until it is fit to become divine. It is also interesting to note that the Yellow Brick Road of Oz begins as an outwardly expanding spiral. In occult symbolism, this spiral represents the evolving self, the soul ascending from matter into the spirit world.

The spirally beginning of the spiritual path

Here's an explanation of the spiral as an occult symbol:

> "Spiral: The path of a point (generally plane) which moves round an axis while continually approaching it or receding from it; also often used for a helix, which is generated by compounding a circular motion with one in a straight line. The spiral form is an apt illustration of the course of evolution, which brings motion round towards the same point, yet without repetition.
>
> The serpent, and the figures 8 and , denoting the ogdoad and infinity, stand for spiral cyclic motion. The course of fohat in space is spiral, and spirit descends into matter in spiral courses. Repeating the process by which a helix is derived form a circle produces a vortex. The complicated spirals of cosmic evolution bring the motion back to the point from which it started at the birth of a great cosmic age."
> - The Encyclopedic Theosophical Glossary

Before undertaking her journey, Dorothy is given the "silver shoes", which represent the "silver cord" of Mystery Schools (Dorothy was wearing ruby slippers in the movie due to a last minute change by the director, who thought that the color ruby looked better against the Yellow Brick Road). In occult schools, the silver cord is considered to be the link between our material and spiritual selves.

> "In Theosophy, one's physical body and one's Astral body are connected through a "silver cord", a mythical link inspired by a passage in the Bible that speaks of a return from a spiritual quest. 'Or ever the silver cord be loosed, says the book of Ecclesiastes, 'then shall the dust return to the earth as it was and the spirit shall return unto God who gave it'.

In Frank Baum's own writing, the silver cord of Astral travel would inspire the silver shoes that bestow special powers upon the one who wears them"
- Evan I. Schwartz, Finding OZ: How L.Frank Baum Discovered the Great American Story

During her journey along the Yellow Brick road, Dorothy encounters Scarecrow, Tin Woodman and Cowardly Lion who are respectively searching for a brain, a heart and courage. Those odd characters embody the qualities needed by the initiates in order to complete their quest for illumination. Baum was probably inspired by these words from Miss Blavatsky:

"There is no danger that dauntless courage cannot conquer, there is not trial that a spotless purity cannot pass through; there is no difficulty a strong intellect cannot surmount"
- H.P. Blavatsky

After surmounting many obstacles, the party finally reaches Emerald city in order to meet The Wizard.

The Wizard

Surrounded by artifices and special effects, the Wizard comes across as cruel, rude and unwise. The Wizard is in fact a stand-in for the personal God of the Christians and the Jews, the oppressive figure used by conventional religions to keep the masses in spiritual darkness: Jehova or Yahwe. It is later discovered that the Wizard is a humbug, a charlatan, who scares people into worshipping his Wizard. He surely could not help the characters complete their quest. If you read literature of Mystery schools, this point of view towards Christianity is constantly expressed.

The wizard exposed as a sleazy fraud.

After all is said and done, the brains, the heart and the courage needed to complete Dorothy, Scarecrow, Tinman and Lion's quests were found within each one of them. Mystery Schools have always taught their students that one must rely on oneself to obtain salvation. Throughout the story Dorothy's dog Toto represents her "inner voice"; her intuition. Here's a description of Toto taken from the Theosophical Society's website:

> *"Toto represents the inner, intuitive, instinctual, most animal-like part of us. Throughout the movie, Dorothy has conversations with Toto, or her inner intuitive self. The lesson here is to listen to the Toto within. In this movie, Toto was never wrong. When he barks at the scarecrow, Dorothy tries to ignore him: "Don't be silly, Toto. Scarecrows don't talk." But scarecrows do talk in Oz. Toto also barks at the little man behind the curtain. It is he who realizes the Wizard is a fraud. At the Gale Farm and again at the castle, the Witch tries to put Toto into a basket. What is shadow will try to block or contain the intuitive. In both cases, Toto jumps out of the basket and escapes. Our intuitive voice can be ignored, but not contained.*
>
> *In the last scene, Toto chases after a cat, causing Dorothy to chase after him and hence miss her balloon ride. This is what leads to Dorothy's ultimate transformation, to the discovery of her inner powers. The balloon ride is representative of traditional religion, with a skinny-legged wizard promising a trip to the Divine. Toto was right to force Dorothy out of the balloon, otherwise she might never have found her magic. This is a call for us to listen to our intuition, our gut feelings, those momentary bits of imagination that appear seemingly out of nowhere."*

As stated above, the fake Wizard invites Dorothy into his balloon to go back to Kansas, her final destination. She however follows Toto (her intuition) and gets out of the balloon, which represents the empty promises of organized religions. This leads to her ultimate revelation and, with the help of the Good Witch of the North (her divine guide), she finally understands: everything she ever wanted could be found "in her own backyard".

In order to obtain illumination Dorothy had to vanquish the wicked witches of the East and the West – who were forming an evil horizontal axis: the material world. She was wise in listening to the advice of the good witches of the North and South – the vertical axis: the spiritual dimension.

The Good Witch of the North representing Dorothy's "divine spark"

At the end of the story, Dorothy wakes up in Kansas: she has successfully combined her physical and spiritual life. She is now comfortable being herself again and, despite her family not really believing the details of her quest (the ignorant profane), she can finally say "There is no place like home".

The Wizard of Oz Used in Monarch Mind Control

Almost all documentation relating to the MK Ultra project and Mind Control mention the importance of the Wizard of Oz. In the 1940's, the story was reportedly chosen by members of the US intelligence community to provide a thematic foundation for their trauma-based mind control program. The movie was edited and given a different meaning in order to use it as a tool to reinforce the programming on the victims. Here are some examples taken from Fritz Springmeier's Total Mind Control Slave:

- The close relationship between Dorothy and her dog is a very subtle connection between the satanic cults use of animals (familiars). A Monarch slave child will be allowed to bond with a pet. The child will want to bond with a pet anyway because people are terrifying to it by this point. Then the pet is killed to traumatize the child.

- Monarch slaves are taught to "follow the yellow brick road." No matter what fearful things lie ahead, the Monarch slave must follow the Yellow Brick Road which is set out before them by their master.

- The rainbow–with its seven colors-has long had the occult significance of being a great spiritual, hypnotic device.

- Dorothy is looking for a place where there is no trouble, which is a place "over the rainbow." To escape pain, alters go over the rainbow. (This is a.k.a. in Alice In Wonderland Programming as "going through the looking glass").

"Somewhere Over the Rainbow" is probably the most dissociative song ever written and is often played in movies during violent or traumatizing events (see the movie Face-Off). The strange effect produced, where the violence doesn't seem real anymore, is exactly how dissociation works on mind-control victims. We may also speculate that the scene where Dorothy falls asleep in a poppy field is a reference to the use of heroin to relax and manipulate the victims of mind-control. Also consider the snow falling from the sky that awakens Dorothy from her slumber. Could this be a reference to cocaine?

In Conclusion

Allegorical stories transmitting spiritual truths have existed since man's beginnings. These simple yet extremely profound stories have been found in all civilizations: Celtic, Indian, Persian, Aztec, Greek, Egyptian and others. Consciously or not, Frank Baum created a classical allegory which, in the same vein as Homer's Odyssey, entertains the masses and also contains mystical messages that can be understood by the "awakened".

The Wizard of Oz's great success confirms America's (and the Western world's) real spiritual dogma. Written during the 1890's, when most Americans were conservative Christians, Baum's story anticipated the population's progressive abandonment of traditional religions and the embrace of a new form of spirituality. Today's New Age movements are gaining many adepts and, even if most of them are total shams, they all claim to be inspired by Theosophy. Could such tales have contributed to the spectacular decline of Christianity in the past decades while other movements continue to gain momentum?

"The Imaginarium of Doctor Parnassus" and Heath Ledger's Sacrifice

Heath Ledger's last movie is a mind-boggling one. From its enigmatic storyline to the mysteries surrounding its production, "The Imaginarium of Doctor Parnassus" deserves to be duly explored. An interpretation of its rich symbolism reveals to the viewers timeless esoteric truths as well as coded references to today's occult cryptocracy. This article looks at the mystical meaning of the "The Imaginarium of Doctor Parnassus" and the sacrificial nature of Heath Ledger's death.

It seems the last movies of actors who die prematurely are often heavily symbolic. A single viewing of the trailer for The Imaginarium of Doctor Parnassus was sufficient to convince me of the movie's deep esoteric undertones. Terry Gilliam's productions have often dealt with occult themes, but this one seemed unusually flagrant. I was therefore looking forward to the movie's reviews and the potential discussions it would engender. However, I found nothing but superficial blurbs and critiques talking about a "fantastic adventure" or something of the sort. So I watched the movie to see if I misjudged the trailer and, after the first minute and a half, all of my doubts evaporated. The movie begins with a man (Anton) dressed as Mercury ("Hermes" of the Greeks and "Thoth" of the Egyptians) announcing Dr. Parnassus, who is dressed as a monk, holding a lotus flower, a symbol of Eastern mysticism. Pretty esoteric. We'll first look at the underlying meaning of the movie and follow with the strange symbols relating to Heath Ledger's death.

The Esoteric Meaning of the Story

The premise of The Imaginarium of Doctor Parnassus conceals a meaning for those who, in the words of Anton playing Mercury, have "eyes to see and ears to hear". Here's a quick summary of the movie.

> "The Imaginarium of Doctor Parnassus is a fantastical morality tale, set in the present day. It tells the story of Dr. Parnassus and his extraordinary 'Imaginarium', a traveling show where members of the audience get an irresistible opportunity to choose between light and joy or darkness and gloom. Blessed with the extraordinary gift of guiding the imaginations of others, Dr. Parnassus is cursed with a dark secret. Long ago he made a bet with the devil, Mr. Nick, in which he won immortality. Many centuries later, on meeting his one true love, D.r Parnassus made another deal with the devil, trading his immortality for youth, on condition that when his first-born reached its 16th birthday he

or she would become the property of Mr. Nick.

Valentina is now rapidly approaching this 'coming of age' milestone and Dr. Parnassus is desperate to protect her from her impending fate. Mr. Nick arrives to collect but, always keen to make a bet, renegotiates the wager. Now the winner of Valentina will be determined by whoever seduces the first five souls. Enlisting a series of wild, comical and compelling characters in his journey, Dr. Parnassus promises his daughter's hand in marriage to the man that helps him win. In this captivating, explosive and wonderfully imaginative race against time, Dr. Parnassus must fight to save his daughter in a never-ending landscape of surreal obstacles – and undo the mistakes of his past once and for all."
- IMDB

The storyline revolves around a classic Faustian theme, in which Dr. Parnassus makes various bets with the Devil (played by Tom Waits) throughout his life. Looking deeper into the symbolism of the story, Dr. Parnassus and his traveling show are a metaphor for the esoteric teachings transmitted through the ages via Mystery schools. He is a human manifestation of the "path to enlightenment" of the Buddhists or the "inner-Christ" of the Gnostics. By inviting people into the magic mirror, he transports them onto the spiritual plane where they can choose between spiritual fulfillment and enlightenment (represented by a pyramid or a ladder, depending on the person) or ignorance and materialism (represented by a pub or a sleazy motel). Dr. Parnassus says "he transmits the story that sustains the universe," which is a poetic way of saying that he is the vehicle for the secret teachings leading to illumination. He provides the path that allows the communion between humanity and divinity. The entire symbolism surrounding Paranassus' theater is inspired by the esoteric teachings of the ancient Egyptians, Greeks, Buddhists and other esoteric schools. The stage contains many interesting occult symbols.

From Janus, the two-faced Roman god to the Masonic twin pillars and the All-Seeing Eye, Dr. Paranassus' stage reveals the spiritual nature of the theater

Parnassus' name is also a reference to occult initiation. His name is derived from Mount Parnassus, the sacred mountain of the Dionysus, the Greek god of mystery religious rites (also known as the roman Bacchus). Mount Parnassus also contained the famed oracle of Delphi, the mystical site where people could obtain spiritual revelations.

Dealing with the Devil

As stated above, the story of the immortal Dr. Parnassus is analogous with the evolution of the Mysteries throughout History. This story was not always perfect and numerous influences have altered its course. There is a constant exchange in the movie between Dr. Parnassus and the Devil and it ultimately becomes evident that they actually need each other in order to exist and to stay relevant. Through their back and forth, they reenact the ancient principle of duality, the constant struggle opposing good versus evil and light versus darkness. This concept is visually represented by the Masonic black and white checkerboard pattern. While explaining his dealings with the Devil to his daughter, Dr. Parnassus explains in coded terms the nature of his essence. It can be found within Buddhist monks, in Jesus Christ and even in Freemasonry. He describes his first bet with the Devil as a competition to see who could first attract twelve disciples. Dr. Parnassus shows his daughter a book containing symbolic images.

The Devil is here shown surrounded by clergymen. Parnassus says he uses the "necessities of danger, fear and the fabled bliss of ignorance" to attract disciples.

Parnassus teaches "the power of the imagination to transform and illuminate our lives". He is here depicted as Jesus Christ with his third eye open, floating under the Eye of the Great Architect. Notice on the left a symbol that is very similar to a Masonic square and compass.

Parnassus won that first bet, but he was tricked: the Devil let him win. The Devil knew that, in due time, "nobody would want to hear Parnassus' stories". In other words, the Devil knew the world would spiral back into ignorance, ultimately finding itself in the spiritual state we are in today. Parnassus' show (a metaphor for the path to Illumination) is now a strange novelty, a road-side curiosity that is ignored by most everyday people who are too busy to ponder on its teachings. Then comes Tony.

Tony Liar

Found by Parnassus' traveling troupe hanging under a bridge, Tony Liar (whose name is based on British Prime Minister Tony Blair) may or may not have been sent by the Devil. Despite his mysterious past, Tony is integrated into to the show and he quickly uses his charming yet dishonest ways to attract more people to the show. He is, however, focused on generating more money and is not interested in people's spiritual salvation. He finally convinces Parnassus to change the style of the show to make it more modern and to change the audience to make it more … rich. Tony tells Parnassus not to hide his "mind control thing", to be bold and to reach the right kind of public. This is the result:

A tri-dimensional Masonic checkerboard pattern leads the way to the "magic mirror", the gateway to the spiritual plane. Did Freemasonry "repackage" the ancient Mysteries in a way that would be attractive to the upper-class?

The new stage is set in an elegant shopping mall. There is also a change of philosophy: instead of asking for donations, there is box filled with money stating "Please Take Generously". The bold marketing ploy pays off and those who experience the "other side of the mirror" come back totally fulfilled, leaving behind their money, fur coats and jewelry.

Tony himself finally experiences the joys of the spiritual plane and finds himself climbing the ladder to Illumination.

Tony is here played by Jude Law, one of the three actors who replaced Heath Ledger after his premature death.

His climb is stopped however by his troublesome past (the Russian mafia) catching up to him, and the ladder breaks. Spiritual enlightenment cannot be obtained by just anyone. He has however tasted the feeling of "being like a god".

Heath Ledger's Sacrifice

While The Imaginarium of Doctor Parnassus communicates an inspiring spiritual message, there is a rather grim side to the movie that relates to Heath Ledger's death. The concept of duality is present within the movie itself where the tales of illumination are mixed with references to black magic and sacrificial death. Good and evil struggle again. The numerous references to death during the movie could be interpreted as a tribute to Heath Ledger, but, as Terry Gilliam states, none of the script was rewritten after the tragedy. Here is an excerpt of the director's interview with Last Broadcast:

> *The film is terribly poignant film to watch now because of the loss of Heath.*
> Yes, it is.
>
> **And there are the references to death in the film that seem terribly poignant in the light of what happened. Did you re-emphasise any of that after his death?**
> The references to death were all in the original script, which people don't understand. They all thought we had written this stuff after Heath had died and no, we didn't change any of the words. And that to me is what's so kind of scary and spooky – why was it so prescient? It seemed to be all about death, it's so much of it.
> - Last Broadcast, Terry Gilliam (The Imaginarium Of Doctor Parnassus) Interview

Not only there are many references to death, there are many references to sacrificial death. Knowing the odd circumstances in which Ledger lost his life, could his death be the result of a ritual sacrifice? Are there codes within the movie relating to it? This might sound improbable to the average person but, to the initiate of the occult practices of the entertainment industry, it is a definite possibility. The observations presented here might be coincidences or they might be signs placed on purpose. One thing is for sure: they are there. The first person that seemed freaked out by this was the director himself, who was apparently a friend of Ledger. In his interview with Sun Media, Gilliam stated:

> *"There are forces at work on this film, don't get me into my mystical mode ... but the film made itself and it was co-directed by Heath Ledger!"*

Why is he implying that other forces were at work during the creation of this movie?

The Hanged Man

Right before the traveling troupe finds Tony hanging under a bridge, Dr Parnassus pulls out the Tarot card of the Hanged Man. It predicted what was about to happen but the occult significance of the card is even more relevant:

> *"Esoterically, the Hanged Man is the human spirit which is suspended from heaven by a single thread. Wisdom, not death, is the reward for this voluntary sacrifice during which the human soul, suspended above the world of illusion, and meditating upon its unreality, is rewarded by the achievement of self-realization."*
> - Manly P. Hall, The Secret Teachings of All Ages

The Hanged Man indeed refers to the myth of the dying god who is committing the ultimate sacrifice in order to attain immortality.

> *"There is present in the rituals similarities of concepts or beliefs. In the ancient tradition it was believed that through the connection of the body and blood of the Slain God that the people became one with the deity. In the "Last Supper" Jesus declare that the bread and wine were his body and blood, which he gave up for the salvation of the people. Blood was believed to contain the life force. The death of the king freed the inner spirit. Through the distribution of his body and blood, heaven and earth were united and his vital energy renewed the kingdom.*
>
> *The appearances of the Slain God have taken on various aspects throughout the ages. His images can be seen in the Jack-in-the-Green, the Hooded Man, the Hanged Man of the Tarot, the Lord of Vegetation, the Harvest, and the free untamed aspect of the forest."*
> - The Mystica, Slain God

Anton and Valentina then find Tony hanging beneath Blackfriars Bridge.

Ledger's previous movie was The Dark Knight in which he played The Joker – The Fool of the Tarot. Did The Fool evolve into the Hanging Man?

This scene is inspired by the actual 1982 hanging of Roberto Calvi (dubbed "God's banker" due to his relations with the Vatican). The hanging took place under the exact same bridge. Although never publicly confirmed, there are strong theories that Roberto Calvi's death was a symbolic and ritualistic murder carried out by the black masonic lodge called Propaganda Due, also referred to as P2. The name of the bridge is very significant:

> "Mr. Calvi's investigation indicates that his father was strangled, before his body was weighted and suspended underneath Blackfriars Bridge, probably by people who were in a small boat. The choice of bridge may have been significant: the P2 members referred to themselves as "frati neri" – black friars."
> - London Evening Standard, A son's quest for truth

Tony's forehead bears strange occult markings, as if to further the sense of ritualistic murder in the minds of the viewers.

Phi is a Greek letter representing the Golden Ratio, a mathematical proportion that is extremely important in Freemasonry.

Why did the directors pay homage to this symbolic murder?

Dying Young

In an eerie scene where Tony (played by Johnny Depp) guides a rich woman through her fantasy world, three boats appear bearing the pictures of Rudolph Valentino, James Dean and Princess Diana, three public figures who died prematurely.

Tony urges the rich woman to follow their path and to embark on a gondola bearing the head of Anubis, the god of the Dead. The woman sees the pictures and says:

> "All these people ... they're all dead."

Tony replies:

> "Yes ... but immortal nevertheless. They won't get old or fat. They won't get sick or feeble. They are beyond fear because they are ... forever young. They're gods ... and you can join them."

He then adds:

> "Your sacrifice must be pure."

All of this is said by Johnny Depp, the actor who replaced Heath Ledger after his premature death. The least I can say is this: strange coincidence. The esoteric meaning of the scene alludes to the dying of the old self in order to give birth to the new, spiritual self. Spiritually, however, this metamorphosis is however obtained through self-sacrifice and personal work, not by dying young. The public figures on the boats all died in "mysterious" circumstances. What is the relation?

I wrote an article last year, Princess Diana's Death and Memorial: The Occult Meaning, in which I explore the possible sacrificial nature of her death and the "goddess" symbolism surrounding her memorial. Did the same thing happen with Ledger?

Occultists believe that occult rituals, by definition, must have an audience. The greater the number of witnesses, the better, as they give those who execute the rituals more power and potency. Was Ledger's death a mega-ritual?

In Conclusion

Many movies in Heath Ledger's career have revolved around occult themes, whether The Order, The Brothers Grimm or The Imaginarium of Dr Parnassus. Despite this last movie's positive moral lesson, it almost seems to have been written with prior knowledge of his death. There is a definite aura surrounding this actor and the mysterious circumstances around his death only further this feeling. Terry Gilliam said about Heath:

> "Everyone said he died young, but I think he was about 150 when he died. This was not a kid. There was wisdom there. I didn't know where it came from – none of us knew – but everybody that was close to him says the same thing."

People close to Ledger observed a strange transformation in him during the filming of Batman: The Dark Knight. Shortly before his death, he posed for this artwork painted by his friend Vincent Fantauzzo.

The artist depicted Heath surrounded by two 'mind spirits' whispering into his ears. Vincent said the whispering spirits represent Heath's inner thoughts. What was going on in his head? Was he victim of mind control or possession? Was he sacrificed by an occult brotherhood? No positive answer can be given at this point and time.

All I can say for now is Heath Ledger's last line in the film, and his last ever as an actor: Don't shoot the messenger.

The Esoteric Interpretation of "Pan's Labyrinth"

"Pan's Labyrinth" is a profound movie telling the story of a young girl's quest to escape the cruelties of Spanish Fascism. The movie also contains a great amount of occult and archetypal symbols telling another story: one of esoteric illumination through test of character and ritual initiation. We will look at the occult and archetypal symbolism found throughout the movie and their relation with Ofelia's quest.

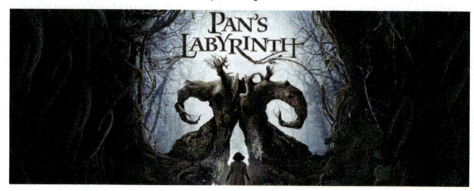

Pan's Labyrinth (Spanish title: El laberinto del fauno) is a Spanish language fantasy film written and directed by Guillermo del Torro, director of The Devil's Backbone, Hellboy and Blade II. The movie's compelling storyline, rich mythological background and strange fantasy world caused many movie critics to consider it as the best movie of 2006.

Like many fairy tales, Pan's Labyrinth is an allegorical story that can be interpreted in numerous ways and on many simultaneous levels. While researching this movie, I came across psychological, sociological and political interpretations of Pan's Labyrinth, but almost none relating to the occult symbolism permeating the work and I've found almost nothing regarding its underlying esoteric story of initiation. This came a surprise as Del Torro himself described the movie as a "parable" and the numerous references to occult mysteries certainly point this way. We will therefore look at the mystical and archetypal symbolism found in the movie and see how they fit into this rich story of esoteric initiation.

One of the reasons why the movie deeply moves its viewers is probably the presence of archetypal myths and symbols that deeply resonate in the collective and personal unconscious:

> "Indeed, once upon a time is a good place to start with a film like Pan's Labyrinth. It is a fairytale above all, an especially dark one too that contains all of those classic mythical archetypes of Jung's collective unconscious. We think of, for instance, the evil king, the heroine in distress, parallel universes, chimerical creatures, and the marching battle between good and evil as portrayed in the story. These are all universal themes, patterns and character types we see in classical fairytales over and over again; the type that led Jungian analyst Donald Kalsched to assert that "When human resources are unavailable, archetypal resources will present themselves." The same can be said of our lead princess, Ofelia. A girl stripped of humanity, crushed by grim realities and forced to draw upon the archetypal myths of the collective human imagination."
> - Psycho-Critical Analysis of "Pan's Labyrinth": Myth, Psychology, Perceptual Realism, Eyes & Traumatic Despondency

Movie Overview

The movie takes place in the mountains of fascist Spain at a military camp fighting against the rebels. Ofelia, a young girl with a wild imagination, obsessed with books and fairy tales, travels with her weak, pregnant mother to meet her new stepfather, a merciless captain of the Spanish army. Upon her arrival, she discovers a labyrinth, and meets a faun that tells her that she is a princess from the "Underworld". He promises her that she can go there and be reunited with her father as long as she completes three tasks for him. In her attempts to complete these tasks, Ofelia is forced to deal with the reality of mortality, the absurdity of war and the meaning of self-sacrifice.

The tale revolves around the juxtaposition of the harsh and oppressive nature of the real world with the magical and sometimes disturbing fairy tale world of the little girl. The faun (named Pan in the English translation) is a horned beast that guides Ofelia through her initiation process and shows her the way to depart from the absurdity of the material world to re-enter the glory of the spiritual plane, where illuminated beings live: the Underworld.

Having "Eyes to See"

Placing back the faun's missing eye

At the beginning of the movie, Ofelia is almost instinctively lead to a mysterious monument depicting the faun with a missing eye. She finds the missing eye and places it back into its socket. A magical insect/fairy suddenly appears: Ofelia's magical quest can begin. There is a great importance placed on eyes and sight in the movie and this scene tells the viewers, right from the start, that Ofelia's quest is occult in nature as not many have the "eyes to see" the invisible world she is about to experience.

> "Having mentioned sight, the film has much to say about it. Guillermo Del Toro almost seems to presuppose that the viewer needs a third "Zen" eye to capture the quintessential truths buried deep within the film's archetypal margins. As Derrida posited, the most important meanings are not in the text itself, but "in the margins," or subtext. In other words, scientists and secularists need to leave the theater. When Ofelia returns the eye of the statue to its rightful place, her fantastical journey immediately begins. Her eyes allow her to see things both visible and invisible, real and unreal, which starkly contrasts with the fascist villain, Captain Vidal, one who punctures the eyes of others and believes not in what cannot be physically seen."
> - Ibid

The importance of the Eye is of the utmost importance in occult symbolism and can be dated back to ancient Egypt with the myth of Horus' eye being restored by Toth. While the right eye is associated with the perception of concrete and factual information (male side of the brain), the left eye of Horus perceives the mystical, the spiritual and the intuition (the female side of the brain). By placing back the eye in its place, Ofelia restores the all-important balance needed to embark into her alchemical transformation.

Ofelia soon realizes however that the adults surrounding her certainly do not believe in what cannot be physically seen, making her quest quite a lonely one.

The Oppressive Father-Dictator and the Cronus Complex

Captain Vidal cursing at Ofelia

Once she has arrived at the war camp, Ofelia meets with her new step-father, the cruel and sadistic Captain Vidal. The character is a representation of Spanish Fascism and, on a philosophical level, of the oppressive material world most people abide in without questioning which prohibits the full emancipation of the being. This phenomena is known as the "Cronus Complex", Cronus being the Greek mythological figure representing time, death and harvesting.

> "The Cronus Complex is not a murderous tendency per say, since Cronus did not just got rid of his offspring, but a destructive ingestive process which hinders the child's capacity to exist separately and autonomously from the parent. In consuming his child, Cronus does not only aim to annihilate him but does so by making him part of himself. According to Bolen, since ancient times, the Cronus Complex is a tendency through which male oriented cultures have maintained power. That is evident is systems such as Fascism, one of the most radical mutations of patriarchy."
> - John W. Crandall, The Cronus Complex

A painting of Cronus devouring his child by Goya

Cronus is also known as "father time". Captain Vidal is often shown looking at and maintaining his watch, time being the most damning limitation of the material world. Ofelia—and everyone around her—is terrified by Captain Vidal but, in order to complete her initiation, Ofelia will need to emancipate herself from this oppressive father figure and, most importantly, get in touch with her oppressed feminine and magical side. Restoring the equilibrium of duality is a necessary step in alchemical transformation.

The Faun and his Labyrinth

Disgusted by her new life, Ofelia is led by a fairy to an overgrown labyrinth where the Faun steps out of the shadows. When she asks him "Who are you?", he replies "I've been called so many names that only the wind and the trees can pronounce. I am the the mountain, the forest, the earth. I am … a faun." He then continues: "It was the moon that bore you. And your real father waits for your return, but first, we must be sure that you have not become mortal".

In ancient mythology, fauns, satyrs and the Greek god Pan were somewhat similar as they all bear the hindquarters, legs, and horns of a goat. Pan is a prototype of natural energy and is undoubtedly a phallic deity, representing the impregnating power of the sun. The faun becomes a sort of spiritual guide to Ofelia, helping her through the actual and figurative labyrinth she must go through. Despite the faun's monstrous appearance—which leads viewers to think at first that he is the "bad guy"—he is actually the only being in Ofelia's life that understands her desire to "become more" and to reach her full potential. The actual "bad guy" in the movie is not the hideous creature, but the cruel step-father.

The Labyrinth

"Labyrinths and mazes were favoured places of initiation among many ancient cults. Remains of these mystic mazes have been found among the American Indians, Hindus, Persians, Egyptians, and Greeks." - Manly P. Hall, Secret Teachings of All Ages

Found in the initiation rites of many ancient civilizations, mazes were symbolic of the involvements and illusions of the lower world through which wanders the soul of man in its search for truth. Pan's Labyrinth is mostly a figurative one as Ofelia must avoid the pitfalls and the dead-ends of the material world in order to be reunited with her true father.

The First Task: Finding the Sacred Feminine

The first task given by the Faun to Ofelia is to retrieve a key from a giant toad who is sucking the life out of an ancient fig tree. There starts the quest of "returning to the womb" and the rekindling the oppressed feminine. The interior of the tree is damp and moist, symbolizing once again the womb-giver of life. The tree itself looks like a uterus.

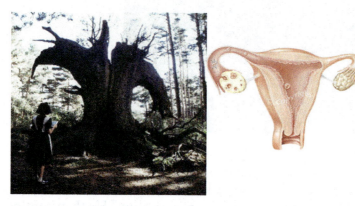

Ofelia wearing a black version of the dress of Alice in Wonderland. Also, a picture of a uterus, in case you forgot what one looks like.

Ofelia's trauma/fascination with the feminine principle is expressed many times in the movie, mainly through her weak and pregnant mother who ultimately has to give her life to give birth. In one disturbing scene, Ofelia sees in her Book of the Crossroads the outline of a uterus that becomes red, predicting her mother's complications.

The Second Task: The Pale Man

Having successfully completed the first task, Ofelia receives a second mission from the faun which is the retrieval of a dagger from the Pale Man. There is however one important condition: She cannot eat anything there.

The immobile Pale Man with his eyeballs on a plate in front of him

The Pale Man is a big flabby creature sitting in front of a great feast. Looking around, Ofelia sees stacks of shoes and depictions of the Pale Man eating children, which is, once again reminiscent of Goya's depiction of Cronus. The Pale Man is a gruesome representation of the oppressive powers of Ofelia's world – Captain Vidal, Spanish Fascism and the Catholic Church. To further this comparison, a scene of Vidal having dinner with his guests, including a Catholic priest, is shown in parallel, in which nobody dares to question the Captain's cruel motives.

Ofelia manages to retrieve the dagger, but on her way out, cannot resist the temptation of eating a big juicy grape, symbolizing the wealth accumulated by the Cronus figures. This awakes the Pale Man, who immediately places his eyeballs in his hands and starts chasing Ofelia.

The pale Man has is eyes in his hands, representing the fact that he can only sees what is palpable. It can possibly represent the stigmata.

Ofelia manages to escape the Pale Man, but at what cost?

The Third Task: The Ultimate Sacrifice

The Faun was furious at Ofelia for giving in to the temptations of the material world and questioned her worthiness to become a true immortal. He therefore leaves her in coldness of the real world, where Ofelia has to witness war, torment and sadness. Shortly after Ofelia's mother's death, however, the faun reappears, to the great joy of the girl. He allows her to complete her initiation, but he demands her complete obedience. For her final task, the Faun asks Ofelia to bring her new born baby brother to the labyrinth at night during the full moon, the prime time to complete a spiritual transformation in occultism.

Ofelia must therefore steal the baby from Captain Vidal by drugging him and runs to the labyrinth, where the faun awaits her.

The faun asks Ofelia to give him the baby so he can prick him with the dagger and obtain a drop of blood from him. Ofelia refuses. The faun loses his patience and reminds her that he requires her full obedience, but she still refuses. At this point, Captain Vidal finds Ofelia, whom, in his point of view, is talking to herself (as he cannot see the faun). He takes the baby from her and shoots her.

Ofelia laying bloody on the ground after being shot by Captain Vidal

Drops of Ofelia's own blood falls into the labyrinth, thus accomplishing the final task required for her initiation: self sacrifice.

The Initiation

While we see Ofelia laying bloody on the ground, she is also shown in another realm, the Underworld, reuniting with her true parents.

Ofelia reuniting with her parents, symbolizing her successful initiation

The entire palace bears the shape of a vesica piscis, an ancient occult symbol representing the vulva, the entrance to the womb and the gateway to another world. Standing on three pillars, the father, the mother and the soon to be princess will complete trinity of the Underworld. The faun greats Ofelia, telling her she did well by going against his orders and sacrificing her life to protect her innocent brother. Indeed, a strong will, sacrifice and rebirth are necessary for the completion of an initiation into occult mysteries. Ofelia is then shown again laying on the floor bloody, making the viewers ask themselves: did this actually happen or is it all in the girl's imagination?

In Conclusion

Pan's Labyrinth describes the quest of a young girl unable to cope with the harshness of the physical world, where dehumanization and repression crush her innocent and playful spirit. It has been shown that children often psychologically respond to an unbearable reality by dissociating into a fantasy world, where magic, adventure and wonder are to be found. Ofelia is often reminded by her mother that "magic does not exist her and no one else". The magical world however seems to exist beyond Ofelia's imagination. One example is the mystical plant given by the faun, the mandrake, which was healing Ofelia's mother from her ills, until she found it under her bed and, disgusted by it, burned it.

Ofelia with the mandrake, the "plant that wanted to be a man". Its presence in the movie is a reminder that all magic is not fairy tales and that occult knowledge can have actual applications in real life.

The mandrake in ancient documents

The mandrake is an important plant in occult lore mainly due to the fact that its roots are often shaped like a human body, complete with arms and feet.

> "The occult properties of the mandrake, while little understood, have been responsible for the adoption of the plant as a talisman capable of increasing the value or quantity of anything with which it was associated. As a phallic charm, the mandrake was considered to be an infallible cure for sterility. It was one of the Priapic symbols which the Knights Templars were accused of worshipping. The root of the plant closely resembles a human body and often bore the outlines of the human head, arms, or legs. This striking similarity between the body of man and the mandragora is one of the puzzles of natural science and is the real basis for the veneration in which this plant was held. In Isis Unveiled, Madam Blavatsky notes that the mandragora seems to occupy upon earth the point where the vegetable and animal kingdoms meet, as the zoophites and polypi do in die sea. This thought opens a vast field of speculation concerning the nature of this animal-plant."
> - Manly P. Hall, The Secret Teachings of All Ages

This movie is one of opposites and reversals: reality versus fiction, good versus evil, innocence versus adulthood, feminine versus masculine, overworld versus underworld, etc. Even the very ending can be interpreted in two opposite ways: either Ofelia created a fairy-tale world in her head to escape real life and ultimately committed a form of suicide or she's simply an awakened being who saw what the masses bound to the material world cannot see and ultimately completed her process of illumination to become a true immortal. The story is also an inversion of the usual paradigm for self-actualization: Ofelia's transformation happens in the shadows and in the dark while enlightenment, as it name says, is associated with light; Ofelia's illumination happens in the Underworld while spiritual transformation is usually associated with "the heavens"; the initiator himself, Pan, is a deity known for getting drunk in the woods and frolicking nymphs (and the odd goat) while illumination is based on the mastery of one's lower impulses; the completion of Ofelia's initiation requires her to crawl in the mud, be chased by a Pale Man and finally spill her blood while the usual path to illumination is based on the master of self and uncorrupted virtue. So what is the true fate of Ofelia? As the last line of the movie states: the clues to the answer can be found by those who have the eyes to see.

The Occult Symbolism of Movie "Metropolis" and its Importance in Pop Culture

Fritz Lang's 1927 movie "Metropolis" is one of those timeless classics that withstand the test of time. Rather than becoming forgotten and obsolete, "Metropolis" is increasingly relevant as many of its predictions are becoming reality. We will look at the underlying occult message of the film and the usage of its imagery in the acts of pop stars such as Lady Gaga, Madonna, Beyonce, Kylie Minogue and others.

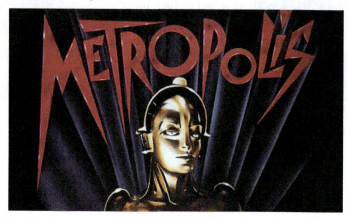

Metropolis is a silent science-fiction movie released in 1927 by Fritz Lang, a master of German Expressionism. Set in a futuristic dystopia divided into two distinct and separate classes—the thinkers and the workers—Metropolis describes the struggles between the two opposite entities. Knowing that it was produced in 1927, viewing this movie today is quite an experience as many "sci-fi" aspects of the plot are eerily close to reality. Metropolis describes a society where the "New World Order" has already taken been implemented and a select elite live in luxury while a dehumanized mass work and live in a highly monitored hell.

As we have seen in previous articles on The Vigilant Citizen, Metropolis is excessively echoed in popular culture, especially in the music business. Whether it be in music videos or photo shoots, pop stars are often portrayed as the character Maria, an android programmed to corrupt the morals of the workers and to incite a revolt, giving the elite an excuse to use violence repression. Are pop stars used by the elite in the same matter, to corrode the morals of the masses?

The Workers

The movie opens by showing the workers and their city, situated deep below the earth's surface. They are shown dressed alike, walking in sync, holding their heads down in submission, resignation and desperation. Throughout the movie, the human cattle is depicted as being physically and mentally exhausted, highly impressionable and, let's say it, all-around dumb. Like a flock of sheep, the workers move in crowds, are very impressionable and can easily be deceived. This description of the masses corroborates those of Walter Lippmann, an American thinker who, five years earlier in Public Opinion, compared the general public to a "bewildered herd" that is not qualified to manage its own destiny. Joseph Goebbels, the head of propaganda of the Nazi regime, was also in accord with the movie's conception of the general public. Hitler famously said "How fortunate for leaders that men do not think".

The workers at shift change

The workers labor in a monstrous machine, a hellish industrial complex where they must accomplish repetitive and dehumanizing tasks. At one point, the machine is compared to Moloch, the ancient Semitic deity honored by human sacrifices.

In one of his visions, Fredersen sees the Machine turning into Moloch. The workers are fed to the beast as human sacrifices.

Moloch the God Baal, the Bull of the Sun, was widely worshipped in the ancient Near East and wherever Carthaginian culture extended. Baal Moloch was conceived under the form of a calf or an ox or depicted as a man with the head of a bull. The sacrifices went through the "belly of the beast".

The tasks assumed by the workers are purely mechanical, needing absolutely no brain power, making them nothing more than an extension of the machine.

The workers accomplish repetitive, mind-numbing tasks, stripping them of their humanity.

The Thinkers

The gleaming city of the Thinkers

If the workers live in a hellish underground dystpia, the thinkers conversely evolve in a gleaming utopia, a magnificent testimony of human achievement. This shiny city could not, however, be sustained without the existence of the Machine (Moloch) and its herds of workers. On the other hand, the Machine would not exist without the need to sustain a city. We find here a dualistic relation where two opposite entities exist in mutual dependence, a concept that has deep occult resonance.

In a thinly veiled reference to the hermetic axiom "As Above, So Below", the movie describes the mirroring yet opposite environments in which in the thinkers and the workers live in.

The hermetic Seal of Salomon visually depicts the concept of "As above, So below" while representing opposites energies mirroring each other to achieve perfect balance. Fritz Lang's world perfectly recreates this concept.

Joh Fredersen, the Demi-God

The city was founded, built and is run by the autocratic Joh Fredersen. As the creator and only ruler of Metropolis, Fredersen is likened to the Gnostic demiurge, a demi-god who is creator and ruler of the material world.

Joh Federsen, plotting his next move. He is holding a compass, reminding viewers of his role as the "great architect" of Metropolis.

William Blake's representation of the gnostic demiurge, creator and ruler of the imperfect lower plane, where sin and suffering prevails. The compass borrows from Masonic symbolism for God as the "Great Architect of the Universe".

Joh's son, named Freder, who, like all sons of managers, was enjoying a life of luxury, discovers the harsh reality of the workers of down under. Wanting to experience the worker's reality first-hand, Freder descends to the lower level and trades places with a worker. Freder therefore becomes a Christ-like figure, a savior who descends from above. He also becomes enamoured with Maria, a saintly young women from the proletariat.

Maria

Maria preaching to the workers.

Maria is a charismatic woman that is highly admired by her fellow workers. Understanding their suffering and despair, and knowing that a revolt is brewing, Maria preaches peace and patience, prophesying the coming of a "mediator", who would become the "heart between the head (the thinkers) and the hand (the workers)

At one point, Maria tells the story of the tower of Babel, upon which would be written:

> "Great is the world and its Creator! And great is Man!"

This statement has a deep resonance in Mystery Schools as it is taught that men have the potential to become gods through enlightenment. Throughout the ages, monuments and architecture were used to communicate the principles of the Mysteries and to celebrate the greatness of the human mind. Partially for those reasons, there are numerous links between Freemasonry and the Tower of Babel.

> "As regards to Masonry, Babel of course represented a Masonic enterprise and early expositors reaped full benefit from the facts. They remembered that the people, who were of 'one language and one speech' journeyed from the East to the West, like those who have been tried and proved as Master Masons. When they reached an abiding place in the land Shinar, it is affirmed that they dwelt therein as Noachide, being the first characteristic name of Masons. It was here that they built their high tower of confusion. Out of evil comes good, however, and the confusion of tongues gave rise to 'the ancient practice of Masons conversing without the use of speech.'"
> - Arthur Edward Waite, A New Encyclopedia of Freemasonry and of Cognate Instituted Mysteries vol. I

> "In several early Masonic manuscripts – for example, the Harleian, Sloane, Lansdowne, and Edinburgh-Kilwinning – it is stated that the craft of initiated builders existed before the Deluge, and that its members were employed in the building of the Tower of Babel."
> - Manly P. Hall, The Secret Teachings of All Ages

> "... at the making of the Tower of Babel there was Masonry first much esteemed of, and Nimrod was a Mason himself and loved well Masons."
> - John T Lawrence, The Perfect Ashlar

However, says Maria, "one man's hymns of praise became the other man's curse". In other words, the monument praising the greatness of the human spirit was built with the blood and sweat of workers who knew nothing of the Thinker's grand vision. And, in the film, the same thing is happening all over again. The name of the demi-god Joh Fredersen's headquarters? Of course … The New Tower of Babel.

Joh Ferdersen's headquarters named the New Tower of Babel.

Rotwang

Rotwang with his trademark mechanical right hand, which replaces the one he lost during one of his experiments. Is this a symbol signifying that the inventor embraces the "left-handed path"?

Upon learning that the workers are planning an uprising, Joh Federsen seeks the advice of Rotwang, an inventor and mad scientist. Although his work utilizes the latest of technologies, many clues within the movie indicate that he also taps into ancient occult knowledge to create his inventions. He is said to live in "a small house overlooked by the centuries," symbolically meaning that the scientist's arcana descended from ancient occult traditions; the basement of his house has a secret trap door leading to 2,000 year-old catacombs, further alluding to the ancient and mysterious sources of Rotwang. Furthermore, the front door of his house bears a pentagram, which refers to the Pythagoreans, occultism and Freemasonry.

If we were to do real-life comparisons, Rotwang is to Joh Fredersen what John Dee was to Queen Elizabeth I: an esteemed advisor immersed in the worlds of science, magic, astrology and Hermetic philosophy. If Fredersen represents our world's rulers, Rotwang is the occult pendant of decision-making, the mystical entity that is hidden from the public but always historically present.

A pentagram on Rotwang's door. Disciples of Pythagoras affixed a pentagram on their door as a secret sign of mutual recognition. The sign and its meaning could remain secret despite that public display because only those initiated into the mysteries of Pythagoras' geometry were able to draw it correctly and to appreciate its deep significance as a symbol for and gateway to those mysteries.

The inventor proudly presents to Fredersen his latest invention, the Machine-Man, which he considers to be the "Man of the Future". The android has the faculty of taking the form of any person and, says Rotwang, "no one will be able to tell a Machine Man from a mortal!". The transhumanist dream was already present back in the early 1920s.

Fredersen then tells Rotwang to give the Machine-Man the likeness of Maria in order to use her credibility and charisma to spread corruption among the workers.

Maria laying down while Rotwang gives her likeness to the android. Notice the inverted pentagram right above the Machine-Man's head. If the upright pentagram represents healing, mathematical perfection and the five elements, the inverted pentagram stands for the corruption of those principles and black magic.

So what do today's pop stars have in common with this android, programmed by the rulers, with a mix of science and occultism? Well ... everything.

Lady Gaga in her Paparazzi video

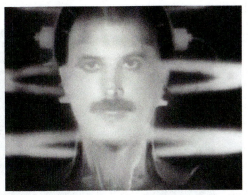

Freddie Mercury from Queen with his face instead of Maria's in Radio Gaga. Lady Gaga's name was inspired by this song and video, which contains a lot of footage from Metropolis.

Beyonce

Metropolis themes are also very prevalent in fashion

Kylie Minogue

Janelle Monae

Lady Gaga in Dave Lachapelle photo shoot that is heavily inspired by Metropolis.

Back to the movie. The android completed, Rotwang tells it:

> "I want you to visit those in the depths, in order to destroy the work of the woman in whose image you were created!"

Robot-maria responds:

One eye closed with devilish grin. You probably know the importance of the single eye from previous articles and the ridiculous amount of pop artists who flash it.

The Maria android is then sent to Yoshiwara, a man's club, where she performs erotic dances. In one of her acts, she is portrayed as Babylon, the Great Harlot from the Apocalypse.

Playing the role of the Great Harlot Babylon of the Book of Revelation. "And the woman was arrayed in purple and scarlet colour, having a golden cup in her hand". She is held up by the seven deadly sins.

Do this scene remind you of a classic music video?

Madonna – Material Girl. How many realized that she was playing the role of Babylon here?

The programmed Maria performs mesmerizing dances in front of an avid public, causing men to fight, to lust, to be jealous and to commit the rest of the deadly sins. When she's with her fellow workers, Maria acts as an "agent-provocateur", inciting the working men to riot and giving Joh Fredersen reason to use force against them. She is basically acting against the best interest of the public and for the interest of the elite.

With the help of their foreman (because they can't really think for themselves), the workers ultimately realize that they have been mislead by the android. Believing that she's a witch, they find robot-Maria and burn her at the stake.

A bunch of things happen after that, but I won't spoil the ending for you (though can you really be mad at someone for spoiling the ending of a 83-year old movie?). The movie finishes with this caption:

> THE MEDIATOR BETWEEN HEAD AND HANDS MUST BE THE HEART!

This "moral of the story" is basically a message to the elite, a tip to keep the masses in check: in order to keep the oppressed content, you must capture their heart. That is what the media accomplish.

Madonna's Express Yourself video heavily borrowed its imagery from Metropolis. In turn, Christina Aguilera's Not Myself Tonight, heavily borrowed from Express Yourself.

The Moral of the Story

The moral of the story of Metropolis is not "let's abolish all inequities and rebuild a world where everyone is equal" and it is certainly not "let's be democratic and vote for who we want as a ruler." It is more "let's send the workers back to the depths where they belong, but with the addition of a mediator, who will be the link between the workers and the thinkers". So, when all is said and done, the movie is intrinsically "elitist," as it still calls for the existence of an elite group of people holding most of the resources and managing a working class. In the end, the workers – and Freder – were duped, believing that their conditions would change. In fact, the status-quo remained and Joh even got his naive son to give the elite a friendly image while reporting everything happening in the depths, resulting in tighter surveillance and control.

Who is the Freder of today's working class? The media. Media is the mediator. That is its function.

Fredersen, the link between "the hand and the head", the Workers and the Thinkers. This role is played today by the media.

Mass media manipulate the masses' thoughts and feelings on a daily basis, tricking them into loving their oppression. Popular culture is the entertainment branch of mass media and pop music is the fun way to communicate the elite's message to the youth. References to Metropolis in pop music are almost winks to those in the know, the initiates, as if to say "this star is working for us". So go ahead and be an ignorant, degenerate and materialistic person, like in the videos … that's what they want you to be.

But why Metropolis? Why has it become the code for "Illuminati star"? If you've read other articles on this site, you've probably realized that the movie touches upon all of the themes of today's "Illuminati agenda": transhumanism, mind control, dark occultism, degradation of morals, police state, all-seeing government. Metropolis is basically a blueprint for population control. Like Maria, today's pop stars are recruited from the working class and literally programmed and reinvented to become the hidden ruler's spokespersons. Notice how many pop stars have wild alter-egos, with a different name and personality. Part of the stars' role is to promote the elite's agenda through music and videos, making it sexy and attractive.

In Conclusion

Metropolis is a definitely a movie "by the elite, for the elite". It tackles the concerns of those managing the world and presents a solution that does not disturb the status-quo. The movie is also permeated with Masonic symbolism and contains many symbols referring to ancient Mysteries which were meant to be decoded by proper initiates. In other words, the movie was primarily aimed at the ruling class.

So why do singers love it so much? Well they probably don't love it as much as those behinds the scenes, the directors and image-makers, those who have power in the music business. They decide what the stars do and stand for. And today's popular culture is elitist, permeated with Illuminati symbolism and promotes moral degradation and the debasement of traditional values. Our pop stars channel Maria, the programmed android, through their acts and accomplish the same functions. Why else would they dress like her? If artists always embodied absolute freedom and creativity, why do singers play the role of a mind-controlled android? Because that's what they are.

Metropolis is indeed a great movie. So great that it is only becoming relevant 80 years after its release. But if the elite have it their way, it will be even more relevant in the years to come.

How the Animated Series G.I. Joe Predicted Today's Illuminati Agenda

G.I. Joe is an iconic cartoon TV show that marked an entire generation of young boys during the 80s. Most fans still recall the main characters and the epic gun fights. But what about the storyline? A look at the TV series in today's context is quite a strange experience: Many of Cobra's "far-out" plots are actually happening today. Could G.I. Joe be a case of predictive programming? We will look at some G.I. Joe episodes describing the replacement of the US dollar and the usage of mind control on celebrities and civilians and see how they relate in today's context.

As a guy who grew up in the 80s, I can personally attest that G.I. Joe was definitely on the menu in my after-school TV cartoon line-up. If you're a younger reader, let me tell you this (at the risk of sounding like a grumpy uncle): G.I. Joe wasn't your wimpy Dora the Explorer cartoon. It was a half-hour full of bad-ass characters face-kicking and laser-gun-shooting their way to victory. And that's pretty much what I remembered of this TV show – laser-gun shootouts – until recently.

A reader of this site recommended I view a particular episode of the series called Money to Burn, which depicts in great detail a vital part of today's NWO agenda (discussed later). I was in shock. So I watched other episodes in the series and this is what I saw: psychological warfare, tapping into occult forces to obtain political power, military research funded by huge corporations and mind control used on civilians and celebrities. The series pretty much summed up the entire contents of the Vigilant Citizen website. Most of the shady things are accomplished by Cobra Commander, the "bad-guy" of the show, who is a ruthless terrorist aiming for world domination. The Joes always managed to stop Cobra, however, dismantling his evil schemes in an orgy of laser-gun fire and spectacular explosions.

Watching the shows today, however, was very unsettling: Because of open-access information laws and the Internet, it is slowly coming to light that today's shadow governments are actually carrying out most of Cobra's plans … in real life. News about these plans come on a daily basis in mainstream news. Did G.I. Joe contain "predictive programming", a technique based on planting ideas and concepts in the brains of viewers in order to make them seem normal and easily accepted when they actually happen?

Show Overview

G.I. Joe: A Real American Hero ran in syndication from 1985 to 1989. The opening title sequence stated: "G.I. Joe is the code name for America's daring, highly-trained Special Mission force. Its purpose: To defend human freedom against Cobra, a ruthless terrorist organization determined to rule the world." The shows ended with a public service announcement, where the Joes gave safety tips to the children. These announcements always concluded with a now-famous saying: "Knowing is half the battle!"

The animated series was designed to promote Hasbro's line of action figures of the same name. In fact, each episode purposely featured a different character in order to boost the associated toy's sales. Maybe this is the reason why the Joes had relatively lame and clichéd dialogue compared to the more complex and interesting Cobras. Other than promoting merchandise, the series pushed an obvious pro-American-military-industrial-complex agenda, a reflection of the Reagan-era dogma happening at the time, which was characterized by a showdown with the Soviet Union. In this context, one might expect the Cobra Organization to represent the "evil communists" as was the trend in so many movies in the 1980s.

Surprisingly, that is not the case. The "bad guys" in G.I. Joe are actually funded by a huge American corporation named Extensive Enterprises and its reptilian leaders (wink to David Icke) carried out their devious plans from hidden "Cobra Temples". These bases, established all across the world with no regard to national borders, were often situated in mystical locations, such as Easter Island or by China's underground terracotta warriors (Cobras apparently believe in the powers of geomancy). In fact, the Cobra Organization bears few characteristics of a communist or "terrorist" organization and many characteristics of an elitist secret society in the style of what we call the Illuminati.

The "Cobra Command" shaped like an unfinished pyramid. This shape can be found in many instances in Cobra Temples.

The unfinished pyramid is today's most famous Illuminati symbol.

Even more significant is the plot of the first G.I. Joe episode ever aired. In the mini-series, titled Pyramid of Darkness, Cobra seeks to take control of the world by shutting down the power grid of the Northern Hemisphere.

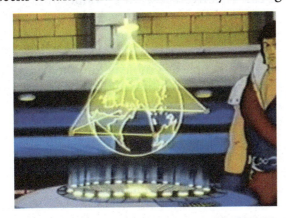

The Cobra elite visualizing their plans for creating a Pyramid of Darkness on earth. Creating a pyramid to keep the world "in the dark" is a powerful symbol for Illuminati control of the masses. The word Illuminati stands for "the enlightened" ... most of its power is based on the masses being as ignorant and dumbed-down as possible. In other words: in the dark.

As we watch later episodes, it becomes noticeable that Cobra Commander's numerous plans to conquer the world are eerily similar to actual events happening today, 25 years after the broadcast of these episodes, in another example of how "science fiction" is indeed becoming reality. Here are some aspects of the Illuminati agenda that were exploited in G.I. Joe:

Making Paper Money Worthless and Taking Possession of People's Gold

In the episode entitled Money to Burn, Cobra finds a way to instantly burn all of America's paper money using a "thermo-molecular ignition transmitter", effectively rendering the American dollar useless.

A scared lady seeing her money bursting into flames.

Cobra then addresses the nation through a TV broadcast (he seems to have easy access to mass media). This is what he says:

> "Attention citizens! Due to the financial irresponsibility and incompetence of your leaders, Cobra has found it necessary to restructure your nation's economy. We have begun by eliminating the worthless green paper, which your government has deceived you into believing is valuable. Cobra will come to your rescue and, out of the ashes, will arise a NEW ORDER!"

This is pretty deep stuff for a show aimed at children under 12. This speech basically outlines the modus operandi of the Illuminati shadow government: create a crisis, cause chaos, claim to have the only solution, get people to beg for that solution, and restore "Order out of Chaos". Furthermore, declaring this New Order to rise out of its ashes is reminiscent of the Masonic concept of a phoenix rising out of the ashes.

There is truth in Cobra's statement regarding the real value of paper money. The American dollar has had no actual value since 1971, when the gold standard was abandoned by the Nixon administration. The American dollar's value used to be based on a fixed weight of gold. Today it can effectively lose all its value and become worthless overnight, as its value is not backed by any tangible goods ... and this is what was happening in this episode of G.I. Joe.

After Cobra's announcement, the dazed and confused American people assemble before the Department of Treasury and shout "We want money!", begging the government to provide a solution to their problem. The Joes see the situation and observe that "buying and selling has been replaced by rioting and looting".

Then Cobra appears on TV again and says:

> "Citizens of the United States, I am pleased to announce Cobra's economic recovery plan! If you want money to buy food for your children, take all your valuables to the nearest branch of Extensive En-

treprises. There, all goods will be exchanged for Cobra currency!"

Cobra presenting the new currency to be exchanged for people's valuables, such as gold.

This exact phenomena is happening today. There is currently a sustained effort to take gold and other valuables off the hands of the public through "Cash for Gold" programs.

In a hidden Cobra Temple, the heads of Extensive Enterprises show a rich client the "largest stockpile of tangible assets ever assembled". Fortunately, the Joes come to the rescue, restored the American dollar and destroyed pretty much everything in sight, including the Cobra Temple. Yo Joe!

Mind Controlling Celebrities to Mind Control the Masses

Many articles on this site discuss the use of mind control in popular culture, a concept that might be hard for some to believe. Well, the Joes were fighting it back in 1986.

Sold Out Singers

In the episode entitled Rendez-Vous in the City of the Dead, Shipwreck and Snake Eyes (two G.I. Joe characters) enter a Cobra-owned night club named "Snake Club" (Cobra obviously knows the power of indoctrinating the youth through entertainment). There, a signer named Satin sings the praise of Cobra in the form of a love song. The singers' backup dancers are dressed alike in Cobra-style costumes.

Backup dancers making Cobra control cool and fashionable.

Now, where did I see a famous singer performing on stage with dancers symbolizing the people's oppression? Oh, right, right, right ...

Beyonce making police in riot gear cool and fashionable at the 2010 Grammy Awards.

MK-Ultra Celebrities

In another episode, titled Glamour Girls, the show describes nothing less than the use of MK Ultra in the entertainment business.

Cobra Commander, with the help of Dr. Mindbender, strikes a deal with an international cosmetic tycoon. Cobra agrees to provide a constant flow of beautiful young girls to the company in exchange for a face-transplant technology developed by the tycoon. Cobra therefore launches "Operation High Fashion", which aims to recruit young models, singers and actresses by catering to their dreams of being famous.

In order to lure these girls, Cobra sends them invitations to a photo shoot, which will appear in an issue of "Glamour Girls" magazine, the most prestigious fashion magazine in the world – a publication that is owned by Cobra's Extensive Enterprises (Cobra of course owns multiple media outlets, like today's Illuminati).
Not surprisingly, all of the girls who received an invitation are ecstatic at the idea of appearing in the magazine

and they gladly present themselves at the Glamour Girls building for the photo shoot. But they are being tricked: The camera's flash sends subliminal hypnotic messages to the models, making them highly suggestible and easily manageable.

Once hypnotized, the models obey any command.

The models are then instructed to go to a "party" and they do so without questioning. In their mind-controlled state, the models dissociate from reality and perceive the party as being a glamorous get-together attended by classy gentlemen. When their hypnotic state wears off however, the harsh reality kicks in.

When the girls snap out of their dissociative state, one of them says "We're not in Kansas anymore". This is a reference to the Wizard of Oz, a movie that is used in actual mind control programming. Being in or out of "Kansas" is in fact a code word regarding a subject's dissociative state.

All of the young girls and celebrities who fall for this trap are manhandled and thrown into a dungeon. The theme of mind control is becoming increasingly prevalent in today's fashion industry and it is often coded with the use

A celebrity trapped in a heavily guarded dungeon. Similar programming facilities are used in actual mind control projects.

of lifeless mannequins and Monarch butterflies. Fortunately, the Joes manage to track down the Cobra's dungeon, punch everybody's lights out and rescue the young ladies. Yo Joe!

Using Mind-Controlled Civilians in Secret Military Missions

In Operation Mind Menace, the theme of mind control is yet again exploited. In this episode, the Cobra Organization kidnaps civilians known to have psychic abilities, in order to harness their power and use them in secret missions.

In Monarch programming terms, this is known as "Theta Programming" and it encompasses the usage of psychic

Kidnapped civilians with psychic powers entering the Cobra Temple. The device on their chests are amplifiers. Similar devices are reportedly implanted in the brains of actual Theta programming victims.

powers, such as extra-sensory perception (ESP), remote viewing, telepathy and psychic killing. Documents have been released proving that the CIA has been conducting experiments to harness these powers and to use them on the battlefield since the 1970s:

> "THETA considered to the "psychic" programming. Bloodliners (those coming from multi-generational Satanic families) were determined to exhibit a greater propensity for having telepathic abilities than did non-bloodliners. Due to its evident limitations, however, various forms of electronic mind control systems were developed and introduced, namely, bio-medical human telemetry devices (brain implants), directed-energy lasers using microwaves and/or electromagnetics."
> - Ron Patton, Project Monarch Mind Control

> "Theta Programming got its name just as the Alpha, Beta, and Delta Programming in part from the four types of EEG brain waves. Theta waves are frequent in children. (...) Psychic warfare became a branch of the Monarch Programming. This is the Theta Programming. It is the marriage of occult practices with state of the art science. The idea to be able to copy what Elisha did to the King of Syria (2 KG 6:11-12) when he "telepathically" spied on the enemy, discovered their plans, and thereby ruined their chances of success. Today this has been called "ESPionage", and the U.S. Army's term is "psychotronics". Of course, the CIA's position is that they couldn't find anything that worked, but that is simply not true, because the co-authors know of many Theta alters and Theta model systems which have Theta programming which is successful. (...)
>
> Whether the public perceives Psychic warfare as viable or not, billions of dollars have been spent on it, and numerous Theta models produced. (...)
>
> Since slaves can not be consistently given Theta programming, a surgical implantation of a sodium/lithium powered high frequency receiver/transducers coupled with a multi-range discharge capacitor was placed into the brains of Monarch slaves. This gives the handlers the ability to signal by remote signals to the victim's brain. When the receiver picks up the signals they electronically stimulate certain areas of the brain which in turn triggers pre-set programming. Implants are now being placed in a high percentage of the Monarch slaves."
> - Fritz Springmeier, The Illuminati Formula to Create an Undetectable Mind Control Slave

These secret programs are slyly being revealed to the public in movies. In Men Who Stare at Goats, the issue is presented as comedy. However, the movie is based on an actual US military project: Lieutenant Colonel Jim Channon's First Earth Battalion.

In G.I. Joe, the mind-controlled civilians talk in a robotic manner and are detained in high-tech facilities. Fortunately, the Joes tracked down the Cobras, rescued the civilians and kicked everyone's ass back to sanity. Yo Joe!

The First Earth Battalion was renamed New Earth Army in Men Who Stare At Goats, a unit using extra-sensory powers (ESP). The movie also vaguely alluded to the dark/satanic side of mind control in some scenes.

In Conclusion

G.I. Joe is an iconic mid-80s television series that undoubtedly impacted the imagination of an entire generation of children. The action-packed battle scenes, the memorable characters and the futuristic, sci-fi plots made the show a sure hit with young boys, especially. Watching these shows today, we discover that many of the Cobra's plots have been a hidden reality and/or are slowly becoming reality. And these plans are not coming from "a shadowy terrorist organization" but from our own "elected" leaders and their elite rulers.

The Joes are presented as a group of all-American soldiers with strong values, fighting with integrity and honesty against an ever-plotting terrorist group. They are what the American army is supposed to be and the ideal image that the military-industrial-complex want us to believe. But the Joe's enemies, the ever-plotting terrorist group is not a foreign menace: It exists within the system. In other words, if the Joes existed today, they would probably be fighting their own government , the hidden part of it … what we call the Illuminati.

So the question remains: Why did the series describe these sophisticated plans with such vivid details to its youthful audience? Was G.I. Joe one of the many TV shows and movies sponsored by the American government and the owners of the mass media companies who broadcast it? Were they preparing the youth to the revelation of realities by exposing it to them at a young age? Were they trying to warn the public? The creators of this show definitely knew the answer to these questions, and we should too. Because knowing is half the battle.

Josie and the Pussycats: Blueprint of the Mind Control Music Industry

"Josie and the Pussycats" is a "girl band movie" aimed at children and young adolescents, especially young girls. At first glance, the flick seems to be one of those generic, God-awful teen movies. However, a closer look reveals how its overall tone and message are in sharp contrast to stereotypes of the genre. "Josie and the Pussycats" is indeed an acerbic critique of a morally bankrupt music industry. The most surprising thing about this 2001 movie is its frighteningly accurate predictions regarding today's pop music and its Illuminati agenda: mind controlled artists, hypnotized masses, subliminal messages… it's all there. This article will examine the movie's themes and their relation to today's music business context.

Josie and the Pussycats was released in 2001 by Universal. In music industry terms, 2001 is ancient history. Just to put you back in the context of the era: N'Sync were still singing Bye Bye Bye, Cisco wanted to see your thong-th-th-thong-thong-thong and everybody was wondering Who Let the Dogs Out. Teens were going crazy for boy bands like the Backstreet Boys and everybody was dancing to Ja Rule. So, yes, it was a long time ago.

Josie and the Pussycats came out during that period, but it seems to foretell the death of the era. The movie starts with members of the boy band "Du Jour," a spoof on the Backstreet Boys, dying in a forced plane crash. The group is then replaced by a girl band with a semi-punky attitude and non-threatening pop rock music. This pretty much reflects what actually happened in the years following the release of this movie: N'Sync and the Backstreet Boys disappeared from the preteen music market and were replaced by Miley Cyrus, Hilary Duff, the Jonas Brothers, and so on.

Despite the movie's apparent lightheartedness, it displays a harsh and sustained judgment of the music business. It is also severely critical of the state of America's youth. Teens and preteens are constantly depicted as a herd of brainless drones who are incapable of independent thinking and prone to hysteria.
But behind the usual "OMG these big corporations are so corporation-y" criticism, Josie and the Pussycats tackles,

Preteens going crazy for the latest manufactured pop sensation.

in an odd and humorous way, some of the darker sides of the music industry. These include the mind control of the masses and entertainers, and even the assassination of artists who rebel or ask too many questions.

The Boy Band That Knew Too Much

As stated above, the movie starts with Du Jour (the boy band "of the day") enjoying their enormous success. In their private jet, the vain and half-witted group of singers complain about petty things to their record executive Wyatt, who acts more like a legal guardian. Or, in mind control terms, a handler.

The band then asks Wyatt about strange sounds they heard in the acapella tracks of their latest song… and they want some answers.

Du Jour asking their exec Wyatt the purpose of the weird background tracks found on their latest song.

Wyatt's answer is quite extreme, for he and the plane's pilot strap on parachutes and jump off, leaving Du Jour to die in what is afterwards called an "accidental" plane crash. This has actually happened in reality numerous times. Artists who start uncovering the darker side of the entertainment business, who ask too many questions, or worse, who plan to reveal these things to the public, are often dropped, publicly humiliated and scorned. And, as in Du Jour's case, they are also sometimes killed for displaying such behavior.

Mega Records

Du Jour was signed with the world's biggest record label, Mega Records. We soon learn that the company is much more than a record label.

Mega Records is, in fact, "in business" with the American government and the FBI to brainwash the "most influential demographic in the entire population": the youth. While giving a tour of the label's headquarters to visitors from foreign countries (who are there to learn how it's done), Fiona, the eccentric CEO of Mega Records, has this to say:

> "I'm sure you're wondering why agent Kelly and the United States government would be so interested in what appears to be a record company. Well, I'm about to show you why."

Fiona's office then turns into an elevator and starts descending into a secret underground facility.

The label's headquarters is, in fact, a control center for manipulating the minds of the American youth. It creates new fads, decides everything from "what clothes are in style to what slang is in vogue," with the ultimate goal of making the youth continually spend money on one temporary trend after another.

Fiona, the CEO of Mega Records, giving a tour of the secret underground headquarters of the label.

Reality is, of course, more complex than that. Trends are (probably) not created in an underground control center in New York City. There is however truth in this near-cartoonish depiction of the music business. The entertainment industry is indeed connected to "higher powers" (as personified in the movie by the FBI agent) in order to sell the youth on the economic elite's agenda. Popular culture not only attempts to sell products and brands to the audience, but also ideas, values and attitudes. In previous articles on the Vigilant Citizen, we have established that today's agenda focuses on concepts such as transhumanism, Illuminati symbolism, premature sexualization, police state/militarization, and so forth.

Continuing her tour, Fiona says:

> "But how, you may ask, can our operation be so effective? Sure these kids have brains like play dough, just waiting to be molded into shape, but something else must be going on, right?"

Fiona then explains that her label inserts subliminal messages in pop music in order to manipulate the youth into buying products and ideas. The label thus goes beyond the simple advertising of products. It conceals hidden messages in the music that bypass the audience's conscious minds in order to directly reach their subconscious.

After the presentation, a foreigner asks Fiona "How can you control the rock bands? What if one of them discovers you are placing hidden messages in their music?" This is what she answers:

> "Ever wonder why so many rock stars die in plane crashes? Overdosed on drugs? We've been doing this a long time. If they start to get too curious, our options are endless. Bankruptcies... shocking scandals... religious conversions!"

There are numerous real life examples of celebrities who have been silenced, one of the most shocking and evident being Michael Jackson. After decades of being controlled by the entertainment business, he attempted to break free in the late 90s. He even spoke out about it (see the article "When Insiders Reveal the Ugly Side of the Entertainment Business"). He then endured years of scandals, trials, public ridicule and financial difficulties. Michael Jackson still managed to keep singing and dancing, even organizing a world tour for 2010. Since previous attempts to destroy him failed, MJ got silenced... by force. So, it would seem that ten years after the release of this movie, shady celebrity sacrifices are still happening.

New 3D Technology

In an attempt to "take things to the next level," Mega Records develops a new technology called "3DX Surround Sound." This new technology "makes the music feel like it is happening all around you." All the kids who attend Josie and the Pussycats concerts or watch them on TV have to purchase this headgear in order to hear the music. Back in real life, we are seeing the commercialization of a very similar technology: 3D Glasses

Hypnotized, mind controlled teens testing the new 3DX Technology in a Mega Records lab. Note that the girl in the middle is a "free thinker" that got kidnapped by the label in order to have experiments conducted on her.

Josie and the Pussycats: From Nobodies to Sex Kittens Stars

After the killing of Du Jour, record exec Wyatt is instructed to find a new band as soon as possible. The movie makes it clear that talent is absolutely irrelevant. The label just needs a good-looking group and it will take care of the rest. Then we are introduced to The Pussycats… and their lack of fans.

The Pussycats performing in a bowling alley, with nobody listening to them. Most overnight successes start from humble beginnings, until the industry takes them, changes them and sells them to the public.

The rock band comprises three young ladies who wear leopard ears as a prop. It is quite obvious that nobody wants to hear their music and even their manager Alexander doesn't seem to like it.

After hearing about Du Jour's plane crash on television, The Pussycats leader, Josie, is motivated to "get out there" and obtain a record contract. At the same time, Wyatt is driving around in the small town of Riverdale, looking for a band to sign. Then it happens.

Wyatt literally runs into The Pussycats crossing the street. Some dudes coincidentally walk behind them holding a sign with "#1 Band in the World" on it. That's pretty much all Wyatt needed to see to sign them.

Wyatt sits down with the girls and tells them how happy he is "to be sitting down with The Pussyhats." He obviously knows nothing about the band and does not care. He then offers them a record contract with Mega Records. Josie wonders briefly why her band is being offered a contract by a label that did not even hear them play. However, her hunger for fame dispels all her doubts and the band signs the contract.

The Pussycats' story is classic: a broke, struggling band attempts to become big by performing gigs; a record label offers a shady contract; the desperate and fame-hungry band signs, not knowing what they are getting into. For the band, it's either taking a chance and signing the contract or going back to eating Ramen noodles in a crappy apartment. So, they sign the contract.

Right after they sign, the label subjects the group to a complete metamorphosis: a make-over to "sexy them up," and a name change, from The Pussycats to Josie and the Pussycats. The group is now completely owned by the label. It has lost control of its image, its name and even its music, as it has been modified to contain subliminal messages. But those changes pay off, as they become a #1 band in less than a week.

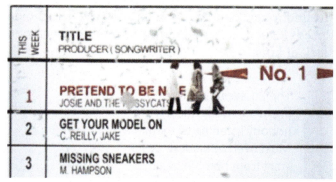

Josie and the Pussycats partying in Billboard's #1 spot

Josie and the Pussycats looking at the "Megasound 8000." On top of "digitally enhancing" the singer's voice (is it the ancestor of Auto-Tune?), the machine inserts subliminal messages in the music in order to convince listeners they love the band and to sell them products and ideas.

Mind Control

The movie also contains numerous references to mind control programming. As stated in previous articles, numerous celebrities have been subjected to mind control in order for them to become more easily manageable by their handlers. In bolder words, they become slaves of the industry.

From wearing cute little kitty ears, the group is now draped in feline prints, a mind control meme signifying a subject's beta programming, also known as Sex Kitten programming. The fact that they wore the ears before they got famous might signify the group's predisposition to this kind of programming.

Monarch mind control includes numerous types of programming, one of them being Beta (or Sex Kitten programming). It is the type of programming that is the most used in the entertainment industry and it is coded with references to "cats," "kitties," "pussycats," and also with the wearing of feline print clothing. This might explain why the producers chose to base the girl band on the Archie Comic of the same name. The symbolism was just too perfect.

So, in less than a week, with the help of subliminal messaging, the group produces a #1 hit and sells out a huge concert. The group even earns the honour of meeting the label's CEO, Fiona.

Fiona's "hang out" room. Notice the painting on the left. Yes, this was years before the creation of the persona named Lady Gaga.

The girls soon realize that Fiona acts in a strange, dissociative matter, as if she were herself under some sort of mind control.

After the meeting, Fiona spies on the group using hidden cameras and learns that two members of the group, Melody and Valerie, are creeped out by her and flat-out do not trust her. So she decides to go with another tactic we often see in the music business: to keep the star of the group and drop the other band members.

In order to carry out this operation, the label proceeds to use mind control on Josie by making her listen to subliminal messages in her own music. The process completely changes her attitude and personality: Josie turns from a sweet and down-to-earth girl into an attention-hungry diva who is convinced that her friends are worthless. This scene subtly describes the hidden, mind control aspect that happens in the music business: label execs use mind control programming to create an alter persona in Josie, which they can control and manage at will.

Josie, in a dissociative state due to her mind control. Everything is "blurry" and "foggy" around her. She is completely dressed in feline prints, still representing her "sex kitten" programming.

Fortunately, Josie manages to snap out of her hypnotic state and learns everything about the 3D, mass mind control concert. Unfortunately, her band mates Melody and Valerie have been kidnapped by the label and Josie must perform in the mind control concert to avoid the "accidental killing" of her friends.

I will spare you the details of the ending, but I can tell you that it involves cat fights and the girls playing generic pop rock in front of a crowd that has learned to think for itself. Thank you Josie!

Fiona shows Josie a pre-taped segment of MTV News announcing the "accidental death" of Melody and Valerie. This is a good example of media manipulation in order to protect the elite's interests.

In Conclusion

The least we can say is that Josie and the Pussycats is an odd movie. It strongly criticizes some aspects of the entertainment business while perpetuating more of the same. One example of this paradoxical situation is the ridiculous amount of product placements in the movie.

As a running gag, the entire movie is filled with over-the-top product placements. Directors say no money was taken for these placements...

Some of those placements are pretty hilarious (see the box of Tide above), but in the end they too perpetuate the market ideology. Imagine me repeatedly punching someone in the face. Then when asked to stop, imagine me replying: "Can't you see that I'm pushing this face punching to an absurd level? You're obviously not getting the brilliant second-degree message here, I'm actually denouncing violence! So sit there and think about violence in society while I keep pounding this guy's face." Despite what is being said, the fact remains that pounding someone in the face is itself perpetuating violence… and this movie keeps punching the viewers in the face with product placements.

In fact, the entire movie's message gives the same odd feeling. Its clever "behind-the-scenes" look of the music industry makes the viewers feel they're "in on the joke," making them comfortable enough to let their guard down. However, at the end of the day, the young viewers are still the butt of the joke: all of the sleazy and gimmicky tactics are being used on real-life viewers in order to sell them mind controlling music. Furthermore, the movie fictionalizes some of the darker aspects of the entertainment business, for example by making mind controlled artists something that one can "only see in the movies."

At the end of the film, Mega Records' mass hypnosis plans are uncovered, and the FBI (who funded the project) immediately attempts to dissociate from the label, even arresting Fiona "on charges of conspiracy against the youth of America." The agent then privately says to Fiona: "We were shutting down your entire project anyways… we found out that subliminal messages work much better in movies!" This is the movie's way of saying that even though it has let you in on the joke, the movie is still part of the plans. In other words, the biggest joke in the movie… is you.

The Occult Interpretation of the Movie "Black Swan" and Its Message on Show Business

"Black Swan" is an intense psychological thriller describing a ballet dancer's metamorphosis into the "Black Swan". Behind the movie's freaky facade lies a profound commentary on the cost of fame, the sacrifice of artists and the hidden forces behind the shady world of high-stakes entertainment. We will look at the occult symbolism of the movie and its themes relating to the dark side of show business.

Directed by Darren Aronofsky, Black Swan follows shy ballet dancer Nina along her path to success in the demanding world of professional ballet. Black Swan can be considered a companion piece to the director's previous movie, The Wrestler, which also describes the ups and downs of a troubled person working in a lesser-known field in the performing arts: professional wrestling. Although both movies explore similar themes (i.e. sacrificing one's self for the good of the performance), the world in which Nina evolves and the obstacles she must endure are diametrically opposed to those of The Wrestler. Randy "The Ram" Robinson is a blue-collar guy living in a blue-collar town and must cope with the physical pain caused by his blue-collar lifestyle. Nina, on the other hand, performs in the refined world of ballet and her struggles are psychological, emotional and even spiritual.

I often point out that great works of art can be interpreted in numerous ways, depending on the knowledge and experiences of each viewer. This movie is no exception … there are indeed numerous ways to interpret the plot of the movie. Through the use of meanings and symbols, however, the movie clearly alludes to many issues previously discussed on The Vigilant Citizen: the dark and occult side of fame, duality, trauma-based mind control, the forced creation of an alter persona and more. The main character, Nina, goes through a metaphysical change – by getting in touch with her "dark side" - in order to become a better performer. This change is imposed on Nina by her "handler", in this case, her ballet director. The movie uses subtle references to trauma-based mind control to explain the creation of an independent alter-person in Nina's psyche.

Although Black Swan is fiction, it nevertheless explores hidden realities of high-stakes art and performance. There are numerous examples of artists who have embraced darker alter egos to take their art to "another level" … and many who ultimately are consumed by them. We will look at the occult and mind-control elements of Black Swan and see how they relate to some of the realities of the world of professional entertainment.

Warning: Major spoilers ahead!

Movie Summary

Black Swan is a modern retelling of Pyotr Ilyich Tchaikovsky's classic ballet, Swan Lake. In the movie, the ballet director, Thomas Leroy (played by Vincent Cassel), describes to his dancers the basic plot of the ballet:

> "We all know the story. Virginal girl, pure and sweet, trapped in the body of a swan. She desires freedom, but only true love can break the spell. Her wish is nearly granted in the form of a prince. But, before he can declare his love, the lustful twin, the Black Swan, tricks and seduces him. Devastated, the White Swan leaps off a cliff, killing herself and, in death, finds freedom".

Nina, a shy and fragile young woman is chosen to play the role of the Swan Queen and must therefore embody both the pure White Swan and the evil Black Swan. Her quest for perfection as a ballet dancer leads her to experience, in her everyday life, the transformation experienced by the White Swan in the ballet's story. The events of Nina's daily life therefore mirror the story of the character she takes on as a ballet dancer, ultimately leading to confusion and, as the line between reality and fiction blurs, to apparent insanity.

The director's use of mirrors and reflections in numerous scenes are a constant reminder of Nina's altered perception of reality. Mirrors in the movie are often misleading and Nina's reflections seem to have a "life of their own". As Nina becomes haunted by the Black Swan, this alternate persona takes a life of its own and acts outside of Nina's conscious control. We will explain later how this relates to trauma-based mind control.

If you have not read other articles on this site, trauma-based mind control – also known as Monarch Programming - is the process in which an individual is subjected to intense trauma and dehumanization in order to cause a mental dissociation. This causes a fragmentation of the slave's personality and enables the handler to create an alternate persona that can be programmed at will. Some researchers claim there are occult elements at work in this process.

> "Project MONARCH could be best described as a form of structured dissociation and occultic integration, in order to compartmentalize the mind into multiple personalities within a systematic framework. During this process, a Satanic ritual, usually including Cabalistic mysticism, is performed with the purpose of attaching a particular demon or group of demons to the corresponding alter(s). Of course, most skeptics would view this as simply a means to enhance trauma within the victim, negating any irrational belief that demonic possession actually occurs."
> - Ron Patton, Project Monarch

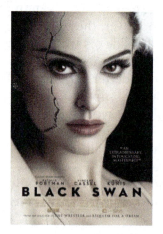

A promotional poster for Black Swan. Nina (played by Natalie Portman) is shown with a crack through her face, representing the fracturing of her personality, an important concept and symbol of mind control.

Nina and her Trauma

Nina lives in a small New York apartment with her mother, Erica, about whom the least we can say is that she is overbearing. Many allusions to trauma-based mind control can be found in Nina's living environment and her mother's controlling behavior.

Nina's bedroom. Notice the butterflies on the wall, a reference to Monarch programming. Next to the window is a big white rabbit, a symbol of mind control originating from Alice in Wonderland – a fairy tale used in the programming of MK slaves. By following the White Rabbit Alice is lead to an alternate world, Wonderland, which, in mind control terms, refers to a slave's dissociative state.

Nina's mother, a retired ballet dancer who failed to become a star, acts more as a mind-control handler than a mother. She obviously has boundary issues and keeps tight control over all aspects of Nina's life. Real-life Monarch slaves often start their difficult lives as victims of ritual abuse in their own household. Symbols relating to mind control in Nina's house probably reflect this sad reality, including her pink, childlike bedroom.

Every night, Erica Sayers winds up the music box next Nina in order to make the little ballerina dance. This is quite symbolic of Nina's mind-controlled state.

Erica Sayers, Nina's mother, forcibly undressing her adult daughter. This unsettling scene depicts to Nina's total submission to her mother and also hints to the unhealthy sexual "familiarity" between the two.

Other people in Nina's life, apparently preying on her weakness and "victim energy", take advantage of her sexually.

An old pervert makes obscene gestures to Nina while riding the train. This disturbing scene tells a lot about Nina's relation to sexuality. Sexual predators sometimes have the sick ability to sniff out and prey on sex-abuse victims.

Nina's mother has subjected her daughter to trauma-based mind control in order to make her a submissive woman who would realize her mother's failed dreams. This has trained Nina to disassociate to make her existence bearable, which in turn makes Nina the perfect subject for the creation of a dark alter persona: the Black Swan.

Bringing out the Black Swan

Getting back to the storyline, Thomas, the ballet director, is looking for a new ballet star play the role of the Swan Queen. Nina's meticulous dancing is perfect to play the role of the White Swan, but she must also be able to play the Black Swan, a role that requires the dancer to be twisted, sexual and dangerous. Nina's frigid style is not suitable for the Black Swan, but Thomas chooses her as the Swan Queen anyway. He knows she has it in her, and he will bring it out.

Thomas bringing out the Black Swan in Nina

At one point, Thomas tells Nina:

> "Perfection is not just about control. It is also about letting go. Surprise yourself so you can surprise the audience. Transcendence. Very few have it in them."

Watching Nina dance, he later says:

> "I knew the White Swan wouldn't be a problem. The real work would be your metamorphosis into her evil twin."

In order to obtain perfection, or in alchemical terms, to accomplish the Great Work, Nina must master both good and evil – light and darkness. The occult concept of duality becomes therefore extremely important (more on this later).

Thomas' job is to create in Nina a new, agressive and sexual alter-ego. He therefore becomes Nina's new mind-control handler. Whereas her mother "programmed" her daughter to be a submissive ballet dancer who never questions her mother/handler, Thomas requires her to embrace the exact opposite. He represents the "big league", the next level of Monarch programming.

After her meeting with Thomas, Nina, dressed in white, crosses the path of another Nina, dressed in black. This symbolically represents the coming of Nina's new, dark alter-ego.

In order to become a Black Swan, Nina must be able to be somewhat comfortable with sex, and even enjoy it. So Thomas gives Nina homework: to "touch herself". Ready to do everything to become a better dancer, Nina tries to masturbate but her mother causes a blockage. Sexual pleasure becomes therefore a form of emancipation from her mother's control and her initiation to the "big league".

As the Black Swan grows in power, Nina starts hallucinating physical mutations on her body. The only other person that can see these mutations are Nina's mother, who, as a handler, has the "key" to her psyche. She is aware of Nina's gradual transformation and tries to repress it, knowing it will cause the lost of her "little girl".

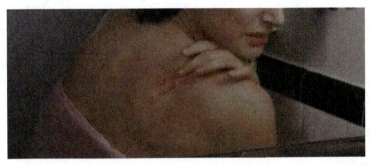

Nina hallucinates all kinds of strange mutations on her body. They represent the gradual coming out of the Black Swan in her.

This situation reflects the ugly truth behind real-life ritual abuse. Children, who are already dissociative due to their parent's abuse, are handed over to "higher instances" who continue the programming process. In this case, Nina is handed over to the entertainment world (known to use Monarch programming on celebrities) to create in her an alter persona destined to be a world-renowned star.

Thomas presenting the new Swan Queen, Nina

In order for Nina to become the new Swan Queen, however, someone must step down.

Beth MacIntyre: The Ageing Star Who Was Pushed Aside

Beth MacIntyre at Nina's crowning ceremony. She has just learned she is no longer the Swan Queen. She is obviously not happy.

Beth MacIntyre (played by Winona Ryder) is the previous star of the ballet company. However, she is growing old and "losing her edge". As a veteran, Beth already went through the "Black Swan process", and, as some people might say, she "sold her soul to the devil". Although this deal gave her years of great performances, in the end, the process completely destroyed her. She has become a bitter, conceited and hateful person who is incapable of existing without being the Black Swan.

There are many real life cases of celebrities suffering the same fate. After being recruited, programmed and primed by the industry to become a superstar, they are suddenly dropped and forgotten. Being psychologically damaged, not knowing who they really are, the fallen stars sink into depression, drugs, alcoholism and even suicide.

Thomas, who was Beth's handler (he called her "my little princess", a mind-control trigger) no longer needs the alter-ego he created in her. It is however impossible to "deprogram" her, so she completely loses her mind. The next day, the ballet company learns she got hit by a car. Thomas says:

> "You know what, I'm also sure she did it on purpose. Everything Beth does comes from within, from some dark impulse. I guess that's what makes her so thrilling to watch … so dangerous … even perfect at times. But also so damn destructive."

So the "spirit", the alter ego that consumed and destroyed Beth, was also the hidden force behind her great performances. The public has always been fascinated by intense and inspired performers who touch them on a primal and visceral level. Depending on the performance, this source of artistic transcendence has been attributed to the divine or to the devil. Controversial and groundbreaking performers have often dwelt between brilliance and insanity – tapping into a mysterious force at the source of artistic greatness and, on the other hand, imminent self-destruction. Religious people might say this force is nothing less than spirit possession; scientists might say that psychological torment leads to creativity. No matter the term one uses for this "force", it certainly exists and it is tapped into by some of the world's most influential artists. Beth hosted this force and it completely destroyed her … and now it can move on to Nina.

The Black Swan Takes Over (Black Wings and Mirrors)

The Black Swan is the artistically brilliant yet spiritually destructive force Thomas wants to see born in Nina. He obviously knows about the Black Swan's devastating powers, but he doesn't care and never did: he is after the ultimate performance. Once Nina has been "used" up by the Swan, he will find another dancer to replace her. He is a representation of the entertainment industry, which manipulates artists into becoming Black Swans, ultimately trashing them when the Swan's effects have faded.

A symbolic movie poster. From the little ballerina rises, as a phoenix from its ashes, a gigantic and menacing Black Swan.

Black Wings

The "force" of the Black Swan is symbolically represented by black wings at different stages of the movie.

Shortly after being crowned "Swan Queen", Nina is fascinated by this creepy statue. Little does she know that it represents what she is about to become.

Black wings on the back of Lily (played by Mila Kunis) while she is "giving pleasure" to Nina. The black wings represent the "force" that is communing with Nina. It is penetrating her, giving her orgasm, but also taking over her life.

Nina at the end of her "perfect" performance as the Black Swan. She is briefly shown with black wings, symbolizing that she has become "one" with the Black Swan.

Mirrors

Mirrors are used throughout the movie to symbolically reflect the true state of Nina's psyche.

Creepy mirror reflection that has a mind of its own. As her metamorphosis advances, Nina realizes that a totally separate entity is living within her. It is completely acting outside of her control. In min-control symbolism, mirror reflections represent a slave's alter-persona that is programmed and manipulated by a handler.

Right before her big performance as the Black Swan, Nina fights against herself in her dressing room. During the fight between Nina and the Black Swan, a mirror breaks, representing the collapse of the psychological boundary separating both entities. By shattering the mirror, Nina becomes the Black Swan.

The Magnum Opus and the Sacrifice

At the show's premiere, Nina gives a stellar performance. She successfully plays the sweet and timid White Swan, and, when the time came, she was overtaken by the "force" to become the twisted, yet thrilling, Black Swan. By marrying the white and the black, the good and the evil, the light and the dark, Nina has accomplished the alchemical Great Work, the occult path to illumination.

The process, however, consumed her. By allowing the Black Swan to completely possess her, Nina gave the performance of a lifetime, but she has become a different person. Thomas and the audiences are in love with Nina as the Black Swan – the same way the prince of the ballet falls in love with the White Swan's evil twin. But this is not the "real" Nina. The Black Swan is a destructive force she cannot live with: it is tormenting her on a physical and psychological level. Not able to go on, the only way Nina can free herself, is by killing herself. And this is what she does. Does this remind you of anyone else's self-sacrificing performance?

Nina dying at the end of her performance. Her last words to Thomas: "I was perfect".

Lady Gaga "sacrificed" in her performance at the 2009 VMA's.

Real Life Black Swans

Beyonce and Sasha Fierce, a pop-music equivalent of the White and Black Swan.

There are real (and tragic) examples of brilliant artists who have been consumed by an intense role. Either they self-destroyed or they HAD to die as a ritual sacrifice. Is Black Swan a commentary on this mysterious phenomena?

A recent example of a self-destructive role is Heath Ledger's Joker in The Dark Knight from the a NY Daily Nesws article entitled "Jack Nicholson warned Heath Ledger on 'Joker' role".

> "Heath Ledger thought landing the demanding role of the Joker was a dream come true – but now some think it was a nightmare that led to his tragic death. Jack Nicholson, who played the Joker in

1989 – and who was furious he wasn't consulted about the creepy role – offered a cryptic comment when told Ledger was dead. "Well," Nicholson told reporters in London early Wednesday, "I warned him."

Though the remark was ambiguous, there's no question the role in the movie earmarked as this summer's blockbuster took a frightening toll.

Ledger recently told reporters he "slept an average of two hours a night" while playing "a psychopathic, mass-murdering, schizophrenic clown with zero empathy ... "I couldn't stop thinking. My body was exhausted, and my mind was still going." Prescription drugs didn't help, he said."
- NY Daily News

Another example of an actor dying in mysterious circumstances after playing the role of a devilish and twisted character is Brandon Lee as The Crow.

People close the Ledger claim his role as the Joker caused his demise.

Brandon Lee mysteriously died DURING the filming of The Crow. The official story of his death is still widely disputed. The scene during which he died was highly symbolic.

In addition to those two extreme cases, there are many cases of artists who, after years of brilliance, mysteriously self-destroyed. Drugs and suicide are often blamed for the tragedies but who really knows what happened with Jimi Hendrix, Kurt Cobain and Jim Morrison, just to name a few?

In Conclusion

Black Swan is a profound movie that can be interpreted on many levels. We looked at the occult and mind-control elements of the movie and examined its messages on the shady world of show business. The movie's commentary on the entertainment world's marriage with occult forces is something that has been discussed numerous times on the Vigilant Citizen. Although the concept is rarely discussed or even noticed by the average person, insiders in the entertainment world often attest to strange forces of varying kinds at work in the industry.

Through Nina's metamorphosis from a shy nobody to a possessed superstar, the viewers experience the dark side of entertainment. Mind control, manipulation and immorality collide with success and recognition. Dark impulses, addictions and self-destruction arise with artistic genius and creative brilliance. Those who are "running the show" know how to bring the Black Swan out of up-and-coming artists ... and they know very well it will destroy them in the long run. And they are OK with that. The same way Beth was pushed aside to welcome a new Swan Queen, the public will always welcome the elite's newest star with applause and acclaim. Because, as they say, the show must go on.

Roman Polanski's "Rosemary's Baby" and the Dark Side of Hollywood

The 1968 movie "Rosemary's Baby" is one of Roman Polanski's most chilling and acclaimed productions. The film describes the manipulation of a young woman by a high-society occult coven for ritualistic purposes. The movie's unsettling quality does not rely on blood and gore but on its realistic premise, which forces the viewers to ponder on the likelihood of the existence of elite secret societies. Even more unsettling are the eerie real life events that surrounded the movie involving ritualistic killings and MK Ultra. We will look at the symbolic meaning of "Rosemary's Baby" and the stranger-than-fiction events that followed its release.

Although articles on the Vigilant Citizen usually pertain to new releases, a look at the past is often necessary to better understand the present. The state of today's Illuminati pop culture is not a spontaneous trend that sprung out of nowhere. Rather, it is the result of years of occult influence on the entertainment industry and the gradual conditioning of the masses to certain messages and symbols. Although pop culture has always been tainted by the elite's agenda to shape and mold young minds, it is during the 60s and the 70s that MK-Ultra stooges and dark secret societies became visible parts of the mix. The need to quell the anti-war and anti-establishment movements of the 60s forced the elite to infiltrate and disrupt the culture. A series of destabilizing events occurred to shock idealistic minds and heroes became enemies. The "Peace and Love" of the 60s became Charles Manson and LSD in the 70s.

Roman Polanski's Rosemary's Baby and its story about the manipulation of a young woman by an elite witch coven to carry and give birth to the Anti-Christ captured the mindset of this era and became symbolic of the irreversible shift that happened in the late 60s. However, it is the real life events surrounding the movie that truly defined this era: Less than a year after the release of Rosemary's Baby, Roman Polanski's pregnant wife was ritualistically murdered by members of the Charles Manson family. This horrific event brought a brutal end to the "good vibrations" of the 60s and is viewed by many historians as pivotal moment in American history. We will look at the symbolic meaning of Rosemary's Baby and analyze the strange events surrounding it, which involve occult secret societies, mind control and ritualistic murders.

Rosemary's Baby

Roman's Polanski's 1968 movie is a faithful adaption of Ira Levin's best-selling novel that appeared only a year before. Although it contains no blood or gore, Rosemary's Baby is considered to be one of the scariest movies of all time. Why? The creepy nature of the film is not in its special effects, but in its realistic premise. The story takes place in a real apartment building (the Dakota) that has a real reputation of attracting eccentric elements of New

York's high society. The evil coven is not composed of stereotypical, pointy-nose witches but of friendly neighbors, prestigious doctors and distinguished individuals. They are elegant, rational and intelligent and are connected to important people. The realism of the movie forces the viewers to ponder on the existence of such groups, to a point that some feared that the movie, after its release would cause an all-out witch hunt. Rosemary's manipulation is also extremely realistic, causing the viewers to think: "It could happen to me".

The Setting

The Dakota Building (dubbed the Bramford in Rosemary's Baby)

The movie starts with a pan-and-glide shot of the New York skyline, showing rooftops of buildings, finally settling on the prestigious Dakota Building (renamed "The Bramford" in the movie).

The Dakota, and other buildings of the Upper West Side, are known to be home of New York's aristocracy (the "old money"). The Dakota has also attracted celebrities such as actors, singers and writers . It is the "place to be" for New York's elite.

In the movie, the Bramford is rumoured to have been the site of numerous strange events involving black magic and ritual killings. Adrian Marcato, a rich man practicing witchcraft was almost killed in the lobby of the building. Ten years later, John Lennon, who lived in the Dakota, was murdered in front of this same building. During the introduction of the movie, the Bramford is just one of New York city's many rooftops, concealing within its austere walls occult rituals the average person would never suspect.

The Young Couple

John and Rosemary Woodhouse visiting the Bramford

Rosemary and Guy Woodhouse (played by Mia Farrow and John Cassavetes) are a young couple who are looking to rent an apartment at the Bramford. Guy is a struggling actor who is not able to obtain recognition or important roles and has to resort to appearing in degrading TV commercials to generate some income. Rosemary is a frail and shy country girl who comes from a strict Catholic background. The name Rosemary has historically been associated with the Virgin Mary, who is said to have spread her cloak over a white-blossomed rosemary bush when she was resting, turning it blue. In the movie, the kind and trusting Rosemary will become a sort of "Black Virgin Mary", bearing within her womb the child of Satan.

The Castevets

Minnie and Roman Castevet, a distinguished yet eccentric elderly couple.

Once settled in their apartment, the Woodhouses meet their neighbors the Castevets, a friendly but nosy elderly couple who invite them for dinner. During this important evening, Roman Castevet compliments Guy on his acting, claiming he has an "interesting inner-quality" and "that is should take him a long way" ... provided he gets those initial breaks (we later learn that those breaks come easier when one is part of their cult). Roman claims his father was a theatrical director and that he worked with all of biggest stars of the time (his father is actually Adrian Marcato, the witch who almost got killed in the building's lobby).

In the kitchen, Minnie asks Rosemary several questions concerning the number of children in her family. She is obviously very interested in the "child-bearing" qualities of Rosemary.

In the living room, Roman is privately discussing with Guy.

Roman and Guy's important discussion

Guy learns about Roman's witch coven and occult rituals. He is also told that his career will succeed if he were to join them. The price of entry is however steep: He must allow his wife to be drugged and impregnated by Satan during an occult ritual.

Under Their Control

Although he did not like the elderly couple at first, Guy joins the coven and becomes good friends with Roman.

Rosemary, who has no idea of these dealings, becomes weary of the couple and their strange behavior. During a pop-in visit, Minnie gives Rosemary a pendant containing tannis root (a fictitious plant), claiming it to be a good luck charm.

The spherical pendant was previously worn by a young woman who was living with the Castevets. The elderly couple found her living on the streets (mind-control handlers prey on such lost individuals). The woman killed herself by jumping out of a window, probably after learning about the Castevets occult plans for her. The pendant becomes symbolic of the coven's mind control.

The same night, Guy obtains the leading role of a play because the original actor suddenly became blind. This strange event convinces Guy of the coven's power, quelling all his doubts regarding its ability to help his acting career. Rosemary soon notices a drastic change in Guy's attitude: Her husband is "suddenly very hot", landing big roles here and there. He is also becoming "self-centered," "vain," "pre-occupied," and "self-absorbed". Funny how this describes the changes seen in celebrities who "sell their soul" for fame.

THE RITUAL

One night, Guy brings flowers to Rosemary and abruptly proposes, "Let's have a baby, all right?". He circles the best days on the calendar to start having sex – October 4th or 5th, 1965. (The coven had determined that these were the prime days for copulation to obtain a numerologically-correct birth). While the couple has a romantic dinner as a prelude to lovemaking, Minnie knocks at their door to drop off a dessert she made. Rosemary finds that the chocolate mousse has a "chalky taste" but Guy insists that she eats it. Her mousse contained drugs and Rosemary becomes dizzy.

During her trance-like state, Rosemary has incoherent hallucinations involving a JFK look-a-like (the only Catholic US President, who died six years before) images of the Sistine Chapel and the Pope (who is wearing Rosemary's spherical pendant, symbol of occult control). She is then seen naked on her bed, surrounded by her husband, the Castevets and the entire witch coven, who are chanting ritualistic hymns while an occult ritual is practiced on her.

Markings on Rosemary's chest, on par with "real" Satanic rituals.

In her dream-like state, Guy begins making love to her, but his appearance changes into a grotesque beast-like figure resembling the Devil, with yellowish eyes and clawed, scaly hands. He strokes the length of her body with his hairy claw. While being 'raped' Rosemary realizes:

"This is no dream, this is really happening!"

There have been persistent rumors claiming that Anton LaVey, the founder of the Church of Satan, played the uncredited role of Satan during the impregnation scene, and also served as a technical advisor for the film. There is no proof of LaVey's involvement in the movie but he was nonetheless linked to the movie's aura in another way: Susan Atkins, the member of the Manson family who later murdered Polanski's pregnant wife Sharon Tate, was an ex-follower of Anton LaVey. Soon after, Rosemary learns that she is pregnant.

The Pregnancy

Right after learning about Rosemary's pregnancy, Guy knocks on the door of the Castevets to inform them of the "good news". Minnie immediately recommends that Rosemary sees "the finest obstetricians of the country", Abe Sapirstein. He is the elite's doctor as he "delivers all high society babies".

Dr. Sapirstein turns out to be part of the Castevet's witch convent. He uses his prestige and authority to manipulate Rosemary during her pregnancy.

The famous real-life April 1966 cover of Time Magazine in Dr. Sapirstein's waiting room. LaVey's "Church of Satan" was established during the same month of the same year.

The doctor orders Rosemary to avoid all pregnancy books and all friendly advice because "no two pregnancies" are alike. In reality, he knows that this unholy pregnancy will be extremely painful. He also requires Rosemary to consume daily drinks made by her neighbor Minnie Castevet. Rosemary becomes therefore totally dependent on members of the coven for all issues regarding her pregnancy. They keep her sheltered from the outside world, monitored and sedated through numerous ways:

Cakes and drinks made by Minnie

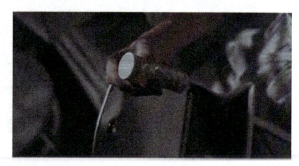

Prescription pills from Dr. Sapirstein

Shots from the Doctor. Rosemary is kept blind to surroundings the same way the general population is: through mind numbing foods, drinks, pills and vaccines.

Even the air Rosemary breathes is controlled by her handlers through air conditioners. At one point Rosemary turns off the air and opens a window – symbolically getting a grip on reality. Rosemary's caretaker immediately says: "Did you turn off the air conditioner? You mustn't do that, dear." She closes the window and turns the air conditioner back on.

Rosemary's pregnancy is extremely difficult. She loses weight and she keeps feeling sharp pains in her stomach. Dr. Sapirstein dismisses her concerns, telling her that the pain would go away. Rosemary becomes weary of her neighbors, who are a little too "interested" in her pregnancy. She then obtains a book from a concerned friend (who mysteriously dies afterwards): All of Them Witches.

The book describes the Castevet's international secret society, which is known to practice blood rituals. Rosemary then buys more books on witchcraft. She is seen reading a passage which might describe the reason why Guy had been obtaining important roles.

> "Many people during that time died supposedly natural deaths. Since then it has been determined that the United Mental Force of the whole coven could blind, deafen, paralyze, and ultimately kill the chosen victim. This use of a United Mental Force is sometimes called a coven."

Rosemary reading Eliphas Levi's Rituals and Dogma. Notice Levi's depiction of Baphomet.

Rosemary attempts to escape the coven's control and seeks help but she is tracked down and brought back home. She is drugged by Dr. Sapirstein and, soon after, she goes into labor.

The Baby

When Rosemary wakes up, she is told that her baby was dead (it was taken by the coven). Guy tries to comfort his wife by telling her that big movie production companies like Paramount and Universal were interested in hiring him. He was also promised a big house Beverly Hills – all rewards for Guy's initiation into the coven and Rosemary's sacrifice.

Determined to find her baby, Rosemary sneaks into the Castevets' apartment and stumbles into a Satanic "Adoration of the Magi" scene, with people from all over the world bringing gifts to the baby.

When Rosemary sees the baby's reptilian eyes, she starts screaming. Roman Castevet tells her:

> "Satan is his father, not Guy. He came up from hell and begat a son of mortal woman. Satan is his father and his name is Adrian. He shall overthrow the mighty and lay waste their temples. He shall redeem the despised and wreak vengeance in the name of the burned and the tortured. Hail, Adrian! Hail, Satan! God is dead! Satan lives! The year is One, the year is One! God is dead"

The birth of Rosemary's baby is the new "Year One." It is also accurate by Church of Satan standards to call 1966 Year One. This is a self-conscious, parallel reference to the year of Jesus Christ's birth, also in Year One, A.D. Another unstated fact: The baby is born in June 1966, which is numerically 6/66.

Roman then asks Rosemary to be a "mother to her child" and to take care of the baby.

Roman asking Rosemary to take care of Adrian, who is in a black cradle and under an inverted cross.

Unable to resist her instinctual, almost animalistic need to respond to her baby's cries, Rosemary starts rocking the cradle. The movies ends with a rather unsettling scene: The coven gathers around Rosemary while she takes care of the monstrous baby. She accepts the reality of the situation and faintly smiles.

The camera moves to the curtained window and then to the outside of the apartment – ending the film with the same, slow pan across the urban rooftops that opened the film ... all of these events happened inside one of New York's many rooftops and no one will ever suspect a thing.

Aftermath of the Movie

While some will consider Rosemary's Baby to be nothing more than a scary movie playing on the sensibilities of devout Christians and young mothers, others see it as Roman Polanski's courageous exposition of high society's occult mind state. Many however see the movie as an occult manifesto, heralding a new era. Rosemary's Baby is Aleister Crowley's "Child of the new Aeon", or Horus the son of Isis – the bringer of a new era in world history. Whether it was intentional or not, Rosemary's Baby did appear at the brink of a new era and became part of an important social change.

> "The movie appeared at a moment of optimum spiritual chaos in American life. Rosemary's Baby

remains an iconic memory trace of a time when anything seemed possible, including the birth of the Anti-Christ".
- Gary Indiana, "Bedeviled", Village Voice

Rosemary is representative of the traditional and naive American society of the 50s and 60s – filled with idealism and hope. But that hope was sold, drugged and manipulated by a hidden cult (formed by prestigious and respectable members of society) to forcefully give birth to a new era. Shocking events left indelible marks on the public mind, including the mysterious deaths of JFK, Marilyn Monroe and Martin Luther King; horrific ritual murders perpetrated by MK-Ultra patsies like Charles Manson and Son of Sam caused fear and horror. These events slapped America out of its ideals and forced it to stare at an undefinable, yet tangible force influencing society. Conspiracies and cover-ups made the news and the masses gradually discovered the existence of a shadow government. Disillusionment and cynicism ensued, causing American society to accept or to ignore the true nature of its rulers. Society became the equivalent of Rosemary who has learned of the evil nature of her baby, but nonetheless accepted the responsibility of mothering it. Today's debased pop-culture is simply the evolution of this system.

Even if one is to overlook the symbolic meaning of the movie itself, the synchronistic occurrences surrounding its production are simply astonishing. To look at the events surrounding Rosemary's Baby is to stare right at the dark side of Hollywood. Here are some of the events:

Murder of Sharon Tate

Roman Polanski with his wife, Sharon Tate

Before settling on Mia Farrow, Roman Polanski originally envisioned his wife, Sharon Tate, as playing the role of Rosemary. She was not cast in the role, but did make an uncredited appearance in the movie, during a party scene. Fourteen months after the release of the movie, Tate (who was 8 months pregnant) was ritualistically killed by members of the Manson family. She was stabbed 16 times and her killers wrote the word "pig" in her blood on the wall of her house.

Charles Manson is described by Fritz Springmeier as "both a Monarch slave and a handler". According to Springmeier, his programmers knew ahead of time what were going to be the next hits. He was basically used by the elite to carry out ritualistic murders.

> "(...) The murders attributed to the Son of Sam, the Manson Family, and numerous other interconnected killings (including possibly the Zodiac murders) were not what they appeared to be. While these killings appeared to be the random work of serial/mass murderers, they actually were contract hits carried out for specific purposes by an interlocking network of Satanic cults ... In other words, these were professional hits orchestrated and disguised to look like the work of yet another 'lone nut'

serial killer."
- David McGowan, "There's Something About Henry"

"The Manson murders sounded the death knell for hippies and all they symbolically represented," Bugliosi told the Observer last week. "They closed an era. The 60s, the decade of love, ended on that night, on 9 August 1969".
- The Guardian, "Charles Manson follower ends her silence 40 years after night of slaughter"

According to numerous observers, Manson's killings were programmed using Beatles songs (Manson himself claimed that the song Helter Skelter contained hidden messages intended for his family).

"Charles Manson was programmed with Beatles' music. (...) They regularly call in slaves and hypnotically make the lyrics to be cues for the slaves before the music comes out. For instance, the lyrics of "Ain't that a Shame" will make certain alters angry. For another slave the lyrics "Everything is relative, in its own way" reminds the person of the cult family & obedience."
- Fritz Springmeier, The Illuminati Formula to Create an Undetectable Mind Control Slave

"The Manson killings were performed according to ancient ritual with hoodwinks and "cords of initiation" around the necks of the sacrifices. A line from a John Lennon Beatles' song was painted on the death house, "Helter Skelter" which was located appropriately on Cielo (Spanish for "sky") Drive (Sharon Tate and Roman Polanski's house).

What we are witnessing in the wake of the public enactment of these alchemical psychodramas, whose spiritual consequences for mankind are far more momentous than most have thus far guessed, is a process of global occult initiation".
- Michael, A. Hoffman, Secret Societies and Psychological Warfare

Speaking of which, the death of John Lennon is another strange piece of the puzzle. The murder occurred as John was walking into the Dakota, the building where Rosemary's Baby was filmed, and where he was living at the time. Mark David Chapman, the "lone nut" who killed Lennon is heavily suspected to be a Monarch mind-control slave.

Lennon in front of the Dakota

Chapman also had ties with high-profile handlers and the strange circle of occult celebrities.

"Lennon's assassin, Mark David Chapman, met LaVey's pal Kenneth Anger, an American disciple of Aleister Crowley, in Honolulu in the late 1970s. In 1967 Anger had directed a film called Lucifer Rising, starring Manson follower Bobby Beausoleil. Another follower and Tate-killer, Susan Atkins, had appeared with LaVey in performances at a Los Angeles area strip club."
- Ibid.

Why was Sharon Tate "chosen"? She was not Hollywood's biggest star and she only enjoyed limited commercial success. Was it the inevitable outcome reserved to stars who go too far into the occult side of stardom? Three years before her death, Tate played the role of a witch in the movie Eye of the Devil. The movie's conclusion: A blood sacrifice was required to "make things right again".

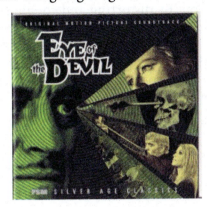

Eye of the Devil, one of Tate's last movies. Another case of a celebrity appearing in a symbolic movie before a strange death.

Did Roman Polanski sacrifice his wife (the same way Guy sacrificed Rosemary) to obtain the favors of Hollywood? Soon after the death, he allowed himself to be photographed by Life Magazine in the living room where Tate had died. Her dried blood was still clearly visible on the floor in front of him. The photo shoot caused him to be heavily criticized.

Other events did not help his credibility. Seven years after Tate's murder, Polanski was arrested and charged with a number of offenses against 13-year-old Samantha Geimer, including rape by use of drugs, perversion, sodomy, lewd and lascivious act upon a child under 14, and furnishing a controlled substance to a minor. According to Geimer's testimony to the grand jury, Polanski had asked Geimer's mother (a television actress and model) if he could photograph the girl as part of his work for the French edition of Vogue. According to author Michael A. Hoffman, Polanski produced snuff films involving minors for sale on the private market, but these allegations remain unproven. Despite all of these accusations, Polanski remains a free man.

Are these events strange coincidences or all part of a big scheme? Is it somewhere in between? Whatever the case may be, they are symptomatic of a hidden force influencing American pop culture.

In Conclusion

Rosemary's Baby can be seen as nothing more than a well-crafted movie that plays on the timeless and archetypal fear of "the Devil". However, when one looks at the movie's precise timing in American history and the incredible series of events that followed its release, the movie becomes a pivotal work symbolizing an important cultural shift in American life. The same way Rosemary discovers the workings of an international witch coven, American society "discovers" a darker side to its entertainment business and internal politics. Mind control slaves are unleashed in the public, shocking mega-rituals occur and pop culture becomes a celebration of depravity.

This era trail-blazed the way to today's Illuminati agenda in popular culture. With the silent consent of the public's indifference, today's cultural industry is still hard at work, molding young minds for a "new eon". The same mind control that was used to kill Sharon Tate and John Lennon has now become a fun way to spice up a music video. The controversies of the past are still echoed today. Should we be surprised to see today's latest Illuminati star Nicki Minaj "channelling" an alter persona called … Roman Zolanski?

That being said, it would be overly simplistic to blame "Satan" for all that happened. In fact, the puppeteers would love to see a scared and confused population blaming everything on a non-human scapegoat, releasing actual men and women from the accountability of their actions. Even LaVey's Church of Satan is a Hollywood-style, theatrical comedy compared to the real actors on the world stage. Secret cabals, evolving at the higher echelons of society, are the true puppeteers here and they avoid media attention. By distorting and corrupting ancient esoteric teachings to fit their needs, the rulers have given themselves a loose moral code to justify their actions. They have usurped "true science", which was inspired by the laws of nature, to create a toxic by-product serving power and greed. The masses, deemed "profane" and unworthy of the Truth, are bewildered spectators at a sick puppet show, not even realizing they are watching puppets. For this reason, it is important to lift the curtain and see what is happening behind the scenes. Once we truly see the sick puppeteers pulling the strings, we will, hopefully, snap out of our hypnotic state and walk out of the show.

"Sucker Punch" or How to Make Monarch Mind Control Sexy

Sucker Punch is an action fantasy thriller that promises its viewers two things: girls and explosions. And it delivers both. But behind the slur of short skirts and CGI effects hides a disturbing underlying story: Sucker Punch is about the life of a mind control slave who dissociates from reality to escape the trauma caused by abuse. This article looks at the hidden meaning and symbolism in Sucker Punch.

Warning: This article deals with disturbing subject matters and contains major spoilers.

Produced by Zack Snyder (Watchmen, 300), Sucker Punch describes the quest of a girl attempting to escape a mental hospital where she was forcibly placed. In order to achieve this goal, our heroine, "Baby Doll", and her friends, must find five items that will be used to escape the institution. Most critics did not appreciate the video game-like plot line of Sucker Punch and were confused its several levels of alternate realities.

The movie does come across as confusing, because there is one important fact about this movie that is not known to most viewers that makes the movie (slightly more) cohesive and coherent: Sucker Punch is about trauma-based mind control. It tells the story of a victim of Monarch Programming (more specifically Beta or Kitten programming) as she becomes increasingly dissociative. The movie takes place in the slave's psyche, where dissociation is a defence mechanism to escape the unbearable trauma of abuse. The deep dark secrets of Monarch mind control are never truly presented on screen yet they are implied in meanings and symbols throughout the movie.

Sucker Punch provides a taste of the confusion lived by actual MK slaves as the film subjects its viewers to some of the same mind twisting: illusion, deceit, reversals and doublespeak. As the movie advances, the line between reality and fiction becomes increasingly blurry and messages become mixed up. At face value, the movie can be perceived as being about the the empowerment of women, but the mind control symbolism of the movie indicates that it is actually about the exact opposite. Our hero Baby Doll is looking for "freedom" but, in the end, "freedom" is definitely not what she thought it would be. In fact, the entire movie can be understood in two completely opposite ways, making it quite a mind bender. Sucker Punch begins with an off-screen voice saying:

> "Everyone has an angel. A guardian who watches over us. We can't know what form they'll take. One day, old man. Next day, little girl. But don't let appearances fool you. They can be as fierce as any dragon. Yet they're not here to fight our battles ... but to whisper from our heart ... reminding that it's us. It's everyone of us who holds the power over the worlds we create."

Like many other parts of the movie, this introduction can refer to guardian angels helping people take charge of their life or to mind control handlers who have the power to manipulate the thoughts of MK slaves. This only one of the several possible double meanings in the movie.

Abuse at home

The movie takes place during the 1950-60s (despite glaring anachronisms), a period during which actual MK-Ultra experiments were known to be taking place. The main protagonist of Sucker Punch is a twenty year old girl known only as Baby Doll. Her name strongly suggests mind control: "baby dolls" do not control their movements or environments. Baby Doll's background and road to mind control mirrors the story of many real life Monarch slaves: an abusive parent caused multiple traumas at a young age, making her predisposed to dissociation. Her "ownership" is then transferred to an institution where the actual programming takes place, under the supervision of specialists (handlers).

The story of Baby Doll is indeed the typical story of real life Monarch slaves, who are often subjected to abuse at a young age. After several years of mistreatment, the ruthless parental figures have then no trouble handing over the children to MK authorities – clearing them of the possible criminal charges they could face for years of abuse.

The movie's introductory sequences presents Baby Doll's source of trauma: an evil step-father.

Baby Doll's drunk step-father looking to abuse her. Many Monarch slaves come from abusive households or multi-generational ritual abuse families.

"*The type of father who is most preferred by the Programmers to offer up their children for programming is the pedophile. If a father will abuse his own little baby girl, then the Programmers know that the man has no conscience. This father's involvement in criminal activity (and thereby his vulnerability) can be continually increased. They want men who they believe will not develop any qualms later on in life about what they have done.*"
- Fritz Springmeier, The Illuminati Formula to Create a Mind Control Slave

The step-father's wounds around the eye produce an emphasis on the "one-eye" symbol, which represents, as seen in other articles, Illuminati mind control. The one-eye symbol appears in other instances during the movie.

The step-father calls the police and accuses Baby Doll of killing her own sister – a crime he committed. She is arrested by the police and immediately drugged. Her ordeal as a Monarch slave begins.

Baby Doll is given a sedative by state officials and taken to the mental institution, which turns out to be a mind-control programming site. Mind-control slaves are constantly drugged by their handlers to facilitate their programming.

The Programming Site

The mental institution in which Baby Doll is placed has all of the characteristic of a mind-control programming site. The threat of physical and sexual abuse is constant during the entire movie and several techniques are used to trigger dissociation.

Music is extremely important in the institution (and in actual Monarch mind control) where it is used as a programming tool. Most of the songs heard during the movie have suggestive lyrics which, in the context of mind control, can to trigger dissociation. As Baby Doll is taken to her cell, Yoav's cover of the song "Where is my Mind" is heard. The lyrics describe the feeling of dissociation:

> With your feet in the air and your head on the ground
> Try this trick and spin it, yeah
> Your head will collapse
> But there's nothing in it
> And you'll ask yourself
>
> Where is my mind
> Where is my mind
> Where is my mind

In the institution, Baby Doll learns that her step-father paid to subject her to the ultimate form of mind control: a complete lobotomy. The administrator of the mental institution tells the step-father: "Don't worry, she won't even remember her name when I'm done with her". The movie then fast forwards to the scene of the lobotomy.

Baby Doll is given a sedative by state officials and taken to the mental institution, which turns out to be a mind-control programming site. Mind-control slaves are constantly drugged by their handlers to facilitate their programming.

Right at the moment where the doctor is about to hammer the orbitoclast into Baby Dolls' brain, dissociation occurs and the viewers are taken to an alternate reality. We are taken to the dissociative, imaginary world created by Baby Doll's psyche, in which she embodies an alter persona: a Sex Kitten.

The Alternate Reality

In Monarch mind control, there are several types of programming, depending on the use the handlers want to make of the slave. In Sucker Punch, it is obvious that Baby Doll and her friends are subjected to Beta Programming – also known as Kitten programming. The emphasis in the beginning of the movie on her step-father's abuse is, in Monarch Programming terms, the anchor.

> "All the programming of each & every slave is anchored upon some type of trauma. One of the first fundamental traumas will be watched, filmed, coded & used as an anchor. For instance, the most brutal abuse of a girl by her father will be used as an anchor upon which to build the Beta programming. (...) Extreme psychosis is created within a child trying to deal with the issues created by the incest from the child's most important figure–their father figure."
> - Ibid.

In Baby Doll's alternate reality, the mental institution becomes a club run by a mobster – who is, in real life, the institution's administrator. The "mental patients" of the institution are dancers…with extras. This distorted version of reality implies one important thing that is not directly mentioned in the movie: If Baby Doll deals in prostitution in her alternate reality, it implies that she is subjected to the same treatment in the mental institution. In actual Monarch programming, repeated and systematic abuse is used to create trauma and dissociation.

In her alternate reality, Baby Doll embodies an alternate persona – what is called a Kitten – who are programmed to give favors. The programming removes inhibitions and, as we'll see, Baby Doll will be trained to "let herself go" and become sensual on demand.

It is during the scene of the lobotomy that we first see Baby Doll dissociating, turning the sordid operation into a sexy dance routine.

Baby Doll being strapped and prepared for the lobotomy.

Baby Doll's alternate world reflecting yet distorting her lobotomy - it is now the premise of an erotic dance routine.

Despite appearances to the contrary, the movie never truly condemns forced prostitution or even mind-control practices. Everything is turned into a fantasy, making the situation cool and attractive. For example, Baby Doll's Kitten alter persona is constantly dressed as a schoolgirl who is brought in by a priest.

Baby Doll's Sex Kitten alter has a different past. Real Monarch programming slaves are programmed to have different alters, who have different pasts, different attitudes and, sometimes, even speak using different accents than the "core" persona. In Baby Doll's case, her abusive step-father becomes a priest.

Sex Kittens

Baby Doll is being told that she is here to please clients. Animal print cushions allude to Kitten programming.

Sweet Pea, another "patient"/slave, practising her dance moves. She is wearing feline print, used in Monarch mind control to identify Beta Kittens.

In her alternate reality, Baby Doll is forced to dance and please clients. Since her alternate world is a product of dissociation, which "sugar-coats" reality to make it bearable, we can deduce that she is forced to do the same actual mental institution, but the movie never actually shows it.

MIRRORS AND BUTTERFLIES

Not unlike other movies on the theme of mind control (see Black Swan), tricky mirror effects and confusing reflections are often used during Sucker Punch to symbolize the blurring of the line between reality and fiction and to give the viewers a small sense of the world of a MK Slave.

Tricky mirrors and camera movements cause viewers realize that they were looking at inverted reflections during an entire scene - warning them to never trust what they see. Notice the butterfly between the mirrors, a symbol of Monarch programming.

Almost all films on mind control feature a shattered mirror at one point - representing the shattering of the slave's personality. In Sucker Punch, the mirror shatters when Blue attempts to assault Baby Doll.

Second Level of Dissociation

So where do the cool action scenes fit in all this disturbing creepy mess? Well, they all happen in Baby Doll's head as a way to escape reality. Each action scene occurs when Baby Doll is forced to perform an alluring dance.

Using music as a programming tool, Vera Grosky (the institution's doctor who becomes the dance instructor in the alternate reality) tells Baby Doll to "let everything go". In other words, she must dissociate. Following Vera's orders, when the music starts, Baby Doll is catapulted into a second level of fantasy world. During the length of the song, the dance turns, inside Baby Doll's head, into an imaginary action scene that vaguely reflects reality. This multiple level of dissociation is Baby Doll's defense mechanism against the cold hard reality: the third level of the action scene means that she is dancing in the second level of the club, which means she is most likely being abused in the first level of the mental institution (I hope this is not too confusing).

During her first dance, Baby Doll dissociates to a world resembling feudal Japan. She is wearing a skimpy school girl outfit, reminding everyone that, behind all of this, the truth is that she is being used for her body.

During this first dissociative action scene, Baby Doll meets the "Wise Man", the guide who will lead her to "freedom" … and I use that word in quotation marks for a reason. While it may appear that throughout the movie, the Wise Man guides Baby Dolls towards liberty, he knows all along that his help will lead her to the exact opposite – total lobotomy. More on this later.

The second action scene takes place in Germany, during WWI. Once again, Baby Doll is forced to dance. The song she must dance to is extremely meaningful: It is a remake of the classic song White Rabbit by Jefferson Airplane. In the context of mind control, the song's lyrics take on a profound meaning:

One pill makes you larger
And one pill makes you small
And the ones that mother gives you
Don't do anything at all
Go ask Alice
When she's ten feet tall

And if you go chasing rabbits
And you know you're going to fall
Tell 'em a hookah smoking caterpillar
Has given you the call
Call Alice
When she was just small

When men on the chessboard
Get up and tell you where to go
And you've just had some kind of mushroom
And your mind is moving slow
Go ask Alice
I think she'll know

When logic and proportion
Have fallen sloppy dead
And the White Knight is talking backwards
And the Red Queen's "off with her head!"
Remember what the dormouse said;
"Feed Your Head"

This classic song can be interpreted in several ways but, in the context of this movie, it perfectly fits into the theme of mind control. As seen in previous articles, the movie Alice in Wonderland is used as an actual Monarch programming tool, where the slave is told to "follow the White Rabbit" through the Looking Glass – the Looking Glass equalling dissociation. For this reason, the symbol of the white rabbit became an important symbol of mind control in popular culture.

In the WWI action scene, the girls ride a "mech" that prominently features the MK symbol of the white rabbit.

The other action scenes follow the same pattern: A dissociative song triggers Baby Doll to go into a fantasy world where she must accomplish a mission. Each mission is a distorted version of the real life mission she and her friends must accomplish to, in the end, escape the institution and find freedom.

The girls succeed and obtain the items required, but not without deaths and sacrifices along the way.

Going to "Paradise"

During the entire movie, Baby Doll's only goal is to "leave this place" and to "be free". At numerous occasions, the process is referred to as "going to Paradise". However, like actual Mind Control slaves, the viewers of the movies are confused with deceitful double-speech and inversions – using attractive words to describe horrible realities. In the movie, "Paradise" and "Freedom" do not equal escaping the mental institution, but rather signify complete dissociation from reality. The Wise Man who seems to be guiding Baby Doll toward "freedom" actually leads her to the acceptance of her lobotomy as the only way to truly "be free".

This disturbing ending reflects the even more disturbing reality of Monarch slaves: even if they escape the grips of their handlers, they cannot escape the suffering and the trauma they have been subjected to. Baby Doll apparently realizes this fact. So, in the end, instead of escaping the institution with her friend Sweet Pea, Baby Doll acts as a true hero and sacrifices herself to free her friend, creating a diversion that allows her friend escape. Baby Doll is seized and taken to be lobotomized.

After the doctor performs the lobotomy, he says:

> "Did you see the way she looked at me? Just in that last moment. It was like … she wanted me to do it".

At least, Baby Doll's sacrifice allowed Sweet Pea to escape the institution and be free, right? Not so sure.

After the escape, Sweet Pea is shown at a bus station about to leave town. When she enters the bus, a boy, who looks oddly familiar, looks at her. Then, when Sweet Pea boards the bus, she realizes that the bus driver is the Wise Man who guided Baby Doll toward her lobotomy. He tells her to get some rest because she has "a long way to go". Is he leading her to freedom or to a dissociative "paradise"?

The weird random kid at the bus station is the same weird random kid that appeared in the WWI scene. Since that scene was a result of dissociation, is the scene of the bus station also imaginary?

As the bus driven by the Guide rolls away, we see a billboard saying "Paradise Diner".

MK Merchandise

Here are some officially licensed Sucker Punch t-shirt designs that contain their fair share of Illuminati mind control symbolism.

The rabbit of the mech with one pupil.

The teddy bear with stitched forehead and buttons instead of eyes represents children MK slaves and their lost of innocence.

Another shirt design featuring an emphasis on one eye. Dangling from the sword is the "key" to Baby Doll's freedom...dissociating into fantasies.

In Conclusion

Most movie goers come out of Sucker Punch believing that its a movie about "empowerment", "women fighting back" and whatever other buzz words they're using these days. While some might perceive Baby Doll as a strong woman fighting back against the oppression of men, others might conclude that the movie caters to the perversions, turning them into a fantasy. The same double-speak can be attributed to the movie when relating to the theme of mind control. While the main message of the movie appears to be about "fighting for freedom", a deeper look at the movie reveals that it might be saying the opposite. In the end, Baby Doll's "battle" was not one of rebellion and freedom, but for escape and dissociation. Her "guide" was not an agent of liberation, but a handler who owned the keys to her psyche, guiding her into the fracturing of her personality.

The final words of the movie, said by an off-screen voice, also play on reversals and double-speak. Is it an empowering speech on self-determination or a description of the handler's complete control of the slave's psyche?

"Who honors those we love with the very life we live? Who sends monsters to kill us and at the same time sings that we'll never die? Who teaches us what's real and how to laugh at lies? Who decides why we live and what we'll die to defend? Who chains us? And who holds the key that can set us free?"

The movie ends with the same words Baby Doll was told before dancing and dissociating the first time.

"It's you. You have all the weapons you need. Now fight."

Through illusion, deceit and double-speech, the viewers witness a subtle promotion and glorification of the very things the movie apparently goes against. I guess this is why they called the movie Sucker Punch.

"Labyrinth" Starring David Bowie: A Blueprint to Mind Control

The 1986 movie Labyrinth, starring David Bowie and Jennifer Connelly, immerses the viewers into a world of fantasy and wonder. Like many other fantastic tales, the movie conceals within its symbolism an underlying meaning and, in this case, it is rather disturbing. Labyrinth describes the programming of a mind control victim at the hands of a sadistic handler. We will look at the occult meaning of the symbolism found in Labyrinth.

Labyrinth is a quintessential 80s movie that contains everything we love from the 80s: 80s synth music, 80s CGI effects and a 80s David Bowie in the same 80s hairdo that your aunt Susan had in the 80s. What's not to love? The movie has, in fact, become a "cult classic" and is still a children's favorite.

But like many of these delightfully twisted fantasy movies, there is more to Labyrinth than meets the eye. By understanding the occult symbolism and references in Labyrinth, the movie becomes a big allegory for mind control, where each scene refers to a particular aspect of the process. What appears to be a young girl's quest through a Labyrinth to find her baby brother becomes a metaphor for the internal world of a mind control victim that is being programmed by a handler. The obstacles that Sarah, the hero of the story, must go through relate to real life ordeals inflicted to mind control slaves to incite dissociation. Mind games, torture, drugs and sexual abuse are all referred to in veiled symbolism during the movie, giving to "those in the know" an entirely different story than what is shown at face value. Labyrinth is therefore constructed like most esoteric works in History: it uses symbolism to conceal from the masses while revealing to the initiates.

Very little prior knowledge is required to understand the underlying meaning of Labyrinth. however. The movie was, in fact, mentioned by a few authors on mind control who described it as one of the most blatant movies on Monarch programming. Fritz Springmeier even states Labyrinth is used by actual mind control handlers as a programming script to train the slaves. This very plausible as the movie bears many similarities to Alice in Wonderland and Wizard of Oz – two movies that are known to be used in mind control programming. The only difference is that Labyrinth was probably specifically constructed to this purpose while, at the same time, exposing the masses to this kind of symbolism.

Since Labyrinth is a blueprint for mind control, it is only fitting that the star of the show is an artist who has served as a blueprint to modern pop stars: David Bowie. Throughout his long and eclectic career, Bowie has touched on many occult and ritualistic themes that are today rehashed by industry-made pop stars. And, for some reason, many of those who touch upon these occult themes also integrate mind control into their works. Maybe it is due to the fact that mind control heavily relies on black magic rituals and Kabbalistic teachings. So, before we look at the symbolism of the movie, let's take a brief look at some of the symbolism used by David Bowie.

David Bowie: The One They All Imitated

Many articles on this site mention modern pop stars and the occult symbolism embedded in their works. It was only a matter of time before David Bowie was mentioned as he is apparently a major source of inspiration for many of them. David Bowie is indeed the prototype of the pop-star/occult icon whose works incorporated concepts originating from Secret Societies. From strange alter-egos, to the occult concept of androgyny, and of course including references to Aleister Crowley and his Thelema, Bowie did decades ago what pop stars are doing now.

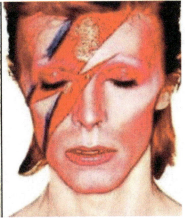

"Bowie's alter-ego named Ziggy Stardust was a representation of the "illuminated man" who has reached the highest level of initiation: androgyny. There was also a lot of one-eye things going on.

Drawing the Kabbalistic Tree of Life

The difference between Bowie and today's pop stars is that he was rather open regarding the occult influence in his act and music. In a 1995 interview, Bowie stated: "My overriding interest was in cabbala and Crowleyism. That whole dark and rather fearsome never-world of the wrong side of the brain." In his 1971 song Quicksand, Bowie sang:

> "I'm closer to the Golden Dawn
> Immersed in Crowley's uniform of imagery"

(Golden Dawn is the name of a Secret Society that had Crowley as member). These are only some examples of the occult influence on Bowie's work and an entire book could be written on the subject.

Since the main antagonist of Labyrinth is a sorcerer who also happens to enjoy singing impromptu pop songs, David Bowie was a perfect fit for the role. Did he know that he played the role of a mind control handler?

Labyrinth

This poster of the movie Labyrinth is full of MK trigger images.

Released in 1986, Labyrinth was a collaborative effort between George Lucas, Jim Henson (his last movie) and David Bowie. Using state-of-the-art effects, the movie quickly became a classic in what we can call the "twisted fantasy" genre. The plot of the movie is simple: A teenage girl named Sarah goes through a strange, magical Labyrinth to recover her baby brother who was kidnapped by a sorcerer named Jareth and his army of goblins.

Some critics did not appreciate the random nature of the events of the movie. Robert Ebert stated that these kind of movies "aren't as suspenseful as they should be because they don't have to follow any logic. Anything can happen, nothing needs to happen, nothing is as it seems and the rules keep changing." By describing the movie this way, Ebert unknowingly describes the inner-world of a mind control slave, which is exactly what the Labyrinth represents. Through trauma, the psyche of the slave is reprogrammed by the handler resulting in a situation where anything can happen, nothing needs to happen, nothing is as it seems and the rules keep changing.

Sarah's quest for her baby brother is, in fact, a quest to recover her innocent core persona (her "real" self) that was taken by the handler. The various events that happen to Sarah are distorted reflections of real mind control trauma – hidden behind a veil of fantasy and imagination.

The Premise

The plot of the movie is very reminiscent of the Wizard of Oz and Alice in Wonderland, two stories that are incidentally known to be used in mind control programming. A young girl, bored and distraught with her normal life, finds herself in a fantasy land, where everything can happen. In order to go back home, she embarks on a dangerous quest to reach a great castle (not unlike the Emerald city of the Wizard of Oz). Along the way, the assertive girl uses her wits, courage and strength to go past the obstacles in a world where no rules are established.

Labyrinth is heavily symbolic from beginning to end, starting from the very first scene. Sarah is at a park, dressed as a princess, practising lines to a play under the watchful eye of an owl that is standing on top of an obelisk.

An owl is standing at the top of an obelisk, watching over Sarah.

We quickly learn that the owl is Jareth, the goblin King (played by David Bowie). The fact that Jareth takes the form of an owl in the "real world" and that he sits at the top of an obelisk is very telling about what he actually represents: The occult elite. The owl is known to be the main symbol of the Bavarian Illuminati and is still used by elite groups such as the Bohemian Grove. It represents "those who act under the cloak of darkness".

Symbol of the Minerval Church of the Bavarian Illuminati featuring a watchful owl.

The owl is at top of an obelisk, a monument that is constantly visible throughout the entire movie. The obelisk has been, for centuries, the ultimate symbol of power of the occult elite. It is found standing at the world's most powerful places and strange occult powers are attributed to them. These tall monuments originate from the ancient Egypt and are said to represent the lost phallus of Osiris – in other words, male energy. The obelisk is therefore a phallic symbol and the fact that this young girl encounters many of them during her quest might be a reminder of the male handler dominating her mentally and sexually (through abuse).

The owl watches Sarah, who is dressed as a princess and practising a role for a play, illustrating her natural tendency to dissociate from reality and to take on other personalities, a characteristic that MK handlers seek when scouting for potential slaves. Sarah is therefore "marked" by the shady Illuminati Mind Control system.

At Sarah's house, we find several clues relating to her predisposition to mind control. She is surrounded by toys, books and posters that foretell the dissociative adventure she is about to embark in. Many of Sarah's toys will be found animated during her adventure, which tells us that everything that will happen will be a result of her own imagination, fuelled by the things that are familiar to her.

Among Sarah's stuff we find a toy version of the obelisk-studded labyrinth she is about to enter and the books of Wizard of Oz and Alice in Wonderland. Both of these fairy tales are used to encourage victims to dissociate from reality. Labyrinth is no different and is probably used in actual mind control programming.

Right above Sarah's bed is Escher's famous drawing named "Relativity".

Escher's "Relativity" (the image with the stairs going in all directions) right above Sarah's bed.

Escher's mind-boggling images contain confusing features that the mind can never compute. For this reason, they are used in actual mind-control programming. This particular painting will become very important later in the movie.

> "If [the child] has artistic brainwaves, then the programmer will use art work in programming. The art work of the european artist M.C. Escher is exceptionally well suited for programming purposes. For instance, in his 1947 drawing "Another World", the rear plane in the center serves as a wall in relation to the horizon, a floor in connection with the view through the top opening and a ceiling in regards to the view up towards the starry sky. Reversals, mirror images, illusion, and many other qualities appear in Escher's art work which make all 76 or more of his major works excellent for

programming."
- Fritz Springmeier, The Illuminati Formula to Create a Mind Control Slave

So Sarah is angry at her parents, especially her step-mother, because she has to stay at home and babysit her little brother named Toby while they go out. Confronted with the child's incessant cries, Sarah wishes for the Goblin King to take him away. An owl then enters the room and turns itself into Jareth, the Goblin King.

Jareth offering Sarah "gifts" represented by the crystal ball

Jareth has taken Toby to his world and will turn him into one of his goblins. In mind control terms, baby Toby represents Sarah's core personality that was taken away by Jareth, her handler. As long as Jareth holds Sarah's core persona, he will be able to make her go through the Labyrinth – which will represent her programming.

When Sarah asks to Jareth to hand back Toby, the Goblin King uses his skills for manipulation and persuasion. He shows Sarah a crystal ball and tells her that it contains "all of her dreams". He however warns that is is "not a gift for an for an ordinary girl who takes care of a screaming baby". In other words, the gift is only for girls who have lost the baby – victims of mind control. Jareth the handler has the power to help Sarah escape the life she loathes but she must allow him to own her core personality – to control her mind. When Sarah refuses Jareth's offer, which is equivalent to the Faustian theme of selling one's soul to the Devil, the crystal ball magically turns into a snake and is thrown at her. Jareth then menacingly says: "Don't defy me". Seeing that she will not forget about the baby, Jareth tells Sarah that Toby is at his castle and that she has 13 hours to find him. They are both transported into the Labyrinth, which is a big image representing Sarah's inner-world under the control of a handler.

Inside the Labyrinth

Sarah must traverse a gigantic Labyrinth in order to reach the castle, which represents her walled-off and compartmentalized core persona. The entire labyrinth is Sarah's inner-world and Jareth is the undisputed master of everything that happens in it. He can also change everything at will. Obelisks are found all across the Labyrinth, a phallic symbol reminding of the sexual control the handlers have over their slaves.

Inside the Labyrinth, Sarah quickly realizes that it does not obey the rules of reality. She finds herself walking never-ending straight paths leading to nowhere.

The Labyrinth appears to be an infinite straight path to nowhere.

Sarah then learns that it is only by mentally picturing an entry towards the castle that one will appear. She must make her own path within her own mind.

Strange plants with eyes on the walls of the Labyrinth reminds us that Sarah is tightly monitored by her handler during the entire process. The symbol of the all-seeing eye is heavily used in actual mind control programming.

While trying to advance through the Labyrinth, Sarah realizes that everything keeps changing around her. She meets strange creatures who say confusing riddles that lead to never-ending loops of circular logic. Her catch-phrase appears to be "It's not fair" as she repeats it numerous time during the movie. This phrase does sum up pretty nicely the life of a MK slave. There are no rules and every kind of unfairness can occur.

Meanwhile, Jareth is in the castle with Toby, monitoring Sarah.

The Ordeals

In her path towards the castle, Sarah goes through all kinds of obstacles, many of which symbolically represent actual traumas lived by mind control victims.

In Sarah's first ordeal, she falls into a pit filled with "helping hands".

Sarah is held and grabbed by countless hands around her. This can refer to the victims being manipulated and abused by hidden handlers.

Later, Sarah finds herself in a forest and surrounded by the Fire Gang, who are strange singing creatures that can remove parts of their bodies at will. The concept of dismembered body parts is central to mind control programming.

The Fire Gang's performance soon turns into a nightmare when they jump on Sarah and try to remove her head.

The Fire Gang trying to remove Sarah's head from her body, representing the MK slave's dissociation from reality.

Upon escaping the Fire Gang, Sarah finds herself in an even worst place, the Pool of Eternal Stench.

The Pool of Eternal Stench is basically a big gassy pond full of feces. It keeps emitting flatulence and belches and is therefore very "bodily" place.

Sarah and her friends are forced to go through the nauseating pond in order to continue the quest. This odd scene can refer to the actual mind control technique to induce trauma which consists in immersing the slaves in feces and urine and/or to consume them. Our natural repulsion to excrements and the foul odor we get from them are our body's way to tell us to stay away from them because they are infested with all kinds of worms and parasites that are toxic to us. Our organisms are so well made that we are instinctively repulsed by the things that are bad for us. The forced consumption of excrements is therefore particularly traumatic as it goes against the human body's most basic instincts. Sarah's episode in the Pool of Eternal Stench is a "imaginative" way to describe Sarah's traumatic experience as a MK slave during programming.

After crossing the pool, Sarah is given a gift – one that is poisoned of course.

Sarah receives a peach that makes her hallucinate - a thinly veiled allusion to the drugs that are given to Monarch slaves during programming.

When Sarah takes a bite from the peach, she feels woozy and starts hallucinating. Monarch slaves are constantly given drugs to amplify the effects of the programming and to incite fear and terror. Laying on the ground, Sarah

Sarah sees doll in princess clothes surrounded by bars - a classic way to portray dissociative mind control slaves.

sees a crystal ball with a symbolic image representing her.

Sarah is then shown at a strange hall with guest wearing masks of goats, pigs and birds (commonly called an Illuminati ball) and finds Jareth, her handler, waiting for her.

Jareth and Sarah find each other and begin waltzing together, with Jareth giving suggestive looks ... to a 15-year-old girl. The scene symbolically portrays the forced Satanic union between the slave (who is said to be the princess of her world) and her handler. The lyrics of David Bowie's song playing during the ball can be interpretative as a "love song" from a handler to a mind control slave.

> "As the pain sweeps through
> Makes no sense for you
> Every thrill has gone
> Wasn't too much fun at all
> But I'll be there for you
> As the world falls down ...
>
> ... It's falling down"

The ball then quickly turns into a nightmare, where all of the masked guests start running after her (is she "bad-tripping"?). Sarah starts running, shatters a mirror and runs through it, another classic symbol of mind control.

To escape the ball, Sarah must shatter a mirror - a symbolic image representing the fracture of her personality.

Confronting Jareth

Despite all of those troubles, Sarah finally reaches the castle and enters it. She finds herself lost in a life-size Escher painting with Toby crawling. Jareth magically appears from everywhere in the scene, the same way handlers ap-

Sarah in a life-size Escher image

pear in the inner-world of Monarch slaves.

Then the entire world around Sarah crumbles, leaving only her facing her handler. Sarah asks Jareth to give her back the baby (her innocent core). Jareth gives her a classic double-speak, mind-bending lecture – the kind MK slaves get from their handlers. He says:

> "I have reordered time … I have turned the world upside down … I have done it all for you. I am exhausted from living up to your expectations of me. Isn't that generous?"

He then offers her the crystal ball again.

> "Look what I'm offering you. Your dreams. I ask for so little. Just let me rule you, and you can have everything that you want. Just fear me, love me, do as I say, and I will be your slave".

This is the classic Faustian "deal with the Devil" proposal, where Jareth says that he "asks for so little" while he is actually asking for Sarah's everything: Her mind, body and soul.

Sarah then starts reciting the lines she was practising at the beginning of the movie and says "You have no power over me". Everything crumbles again, Sarah leaves her internal world and finds herself back in the external world, the real world, her house. Toby is back in his crib and everything is apparently back to normal.

In her room, sees some of the creatures she has met in the Labyrinth and is apparently happy to see them. She tells them:

> "I don't know why, but … every now and again in my life, for no reason at all, I need you."

In other words, Sarah has accepted the internal world that was programmed into her by her handler. It now can be triggered by him at any time during her life.

Sarah and her friends party in her room under the watchful eye of an owl, Jareth, who has never lost control of her. He is actually the winner of the duel with Sarah. Her programming is complete.

The movie closes with David Bowie's song "Underground". The song has very church-y feel (with a loud a gospel choir accompanying him) and talks about a place with "no pain". That place is not heaven, but "Underground", which can be equated to hell, which, in mind-control terms, is the trauma-filled life of a MK slave.

So, in perfect continuation with the movie, Bowie leaves the viewers with one last inversion of good and evil, heaven and hell and pleasure and pain, with this song:

> "No one can blame you
> For walking away
> Too much rejection (na na)
> No love injection

Life can be easy
It's not always swell
Don't tell me truth hurts, little girl
'Cause it hurts like hell
But down in the underground
You'll find someone true
Down in the underground
A land serene
A crystal moon, ah, ah

It's only forever
Not long at all
Lost and lonely
That's underground
Underground

Daddy, daddy, get me out of here
Ha ha I'm underground
Heard about a place today
Nothing ever hurts again
Daddy, daddy, get me out of here
Ah ha I'm underground
Sister sister, please take me down
Ah ah I'm underground
Daddy, daddy, get me out of here"

While most viewers interpret the story of Labyrinth as a tale about "the importance of imagination" or something of the sorts, the symbolism of the movie gives it a deeper meaning. While the story could be interpreted in numerous ways (another article could be written about Sarah's quest being a metaphor for esoteric initiation) references to mind control are definitely present. Once the imagery and the triggers relating to mind control are understood, the movie becomes a vivid description of the internal world of a Monarch slave during programming. Totally at the mercy of her handler and the twisted world he created in her mind, the slave attempts to return to reality, where things make sense. The task is difficult as the handler controls time (hence the 13-hour clock that keeps popping up during the movie) and space (secret passages in the Labyrinth). During the quest, the slave meets friends who appear to be helping her, but who are, in actuality, leading her to exactly where her handler wants her to be. In fact, Sarah's entire "quest for liberation" is actually her being manipulated towards the acceptance of her programming. By going through the Labyrinth, Sarah went through all of the trauma necessary to program her. What appears to be the defeat of Jareth is actually a victory as he successfully programmed Sarah's internal world. It can be used, in her words "every now and again in her life".

In Conclusion

Like Wizard of Oz and Alice in Wonderland, Labyrinth is an imaginative fairy tale whose story can be used as a programming script in mind control programming. Unlike the older tales however, Labyrinth might have been specifically constructed for mind control purposes. The story, the symbolism and the music of the movie all form a cohesive sensory-overload, where the viewers are totally immersed in the strange world of mind control. There is however one hitch: like mind-control victims, most viewers are completely duped by the movie and its message. While it appears to be about the triumph of a girl's mind over evil, its is actually the triumph of evil over a girl's mind. In the words of Bowie, "Don't tell me truth hurts, little girl, 'Cause it hurts like hell."

'Contagion' or How Disaster Movies "Educate" the Masses

Hollywood movies are usually presented as a form of entertainment, but their plots often conceal a specific agenda. "Disaster movies", films about the end of the world through various mass crises, are particularly interesting as they all follow the same basic formula and glorify the same entities. In this article, we'll look at the disaster movie 'Contagion' and how it "teaches" its viewers who to trust and who not to trust during a crisis.

Most people watch movies to be entertained. Well, I for one can say that there was absolutely nothing entertaining about Contagion. In fact, the only difference between this movie and state-sponsored educational movies shown in schools is that with Contagion you actually have to pay to be indoctrinated ... and to see Matt Damon. During the cold war, students were shown videos instructing them to "Duck and Cover" in case of a nuclear attack. Contagion conditions the masses to expect martial law and to throw themselves at the first available vaccine in case of a crisis.

Featuring Hollywood mega-stars like Matt Damon, Laurence Fishburne, Jude Law and Gwyneth Paltrow, Contagion is a big-ticket Hollywood movie, but also an infomercial promoting specific national and international agencies while encouraging specific behaviors from the public. The plot of the movie appears to follow the big H1N1 scare of 2009 that left many citizens uncertain about the actual risk of the virus. Indeed, after months of terrifying news crowned by a massive vaccination campaign, an important portion of the population concluded that the H1N1 scare was grossly exaggerated and and thought that a vaccine was unnecessary.

In the wake of this "crisis", the UN's World Health Organization (known as the WHO) was harshly criticized and even accused of colluding with Big Pharma to sell vaccines. The U.S. Centers for Disease Control and Prevention (the CDC) also had its credibility tarnished as investigations revealed that the agency misled the public regarding the number of actual cases of H1N1. As a result, these two agencies needed a good PR stunt to restore their credibility and to scare the hell out of the public. This is where Contagion comes in.

Directed by Steven Soderbergh, Contagion was produced with the active cooperation of the CDC, the WHO and other governmental organizations and its function is clear: To present a hyper-realistic disaster scenario to justify the vaccination campaigns promoted by these agencies while discrediting those who criticize them.

Nothing in the movie hints that it is a work of fiction. Quite to the contrary, everything in Contagion is made to be as realistic as possible, using actual locations and governmental agencies, to make the story as plausible – and as frightening to the masses – as possible. As the slogan of the movie says: "Nothing spreads like fear" and, boy, does it try to spread fear. This movie's message is: "Nothing was exaggerated, and next time there's a virus outbreak, listen to us … or you'll die".

The Function of Disaster Movies

Disaster movies are often action-packed thrill rides that venture in the sometimes fascinating "what if that happened" side of things. While some are very over-the-top and border on fantasy, others, like Contagion, emphasize realism and actual events. These movies tend to "hit home" with the viewers because they lead them to think "this could happen to me". Disaster movies exploit the latent fear that recent events caused on the psyche on the masses, tapping into the anxiety and trauma they cause in order to create tension and terror in the viewers. Then, the "agenda" aspect of these movies kick in as they propose to the viewers the best (and only) way these issues can be resolved. Specific groups and agencies are cast as honorable, helpful and trustworthy during the time of crisis, while others are portrayed as hindrances and even traitors. The drama that follows becomes a case of predictive programming, as the steps taken in the movie to resolve the problem will thereafter appear normal to the masses if they ever occur in real life.

In his book Propagandes Silencieuses (Silent Propaganda), the journalist and writer Ignacio Ramonet describes the always present underlying message found in disaster movies:

> "In all cases, the disaster causes a kind of 'state of emergency' that hands all powers and modes of transportation to state authorities: the police, the army or "the crew". Portrayed as the ultimate recourse, these institutions are the only ones capable of facing the dangers, the disorder and the decay threatening society thanks to their structure and technical knowledge. (…) As if it was impossible to present to the general public a disaster that is not resolved by state authorities and governmental powers."
> - Ignacio Ramonet, "Propagandes Silencieuses" (free translation)

Along with the all-importance of authorities, the masses are inevitably presented as a herd of idiots prone to panic that must be kept in the dark.

> "Another constant found in disaster movies is the infantilization of civilians. The full amplitude of the catastrophe and the danger the masses are facing is often hidden from them. They are kept out of any decision making process, with the exception of managers and technical specialists (engineers, architects, entrepreneurs) who are sometimes called to intervene in the crises, but always through state authorities.
>
> The general public is often distracted with pointless entertainment and encouraged to obey without question to a 'paternal and benevolent' elite that is doing everything (to the point of self-sacrifice) to protect them.
>
> These aspects, along with others, prove that disaster movies, beyond their entertaining value, also present a 'political response' to a crisis. Behind a naive mode of fantastic storytelling, a silent message is communicated to the public: the ruler's profound desire to see entities such as the army, the police or 'prominent men' take charge of the restoration and the rebuilding of a society in crisis, even if this means partially sacrificing democracy".
> - Ibid.

Contagion follows Ramonet's blueprint of disaster movies to a tee. Right from the start, specific organizations are identified as the go-to guys and are automatically given the power to act on a massive scale, namely FEMA, the WHO, the American Red Cross and the CDC.

So what solution does Contagion propose in case of the outbreak of deadly disease? Martial law and mass vaccinations. What will happen if ever an actual disease would break out? Martial law and mass vaccinations. Would the masses questions this type of drastic response to a crisis which might or might not be necessary? No, because hundreds of hours of media content have prepared the masses for this kind of situation. Let's look at the main components and messages found in Contagion.

Fear Spreads Faster Than Germs

The movie starts by showing how a few sick people, who go about their daily routine, can easily contaminate thousands of people. The point of the introduction is simple: A deadly virus can spread around the world in a matter of days. This realistic yet terrifying scenario is a very effective way to grip the audience and to cause a state of fear. During these scenes, the camera focuses for a few extra seconds on common objects that can transmit germs such as drinking glasses, just long enough for the viewer to realize: "Hey, I sometimes touch these things! That could be me! Aaaah!"

This sick guy could infect the entire bus. To add to the drama and scare factor, they name big cities and their population.

Beware of glasses of water being handed to you...

Not even a mother's hug is safe.

Most of those who are infected with the virus do not live long. In a series of heartbreaking scenes, one of the main characters, Mitch Emhoff (played by Matt Damon), sees his wife and his son lose their lives to the virus. Viewers watching this tragedy play out are led to think "Hey, that's the most terrible thing could happen to me! Aaaah!"

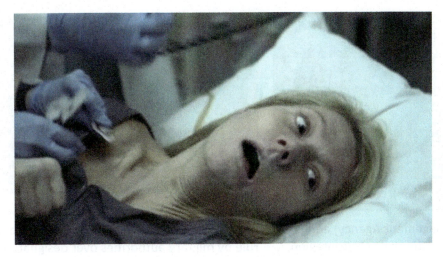

Watching Beth Emhoff (played by Gwyneth Paltrow) die from the virus is quite disturbing and certainly helps create a climate of fear.

This movie was released only a two years after the outbreak of H1N1 and the media hype that surrounded it, so that fear is still latent in many people. These scenes from Contagion reactivates the "fear virus" that was planted in people … and adds some. After a few minutes of panic-inducing scenes, most viewers will say "Oh my God, someone do something about this virus! This guy lost his wife and child, that's awful! AAArgh!". Heroes do step up to the plate and take charge of things … and it just so happens that they were involved in the making of the movie.

The Organizations That Take Charge

In Contagion, as soon as the virus becomes a threat, the entire American government escapes to an "undisclosed location" and "looks for a way of working online". Meanwhile, specific real-life non-government organizations (NGOs) are identified by the movie as the "heroes" and the go-to people to handle the crisis. These organizations are promoted to the viewers and are given automatic legitimacy and trustworthiness. However, those who are educated about the world elite's agenda for a New World Order know that these organizations have been know to push that agenda and everything that goes with it. In short, the movie says: "If a crisis like this happens, the government will disappear, democracy will be suspended and NGOs will take over".

The agencies identified by the movie are:

The CDC (Center for Disease Control), which has always heavily promoted vaccinations campaigns.

The World Health Organization (WHO) - which was accused, in the wake of the H1N1, of spreading "fear and confusion rather than immediate information". In the movie however, the WHO is an important factor in the resolution of the problem.

FEMA (Federal Emergency Management Agency) and the American Red Cross manage the civilians. Contagion, shows viewers how emergency situations could quickly lead to martial law, which would automatically lead to the creation of civilian camps ran by FEMA, who needed some good PR after Hurricane Katrina.

Of course, the U.S. army is all over the place since martial law is defined as the "imposition of military rule by military authorities over designated regions on an emergency basis".

So, in the wake of a "biological crisis", the democratically elected American government basically dissolves and specific organizations (CDC, WHO, FEMA, the U.S. Army) take charge of all aspects of society. And this "taking charge" proceeds in a very specific way: Martial law and civilian camps.

Martial Law

In Contagion, the deadly virus is called MEV-1 and the social result of the outbreak is portrayed in a specific way. First, the general population, always depicted as idiotic, cattle-like and prone to violence, spirals out of control. The masses are always shown panicking, yelling, stealing, fighting and looting. This leads to a general breakdown of social order and a state of lawlessness.

A bunch of rude people looting a pharmacy to obtain medication.

Wherever regular people are put together, all sort of crap ensues. This goes along with the concept of "infantilization" of the masses, who require to be taken charge by "fatherly" authorities. And boy do the authorities take over.

The US Army imposes Martial Law and places the State of Minnesota in quarantine, blocking all traffic out of the state. Those who seek to leave the state are told to turn around and go back home.

This stadium has been turned into a FEMA camp.

Civilians (even healthy ones) have their rights revoked and are directed to FEMA camps where they are fed and lodged. In this scene, the lack of "individual meals" to feed all of the camp's population causes a small riot.

The Conspiracy Theorist

If specific groups and organizations are identified by the movie as "competent" and "trustworthy", other groups get a very different treatment, namely alternative media. Personified by a blogger named Alan Krumwiede (played by Jude Law), alternative media are presented as unreliable sources bent on sensationalism and profit. In other words, the movie implies that information that does not come from "official" sources is invalid and potentially dangerous. Not exactly a pro-free-speech message.

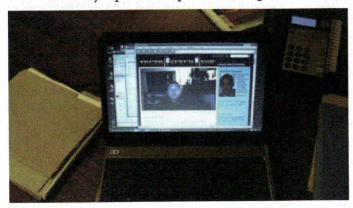

"Truth Serum", a blog run by Alan Krumwiede, resembles the many "alternative news" website around the web. This type of information, which does not come from mass media or governmental sources, is definitely not portrayed in a positive light.

Right from the start, Alan Krumwiede is portrayed as a somewhat dodgy blogger with a questionable work ethic and who does not get much respect from the journalistic nor the scientific community. When he tries to get one of his stories published in a newspaper called The Chronicle, he gets rejected due to lack of evidence behind his story. When he contacts a scientist regarding the virus, the scientist replies: "Blogging is not writing, it's graffiti with punctuation".

Despite this lack of respect from "competent" bodies, Alan Krumwiede has a wide audience and proudly boasts "millions of unique visitors per day" on his website. On it, he claims that a cure for the MEV-1 virus exists and is named Forsythia but it is repressed by the powers that be to sell vaccines. He also urges his readers not to take the vaccine that is given out by authorities.

The government apparently does not tolerate this kind of dissent. Krumwiede gets set up by an undercover agent to get him arrested. When he discovers the ploy against him the agent tells Krumwiede: "Alan, I didn't have a choice, they've seen your blog". Government agents then appear out of nowhere and arrest Krumwiede for "security fraud, conspiracy and most likely man slaughter".

Krumwiede is arrested due to the contents of his blog. Contagion sends out a powerful message against "alternative" information sources: Diverging from "official sources" is dangerous and against the law.

It is later learned that Forsythia was a lie and that Krumwiede made 4.5 million dollars by promoting it to his readers. The chief of Homeland Security wants to put him in jail for a "long, long time". However, due to his popularity, Krumwiede makes bail because, as the chief of Homeland Security states: "Evidently, there are 12 million people as crazy as you are".

The character of Alan Krumwiede and the way he is portrayed is interesting for several reasons. First, he reflects the growing influence of blogs and alternative websites on public opinion – a recent phenomena that does not sit well with the elite that seeks to have the monopoly of information. By depicting this character as dishonest, corrupt and even dangerous to the public, the movie justifies the shunning of such writers and even their arrest. Nobody in the movie seems to mind that all of this is in direct violation of the First Amendment.

Second, when the H1N1 vaccine was released in 2009 and mass vaccination campaigns were organized, many citizens and authoritative figures including public health officials, doctors and specialists spoke against it. They claimed that the vaccine was unnecessary, insufficiently tested and that it had negative side-effects. By associating the corrupt figure of Alan Krumwiede with the "anti-vaccine movement", the movie discredits all of those who question the necessity of mass vaccination campaigns. If another virus should strike, viewers of Contagion might be more prone to ignore these movements. In other words, the movie says: "Conspiracy theorists are corrupt liars that are dangerous to public safety and they should be arrested. Do not listen to them. They make money off phony cures. HOWEVER, those who make even more money off phony vaccines are good. Listen to authorities and get the vaccine … or you'll die."

The Ultimate Solution

After months of horror and hundreds of millions of deaths, a final solution emerges and saves humanity: Mass vaccination.

The only solution to do virus problem? A mass vaccination campaign.

Those who receive the vaccine get the privilege of wearing a scannable wristband. This allows them to go to public places such as shopping malls.

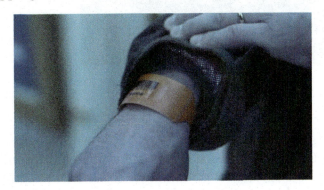

You get vaccinated, you get a barcode and go places. You don't get vaccinated, you stay at home ... and you die.

In Conclusion

Contagion may be presented as a work of fiction, but it communicates several important messages that authorities need the public to accept. To do so, the movie defines a specific problem that has actually occurred in the past, it identifies the agencies that have the right to take charge of the situation and proposes the only solution required to fix the problem. That solution is not pretty: The dissolution of the government, the imposition of martial law, the creation of civilian camps, forced vaccination campaigns and the suppression of free speech. Democracy and civil rights are summarily suspended and we witness the establishment of a highly controlled and monitored society (using barcodes).

Are disaster movies such as Contagion solely created for entertainment or are they also used to teach the public about what is acceptable and what is not when a disaster occurs? Would the World Health Organization participate in a movie simply to entertain people? Interesting fact: The movie was released on DVD at the same time the WHO got accused of exaggerating the death rate of the new H5N1 bird flu. The WHO has also recently allowed the publication of controversial research describing the creation of a mutant and highly contagious version of the virus. Could a weaponized version of the virus be purposely released on the public to justify martial law? Wait, maybe I shouldn't say things like that. I don't want to get arrested for "security fraud, conspiracy and most likely man slaughter".

"They Live", the Weird Movie With a Powerful Message

'They Live' is a science-fiction movie from the Eighties that features aliens, a WWF wrestler and a whole lot of sunglasses. What's not to like? While, at first glance, the movie appears to be a bunch of nonsense, 'They Live' actually communicates a powerful message about the elite and its use of mass media to control the masses. Is the movie describing what we call the Illuminati? This article looks at the deeper meaning of John Carpenter's strange but fascinating movie 'They Live'.

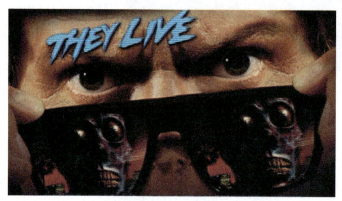

Warning: Major spoilers ahead

Watching They Live is a conflicting experience. It is an odd combination of eye-opening messages with lackluster acting, powerful social commentary with 1950's B-movie special effects and gripping satire with odd punchlines. Constantly making viewers oscillate between "Wow, that was genius!" to "Wow, that was corny!", it is difficult to properly evaluate the movie from a cinematographic point of view. However, from a "message" point of the view, They Live is gold. Based on Ray Nelson's short story Eight O'Clock in the Morning, the movie is one of those rare subversive stories that forces viewers to question their world and their surroundings. Because, despite the fact that the movie is about ghoulish aliens, it communicates truths to the viewers that are only alluded to in mainstream movies. In fact, looking deeper into the storyline, one might realize that there's probably more "science" than "fiction" in the story of They Live ... especially when one has "truth-seeing sunglasses".

The hero of the movie, played by WWF wrestler Rowdy Roddy Pipper, is a drifter that is apparently nameless. In the short story and the movie's credits, he is referred to as Nada, which means 'nothing' in Spanish. While this nameless nothing is broke and homeless, he still manages to expose the alien's hidden rule of the world. How did he accomplish that? With the only thing he'd ever need: The Truth. Oh, and also guns. He used a lot of guns. Most importantly, despite the fact that Nada was tempted several times to shut up in exchange for "generous compensation", he kept his integrity and never agreed to sell out to the aliens. Now, that's a role model. To top it off, he says the best things ever.

"I'm here to kick ass and chew bubble gum ... and I'm all out of bubble gum".

Are the aliens in the movie an imaginative way to portray the world's elite, those who secretly run the world, those we call the Illuminati? Let's revisit this cult classic and see how it describes the hidden rule of the elite.

The Premise

Right from the beginning, as we see Nada walking around Los Angeles with his backpack, the movie sets a particular mood: Something is not quite right. While Nada appears to be a happy-go-lucky kind of guy, the city is not happy and it is not too kind to happy-go-lucky kind of guys. Quite the contrary, there is a sense of impending doom in the air: Poverty is rampant, helicopters fly around the city and street preachers speak of soulless beings ruling the world.

"The venom of snakes is under their lips. Their mouths are full of bitterness and curses. And in their paths, nothing but ruin and misery. And the fear of God is not before their eyes! They have taken the hearts and minds of our leaders. They have recruited the rich and powerful, and they have blinded us to the truth! And our human spirit is corrupted. Why do we worship greed? Because outside the limit of our sight, feeding off us, perched on top of us from birth to death are our owners. Our owners -- they have us. They control us. They are our masters. Wake up. They're all about you, all around you!".

Is the preacher's description of the "masters" applicable to the Illuminati? I believe so.

As we follow Nada's aimless drifting across the city, the camera often focuses on people gazing blankly at television screens, mindlessly absorbing the vapid messages it communicates. Regular Joes appear to truly enjoy their television shows … until an obscure organization hacks the airwaves to broadcast subversive messages about the hidden rulers of the world.

"Our impulses are being redirected. We are living in an artificially induced state of consciousness that resembles sleep. (...) The poor and the underclass are growing. Racial justice and human rights are nonexistent. They have created a repressive society, and we are their unwitting accomplices. Their intention to rule rests with the annihilation of consciousness. We have been lulled into a trance. They have made us indifferent to ourselves, to others. We are focused only on our own gain. Please understand. They are safe as long as they are not discovered. That is their primary method of survival. Keep us asleep, keep us selfish, keep us sedated."

Can the above statement be applied to the Illuminati? I believe so.

The Average Joes who watch this pirated TV broadcast all get a massive headache – the raw truth is indeed too much for most people to bear. One such viewer switches the channel after telling the guy on TV: "Blow it out your ass". Just like today, most people do not want to hear about this kind of stuff … they just want to go back to their mindless TV viewing.

Nada realizes that the street preacher and the man on television are connected through a local church. When he sneaks into the church, he discovers that it is actually the headquarters of an underground organization.

On a wall inside the church is written "They Live We Sleep", a phrase that describes the fundamental difference between the elite and the masses. Those in power know the truth about the world and possess the means and the power to truly "live". The rest of the population is sedated, dumbed-down and manipulated into a zombie-like status in order for it to be as easily manageable as possible by the masters. The masses' ignorance equals a state of endless slumber.

Nada learns that the rebellious organization is attempting to recruit people to take down the rulers. However, a few days later, Nada discovers what happens to those who plot against those in power.

Helicopters, bulldozers and police in riot gear raid the place, destroy everything and violently arrest the members of the underground organization. That is how the elite responds to contrary views.

After witnessing the violent police shakedown, Nada begins to realize that something is wrong in America. The happy-go-lucky guy who believed in working hard and following the rules is starting to believe that something is amiss here.

Determined to learn more, Nada re-enters the church and finds a few interesting things.

The police painted over "They Live We Sleep". Obviously, "They" don't want that message to be known.

More importantly, Nada discovers a box full of sunglasses that allows his to see the world as it is. Added bonus: They also look pretty cool.

Seeing the Truth

While the sunglasses found by Nada appear on the surface to be worthless, they actually provide him with the greatest gift of all: The Truth. When Nada first puts on the sunglasses, the experience is shocking.

When he has his sunglasses on, Nada sees through the smoke and mirrors projected by advertisement and mass media . He only sees the core of their message and the only reason why they exist.

No matter which magazine Nada flips open, he sees the same subliminal messages, which tells a lot about the true function of "celebrity" and "fashion" magazines. Despite the fact that they are all different, they all ultimately serve the same purpose: To reinforce messages from the elite to the masses.

Nada also quickly understands the truth about money.

"In God We Trust"?

Nada's most shocking discovery concerns people around him.

Some people are not human. They are from another race that has infiltrated society.

Nada realizes that they are everywhere and that they hold positions of power, like this politician giving a typical "politician" speech on television. Is this a way to portray the Illuminati?

Upon discovering this truth, Nada became pissed off. REALLY pissed off. How did he react to the situation? He did not go home and write a poem about it. Nope, he grabbed a shotgun and started shooting aliens.

When the aliens realize that Nada can see through their disguise, they immediately alert the authorities saying "I've got one that can see". Being able to "see" is obviously frowned upon by the aliens – they do not like to be exposed. Nada quickly becomes a social pariah and aliens start closing in on him. Confronted with this situation, Nada says profound and timeless words: "I don't like this oooooooone bit".

Many aliens are part of the police force as its sole purpose is to ensure that the alien's rule is not disturbed. Most policemen are however regular humans and just follow the orders because that's their job ... a little like actual policemen who do the Illuminati's work.

Nada and everyone in the city are constantly monitored by flying surveillance cameras that are oddly similar to the new unmanned drones that are currently appearing around the world.

Flying surveillance cameras were considered science fiction in 1988. They are reality today.

An actual, modern unmanned drone mounted with a video camera.

The concept of truth-seeing sunglasses is an interesting way to illustrate the importance of knowledge in one's world perception. Two people can be looking at the exact same thing yet perceive two very different realities, depending on the level of information and awareness possessed by each person. Nada's sunglasses can therefore represent one's knowledge of the truth, which allows a clear perception of reality.

Looking for Others Who Know the Truth

Upon learning the shocking truth about the world, Nada feels the need to share this vital information with his friend Frank Armitage. Nada however quickly realizes some people do not want to hear about it. In fact, many actually get angry and offended at the simple mention of something that alludes to it. When Nada asks Frank to put on his sunglasses so he can see what he sees, Frank firmly refuses and calls him a "crazy motha…". Nada replies with another classic line "Either you put these sunglasses on or start eating that trash can".

Then ensues one of the longest one-on-one fight scene I ever seen (eight minutes of punching and kicking), a scene that is dragged out for so long that it becomes utterly absurd and even comical. While the scene maybe appear ridiculous, it says something about the difficulty of making regular, average people wake up from their blissful ignorance.

Frank finally sees the truth. All it took is Nada beating the crap out of him, sticking the sunglasses on his face against his will and forcing him to look around. Yes, convincing other people of the truth can be a hard task.

It takes a lot of effort on Nada's part, but Frank finally sees the aliens controlling the world. The two pals are then

During the meeting, Nada and Frank are given truth-seeing contact lenses. The sunglasses gave truth-seers a nasty headache, especially when they are taken off. When first exposed to the truth, adapting to the new reality can indeed be difficult, and even painful. However, after a while, it becomes seamless part of the person. A little like wearing contact lenses.

invited to a secret meeting of the underground organization that is attempting to rid the earth from the aliens. During the meeting, Nada and Frank learn that humans are being recruited by the aliens in exchange for wealth and power. As the leader of the underground organization says: "Most of us just sell out right away". It is rather easy to make a correlation between the movie and actual politicians and celebrities we've seen in previous articles on this site who readily sell out to the Illuminati in exchange for wealth, power and celebrity.

The meeting doesn't last long, however, as police barge in the place and start shooting everyone there. They are designated a "terrorist organization" by the elite. Nada and Frank manage to escape and accidentally find themselves behind enemy lines, in the alien's underground base.

Movies and TV

Behind Enemy Lines

While exploring the aliens' underground base, Nada and Frank stumble upon a party thrown by the aliens for human collaborators to thank them for their "partnership". Although humans will never be considered equals to the

"Our projections show that by the year 2025, not only America but the entire planet will be under the protection and the dominion of this power alliance. The gains have been substantial, both for ourselves and for you, the human power elite."

aliens, those who sell out to them get monetary benefits … much like those who are not part of today's elite who nevertheless sell out to push the elite's New World Order Agenda.

The TV station 'Cable 54' is used by the aliens to hypnotize humans. Is this science-fiction? Barely.

Frank and Nada then discover the source of the aliens' brainwashing signals: A television studio. The aliens use the network to broadcast hypnotic and subliminal signals to humans, blinding them from the truth about their rulers and the world. The message that is communicated here: Mass media is the elite's favorite tool indoctrinate the masses and to keep them in servitude.

Nada realizes that the only way to save humanity from the grips of the aliens is to go to the roof of the TV station's building and to take down the emitter of the subliminal messages, disguised as a satellite dish. Indeed, without an elite-controlled mass media, indoctrinating the masses will be a lot more difficult. So Nada and Frank start shooting their way towards the roof, not an easy task.

The Disinformation Agent

Nada met Holly Thomspon, a Cable 54 network executive, at the beginning of his wild rampage. While Nada appears to be somewhat enamoured with her, she always somehow brings trouble. During the "terrorist organization" meeting, Holly infiltrated the group, posing as a sympathizer and claiming that Cable 54 "was clean" and was not the source of aliens' signal, which was false and misleading. Today, disinformation is widely used by the elite to confuse and mislead those who attempt to discover the truth about the world.

During Nada's rush towards the roof of the network's building, Holly appears again, claiming that she wants to

While this lady appeared to be nice at first, she tried to mislead, deceive and even kill Nada during his quest. She ends up shooting his pal Frank in the head.

help him. However, she is simply trying to kill him before the mission is accomplished. She is therefore another human that sold out to the aliens being used to disrupt non-corrupted humans attempting to liberate themselves and others.

Taking Down the Aliens

Here's the biggest spoiler of them all: Nada manages to take down the aliens' transmitter and saves humanity. This heroic move gets him killed, however, as a policeman inside a helicopter shoots him dead. Nada therefore becomes

Even though it cost his life, Nada visibly does not regret exposing the aliens to the world. With his last once of strength, Nada gives the aliens a uniquely human parting gift: the finger.

the quintessential hero, sacrificing his life for the good of humanity – a martyr for human freedom from soulless rulers.

TV viewers around the world now realize that those giving the daily news were also those who controlled them.

Once the aliens' satellite dish is down, the masses are able to see the world as it is: the alien's ugly faces are exposed to the world.

In Conclusion

Although They Live is usually described as "a science-fiction movie that criticizes consumer culture", the scope of its message actually goes way beyond the usual "consumerism is bad" lecture. They Live can indeed be interpreted as a treatise on the thorough and systematic conditioning of human experience in order for a hidden elite to covertly control, manipulate and exploit the masses. In the movie, the rulers are portrayed as a completely different race that perceives humans as inferior – something that can easily be correlated to the attitudes about the bloodlines of the Illuminati. The presence of these strong messages in the movie is one of the reasons They Live became somewhat of a cult-classic, despite the fact that it was panned by movie critics. As the years go by, the movie's message is becoming increasingly relevant … and freakishly realistic.

Many of those who seek the truth about the world realize that it's reins are held by an un-elected elite, one that is essentially hidden from the public eye. As the movie's promotional poster says: "You see them on the street. You watch them on TV. You might even vote for one this fall. You think they're people just like you. You're wrong. Dead wrong." Working behind the scenes, this secretive elite constantly works towards the creation of a global system that would serve its interests: a New World Order, ruled by one world government. As a human collaborator says in the movie to justify his selling-out: "There ain't no countries anymore. No more good guys. They're running the whole show. They own everything. The whole goddamn planet!" To facilitate the rulers' work, the masses are kept in the dark and are distracted with the fake puppet show that is politics and the "no independent thought" programming that is mass media. Apathy, ignorance and indifference are the elite's best friends.

Despite its unimpressive special effects and odd dialogue, They Live manages to describe the world elite's motives and strategy in a way that can be understood by all. And that is no simple task. However, in order to fully understand the movie's message, one must be wearing truth-seeing sunglasses. Do you have yours on?

The Hidden Symbolic Meaning of the Movie "2012"

The disaster movie "2012" is about the near-total destruction of planet Earth in accordance with predictions made by Ancient Mayans, thousands of years ago. While most of the movie is centered around spectacular explosions and impressive special effects, "2012" also communicates messages and symbolism about the elite's plans for a New World and the coming of the Age of Aquarius.

Warning: Major spoilers ahead

Released in 2009, Roland Emmerich's film 2012 plays on the fears and panic engendered by the "OMG-the-Mayans-said-we're-gonna-die-in-2012" scare. The movie's apocalyptic scenario depicts in vivid detail people's worst fears regarding 2012: The destruction of everything and the killing of everyone … well, almost everyone. While a good portion of the two-and-a-half hour movie is dedicated to CGI destruction, 2012 contains many Biblical, mythological and historical references that gives the story a deeper underlying meaning. Furthermore, a specific message can be understood by the way the crisis has been handled in the movie. It basically says: "If something happens, the rich and powerful will live and the rest of you suckers will die".

In the article entitled 'Contagion' or How Disaster Movies "Educate" the Masses, we discussed how disaster movies are an important indoctrination tool that present and sell specific "political responses" to major crises. In 2012, the political response to the mega-cataclysm that is threatening Earth is rather unsettling: The world elite learns about 2012 a few years in advance, secretly plans its own rescue mission (while keeping the masses in the dark) and leaves the world to die while creating a new world that is only populated by the elite. A few "regular" people do manage to infiltrate the elite's ships. Apparently their survival, along with the world's rich and powerful, constitutes a happy ending.

When I first finished watching the movie, I wasn't exactly feeling happy having just paid a few bucks to basically watch a flick that predicts my death and the death of everyone I know while the elite embark on giant ships to start a new world by themselves. It's a little insulting.

Does the movie accurately predict what will happen on December 23rd, 2012? Probably (hopefully) not, but I do believe that the movie uses the 2012 scare tactic to communicate specific messages to the masses about the elite's plans for a New World Order and the coming of the Age of Aquarius. Let's look at the movie's most symbolic scenes.

The Preparations

The movie takes place in 2009 and begins with a cosmic event that triggers the cataclysm: A planetary alignment.

The alignment of astronomical bodies causes a series of events that lead to the destruction of Earth. On an esoteric level, the alignment of astral bodies is representative of the dawning of a new era - what some may call the Age of Aquarius.

On Earth, a few scientists discover that massive solar flares are causing the planet's core temperature to rise. Adrian Helmsley, an American geologist, realizes that the end of the world is rapidly approaching. He rushes to Washington D.C. to inform the highest level of power that action must be taken, but it turns out that the world's ruling elite is not only well-aware of the coming disaster, but have been secretly working on a rescue plan for years. The elite are taking steps to preserve the lives of those that are deemed "worthy" and collecting the Earth's most important artifacts to bring to the new world.

In this scene, the Mona Lisa at the Louvre is fake. The real painting will be brought into "post-apocalypse" world.

The only people that know about the 2012 rescue plan are the world's most powerful people. Tickets were also sold to private individuals. The price? 1 billion Euros … per person. In other words, there is no way that a regular person would survive. And that's all part of the plan.

Meanwhile, as usual, the masses are portrayed as a herd of idiots, prone to panic and violence.

As it is the case in most disaster movies, the masses are portrayed as a "bewildered herd" that cannot act civilized. While the elite is planning its secret escape from the 2012 cataclysm, the masses are shown rioting during a G8 Meeting. Seeing how people are portrayed to act in times of crisis, one might be inclined to think: Maybe the elite is doing the right thing by hiding the truth from the masses …

This massive conspiracy against the public is not an airtight secret. Some prominent figures discover the ugly truth and attempt to warn the public, but they are rapidly silenced.

When the director of the Louvre discovered the elite's plans, he called a press conference to disclose the truth to the entire world. He then dies in a "mysterious" car accident, right before he makes his announcement.

There are interesting facts about the above car "accident" that killed the French museum director. First, it is clearly stated in the movie that the accident occurs in the Pont d'Alma tunnel … the same tunnel where Princess Diana lost her life in a odd car accident. In my article Princess Diana's Death and Memorial: The Occult Meaning, I've explained the symbolic meaning of the Pont d'Alma tunnel and how the death of Lady Di had all of the markings of a ritual sacrifice. The death of the Museum director at the exact same spot might be the movie's way of saying that his death was a ritual sacrifice by the elite. The movie might also be indirectly saying: "If the death of the Museum Director inside the Pont D'Alma tunnel was a murder disguised as an accident, what do you think happened to Lady Di?".

It is later discovered that the museum director is not the only whistle-blower that has "mysteriously" lost his life. Many other people who had the public's well-being in mind also died in strange circumstances during the elite's secret preparations.

A conspiracy theorist dedicated an entire wall to news clippings of people who got killed by the elite.

All of the elite's decision-making is done in secret and secluded meetings and involving only the world's most powerful people.

Meanwhile, the public is restless, to the point that the London Olympics are suspended. Is the movie predicting events to come?

While all of this is happening, the Chinese government has been put in charge of building the gigantic boats named "Arks" that would allow the elite to survive 2012.

Farewell Atlantis

The hero of the movie is Jackson Curtis, a regular divorced father, that discovers the truth and attempts to embark on one of the Arks in order to survive 2012.

Jackson Curtis and his kids are told by the US Army that they must leave the national park. They are not told why because the public is not allowed to know about the upcoming 2012 disaster.

Jackson Curtis is a not-too-successful writer of a book entitled Farewell Atlantis, which is very symbolic in the movie's context. Atlantis is the name of a fabled continent that got submerged by a massive flood several millenia ago. Legend holds that the highly advanced civilization that flourished on that continent disappeared, but some survivors of Atlantis managed to sail to places like Egypt, America and Asia, where they became great teachers to the natives. Atlantis is of a great importance in the occult elite's Mysteries as it is believed that the continent actually existed and was the origin of the world's occult knowledge. Atlanteans who sailed to far-away lands in order escape the Great Flood are considered the teachers of esoteric knowledge to the Ancient Egyptians, Mayans and possibly even the Celts. Mystery schools often state that the Biblical story of the Great Flood is, in fact, the story of the disappearance of Atlantis. They also claim that many other ancient cultures have similar stories within their folklore.

Today's secret societies perceive and refer to America as the "New Atlantis", a country that was founded on the principles of Freemasonry and Rosicrucianism, the supposed descendants of Atlantean Mysteries.

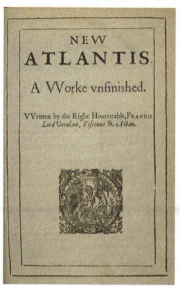

Francis Bacon's 1605 book "New Atlantis" describes an ideal society where science and reason would rule, according the principles of Freemasonry and Rosicrucianism. The book is said to be the blueprint of the founding of America. Bacon is known for writing "Knowledge is Power", a famous phrases that has deep resonance in Rosicrucianism and that is prominently featured in the US Library of Congress.

While Sir Francis Bacon's New Atlantis appeared to be foreshadowing the founding of America, Jackson Curtis' novel Farewell Atlantis appears to be foreshadowing its destruction. The same way Atlantis was completely submerged by water, America, the home base today's occult elite, will suffer a similar fate. The lucky few that will embark in a modern version of Noah's Ark will be given the task to found a New World – and the movie subtly states which institutions will carry on and which will disappear.

The Disaster

As the film progresses, the Earth begins to heat up and fissures start to appear in Los Angeles. Although it is obvious that a major disaster is about to happen, mass media (which is in collusion with the elite, in the movie and in real life) downplays everything in order to keep the population calm and oblivious to the fact that the world is ending. The only non-elite guy that appears to know what's going on is a nut-job conspiracy theorist living in the woods (apparently, according to Hollywood movies, truth seekers cannot be level-headed, rational people).

Charlie Frost is a near batcrap crazy conspiracy theorist that hosts a radio show and that runs a not-so-great-looking website. He actually knows the truth and he is right about everything, yet, in the end, he is still depicted as a complete nutjob. Knowing the truth is not "cool" in Hollywood movies.

Charlie Frost describes everything that is about to happen to Jackson Curtis and even provides him a map to the Arks.

The map to the Arks are conveniently placed in Charlie Frost's "conspiracy files", right next to his documents on Marilyn Monroe. A little wink to the ultimate mind-controlled Presidential slave?

As the world is crumbling apart, members of the elite receive an important and top-secret message on their mobile phones.

When things get serious, members of the elite are notified that it is time to embark on the Arks and to leave the rest of the world to die.

When hell breaks loose on Earth, several important monuments are shown being destroyed. These scenes are not only spectacular to watch but they also represent the fall of important institutions as the world enters the Age of Aquarius. In one scene, the famous Brazilian monument "Christ the Redeemer" is shown falling down in a matter similar to the way statues of Saddam Hussein fell after the Gulf War.

Does this symbolize the fall of Christianity in the wake of a new era?

In another scene, St. Peter's Basilica in the Vatican, the "epicenter" of Catholic faith, is shown crashing down on faithfuls and killing thousands of people who assembled to pray.

In this symbolic scene, a crack appears on Michelangelo's iconic painting in the Sistine Chapel, right between the fingers of God and Adam - which can represent the break of the connection between humanity and the divine. Is the elite's New World devoid of the touch of God?

Other religions are also shown being destroyed during the movie. According to an article in The Guardian, 2012 was supposed to contain a scene depicting the destruction of the Kabaa, the holiest site of the Muslim faith. However, the scene was axed for fear of backlash from Islamic groups. The elite's new world, is therefore not only devoid of Christianity, but of all major religions – one of the goals of the New World Order.

2012 does not only show the destruction of religious monuments, but also of political landmarks. These scenes symbolize the fall of regular nation states before the formation of a single world government.

The White House, symbol of US power, is shown being hit by one of its own war ships and taken away by a gigantic wave. In the elite's new world, it is not about National powers and military might: It is about a single world government and a single military.

The American President addressing the Nation for the last time. The "leader of the free world" symbolically stays in Washington D.C. to die with regular people. In other words, the (supposedly) democratically elected representative of the people has no place in the elite's new world government.

The Noah's Ark of the Elite

Several of these gigantic Arks were secretly built in China.

While most of the world's population is getting killed by floods and earthquakes, the "chosen ones" are taken to China to embark in gigantic Arks.

In this clear allusion to the Biblical story of Noah's Ark, animals are shown carried to the ships by helicopter.

Entry to those Arks is far from fair and is reserved for those that are "one of them". For example, the Indian scientist that discovered the coming of the 2012 cataclysm is left to die, while greedy Russian billionaires are granted access.

Of course, as a member of the world's occult elite, the Queen of England and her dogs are granted access to the ships. Because her hat-wearing skills will be very useful to humanity in the future.

A bunch of pointless "suspenseful" scenes happen as Jackson Curtis and his family attempt to illegally enter one of them. Seeing how many people were left to die, the scientist Adrian Helmsley makes a unavoidable speech about how us humans must stick together and whatnot. However, we don't see him giving up his place for anyone and everyone still dies ... except for the elite. So, despite the moralizing monologues about caring for each other, the elite's plan carries on right on schedule and only those that were chosen to survive do.

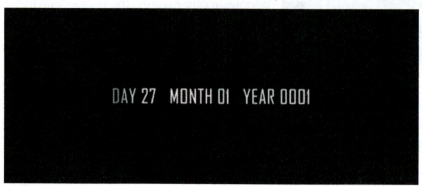

After the disaster, humanity enters a new era and resets its calendar to year 0001. The previous calendar was based on the birth of Jesus Christ - which is esoterically associated with the Age of Pisces. The resetting of the calendar signifies that Christ's era is over. It is the beginning of the Age of Aquarius.

At the end of the movie, the entire world is completely submerged by water, except for the African Continent. The Arks set sail to the cradle of Civilization to start anew in a place symbolically called "Cape Hope". Is this a happy ending? Depends if you're in the elite or part of the 99% of the rest of the world that died.

The Age of Aquarius

Esoteric schools teach that a "Great Solar Year" is the period of time during which the sun cycles through all of the zodiacal constellations, lasting about 25,000 years. Every 2,000 years (more or less) the sun enters a new zodiacal constellation and humanity, somewhat unconsciously, adopts symbolism that relates to that zodiacal sign. For nearly the past 2,000 years the sun was in the constellation of Pisces (represented by Two Fishes), meaning that we are in the Piscean Age. Oddly enough, Christianity has always been represented by the symbol of a fish (i.e. the Jesus Fish). Every 2,000 years, the sun migrates to the previous sign of the zodiac, which means that the world is set to enter to Age of Aquarius.

By showing the fall of Christian symbols and the emerging of a new world after a massive flood, the movie 2012 appears to be announcing the coming of the Aquarian Age.

The astrological sign of Aquarius consists of a cup-bearer pouring water. In Greek mythology, the cup-bearer is said to be the cause of the Great Flood that probably caused the disappearance of Atlantis.

Since the symbol of the sign of Aquarius is a man pouring water and is methodologically associated with the legendary Great Flood, it is rather appropriate to depict the coming of the Aquarian Age with a flood that submerges New Atlantis, aka America.

In Conclusion

While 2012 is often described as a big orgy of explosions and special effects, the movie nevertheless contains a great deal of messages and symbolic moments. Its references to historical, Biblical, mythological and esoteric concepts give the movie a deeper meaning, one that fits with the world view of today's occult elite. While the world will probably not crash and burn on December 23rd 2012, the movie uses the scare relating to the Mayan Calendar to communicate its plans for the future: The fall of religions, dissolution of Nations and the glorification of a select elite on the backs of the clueless masses. Everything that happens in the movie is remarkably on-par with "ten commandments" found on the Georgia Guidestones (see the article Sinister Sites – The Georgia Guidestones). Here are some of them: "Maintain humanity under 500,000,000 in perpetual balance with nature", "Unite humanity with a living new language" and so forth. The way things go down is also reminiscent of the symbolic stories told on the prophetic murals found at the Denver International Airport (read the article here) and the murals at the Bank of America (read the article here). Both of these pieces depict a period of great tribulation, destruction and oppression that is followed by the founding of a new world based on the elite's principles.

On a more esoteric level, the movie equates America with Atlantis, an advanced civilization that was destroyed by a great flood. The survivors of ancient Atlantis, who are said to be the originators of the occult lore of secret societies, went on to perpetuate their knowledge across the world.

And while solar flares are said to be cause of the 2012 disaster, major floods are the cause of the Earth's destruction. Through this symbolism, the movie appears to announce the end of the Age of Pisces and the coming of the Age of Aquarius.

There is therefore much more to 2012 than originally meets the eye. Unfortunately, as it is often the case in mass media, the messages being communicated are neither enlightening nor inspiring. Quite the contrary, the movie basically tells the story of gigantic conspiracy against the public, complete with cover-ups and murders. In the end, the elite saves its own ass and leaves billions of people to die. To top it off, this conspiracy is presented as the only viable solution to such a crisis. Is the public being prepared for a major crisis that will be resolved with the heralding of a New World Order? As the movie's promotional poster clearly states: "We Were Warned".

The Movie "Videodrome" and The Horror of Mass Media

"Videodrome" is an 80s science fiction horror film that contains some gore, James Woods and Betamax videotapes. Above all, the movie communicates a strong message on the perversity of mass media, its dangers to the human psyche and how it is used to manipulate the masses. This article will look at the meaning of the movie "Videodrome" and how it reveals the shadier aspects of mass media.

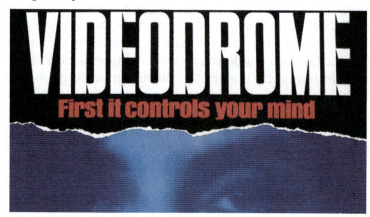

Warning: This article contains spoilers and disturbing subject matters.

Videodrome is a dark Canadian movie about a sleazy CEO of a small cable TV station and his discovery of a broadcast signal featuring live torture and murder. As fascination turns into obsession, then into physical illness, the movie symbolically describes, in a very extreme and graphic way, the impact of mass media perversity on the human psyche, as well as the dark forces behind it.

The movie's odd mix of gore, taboo subject matters and social commentary make it an original, but disturbing film to watch. I am glad I did not watch the movie as a child because I'd probably have gotten nightmares for days. Thirty years later, though Videodrome's horror special effects appear quite corny and laughable, one thing is for sure: Its message hasn't aged a bit. In fact, the metaphorical meaning behind the twisted scenes in the movie is as real, relevant and shocking as it ever was, which probably explains why it became somewhat of a cult classic.

Videodrome was produced in 1983 but one can argue that it was decades ahead of its time. It successfully predicted the growing control of mass media by shady forces, the coming of reality television and the propagation, through various mediums such as the Internet, of all kinds of extreme underground films.

While many perceive the movie as a criticism of the effect of mass media, some claim that it is nothing less than a manifesto from the elite to reveal the way it functions.

> *"This writer submits that part of the ongoing "Revelation of the Method", the cryptocracy recently issued a kind of Rosicrucian manifesto, revealing precisely what television is doing to us and what the future of the video imperium they are planning for us will be like. The name of this manifesto is Videodrome, directed by the Canadian David Cronberg whose other works include two films about psychic assassins, Scanners which features the Kennedy-sigil exploding head and the Dead Zone".*
> - Michael A. Hoffman, Secret Societies and Psychological Warfare

Let's look at the movie's plot and how it relates in the context of today.

Discovering the Videodrome

Max Renn is the president of CIVIC-TV, one of those sleazy television stations that specialize in low-grade programming such as soft "adult" shows and low grade violent movies. He is convinced that the public is hungry for more extreme TV experiences and that his network must bring this to its viewers.

During a TV interview, Max Renn argues that TV acts as a catharsis, meaning that it is a healthy outlet for our violent and sexual needs. He soon discovers first hand that his theory is completely false.

Harlan shows Renn a television signal broadcasting nothing but ultra-realistic torture, abuse and murder performed by masked individuals. Renn believes that it is all staged and that it is exactly the kind of programming his network needs.

Renn is actively looking for something new and exciting to propose to his viewers. To do so, he has a secret contact: A TV pirate named Harlan who can intercept satellite signals from across the world. The pirate shows him a television show that will change his life.

Renn discovers later in the movie that nothing in Videodrome is staged and that it is, in fact, snuff TV, which is real live footage of violent acts.

In the "real world", the concept of snuff videos is taboo and controversial. However, some researchers have exposed the existence of underground networks distributing snuff videos in elite organizations. Everything from blood rituals to abuse involving mind-controlled slaves and minors is distributed and consumed by high-placed circles operating above the law. Also, high-profile crimes that bear a ritualistic aspect are sometimes recorded and sold at high price.

> "Some of the Son of Sam murders were videotaped by cult-members and copies command high prices
> in cash, drugs and other commodities on the underground snuff-film circuit."
> - Michael A. Hoffman, Secret Societies and Psychological Warfare

The masses are introduced and desensitized to the occult elite's taste for the violent and perverse through mass media.

> "None of this ought to be too shocking to any American TV watcher since a version of this process can
> be seen in those glimpses of actual murders and other horrors we are shown on broadcast TV, on the
> "news" and in "specials", right in the "Videodrome". Simulated snuff-videos are already available at

many of our cheery neighbourhood video-rental stores. Cable and network television broadcast the highest grade of brutalizing voyeurism."
- Ibid.

In the movie, Max Renn is somewhat representative of the masses. Even though he knows that Videodrome is not the most engrossing show on TV, he still irresistibly attracted to its graphic material. Fascination with blood and lust is a primal and instinctive reflex and has been used as a tool to capture attention and to control since ancient times (see Circus and Gladiatorial Games in the Roman Empire). Furthermore, when no moral objections are involved, some are willing to be exposed to truly evil and twisted deeds to satisfy a craving that often turns into an obsession.

In the movie, Nicki, the woman Max is dating, gets sexually aroused by the violence in Videodrome. Completely submitting to the call of their lowest impulses, the couple gets "busy" while watching some guy getting tortured. While blood and lust are primal instincts that are meant to insure survival, we see here that they've been twisted and distorted by mass media to manipulate weaker minds.

Watching Videodrome quickly produces negative effects on Renn. His interest for the show quickly turns into an obsession. The tape he uses for entertainment soon begins to consume him.

Max's obsession for Videodrome causes a blurring between reality and fiction. Here, TV takes life and literally calls him.

Max begins to experience intense hallucinations. He doesn't see a difference between television and reality. He soon realizes that Videodrome is not just "entertainment".

More Than a TV Show

While researching the origin of Videodrome in order to broadcast it on his TV station, Renn learns that it is much more than a TV show. One his friends tells him that the action on Videodrome is not staged and that those behind it are powerful and dangerous. While the show simply appears to be about violence, there is much more behind it. Max's friend tells him:

> *"It has something that you don't have, Max. It has a philosophy. And that's what makes it dangerous".*

This concept is very true in mass media. While most people do not live according to a specific philosophy and do not put a lot of thought about what they watch on TV, those in power and those controlling the airwaves are often motivated by strong philosophical and political motives. This results in the communication of propaganda to people who do not even realize they are watching propaganda.

The man behind Videodrome is Professor Max Oblivion, who only communicates through TV screens.

Oblivion is an idealist convinced that technology, particularly television, would help lead humanity to a better tomorrow. He runs "Cathode Ray Mission", a homeless shelter that provides a "healthy dose" television to those who cannot afford it.

"The battle for the mind of North America will be fought in the video arena. The Videodrome. The television screen is the retina of the mind's eye. Therefore, the television screen is part of the physical structure of the brain. Therefore, whatever appears on the television screen emerges as raw experience for those watching. Therefore, television is reality. And reality is less than television."

Oblivion's office is full of items relating to religion and philosophy. He believes that mass media can bring near-spiritual salvation and promise eternal life through television.

As it is the case in the real world, Professor Oblivion's altruistic dream got taken over by people who mean business. He is killed by a shady yet powerful organization that wants to use Videodrome to control and manipulate the masses. And Max soon discovers who they are.

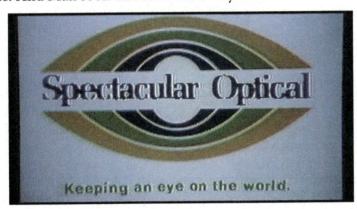

The organization runs behind a front company named Spectacular Optical. The eye logo and the ominous slogan "Keeping an eye on the world" is rather Illuminati-ish.

When Renn meets to head of Spectacular Optical, he is shown an introductory video that describes the organization an "enthusiastic global corporate citizen that makes inexpensive glasses for the Third World and missile guidance systems for NATO". In other words, it is the type of mega-corporation that would be part of our world's global elite. Spectacular Optical also makes Videodrome.

The head of Spectacular Optical, Barry Convex, tells Max that Videodrome is extreme because exposure to violence affects the nervous system and "opens receptors in the brains and the spine which allow the Videodrome signal to sink in" – and mess with people's minds. One can wonder if there is some factual basis behind this theory:

Do sex and violence create a primal response in our bodies that makes us more receptive to other messages and signals? Even if there were serious studies on the subject, I doubt they would be divulged to the public.

Max then learns that he was purposely deceived into watching Videodrome because Spectacular Optical needs to take over his TV station to broadcast its signal to the masses. To do so, Max will be used as a mind-controlled patsy to kill his partners and hand over Channel 83 to Spectacular Optical.

When the Program Programs You

Although Max realizes that weird stuff is going on, his exposure to Videodrome has rendered him utterly powerless and at the mercy of those broadcasting the signal. The movie illustrates in a rather graphic matter how individuals can easily be brainwashed and controlled by mass media.

The head of Spectacular Optimal literally jams inside Max a tape in order to program his mind and control his actions. This is a rather graphic way of representing how the elite-controlled mass media programs its viewers, figuratively inserting a tape into people to get its Agenda and messages accepted.

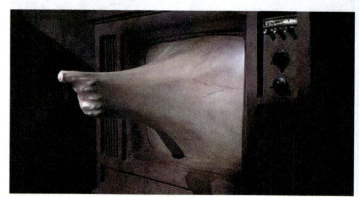

Bianca's TV points back at Max the gun he is holding. Media therefore became a reflection of him and him, a reflection of media. The TV then shoots Max which allows him to be free from the Videodrome tape and to be "reborn" in an almost religious way. Max's new mantra: "Death to Videodrome, Long Live the New Flesh".

Controlled by the tape, Renn enters the office of his TV station and takes out his partners. He is then told to go take care of Bianca Oblivion, the daughter of Professor Oblivion. There, he is stopped short and Bianca uses a TV screen to "deprogram" him. He is however quickly reprogrammed to kill the head of Spectacular Optical, Barry Convex. Max has become a blank slate that can be programmed and re-programmed at will.

Max then goes to take care of Barry Convex, who is in an optical trade show for reading glasses and such. The theme of the show is de Medici, Florence's prominent political dynasty, banking family and royal house of the 14th century. This choice of theme is rather interesting considering the fact that Spectacular Optical can easily be related to the occult elite we call the Illuminati.

The de Medici family can be seen as a prototype of today's Illuminati bloodlines, as it had a stronghold on the monetary, cultural and even religious affairs of their subjects (the family produced four popes). From an occult point of view, de Medici's translated classical works on Mystery teachings (such as the Corpus Hermeticum) are often credited for having revived hermeticsm, the Kabbalah and Gnosticism in Europe – all basic teachings of today's secret societies. The theme of the trade show can therefore further associate Spectacular Optical with the occult elite.

The stage of the trade show contains two quotes: "The eye is the window to the soul" and "Love comes in at the eye". Considering the fact that this organization controls people by making them watch acts of cruelty, these sayings conceal a disturbing meaning. Then again, doublespeak is a specialty of the elite.

When Renn shoots Convex, we find out that he's some kind of alien or monster, which is somewhat reminiscent of the movie They Live (read my article about They Live here).

Dazed and Confused

After carrying out his murderous mission, Renn hides in an abandoned place. He once again finds himself in front of a TV that directly talks to him. It tells him that "death is not the end" and that it can "help him". Is it proposing eternal life through appearing on television? Max then tells the TV what many people unconsciously feel.

> "I don't know where I am now. I am having trouble finding my way around."

His exposure to Videodrome (mass media) has caused him to lose his thoughts and even his free will. The TV, which uses the image of Nicki to seduce him and attract his attention, replies:

> "Videodrome still exists. Its very big, very complex. You've hurt them, but you haven't destroyed them. To do that, you'd have to go on to the next phase."

The TV then tells him that he needs to go "all the way" and become the New Flesh. To do that, he has to kill himself. We see here how mass media can be a manipulative force, using seduction and rhetoric to influence behavior, even if it involves shooting oneself in the head. Then, the TV says: "Here, I'll show you".

The TV shows Max how to shoot himself.

Right after, Max imitates what he saw on television, says "Long live the New Flesh" and shoots himself in the head

… and the movie ends on that unsettling note.

Did Max truly "complete his transformation" and become New Flesh? Probably not. Like most of what is said on television, all of this New Flesh story was most likely a bunch of BS used to manipulate his confused mind and to push him towards suicide. By shooting Convex, Max became an enemy of Videodrome and, like most mind-controlled patsies, he was pushed into a "self-destruct mode" once he stopped being useful to the organization.

On a larger scale, the ending of the movie communicates a strong statement about the influence of mass media on the world. Does it directly influence people's thoughts and actions, even if it goes against their best interests? This movie says yes.

In Conclusion

While the premise of Videodrome is over-the-top science fiction, its underlying message rings even truer today than it did in 1983 when it was released. With the advent of new technologies such as the Internet and mobile devices, we are today, more than ever, surrounded by the signals of the real-world Videodrome that is mass media. Its images and message can now reach us in a variety of ways, following us anywhere we go. While not as in-your-face and extreme as the movie's Videodrome, today's mass media still tap into these two primal urges humans that are difficult for human to ignore: blood-lust and reproduction. These two instincts were encoded in our DNA for the survival of individuals and the propagation of the species, but they are now "soft spots" that can easily be triggered with specific stimuli, causing an immediate and powerful reactions. As people get desensitized to sexual and violent imagery, mass media constantly pushes the envelope to bring new, distorted and twisted ways to capture their viewer's attention. While the showing of a woman's ankle caused quite a stir a few decades ago, today Internet users keep demanding for more extreme footage to get excited. As Max says in the movie: "They need something rough". How long will it take until all-out snuff movies become acceptable for mass consumption? Some say that we are already being introduced to the Illuminati twisted underground world as a lot of snuff is actually already in mass media and we don't even realize it.

However, as the movie states, blood and lust are not the ultimate end, but merely a vehicle to communicate the most important aspect of it all: the Agenda. This is what it is all about. It is about materialism, superficiality, the sexualization of anything, the destruction of family values and much more. All of the articles on Vigilant Citizen show that behind the bells, the whistles, the sexiness and the eye candy, a message is being communicated – one that goes with the best interests of the elite. Watching Lady Gaga in a music video wearing a bikini and whipping some guy (which oddly resembles a scene in Videodrome) is a good attention-grabber but, as we've seen in many articles, there are many messages that also being communicated. The Videodrome signal that causes everything from hallucinations and brain tumors is the constant conditioning that is exerted by mass media to force the world accept a specific world vision – which is a fake as a hallucination.

In the Illuminati's Videodrome, the masses are constantly exposed to the values that need to be accepted, the mindset that needs to be adopted and the symbolism that needs to be embraced. From mega-rituals disguised as current events to propaganda disguised as entertainment, TV viewers find themselves like Max Renn, with tapes inserted right in their belly. Don't want your mind to end up like Max's? Remove that tape, throw it in the garbage and think for yourself.

"The Cabin in the Woods": A Movie Celebrating the Elite's Ritual Sacrifices

"The Cabin in the Woods" is a widely successful horror film that also obtained great critical acclaim. While many appreciated the movie for its wit, humor and originality, the movie's storyline is nevertheless serious and very real: It depicts the elite's use of occult rituals on the unsuspecting masses. We'll look at the symbolic meaning of "The Cabin in the Woods".

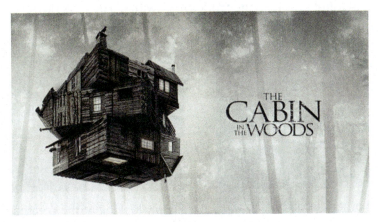

Warning: Major spoilers ahead!

Considered to be "groundbreaking" and a "game changer" by movie critics, The Cabin in the Woods contains many elements of classic horror films while adding interesting new elements to the mix. It continually refers to and comments on the horror movie genre, praising some aspects of it while poking fun at the many clichés that are found in the genre. The basic plot has been seen many times as it involves zombies running after teenagers that are so dumb and generic that you almost want them to die. But there is more to the story than hack and slash: It is about elite puppeteers overseeing a massive blood ritual using mind control and high tech monitoring. In the end, The Cabin in the Woods is a metaphor for our heavily controlled society that is under the control of dark, hidden forces. The movie was co-written and directed by Joss Whedon, who also created Dollhouse a TV series that tackled the concept of mind control in a rather obvious way.

At first glance, the characters of the movie are heavily clichéd, to the point that it is absurd. We have the typical jock, the typical slutty girl, the typical stoner, the boring smart guy and the timid prude virgin. These teenagers are purposely generic to comment on the boringness of characters in bad horror movies, but, as the story unfolds, we also discover that they were selected and manipulated by an organization to fully embody specific archetypes in order to complete a ritual.

The heroes (or the victims) of the movie are somewhat uni-dimensional. We soon learn that they were manipulated to become that way.

As the movie progresses, many key aspects of the occult elite and its way of functioning are described in vivid detail: Mediatised mega-rituals, occult secret societies, mind control, high-tech monitoring and so forth. At the end of the movie, one might realize that these scared and confused teenagers running around and falling into traps are…us, aka the masses. Let's look at the elements found in the movie and analyze their full significance.

The Nameless Organization

At the beginning of the movie, we see five friends hoping into van and driving to a cabin in the woods (hence the title of the movie) where fun, alcohol and teenage frolicking awaits. The pals however don't know that this weekend of apparent partying is, in fact, a big ritual sacrifice conducted by a high-level, international organization.

Never named in the movie, the organization behind the blood sacrifice utilizes high-tech facilities across the world and appears to have a great amount of resources and employees. Can we associate this organization with the occult elite, the NWO and its secret facilities? Yes, yes we can.

Simply looking at the command center, we understand that is not a small, clandestine operation, but a highly sophisticated organization dealing with military tracking equipment that is only available at the highest governmental levels.

The organization's sole purpose is to set up high-profile mega-rituals involving the deaths of civilians across the world in order to appease dark forces beneath the Earth. These rituals are made possible through the manipulation of certain individuals into doing certain things, causing them to unknowing become participants in an occult ritual. This concept has been discussed several times on this site as mega-rituals involving symbolic elements and blood sacrifices do happen in real life, where everything is staged and set up to obtain maximum exposure and magickal potency.

Although this is a very obscure and taboo subject, some occult researchers have determined that many mediatised events are actually mega-ritual carried out to fulfill specific occult objectives. Whether we go as far as Jack the Ripper or as recently as the Batman killings, some murders are actually set up to follow specific rules and to imprint society with specific symbols.

> *"Of course, many serial murders are nothing more than the work of a single individual acting out a graphic horror movie he saw, or responding to powerful "psychotic" impulses for aggression and predation. But many other serial murders involve a cult protected by the U.S. government and the corporate media, with strong ties to the police. These murders are actually intricately choreographed rituals; performed first on a very intimate and secret scale, among the initiates themselves in order to program them, them on a grand scale, amplified incalculably by the electronic media. In the end what we have is a highly symbolic, ritual working broadcast to millions of people, a Satanic inversion; a Black mass, where the "pews" are filled by the entire nation and through which humanity is paganized, brutalized and debased in this, the "Nigredo" phase of the alchemical process.*

The French adept Antonin Artaud, architect of the theory of the "Theater of Cruelty" with its transformative power, and the inspiration for the extreme sex-and-death media of our time, had this to say about the processing of the Group Mind: 'Aside from trifling witchcraft of country sorcerers, there are tricks of global hoodoo in which all alerted consciousnesses participate periodically... That is how strange forces are aroused and transported to the astral vault, to that dark dome which is composed above all of... the poisonous aggressiveness of the evil minds of most people... the formidable tentacular oppression of a kind of civic magic which will soon appear undisguised.'

The issue of controlling humanity with esoteric words and symbols encoded within a play, a media spectacular or a ritual is one of the most difficult for people to comprehend. That is why most people are viewed with utter contempt as "cowans," "the profane," the "gentiles" and the "goyim" (cattle) by secret society initiates. "I think we are farmed," Charles Fort said of humanity. It was Fort who also suggested that man deliberately invented the dogma of materialism in order to shield himself from the evidence of what was being done to him by means of psycho- spiritual warfare methods hyped by "coincidence," symbolism and ritual."
- Michael A. Hoffman, Secret Societies and Psychological Warfare

Although the above quote was written more than 20 years ago, it perfectly describes the plot of The Cabin in the Woods which, in turn, describes mega-rituals in a direct but very caricatural matter. By doing so, the movie reveals the elite's way of functioning while fictionalize it – it puts everything out in the open while making people believe that "it's just a movie". While there is a lot of satire and foolishness in the movie, it underlying concept is truer than most would believe.

This elite organization, as powerful as it is, only obeys the will of dark forces called "The Ancients" and "the gods". The "technicians" overseeing the ritual are actually members of an occult brotherhood and their job is to make sure rituals are complete.

The shady organization carries out rituals across the world, some of which succeed and others fail. Most are made to appear as "accidents" and those that succeed are widely publicized across the world.

After the death of the first victim, we see one of the technicians reciting a dark prayer and then kissing a pendant bearing the secret society's magical symbol. Like in real life, some operations that appear to be about science and pragmatism are actually motivated by very obscure and occult reasons.

So the U.S. branch of this shady Organization manipulates five all-American students to go spend a weekend in a remote cabin in the woods. The cabin is set up in an environment that is totally artificial and controlled by the puppet masters. In fact, the cabin and its surrounding is one big TV recording studio, complete with mics and cameras, mind altering drugs to control the actors and remote controlled doors and light effects.

The Sacrificial Lambs

Once arrived at the cabin, the teenagers are made to embody specific archetypes in order to complete the ritual drama required by the gods. It therefore needs to be carried out in a specific matter and it needs to completely recorded and televised. The "gods" require the death of five specific archetypes in the ritual drama: The whore, the athlete, the fool, the scholar and the virgin.

THE WHORE

Right from the start of the movie, the character named Jules Louden plays the role of a s-bomb that appears to be aroused by anything. During her (short) stay at the cabin, she constantly feels the urge to talk about doin' it or to dance like a stripper. We however learn that Jules is not being herself: She was drugged and manipulated to become the proverbial whore. Upon closer look, an astute viewer might realize that Jules Louden bares many characteristics of a Sex Kitten mind control slave.

In the brotherhood's temple are displayed stone tablets representing each archetype that needs to be slain. This one represents the whore.

The first scene involving Jules emphasizes the fact that she dyed her hair blond. In Mind Control symbolism, blond hair is used to identify Beta Kittens – Marylin Monroe programming. We then learn that the "puppet masters" laced her hair dye with chemicals to reduce cognition and to augment her libido.

So Jules is not usually a whore – she was manipulated and drugged into becoming one, the same way the elite uses mind control to make regular girls become Beta Kittens (think of the many slutty "celebrities" that started off "normal"). In the cabin, Jules displaying typical behavior of a MK slave, victim of Beta programming.

> "BETA is referred to as "sexual" programming (slaves). This programming eliminates all learned moral convictions and stimulates the primitive instinct, devoid of inhibitions. "Cat" alters may come out at this level."
> - Ron Patton, Project Monarch

The most obvious example of Beta Kitten behavior occurs when Jules is "dared" to make-out with a wolf head mounted on the cabin wall. She engages in a disturbingly long make-out session with the wolf head, as her friends awkwardly watch. The scene ends with Jules saying "thank you" to the wolf, confirming that the drugs she was given completely eliminated her inhibitions.

The puppet masters make it clear that Jules needs to be sacrificed first – because she is a whore and therefore corrupted. This needs to happen in a very specific matter in order to follow dark occult principles. The technicians want her to be killed during coitus and, more specifically, when she is nearing climax. Magick principles stipulate that individuals accumulate the most "life force" during the moments right before climax. Sacrificing a person right at that moment would therefore insure the most magickal potency to a ritual.

Jules is getting a lot of pleasure making out with this wolf head because she was programmed to accomplish such tasks. Bestiality is only one of the twisted things actual Beta Kittens are ordered to do by their handlers.

The technicians closely monitor Jules copulating with the jock, hoping that she will take her shirt off. Explaining the ritual to an "outsider" who doesn't understand why she MUST undress herself, a technician says: "We're not the only ones watching…Got to keep the customer satisfied. You understand what's at stake here?" In other words, the ritual needs to be graphic and fully broadcasted to be considered a success, something we see in real life without even realizing it.

After a few minutes of frolicking, which gets the teenagers (and the viewers) excited, Jules gets viciously attacked by a zombie right when she nears climax. The odd combination of copulation and death is characteristic of the dark rituals and is also featured be in underground snuff films circulated in elite circles. In short, Jules' death was planned according the occult elite's way of functioning.

The Fool

Like in most horror movies involving teens, there is some kind of stoner in the pack providing comic relief. Always smoking a joint, the character named Marty Mikalski plays that role. Interestingly enough, the "fool" is also quite the conspiracy theorist.

Inside the van, Marty explains how society is being heavily monitored through cameras and "chips inside children's heads". He states that one must sometimes "go off the grid" to escape the madness. Of course, he says all of these things while rolling a joint, subtlety telling the viewers: "Only paranoid pot heads are against microchips and state monitoring". To make things worse, Marty then shows a finished joint to Jules and tells her "I'll make you see things my way", meaning that being "aware" equals being on drugs.

As discussed in my articles on the movies Contagion and 2012, "conspiracy theorists" (or anyone with non-mainstream views) are always depicted as loons with little to no credibility. Marty in The Cabin in the Woods accomplishes the same function. While he says things that are believed by many people, we still almost hear a "coo-coo" sound effect in the background while he discusses microchips and such.

The fool however turns out to be right about a lot things and tries to convince his friends about the conspiracy they are involved in. As it is often the case, nobody believes him until it is too late, because, after all, he is the fool. We'll later see how he'll turn out to be an unlikely hero (while also destroying the world).

The Virgin

In most cultures that practiced ritual sacrifices, virgins were considered to be the "highest quality" offerings due to the fact that they were considered pure, clean, uncorrupted and innocent. They were untainted by man and the world and were therefore perceived as holy and the most spiritually potent. The character named Dana Polk was made to play that role in the ritual drama, although she isn't actually a virgin (there's apparently not many teenage virgins available nowadays).

Although she appears to be the weakest and the most vulnerable of the victims, the virgin ended up being an unlikely hero.

For the ritual to be complete, Dana needed outlive all of her friends and her death was optional. The important thing is that she suffered as the puppet masters need capture pain and punishment on camera, a fetish of the real life dark forces behind the Illuminati. In fact, the ritual in The Cabin in the Woods follows a specific protocol that is similar to the actual rituals carried out by the occult elite. Here are some of them.

Rules of the Ritual

Most mega-rituals follow specific rules that are clearly spelled out in the movie. These rules are made to give the rituals more potency while allowing the powers that be to avoid the negative effects of bad karma (according to their weird interpretation of it).

1st Rule: Announcing What Will Happen Beforehand.

On their way to the cabin, the teenagers meet an unsavory character dubbed "The Harbinger" that warns them in not-so-subtle ways that they will be killed. Despite the warnings, the friends resolutely carry on.

As seen in previous articles on this site, mega-rituals are often preceded by "clues" in mass media warning or preparing the victims (and the world) for what's coming. If after being warned, victims go on by their own free will, then the puppeteers are liberated from karmic responsibility. During the movie, one technicians says:

> "They have to make the choice of their own free will. Otherwise, the system doesn't work. Its like The Harbinger…this creepy old fuck who is practically wearing a sign saying 'You Will Die'. Why do we put him there? The System. They have to choose to ignore him. They have to choose what happens in the cellar. Yeah, we rig the system as much as we need to but, in the end, if they don't transgress, they can't be punished."

This concept is often seen in real life where victims of ritual sacrifice place themselves in a specific situation, although they have been thoroughly manipulated to do so (see MK victims dying from an "overdose").

In one of the cabin's rooms is a painting depicting a lamb being torn to pieces by all kinds of vicious creatures. This is yet another way the victims are subtly "warned" of what is bound to happen. However, since the kids have no idea of what's happening, they simply ignore it. This can be compared the elite hiding in plain sight warnings and predictions about the NWO in public places (see the murals at the Denver International Airport).

2nd Rule: The Victims Must Seal Their Own Fate

Although every aspect of their environment is tightly controlled and manipulated by the puppet masters, the victims are still made to choose their fate by their own free will.

By reading cryptic Latin phrases inside a book, the 5 friends summoned themselves the redneck zombies that will tirelessly want to kill them. By triggering the killers themselves, the puppeteers are freed from karmic responsibility.

Although the above concepts are extremely obscure, they are clearly defined and communicated in the movie. They are a reflection of the occult elite's (aka the Illuminati's) particular way of functioning, where nothing is obvious and everything is manipulated behind the scenes in order to obtain a specific result. Ancient blood sacrifices were accomplished out in the open with participants that knew what was happening (not that I'm idealizing those days) but today, it is about deceit and manipulation, with an emphasis placed on suffering and anguish, something that only those dealing in black arts would revel on. Upon discovering exactly what was happening, Marty (the stoner) says:

> "A ritual sacrifice? Great. You tie someone to a stone, get a fancy dagger and a bunch of robes. It's not that complicated."

To which the virgin replies:

> *"Tt IS simple. They don't just want to see us killed. They want to see us punished".*

Who Wins in the End?

The ending of the movie is very telling, yet very unsettling. In order for the ritual to be complete, Marty must die before the virgin. If this doesn't happen, the "ancient evil gods" will rise and kill everyone on Earth. When asked to kill himself to save the world, Marty refuses – knowing very well he'll be killed anyways by the evil gods.

Dana and Marty then light up a joint and wait for the gods to rise. Dana says:

> *"It's time to give someone else a chance…Giant evil gods".*

Then a giant hand rises up from beneath the Earth, kills everyone and then reaches out to grab the movie viewers. And that's how the movie ends…with an evil god grabbing the viewer.

So, in the end, the only winner of the movie is a "giant evil god" rising up straight from hell, one that could be equated to Satan in Abrahamic religions. Dana and Marty, the "heroes" of the story, therefore willingly allowed the evil god to rise up and to take over the Earth. The "heroes" brought about the worst ending possible, one of the movie's original twists that kept the audiences guessing. It nevertheless has an important symbolic meaning and tells a lot about those who are behind the movie. In retrospect, were the puppeteers the good guys or the bad guys? They were sadistic jerks carrying out an occult ritual but they were also trying to save the world from the wrath evil gods. Hmmm…

In Conclusion

The Cabin in the Woods is a hit with movie fans due to its wit and its study of the horror film genre. However, going past these obvious remarks, the story of the movie conceals another layer of interpretation: It reveals the Illuminati's occult way of functioning in order to maintain power and to imprint the group mind with symbols using rituals and sacrifices. The "organization" in the movie uses an odd mixture of scientific knowledge with "old world" occult rituals to carry out its plans. While this story is pure fiction, it also reveals (in a strange way) how the occult elite truly functions.

That being said, can we equate the clueless teens in the movie to the clueless masses? Can we equate the cabin in the woods to today's highly monitored and controlled society? Are our perceptions being purposely modified through mind control, mass media and meds to make us fall into traps? Are we being purposely dumbed-down like these kids in order for us to do the elite's bidding by our own free will? Is the movie The Cabin in the Woods an equivalent to the Harbringer in the movie, who communicates a grave warning to people that are too clueless to understand any of it? As Marty the stoner says: "You are not seeing what you don't want to see".

"Prometheus": A Movie About Alien Nephilim and Esoteric Enlightenment

The science fiction movie "Prometheus" explores theories on the origins of humanity and their relation to extra-terrestrial visitors. While most might find this premise very "fictional", many aspects of the movie actually symbolically reflect some beliefs and philosophies of the occult elite. We'll look at the esoteric meaning of the movie "Prometheus".

Warning: Major spoilers ahead!

There is no shortage of movies involving angry aliens these days and we can definitely add Prometheus to the list. However, while most of these alien flicks are centered around shooting them in their ugly faces before they destroy Earth, Prometheus has a back story dealing with timeless questions puzzling humanity such as "Where do we come from?" and "Why are we here?"… plus a healthy dose of shooting aliens in their ugly faces.

Directed by Ridley Scott, the movie was originally intended to be a prequel to the classic 1979 movie Alien, but the final product has little relation to it. The movie tells the story of scientists that discover ancient artifacts depicting visitors from another planet. To investigate this discovery, the scientists get the backing of a giant corporation and embark on space mission to find the planet the aliens came from and to ask them important questions. The premise is based on the Ancient Astronauts theory, which stipulates that thousands of years ago, early humans were in contact with a superior alien race.

As the movie's name suggests, Prometheus is also filled with mythological references and symbolism that give the movie an underlying esoteric meaning. While the movie is, at face value, about humans going into space to find their alien creators, Prometheus can also be viewed as a metaphor for spiritual illumination as it is portrayed by occult secret societies. Let's look at the concepts explored in the movie.

The Engineers?

At the beginning of the movie, a humanoid alien debarks on Earth and drinks a strange liquid. After drinking the liquid, the alien completely disintegrates and falls into the water. In the water, the DNA triggers a biogenetic reaction and, on a microscopic level, we see single cells beginning to multiply themselves. This is the movie's theory on how human life appeared on Earth.

An alien is dropped off on Earth by a massive spaceship.

The alien is disintegrated at its very core, at the DNA level and interacts with the Earth's water to create a new life form.

The movie then fast forwards to 2089, where two archeologists, Elizabeth Shaw and Charlie Holloway, are searching a cave in Scotland. There, they discover a painting drawn by a caveman that depicts humans looking towards a star formation in the sky. The researchers discover that this particular star formation can be found in the art of several ancient cultures.

The star formation in this cave painting is similar to star formations found in ancient Egyptian, Sumerian and Mayan art.

The archeologists believe that aliens (whom they call the "Engineers") came from this particular star formation and spread human life on Earth. This causes them to embark on a space mission to find that planet and seek answers from the Engineers.

The premise of the movie is heavily inspired by the "Ancient Astronauts" theory originally proposed by authors such as Eric Von Daniken and Robert Temple. According to those theories, humanity was either created or "helped" by visitors from another planet, who left lasting traces on human history.

The director of Prometheus, Ridley Scott, appears to believe this theory. In an interview with Hollywood Reporter, he stated:

> "NASA and the Vatican agree that it is almost mathematically impossible that we can be where we are today without there being a little help along the way ... That's what we're looking at (in the film), at some of Eric Von Daniken's ideas of how did we humans come about".
> - Hollywood Reporter, "Ridley Scott's New Alien Movie Influenced by Ancient Astronaut Theory

Let's take a closer look at the Ancient Astronauts theory.

Ancient Astronauts

Proponents of the Ancient Astronauts theory believe that much of human knowledge, culture and religion are remnants of an alien "mother culture". Ancient monuments considered to be too advanced for the technology of the time such as Stonehedge, Easter Island and the Great Pyramid of Giza are considered to be proof of alien contact. Eric Von Daniken also claims that ancient art and iconography throughout the world contain depictions of space vehicles, non-human intelligent creatures and advanced technology. He claims that cultures that had no contact with one another had similar themes in their art, proving that there was a common source for their knowledge.

An actual cave painting found in Italy that is said to depict Ancient Astronauts visiting earth. This image was probably the inspiration for the cave painting found in Prometheus.

In Prometheus, similarities between Egyptian, Mayan, Sumerian and other civilization's artifacts prompt the research team to travel to space and seek humanity's "Engineers".

Proponents of the Ancient Astronauts theory claim that many ancient religious texts contain references to visitors from outer space. Two of the main works often cited are the Book of Genesis and the Book of Enoch, which both mention the existence on Earth of enigmatic giant beings named the Nephilim.

The Watchers and the Nephilim

The Book of Genesis mentions the presence on Earth of beings named Nephilim (the King James version uses the term Giants). These beings are described as hybrids that are the result of procreation between human females and "sons of Gods".

> "When human beings began to increase in number on the earth and daughters were born to them, the sons of God saw that the daughters of humans were beautiful, and they married any of them they chose. (...) The Nephilim were on the earth in those days—and also afterward—when the sons of God went to the daughters of humans and had children by them."
> - Genesis 6:1-4 (New International Version)

In Numbers 13, the Nephilim are mentioned again, described as giant destructive beings that appeared quite different from regular humans.

> "And they spread among the Israelites a bad report about the land they had explored. They said, "The land we explored devours those living in it. All the people we saw there are of great size. We saw the Nephilim there (the descendents of Anak come from the Nephilim). We seemed like grasshoppers in our own eyes, and we looked the same to them".
> - Numbers 13:32-33

The apocryphal Book of Enoch greatly expands on the Nephilim and their originators, the Watchers. According to the text dating from 300 BC, the Watchers were a group formed of 200 "sons of God" who disobeyed God and descended to Earth to breed with humans. They were said to have taught humans advanced skills such as metallurgy, metal working, cosmetics, sorcery, astrology, astronomy and meteorology. Because the Watchers disobeyed God, they were also called the Fallen Angels.

The offspring of the Watchers were the Nephilim, described as giants who lived among humans. They ultimately became a destructive presence on Earth and were said to have consumed "all acquisitions of men". In order to rid these beings from Earth (along with the humans who mixed with them) God created the Great Flood. In order ensure the survival of humanity, however, Noah was forewarned by God to build his ark.

Another ancient Jewish text, The Book of Jubilees, states that ten percent of the disembodied spirits of the Nephilim were allowed to remain on Earth after the flood, as demons, to try to lead humans astray until the Final Judgement. Is this why the occult elite is so bent on corrupting the masses with materiality and perversion?

So who were the Watchers and the Nephilim? Many different researchers have proposed many different interpretations, including a class of rich humans, demons or an ancient super-race. Proponents of the Ancient Astronaut theory believe that they were actually aliens that were sent to Earth to oversee the evolution of humanity – hence their name "the Watchers".

The premise of Prometheus is greatly influenced by this theory as the aliens in the movie are giant beings who came to Earth to create and teach humanity.

The crew finally meets one of its "Engineers", a giant alien. Unfortunately, the alien didn't feel like having a discussion on the origins of humanity and ripped David the Android's head off (the guy on the left).

Discovering that aliens were part of human evolution is not important from a scientific standpoint alone, but also from a spiritual one, as it could potentially render many religions completely obsolete. All belief systems would be thoroughly questioned, or at least revised to include the "alien angle".

Spiritual Dilemma

The spiritual implications of the space mission are subtly reflected in the movie, through various scenes questioning the relevancy of Christianity in this alien-engineered context.

When the ship arrives at its destination, the crew discovers a deserted building built by an alien civilization containing … dead aliens. After running tests on one of the bodies, the crew realize that aliens are indeed the originators of human life on Earth. In other words, the Ancient Astronauts theory is correct and being from another planet were indeed the "Engineers" of humanity. Once Elizabeth confirms this discovery to her boyfriend Charlie, he immediately questions her on the validity of her cross pendant:

"- OK, I guess you can take your father's cross off now.
- Why would I want to do that?
- Because THEY made us."

Elizabeth then gives a "whoa"-worthy reply:

"- And who made them?"

She therefore does not see a contradiction between believing in Christianity and in the Ancient Astronauts theory simultaneously. She still believes that God is the first creator of everything … but now she has to add aliens to the equation.

At the beginning of the trip, the Captain of the ship installs a Christmas tree. He is asked by his superior "What the hell is that?", to which the Captain answers: "It's Christmas!". The fact that this history-altering space mission takes place during Christmas time (the holiday that celebrates the birth of Jesus Christ) gives it a religious meaning.

Elizabeth, the hero of the movie, proudly and prominently wears a Christian cross around her neck. This pendant becomes symbolic of the spiritual dilemma that results from the findings of the mission.

After this profound discussion, Elizabeth and Charlie get horny and have spaceship sex. What the couple doesn't know is that Charlie was injected with alien DNA by David, an android.

Before Charlie visited Elizabeth in her quarters, David, a robot with an inquisitive mind, tricks Charlie into drinking a beverage containing alien DNA, knowing that he would copulate with Elizabeth and she would therefore give birth to a half-alien child. Notice the Christmas tree in the background.

The couple copulates without protection and Elizabeth soon learns that she is pregnant. She immediately realizes that her pregnancy is very, very wrong, as her child is not human and very hostile. Considering the fact that the mission takes place during Christmas time, Elizabeth becomes a kind of anti-Virgin Mary. Instead of giving birth to the Christ, she will give birth to a half-alien creature … not unlike the Nephilim.

Elizabeth manages to "abort" the monstrosity. Then, the mission goes terribly wrong and everyone dies except her. After almost giving up, Elizabeth apparently has an epiphany and becomes determined to discover the truth about the aliens. Apparently, they abandoned humanity a long time ago and they were even planning to destroy earth.

Something must have gone very wrong with human evolution.

Upon discovering her pregnancy, Elizabeth's cross pendant is removed and stored away, symbolically meaning that her Christian faith is not valid anymore.

At the end of the movie, she puts the cross back around her neck, signifying that she did not lose faith and that her quest for truth is now greatly spiritual. It is not about science anymore, but about the basic human need of having existential questions answered.

Elizabeth puts back her cross and is determined to find the truth about the alien Engineers.

The entire movie can be interpreted as a spiritual metaphor – a quest for enlightenment. The title of the movie itself, Prometheus, is greatly indicative of the underlying esoteric meaning of the movie.

Prometheus and the Quest for Enlightenment

In Greek mythology, Prometheus is a Titan, the primeval race of deities that came before the Olympians. He stole fire from the gods in order to give it to humanity – an act that enabled progress and civilization. For accomplishing the act of bringing fire (a symbol of divine knowledge) to humanity, Prometheus became an important figure in the mythology of Mystery schools, such as Freemasonry and Rosicrucianism, which are based on the usage of occult knowledge in order to achieve godhood.

Prometheus, a favorite figure of the Illuminist elite, is prominently displayed in the Rockefeller Center.

The Judeo-Christian equivalent of Prometheus is Lucifer, a "fallen angel" of great intelligence who, once a favorite of God, then defied him and brought a new form of knowledge to mankind. The name Lucifer is Latin for "light-bringer", which is exactly what Prometheus accomplished by bringing fire to man. This "light" is said to be the occult knowledge taught in Mystery Schools, as it allows "enlightened humans" to ascend back to godhood.

The story of the Watchers and the Nephilim described above also appear to follow the same archetype as it tells the story of "sons of God" rebelling against his rule and descending to Earth, teaching humanity important knowledge. Also, like Lucifer, the Watchers are dubbed "Fallen Angels". Where therefore see that there's a lot of interconnectivity in these mythos and in the movie's symbolism,.

At the beginning of the space trip, the president of the corporation funding the mission holds a briefing and gives a speech regarding the importance of the mission:

> "The Titan Prometheus wanted to give mankind equal footing with the gods and for that, he was cast from Olympus. Well, my friends, the time has finally come for his return".

In the movie, Prometheus is the name of the spaceship that transports humans to their alien Engineers. It symbolically represents humans using the "fire" (knowledge) that was given to them to ascend back to godhood (their alien creators) by their own means. This metaphor of spiritual initiation is reminiscent to the many mythological stories found throughout History that hide a similar esoteric meaning.

However, Mystery Schools believe that illumination is not given to all, but only to a chosen few and this is aptly reflected in Prometheus. In the movie, all of the people who were on board for selfish, monetary or insincere purposes died. Only the one that was there for the truth and with a strong spiritual faith survived. This type of narrative is on-par with allegorical stories of spiritual illumination stating that only the true of heart will reach that higher state of being.

Other than Elizabeth, another non-human character survived, David the Android.

Towards the end of the movie, David gets his head cut off but, since he's a robot, he stills functions. Elizabeth takes the head and continues her journey, symbolically meaning that she needs pure intellect and technology to reach enlightenment.

David has great intellectual capacity, making him believe that he is superior to his human colleagues. Despite this fact, he is nevertheless crucial to Elizabeth's quest – a subtle message stating that transhumanism is important in human evolution.

At the end of the movie, David does not understand why Elizabeth desires to continue her search for her creators. The difference is that she has a soul and he doesn't. It is for this reason that she put back the cross around her neck. Her quest is not simply a space mission, it is a spiritual pilgrimage to discover where she comes from.

In the final scene of the movie, Elizabeth decides to not go back to Earth (representing materiality and the lower self) and continues to search for the Engineers (representing illumination and godhood). Her quest is therefore not over ... and there might be a sequel.

In Conclusion

While most moviegoers probably stepped out of the Prometheus thinking that it was a "decent alien movie", digging a little deeper into its meaning and symbolism reveals an entire other layer of interpretation. Drawing inspiration from the Ancient Astronauts theory, Prometheus proposes a radical rewrite of history and theology, one that makes humanity a product of extra-terrestrial "creator gods". The movie also intermixes this quest for scientific knowledge with spiritual and metaphysical questions, making this story not only about angry aliens, but about timeless existential questions.

As the title of the movie suggests, the story of humans going into space to find their creators has an underlying esoteric meaning, as it can be interpreted as a metaphor for spiritual enlightenment. The Titan Prometheus is a central figure in occult mystery schools, an archetypal figure of a "rebel from above" that brought divine knowledge to humanity – with all the benefits and pitfalls it engenders. Occult secret societies believe that this knowledge provides the path back to divinity. The same way the spaceship Prometheus leaves earth to find the Engineers, occult initiates look to leave the material plane to reach illumination and "be one" with the Great Architect of the Universe.

That being said, is there any truth to the many stories and mythologies referring to a divine figure coming from above to impart knowledge to humanity? Do the figures of Prometheus, Lucifer, and the Watchers of the Book of Enoch have factual basis to them? Is there an "outside" source for humanity's advanced and esoteric knowledge? Was there once a Nephilim-type "super-race" on Earth helping humanity develop itself, but ultimately corrupted it? Is this the "missing link" in human evolution? Is it the reason why humanity is self-destructive and somehow out-of-synch with the rest of the planet? Does this outside source come from aliens as suggested in Prometheus or from fallen angels and/or demons as written in ancient texts? Is this outside source behind the teachings of secret societies and behind ... the Illuminati?

"Hide and Seek": The Most Blatant Movie About Monarch Mind Control Ever?

"Hide and Seek" is a 2005 thriller movie that did not get great reviews at the time of its release. However, chances are most critics did understand its symbolism and its underlying theme which is all about Monarch Programming. In fact, "Hide and Seek" is probably one of the most blatant movies about Monarch Mind Control in Hollywood's history. We'll look at the hidden meaning of the movie.

Warning: Gigantic spoilers ahead.

Hide and Seek is not going down in history as Robert De Niro's most memorable movie. It was bashed by movie critics for its derivative nature and because its ending was deemed "nonsensical". While it is true that the plot of Hide and Seek has a fair share of logical fallacies, the movie simply cannot be fully understood without knowing about the key element at its core: Trauma-based Mind Control. From the first frame to the last, almost every line and every symbol found in the movie directly refers to concepts associated with mind control, specifically Monarch Programming.

In this particular brand of mind control, children are subjected to trauma so intense that it causes them to dissociate from reality. The slave's handlers can then program into the children's minds alter personas that can be triggered at will. In a symbolic and theatrical way, Hide and Seek describes the horrible procedure behind Monarch Programming and hints to the more sadistic aspects of it. The fact that Monarch butterflies appear in key parts of the movie confirm that the whole storyline is based on Monarch Mind Control.

Further, when one understands the handler/slave relationship that is happening in the movie, the "nonsensical" ending becomes a little more "sensical" as it fits precisely with the way Monarch Programming works . Let's look at the story of Hide and Seek and the MK symbolism it contains.

Brief Summary

After witnessing the apparent suicide of her mother, a young girl named Emily Callaway (played by Dakota Fanning) displays symptoms of severe trauma. Her father David Callaway (played by Robert De Niro) attempts to help his daughter snap out of her trauma by leaving his job as a psychologist and by moving to a small town outside of New York.

There, he realizes that his relationship with Emily is extremely difficult and that her behavior is increasingly worrisome. Emily claims to have a new friend named Charlie who is "lots of fun" and plays with her, but Emily tells her father that Charlie doesn't like him at all. David believes that Charlie is an imaginary friend Emily created to help cope with her trauma. Things however become unsettling when horrible things begin to occur around the house (i.e. the cat gets drowned in the bathtub) that Emily then blames on Charlie. When David discovers his potential new girlfriend has been murdered in the bathtub, he realizes that Charlie is a real person and that he's extremely dangerous. After running around the house for a few minutes, David has a moment of clarity and realizes that HE is Charlie. Charlie is indeed David's alternate personality, one that he didn't know even existed. This alter personality has been manipulating poor traumatized Emily and has been committing horrible crimes. After this epiphany, Charlie takes control of David's body and goes on a murderous rampage. Charlie is then stopped, and shot dead, by Katherine, a psychologist who worked with David in New York and who came to see if Emily was alright. After the ordeal, Emily goes to live with Katherine and that's that.

As stated above, for most movie viewers, the internal logic of the script is somewhat unbelievable. However, once the MK symbolism of the movie is recognized, one understands that Hide and Seek is about a handler traumatizing and programming an MK slave. The fact that the father/handler has two personas is consistent with the fact that handlers are often dissociative slaves themselves who've been programmed to carry out someone else's dirty deeds. Let's look at the deeper symbolism of the movie.

Emily, the Traumatized Child

Emily is a regular and playful child who appears to be very happy. In the first scene of the movie, we see her playing hide-and-seek with her mother, who then lovingly tucks her into bed.

The movie begins with a symbolic image: Emily playing with her mother, spinning around in the bliss of childhood and innocence. Notice the doll: she holds this constantly in the first part of the movie.

Emily constantly holds a doll that takes on an important meaning later in the movie. The doll represents Emily's innocent, core personality: her "real" self.

Later that night, Emily witnesses a horrifying scene: Her mother dead in a bloody bathtub. Seeing her mother dead is Emily's first mind-altering, life changing traumatic event ... but not the last.

While the death appears to be a suicide, we later learn that Charlie (the alter personality of David – Emily's father) killed the mother and placed her in the bathtub to make it look like a suicide. Did he do this on purpose to traumatize Emily and begin her Mind Control programming?

Emily is then placed in a mental hospital for children. David (or was it Charlie) decides to leave his job and moves to a small town named Woodland. He says to Katherine, another psychologist who works with him:

"Right now I need to be doing what's right for Emily. I need to be a full time dad".

Did he mean: "I need to be a full time handler"?

Emily displays the classic signs of a traumatized person: Shock, isolation and withdrawal.

Right before leaving, Katherine, gives Emily a gift.

Katherine gives Emily a music box that plays the Mockingbird song. As the movie progresses, the Mockingbird song plays whenever a traumatic event happens, which makes it a programmed trigger song. Upon giving the gift, Katherine tells Emily: "Whenever I was feeling sad, I would open the lid and all my sorrows went away" – essentially telling Emily that she should dissociate from reality whenever she hears that song to avoid trauma.

Once in their new home, Emily goes into a wooded area behind the house. There, she follows a Monarch butterfly that leads her to a cave.

This mysterious cave is in fact the programming site where Charlie programs and traumatizes Emily.

The fact that a Monarch butterfly leads Emily to the cave is a coded way of telling viewers "in the know" that this is all about Monarch Programming and trauma-based mind control.

When Emily discovered the cave, she does something that ends up being extremely symbolic.

Emily drops her beloved doll, signifying that she lost her core, innocent persona. Mind Control handlers seek to "lock away" this core persona to be able to program new alter personas within their psyche.

Emily however did not simply "drop" the doll that represents her innocence. She literally mutilates it.

David finds Emily's doll completely defaced in a garbage can. The mutilation represents how Emily's mind is being mutilated by the torture and programming happening in the cave.

As Emily "plays" with her friend Charlie (handlers manipulate their slaves to believe they are their friends), she develops a disturbing taste for the morbid. A growing likeness for the dark side of things is often seen in Monarch slaves who become disillusioned with life. Starting with innocent children, handlers seek to create an opposite "mirror image" of their slave who become dark, twisted and disturbed (for this reason, the dualistic, black and white imagery in MK symbolism is extremely important). While we don't ever see Charlie actually "programming" Emily during the movie, we clearly see the symptoms and the switch in Emily's behavior.

While fishing with her father, Emily cold-hardheartedly inserts the hook inside a live insect to use as bait. Her lack of reaction to what is usually considered to be repulsive indicates that she might have been "desensitized" to pain, suffering and the repulsive due to the torture she received while being programmed by her handler.

Emily's programmed dark side becomes more evident when she is set up to play with a "normal" girl.

While fishing with her father, Emily cold-hardheartedly inserts the hook inside a live insect to use as bait. Her lack of reaction to what is usually considered to be repulsive indicates that she might have been "desensitized" to pain, suffering and the repulsive due to the torture she received while being programmed by her handler.

Emily reacts rather badly to the playfulness of this girl and finds a way to show that to her.

Emily takes the girl's doll and mutilates it – hence reflecting her own distorted soul and her loss of innocence. Notice that the mouth was melted away (symbolizing the slave's inability ask for help) and has one eye (symbol of Illuminati Mind Control). She also holds her by the neck as if shocking her (shocking is a form of torture used in MK programming).

As things progress in the movie, Emily realizes that the "fun" Charlie is actually evil and sadistic. While playing hide-and-seek with Charlie, Emily gets lured into a dark and scary room in the basement of the house. Then, the lights go out and Emily screams.

David (who has switched back to his core personality) finds Emily in the basement in tears and in state of shock. We can deduce that, while the lights were out, some kind of traumatizing event occurred in that creepy basement – probably torture or abuse.

We then see her in bed with the "face of trauma", hinting that something horribly wrong happened in that basement – and that Emily's trauma-based mind control is continuing.

Towards the end of the movie, Charlie loses it, kills some people and starts running after Emily. In a classic "horror movie dumb move", Emily decides to go hide in the cave where she gets tortured. There, we see a disturbing yet symbolic display of Emily's stuff.

Inside the cave are Emily's dolls – mutilated, decapitated and dismembered – representing the powerless state of MK slaves and the abuse they are subjected to. We also see the music box that plays the Mockingbird song, the song Katherine told her to dissociate to when "she was feeling sad". In MK terms, the song was a trigger to engender dissociation.

In the movie, everything relating to childhood and innocence is twisted, perverted and destroyed, which goes in line with how Monarch programming works on children.

In the final scene of the movie, Emily is living in Katherine's house and drawing a picture. While everything appears to be well, the last shot of the movie shows Emily's drawing. Everything is not well at all.

Movies and TV

Emily drew two heads on herself, representing that she has an alter persona.

The final frame of the movie basically confirms that the entire programming process succeeded. Emily has an alter persona and is living with another psychiatrist who may or may not be continuing the process. Is Katherine there to help her or is there to continue her programming?

The movie's DVD features an alternate ending, where Katherine appears to be continuing Emily's programming.

In the alternate ending, Emily is locked up in a room in a psychiatric institution.

In a deleted scene featured from the DVD, we see Emily acting extra creepy around her babysitter. She is wearing a shirt with a big butterfly on it. Monarch programming.

David the Father / Charlie the Handler

The big "whoa" moment of the movie is when we discover that Charlie is David's alter persona. While this plot twist was a major let down to most viewers, it falls right in line with how MK programming works. Many handlers are dissociative slaves themselves who are programmed to do someone else's dirty work. At the end of the movie, we learn that David was deeply traumatized when he caught his wife cheating on him – and that's when Charlie was born. I guess this is a clunky way of conveying to the viewers that he is also a product of trauma-based mind control.

David is a psychologist with intricate knowledge of the effects of trauma on the human psyche. One can therefore say he is qualified to do some Mind Control programming.

During the first part of the movie, whenever the Charlie alter is triggered, we see David sitting in his study, wearing headphones and listening to music. This symbolizes his core/real persona being "put on hold" while Charlie is in control of his body. David is "out of service" and oblivious to what is going on – hence the headphones.

While in his study, David notices a black mark on his hand.

We then learn that its because Charlie, while in the cave, was holding Monarch butterflies in his hand. Get it? Monarch ... in his hand ... ? Monarch ... handler? While most viewers might perceive this scene as being very random, it is extremely clear to those who know about Monarch programming.

We therefore understand that David never actually sat in his study: It was a way of symbolically showing that his core persona was on hold while Charlie was triggered.

Other random scenes in the movie explain what is happening with David.

David's head is torn off family pictures, hinting that his "real" self has been taken over and removed from the family.

David's head is found in the song box, symbolizing his dissociation from reality while the Charlie alter persona is triggered.

At the end of the movie, Charlie is shot dead by Katherine, who takes custody of Emily and brings her back to New York City. Considering the Mind Control interpretation of this movie, we can ask ourselves: Was David and his programmed alter Charlie used by higher ups to traumatize and program Emily? Was he ultimately a disposable, mind controlled pawn who needed to be eliminated? Was his death the final, major traumatic event to completely break down Emily – and to make her an orphan that is completely dependent on the state? These are all questions that arise when one understands the Mind Control symbolism in the movie.

Most people in Woodland are extremely creepy and strange. Every man made it a point of saying that Emily was "very beautiful" – with an unsettling, perverted look on their face. These scenes might refer to a child abuse ring going on in the town. Or maybe it was an odd way to add some suspense to the movie.

Also, were the people in this friendly town "in on it"? Is Woodland a kind of government-owned remote location used for MK programming?

In Conclusion

Hide and Seek is a deeply symbolic movie that depicts, in careful detail, the process behind Trauma-based Mind Control. While the meaning of the MK symbolism of the movie probably flew about a mile above most viewer's heads, a only a little knowledge of the subject is required to make the entire thing extremely overt and blatant. This story of a traumatized child who followed a Monarch butterfly into a dark cave full of pain and horror sums up the entire plight of Monarch slaves. But it played out before the eyes of most viewers without them even realizing it.

The same way Charlie stood in the dark in his deadly game of hide-and-seek with Emily, the truth about the movie is hidden in the darkness of people's ignorance. However, simply flicking on the light of knowledge reveals the movie's true meaning: A description of the ugly, disgusting world of Monarch Programming. Playing hide-and-seek with the truth? VCs ain't got no time for that.

The Hidden (And Not So Hidden) Messages in Stanley Kubrick's "Eyes Wide Shut" (pt. I)

"Eyes Wide Shut" was promoted as a steamy, suspenseful movie starring the "It" couple of the day: Tom Cruise and Nicole Kidman. While the actors were prominently featured in the movie, it is everything around them that told the true story of "Eyes Wide Shut". Stanley Kubrick's attention to detail and symbolism gave the movie an entire other dimension – one that cannot be seen by those who have their eyes wide shut. This multiple-part series will look at the hidden symbolism of Kubrick's final film.

I remember when I first watched Eyes Wide Shut, back in 1999. Boy, did I hate it. I hated how slow everything was, I hated how Nicole Kidman tried to sound drunk or high and I hated seeing Tom Cruise walk around New York looking concerned. I guess I reacted the same way critics did at the time the movie came out and thought: "This movie is boring and there is nothing hot about it." More than a decade later, equipped with a little more knowledge and patience, I re-watched the movie … and it blew my mind. In fact, like most Stanley Kubrick films, an entire book could be written about the movie and the concepts it addresses. Eyes Wide Shut is indeed not simply about a relationship, it is about all of the outside forces and influences that define that relationship. It is about the eternal back-and-forth between the male and female principles in a confused and decadent modern world. Also, more importantly, it is about the group that rules this modern world – a secret elite that channels this struggle between the male and female principles in a specific and esoteric matter. The movie however does not spell out anything. Like all great art, messages are communicated through subtle symbols and mysterious riddles.

Stanley Kubrick unexpectedly died only five days after submitting the final cut of the movie to Warner Bros, making Eyes Wide Shut his swan song. Considering the fact that Eyes Wide Shut is about an occult secret society that eliminates those who cross its path, some theories arose about Kubrick's death and its suspicious nature. Did he reveal to the public too much, too soon? Maybe. Let's look at the main themes of Kubrick's last creation.

The Modern Couple

The stars of Eyes Wide Shut were the "It" couple of 1999: Tom Cruise and Nicole Kidman. Those who were expecting the movie to be a sort of voyeuristic experience showing hot scenes of the couple were probably very disappointed. The audience rather got a cold, egoistic and profoundly unsatisfied couple, one that seems to be tied together not by pure love, but by other factors, like convenience and appearances. While the couple is very "modern" and "upper-class", the forces that keep it together are the result of basic, primal and almost animalistic behavior. If we look at the instinctive behavior of humans and animals, males primarily look for females that have good childbearing qualities while females look for a strong provider. Remnants of this behavior still exist today as males tend to display wealth and power to attract females while females showcase their beauty to attract males. In Eyes Wide Shut, the couple perfectly follows that instinctive script.

Tom Cruise's character is called Dr. Bill ... as in dollar bill. Several times during the movie, Dr. Bill either waves his money or his "doctor badge" at people to get them to do what he wants. Bill is part of the upper class and his dealings with people of the lower class are often resolved with money.

In order to get this taxi driver to wait for him in front of the elite mansion, Dr. Bill tears up a hundred dollar bill and promises him to give him the other half when he comes back. Dr. Bill's motto is probably "Everybody has a price". Does his own wife have a price?

Played by Nicole Kidman, Alice lost her job in the art world and is now fully supported by her husband's salary. While she lives very comfortably, Alice appears to be extremely bored with her life as a stay at home mother. The name Alice is most likely a reference to the main character of Alice in Wonderland – a fairy tale about a privileged girl who is bored with her life and who goes "through the looking glass" to end up in Wonderland. In Eyes Wide Shut, Alice is often shown staring at the looking glass – grooming herself or ... maybe looking for something more to life.

Alice is often shown in front of the mirror and making herself pretty. At the beginning of the movie, almost everyone who talk to her mention her appearance. Her daughter Helena (maybe named after Helena of Troy, the most beautiful woman in the world) follows in her footsteps.

Promotional images for the movie feature Alice kissing Bill but looking at herself in the mirror, almost as if she was seeing an alternate reality.

While the couple shows signs of fatigue, Bill and Alice put on their "happy masks" when it is time to attend social events. Like the elite people they socialize with, there is a big difference between the facade they put on and reality.

Brushing With the Elite

Bill and Alice go to a classy party given by Victor Ziegler, one of Bill's wealthy patients. Judging from Victor's house, he is not simply rich, he is part of the ultra-elite. While his party is very elegant and is attended by highly cultured people, it doesn't take long for the viewers to realize that this facade hides a disgusting dark side. Also, small details inserted by Kubrick hint to a link between the party and the occult ritual that occurs later in the movie.

When entering the party, the first thing we see is this peculiar Christmas decoration. This eight-pointed star is found throughout the house.

The star at Zeigler's house is nearly identical to the ancient symbol of the star of Ishtar.

Knowing Kubrick's attention to detail, the inclusion of the star of Ishtar in this party is not an accident. Ishtar is the Babylonian goddess of fertility, love, war and, mostly, sexuality. Her cult involved sacred prostitution and ritual acts – two elements we clearly see later in the movie.

> "Babylonians gave Ishtar offerings of food and drink on Saturday. They then joined in ritual acts of lovemaking, which in turn invoked Ishtar's favor on the region and its people to promote continued health and fruitfulness."
> - Goddess Ishtar, Anita Revel

Ishtar herself was considered to be the "courtesan of the gods" and had many lovers. While inspired in bed, she was also cruel to the men that got attached to her. These concepts will constantly reappear in the movie, especially with Alice.

During the party, Bill and Alice go their separate ways and are both faced with temptation. Alice meets a man named Sandor Szavost who asks her about Ovid's Art of Love. This series of books, written during the times of Ancient Rome, was essentially a "How to Cheat on Your Partner" guide, and was popular with the elite of the time. The first book opens with an invocation to Venus – the planet esoterically associated with lust. Interestingly enough, Ishtar (and her equivalents in other Semetic cultures) was considered to be the personification of Venus.

Sandor's name might be a reference to the founder of the Church of Satan: Anton Szandor Lavey. Is this Kubrick's way of saying that this man, who urges Alice to cheat on her husband, is a part of the occult elite and its decadent ways? The Hungarian man is apparently skilled in neuro-linguistic programming (NLP) as he nearly hypnotizes Alice with well calculated phrases about the futility of married life and the necessity of pursuing pleasure.

Movies and TV

Sandor drinks from Alice's glass. This trick is taken right out of Ovid's The Art of Love. It sends Alice a message that is not very subliminal: "I want to exchange fluids with you".

Meanwhile, Bill is discussing with two flirtatious models who tell him that they want to take him to "where the rainbow ends". While the meaning of this enigmatic phrase is never explicitly explained in the movie, symbols talk for themselves.

Rainbows Everywhere

Rainbows and multicolored lights appear throughout the movie, from the beginning to the end.

The name of the store where Bill rents his costume is called "Rainbow". The name of the store under it: "Under the Rainbow". Kubrick is trying to tell us something…Something involving rainbows.

As if to emphasize the theme of multicolored rainbows, almost every scene in the movie contains multicolored Christmas lights, giving most sets a hazy, dreamy glow.

Almost every time Bill enters a room, the first things we see are multicolored Christmas lights.

Sometimes Christmas lights are the focal point of attention.

482

These lights tie together most scenes of the movie, making them part of the same reality. There are however a few select scenes where there are absolutely no Christmas lights. The main one is Somerton palace – the place where the secret society ritual takes place.

Sharply contrasting with the rest of the movie, Sommerton is completely devoid of multi-colored lights. Everything about this place is in sharp opposition with the "outside world".

In Eyes Wide Shut, there are therefore two worlds: The Christmas lights-filled "rainbow world", where the masses wander around, trying to make ends meet and the other world… "where the rainbow ends"- where the elite gathers and performs its rituals. The contrast between the two world give a sense of an almost insurmountable divide between them. Later, the movie will clearly show us how those from the "rainbow world" cannot enter the other world.

So, when the models ask Bill the go "where the rainbow ends", they probably refer to going "where the elite gathers and performs rituals". It might also be about them being dissociated Beta Programming slaves. There are several references to Monarch mind control in the movie. Women who take part in elite rituals are often products of Illuminati mind control. In MK Ultra vocabulary, "going over the rainbow" means dissociating from reality and entering another persona (more on this in the next article).

The models ask Bill to leave the "rainbow world" (there's a Christmas tree right behind them) to indulge in the debaucherous rituals of the occult elite.

Behind the Curtain

Bill's flirting with the models is interrupted when Ziegler calls him to his bathroom. There, we get a first glance of "where the rainbow ends" – the dark truth about the elite.

If we rewind a little, when Bill and Alice first entered the party, they were welcomed by Ziegler and his wife in a room filled with Christmas lights. We saw two respectable couples talking about respectable things in room full of enchanting lights. But when Bill goes "where the rainbow ends" (notice there are no Christmas lights in the bathroom) we see reality: Ziegler with a Beta programming slave who overdosed on goofballs. When the woman gains consciousness, Ziegler talks to her in an odd, paternal matter, highlighting the fact that he's the master and she's the slave. The luxurious setting of this scene is Kubrick's way of saying that extreme wealth does not necessary equal high morals.

Bill meets Ziegler in his gigantic bathroom. The man is dressing up and is with a naked unconscious woman... who is not his wife.

Ziegler then urges Bill to keep everything he just saw a secret. The world "where the rainbow ends" must never be revealed to the outside world. It operates in its own space, has its own rules and depends on the masses' ignorance.

Questioning Marriage

While Alice ultimately rejected Sandor's advances, she was nevertheless enticed by them. The next day, Alice tells Bill that she could have cheated on him at the party. When Bill tells his wife that he loves and trusts her, she completely loses it. She then proceeds to tell him a story about how she was once ready to cheat on him with a naval officer she met in a hotel. This cruel story highlights the "Ishtar" side of Alice as she brings up in her husband feelings of jealousy, insecurity, betrayal and even humiliation. In short, Alice purposely summoned everything that is negative in relationships to pop Bill's "love bubble". This wake-up call prompts Bill to embark in a strange journey around New-York city, one that has multiple level of meanings. That strange night will ultimately lead him to the exact opposite of a monogamous relationship: Anonymous, masked copulation with strangers in a ritual setting. Bill's journey will be further analyzed in the second part of this series of articles.

Conclusion of Part One

The first part of this series about Eyes Wide Shut took a broad look at Bill and Alice, a modern couple that has the "privilege" of brushing with the upper-echelon of New York. While everything appears great on the surface, Kubrick quickly tells the viewers to not be deceived by appearances and to not be impressed by exhibitions of wealth. Because, behind the "rainbow world", exists a dark and disturbing reality, one that Kubrick exposes in many subtle ways throughout the movie.

While Bill and Alice are simply "guests" in the elite circle, they are nevertheless fascinated and attracted by it. They see in this lifestyle a way of fulfilling their dark and secret needs. In the next part of this series, we'll look at the occult meaning of Bill's journey – a story told by subtle symbols peppered throughout the movie.

The Hidden (And Not So Hidden) Messages in Stanley Kubrick's "Eyes Wide Shut" (pt. II)

The second part of this series of articles on Eyes Wide Shut takes a closer look at the elite secret society discovered by the film's main character, Bill Harford, and how it resembles real life organizations. Was Stanley Kubrick trying to warn the world about the occult elite and its depraved ways?

In the first part of this series on Eyes Wide Shut, we looked at main characters of the film and the symbolic world Kubrick created around them. We saw that Bill and Alice Harford are a married upper-class couple that was not immune to the temptations of adultery. We also saw that the couple was in contact with the upper-echelon of New-York and its decadent ways – a world that fascinates Bill, but that has a dark side, one that is kept from the public. In this article, I will jump straight to the most unsettling part of the movie: The secret society ritual.

When Bill learns that his wife has considered cheating on him, he embarks in a strange series of encounters (which I will analyze in the third and final part of this series), eventually ending up in a luxurious house in Long Island where he encounters a large gathering of masked individuals partaking in an occult ritual. Since he was never initiated into that secret society, Bill was not even supposed to know that it existed, let alone bear witness to one of its "meetings". So how did he find out about this thing? Well, a little birdie told him.

Nick Nightingale

At one point during his strange night out, Bill meets his old friend Nick Nightingale at a jazz cafe. The professional piano player reveals to Bill that he is sometimes hired by mysterious people to play, blindfolded, during mysterious parties that are full of beautiful women. This juicy piece of information intrigues Bill to the highest degree because, since his talk with his wife, he is appears to be looking for some kind of … experience. Nick ultimately makes a big mistake and agrees to provide Bill with all of the information needed to access the venue.

A nightingale is type of bird that is known for singing at night, just like Nick Nightingale "sings" secret information at the start of Bill's fateful night.

The password to enter the ritual is "Fidelio", which means "faithfulness", a main theme of the movie. More importantly, as Nightingale points out, "Fidelio" is the name of an opera written by Beethoven about a wife who sacrifices herself to free her husband from death as a political prisoner. This password actually foreshadows what will happen during that ritual.

After getting the details from Nightingale, Bill rents a costume at a store named "Rainbow" (more about the store in the next article) … and then proceeds to go to Somerton, the estate where the party is being held.

The Occult Elite

The occult ritual takes place at Somerton, in Long Island. The building used to film the outside scene is Mentmore Towers in UK.

The location selected to film the elite scenes is quite interesting. Mentmore Towers was built in the 19th century as a country house for a member of the most prominent and powerful elite family in the world: The Rothschilds. By selecting this location, was Kubrick trying to show his audience the "real world" equivalents to the ultra-elite shown in the movie? Incidentally, the name of Bill's connection to the elite, Victor Ziegler, is of German-Jewish origin, like Rothschild.

It has been documented that the Rothschilds do actually partake in masked events very similar to those shown in Eyes Wide Shut. Here are rare images taken from a 1972 party given by Marie-Hélène de Rothschild.

Baroness Marie-Hélène de Rothschild and Baron Alexis de Redé at a 1972 party. Invitations were printed in reversed writing. One wonders if this party "degenerated" into something resembling what is shown in Eyes Wide Shut.

A couple wearing Venetian masks (more specifically "female jester" and "bauta" masks) slowly turn towards Bill and nod in a very creepy matter. Is this Ziegler and his wife? Perhaps. Kubrick likes to keep things mysterious.

In the movie, when Bill enters the mansion, he mixes with a crowd of masked people silently watching the ritual. One of these people appear to instantly recognize Bill (or the fact that he doesn't belong here).

Venetian masks were originally worn during the Italian Renaissance in Venice and were a way for the powerful elite of the time to indulge in debauchery without reprisal.

> *"Though the precise origin of the mask-wearing tradition can't be known for certain, the prevailing theory goes something like this: beginning in the Italian Renaissance, Venice was an extremely wealthy and powerful merchant empire. Its position on the Mediterranean sea opened it up to a myriad of trading opportunities across Europe, North Africa and Asia Minor, and its powerful navy allowed it to exert the military force necessary to defend its vast wealth. In a city-state so prosperous, it's a small wonder that Venetian society was class-obsessed and rigidly stratified. One's individual standing was immensely important for the perception of his or her entire family, and so naturally the pressure to act in accordance with the social morays governing one's social standing was immense and stifling. The Venetians, the theory goes, adopted the practice of wearing masks and other disguises during the Carnival season as a way of suspending the rigid social order. Under the cloak of anonymity, the citizens of Venice could loosen their inhibitions without fear of reprisal. Masks gained so much popularity that the mascherari (mask makers) became a venerated guild in Venetian society. However, as word of the famed Venetian Carnival spread, more and more outsiders flocked to the city every year to take part in the festivities. The Carnival celebrations became increasingly chaotic and debaucherous as the years progressed until their decline in the 18th Century."*
> - Geoffrey Stanton, Guide to Venetian Carnival Masks

Since then, Venetian masks have been used in elite circles and have somewhat become a symbol of its dark occult philosophy. Even The British Royal Family appears to enjoy the same type of masks and events. It seems evident that Kubrick carefully selected the Rothschild-owned location and hand-picked the masks worn by participants of the ritual, echoing real-life families and events.

Setting of the Ritual

When Bill enters Somerton, everything about the movie changes. There are no more colorful Christmas lights and no tacky decorations. Instead of incessant chatter between needy people, it is all about stillness and silence.

Staring right at the camera (and at the movie viewers), the creepy masks are silent yet disturbing reminders showing the "true faces" of the elite. Note that the multi-faced mask on the left which is similar to the one worn at the Royal party above.

The music in the movie also changes drastically. The song heard in the background is called "Backwards Priests" and features a Romanian Orthodox Divine Liturgy played backwards. The reversal or inversion of sacred objects is typical of black magic and satanic rituals. By having this Christian liturgy played backwards right before widespread fornication is Kubrick's way of stating that the elite is nothing less than satanic.

Movies and TV

Here we see Nick Nightindale playing the song "Backwards Priest", meaning that people in the ritual actually hear that music and that the whole thing is choreographed to it. Nightindale is blindfolded because the "profane" cannot witness the occult rituals of the elite.

The interior scenes of the party were shot at Elveden Hall, a private house in the UK designed to look like an Indian palace. When the "festivities" begin, a Tamil song called "Migration" plays in the background, adding to the South-Asian atmosphere (the original version of the song contained actual scriptural recitation of the Bhagavad Gita, but the chant was removed in the final version of the movie). This peculiar Indian atmosphere, combined with the lascivious scenes witnessed by Bill as he walks around the house, ultimately points towards the most important, yet most hidden part of the movie: Tantric Yoga and its Western occultism derivative, Sex Magick. This last concept was "imported" by British occultist Aleister Crowley and is now at the center of the teachings of various secret societies:

> "Aleister Crowley's connections with Indian Yoga and Tantra were both considerable and complex. Crowley had direct exposure to some forms of these practices and was familiar with the contemporary literature of the subjects, wrote extensively about them, and – what is perhaps the most important – he practiced them. In his assessment of the value of Tantra, he was ahead of his time, which habitually considered Tantra a degenerate form of Hinduism. Instead, he claimed that, "paradoxical as it may sound the Tantrics are in reality the most advanced of the Hindus". Crowley's influence in bringing Eastern, primarily Indian, esoteric traditions to the West extends also to his incorporation of the elements of Yoga and Tantra into the structure and program of two influential magical orders, the A.:A.: and the OTO."
> - Martin P. Starr, Aleister Crowley and Western Esotericism

The above quote stipulates that Tantric concepts were incorporated in two important secret societies: the A.:A.: and the OTO (Ordo Templi Orientis). The OTO is still extremely influential in elite circles and reaches the highest levels of politics, business and even the entertainment industry. At the core of these orders is the Thelema, a philosophy created by Aleister Crowley that he summed up with the saying "Do What Thou Wilt". This saying is actually a translation of "Fais ce que tu voudras" the motto of an 18th century secret society, the infamous Hellfire Club.

Hellfire Clubs were said to be "meeting places of 'persons of quality' who wished to take part in immoral acts, and the members were often very involved in politics". According to a number of sources, their activities included mock religious ceremonies, devil worship and occult rituals. Although details are vague regarding that elite club, they were known for performing elementary Satanic rites as a prelude to their nights of fornication. These acts were however not just "for fun" or to "shock people" as some sources might claim, the members were initiates of occult mysteries and their rituals were based in ancient rites involving invocations and other forms of black magick.

In short, although Kubrick never actually names the secret society infiltrated by Bill, there are enough clues to understand what kind of club he is referring to. Most importantly, he is telling his viewers: These societies still exist

… and they are more powerful than ever.

The Ritual and its Participants

The ritual begins with the High Priest, dressed in red, performing a ceremonial routine. He is at the center of a "magic circle" formed by young women who are very likely to be Beta Kitten slaves. Later, when Bill is unmasked, another magic circle is formed.

Magic circles is concept used in ritual magic during invocations. The placement of the people in this scene recalls magic circles. Right: A magic circle as pictured in an ancient grimoire.

The last scene of the movie takes place at a toy store – a place full of highly symbolic items (more on it in the next article). Here, Helena Harford walks by a toy called Magic Circle – showing that the occult elite's ways seep through popular culture, but are not noticed by those who have their eyes wide shut.

AMANDA

At the beginning of the ritual, one of the Beta slaves goes to Bill and urges him to leave the house before he got caught. We ultimately learn that it was Amanda, the girl that was passed out in Ziegler's bathroom. When Bill gets caught and gets (literally) unmasked by the High Priest, Amanda appears at the balcony in a very dramatic fashion and tells the High Priest she wants to "redeem" him, in a tone that approaches ritual drama. The Priest then replies "Are you sure you understand what you're taking upon yourself in doing this?" This implies that she will be repeatedly abused and then sacrificed.

The next day, Bill discovers the true power of that secret society.

Bill discovers in the newspaper that Amanda was found dead in a hotel room due to an overdose. The way in which this ritualistic murder is disguised as an overdose is highly similar to the many celebrity ritual deaths disguised as overdoses that occur in real life.

By freeze-framing and actually reading the above news article about Amanda, we learn important details about Amanda's background (classic hidden sub-plot integration by Kubrick). To those "in the know", the article perfectly describes the life of an entertainment industry Beta Programming slave (i.e. Marilyn Monroe). We indeed learn that Amanda was "emotionally troubled" as a teen and underwent "treatments" (a code word for MK Programming perhaps?), she had "important friends in the fashion and entertainment worlds", and she had an "affair" with a powerful fashion designer who got "wowed by her private, seductive solo performances" (typical behavior of a Beta Kitten). What the article however conveniently doesn't mention is that she was selling her body to elite people and being used in their occult rituals.

As it is the case for Beta Kittens who've gone "rogue", she was eliminated by the people who controlled her life. The article states that she was last seen being escorted to her hotel room by two men and that she was "giggling" (drugged and dissociated?). Like "real life" elite sacrifices, "overdose" is cited as the cause of her death.

The High Priest

Cloaked in red, the High Priest sits on a throne which features a very important symbol: A double-headed eagle topped by a crown.

The double-headed eagle is one of the most ancient and prominent symbols of Freemasonry. A crowned double headed eagle is representative of the 33rd degree of Freemasonry, the highest degree attainable. Is Kubrick implying that the High Priest is a 33rd Degree Freemason?

Like other participants of the ritual, the true identity of the High Priest is never revealed. However, Kubrick left a few clues hinting to his identity and his relationship with Amanda.

In the movie's end credits (and sources such as IMDB), it is listed that the role of the High Priest was played by "assistant director" of the movie, Leon Vitali. If one carefully reads the news article mentioned above, Leon Vitali is the name of the London fashion designer Amanda had an "affair" with. Furthermore, the High Priest has an unmistakable English accent. We can therefore deduce that the High Priest is the fashion designer.

This hidden subplot is interesting as it reveals the true nature of the fashion and entertainment industry. High-ranking individuals in these fields are initiated in occult secret societies and deal with MK slaves.

The Power of the Secret Society

When Bill is uncovered by the High Priest, he gets told that he and his family would pay for any transgression. The next day, he realizes that he is being followed by strange people and becomes paranoid.

The headline of this newspaper is "Lucky to be alive". This applies to Bill.

Right after Bill leaves the morgue to confirm that Amanda died, Ziegler calls him and invites him over.

Although Bill is a rich doctor, he is not part of the elite. Ziegler's attitude towards Bill makes it very clear. While Ziegler appears to want to be honest and straight with Bill, we realize that he is simply trying to cover the ugly truth. After all, Bill is an "outsider". He tells Bill:

> "I don't think you realize what kind of trouble you were in last night. Who do you think those people were? Those were not just ordinary people there. If I told you their names – I'm not gonna tell you their names – but if I did, I don't think you'd sleep so well."

Ziegler therefore admits that people attending the ritual were high-level, well-known and powerful people. Kubrick is therefore making clear that the richest, most powerful deciders of the "real world" meet in these types of rituals … and that these rituals are off-limits for the profane.

When Bill mentions Amanda, Ziegler gets more defensive and replies: "She was a hooker" – meaning that she was an Beta slave that could be easily disposed of. Then Ziegler tells Bill that everything that happened at the ritual was a charade to scare him, Bill answers:

> "You called it a fake, a charade. Do you mind telling me what kind of f—-cking charade ends with someone turning up dead?"

This highlights the fundamental difference between the public's perception of occult rituals and what actually happens. Regular people are lead to believe that these elite rituals are nothing more than goofy meetings of people with too much time on their hands. In reality, these elaborate rituals often incorporate real attempts at Black Magick and include real blood sacrifices and other terrible acts.

Then Ziegler proceeds to telling Bill the same stuff media tells the masses when someone has been sacrificed by the elite: She OD'ed, she was a junkie, it was only a matter of time, and the police did not see any foul play.

Conclusion of Part II

The second part of this analysis focused exclusively on the unnamed secret society Bill stumbles upon and its ritual. Although nothing is explicitly spelled out to the viewers, the symbolism, the visual clues and even the music of Eyes Wide Shut tell reveals a side of the occult elite that is rarely shown to the masses. Not only does the movie depict the world's richest and most powerful people partaking in occult rituals, it also shows how this circle has also the power to exploit slaves, to stalk people, and even to get away with sacrificial murders. Even worse, mass media participates in covering their crimes.

The secret society in the movie closely resembles the infamous Hellfire Club, where prominent political figures met up to partake in elaborate Satanic parties. Today, the O.T.O. and similar secret societies still partake in rituals involving physical energy as it is perceived to be a way to attain a state of enlightenment. This concept, taken from Tantric yoga, is at the core of modern and powerful secret societies. Although none of this is actually mentioned in Eyes Wide Shut, the entire movie can be interpreted as one big "magickal" journey, characterized by a back-and-forth between opposing forces: life and death, lust and pain, male and female, light and darkness, and so forth … ending in one big orgasmic moment of enlightenment. This aspect of the movie, along with other hidden details, will be analyzed in the third and final part of this series of articles on Eyes Wide Shut.

The Hidden (And Not So Hidden) Messages in Stanley Kubrick's "Eyes Wide Shut" (pt. III)

In the third and final part of this series on Eyes Wide Shut, we'll look at Bill's journey as a whole and at its underlying esoteric meaning. We'll see how symbolism placed by Kubrick connects all of the women in the movie, making Bill's encounters a multi-faceted exploration of the feminine principle.

The previous parts of this series of articles on Eyes Wide Shut was solely dedicated to the secret society discovered by Bill. This elite club, attended by the world's most powerful people, deals with Satanism, black magick and even ritual sacrifices. Aided by his friend Nightingale, Bill infiltrates one of the secret society's occult rituals and witnesses a ceremony presided over by a high priest. Then an orgy ensued.

In the second article, I explained how real life secret societies, such as the Hellfire club and the O.T.O., actually practice these kinds of rituals. The occult principles behind them derive from Tantric yoga, where the energy generated by physical arousal is used to reach a "higher state". This concept was reused (and maybe corrupted) by Aleister Crowley who called it "Sex Magick". According to him and his peers, knowledge of this type of magick was the biggest secret of past secret societies and was only disclosed to the highest initiates.

There is, however, no (direct) mention of any of this in Eyes Wide Shut. In fact, the ceremony witnessed by Bill, with its elaborate choreography and its creepy music, appears to be one big, empty, phony piece of dramatic theater that simply exists to give the rich people some kind of mystical reason to engage in gratuitous debauchery. While Kubrick stripped the occult ritual of all of its esoteric, "magickal" meaning, he did infuse the entire movie with it. If one looks at the pace of the movie, at Bill's journey and the people he encounters, it becomes somewhat apparent that the "magick" does not occur during the ritual itself but during the movie as a whole. Was Kubrick somehow initiated to occult secrets? Was he trying to communicate them through his movie? Let's look at the concepts behind the ritual.

Kundalini Rising

The concept of magick through reproductive forces is said to originate from ancient ritual practices, as traces of it can be found in Hinduism, Taoism and in Medieval secret societies, such as the Knight Templars. In today's Western world, the O.T.O is said to be the heir of this path as it claimed by Aleister Crowley and his acolyte, Theodor Reuss.

> "Theodor Reuss was quite categoric: the OTO was a body of initiates in whose hands was concentrated the secret knowledge of all oriental orders and of all existing Masonic degrees.(…) The order had "rediscovered" the great secret of the Knights Templar, the magic of sex, not only the key to ancient Egyptian and hermetic tradition, but to all the secrets of nature, all the symbolism of Freemasonry, and all systems of religion."
> - Peter Tomkins, The Magic of Obelisks

The basic principle behind this "great secret" is the raising of the Kundalini or "life force", an energy that can be used for magickal purposes.

> "In all Tantric magic, the essential requirement – whether in the ecstasy of couples or the solo ritual of a priestess – involved the raising of the energy known as the serpent of fire, or kundalini. This mysterious energy described as lying dormant in the lowest of the seven chakras, can be aroused by two distinct methods, called, traditionally, the right- and the left-hand path. The right hand allots supremacy to the male principle, the left to the feminine. As the serpent power is aroused, according to clairvoyants, it climbs up the backbone of the adept, energizing each chakra, till it emerges from the skull – symbolically as the snake's head like those so clearly depicted in Egyptian statuary.
>
> As adepts describe the rising of the serpent, it unites with the "many-petaled louts of the cerebral region" to bring about illumination – or the highest form of initiation -as the current "climbs from the duality to unity by reversing the path it originally took the chakras to procreate humanity."
>
> Details of the OTO's initiation into Hindu and Tibetan Tantra, including ceremonies involving the use of "exudation" from specifically trained priestess were brought to a wider public by Crowley's follower Kenneth Grant. Sacred courtesans, experts in ritual eroticism, known in India as nautch girls (…) were exceptionally honored."
> - Ibid.

While sacred courtesans were "exceptionally honored" in Eastern esotericism, today's twisted black magic orders use Beta Programming slaves and dispose of them when they are through with them. In short, the exact opposite of being "exceptionally honored".

Kundalini rising, the concept behind Tantric magic is wholly represented in a single image, Eliphas Levi's depiction of Baphomet.

This famous depiction of Baphomet includes all of the symbols behind Sex Magick – the rising of the kundalini (represented by the phallic pole wrapped by two serpents) through the union of opposite forces. The torch above the goat head represents illumination.

So what does all of this have to do with Eyes Wide Shut? At first glance, nothing much. While we see a ritual involving "sacred courtesans" in the movie, there is absolutely no mention of "kundalini rising" during the whole thing. However, if we take a closer look at Bill's journey as a whole, from the beginning of the movie to the end, we realize that the real ritual does not occur at the elite mansion, but within Bill's head. As he encounters new women and is exposed to new opportunities, his kundalini rises – and Kubrick added clues to denote this fact.

The Movie as a Ritual

While Eyes Wide Shut appears to be all about sexuality, nobody in the movie ever reaches climax. While Bill has many chances of satisfying his urges with attractive women, it never actually happens. However, as the movie progresses, there's a definite increase in desire and lust, but Bill manages to keep it under control. Managing this "life force" is at the core of Tantric magic. Viewers are constantly reminded of this process several times during the movie when Bill imagines his wife with a naval officer. Each flash is increasingly intense – going from kissing to all-out copulating.

As the movie progress, Bill's flashes of Alice cheating on him become more intense. Towards the end of the movie, she's about to reach climax. These scenes reflect Bill's kundalini rising. Having these flashes would be hurtful and painful and they remind the viewers that Bill's journey started out of pain and humiliation.

Towards the end of the movie, Bill is so horny that he gets flirty and grabby with a complete stranger, minutes after he met her. While that scene was rather odd and surreal, it reflects his "progress" in the ritual.

The very last lines of the movie conclude and define Bill's journey. After running around New York and getting aroused by all kinds of stuff, Bill stands face-to-face with his wife and talks about how "awake" he is now. With his "life force" fully charged, Alice ends the movie with a phrase completing the ritual:

> "- I do love you. And you know, there is something very important that we need to do a soon as possible.
> - What's that?
> - F*ck."

Ending the movie on that particular note suggests that the entire journey was one of increasing intensity, one that ultimately lead to a "magickally charged" climax, the goal of Crowleyan-magick.

Bill's journey was not all fun and games, however. As the movie progresses, there is a constant back-and-forth between pleasure and pain, attraction and repulsion, life and death, and so forth. The path is all about duality and, just like the floors of Masonic lodges are checkered in black and white, Bill's journey consists on his alternatively stepping on black and white tiles – seeing the dualistic nature of all things.

Eros and Thanatos

Bill's night out in New York City is characterized by numerous encounters with the female gender – each one of them offering a "cure" to a broken heart. However, each encounter also bears a potentially destructive aspect to it, one that counterbalances its appeal and attraction. While Bill is looking to procreate, he sees that his urges engender pain and even death. Bill's journey is therefore a back-and-forth between man's two basic impulses as defined by Freud: Eros and Thanatos.

Freud saw in Eros the instinct for life, love and sexuality in its broadest sense, and in Thanatos, the instinct of death, aggression. Eros is the drive toward attraction and reproduction; Thanatos toward repulsion and death. One leads to the reproduction of the species, the other toward its own destruction. While each one of Bill's encounters promise the sweet temptation of lust, they also have a destructive counter side.

Bill's first encounter occurs when he visits one of his regular patients that died. The dead patient's daughter kisses Bill and tells him that she loves him. We therefore see in this scene a juxtaposition of concepts of lust and desire with death. Also, if Bill went with this woman, it would ultimately hurt her husband – another bad side of succumbing to lust.

Each one of Bill's female encounters promises gratification, but ends up being interrupted by something negative, such as guilt or potential danger. Also, every time Bill is in contact with the sleazy-yet-tempting aspects of lust (prostitution or slavery), he quickly discovers the dark, exploitative and destructive side of it.

For instance, right after Bill enjoyed the "delights" of seeing MK Kittens at work at the elite ritual, when returning his costume, he immediately sees the dark side of it all. The shop owner, who previously caught his underage daughter with two Asian businessmen and was outraged by it, had a sudden change of heart.

Standing behind his business counter, the shop owner sells his underage daughter as if she was another product. After enjoying masked slaves in lavish rituals, Bill sees the other side of the "trade": Young girls being sold by exploitative people to a system feeding on minors, turning them into MK slaves. Is that why this store was called "Rainbow"?

Bill's journey is therefore one that continually alternates between the primal allure of lust and the destructive social constructs that are erected around it. There is nothing more basic and instinctual than carnal attraction, but our modern world has made these relations complex, bound by rules, and prone to exploitation. While lust is nature's way of pushing humans to procreate, social constructs have created all kinds fetishes, distortions, games, and perversions around this primal urge … to the point that it has been denatured and debased into an unhealthy obsession.

As Bill navigates between joy and pain, monogamous marriage and anonymous debauchery, we notice that there's a common thread uniting his various encounters.

Red-Headed Women

The most important women in the movie are Bill's wife, his daughter Helena, Amanda (the Beta slave who was sacrificed at the ritual) and Domino (a prostitute he met on the street). All three adult women are somewhat physically similar as they are tall, well-proportioned, and red-headed. They also appear to be connected on "another level".

While Alice is a respectable, upper-class lady, she makes a living using her looks in loveless relationship, a little like what a prostitute would do. On the other hand, the time spent between Bill and Domino is sweet and tender, a little with what happens in a loving relationship. Alice is therefore not very different from Domino, and vice-versa.

There are also links with Amanda. While Alice was (probably) not at the occult ritual attended by Bill, when he comes back from it, she describes to him a dream that is similar to what he just witnessed and what Amanda just experienced.

> "He was kissing me. Then we were making love. Then there were all these other people around us, hundreds of them, everywhere. Everyone was f-cking. And then I …I was f-cking other men. So many. I don't know how many I was with. And I knew you could see me in the arms of all these men … just f-cking all these men."

Alice's dream "connects" her with Amanda who was at the ritual and who actually lived Alice's dream. Was Domino at the ritual? It is also interesting to point out that "Domino" is a type of mask used in these types of gatherings.

Was Domino at the ritual? It is also interesting to point out that "Domino" is a type of mask used in these types of gatherings.

A Domino mask

Looking closer at the "magic circle" formed by the women of the ritual, we can identify a few women who could be

Domino. The day after the ritual, Bill shows up at Domino's house with a gift, but her roommate informs him that she is HIV-positive ... and that she might never be back again. Is this true or was Domino yet another "casualty" in Bill's journey? Like Amanda and Nightingale, Domino mysteriously disappears after the ritual.

The fact that these women are all connected reveals one fundamental fact: Bill's journey is not about a specific woman, it is about the feminine principle as a whole. It is an esoteric quest to understand and "be one with" the feminine principle that is opposite to his.
Helena Down the Same Path?

Throughout the movie, Helena (Bill's daughter) is shown to be groomed to be another Alice. There are also some cues linking Helena to Domino. For instance, there's a stroller in front of Domino's apartment and, at the end in the movie, in the toy store, Helena is very interested by a stroller and shows it to her mother.

Domino on her bed with a stuffed feline, a symbol of Beta Kitten programming.

An entire row of this exact same toy is at the store where Helena shops in the final scene of the movie.

There is also something strange about the scene above: the two men behind Helena happened to be at Ziegler's party at the very beginning of the movie.

The two same men at Ziegler's party: same hair, same physical stature and the guy on the right wears similar glasses.

Why are these two men in the store, looking at toys? Is New York City such a small town? Was Kubrick lacking extras to appear in that scene? Unlikely. Could it be that they're part of the secret society that's been following Bill and his family? Strange fact: When the men walk away and disappear from the shot, Helena appears to follow them ... and we don't see her for the rest of the movie. The camera indeed zooms onto Alice and Bill, who are completely absorbed with themselves. Is this a VERY subtle way of saying that their daughter will be sucked in by the Beta slave system of the secret society? Another enigma.

In Conclusion

Stanley Kubrick's works are never strictly about love or relationships. The meticulous symbolism and the imagery of all of his works often communicate another dimension of meaning–one that transcends the personal to become a commentary on our epoch and civilization. And, in this transitional period between the end of 20th century and the beginning of the 21th century, Kubrick told the story of a confused man who wanders around, desperately looking for a way to satisfy his primal urges. Kubrick told the story of a society that is completely debased and corrupted by hidden forces, where humanity's most primal urge–procreation–has been cheapened, fetishized, perverted, and exploited to a point that it has lost all of its beauty. At the top of this world is a secret society that revels in this context, and thrives on it. Kubrick's outlook on the issue was definitely not idealistic nor very optimistic.

His grim tale focuses on a single man, Bill, who is looking for an undefined something. Even if he appears to have everything, there is something missing in his life. Something visceral and fundamental that is never put into words, but that is quite palpable. Bill cannot be complete if he is not at peace with the opposite of him: the feminine principle. Bill's quest, therefore, follows the esoteric principle of uniting two opposite forces into one. As suggested by the last lines of the movie, Bill will ultimately "be one" and get physical with his wife. After that, the alchemical process and the Tantric ritual would be complete. However, as Kubrick somehow communicates in the final scene, even if these two extremely self-absorbed, egoistical and superficial people believe they've reached a some kind of epiphany, what does it really change? Our civilization as a whole still has its eyes wide shut … and those were Kubrick's last cinematographic words.

"Now You See Me": A Movie About the Illuminati Entertainment Industry?

"Now You See Me" is about big-time magicians doing incredible magic tricks ... and some kind of a bank heist. But mostly, "Now You See Me" is about a shady organization named "The Eye" that controls these entertainers. While most viewers are dizzied with the senseless action of the movie, an important message is being communicated: The occult elite controls the entertainment business ... Do you see it?

Warning: Gigantic spoilers ahead!

Most critics had the same complaint about Now You See Me: The story makes absolutely no sense and is completely illogical. I wholeheartedly agree with them. Almost everything that happens during the entire movie is implausible. Even the mind-blowing overarching "master plan" of the movie actually depends on so many variables that could go wrong that it is, in fact, a horrible plan.

While most viewers will try to make sense of the action in Now You See Me, the movie simply keeps repeating to the viewers "The closer you look, the less you see". It also constantly repeats that magicians always do something to distract the audience while the real magic happens elsewhere. Does this apply in the movie itself? Of course it does. The police chase, the bank heist plot, the explosions are there to keep the viewers' eyes occupied while the real underlying story unfolds: It is about the entertainment industry, the forces that rule it and those that are used by it. It is also about the audience, the masses that are being fooled by master illusionists. The first lines of the movie say it all:

> "Come in close. Closer. Because the more you think you see, the easier it'll be to fool you. Because what is seeing? You're looking, but what you're really doing is filtering, interpreting, searching for meaning. My job? To take that most of gifts you give me, your attention, and use it against you."

These lines, said while a magic card trick is being performed, sum up the true role of mass media and the entertainment industry. The rest of the movie aptly describes who rules the industry and even the methods it uses. The magicians are recruited by a secret society named "The Eye" (this might ring a bell for readers of this site) that uses the entertainers to further its agenda and make its symbolism a part of popular culture. Take a step back and realize this: The movie IS the magician. Let's take a look at the themes of Now You See me.

Approached

At first, we see the four magicians doing their own little thing separately. They are all trying to make a living doing their magic tricks. They are however far from being big-time celebrities. They are watched and followed by a hooded figure who leaves an invitation in the form of a tarot card.

On the back of the invitation card is the symbol of the All-Seeing Eye. In this particular shot, the card is held above a photo of one of the magicians and hides one of its eyes – hinting that he's about to be part of the occult elite's entertainment industry. The fact that one eye is replaced by the all-seeing eye also implies that he is about to lose a whole lot sight ... and freedom.

The four magicians are selected because they excel in their particular field of magic and, mostly, because they sometimes appear to be using real, occult magic.

From left to right: Henley Reeves is an escapist (High Priestess tarot card); J. Daniel Atlas is an illusionist (Lovers card); Merritt McKinney is a mentalist (Hermit card); Jack Wilder is a sleight-of-hand illusionist (Death card).

Jack Wilder, the youngest of the crew received the Death card for a reason: It foreshadows his upcoming ritual sacrifice.

The magicians are invited to a strange apartment with strange contraptions in it. After figuring out the riddles that were placed there (an initiation process), they see the elite's plans laid out for them. Then, just like magic, they become big-time entertainers.

Puppets of Their Rulers

After joining The Eye, the magicians are in Las Vegas, surrounding by a roaring crowd while we hear big boisterous music that basically screams "This is showbiz, baby!". The four magicians, who were four solo, independent acts, have now joined into a group to become the Four Horsemen. This name is taken the Bible's Book of Revelation, where the Four Horsemen are harbingers of the Apocalypse and the tribulations that come with it. The Four Horsemen of the Apocalypse are often said to be associated with pestilence, war, famine and death. This is a rather grim name for a bunch of magicians, but it makes sense when we know that they are working for the occult elite. The Book of Revelation is of great importance in secret societies as it is believed to conceal an occult meaning to be only deciphered by the initiates. A lot of their symbolism derives from it and this is no exception.

Not unlike "real" performers in the entertainment industry, the Four Horsemen are only there to obey orders coming from The Eye. Everything about them relates to the secret society that controls them.

The stage on which the Horsemen perform is a giant eye. That's a scale model of the stage.

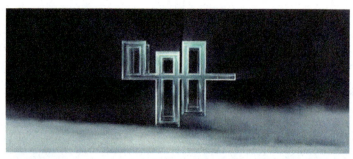

The logo of the Four Horsemen is quite enigmatic.

In one scene however, we see a strange decoration that says "Eye". It appears consist of a combination of two 3D versions of the Horsemen logo. In short, the logo is another hidden way of hiding Eye symbolism in plain sight.

When the group completes its most spectacular magic trick, the symbol of the Eye flashes on Times Square. While most people believe that The Eye is a myth, its symbolism is everywhere ... just like in real life.

Everything about the Four Horsemen is therefore stamped with the seal of the Eye.

It is interesting to note that the people behind the movie did not create a fictional symbol to represent the secret society. They used the most important symbol of today's occult elite – one the most important symbols of various powerful secret societies. As we often see on this site, this symbol is also already used all around mass media. Why is that? Is it because the movie plays the role of the Four Horsemen – a vehicle for the symbolism of the occult elite?

The Eye – Based on the Actual Secret Society that Runs Hollywood?

As the movie progresses, we discover some information The Eye and its history. Everything about it closely resembles an actual secret society that is powerful in Hollywood: the OTO, a self-described "magickal Order".

In the movie, the Eye is:

> "keepers of real magic and protectors of those who practice it. Candidates for initiation must follow a series of commands with blind obedience".

It is clearly stated that the symbol of the Eye originates from the Ancient Egyptian symbol of the Eye of Horus. The characteristics of the Eye closely resemble the OTO. The OTO is based on Aleister Crowley's Thelema – a philosophy that was "communicated" to him while inside an Egyptian pyramid. Like The Eye, the OTO primarily focuses on "real" magick and its near-scientific application. Crowley added the letter "k" at the end of magick to distinguish it from stage magic. Therefore, like The Eye, the OTO considers itself "keepers of real magic".

A documentary on the Eye shows its occult origin.

This is a page of the notepad of the researcher investigating the Four Horsemen. They Eye of Horus is one of the most important symbols of the Freemasons, OTO and the Illuminati. The use of this symbol in this movie was not random.

The symbol of the Eye of Horus is of the extreme importance for the OTO because the OTO is all about bringing about the Aeon of Horus – an era ruled by the Thelema. Is it surprising to see that, in this Aeon of Horus, mass media is literally flooded with the symbol of the Eye of Horus?

In the movie, one of the book used to research The Eye is called "The Guardians of Horus".

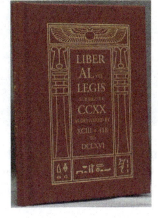

The layout of its cover closely resembles the cover of actual OTO books, complete with rectangular borders and a title in golden, embedded, capitalized letters.

Just like The Eye, the OTO exerts a great influence in Hollywood. One of its mission statements is to bring about Thelema and the Aeon of Horus to the masses. What better tool than mass media to do so?

Inside the Industry

As we witness the Four Horsemen rise to fame, we also see how the entertainment industry functions. For instance, there are a few allusions to the usage of mind control on various people.

This supposedly "randomly selected member of the audience" for a magic trick is actually a mind-control slave.

Thaddeus (the guy who attempts to debunk the Horsemen and the Eye) describes how this guy ended up on stage:

> "He was selected. Programmed his mind to make it to Las Vegas. And then they kept reinforcing it until he did. They trailed him. They studied him. Nothing was left to chance. He had no idea he was their target. And they simply activated him in Las Vegas."

This FBI agent (played by Common) starts playing an air violin after he hears the word "bullshit". We later learn that he was programmed by the magicians and that the word "bullshit" triggers him into playing air violin. This is a way of letting us know that law enforcement can also be programmed by the elite.

Another key aspect of the Illuminati industry is the use of ritual sacrifices in order to bring about transformation. The illusionist Jack Wilder was given the tarot card of Death at the beginning of the movie because he was chosen for a ritual sacrifice.

Jack, one of the Four Horsemen, dies (kind of) in a car crash – an event that is broadcast on live TV.

The event causes shock and brings sympathy towards the elite-backed magicians. We later discover that the car crash was a set up and that Jack is still alive – but the public doesn't know that. The event is an example of a ritual sacrifice played out on a mass scale by the occult elite. It was also a diversion.

The movie also shows what happens to those who fall out of the elite's good graces. Thaddeus, an ex-magician, now makes a career out of creating DVDs "debunking" magicians. When he goes against the elite-backed Horsemen, things do not end well for him. Thaddeus is framed by The Eye and thrown in jail.

When asking the police officer (who turns out to be part of The Eye) why this is happening to him, here's the reply.

> "The legend is that The Eye is everywhere. Waiting for the truly great magicians to distinguish themselves from the mediocre ones. Maybe that was you. Deep down inside you wanted nothing more than be part of The Eye, but you were never invited."

Duped?

As the movie progresses, it becomes obvious that the members of the Four Horsemen have no idea what's really going on. Like real life artists in the industry, they are mere puppets trying to fulfill the tasks given to them. They however know one thing for sure: They desperately want to be part of The Eye.

Once they complete their entire mission, the Horsemen meet up in Central Park.

The magicians are greeted by Dylan Rhodes, the FBI agent that was trying to arrest them during the entire movie ... *cough*... While this plot twist makes little to no sense, it does convey the meaning that The Eye own mass media AND law enforcement.

Rhodes tells the magicians "Welcome to The Eye" and brings them to a carousel that starts turning. The magicians mount on a little horsie and start spinning around. This leads us to think: Were the magician taken for a literal ride during the whole time? Does The Eye even exist?

Judging by the magnitude of the schemes the Horsemen were involved in, there is no doubt that a VERY powerful entity was behind them. However, like in real life, outsiders can never be part of the "inner-circle". While the Horsemen did everything required from them, they will never be part of the elite. This fact is reinforced in a semi-hidden scene at the end of the movie.

A few minutes after the credits roll out, there's a scene that I'm sure many people missed. It shows the ultimate fate of entertainers used by the occult elite.

The Horsemen are told to go to a place in the desert where old Las Vegas signs are thrown away. This neon sign graveyard pretty much represents their own career.

The magicians realize that the boxes stamped with the sign of The Eye are locked. The Horsemen do not have access to Eye-related privileges anymore.

Thinking that maybe their magical tarot cards might be able to unlock their crates, the magicians look in their pockets. Their tarot cards are gone. The Eye does not need these performers anymore so their pass was revoked. They were used and now they were thrown away in the desert amongst discarded neon signs.

So to answer questions many ask me: Are artists like Jay-Z actually part of the Illuminati? There's your answer.

The Big Picture

Throughout the movie, investigators ask themselves "Why do they go through all of this trouble"? Why do the magicians and, by extension The Eye construct these elaborate schemes? It makes no sense. And, to many viewers, the movie doesn't make sense. Most of the action is based around moronic police officers running around, pointing their guns, trying to catch smug-faced magicians. However, behind the action scenes and the loud music, there's a message there. The movie itself repeatedly tells the viewers: "The closer you look, the less you see". The closer you try to understand and make sense of the action going on screen, the less you see the "big picture".

Now You See Me is definitely not about a bank heist. It is about the "magic" of the entertainment industry. Crowley defined magick as "the Science and Art of causing Change to occur in conformity with Will". The goal of the entertainment industry is to cause change. But that change takes time … years, decades and generations. The movie describes the process in a very metaphorical matter.

The interpol agent researching The Eye describes the most famous trick of a magician named Lionel Shrike

> "When he was 14, he saw a hole in a tree in Central Park. He had a guy, who worked at the carousel, sign a card for what looked like a routine little trick. At the guy's retirement, 18 years later, Shrike performs, has the guy sign a card and presto! The card is in the tree. It was in the tree for 18 years. The trick was not to look closely. It was to look so far that you see 20 years into the past."

After the Horsemen completed all of their tasks, they were asked to meet at Shrike's tree because it represent what the Eye is all about. Just like the card inside the tree trick, the elite's transformative "magic" is about the long-term big picture.

At one point, Thaddeus says:

> "This is a magic trick played out on the global scale. And you are the abracadabra, the distraction".

While the viewers are hypnotized with explosions and car chases, they are missing the real magic: The elite transforming society to fit its needs through mass media.

Most of the "magic" we see during the movie is CGI. The entertainment industry is the real master of illusion.

The movie ends with a call from the Illuminati to the public, letting them know that they are the ones being duped by the real magicians.

> "Come in close. Closer. Because now you know our secret. We could be anywhere. Watching you. We're looking for someone to help us with our next trick. On the count of three, open your eyes and tell me what you see. One. Two …"

Fade to black…

In Conclusion

While there is absolutely nothing "realistic" about Now You See Me, it does aptly describe what actually happens in the entertainment industry. The magicians in the movie represent the various artists and performers that are recruited by the elite to advance its agenda. The Eye is based on actual secret societies that exert influence in Hollywood. While these facts might be crystal clear to some, most viewers probably miss these messages as they try to understand what the hell is going on.

In fact, during the entire time, the movie kind of laughs at the audience. At one point, a member of the Horsemen says: "The magician must be the most intelligent person in the room". The movie is so Hollywood that it is almost a parody of it. It is almost telling the viewers: "Look at the moronic stuff you're consuming to be entertained". But, behind it all, there's a powerful message coming straight from The Eye. Either you see it … or you don't.

The Esoteric Interpretation of the Movie "9": Heralding the Age of Horus

Tim Burton's "9" is a computer animated movie that was released on 9/9/09. While some critics claimed that the movie "lacked substance", it nevertheless conveyed powerful messages through symbolism. It even defines a "new age" for humanity as seen by occult secret societies. We'll look at the esoteric meaning of "9".

Warning: Gigantic spoilers ahead!

9 takes place in a dark, post-apocalyptic world where intelligent, self-reproducing machines destroyed all life on Earth. In this desolate setting, a small relic of humanity remains: Nine rag dolls animated by a scientist's soul. These dolls, however, are constantly targeted by the machines that are determined to eradicate anything resembling life on Earth. The dolls must therefore band together to fight and destroy these evil robots.

The above paragraph pretty much sums up the plot of 9 in its entirety – and that is probably what most viewers got out of the movie. However, like all works infused with an esoteric dimension, there is more to the movie than meets the eye. Through symbolism and references, the movie describes humanity as a whole and the transitional phase it is going through. More precisely, 9 describes the world as seen by occult secret societies and the "new age" they are all predicting: the Age of Horus or the Age the Aquarius.

Before we look at the movie, let's look at the occult philosophy behind it.

The Age of Horus

The occult elite believes that humanity needs to go through a period of great tribulation in order for it to "purge its impurities". According to occult writers, these "impurities" include traditional religions and governments as we know them. Manly P. Hall, a 33rd degree Freemason, describes what should happen in the next phase of humanity. We'll later see how this fits perfectly with the vision portrayed in 9.

> "The criers of the Mysteries speak again, bidding all men welcome to the House of Light. The great institution of materiality has failed. The false civilization built by man has turned, and like the monster of Frankenstein, is destroying its creator. Religion wanders aimlessly in the maze of theological speculation. Science batters itself impotently against the barriers of the unknown. Only transcendental philosophy knows the path. Only the illumined reason can carry the understanding part of man

upward to the light. Only philosophy can teach man to be born well, to live well, to die well, and in perfect measure be born again."
- Manly P. Hall, The Secret Teachings of All Ages

The most prominent occultist of the 20th century, Aleister Crowley, stated that the last 2,000 years were the "Age of Osiris". Osiris was the "king of the living and ruler of the dead" and his Age was characterized by strong governments and religions, notably Christianity's "emphasis on death, suffering, sorrow and the denial of the body". However, since the 20th century, Crowley claims that humanity entered the Age of Horus, who is the child of Osiris. In this phase, humans would learn to become their own gods.

> *"In plain language, the Aeon of Horus means that the Godhead is being passed down to the individual who needs to learn to activate and find the God-Within themselves. This latest Aeon sees the beginning of the end of Divine Power and authority being owned by kings, queens, religions, governments, big institutions and dictatorships, which will increasingly all begin to fail spectacularly. The individual will have the opportunity to become fully liberated, in charge of their own spiritual destiny."*
> - Paul Dunne, The Magic of the New Aquarian Age and the New Aeon of Horus

Through subtle symbolism, 9 describes the fall of authority (mainly the Christian Church) in an new era ruled by the Luciferian philosophy of obtaining godhood through one's own powers. Using rag dolls and very little dialogue, 9 describes the basis of this occult philosophy and shows how it will prevail.

The heroes of the movie are themselves the product of an ancient occult concept: They are homunculi, "little men" artificially created through a magical process. They are the epitome of man playing God and giving life.

Homunculi

Scientist creating 9, the last of the 9 homunculi that remain on Earth.

Homunculi (Latin for "little men") is a concept that can be found in several ancient alchemical documents. In Jewish folklore, the Golem, an animated anthropomorphic being created entirely from inanimate matter, is documented in the Talmud and the Sefer Yetzirah (there are even accounts of Kabbalist rabbis successfully animating such Golems).

For a brief moment, the movie acknowledges the occult roots of its premise. The title of the book, "Annuls of Percelsus", basically tells the viewers: "This movie is based on hermetic philosophy and alchemy". Paracelsus was one of the most renowned occultists of the Renaissance. His work in the field of Hermetism, alchemy and medicine are still thoroughly studied to this day, in practically all occult circles.

Movies and TV

Visible for about a half a second, the cover of this book explains the origins of the rag dolls and indicates the occult meaning behind the entire movie. You might recognize the ubiquitous symbol of the All-Seeing Eye inside a triangle. However, the title of the book is even more telling.

"In any matter of Realization and Ritual, Paracelsus is an imposing magical authority. No one has accomplished works greater than his, and for that very reason he conceals the virtue of ceremonies and merely teaches in his occult philosophy the existence of that magnetic agent which is omnipotence of will; he sums also the whole science of characters in two signs, the macrocosmic and microcosmic stars. It was sufficient for the adepts, and it was important not to initiate the vulgar. Paracelsus therefore did not teach the Ritual, but he practised, and his practice was a sequence of miracles."
- Eliphas Levi, Rituel de la Haute Magie

Paracelsus' work De natura rerum (1537) is the first alchemical work that mentions the creation of homunculi. It actually describes a technique to create a "little man" using horse dung and human sperm.

The concept of creating homunculi subsequently appeared in other seminal occult texts, such as the Rosicrucian work Chymical Wedding of Christian Rosenkreutz (1616) and Johann Wolfgang von Goethe's Faust, Part 2 (a German legend about a man making a pact with the Devil). More recently, Aleister Crowley and his followers were obsessed with the creation of a homunculus (Crowley used the term "Moonchild"). Crowley even added the creation of a homunculus as a "secret instruction" when one is initiated to the O.T.O's (an occult secret society) 10th degree.

With this reference, 9 therefore taps into a crucial part of Western Occultism.

19th century engraving depicting the creation of a homunculus from Goethe's "Faust part II"

In 9, the rag dolls read "Annuls of Peracelsus" and find a drawing documenting their creation. That drawing was probably inspired by the Faust engraving above.

In addition to the creation of homunculi, the movie also includes other parts of Paracelsus' research, such as the use of magically charged Talismans, a tool Paracelsus used to treat his patients.

Understanding that the backstory of 9 is steeped in ancient occultism gives the movie's storyline a specific color: It describes the world as seen by members of occult secret societies. The evolution of the characters in 9 tells it all.

The Characters

The heroes of the movie are nine rag dolls created by a scientist who infused his soul into them in order to give them life. He then died, along with the rest of humanity. Each one of the rag dolls embodies a part of the scientist's soul and personifies one of his traits. On a larger scale, each one of these rag dolls represents a group within humanity as a whole. The fate of each doll represents what occultists predict will happen in the Age of Horus.

1: The Pope

The rag dolls are named and numbered in the order they are created, so 1 is the oldest one of the bunch. His position of authority and his distinctive garments make him the leader of the group. Given his attire, it is quite clear that 1 represents the power and authority of the Catholic Church (and religions in general).

1 wears a cape and holds a scepter, symbols of power. On his hat is strapped a coin, symbolizing the wealth of the Church.

1 is stubborn, fearful, dogmatic, cowardly, and close minded. In short, he represents all of the Church's shortcomings as perceived by elite occult groups. In the first part of the movie, 1 forces all of the dolls to hide in a decrepit Cathedral, discouraging his followers to venture outside of it. He wants his followers to stay hidden and ignorant as he believes that it is the best way to stay alive.

As the movie progresses however, 1 loses his authority, his scepter and his cape. He even loses the coin on his hat. In this transitional period, 1 ultimately represents the fall of religions in the Age of Horus and their loss of power, wealth, and authority.

At one point, 1's Cathedral is attacked by one-eyed robots and burns down, forcing the group to hide in the Library instead. It is difficult to find a more telling image representing the fall of religions at the brink of a new era.

After the Cathedral burns down, the group hides in the Library. There they discover "Annuls of Peracelsus", an occult book describing the creation of the rag dolls. 1 is against the dolls reading this book.

When the dolls open up Peracelsus' book, 1 tears up the page describing their creation.

At one point 1 says:

"Dark Science. What does this useless rubbish do for us? Forget it!"

To which 9 replies:

- You know something. What do you know?"

1 answers:

- I know enough to leave their ancient evil to moulder. Look what they left us with."

Does this scene represent religious elites holding occult knowledge while forbidding their followers from seeking it? 1 is therefore exactly how secret societies perceive the Church and how they want the world to perceive the Church … in order to abandon it.

9: The Light Bearer

9 is the hero of the movie. Not unlike 1, he is also associated with an object that holds a heavy significance: A lightbulb on a stick.

The movie poster depicts 9 holding his electric torch. Note that the release date of the movie was 9-9-09, a nod to occult numerology and one of the movie's flirts with the number of the beast, 666.

"Prometheus Brings Fire" by Heinrich Friedrich Füger.

The Judeo-Christian version of Prometheus is Lucifer, which is a Latin word meaning "light-bearer". 9 represents the Mystery Schools' interpretation of Lucifer: A savior who "initiated" humanity to divine knowledge and opened a path to godhood (Lucifer gave Adam and Eve knowledge of good and evil).

While 1 apparently awaits a divine intervention to save the world, 9 represents the Promethean/Luciferian concept of attaining godhood through one's own means. In the end of the movie, 9 does just that and even brings life back on Earth.

In this movie that takes place in a transitional period of humanity – between the Age of Osiris and the Age of Horus – 9 symbolically represents the Luciferian principle overthrowing traditional religions … and saving the world.

Other Notable Characters

6 is a visionary obsessed with a symbol that turns out to be the talisman needed to save the dolls. If you look closely at 6's sketches, you might notice that they contain three 6s.

5 is an inventor who lost an eye. He actually says during the movie: "Actually I don't mind having one eye. It's easier for me. I can concentrate on one thing at a time., you know?" He is one of many nods to the one-eye signs throughout the movie. ALL of the evil robots in the movie also have one eye.

Here's an evil one-eyed robot.

Here's another evil one-eyed robot. In short, whether you're looking at the rag dolls or the robots, there's some one-eyed action going on. Is it a way of saying that the entire movie is a message from the occult elite?

3 and 4 are twins who serve as historian and archivist. 7 is a fearless warrior and the only female of the group. These three characters rejected 1's rule at the Cathedral and sought refuge at the Library, the place where all knowledge (including occult knowledge) is stored. When the Cathedral burns down, all of the dolls (including 1) hide in the Library. Once again, knowledge and courage are portrayed as the opposite of 1, the representative of religion.

A Purge to Save Humanity

The dolls flee the burning Cathedral and seek refuge in the Library, where 3, 4 (the historian and archivist) and 7 (the warrior) already live.

This part of the story is telling because it represents the "evolution" that occult secret societies want to see in the world. Ever since the time of the medieval Knight Templars, occult secret societies have accused the Church of stifling knowledge, science and progress. It is difficult to find an occult writer who doesn't extensively denounce the Church's role in censoring occult knowledge and punishing those who teach or practice it. The move from the Cathedral to the Library therefore represents the abandonment of religions for knowledge.

Moving to the Library is however not enough. The robots still find the dolls and attack them. In the end, sacrifices must be made and some elements must be "purged" in order for the group to survive.

The occult elite perceives the evolution of humanity as an ongoing alchemical process. The goal of alchemy is to turn crude metals into gold and it is believed that humanity needs to transform using the same process. The first phase of the alchemical Great Work is called Nigredo – blackening. This phase represents the process of burning, turning the base material into black ashes in order to break it down and remove its impurities. In 9, the world is definitely going through the Nigredo phase: It is dark, burnt down and in ruins.

9 creates a bonfire that will release the souls of 1, 2, 5 and 8. In the New Age, occultists believe some elements of humanity must be "purged". While they may have been useful during the previous period, they are now thought to be outdated.

The four dolls who remain alive to see the New Age are 9, 7, 3, and 4 ... coincidentally, the four who defied 1's rule. This is pretty much up the message of the entire movie.

The end of the movie is also extremely symbolic. 9 creates a bonfire in the shape of a five-pointed star to liberate the souls of the dolls who were killed by the robots.

After the bonfire, 7 asks 9:

> "What happens next?"

> "I'm not sure exactly. But this world is ours now. It's what we make of it".

Then it starts raining and we see living organisms in the drops of water. The purge has allowed life to be brought back to Earth and only the representatives of the Luciferian principle have survived.

In Conclusion

When one takes a first, superficial look at 9 and its promotional material, one is inclined to think that it is a children's movie, with a slightly darker feel. Critics summed up the movie as being "eye candy with little substance"They may have understood the in-your-face "too much technology is bad, m'kay" message, but its deeper, esoteric message was probably missed by most.

However, once one understands the background knowledge used to build the storyline, the occult references, and the movie's overarching philosophy, it is easy to see an entirely different dimension to the movie. 9 is about humanity going through a transitional period, embracing a Promethean/Luciferian savior, and destroying the rule of traditional powers, such as religion.

Aleister Crowley believes that this transitional period is now. He called this new age the Aeon of Horus. Horus was the child of Osiris and Isis and, for this reason, it is believed that humanity is currently taking the traits of a child. After finding the "Stele of Revealing" in an Egyptian museum (it was exhibit #666), Crowley wrote this about the coming New Aeon:

> "Horus rules the present period of 2,000 years, beginning in 1904. Everywhere his government is taking root. Observe for yourselves the decay of the sense of sin, the growth of innocence and irresponsibility, the strange modifications of the reproductive instinct with a tendency to become bi-sexual or epicene, the childlike confidence in progress combined with nightmare fear of catastrophe, against which we are yet half unwilling to take precautions.
>
> Consider the outcrop of dictatorships, only possible when moral growth is in its earliest stages, and the prevalence of infantile cults like Communism, Fascism, Pacifism, Health Crazes, Occultism in nearly all its forms, religions sentimentalized to the point of practical extinction. Consider the popularity of the cinema, the wireless, the football pools and guessing competitions, all devices for soothing fractious infants, no seed of purpose in them. Consider sport, the babyish enthusiasms and rages which it excites, whole nations disturbed by disputes between boys. Consider war, the atrocities which occur daily and leave us unmoved and hardly worried. We are children."

- Aleister Crowley, Book of the Law on the New Aeon / Age of Horus

This is what 9 is about. But there is one question the movie doesn't answer: Is humanity organically entering this phase of History or is it being forced and provoked by the powers that be in order for it to achieve its own "Great Work"?

Movies and TV

THE HIDDEN MEANING OF THE MOVIE "CORALINE"

Coraline is a popular stop-motion movie released in 2009. While the film appears to be aimed at young people, Coraline's imagery tells a hidden story: The programming of a mind control slave at the hands of a sadistic handler. We'll look at the hidden meaning of the movie Coraline.

Warning: Gigantic spoilers ahead!

Coraline was the first animated movie released by Focus Pictures, the same company that later released 9, another animated movie with a dark underlying meaning. However, unlike 9, Coraline received rave reviews and almost universal praise for its story and visuals. Part of the movie's appeal is its simple, child-friendly premise interlaced with twisted imagery and psychological depth. And, for those who know about Mind Control symbolism, the movie goes even deeper: It symbolically depicts the process of programming of a mind control slave at the hands of a manipulative handler.

In fact, the very first scene of the movie is basically a "Mind Control 101" summation of the entire process. It shows a pair of creepy metallic hands transforming an old doll into a new one. If one examines this scene closely, "with eyes to see", it symbolically (and creepily) depicts how MK slaves are taken, traumatized, and programmed by a handler–represented throughout the movie by a metallic hand.

The creepy hands of an unseen creep are about to get to work on this doll (which represents an MK slave).

Its clothes are removed using scissors (a reference to abuse?)

The insides are forcibly removed (representing the removal of the slave's core persona?)

The doll is then refilled by the handler and made to look like Coraline. The creation of the alter persona is symbolically complete.

The first scene of the movie sums up what will happen during the entire movie: The programming of a young girl by a sadistic handler. Before going into the details of the movie, let's look at its general premise.

The Premise

Coraline is a little girl who moved into a new house with her parents. She is constantly bored and unhappy and her parents do not give her the attention she wants. While exploring her new house, Coraline finds a small door that leads to an alternate version of her reality where her parents are fun and attentive and where everything is magical and wonderful. In this sense, the premise of Coraline is similar to stories such as The Wizard of Oz, Alice in Wonderland and Labyrinth. All of these movies, including Coraline, follow the same basic blueprint: 1) The protagonist is a young girl that is curious, fearless, resourceful, and not afraid to speak her mind; 2) She is bored with her life and wishes for fun and adventure; 3) She magically enters a world that is strange, but wonderful; and 4) She gets "hooked" into the alternate world and doesn't want to go back to reality.

For this reason, these story are used as programming tools in actual Mind Control sessions. These storylines encourage slaves who are being tortured to escape the trauma by dissociating from reality and entering an alternate reality (programmed by the handler). By doing so, the brain "disconnects" from the body and the sensation of pain disappears. While watching The Wizard of Oz, slaves are told to "go over the rainbow" and while watching Alice in Wonderland, they must "walk through the looking glass". Coraline follows a similar script as the protagonist goes through a small door to access the "wonderful" alternate reality. This world is everything Coraline wishes for, but there is one small hiccup: It is fake, created by a sadistic handler to manipulate her. Let's look at the movie's protagonist.

Coraline

Coraline is voiced by Dakota Fanning, a child star (she was about 15 years old when working on Coraline) who has appeared in other MK-themed movies (see my article on Hide and Seek). The character appears to have a "magical" side. At the beginning of the movie she is shown practicing the ancient occult activity of dowsing or "water witching".

Coraline looking for a secret well using her dowsing rod. Because of this, her friend Wybie will call her a "water witch".

A water witch or dowser, redrawn from a sixteenth-century woodcut.

Later in the movie, Coraline's father calls her a "twichy, witchy girl" while singing to her. Throughout the movie, magical, supernatural things happen around her. However, we later discover that these things are traps meant to lead Coraline to her handler. All of these scenes allude to the witchcraft aspect involved in MK programming.

At one point, Wybie gives Coraline a strange gift: A doll that looks just like her.

In MK symbolism, dolls represent the slave's alter persona. Coraline will call this doll "Little Me".

Coraline brings this dolls everywhere she goes. However, sometimes, the doll appears to lure Coraline to places where her handler wants her to go: The alternate world or, in MK terms, dissociation.

Coraline finds a small locked door in her house. When her mother unlocks it, the door leads nowhere.

However, at night, Coraline is "magically" lead back to the door and she finds out that it leads to an alternate reality.

The Other World

When Coraline goes through the door, she enters back into her house – but everything is slightly different.

Coraline finds her "Other Mother" who is warmer, more attentive and a better cook than her real mother. Also, she has buttons instead of eyes. The symbolism of buttons instead of eyes is extremely important in this movie: it illustrates that the characters in the alternate world are puppets fabricated by the handler. It is later revealed that the Other Mother is the handler in disguise.

Everything in the Other World is tailor-made to charm Coraline and to fulfill her needs (which are the needs of all children): Receiving attention from parents, having fun and discovering wonderful things. The handler therefore knows exactly which "buttons to push" to get a positive response from Coraline. Knowing that Coraline is upset with the disgusting food of her real parents, the Other Mother projects the warm and comforting sight of a mother preparing a home cooked meal for her family.

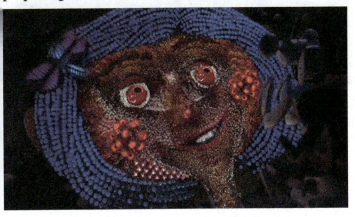

In the Other World, Coraline's father created an entire garden that looks like Coraline's face when seen from above. This is another way to win over Coraline, by tapping in children's need of being the center of the world. Everything is made especially for her and everything is made to make her feel special.

As expected, Coraline realizes that she likes it better in the Other World. But things get creepy very quickly. While, at first, the movie caters to everything children like, it then turns to everything that scares children (many parents reported that this seemingly child-friendly movie terrified their children and gave them nightmares).

The Other Mother asks Coraline to stay with her forever. To do so however, Coraline must let the Other Mother sew buttons over her eyes.

Coraline's other parents proposing her to sow buttons on her face. Notice the two horned (Baphomet-like) heads in the background. They are prominently lit to emphasize the black magic/occult transformation of the MK process happening in the alternate world. These horned heads are not there in the kitchen of the real world.

The Other Parents ominously call Coraline "our little doll" and tell her that "soon you will see things our way". Sewing buttons onto her eyes means that she would permanently become the handler's puppet, who would then, as the movie states, "devour her soul". In MK terms, she would lose control of her core persona by staying stuck in the dissociative world created by her handler (the equivalent of devouring her soul).

The concept of eyes (and the lack thereof) is extremely important in this movie, as it is in actual MK Programming symbolism. While the occult elite represents itself with the All-Seeing Eye, Mind Control is represented by removing eyes – causing the slave to lose sight of reality. When Coraline refuses the button deal, the Other Mother gets angry and we see her true form.

The illusion of the Other World is broken. Coraline sees the true form of the other mother, a skeletal spider-like monstrosity. When MK slaves give in to dissociation, the "relief" it causes at first quickly turns into a nightmare.

Coraline is then locked in a room where she finds the ghosts of other kids who became the handler's slaves. In this scene, the ghosts are hiding one eye while asking Coraline to find their eyes, the only way their souls will be freed.

The three ghosts call the Other Mother "Beldam", which means "ugly, evil-looking old woman". The word also resembles the term Grand Dame, the title given to important women in the Illuminati mind control system.

> "An Illuminati Grande Dame will assist the programmers to insure that the proper script is given to the child and that a psychotic break doesn't occur causing the victim to lose their mind."
> - Fritz Springmeier, The Illuminati Formula to Create a Mind Control Slave

Not so coincidentally, the Beldam in Coraline basically plays the role of a Grand Dame in mind control programming.

> "A close loving bond is needed between a child and the initial abuser so that a clean split is created when the initial mind-splitting trauma is carried out. The clean split occurs when the child is confronted with two irreconcilable opposing viewpoints of someone who is important to them. The child can't reconcile the two extremely opposite views of the same person, one being a loving caretaker, and the other being the worst kind of abuser. The person the child trusted the most is the person the child fears the most. Some professional therapists have come to realize that this is how the core is split."
> - Ibid.

In Monarch Mind Control, the Grand Dame is one of the three people that assist in the programming of young slaves. Like in Coraline, the Grand Dame is somewhat of a (twisted) mother figure.

> "As a child of the Illuminati progressed through its programming, three people had oversight over its programming: its Grande Mother, its Grande Dame, and the Programmer."
> - Ibid.

Throughout the movie, Coraline is told that there is "only one key" that can open and lock the door to the alternate world – and the Beldam desperately wants it. This key represents access to Coraline's psyche. Either Coraline has control of it or the Beldam does. For this reason, there is "only one key".

In her quest for freedom, Coraline is not alone. She is helped by a strange character.

The Black Cat

A nameless black cat becomes Coraline's guide and mentor throughout her journey.

The black cat first appears to Coraline while she's "water witching" at the beginning of the movie. In European folklore, black cats were believed to be witches' "familiars"- spirits who aid and protect them while they accomplish their magical work. In Coraline, the black cat basically plays the same role and becomes vital to her succeeding.

While the cat appeared to Coraline in the real world, he also appears in the Other World – and with no buttons on his eyes. Furthermore, when in the Other World, the cat can speak with her. The cat also seems to know a lot about the Beldam and the world she created. While the black cat appears to be of great help, he also tends to lead Coraline into Beldam's traps.

In this scene, the black cat shows Coraline how the Other World is a fake construct created by the Beldam to lure Coraline. In MK terms, the black cat is showing Coraline the confines of the dissociative world.

In this scene, the Black Cat leads Coraline back to the portal to the Other World, causing her to dissociate again.

So is the black cat helping or manipulating Coraline? The very end of the movie might provide an answer.

After some adventuring, Coraline saves the ghosts by finding their eyes and destroying Beldam's constructed world. She then throws the key to the Other World (which represents her psyche) down the magical well she found while water-witching. Coraline then happily goes back to her real world and tries to make the best of real life. Her family organizes a party in their garden – the same garden that was made to look like Coraline in the Other World. As the view of the garden pans out, observant viewers might realize something odd.

The garden is shaped like the face of Beldam.

While many viewers probably did not notice this almost-subliminal tidbit, it has a heavy meaning. It represents the Beldam imprinting Coraline's forever – even if she was apparently defeated.

In fact, was the Beldam truly defeated? Was Coraline actually manipulated by the cat? Was throwing the key to her psyche down that well a good move? Can the Beldam now "trigger" Coraline back into her world whenever she needs to? Like in other MK-themed movies (such as Labyrinth), while the final scene of the movie appears to be a celebration, the celebration is dampened by creepy little details that hint that all might not be "well and good".

The movie ends with the black cat magically disappearing behind a pole.

Does the cat magically disappear because his job as a guide is complete? Or his job as a programmer is complete? It's not clear.

In Conclusion

While, at first glance, Coraline appears to be a cautionary tale about appreciating what you've got and not falling for things that are too good to be true, the movie's dark and twisted imagery hints to deeper concepts. As proved by the number of screenshots used in this article, the movie contains a wealth of subtle symbols that tell their own story, one that is laced with occultism and the dark process of Monarch mind control.

The entire movie is based on the symbolism of a menacing hand (representing the handler) manipulating a young girl, luring her into a world created to appeal to her psyche. When Coraline escapes (dissociates) to the Other World, the concept of buttons replacing eyes represent the illusory nature of this world and the blindness of those trapped in it. In the end, Coraline appears to vanquish her foe but, as subtle symbolism suggests, she might have simply done exactly what was expected from her all along.

This movie, which features visuals based on the comforting feel of arts and crafts, nevertheless alludes to mind control, the most sadistic practice known to man. In short, it is deception at its finest. As it is the case with many other works in mass media, Coraline's hidden meaning can only be understood by those who have "eyes to see". Unfortunately, most people still have buttons.

The Esoteric Meaning of the Movie "Prisoners"

"Prisoners" is a 2013 thriller film about the abduction of two girls in Pennsylvania. Behind this crime story is an underlying spiritual subtext and subtle symbolism that gives the movie another layer of meaning – one that comments on religion, morality and the hidden forces at play in society. This article will look at the esoteric meaning of "Prisoners".

Warning: Gigantic spoilers ahead!

Prisoners is the kind of movie that stays in your mind long after the ending credits roll. This is not only due to its gripping, dramatic story but to the spiritual subtext that underlies it all. As the film unfolds and the crime investigation progresses, esoteric concepts and symbolism are also introduced, giving the movie an entirely new dimension. What appears to be a story about the abduction of two little girls turns into a profound spiritual journey of humans facing adversity and finding themselves lost between good and evil, right and wrong, and morality and immorality.

Prisoners takes place in an average American town, Conyers, Pennsylvania during the time of Thanksgiving. The grey, gritty and unglamorous setting of the movie allows the characters to shine through, as the story is driven by their pains, struggles and dilemmas. Through the background and evolution of each character, the movie comments (and sometimes condemns) some aspects of American society. Some items that are touched upon: Christianity, "preppers", secret societies and mind control. Let's look at the most important characters of the movie.

Keller Dover, the Father

Played by Hugh Jackman, Keller Dover is a family man, a devout Christian and a "prepper" – someone who maintains a massive stockpile of various goods in his house in case of a major disaster. He is also very patriotic, for example, his favorite song is Star Spangled Banner. While not specifically stated in the movie, Keller somewhat has the profile of a Libertarian or close to the Tea Party movement. However, we quickly realize that in the context of this movie, these traits are far from helpful. In fact, they pretty much lead him to his downfall.

In the very first scene of the movie, Keller Dover recites a prayer right before his son shoots a deer. This sets the awkward tone of the movie where religion is associated with the death of an "innocent animal".

Keller Dover is a "Jesus fish on the truck" and "cross hanging from the mirror" kind of guy. To make things more Jesus-related, Keller is a carpenter.

We also quickly learn that Keller is a "prepper". On the way back from hunting, Keller gives his son the same advice his father gave him:

> "Be ready. Hurricane, flood, whatever ends up being. No more food gets delivered to the grocery store. Gas stations dry up. People just turn on each other. All of a sudden, all that stands between you and being dead ... is you."

Keller's basement is a well-organized stockpile of food, tools, weapons and even gas masks.

Although there is nothing wrong or illegal about stockpiling items in one's basement, people around Keller act weirdly about it. We get the feeling that it is a taboo subject. When the detective visits Keller's basement and discovers his "prepper" secret, Keller immediately becomes a suspect. In short, the movie communicates the idea that this type of person is suspicious and not trustworthy.

Upon learning that his little girl has probably been abducted, Keller becomes distraught. As the movie progresses, his desperation turns into madness and Keller kidnaps a guy whom he believes is the culprit and proceeds to torture him.

Although Alex Jones kind of looks and acts like a child molester, we find out that he is innocent. Even worse, it turns out that he himself was abducted as a child and his odd behavior is the result of years of mind control that impaired his intellectual development (he has the IQ of a ten year old boy). The name choice of Alex Jones is interesting because, as many of you might know, it is also the name of the "conspiracy" radio host who promotes the "prepper" movement, constitutionalism and other elements Keller Dover probably agrees with. However, in the movie, Alex Jone's name is associated with a mentally deficient boy who gets beaten up by Keller. Is this a way to "diss" Alex Jones and the people who agree with him?

Whatever the case may be, by kidnapping and torturing Alex Jones, Keller only further traumatizes an already-damaged person.

Going further into madness, Keller builds a custom torture chamber where Alex is confined in a little dark space and is occasionally showered with scolding hot water.

For the rest of the movie, all we see of Alex is one eye (perhaps representing his perpetual state of mind control), lighted by the hole in his chamber.

So, instead of helping authorities find his daughter or even comforting his family, Keller lashes out at an innocent person and becomes a kidnapper himself.

While Keller's actions may have stemmed from a noble purpose, he distinctly crosses the boundary between right and wrong. This conflict is further emphasized when Keller turns to prayer to find strength and, perhaps, answers. At one point, during a torture session, Keller recites the Lord's Prayer:

> "...and forgive our trespasses as we forgive ..."

But he stops at the point where he is supposed to say "those who trespass against us" - indicating that he cannot live up the Christian ideals described in the prayer he is reciting.

In short, Keller reacted to his daughter's abduction in a violent matter, stubbornly focusing on a sole (innocent) person. Instead of providing comfort or seeking actual facts about his daughter's abduction, Keller relied on instinct mixed with ignorance and anger. Through Keller's response to the family crisis, the movie does not shine a favorable light on the "religious, patriotic, prepper" profile. Far from being prepared for disaster, Keller became paranoid, irrational, and prone to madness. Furthermore, behind his "good Christian" surface hides an infinite "stockpile" of anger, hate and rage.

Luckily, the detective in charge of the investigation is the exact opposite of Keller.

Detective Loki

Unlike Keller Dover, Detective Loki is rational, methodical, and never strays away from the law. He does not appear to have any kind of family and is portrayed as a loner dedicated to his job. Despite receiving constant verbal abuse from Keller, Loki stays focused on his task and manages to save pretty much everyone involved in this drama.

Loki is the name of a Norse god known to be crafty, quick-witted and sometimes heroic. He is also known to be a trickster, a shape-shifter who eventually turns against the gods. Does Detective Loki share traits with the Norse god he's named after? It does symbolically represents the anti-thesis of the monotheistic, Judeo-Christian beliefs of Keller Dover. Furthermore, Loki definitely uses his intellectual powers to achieve his aims.

While Keller is associated with Jesus fishes and crosses, Loki is covered in occult symbols:

Detective Loki's Masonic ring is clearly displayed throughout the movie. It is most visible during scenes where he is researching clues or reflecting on what is happening. Loki represents the Masonic ideal of obtaining truth through one's own means and intellect.

On his right hand are tattooed astrological symbols which are also extremely important in occult Mysteries.

On his neck is tattooed an eight-pointed star. In occult symbolism, this is known as the Star of Ishtar, a Babylonian goddess associated with the planet Venus.

In short, Loki is associated with the rationality and enlightenment claimed by occult secret societies. In this sense, he is the opposite of the irrational, emotion-based Keller.

Merely through the varied symbolism associated with the characters of Keller Dover and Detective Loki, the movie criticizes the "religious prepper" type while glorifying members of secret societies. But Keller is not the only negative representative of Christianity in the film. While going through a list of sex offenders living in the area,

Detective Loki ends up visiting a local priest … and finds him passed out on the floor, drunk. Then Loki finds a dead body in his basement (although it's the body of a child abductor).

Prisoners also features another poor representative of Christianity: Holly Jones, the kidnapper.

Holly Jones the Child Abductor, Mind Control and the War on God

Holly Jones stands next to an ironic painting of an angel watching over two children.

Toward the end of the movie we learn that Holly Jones (Alex Jones' "aunt") is the one who kidnapped the two little girls. She claims that she and her late husband used to be devout Christians and that they used to drive around "spreading the good word". However, since they lost their son to cancer, they turned against God. She tells Keller:

> "Making children disappear is the war we wage on God. Makes people lose their faith. Turns them into demons like you".

As we learn about the modus operandi of the Jones couple, we discover that they use basic mind control techniques on the children: They drug the captives, traumatize them by throwing them in dark holes and subject them to crazy mind games. This system is represented with one important symbol: the maze.

The Maze

The symbol of the maze is extremely important throughout the movie. It represents the system that abducts children and, more importantly, the state of mind control these children are forced to live in.

Detective Loki observes a picture of Holly's late husband who is wearing a maze pendant.

On this maze book is written "Finish all the mazes and you can go home". This is given to the abducted children to mess with their minds.

After days of torture, Alex Jones finally says to Keller: "I am not Alex Jones", implying that he was abducted by Holly and that he was given an alter persona. When Keller asks him where the kidnapped children are, Jones replies: "They're in the maze. That's where you'll find them." Of course, Jones does not refer to an actual maze but to the state of mind control the children are subjected to.

Later, Detective Loki finds a suspect named Bob Taylor who acts in bizarre matter and who was also a victim of Holly Jones. He stayed at her house for three weeks and was drugged with a LSD/Ketamine drug cocktail, which is classic a mind control technique. Bob managed to escape from the house, but while Bob is free, his mind is definitely not. We quickly realize that he is still "stuck in the maze".

Bob's house is covered with never-ending mazes.

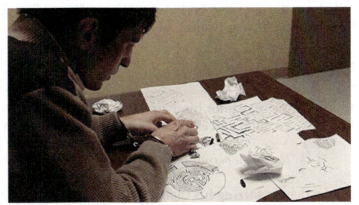

While being interrogated by the police, Bob obsessively draws mazes which he claims are "maps" to the kidnapped children.

While Bob's "maps" do not actually lead to the physical location of the children, it leads to their psychological state: Trapped in the mind control maze of their handler. In actual mind control, mazes are an important trigger image that accurately represents a slave's mind state. "Maze maps" are programmed into the victim's internal world to keep them from accessing their core/true personality.

Bob tries to help the police, but his damaged mind does not allow him to give out actual information. When Loki gets aggressive during interrogation and asks for specific answers, Bob says "I can't ..." and kills himself. Actual MK slaves are often programmed to commit suicide in these types of situations.

As Loki examines Bob's house, he discovers that Bob is completely obsessed with the child abductors and their tactics (he recreates child abductions using dummies as a hobby). While searching Bob's stuff, Loki finds a book that appears to be written about the Jones.

At Bob's house, Loki examines a book called "Finding the Invisible Man" which was written by an ex-FBI agent.

According to Loki's colleague, the book is about a "theoretical suspect believed to be responsible for a bunch of child abductions". He adds that the book was "totally discredited". The last page of the book contains an unsolvable maze, which was used by the Jones' as a sick game to traumatize children.

While the book was discredited, "The Invisible Man" appears to accurately describe the Jones and their system of mind control. However, one can ask: Do the Jones work for a higher organization? Is "The Invisible Man" actually the MK Ultra system of the occult elite? Does the fact that the book was discredited imply that powerful people covered up that story?

Whatever the case may be, the movie has a "happy" ending: The children are rescued and returned to their family. So who is the true prisoner?

The Prisoner

In his frantic search for his daughter, which leads him to kidnap and torture Alex Jones, Keller Dover crosses the line between good and evil. He tries to justify his actions by claiming:

> *"He's not a person anymore. He stopped being a person when he took our daughters."*

But by dehumanizing his captive in that manner, Keller stooped to the same level as the child abductors. He became one of them.

Later, when Keller realized that his daughter was at Holly Jones' house, he rushed there in order to torture her. However, Holly had a gun and forced him to jump in a dark hole. Instead of saving his daughter, Keller is thrown in the same hole his daughter was previously trapped in.

Therefore, Keller himself turns into a captive. After a period of moral tribulation, his time in the dark hole can represent his spiritual death, and can be compared to the three days spent by Jesus Christ in his tomb before being resurrected. In ancient occult secret societies, candidates for initiation were held in darkness for several days to represent the death of their "old self" before they were "spiritually reborn".

Guess who ultimately saves Keller from the hole? Detective Loki. In a sense, Loki is Keller's savior, the one who frees him from spiritual death and toward a second life. Loki, a representative of Masonic-like occult secret societies, is therefore portrayed as the one who pulls Keller, along with his irrational and hypocritical fervor, out of the hell he put himself into.

While Loki probably saved his life, Keller will nevertheless have to go to prison for the crimes he committed. In the end, there's only one true prisoner in the movie: Keller Dover.

In Conclusion

Through the characters of Keller Dover and Detective Loki, Prisoners comments on specific elements of society, casting them in either a favorable or unfavorable light. Keller is a family man that is religious, patriotic, and prepared for disaster. While at first, he appears to be the hero of the story, he somewhat turns into a "bad guy". The attributes that positively defined him in the beginning turn into gigantic flaws causing him to become irrational, sadistic and paranoid. The one who saves the day is Detective Loki, a character literally covered in occult symbolism, hinting that the way of secret societies is the "true light". Loki's enlightened ways ultimately give Keller a chance to be reborn.

Prisoners' narrative and treatment of its characters reflects the direction of mass media today. The Keller Dovers of this world, who are either openly religious, patriotic, or prepared for disaster, are often deemed suspicious and prone to negative action. The values represented by Keller Dover are increasingly being frowned upon by mass media. Are these traits not desirable in the America of the New World Order? In an America where fundamental rights and freedoms are being slowly and steadily revoked, people like Keller Dover are the most likely to take action about it. And the elite does not want that. Perhaps that is why the Department of Homeland Security creates training videos portraying "constitutional, patriotic militias" as terrorist groups. Perhaps they want to find a way to turn them, like Keller, into prisoners.

SECTION 4
SINISTER SITES

Encoded within buildings and monuments, the elite's philosophy is told in symbols and hidden in plain sight.

Sinister Sites: The Georgia Guidestones

The Georgia Guidestones is a mysterious monument on which are carved ten "commandments" for a "New Age of Reason". The first commandment? Maintaining the world population under 500 million people. Another sinister fact: the authors of what we now call the American Stonehedge are still a "mystery"... except for those in the know. We will look at the numerous features of this monument, its message calling for a New World Order and explain how it is the work of an occult secret society.

The Georgia Guidestones is an enigmatic granite monument situated in Elbert County, Georgia. Also known as the American Stonehedge, the gigantic structure is almost 20 feet high and is made of six granite slabs, weighing in total 240,000 pounds. The most astonishing detail of the monument is however not its size but the message engraved into it: Ten rules for an "Age of Reason". These guides touch upon subjects that are associated with the "New World Order", including massive depopulation, a single world government, the introduction of a new type of spirituality, etc. The authors of those rules have requested to remain totally anonymous and, until now, their anonymity has been duly preserved. However, this mysterious group left a text explaining the reasoning behind the rules, a text that was not discussed online before. With this new information, the purpose behind the Guidestones become very clear, leaving little room for hypotheses. The Guidestones describe the ideal world, as envisioned by occult Secret Societies. The monument is therefore proof of an existing link between secret societies, the world elite and the push for a New World Order.

The Monument

Made of Pyramid blue granite, the Georgia Guidestones are meant to withstand the test of time and to commu-

Quietly standing in Elberton county, the Guidestones will probably gain in relevancy in the next years

nicate knowledge on several levels: philosophically, politically, astronomically, etc. It consists of four major stone blocks, which contain ten guides for living in eight languages: English, Spanish, Swahili, Hindi, Hebrew, Arabic, Chinese, and Russian. A shorter message is inscribed at the top of the structure in four ancient languages' scripts: Babylonian, Classical Greek, Sanskrit, and Egyptian hieroglyphs. It is important to note that those last four ancient languages are of a great importance in the teachings of occult mystery schools, such as the Freemasons and the Rosicrucians, organizations I will discuss later.

The four major stones are arranged in a giant "paddlewheel" configuration which are oriented to the limits of the migration of the sun during the course of the year and also show the extreme positions of the rising and setting of the sun in its 18.6 year cycle. The center stone has two special features: first, the North Star is always visible through a special hole drilled from the South to the North side of the center stone; second, another slot aligns with the positions of the rising sun at the time of the summer and winter solstices and at the equinox.

At the base of the Guidestones lies an explanatory tablet listing some of the details of the structure. It also mentions a time capsule buried underneath it. The contents of this time capsule (if it exists) are a total mystery.

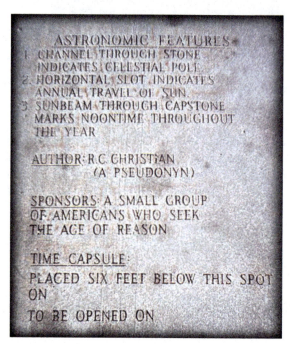

The explanatory tablet explains some of the features of the monuments and its authors (more on them later). The opening date of the time capsule has been left blank.

Astronomical features are of a great importance in the design of the Guidestones. In a relatively "new" nation such as the United States, monuments that are aligned with celestial bodies are often the work of secret societies, such as the Freemasons. Drawing their teachings from the Mystery schools of Ancient Egypt, Greece or the Druidic Celts, they are known for embedding into monuments some of their "sacred knowledge".

The 10 Commandements

The ten guides for a new Age of Reason are as follows:

1. Maintain humanity under 500,000,000 in perpetual balance with nature.
2. Guide reproduction wisely – improving fitness and diversity.

3. Unite humanity with a living new language.
4. Rule passion – faith – tradition – and all things with tempered reason.
5. Protect people and nations with fair laws and just courts.
6. Let all nations rule internally resolving external disputes in a world court.
7. Avoid petty laws and useless officials.
8. Balance personal rights with social duties.
9. Prize truth – beauty – love – seeking harmony with the infinite.
10. Be not a cancer on the earth – Leave room for nature – Leave room for nature.

As you can see, the guidelines call for a drastic reduction of the world population, the adoption of new a world language, the creation of a world court and a vague allusions to eugenics. In other words, a blueprint for a New World Order.

DEPOPULATION, PLANNED PARENTHOOD AND EUGENICS

The first "commandment" is particularly shocking, since it basically stipulates that 12 out of 13 people on Earth should not exist; basically, that would mean everybody in the world would disappear except half of India. If today's world population is 6,7 billion, then that is a 92.54% surplus. To consider these figures is mind-boggling. But then, how many people survived in the movie 2012? Not many. Who were they? The earth's wealthiest people. Is this predictive programming?

The last rule of the Guidestones, "Be not a cancer on the earth – leave room for nature – leave room for nature" is particularly disturbing as it compares human life to cancer on earth. With this state of mind, it is easy to rationalize the extinction of nearly all of the world's population.

Massive depopulation is an admitted goal of the world's elite and many important people have openly called for it:

In 1988, Britain's Prince Philip expressed the wish that, should he be reincarnated, he would want to be "a deadly virus" that would reduce world population. More recently, Bill Gates said "The world today has 6.8 billion people ... that's headed up to about 9 billion. Now if we do a really great job on new vaccines, health care, reproductive health services, we could lower that by perhaps 10 or 15 percent." Along with tax-deductible donations of enormous amounts of money to help the depopulation cause, "secret meetings" of the world's elite have been taking place to discuss those issues:

> "Some of America's leading billionaires have met secretly to consider how their wealth could be used to slow the growth of the world's population and speed up improvements in health and education.
>
> The philanthropists who attended a summit convened on the initiative of Bill Gates, the Microsoft co-founder, discussed joining forces to overcome political and religious obstacles to change.
>
> Described as the Good Club by one insider it included David Rockefeller Jr, the patriarch of America's wealthiest dynasty, Warren Buffett and George Soros, the financiers, Michael Bloomberg, the mayor of New York, and the media moguls Ted Turner and Oprah Winfrey."
> - The Sunday Times, May 24th 2009

The second rule ("Guide reproduction wisely – improving diversity and fitness") basically calls for the inference of lawmakers into the management of family units. If we read between the lines, it requires to creation of laws structuring the number of children per family. Furthermore, "improving diversity and fitness" can be obtained with "selective breeding" or the sterilization of undesirable members of society. This used to be called "eugenics", until it became politically incorrect because of the Nazis.

ONE WORLD GOVERNMENT

> "Some even believe we are part of a secret cabal working against the best interests of the United States, characterizing my family and me as 'internationalists' and of conspiring with others around the world to build a more integrated global political and economic structure – one world, if you will. If that's the charge, I stand guilty, and I am proud of it."
> - David Rockefeller, "Memoirs of David Rockefeller" p.405

Most of the other rules of the Guidestones basically call for the creation of a world government, ruled by an "enlightened few", who would regulate all aspects of human life, including faith, social duties, economy, etc. This idea is far from new, as it has been entertained by Mystery schools for centuries. Manly P. Hall wrote in 1917:

> "When the mob governs, man is ruled by ignorance; when the church governs, he is ruled by superstition; and when the state governs, he is ruled by fear. Before men can live together in harmony and understanding, ignorance must be transmuted into wisdom, superstition into an illumined faith, and fear into love. Despite statements to the contrary, Masonry is a religion seeking to unite God and man by elevating its initiates to that level of consciousness whereon they can behold with clarified vision the workings of the Great Architect of the Universe. From age to age the vision of a perfect civilization is preserved as the ideal for mankind. In the midst of that civilization shall stand a mighty university wherein both the sacred and secular sciences concerning the mysteries of life will be freely

taught to all who will assume the philosophic life. Here creed and dogma will have no place; the superficial will be removed and only the essential be preserved. The world will be ruled by its most illumined minds, and each will occupy the position for which he is most admirably fitted."
- Manly P. Hall, The Secret Teachings of All Ages

In "The Secret Destiny of America", Hall explains the ancient dream of a world government, as entertained by Secret Societies:

"World democracy was the secret dream of the great classical philosophers. Toward the accomplishment of this greatest of all human ends they outlined programs of education, religion, and social conduct directed to the ultimate achievement of a practical and universal brotherhood. And in order to accomplish their purposes more effectively, these ancient scholars bound themselves with certain mystic ties into a broad confraternity. In Egypt, Greece, India, and China, the State Mysteries came into existence. Orders of initiated priest-philosophers were formed as a sovereign body to instruct, advise, and direct the rulers of the States."
- Manly P. Hall, The Secret Destiny of America

Explanations Directly from the Anonymous Authors

Since the monument's erection on March 22, 1980, numerous authors and researchers have attempted to interpret the rationale behind these ten guidelines. Do they truly consist of a blueprint for a New World Order? Are they simply rules to apply in case of a major catastrophe? The best place to get an accurate answer is to ask the authors of the rules themselves. However, since they have chosen to remain anonymous, it is impossible to do so. They did, however, leave an all-important statement, which has been overlooked by nearly all researchers of the Guidestones. This astonishing text, which describes their motives in great detail, can only be found in The Georgia Guidestone Guidebook, a pamphlet produced by the Granite Company, which produced the monument. Right from the start, it is obvious that the authors of the monument do seek the creation of a New World Order. This is not a "conspiracy theory" or hypothesis. It is written in clear and unequivocal terms. So here is, directly from the pen of the secret authors, the explanation of the 10 rules of the Guidestones (parts in bold have been highlighted by myself, to emphasize noteworthy parts).

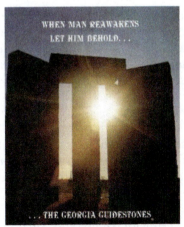

Cover of the Georgia Guidestones Guidebook

"It is very probable that humanity now possesses the knowledge needed to establish an effective world government. In some way that knowledge must be widely seeded in the consciousness of all mankind. Very soon the hearts of our human family must be touched and warmed so we will welcome a global rule of reason.

"The group consciousness of our race is blind, perverse, and easily distracted by trivia when it should be focused on fundamentals. We are entering a critical era. Population pressures will soon create political and economic crisis throughout the world. These will make more difficult and at the same time more needed the building of a rational world society.

"A first step will be to convince a doubting world that such a society is now possible. Let us keep in view enduring appeals to the collective reason of humanity. Let us draw attention to the basic problems. Let us establish proper priorities. We must order our home here on earth before we reach for the stars.

"Human reason is now awakening to its strength. It is the most powerful agency yet released in the unfolding of life on our planet. We must make humanity aware that acceptance of compassionate, enlightened reason will let us control our destiny within the limits inherent in our nature.

"It is difficult to seed wisdom in closed human minds. Cultural inertias are not easily overcome. Unfolding world events and the sad record of our race dramatize the shortcomings of traditional agencies in governing human affairs. The approaching crisis may make mankind willing to accept a system of world law which will stress the responsibility of individual nations in regulating internal affairs, and which will assist them in the peaceful management of international frictions.

"With such a system we could eliminate war, We could provide every person an opportunity to seek a life of purpose and fulfillment.

"There are alternatives to Armageddon. They are attainable. But they will not happen without coordinated efforts by millions of dedicated people in all nations of the earth.

"We, the sponsors of The Georgia Guidestones®, are a small group of Americans who wish to focus attention on problems central to the present quandary of humanity. We have a simple message for other human beings, now and in the future. We believe it contains self-evident truths, and we intend no bias for a particular creed or philosophy. Yet our message is in some areas controversial. We have chosen to remain anonymous in order to avoid debate and contention which might confuse our meaning, and which might delay a considered review of our thoughts. We believe that our precepts are sound. They must stand on their own merits.

"Stonehenge and other vestiges of ancient human thoughts arouse our curiosity but carry no message for our guidance. To convey our ideas across time to other human beings, we erected a monument — a cluster of graven stones. These silent stones will display our ideas now and when we have gone. We hope that they will merit increasing acceptance and that through their silent persistence they will hasten in a small degree the coming age of reason.

(...)

"We believe that each human being has purpose. Every one of us is a small but significant bit of the infinite. The celestial alignments of the stones symbolize the need for humanity to be square with External principles which are manifest in our own nature, and in the universe around us. We must live in harmony with the infinite.

"Four large stones in the central cluster are inscribed with ten precepts, each stone carrying the same text in two languages. In the English version the message totals fewer than one hundred words. The languages have been selected for their historical significance and for their impact on people now living. Since there are three thousand living languages, not all could he chosen.

"We envision a later phase in the development of the Georgia Guidestones®. It is hoped that other *stones can be erected in outer circles to mark the migrations of the sun and perhaps certain other celestial phenomena. These stones would carry our words in the languages of other individuals who share our beliefs and will raise similar stones at international boundaries in the languages of friendly neighbors. They would serve as reminders of the difficulties which all humanity must face together, and would encourage mutual efforts to deal with them rationally and with justice.*

"*We profess no divine inspiration beyond that which can be found in all human minds. Our thoughts reflect our analysis of the problems confronting humanity in this dawning of the atomic age. They outline in general terms certain basic steps which must be taken to establish for humanity a benevolent and enduring equilibrium with the universe.*

"*Human beings are special creatures. We are shepherds for all earthly life. In this world, we play a central role in an eternal struggle between good and evil–between the forces which build and those which would destroy. The Infinite envelops all that exists, even struggle, conflict and change, which may reflect turmoils in the very soul of God.*

"*We humans have been gifted with a small capacity to know and to act– for good or for evil. We must strive to optimize our existence, not only for ourselves but for those who come after us. And we must not be unmindful of the welfare of all other living things whose destinies have been placed in our trust.*

"*We are the major agency through which good and evil qualities of the spirit become actors in our world. Without us there is very little of love, mercy, or compassion. Yet we can also be agents of hate, and cruelty and cold indifference. Only we can consciously work to improve this imperfect world. It is not enough for us to merely drift with the current. The rational world of tomorrow lies ever upstream.*

"*In 1980, as these stones were being raised, the most pressing world problem was the need to control human numbers. In recent centuries technology and abundant fuels have made possible a multiplication of humanity far beyond what is prudent or long sustainable. Now we can foresee the impending exhaustion of those energy sources and the depletion of world reserves of many vital raw materials.*

"*Controlling our reproduction is urgently needed. It will require major changes in our attitudes and customs. Unfortunately, the inertia of human custom can be extreme. This is especially true when those for whom custom is a dominant force are uninformed of the need for change.*

"*Nearly every nation is now overpopulated in terms of a perpetual balance with nature. We are like a fleet of overcrowded lifeboats confronted with an approaching tempest. In the United States of America we are seriously overtaxing our resources to maintain our present population in the existing state of prosperity. We are destroying our farmland and we have grown dangerously dependent upon external sources for oil, metals and other nonrenewable resources. Nations such as Japan, Holland and Haiti are even more seriously overpopulated and, therefore, in greater jeopardy.*

"*In these circumstances, reproduction is no longer exclusively a personal matter. Society must have a voice and some power of direction in regulating this vital function. The wishes of human couples are important, but not paramount. The interests of present society and the welfare of future generations must be given increasing consideration as we develop mechanisms to bring rational control to our childbearing.*

(…)

"*Irresponsible childbearing must be discouraged by legal and social pressures. Couples who cannot provide a decent income and support for a child should not produce children to be a burden for their neighbors. Bringing unneeded children into an overcrowded lifeboat is evil. It is unjust to those children. It is harmful for the other occupants and all living things. Society should not encourage or subsidize such behavior.*

"Knowledge and techniques for regulating human reproduction are now in existence. Moral and political leaders throughout the world have a grave responsibility to make this knowledge and these techniques generally available. This could be done with a fraction of the funds which the world now devotes to military purpose. In the long run, diverting funds into this channel could do more than anything else to reduce the tensions which lead to war.

"A diverse and prosperous world population in perpetual balance with global resources will be the cornerstone for a rational world order. People of good will in all nations must work to establish that balance.

(...)

"With the completion of the central cluster of The Georgia Guidestones our small sponsoring group has disbanded. We leave the monument in the safekeeping of the people of Elbert County, Georgia.

"If our inscribed words are dimmed by the wear of wind and sun and time, we ask that you will cut them deeper. If the stones should fall, or if they be scattered by people of little understanding, we ask that you will raise them up again.

'We invite our fellow human beings in all nations to reflect on our simple message. When these goals are some day sought by the generality of mankind, a rational world order can be achieved for all."

Who Are the Authors?

So who was is this "small group of Americans who seek the Age of Reason"? Although their identity is secret, they have left some telling clues to the initiates, unmistakably pointing towards the occult nature of their group. For starters, the text above bares the unmistakable mark of western occultism. We can find references to "As Above, So Below" (The celestial alignments of the stones symbolize the need for humanity to be square with External principles which are manifest in our own nature, and in the universe around us) and to duality (We are the major agency through which good and evil qualities of the spirit become actors in our world. Without us there is very little of love, mercy, or compassion. Yet we can also be agents of hate, and cruelty and cold indifference). I believe this text alone provides enough proof to conclude that the authors are either Freemasons, Rosicrucians or another hermetic Secret Society. There are however even more obvious clues pointing to the esoteric leanings of the authors, starting with R.C. Christian, the mysterious man who ordered the monument.

The unveiling of the Georgia Guidestones. Could one of these people be the mysterious R.C. Christian?

R.C. Christian

Here is the story of the ordering of the Guidestones as told by the official guidebook.

> "What started out as a usual Friday afternoon in mid-summer has ended in the production and erection of one of the world's most unusual monuments, produced under the most unusual conditions. Joe Fendley, president of Elbert Granite Finishing Company, Inc. in Elberton, Georgia, was spending this Friday afternoon in June 1979 like he spends most Friday afternoons … studying his weekly reports and generally closing up shop for a weekend … and then it all started.
>
> A neatly dressed man walked into Fendley's Tate Street office and said he wanted to buy a monument. Since everyone else in the office was busy, Fendley decided to talk to the stranger himself and explained that his company does not sell directly to the public, but only on a wholesale basis.
>
> Not to be discouraged, the middle-aged man who identified himself only as Mr. Robert C. Christian, said he wanted to know the cost of building a monument to the conservation of mankind and began telling Fendley what type of monument he wanted. With this he outlined the size in metric measurements.
>
> Fendley admitted that his first reaction to Mr. Christian was not very good, but after listening for about 20 minutes and learning the massive size of the monument he wished to purchase and have erected, Fendley decided he should take this man seriously."
> - Ibid.

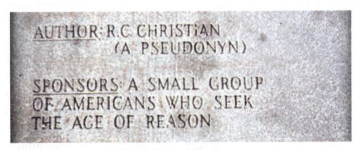

The name of R.C. Christian on the explanatory tablet with a nice typo in "pseudonyn"

If the name R.C. Christian was simply a meaningless pseudonym, why would it engraved on to the monument for posterity? Could the name be of any significance? Well, it is. R.C. Christian is a clear reference to Christian Rosenkreuz whose English name is Christian Rose Cross, the legendary founder of the Rosicrucian Order. Some might say that the resemblance between R.C. Christian and Christian Rose Cross is the result of an odd coincidence. As we will see, it is however only one of the MANY references to Rosicrucianism associated with the monument. This is only one piece of the puzzle, but an important piece nonetheless.

The Rosicrucians

The Rosicrucians are known for publishing three Manifestos, published at the beginning of the 17th century: Fama Fraternitatis Rosae Crucis, Confessio Fraternitatis and Chymical Wedding of Christian Rosenkreutz.
These anonymous works, surrounded by mystery, cryptically introduced the general public to the Rosicrucian philosophy, while announcing a great transformation of the political and intellectual landscape of Europe. The Age of Enlightenment soon followed, accompanied with the fall of feudal Monarchies. The Georgia Guidestones seem to accomplish the same functions as the Rosicrucian manifestos, by calling for an important world transformations and maintaining a climate of mystery.

Seeking entry into the Rosicrucian mysteries. Notice the candidate is showing the hand sign of secrecy. Also notice the letters "RC", as in R.C. Christian.

The Age of Reason

There are numerous references to the concept of "Age of Reason" within the Guidestones. Could they be a reference to the classic work of Thomas Paine entitled … Age of Reason?

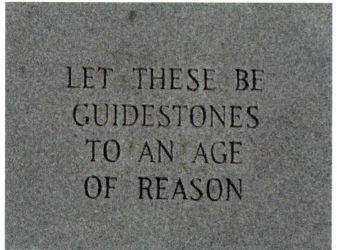

Does "Age of Reason" refer to Thomas Paine, a prominent Rosicrucian?

The Age of Reason: Being an Investigation of True and Fabulous Theology, is a deistic treatise written by eighteenth-century British radical and American revolutionary Thomas Paine. The work critiques institutionalized religion and challenges the inerrancy of the Bible. Its tenets advocate reason in place of revelation, a viewpoint that is obviously shared by the authors of the Guidestones.

It is a known fact that Thomas Paine was a leading member of the Rosicrucian Fraternity in America.

> "The Rosicrucian Fraternity existed in America prior to the First American Revolution. In 1774, the great Council of Three (the Fraternity's ultimate governing body) was composed of Benjamin Franklin, George Clymer and Thomas Paine."
> - The Fraternitas Rosae Crucis, soul.org

In The Secret Destiny of America, Manly P. Hall describes Thomas Paine as an important crusader for the march towards an ideal world government.

> "Of Thomas Paine it has been said that he did more to win the independence of the colonies with his pen than George Washington accomplished with his sword, Only complete reorganization of government, religion, and education would bring us even today to the perfectionist state Tom Paine

envisioned".
- Manly P. Hall, The Secret Destiny of America

This thinly veiled to Thomas Paine is another piece of the Rosicrucian puzzle, which leads me to believe that the authors were either Freemasons (who have incorporated Rosicrucian teachings into their degrees) or members of the Rosicrucian fraternity.

Furthermore, as if to make things more obvious, the Georgia Guidestone booklet mentions that Joe H. Fendley Sr., the president of Elberton Granite, as well as many other people involved with the building of the monument, were Masons. Was this the reason of the selection of these men by the anonymous sponsors of the monuments?

> *"Fendley is also involved in fraternal activities. Raised a Master Mason in 1958, he is now a member of Philomathea Masonic Lodge #25 in Elberton, is a York Rite and Scottish Rite 32° Mason, and was admitted in the Yaarab Shrine Temple in Atlanta in 1969. He was President of the Savannah Valley Shrine Club from 1972 through 1973. The Potentate of the Yaarah Shrine Temple awarded Fendley the "Divan Degree of Distinction" in 1973, and appointed Ambassador in 1975."*
> - The Georgia Guidestones Guidebook

In Conclusion

The Georgia Guidestones are a modern day Rosicrucian manifesto calling for (or announcing) a drastic change in the way the world is managed. The monument is of a great importance in the understanding of the forces covertly shaping today and tomorrow's world. It materializes into stone the crucial link between secret societies, the world elite and the agenda for a New World Order. The push for a world government, population control and environmentalism are issues that are today discussed on a daily basis in current events. They were not in 1981, when the Guidestones were erected. Can we say that great progress was made?

Many of the rules of the Guidestones do make sense for the preserving of Earth on a long-term basis. But between the idealistic words of the Guidestone's authors and the actual way these policies would be applied on the masses – by power-hungry and greedy politicians – there is a world of difference. Reading between the lines, the Guidestones require from the masses the loss of many personal liberties and to submit to heightened governmental control on many social issues … not to mention the death of 92.5% of the population…and probably not those of the "elite". Is the concept of a democracy "by and for the people", as idealized by the Founding Fathers a mere illusion, a temporary solution until the introduction of socialist world government? Why are the world's citizens not being consulted in a democratic matter? I guess it is easier for the elites to manufacture consent through mass medias.

Sinister Sites – Israel Supreme Court

The Israel Supreme Court is the creation of one elite family: the Rothschilds. In their negotiations with Israel, they've agreed to donate the building under three conditions: the Rothschilds were to choose the plot of land, they would use their own architect and no one would ever know the price of its construction. The reasons for those conditions are quite evident: the Supreme Court building is a Temple of Masonic Mystery Religion and is built by the elite, for the elite.

Built in 1992, the Israel Supreme Court sits in Jerusalem, in front of the Knesset (Israeli legislature). Its peculiar architecture has earned critical praise due to the architects' opposition of old versus new, light versus shadow and straight lines versus curves. Almost all critics and journalists have however omitted to mention the blatant occult symbols present all over the building. Masonic and Illuminati principles are physically embodied in numerous instances, proving without a doubt who runs the show in there.

House of the Rothschilds

The Rothschild family is an international dynasty of Germans of jewish descent who established a worldwide banking and finance operation. The offsprings of Mayer Amschel Rothschild (1744-1812) have spread all over Europe and became major actors in the social, political and economic life of the continent. By knitting close ties with the elite of England, Austria, France and Italy, the Rothschilds became a hidden force in most political events of the last centuries. Alternative historians say they are part of the infamous 13 bloodlines of the Illuminati, along with the Rockefellers and the Duponts.

The Rothschilds are one of the originators of the Zionist movement and the most active actors in the creation of the state of Israel. James A. de Rothschild financed the Knesset, Israel's main political building. Right in front of it sits the Israeli Supreme Court, donated by another member of the dynasty: Dorothy de Rothschild.

Painting at the entrance of the Supreme Court – The Rothschilds with Shimon Perez and Isaac Rabin

In the same general area of Jerusalem we can therefore find the Knesset and the Supreme Court, built by the Rothschilds and, following a perpendicular layline, several blocks away, sits the Rockefeller Museum (other elite family). You might start to understand who owns this area now.

Jerry Golden wrote several years ago on the Israeli Supreme Court, appropriately pointing out its occult concepts. When you study those types of buildings, you quickly realize that the same themes inevitably reappear: illumination, pyramid, ascent, the number 13 or 33 , phallic/yonic symbols, etc. This building has it all and more.

Path to Illumination

A journey through the Supreme Court is in fact a symbolic course towards Illumination. The ultimate "goal" of the journey is to reach the top of the pyramid which is located on the roof of Supreme Court, atop of an area where the "holy of holies" would be in a Jewish Temple.

On each side of the pyramid's apex is a hole representing the "All-Seeing Eye" of the masonic Great Architect (see the reverse of the Great Seal of the United States).

Pyramid with All-Seeing Eye

Let's go through the path of the "profane" to reach illumination.

Darkness to Light Stairway

One who enters the Supreme Court finds himself in a dark area, in front of a stairway leading to a source of light.

By climbing those stairs, the visitor gradually leaves the depths of darkness to finally reach glorious sunlight. There are exactly three times 10 steps, totaling 30. They represent the 30 first degrees of Freemasonry, where the profane is gradually taken from the depths of material life (darkness) to wisdom and illumination (light). We know that Freemasonry comprises a total of 33 degrees and we'll later see where we can find those last three degrees in the structure. On the right side of the stairs are old rocks reminiscent of walls of ancient Jerusalem while on the left is a smooth and modern wall. This represents the timeless nature of occult teachings, who have been transmitted since ancient times to this day.

Once having climbed the stairs the visitor can admire a great view of Jerusalem. In a symbolic way, the enlightened person gained "spiritual sight". Embedded on the floor is a layline, guiding the traveler to the entrance of the library, which is conveniently placed right under the pyramid.

The Library

The second floor of the library

The library is divided in three levels, symbolically representing the last three degrees of Freemasonry (31st, 32nd and honorary 33rd) . The first level is reserved for lawyers, the second is reserved for judges and the books on the third level can only be read by retired judges. The library's way of functioning – where some information is the exclusive privilege of a selected few – directly correlates with the functioning of occult orders, where teachings of a certain degree can only be given if the initiates have successfully cleared the previous degrees.

The three levels of the library

The library contains legal, judicial, philosophical and spiritual works. There is no doubt that the "reserved" books contain a wealth of esoteric knowledge. Right above the higher level of the library (representing the 33rd level of Masonry) is the base of the pyramid. This is where Freemasonry symbolically ends and the hidden order of the Illuminati begins.

View of the pyramid from inside

Right under the apex of the pyramid, on the floor, we can find patterns of sacred geometry

Jerry Golden has mentioned that a crystal is embedded right in the middle of the pattern, right under the eye of the pyramid. What does it signify?

Judges Bringing Illumination

The entrances of the courtrooms are said to resemble ancient Jewish tombs. The holes atop the doors are meant to permit the soul to leave the room. Also notice the contrast between old and new.

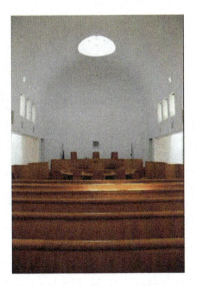

Courtroom

The prison cells, the courtroom and the judge's quarters are placed one on top of the other, symbolizing the threefold nature of the world. The inmates are stuck in cells, symbolizing the the lower material world. The courtrooms, placed right over the prison cells, represent the "higher world" where divinity gets in touch with humanity.

In the courtrooms, the judges are illuminated by a natural source of light. So the judges, hearing the pleads of the masses sit there with divine light constantly shining upon them. After the hearings, the judges retire to their quarters, situated right over the courtroom. They symbolically "ascend" to the divine world. When a decision is taken, they "descend" to bring illumination to the lower world.

Fertility Symbol

Outside the courtrooms is a stairway leading to a lower level. No occult temple would be complete without those next two features.

In the middle of the stairway is the shape of a vesica piscis (representing female genitals) "penetrated" by a column (phallic symbol). This is an obvious fertility symbol, a union of the male and female principles. Numerous occult temples insert a fertility symbol in their lower floor (see Washington Capitol). But wait, there's usually a rotunda along with the fertility symbol. Oh, there it is.

Some occult buildings hide the star of Ishtar (fertility symbol) at the center on the lower rotunda. Is hidden there?

Outside

The exterior of the Supreme Court contains loads of symbolic features. Just follow the "Dorothy de Rothschild" stone to see where it leads you.

OBELISK

This is the Dorothy de Rothschild grove. The obelisk is the most commonly used and the most blatant occult symbol used throughout the world. In ancient Egypt, the cult of this phallic symbol was associated with the god Osiris, who was cut in 13 pieces by Seth. Isis traveled far and beyond to retrieve all of Osiris' body parts and was successful, except for one body part, the penis, which was swallowed by a fish. "The lost phallus" is thus representative of male energy, and is almost always placed (as in this case) inside a circle, which represents female genitalia and energy. The obelisk in the middle of a circle represents the sexual act and the union of opposite forces. In our modern world, obelisks are found on nearly all important landmarks, and thus became and symbol of the occult elite's power.

COURTYARD

The courtyard has beautiful zen-like feel. A source of water is constantly bubbling and streaming through a narrow path towards a strange stone. Official Supreme Court documentation say that the courtyard is a physical representation of the verse from Psalm 85:11:

> *"Truth springs from the earth, And righteousness looks down from heaven"*

The judge's offices overlook the courtyard, so they are symbolically "looking down from heaven". The stream of water goes straight and ends up right under a strange and enigmatic stone.

What is this thing and why is "truth who sprung from earth" leading towards it? The stone's polished surface reflects a distorted image of the courtyard. What does it represent?

Trampled Cross

At the center of the parking facilities are pathways shaped like Christian cross. Jerry Golden has mentioned that this cross has been specifically placed to be trampled on by visitors. He is most probably right. In a building where spiritual symbolism reigns supreme, there are effectively little chances that the layout of those pathways haven't been thoroughly thought out by the architects. In other words, this can't be just a coincidence. The visitors have to go down the stairs – symbolically "descend" to lower spheres – to reach the cross. As you might have noticed, the importance of the act of ascending and descending in this building is very important. This is not an exception.

Occult secret societies have historically been at odds with the Christian church who repeatedly persecuted and accused them of all sorts of heresies. During the Middle-Ages the Knights Templar (ancestors of Freemasonry) have been accused by the Archbishop of Canterbury of numerous anti-Christian deeds, including "trampling the Cross under foot" during their initiation processes. Are they poking back at Christianity with this symbol?

Pomegranates

These pomegranates placed on the floor might seem extremely insignificant to the average onlooker. They however hold a special signification for students of the Mysteries and of Freemasonry.

> "Among the ancient Mysteries the pomegranate was also considered to be a divine symbol of such peculiar significance that its true explanation could not be divulged. It was termed by the Cabiri "the forbidden secret." Many Greek gods and goddesses are depicted holding the fruit or flower of the pomegranate in their hands, evidently to signify that they are givers of life and plenty. Pomegranate capitals were placed upon the pillars of Jachin and Boaz standing in front of King Solomon's Temple; and by the order of Jehovah, pomegranate blossoms were embroidered upon the bottom of the High Priest's ephod"
> - Manly P. Hall, Secret Teachings of All Ages

As stated by Hall, pomegranates were placed on top of the two pillars standing in front of Solomon's Temple. If you have minimal knowledge of Masonic teachings, you know that the Temple of Solomon and the pillars named Jachin and Boaz are of an utmost importance.

> "The capitals were enriched by pomegranates of bronze, covered by bronze net-work, and ornamented with wreaths of bronze; and appear to have imitated the shape of the seed-vessel of the lotus or Egyptian lily, a sacred symbol to the Hindus and Egyptians."
> - Albert Pike, Morals and Dogma

We know that the Masons patiently look forward to the day they'll rebuild the Temple of Solomon on its original grounds – Temple Mount, Jerusalem. Are those pomegranates waiting to be placed on the pillars of the next Temple?

In Conclusion

This article barely scratches the surface of the occult symbolism of the Israeli Supreme Court. It is however clear that the building's architecture carries important symbolism relating to spirituality and the attainment of illumination. There are no religious monuments relating to Judaism or any organized religion. The Supreme Court is a temple of the Mysteries, which are an amalgamation of pagan rituals interlaced with an esoteric interpretation of the Scriptures. The teaching of the Mysteries is reserved to members of occult secret societies, which the Rothschilds are obviously part of. The esoteric meaning of this building is concealed from the public but it unmistakably reveals to the initates who possesses real power in the world.

Sinister Sites – The Denver International Airport

An apocalyptic horse with glowing red eyes welcoming visitors? Check. Nightmarish murals? Check. Strange words and symbols embedded in the floor? Check. Gargoyles sitting in suitcases? Check. Runways shaped like a Nazi swastika? Check. OK, this place is evil.

But seriously, there are so many irregularities surrounding the DIA, that a voluminous book could be written on the subject. The facilities and the art displayed lead many observers to believe that the DIA is much more than an airport: it is literally a New-Age cathedral, full of occult symbolism and references to secret societies. The art at the DIA is NOT an aggregation of odd choices made by people with poor taste, like many people think. It is a cohesive collection of symbolic pieces that reflect the philosophy, the beliefs and the goals of the global elite. The DIA is the largest airport in America and it has cost over 4.8 billion dollars. Everything regarding this airport has been meticulously planned and everything is there for a reason.

The Airport

The airport facilities themselves raised a ton of questions regarding the true purpose of the mega-structure. Numerous "creative" theories are floating around the DIA regarding underground military bases, aliens and/or reptilian creatures. While I'm aware that anything is possible, we will stick to the documented facts.

The airport was built in 1995 on 34,000 acres. Its construction forced the Stapleton International airport to shut down, although it used more gates and runways than the DIA. The initial cost of construction was 1.7 billion $ but the final project elevated the bill to 4.8 billion: 3.1 BILLION $ over budget. Numerous irregularities have been reported regarding the construction of the site:

Different contractors have been hired for different parts of the airport. They've all been fired after their job was done. This lead observers to believe that it was a strategy to make sure nobody had the full scope of the project.

- 110 million cubic yards of earth have been moved, way more than usually required. This arose suspicion of construction taking place underground.

- 5300 miles of fiber optics were installed for communications (USA coast to coast is 3000 miles in comparison).

- Fueling system that can pump 1000 gallons of jet fuel per minute. This amount is totally absurd for a commercial airport.

- Granite imported from all over the world even if the project was already grossly over budget.

- Construction of a huge tunnel system (trucks can circulate in them) and underground trains. Most of those aren't used at the moment.

Analysis of the data available makes me reach at least one conclusion: this gigantic structure will eventually become much more than a regular commercial airport. It has the capacity to handle a huge amount of people and vehicles, leading observers to think that the structure might be used as military base and others even add that it will be used as a civilian concentration camp in the near future. I will not advance on this subject because I do not have proof of those claims. I however would understand why such plans would be top secret. Let's look at the soothing, traveler-friendly art on display at the DIA.

Horse of the Apocalypse

So this is what welcomes you when you enter the gates of hell…sorry, I meant the gates of the airport. A 32 foot high fibreglass stallion with veins popping out of its whole body and demonic eyes that glow red. Nice. I heard the children love it. Interesting fact: the horse killed his creator, Luis Jimenez, while he was working on it. A portion of the sculpture came loose and smashed him, causing fatal injuries. His friends now say that the horse is cursed.

What does it represent? The 1st thing that came to mind when I saw this horrendous piece (for an aiport anyways) is: the Pale horse of the Apocalypse. It is the fourth horse in the book of Revelation in the Bible and is appropriately called "Death".

> "And I looked, and behold a pale horse;
> and his name that sat on him was
> Death, and Hell followed with him. And

*power was given unto them over the
fourth part of the earth, to kill with
sword, and with hunger, and with
death, and with the beasts of the earth".*
- Revelation 6:7-8

In other words, the horse "Death" brought killing with weapons, with hunger, and with disease. That's pretty extreme a family airport, right? Doesn't seem like that horse should be there. You will soon realize that it fits perfectly with the rest of the DIA. By the way, this is one scary horse anus!

2- Masonic Capstone

The stone is situated in the "Great Hall" of the airport (term that is also used by masons to refer to their meeting hall). There's Freemason symbols on the stone and on the "keypad" which seems to be written in braille. Notice on the capstone the mention "New World Airport Commission". This particular commission does not exist, so it most likely refers to the New World Order. There is also a time capsule buried under the stone to be opened in 2094.

Prophetic Murals

Divided into four walls, the murals painted by Leo Tanguma are supposed to represent peace, harmony and nature. But I'm not getting these messages at all. When you analyze the symbolism of the murals, you realize that they tell a terrifying story of future events about to happen, as if it was some sort of prophecy. There are specific social and political references and other occult details that basically turn those paintings into a New World Order manifesto. Tanguma reportedly confirmed that he was given guidelines for the paintings and was paid 100 000$ for the first ones. He later denied he was given instructions and refuted any questions regarding hidden meanings in his paintings. Previous Leo Tanguma murals were typical Chicano art, politically charged and community oriented. However, his work at the DIA sends a totally different "vibe", giving me the gut feeling that he simply drew someone else's vision. Let's look at the paintings one by one:

1) "Peace and Harmony with Nature"

So the airport's official website says that the name of the mural is called "Peace and Harmony with Nature". Really? At the center of the piece, saddened children with extinct animal and plant species. In the background, a forest on fire and further back, a city on fire.

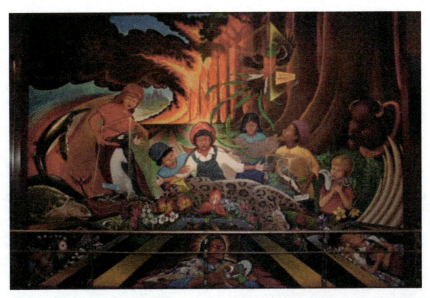

An interesting fact about that city is that it has been retouched and painted over many times during the years, as if it represents something important for the creators. It seems surrounded by an ill colored haze, as if it was attacked by a bio-chemical weapon. One of the children holds a Mayan tablet depicting the end of civilization.

At the bottom, of this peaceful painting, we see three open-caskets containing dead girls from different cultures. Left is a Black woman, center is a Native woman. Why are they laying there with the other animals? Are we predicting the extinction of those races? We already know that the military has developed race-specific chemical weapons. Here's what the Project for New American Century (PNAC), a think tank that defines the foreign and defence policy of the US has to say about this:

> "... the art of warfare ... will be vastly different than it is today ..."combat" likely will take place in new dimensions ... advanced forms of biological warfare that can "target" specific genotypes may transform biological warfare from the realm of terror to a politically useful tool."

The girl on the right holds a Bible and a yellow "Juden" star used by the Nazi to identify jews. It seems to symbolize the death of Judeo-Christian beliefs. The group at the origin of the imagery of this airport are definitively NOT Christian or Jewish. Secret societies have their own belief system that is way too complex to explain here. I can however tell you that caskets are an important part of masonic symbolism as you can see in the next image depicting the main symbols of freemasonry. Tombs are also a big part of the Skull and Bones' rituals.

2) CHILDREN OF THE WORLD DREAM OF PEACE

The 2nd mural is a two part piece. We read from left to right, so I will analyze it from left to right.

Children of all colors, dressed in folkloric costumes give weapons wrapped in their country's national flag to a... German boy? Huh? Yes the Bavarian costume leaves no doubt. The boy at the center of the image, holding the hammer and apparently building something is German. Even the American kid (dressed as a boyscout) seems eager to give his weapons and flag to the German boy. You're in the largest airport of America, in the middle of the USA, and this is the mural we display. America joyfully submitting to Germany. It's just too odd to compute. This obviously represents countries of the world giving up their military might and their national identity for "the common good". Another reference to a New World order, with one government and one army.

But why is the German boy at the center of everything? There are so many allusions to Germany and Nazism in this airport, there is NO WAY it can be a coincidence. I can't help but to think of "Operation Paperclip", which brought prominent Nazi scientists and researchers to the USA after WWII. Laying at the bottom of the mural is a broken figure holding a riffle (representing war) with two doves sitting on top of it (representing peace). Heartwarming. Now follow the movement the of the rainbow that starts underneath that statue, going around the children and leading you to part II of the mural (which has recently painted over).

The monster has awakened! This big and aggressive militaristic figure is dressed in a Nazi uniform (notice the symbol on the hat) with a face shaped like a gas mask. His hands are holding a rifle and a scimitar that is rather violently molesting the peace bearing dove. On the left is depicted an endless lineup of crying parents holding their limp, dead baby. This is a truly atrocious painting, with no redeeming message or moral. The fact that this was displayed at the main gate of the largest airport of America, during the age of political correctness (the nineties) is totally aberrant. The militaristic figure is glorified and all-powerful, situated at the center of the action. It has regained its powers that it seemed to have lost after WWII. It is back in full force and its leading the way to a new holocaust.

Look closely at the people on the left and the dead children sleeping on bricks. There is no traces of violence on them. They're simply devoid of life, as if they were poisoned by the deadly gas emanating from the rainbow above them. The monster, protected by his gas mask, is pointing the lineup of victims towards the letter on the bottom left.

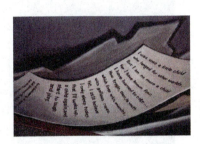

It is an actual letter written by a Hama Herchenberg, 14 years old, that died December 18, 1943 in Auschwitz Concentration camp (as written at the bottom of the letter). A little disturbing isn't it. Auschwitz was infamous for it use of toxic gas.

> *The camp commandant, Rudolf Höß, testified at the Nuremberg Trials that up to 3 million people had died at Auschwitz, about 90 percent of whom were Jews. Most victims were killed in Auschwitz II's gas chambers using Zyklon B.*
> - Wikipedia

The presence of a colorful rainbow and a teddy bear in this image, symbols our minds instantly associate with youth and innocence, is totally sickening and twisted.

3) Peace and Harmony with Nature

What do you do when you've killed most of the world population with toxic gas? You celebrate around a genetically-modified-glowing plant of course! Happy people from all over the world irresistibly heading towards that plant, some are almost flying towards it. Right above this plant (that doesn't exist in real life) is a Jesus-like figure but is definitively not Jesus.

All of the extinct species of the 1st mural are all back in action and you even see a little dove appearing in the plant. How nice. They feel so much better now that there's much less people on earth now. The animals are happy too and they thank you for dying. People can now use high levels of scientific knowledge to live in a state of synthesized happiness provided by genetically modified plants. Good for them. The whales are jumping in the air, high-fiving humans. If you look closely at the baby tigers, they have faces of human children. Its it quite bizarre. This whole piece reeks of genetic modification and magick.

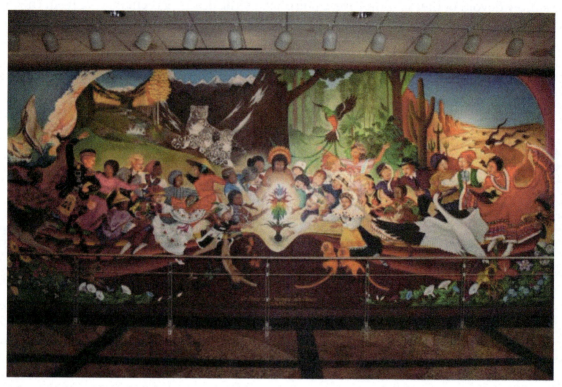

To sum up, those murals clearly depicted admitted goals you can read in documents calling for a New World Order:

    Massive depopulation of the earth
    Death of Judeo-Christian beliefs
    One World government
    Restoration of nature

If you've read my piece about the Georgia Guidestones, you might notice that the themes are strikingly similar. Coincidence? The Georgia Guidestones also feature a capstone with a time capsule buried under it. There is no "conspiracy theory" here, those are facts. Everything is written in stone for you to see. The elites own this place and they build monuments to celebrate their culture. Their "divine knowledge" is however inaccessible to you unless you're a high ranking member. There is so much to interpret in those murals that I'm convinced I've missed a lot of details (colors, shapes, movement, symbols).

Other weirdness

Like I've said before, a book could be written on the DIA, so I'll leave you with unsorted oddities you can see at the DIA.

Garoyles

The symbolism of gargoyles has always been a mystery. Nobody can really explain the reason of their presence, specifically on religious buildings. Are they remnants of past pagan beliefs that never went away? Do they represent something only "illuminated" people know about?

"What are these fantastic monsters doing in the cloisters under the very eyes of the brothers as they read? What is the meaning of these unclean monkeys, strange savage lions and monsters? To what purpose are here placed these creatures, half beast, half man?
- St Bernard of Clairvaux, 12th century

THE FLOOR

The following pictures are of a strange set of symbols that run in the floor from the south end of The Great Hall on Level 5 and progress to the north end of The Great Hall. Note the black disk which is occulting the sun. There is no mistaking the architecture in the floor as depicting the sun, and the black disk is beginning to eclipse it. When we arrive at the north end of The Great Hall, there is a statue of Jeppesen which is covering the sun. Is it a reference to the black sun, as revered by the Nazis?

CURIOUS PAINTING

Is it supposed to be "native" art representing mother earth? Looks like an alien "sprinkling" life on earth. Whats with the little faces at the top of the painting? Are they alien watching us from space? I don't know, I can't find any information about this piece. It makes me think of crop circles for some reason.

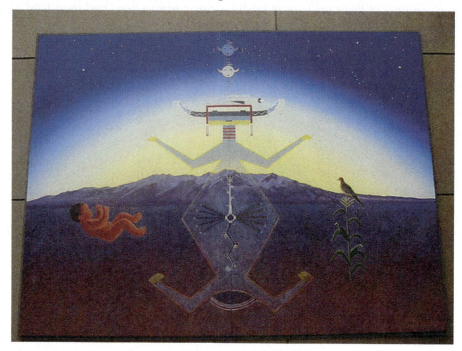

I hope you've enjoyed this virtual tour of the DIA and that you currently have a huge question mark on top of your head at the moment. The only way to answer these questions is to further your research on the philosophy, the beliefs and the long term projects of who are called the "elite".

Sinister Sites – Illuminati Pyramid in Blagnac, France

Located in a suburb of Toulouse, the "Place de la Révolution" is probably one of the most blatant displays of Illuminati designs in existence: a huge pyramid hovering atop a map of the world. The symbolic meaning of this structure reveals a rather grim and elitist ideology and seems to confirm the conspiracy theorist's claims: the world is lead by a secret cabal named the Illuminati.

The Place de Revolution is situated on a roundabout in the rather quiet commune of Blagnac in Toulouse, and a constant flow of cars drive around the monument every day. As is the case in diverse parts of the world, most locals find the monument that adorns their town "nice" and "decorative" without having the slightest idea of its deep occult meaning. To those who have "eyes to see" however, the Place de la Révolution clearly and unequivocally reveals the hidden force which shaped the past and is relentlessly working to mold the future. In this apparently simple structure are embedded the goals, the aspirations, the philosophy and the beliefs of the hidden elite who guide the clueless masses towards a New World Order.

Historical Considerations

The Place de la Révolution was built in 1989 to commemorate the bicentennial anniversary of the French Revolution. Modern Historians agree that Freemasonry played a critical role in the unfolding of the revolution.

> "If one desires to point to a major world event proven to have been inspired by secret society machinations, one need look no further than the French Revolution, which devastated that nation between 1787 and 1799. Revolutionary leaders, in seeking to overthrow the decadent monarchy of King Louis XVI, launched the first national revolution of modern times.
>
> Although popularly believed to have begun due to a public uprising over lack of food and government representation, the record is quite clear that the revolution was instigated by cells of French Masonry and the German Illuminati.

> *The New Encyclopedia Britannica tells us that in France there arose a political system and a philosophical outlook that no longer took Christianity for granted, that in fact explicitly opposed it... The brotherhood taught by such groups as the Freemasons, members of secret fraternal societies, and the Illuminati, a rationalist secret society, provided a rival to the Catholic sense of community."*
>
> *Secret society researcher and author Nesta H. Webster was even more pointed, writing in 1924, "[The Masonic book A Ritual and Illustrations of Freemasonry] contains the following passage, 'The Masons... originated the Revolution with the infamous Duke of Orleans at their head.'"*
>
> *Author Bramley wrote, "During the first French Revolution, a key rebel leader was the Duke of Orleans, who was grand master of French Masonry before his resignation at the height of the Revolution. Marquis de Lafayette, the man who had been initiated into the Masonic fraternity by George Washington, also played an important role in the French revolutionary cause. The Jacobin Club, which was the radical nucleus of the French revolutionary movement, was founded by prominent Freemasons."*
> - Jim Marrs, Rule By Secrecy

Far from hiding this fact, French Masons take great pride in this historical accomplishment. Many Masonic monuments were erected in France in 1989 to celebrate Freemasonry's role in the French revolution. The one in Blagnac is however particularly revealing. It is modern, slightly futuristic even and focuses on "what is left to do" rather than "what has been done". It describes a world united under the rule of a giant floating pyramid, representing secret societies inside the realm of the Great Architect.

The Pyramid

The pyramid is composed of a total of thirteen layers, the top two layers of which are separated by a metallic divider. If you have studied any of the works of art or monuments that were inspired by Masonic teachings, you will already know that the number thirteen is constantly represented in various ways. The bottom layers of the pyramid represent the lower degrees of Masonry while the top two, which are separated by the divider, represent the Illuminati – the "hidden degrees", the capstone of the pyramid. Every single time I talk about Freemasonry on this website, I always refer to those hidden degrees. This is where the "Truth" is revealed and where the decisions are taken. The bottom layers are simply a school of hermeticism and are a means to recruit "those who are worthy". If you are a Mason and you are not at the top of the hierarchy, represented by the capstone of the pyramid, I am not referring to you and I never did (just had to make this point clear). It is interesting to note that the pyramid on the back of the American dollar bill also contains thirteen layers.

The symbolism here could not be more blatant. The pyramid, this symbolic structure representing secret societies operating on every continent, floats above the whole world, dominating it (some might say overshadowing it) and owning it.

Water in this structure also bears an important symbolic and spiritual meaning. Emanating from the top of the pyramid, water slowly trickles down each layer to finally end up on the map of the world. Water, a representation of divine wisdom, starts by gracing the top of the pyramid, which represents the "illuminated", the elite of the world. From the capstone, water descends from one layer to another, "feeding" each Masonic degree with its share of wisdom. The symbolic end result is that the entire world is filled with (or drowning in, depending on the point of view) this knowledge.

When viewed in kabbalistic terms, water flowing through thirteen layers or "channels" is a reference to Mem, the Fountain of Wisdom.

"Just as the waters of a physical fountain (spring) ascend from their unknown subterranean source (the secret of the abyss in the account of Creation) to reveal themselves on earth, so does the fountain of wisdom express the power of flow from the superconscious source. In the terminology of Kabbalah, this flow is from Keter ("crown") to Chochmah ("wisdom"). The stream is symbolized in Proverbs as "the flowing stream, the source of wisdom."

In particular, we are taught that there are thirteen channels of flow from the superconscious source to the beginning of consciousness. These channels correspond to the Thirteen Attributes of Mercy revealed to Moses at Sinai, as well as to the thirteen principles of Torah exegesis, the (superrational) "logic" of Torah."
- Rabbi Yitzchak Ginsburgh, "Mem: Fountain of Wisdom"

The Bronze Tablets

In front of the pyramid are two bronze tablets, which are very reminiscent of Moses' 10 Commandments in shape, but engraved with astronomical and planetary glyphs instead of words. The rectangle slab of bronze uniting the two tablets bears the biggest accomplishment of modern illuminism: the Declaration of Human Rights.

The Declaration contains many Masonic, Illuminist and alchemical symbols such as (starting from the top): the Eye of the Great Architect in glory, the Orobouros (snake eating its tail), the Phrygian cap (the red hat under the Ouroboros) and the fasces. Let's not forget the two Masonic pillars on each side sustaining everything.

> *"At the visual focus of this illuminated document (and its copies), and set apart with striking contrast, we find a familiar Mithraic motif—a red Phrygian cap set atop the shining white steel of a weapon, itself braced vertically, Excalibur-like, into the presumed bedrock. Should one doubt the symbolic significance of this spear and its Mithraic equivalent, the sword or harpe, attention is directed to the fasces, or barsom,, which otherwise would remain inexplicable in this context. Also, the red tassel situated above the fasces is an important Masonic symbol for the 'Mystic Tie' that binds Masons, although they might be of diverse opinion and perspective, into a sacred band of Friends and Brothers; the knot or tie, however, is a more ancient symbol of cosmic trans-terrestrial Union."*
> - Mark Hoffman, Freemasonry and the Survival of the Eucharistic Brotherhoods

In a documentary on Masonic monuments in Paris, Jacques Ravenne, a French author and high level Freemason said:

> *"The Declaration of Human Rights, which was created in France and gradually adopted around the world, was conceived, discussed and written in Masonic lodges before being released to the public. One can retrace those Masonic origins by the use of symbols, which bear little significance to the profane but are extremely important to the initiate."*
> (Translated from French)

The most significant symbol is the Eye within the triangle, also found on the reverse of the Great Seal of the United States. It is an unmistakable symbol of the Mysteries of secret societies and became the most universally recognized symbol of Illuminism in pop culture. The entire structure is meant to resemble this Eye within a triangle.

Lequeu's Quote

The creators of this structure inscribed at the base of the pyramid its true meaning. One inscription says:

LE BONHEUR EST DANS L'ANGLE OÙ LES SAGES SONT ASSEMBLÉS.

which can be translated to:

HAPPINESS IS IN THE ANGLE WHERE THE WISE ARE GATHERED.

Lequeue's quote on the Pyramid.

This phrase is a quote from Jean-Jacques Lequeu, a French architect from the revolutionary era who mixed Masonic principles with visionary designs.

The "angle" mentioned in Lequeu's enigmatic quote is a direct reference to Freemasonry, where architecture and geometry are at the basis their spiritual allegories. The Masonic symbols of the compass and the square and considering God to be "the Great Architect" are proof enough of this fact. In the context of the pyramid however, the quote takes on a specific meaning. The "angle where the wise are gathered" most probably alludes to the divider placed towards the top of the pyramid, at the level of its capstone. As mentioned previously, the top of the pyramid represents the Illuminati, the hidden order which is only accessible to a select few. So the quote says: "True happiness is at the top of the pyramid, the Illuminati, where the wisest unite". On the other side is another engraving saying:

"TEMPLE DE LA SAGESSE SUPREME"

which can be translated to:

"TEMPLE OF SUPREME WISDOM"

This is most probably the name of the actual structure, which contains obvious Masonic terminology and confirms the above interpretation of its meaning.

The "House"

The metal frame of a house surrounds the pyramidal structure. This represents the metaphorical creation of the "Great Architect", a great temple, inside which divine wisdom flows freely. On the other hand, one can interpret this thing as a kind of prison. Notice how the tip of the pyramid reaches above the house.
Are the Illuminated the only ones able to escape the prison of the material world?

The Phrygian Cap

In the plaza surrounding the pyramid there are numerous columns, including this one, which bears a stylized Phrygian cap. This red hat, with its tip pointing forward, became the symbol of revolution in France and the USA. Once again, the origins and the significance of this hat can be found in occult mysteries.

> *"During the 18th century the 'Mithraic Mysteries' and its symbolism was of great interest to the Freemasons, and the conflation of the cap used in Mithraism with the Pileus led to the red Phrygian cap evolving into a symbol of 'freedom', held aloft on a Liberty Pole during both the American Revolutionary War and the French Revolution ."*
> - Mark Hoffman, Freemasonry and the Survival of the Eucharistic Brotherhoods

> *"As a Phrygian Cap, or Symbolizing Cap, it is always sanguine in its colour. It then stands as the 'Cap of Liberty', a revolutionary form; also, in another way, it is even a civic or incorporated badge. It is always masculine in its meaning. It marks the 'needle' of the obelisk, the crown or tip of the phallus, whether 'human' or representative. It has its origin in the rite of circumcision–unaccountable as are both the symbol and the rite.*
>
> *The real meaning of the bonnet rouge, or 'cap of liberty', has been deeply obscure since time immemorial, notwithstanding the fact that it has always been regarded as a most important hieroglyph or figure. It signifies the supernatural simultaneous 'sacrifice' and 'triumph'. It has descended from the time of Abraham, and it is supposed to be an emblem of the strange mythic rite of the 'circumcisio preputii'. The loose Phrygian bonnet, bonnet conique, or 'cap of liberty' may be accepted as figuring, or standing for, that detached integument or husk, separated from a certain point or knob, which has various names in different languages, and which supplies the central idea of this 'sacrificial rite–the spoil or refuse of which (absurd and unpleasant as it may seem) is borne aloft at once as a 'trophy' and as the 'cap of liberty'. It is now a magic sign, and becomes a talisman of supposedly inexpressible power–for what particular dark reason it would be difficult to say. The whole thing is a sign of 'initiation', and of a baptism of a peculiar kind. The Phrygian cap, ever since this first inauguration, has stood as the sign of the 'Enlightened'."*
> - Hargrave Jennings, Rosicrucians: Their Rites and Mysteries

Phrygian cap on the seal of the United States Senate

In Conclusion

The Place de la Révolution of Blagnac is one of those monuments which simply does not lie. It celebrates simply, and without any political correctness, the nature of the works of secret societies. The "Temple of Supreme Wisdom" is permeated with symbolism and messages directly alluding to Freemasonry and the Illuminati and hides in plain sight the true philosophy of our world leaders.

The French Revolution was mainly carried out by Freemasonry and resulted in a great political success – the creation of the French Republic – the ideals of which radiated across the world. Is it realistic to think that the work of secret societies stopped there? Masonic scholars believe that these events were only the beginning, the first necessary step towards an "enlightened world". Is the New World Order the next step?

Analysis of the Occult Symbols Found on the Bank of America Murals

Prominently displayed in the lobby of the Bank of America's Corporate Center are "creepy" frescoes, filled with occult symbols. Even more unsettling is the fact that those images seem to predict events of a radical world change in the not-so-distant future. Are those murals predicting the coming of an occult New World Order? We will look at the occult meaning of the symbols found on the Bank of America frescoes.

A reader sent me pictures of some very odd murals displayed at the Bank of America Corporate Center in Charlotte, NC. Needless to say they immediately caught my attention, as I was flabbergasted by their symbolism and their message. I also couldn't help relating them to the ominous murals of the Denver International Airport.

Painted by Benjamin Long, the paintings are said to revolve around the themes of "making/building, chaos/creativity, and planning/knowledge in a "daring blend of abstract and realism, set off with touches of gold".

The three frescoes ruling over the lobby of the Bank of America Corporate Center.

Although we normally read from left to right, there are clues within the frescoes hinting the viewers to read the paintings from right to left. The "planning" stage (visually represented by the fresco on the right) is normally the first step of any process so it would make sense to start from there. There is also alchemical symbolism hinting towards the chronology of the frescoes, so we will begin with the one on the right:

Right Fresco

The fresco on the right is dubbed Planning/Knowledge. An esoteric read of its symbolism reveals exactly what is being planned and what knowledge it is referring to.

Masonic Boy on Masonic Floor

We see here a young blond boy standing on a standard Masonic checker-board pattern floor. His feet are placed at a 90 degrees angle, in accordance to Masonic initiation ritual:

> "Q. On your return to the Lodge, where were you placed, as the youngest Entered Apprentice?
>
> A. In the northeast corner, my feet forming a right angle, my body erect, at the right hand of the Worshipful Master in the east, an upright man and Mason, and it was given me strictly in charge ever to walk and act as such."
> - Malcolm C. Duncan, Duncan's Masonic Ritual and Monitor

Seemingly underneath the boy are people dressed in business suits, seemingly strategizing while pointing at the Masonic boy. Does the boy represent the "new generation"?

This blond boy is very reminiscent of the blond boy featured at the center of one of the murals of the Denver International Airport.

Blond boy hammering a sword into a plowshare. Note that the boy is wearing a traditional Bavarian costume ... perhaps as in Bavarian Illuminati?

Burning Bush, Woman in Cube and Pyramid

Behind the boy is a tree on fire, which is a reference of the Burning Bush of the Old Testament. The Burning Bush is of great importance in Masonic ritual, especially for the 33rd degree, whose members are considered to be "near the Burning Bush".

> "In the third Exodus it is record that, while Moses was keeping the flock of Jethro on Mount Horeb, "the angle of Lord appeared unto him in a flame of fire out of the midst of a bush", and there communicated to him for the first time his Ineffable Name. This occurrence is commemorated in the Burning Bush of the Royal Arch Degree. In all systems of antiquity, fire is adopted as a symbol of Deity; and the Burning Bush, or the bush filled with fire which did not consume, whence came forth the Tetragrammaton, the symbol of Divine Light and Truth, is considered in the advanced degrees of Freemasonry, like the Orient in the lower, as the great source of true Masonic light; wherefore Supreme Councils of the Thirty-Third Degree date their balustres or official documents, "near the B.B." or Burning Bush, to intimate that they are, in their own rite, the exclusive source of all Masonic instruction".
> - Albert G. Mackey, Encyclopedia of Freemasonry, Part 1

In the background is an Egyptian pyramid, the ultimate symbol of the Mysteries in occult teachings.

A strange feature of the painting is the woman apparently trapped inside a transparent cube, hanging from threads coming from the sky. Does she represent the common man, stuck in the confines of the material world (occultly represented by the cube) and manipulated by unseen the forces from above?

Stairs and Black Sun

On the left of the image are stairs, apparently leading to the heavens, a classic symbol representing the path to illumination/Illuminati through the mysteries of Masonry.

In the sky is a black sun, another symbol of an esoteric significance. Hermetic traditions teach the existence of two suns, an invisible and etheric one made of pure "philosophical gold" and the material one, the only one the profane can perceive, known as the Black Sun.

In alchemy, the black sun (Sol niger) is the name of the result of the first stage of the Opus Magnum. The alchemical Magnum Opus (or Great Work) starts with the "blackening" – the calcination of crude metals – and ends with their transmutation into pure gold.

Today, the symbol of the Black Sun is mostly associated with esoteric Nazism and cults such as the Temple of Set. It is also found in odd places such as:

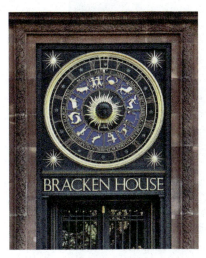

Bracken House, London. The Black Sun beares the face of Winston Churchill.

The right fresco therefore seems to portray the first step of a "Great Work" that needs to be accomplished, as symbolically represented by the black sun. Men dressed in suits (one of them oddly looks like Adam Weishaupt), seem to be preparing a new generation of Masonic youth. Meanwhile, the "profane" seem to be idling in an translucent cube, controlled by invisible puppeteers.

Middle Fresco

The middle fresco, Chaos/Creativity, depicts a turbulent transitional period. Many details within the painting describe this profound turmoil, which seem to be affecting all part of society and civilization. We find military and religious figures, people protesting and much more.

Barb wires, nets and soldiers on the streets tell the viewers that this period of turmoil is also one of oppression. The nun does not seem very pleased either.

At the left of the painting is a person wearing a biohazard suit, hinting to some kind of chemical warfare. For this reason, and many more, I find this painting very similar to one of the Denver Airport's murals … the most infamous one.

Person in gas suit

This mural of the DIA portrays a militaristic figure wearing a gas mask and oppressing an endless line of sad people. Chemical warfare, military repression, dead babies … what is there not to like about this image?

If we look at the top of the fresco, we see translucent beings spinning with fire, perhaps implying that the turmoil is also happening on a metaphysical, cosmic or astral level.

Spinning naked bodies in a vortex of fire

This round fiery shape can also be likened to a sun. Its pale golden color and the transparency of its figures can be associated with the intermediate step of the great alchemical work named "Whitening". Jung compared this step with daybreak, the preparation for the next and final stage, which is the sunrise, characterized by the color red. Which is, of course, the most prominent color of the left fresco.

Left Fresco

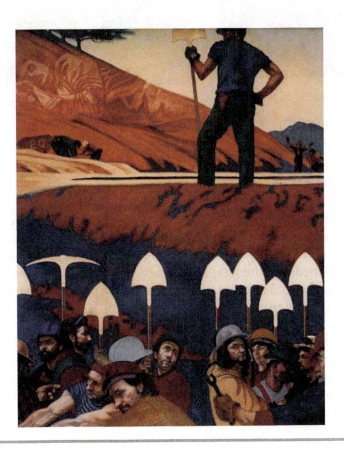

The fresco on the left is said to focus on the theme of "Making/Building". The main figure of the fresco is a worker holding a shovel, contemplating the work done. In his back pocket is a red piece of cloth, a symbolic detail in the context of this image. There is indeed a great emphasis on the color red in this fresco, which, as mentioned above, is the also the color associated with the final step of the alchemical Magnum Opus: Rubedo, the "Red Work".

In occult teachings, alchemical transformation can happen on numerous levels: a material level, where crude metals are transmuted to pure gold, but also on a spiritual and philosophical level, where the profane man becomes a "regenerated man". In secret-society lore, the entire world is considered to be the subject of alchemical transformation; it is said to be an imperfect plane needing to be "transmuted into gold" in order to mirror the heavens, in accordance with the hermetic axiom "As Above, So Below". Is a New World Order the "Great Work" of the occult elite?

Sleeping Giant

An odd detail of the fresco is this man blending with the earth, apparently in deep sleep … or is he buried? This is also reminiscent of the (unsettling) sleeping little boy on the DIA murals.

Is he dead or sleeping? And what does "EQ" mean?

A helpless little boy sleeping (or dead) under a red blanket at the DIA Airport

What Is The Meaning of the Frescoes?

Like most elitist art, the frescoes on display at the headquarters of Bank of America, the largest bank in America, tell a story intended to be decoded by those in the know. The frescoes seem to depict three stages of world transformation – planning, chaos and achievement – and are color-coded to be analogous to the three stages of hermetic alchemy: Nigredo (blackness), Albedo (whiteness) and Rubedo (redness). The frescoes bear many resemblances to the murals of the Denver International Airport, which also depict progressive phases of a profound transformation of society after a period of intense turmoil.

The first fresco displays a wide array of occult symbols, some directly referring to Freemasonry. This is quite astonishing as the painting is in the lobby of the headquarters of the United States' most predominant bank and not in a Masonic lodge … but perhaps there is some overlap. Those who are "in the know" and initiated to the Mysteries are those who are qualified to accomplishing the planning process, which in this painting seem to be the men in suits, whose ties match the red and white checker-board floor, and who make plans for the future generation, represented by the blond Masonic boy.

In the second fresco, civil unrest, riots, protests and repression are all taking place. Historically, the masses only usually go into an outright revolt when their living conditions deteriorate significantly or when hugely unpopular policies get adopted. Does this piece refer to the loss of civil liberties and the rise of a police state? There is also a metaphysical aspect to the image, represented by the spinning naked bodies that appear as the sun, implying that the period turmoil is also happening on a cosmic level.

The last fresco gives a sense of "mission accomplished", with the dominant figure surveying the work, while also conveying the message that "the work is never totally done" as labourers are still hard at work in the underground. This is reminiscent of the movie Metropolis, where a class of workers silently slave away underground to sustain the elite's utopia. I also can't help but being reminded of the 33 Chilean miners while looking at those workers …

In Conclusion

The Bank of America frescoes are yet another example of the elite's agenda being "hidden in plain sight". These giant images, on display for all to see, but designed to be understood by few, describe the philosophy of the elite rulers, their occult knowledge and their plans for the future. As it is the case for all works of art, it is possible to interpret these paintings on numerous levels and to come up with different conclusions. It is, however, difficult to ignore the recurrent themes found in the"Sinister Sites" described on The Vigilant Citizen: prevalent occult symbolism, the heralding of a "new era", contempt for the profane masses, celebration of repression and war, etc. When comparing the Bank of America frescoes with the art of the DIA and the Georgia Guidestones, we can find a definite consistence in their symbolism, their tone and their message. This leads me to believe that the same group is behind all of those sites and many more. Whoever they are, we know a few things for sure: they are extremely rich, extremely powerful and they don't really like you … because you are not one of Them.

The Occult Symbolism of the Los Angeles Central Library

Throughout the history of Western Civilization, libraries have been the repositories of nations' accumulated knowledge and the epicenters of their culture. Central libraries, more than being big buildings containing books, are important landmarks designed with impressive architecture and filled with symbolic art. The Los Angeles Central Library is certainly no exception. An in-depth look at the art found at the Library is quite a revealing one: It describes the occult philosophy of those in power. We will look at the Central Library's history and the hidden meaning of its architecture.

Built in 1926, the Central Library is an important landmark of downtown Los Angeles. It is the central piece of one of the largest publicly funded library systems in the world, the Los Angeles Public Library (LAPL). Most touristic pamphlets describe the building's design to be inspired by ancient Egyptian and Mediterranean Revival architecture. As we will see, this choice of design is not simply an aesthetic one, it rather recalls the teachings and the symbolism of the ancient mystery schools of Antiquity. In fact, after decoding the library's many esoteric features, we can safely say that the building is mainly inspired by Freemasonry, which is, in turn, heavily steeped in ancient Egyptian and Mediterranean mysteries.

The Library's tiled pyramid, two sphinxes, celestial mosaics and other details turn this public space into a true occult temple. Furthermore, the library is definitely built with an elitist state of mind. The true meaning of the art on display seems to be solely intended for initiates of secret societies and not the masses. Before we examine the building's most important features, let's look at the background of its builders.

Elite Architect: Bertram Goodhue

The LA Central Library was designed by Bertram Grosvenor Goodhue, a prominent architect who was recognized and hired by America's most powerful people. His works include governmental and military buildings, churches, libraries and the private houses of politicians.

One of the most recognized elite buildings designed by Goodhue is the headquarters of the Wolf's Head Society – a secret society of Yale University. Along with the notorious Skull & Bones and Scroll & Key – the two other secret societies found at Yale - Wolf's Head functions are quite similar to Freemasonry: It is a discreet yet major force influencing one of America's most elite universities. It has held within its ranks members who went on to become prominent politicians, diplomats, lawyers and athletes.

Bertram Grosvenor Goodhue, architect of numerous buildings of power.

Perhaps Goodhue's most notable project is the Rockefeller Memorial Chapel of the University of Chicago. Commissioned by America's most powerful tycoon, John D. Rockefeller, the ecumenical Chapel is used for various religious celebrations. Rockefeller stated that the Chapel was meant to be the campus' "central and dominant feature"

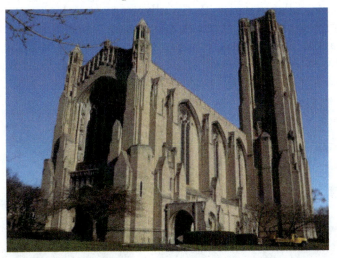

The Rockefeller Memorial Chapel.

The Chapel was designed in collaboration with Lee Lawrie, America's foremost architectural sculptor. The duo worked on several other important projects such as Nebraska's State Capitol and the Los Angeles Central Library, the subject of this article.

Sculpture of Bertram Goodhue holding the Rockefeller Chapel by the Rockefeller's favourite sculptor, Lee Lawrie.

Elite Sculptor: Lee Lawrie

Born in Germany in 1877, Lawrie came to the United States at the age of 5. After learning the craft from some of America's leading artists, Lawrie collaborated with Goodhue on several projects and became America's leading sculptor. His unique style and his knowledge of occult symbolism, ancient mysteries and Masonic principles apparently made him the elite's artist. Some of his high-profile commissions include: the allegorical relief panels of the United States Senate, the Louisiana State Capitol, the statue of George Washington at the National Cathedral in Washington D.C and the Harkness Tower of Yale University.

Lawrie's statue of George Washington at the National Cathedral. Notice the Masonic Square and Compass behind him.

Lawrie's Wisdom, above the main entrance of 5, Rockefeller Center, NY. The sculpture, depicts a gnostic demi-urge holding a Masonic compass.

The complex built by John D. Rockefeller is filled with symbolic art describing the elite's Luciferian philosophy based on the acquisition of divine knowledge (more on this later). Another important piece conceived by Lawrie at the Rockefeller Center is the statue of Atlas.

Atlas is used by the ruling class as a metaphor "for the people who produce the most in society", and therefore "holding up the world" in a metaphorical sense. Not surprisingly, Atlas is associated with some of the most important works of fictions describing the point of view of the elite.

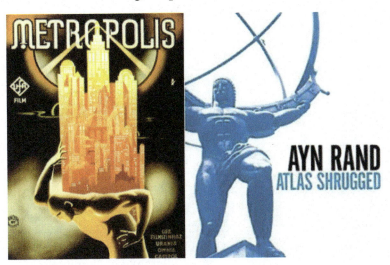

Fritz Lang's Metropolis and Ayn Rand's Atlas Shrugged: two classic works of fiction describing the vision of the world's occult elite. Both work's promotional material feature Atlas, a metaphor for the elite "upholding the world".

Knowing that Goodhue and Lawrie produced symbolic architecture for America's most prominent tycoons, politicians and institutions, would you be surprised if the Central Library contained the same?

The Central Library

Facade of the Los Angeles Central Library

The library was originally built in 1926 by Bertram Goodhue. According to the Library's documentation, the architecture's central theme revolved around "illumination through the light of learning". Due to an arson fire in 1986, the building underwent extensive renovations and expansion – but the central theme was faithfully respected. The artwork's spiritual and esoteric undertones make the entire complex a "temple of illumination". It is replete with profound mystical symbolism, sacred geometry, proportions and allusions to important occult works. The Los Angeles Central Library and the Rockefeller Center are very similar in this regard – not surprising, as Lee Lawrie masterminded both complexes. As it is the case for the Rockefeller Center, the torch of Illumination, representing divine knowledge, is the most important symbol of the Library.

The Pyramid of Illumination

Pyramid of Illumination at the top of the Library

Throning at the top of the Library is probably the complex' most distinctive feature: A tiled pyramid topped by a golden hand holding a torch. Other than being beautiful and decorative, the Library's apex has a deep occult meaning, clearly inspired by Freemasonry.

First, in occult lore, the pyramid is considered to be the ultimate symbol of the Mysteries. It represents the transition from the material plane to the spiritual world. From the square-shaped base of the pyramid (representing the material world) rise, in mathematical perfection, four triangles (representing divinity). According to many occult researchers, the pyramids of Ancient Egypt were most likely used for the purposes of initiation, where candidates were led to the path of Illumination.

> *"The more the great Hierophants were at pains to conceal their absolute Science, the more they sought to add grandeur to and multiply its symbols. The huge pyramids, with their triangular sides of elevation and square bases, represented their Metaphysics, founded upon the knowledge of Nature."*
> - Albert Pike, Morals and Dogma

On each side of the pyramid is a sun symbol, the most visual ancient representation of deity.

> *"The adoration of the sun was one of the earliest and most natural forms of religious expression. Complex modern theologies are merely involvements and amplifications of this simple aboriginal belief. The primitive mind, recognizing the beneficent power of the solar orb, adored it as the proxy of the Supreme Deity."*
> - Manly P. Hall, The Secret Teachings of All Ages

Although the sun (or sunburst) is the most common occult symbol to represent the divine, it is however not directly worshiped as a god. It is a visual representation of the divinity. For this reason, the Central Library is replete with references to the sun.

> "In all the histories of the Gods and Heroes lay couched and hidden astronomical details and the history of the operations of visible Nature; and those in their turn were also symbols of higher and profounder truths. None but rude uncultivated intellects could long consider the Sun and Stars and the Powers of Nature as Divine, or as fit objects of Human Worship; and they will consider them so while the world lasts ; and ever remain ignorant of the great Spiritual Truths of which these are the hieroglyphics and expressions."
> – Albert Pike, Morals and Dogma

The Luciferian Torch

Above the pyramid is golden hand holding a torch. There is a reason why this symbol is sitting above all others in the building: It is a perfect representation of the building's philosophy, Luciferianism.

The original torch is on display inside the Library. There, we can see more of the torch's detail, including the serpent of knowledge intertwining its base.

In Latin, the word "Lucifer" means "light bearer". In occult symbolism, light and fire esoterically represent divine knowledge and enlightenment. A hand holding a lit torch therefore represents man's ascent to divinity through the teachings of the Mysteries. The Gnostic interpretation of the story of the Genesis considers the snake (Lucifer) as a positive figure. It has given humans the intellectual faculties to reason and to ascend to divinity by their own means.

> "Luciferianism represents the ultimate inversion of good and evil. The formula for this inversion is reflected by the narrative paradigm of the Gnostic Hypostasis myth. As opposed to the original Biblical version, the Gnostic account represents a "revaluation of the Hebraic story of the first man's temptation, the desire of mere men to 'be as gods' by partaking of the tree of the 'knowledge of good and evil."
> - Carl A. Raschke, The Interruption of Eternity: Modern Gnosticism and the Origins of the New Religious Consciousness

In occult teachings, Lucifer is not an existing being and is not equal to Satan. While Satan is esoterically associated with the descent to materiality, Lucifer represents the ascent to divinity using the cognitive powers of man. Through the acquisition of the knowledge of the Mysteries, an initiate has the:

> *"opportunity to erase the curse of mortality by direct encounter with the patron deity, or in many instances by actually undergoing an apotheosis, a transfiguration of human into divine".*
> - Ibid.

Masonic authors such as Albert Pike and Albert G. Mackey have referred to the "luciferian path" and the "energies of Lucifer" to describe the "search for light". The term "luciferian" is therefore used in the scholarly sense of "bringing enlightenment". Masonic scholars often invoke Prometheus, who stole fire from the gods to bring to man, to describe this concept. For this reason, Prometheus is the central figure of the Rockefeller Center.

Prometheus, the Hellenic equivalent of Lucifer, bringing divine knowledge to humanity at Rockefeller Center.

The references to Lucifer in this library do not stop here.

The Western Facade – Phosphor and Hesper

The Western facade of the Library

Conceived by Lee Lawrie, the Western facade of the Library is another nod to the Mystery schools. Two human figures are depicted with the names "Phosphor" and "Hesper" underneath them. This apparently minor detail is perhaps the most significant.

Phosphor (or phosphorus) is the Latin word for the planet Venus in the morning, also referred to as the "Morning Star" or the "bringer of light". Those terms are synonymous with Lucifer.

> "Believing Venus to be two bodies, the Ancient Greeks called the morning star Φωσφόρος, Phosphoros(Latinized Phosphorus), the "Bringer of Light" or Ἑωσφόρος, Eosphoros (Latinized Eosphorus), the "Bringer of Dawn". The evening star they called Hesperos (Latinized Hesperus) (Ἕσπερος, the "star of the evening"). By Hellenistic times, the ancient Hesperos would be translated into Latin as Vesper and Phosphoros as Lucifer ("Light Bearer"), a poetic term later used to refer to the fallen angel cast out of heaven."
> - William Sherwood Fox, The Mythology of All Races: Greek and Roman

Hesper (or Vesperus) refers to Venus in the evening, the evening star.

> "The disciples of Pythagoras also highly revered the planet Venus, because it was the only planet bright enough to cast a shadow. As the morning star, Venus is visible before sunrise, and as the evening star it shines forth immediately after sunset. Because of these qualities, a number of names have been given to it by the ancients. Being visible in the sky at sunset, it was called vesper, and as it arose before the sun, it was called the false light, the star of the morning, or Lucifer, which means the light-bearer".
> - Manly P. Hall, The Secret Teachings of All Ages

So Phosphor and Hesper are two words signifying the same entity, Venus, a celestial body occultly associated with Lucifer, at different stages of evolution. The figure representing Phosphor holds the names of Eastern philosophers such as Moses, Zoroaster and Buddah, while Hesper holds the name of Western thinkers such as Socrates, Francis Bacon and Immanuel Kant. These historical figures have not been chosen at random: they all play important roles in the teachings of the Mystery Schools. In fact, Francis Bacon, René Descartes and Immanuel Kant are central figures of the revival of modern Rosicrucianism and Freemasonry in Western civilization.

At the top of the wall is the Latin saying "et quasi cursores vitai lampada tradunt". This is a quote from the Roman poem De Rerum Natura (On the Nature of the Universe) written by Lucretius and can be translated to "And like runners they pass on the torch of life". The "torch of life" can be equated to the occult Mysteries, the hidden knowledge passed down from generation to generation through secret societies. Between Phosphor and Hesper, we see a cavalier passing the "torch of life", or occult knowledge, to the next generation and from the East to the West.

The western facade of the Library, which also serves as the main entrance, is therefore a very significant piece representing the enduring existence of mystery schools through luciferian philosophy. All of this, and we haven't even stepped inside the building.

Illuminated Globe

Situated right under the pyramid on the top of the building, this globe chandelier is composed of cast bronze and, according to the Library's documentation, weighs one ton. It was designed by Goodhue associates and modelled by Lee Lawrie.

The globe is surrounded by a ring containing the signs of the zodiac and is illuminated by 48 lights. The ring is attached to chains leading to the sunburst on the ceiling. As seen earlier, the sunburst is an ancient symbol representing divinity. This design is reminiscent of qabbalistic engravings representing the 72 names of God.

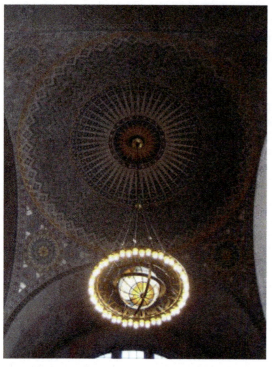

9-Feet wide globe chandelier

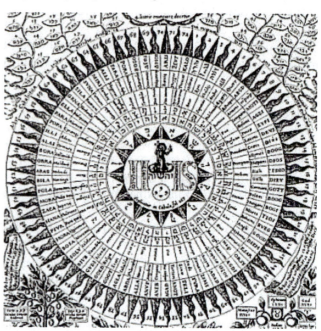

The seventy-two names of God from Kircher's OEdipus Ægyptiacus. Like the library's globe chandelier, this qabbalistic engraving bears the symbols of the planets and the signs of the zodiac.

Do the lights surrounding the globe represent the "circle of the illuminated", the hidden rulers of the earth, who are connected to divinity through Gnosis? Do the 48 lights, mirroring the 48 sunrays, represent the hermetic axiom "As Above, so Below"?

> "Despite statements to the contrary, Masonry is a religion seeking to unite God and man by elevating its initiates to that level of consciousness whereon they can behold with clarified vision the workings of the Great Architect of the Universe. From age to age the vision of a perfect civilization is preserved as the ideal for mankind. In the midst of that civilization shall stand a mighty university wherein both the sacred and secular sciences concerning the mysteries of life will be freely taught to all who will assume the philosophic life. Here creed and dogma will have no place; the superficial will be removed and only the essential be preserved. The world will be ruled by its most illumined minds, and each will occupy the position for which he is most admirably fitted. (...)
>
> The perfect government of the earth must be patterned eventually after that divine government by which the universe is ordered."
> - Manly P. Hall, The Secret Teachings of All Ages

The Statue of Civilization

In a remote alcove at the end of a checker board-patterned floor, the Statue of Civilization stands above a staircase flanked by two sphinxes. According to library documentation, the Lee Lawrie's statue "symbolizes everything the library represents".

Her left hand holds a torch tipped with a flame and her right hand holds a book containing quotes which are, incidentally, quite important in Freemasonry:

"In the beginning was the word." (Greek)
"Knowledge extends horizons." (Latin)
"Nobility carries obligations." (French)
"Wisdom is in the truth." (German)
"Beauty is truth – truth beauty." (English)

On the statue is a carved panel containing symbols of ancient and modern civilizations.

Panel on the Statue of Civilization's robe

From bottom to top:

- Blank for unknown ages of man
- Pyramids of Egypt
- Ship for Phoenicia
- Winged Bull for Babylonia & Tablets for Judea
- Lion Gate of Palace of Ninos & Parthenon for Minoan and Grecian civilizations
- Wolf with Romulus and Remus for Rome
- Dragon for China
- Siva for India
- Notre Dame for Medieval Christian Europe
- Plumed Serpent Head for Maya
- Buffalo, Covered Wagon, and Liberty Bell for United States of America

Once again, these civilizations were chosen for their importance in Masonic history as they are known to have passed down occult mysteries. The blank space at the bottom most probably refers to Atlantis, the lost civilization, which, according to occult texts, was at the origin of Hermetism. The building representing Medieval Christian Europe, Notre Dame de Paris, was built by the Knight Templars, the order considered to be the ancestors of modern Freemasons.

The Sphinxes

One of the Sphinxes guarding the Statue of Civilization

In occult symbolism, sphinxes are the guardians of the Mysteries, protecting esoteric secrets from the eyes of the profane. The official website of the Library describes the sphinxes:

> *"In black unveined Belgian marble with bronze headdresses, the sphinxes symbolize the hidden mysteries of knowledge and guard the approach to the Statue of Civilization."*

Each sphinx carries a book containing quotes from Plutarch's Morals ("On Isis and Osiris")

Left Sphinx – "I am all that was and is and is to be and no man hath lifted up my veil."

Right Sphinx – "Therefore the desire of Truth, especially of that which concerns the gods, is itself a yearning after Divinity."

The first quote is incredibly significant in Masonic mysteries as Illumination is metaphorically equated to the "lifting of the veil of Isis". For this reason, Freemasons dub themselves the "Widow's Sons", the widow being Isis, the goddess who lost her husband Osiris.

"Though few ever discovered her identity, she was Sophia, the Virgin of Wisdom, whom all the philosophers of the world have wooed. Isis represents the mystery of motherhood, which the ancients recognized as the most apparent proof of Nature's omniscient wisdom and God's overshadowing power. To the modern seeker she is the epitome of the Great Unknown, and only those who unveil her will be able to solve the mysteries of life, death, generation, and regeneration."
- Manly P. Hall, The Secret Teachings of All Ages

The second quote sums up the entire purpose of occult secret societies: to seek godliness through the knowledge of the Mysteries.

The symbolism of these sculptures is therefore extremely powerful and revealing: Civilization, the force behind nations, politics, culture, economics and citizenship is guarded by the symbol of the Mysteries. The statue basically says: Secret societies have guided the evolution of civilization since ancient times and will continue to do so.

The Star of Ishtar

Embedded in the floor, at a central point of the Library, is an eight pointed star, a symbol known as the star of Ishtar.

A version of the ancient Mesopotamian eight-pointed star symbol of the goddess Ishtar (Inana/Inanna), representing the planet Venus as morning or evening star.

Ishtar is the Assyrian and Babylonian goddess of fertility, love, war, and sexuality and is considered by the Babylonians to be "the divine personification of the planet Venus. The story of her descent into the underworld in search presumably for the sacred elixir which alone could restore Tammuz to life is the key to the ritual of her Mysteries. Perhaps for this reason, the symbol of the star of Ishtar is often found in the lower levels of occult buildings, such as the Manitoba Legislative building. Does this symbol represent the underworld?

The star of Ishtar at the Manitoba Legislative Building

In Conclusion

To most people, the Los Angeles Public Library is nothing more than a functional building, which happens to be beautifully ornamented. When one understands the occult symbolism displayed around the complex, the Library turns into a temple of illumination, dedicated to occult mysteries and Masonic principles. It is a celebration of the accomplishments of the luciferian elite and of the prevailing of its occult philosophy. The fact that the library is dedicated to secret societies, despite the fact that the LAPL is publicly funded, tells volumes about the true nature of America's power.

After reading this article, some might ask: "If seeking knowledge is a Luciferian trait, and if Lucifer is traditionally associated with evil, does it mean that seeking knowledge is wrong?". Heck no. Seeking knowledge will never be wrong and being ignorant will never be right. Knowledge leads to wisdom and discernment while ignorance leads to confusion and bewilderment. Furthermore, it is only by fully understanding the forces at work in the world that one becomes in a position to truly accomplish good in society. Conversely, an ignorant person can easily be manipulated by deceivers to become their unknowing accomplices. No matter what term is used to describe the search of Truth, it will always be the noblest of deeds, regardless of one's creed or religion. The faculties of learning and understanding are not the exclusivity of one group of people. They are gifts endowed to all humans and it is our duty to make the most of them. The most important thing to consider is this: Do you use knowledge to guide, inspire and enlighten or do you use it to control, manipulate and deceive? We have seen in previous articles how the elite uses their knowledge to manipulate the masses. What will you do with yours?

Sinister Sites: IRS Headquarters, Maryland

The IRS headquarters in New Carrollton, Maryland is a government building that, despite being constructed with public funds, contains art referring to elite secret societies. More importantly, the art conveys a strange message about the U.S. Constitution, and the American people in general. We'll look at the symbolic meaning of the art found in front of the IRS headquarters in Maryland.

The IRS is probably the most hated institution in America – mainly because its primary role is to force people to hand over their hard-earned cash. This modern equivalent of the proverbial tax collector indeed collects money from American workers and gives it to a government that will, in turn, use this money to send drones abroad or to build information superstructures to better monitor these same workers. What's not to like?

The IRS was originally created as a "temporary measure" during wartime (funny how the Canadian Revenue Agency was also supposed to be "temporary"), but there is nothing temporary about it now. In fact, the gigantic IRS complex in New Carrollton, Maryland was built in 1997 and is still growing today, indicating that this institution is indeed here to stay. This modern building has all of the state-of-the-art amenities one can think of, but it is the odd public art in front of it that is the most noteworthy. As is the case for many government buildings, the art displayed means absolutely nothing to most people, but to those who are versed in secret society symbolism, its implications are manifold and profound. In fact, fully understanding the origins and the meaning of the symbols in front of the IRS building means understanding who are truly in power in America (and around the world), what they believe in and what they truly think about us, the masses.

The IRS is not known to be a very artistic institution and likewise there is not much art present at its headquarters in Maryland. However, the few pieces that are on display manage to convey everything that needs to be known about the occult elite.

General Layout

The entrance to the IRS headquarters is guarded by two black and white pillars made of the highest quality marble, topped with white hands. Between the two pillars is a dark pyramid with a metallic capstone on which is written "We the People". What does all of this represent? Here's an "official" description:

> "The most striking elements are the huge, white marble hands atop each column. Each hand points skyward, one with the forefinger extended; the other is an open hand, the fingers ever so slightly

cupped.

The 1997 work is called "Vox Populi," which is Latin for "the voice of the people." The hand with the raised index finger represents deliberation, argument, the gesticulation of a speaker giving his or her opinion. The hand with an open palm represents the act of voting or taking an oath."
- The Washington Post, "The Big Hands of the Law"

That is all well and good, but what does "Vox Populi" have to do with the IRS? Can citizens weigh in or vote on anything about the IRS? Why are the pillars black and white? Why is there a pyramid with a capstone between them? As it is the case for most occult symbols, there's as basic (and unsatisfactory) interpretation given to the masses and a "real" meaning for those in the know. For those in the know, the art is a nod to the highest degrees of Freemasonry, the true source of power in America – not unlike what the Washington monument stands for.

The art in front of the IRS Headquarters features a pyramid with a capstone between two pillars. The black and white stripes refer to the Hermetic concept of duality.

This Masonic monument in Israel bears exactly the same elements: A pyramid with a capstone between two pillars. The stripes on the ground represent duality.

Let's look at each element of this (not so) public art.

Twin Pillars

The symbolism of the twin pillars is ancient and very meaningful as it refers to the core of hermetism, the basis of secret society teachings. In short, the pillars represent duality and the union of opposites:

> "The right Tablet of the Law further signifies Jachin – the white pillar of light; the left Tablet, Boaz – the shadowy pillar of darkness. These were the names of the two pillars cast from brass set up on the porch of King Solomon's Temple. They were eighteen cubits in height and beautifully ornamented with wreaths of chainwork, nets, and pomegranates. On the top of each pillar was a large bowl – now erroneously called a ball or globe – one of the bowls probably containing fire and the other water. The celestial globe (originally the bowl of fire), surmounting the right-hand column (Jachin), symbolized the divine man; the terrestrial globe (the bowl of water), surmounting the left-hand column (Boaz), signified the earthly man. These two pillars respectively connote also the active and the passive expressions of Divine Energy, the sun and the moon, sulphur and salt, good and bad, light and darkness. Between them is the door leading into the House of God, and standing thus at the gates of Sanctuary they are a reminder that Jehovah is both an androgynous and an anthropomorphic deity. As two parallel columns they denote the zodiacal signs of Cancer and Capricorn, which were

formerly placed in the chamber of initiation to represent birth and death – the extremes of physical life. They accordingly signify the summer and the winter solstices, now known to Freemasons under the comparatively modern appellation of the "two St. Johns."

In the mysterious Sephirothic Tree of the Jews, these two pillars symbolize Mercy and Severity. Standing before the gate of King Solomon's Temple, these columns had the same symbolic import as the obelisks before the sanctuaries of Egypt. When interpreted Qabbalistically, the names of the two pillars mean "In strength shall My House be established. "In the splendor of mental and spiritual illumination, the High Priest stood between the pillars as a mute witness to the perfect virtue of equilibrium – that hypothetical point equidistant from all extremes. He thus personified the divine nature of man in the midst of his compound constitution – the mysterious Pythagorean Monad in the presence of the Duad. On one side towered the stupendous column of the intellect; on the other, the brazen pillar of the flesh. Midway between these two stands the glorified wise man, but he cannot reach this high estate without first suffering upon the cross made by joining these pillars together. The early Jews occasionally represented the two pillars, Jachin and Boaz, as the legs of Jehovah, thereby signifying to the modern philosopher that Wisdom and Love, in their most exalted sense, support the whole order of creation – both mundane and supermundane."

The same way Masonic pillars guard the entrance of Masonic temples, two pillars guard the entrance of the IRS building.

- Manly P. Hall, The Secret Teachings of All Ages

Masonic art depicting the twin pillars named Jachin and Boaz guarding the entrance of a Masonic temple.

While not all pillars are necessarily Masonic, those in front of the IRS building contain other features that leave

The IRS pillars feature exactly 13 black and white stripes and a very significant hand sign.

no doubt regarding their secret society connection.
Sharply contrasting with the rest of the building, the pillars are stripped in black and white, a pattern evoking duality, a concept that is visually represented on the Masonic mosaic pavement.

Probably the most important feature in Masonic lodges, the black and white checkerboard pattern is meant to be a visual representation of the concept of duality. Variations of this pattern do exist.

To make things even more explicitly Masonic (for those in the know) each pillar is comprised of exactly 13 stripes, a number that is of the utmost importance in Masonic lore (research the omnipresence of the number 13 on the American dollar bill). Considering the constant attention to occult numerology in Masonic art, this fact alone should be very telling.

Above each pillar are white marble hands. It is interesting to know that formal Masonic attire requires white gloves. One of the hands points upwards, towards the sky. While the official meaning claims that it refers to the act of public discussion and discourse, this hand sign, place in the esoteric context of the artwork, takes on a much more ancient and mystical meaning.

Named the "hand to god", the "sign of Preservation" or the "hand of the Mysteries", the sign of the hand pointing upwards can be found in many works of art that bear an esoteric meaning. It appears to be always associated with

The classic depiction of Hermes always depicts him pointing towards the heavens. Known as the "messenger of God", Hermes is a central figure in Masonic lore. He is considered to be the teacher of theurgic sciences, therefore helping humanity ascend towards godhood (the word Hermetism derives from Hermes).

"Plato, an initiate of one of these sacred orders, was severely criticized because in his writings he revealed to the public many of the secret philosophic principles of the Mysteries." – Manly P. Hall. In this classic depiction of Plato by Raphael, he is pointing upwards – probably because he "initiated" the world to some of the secret teachings of Mystery schools.

figures that are seen to possess "knowledge from the gods".
In the context of esoteric teachings, a human pointing towards God can represent the ultimate goal of the Myster-

ies: Ascending from the state of mere mortal to achieve godhood.

The hand above the other pillar does not point towards the sky, but is rather opened. While pointing towards somewhere means moving into that direction, an opened palm is traditionally associated with "stop" or "halt". In Masonic symbolism, the twin pillars are often topped with contrasting symbols (the sun and the moon or globes representing earth and heavens). Could the white hands above the pillars represent the same opposite notions of godhood (pointing towards god) and earthly materiality (halt sign)?

On these Masonic pillars are etched various quotes regarding the U.S. Constitution and the Bill of Rights. Some of

"The Bill of Rights was not ordained by Nature or God. It's very human, very fragile." Hmmm, that's ... unsettling.

them are quite odd in the context of today, such this one by Barbara Jordan:
Considering the fact that a bunch of laws blatantly violating the Bill of Rights (notably the First and Fourth Amendment) were enacted shortly after this building was erected, one can ask if this quote wasn't some kind of a warning. As we see new police-state-style laws violating privacy, free speech and encouraging oppression, we can definitely conclude that the elite views the Bill of Rights as something "very human, very fragile" that can easily be violated. While the above quote can be interpreted as a reminder to not take the Bill of Rights for granted, in the context of its location, it conveys an unsettling message about how it can easily be tampered with ... and even disappear. Think I'm going too far? Check out this next piece.

The Pyramid

Between the two pillars is the most recognizable symbol representing the occult elite: A pyramid with a shiny capstone. On the pyramid is written the US Constitution, which famously starts with "We the People". Looking closer at this sculptures, several questions come to mind.

First, why is the U.S. Constitution etched on a symbol that is associated with occult secret societies whose highest degrees are restricted to "elite men"? Isn't there a contradiction here? Second, it is somewhat clear that the charcoal-colored base of the pyramid represents the masses (it is written "We the People" right on it), while the shiny, illuminated capstone represents the "illuminated" elite. Isn't this … elitist? Does the capstone that is standing above the pyramid and the U.S. Constitution mean that the elite is above the law? Finally, why isn't the Bill of Rights on the pyramid? Is it because it is "very human, very fragile"? Is it considered outdated by the NWO elite? As it is the case for many Sinister Sites described on Vigilant Citizen, this barely noticeable artwork contains an infinitely of dark implications.

In Conclusion

In this edition of Sinister Sites, we looked at a relatively small amount of items that nonetheless conveyed a massive amount of symbolism. Far from being merely decorative, the art in front of the IRS building in Maryland describes in a symbolic matter the true source of power behind the American (and world) government, its spiritual and political philosophy, its perception of the masses and so forth. But while the symbolism is unmistakably Masonic, your local front-porch Freemasons have nothing to do with the occult elite. Those in power are part of the highest, hidden levels of the order – what we like to call the Illuminati.

While the IRS doesn't shy away from collecting money from every single American worker in the United States the occult symbols in front of its headquarters is not definitely not meant for every single American worker. It is meant to be understood by a very few "select" ones – the same way real power is owned by a very few "select" ones. Why are there symbols associated with secretive and elite groups displayed on buildings that are supposedly public? Isn't this a contradiction?

While some might say that the true, mystical meaning behind these symbols is not inherently evil, the real upsetting part is that those "in the capstone" are clearly telling us that those at the base of the pyramid are not meant to understand these things. They are meant to be distracted and controlled in order to fund the elite while not causing too much damage … and that's about it. And the IRS is part of the equation.

Contrarily to the "official" meaning of the pointing hand, no citizen has a say on the policies of these institutions or even what they display in front of their building. It is rather those in the capstone that dictate what will happening to "We the People" … even if it means making the Bill of Rights disappear. As the official IRS motto goes: Service plus Enforcement equals Compliance. In short, maybe the finger that is pointing upwards should be the middle one.

Section 5
Secret Arcana

Secret Arcana means "hidden knowledge". Explore the unknown forces shaping our world...

Aleister Crowley: His Elite Ties and His Legacy

The man who revelled in being called "Great Beast 666" and dubbed by the press as the "Wickedest Man in History" was more than a theatrical occultist: Aleister Crowley is at the heart of one of the most influential movements of the 20th and 21st centuries. He also had ties with some of the world's most powerful figures, even working with the British Intelligence Agency MI-5. This article describes the life and works of occultist Aleister Crowley and looks at his ties with the world elite which facilitated the propagation of the Thelema.

Although he is considered to be the most influential occultist of the 20th century and was recognized by the BBC as the 73rd "greatest Briton of all time", most people have never heard of Aleister Crowley. The English occultist, mystic and ceremonial magician is incredibly popular in some circles (occultists, artists, celebrities, etc.) but completely unknown to the average person. And why should he be known? What did he accomplish? Simply put, he foreshadowed the radical philosophical change that would sweep the Western civilization during the 20th century. By founding the philosophy of Thelema and announcing the coming of a New Aeon, Crowley did not only formulate the major philosophical precepts of the 21st century, he was part of the Illuminist motor that promoted it.

Because of Crowley's sexual rituals, drug consumption and dabblings in Black Magick (he introduced the letter "k" at the end of "magic" to differentiate it from the entertainment kind) , Crowley was maligned and heavily criticized by the press during his lifetime. However, declassified documents have since revealed that the "Great Beast 666" led a double life: Crowley apparently maintained ties with the British Government and worked with the British intelligence and high-ranking members of the American Government. The O.T.O.–the secret society he popularized–held within its ranks some of the most influential people of the time, who in turn used their power to further the advancement of its main philosophy: the Thelema.

His Youth

Crowley was born to a wealthy and religious family. His parents were part of the Exclusive Brethren, a conservative faction of the Christian denomination called the Plymouth Brethren. His father, a travelling preacher for his sect, was particularly devout and was said to read a chapter from the verse to his wife and son every day after breakfast [1]. While Crowley maintained a good relationship with his father, he despised his mother, who described him as "the beast" – a name he later adopted as his life-long moniker.

After losing his father to lung cancer at age 11, Crowley inherited the family fortune and went on studying English

Young Crowley

literature at Trinity College in Cambridge. It is during those academic years that Crowley began renouncing and even rebelling against his Christian background. He seriously questioned the Bible, partook in sexual activities with local girls and prostitutes and developed an acute interest in occultism. Another symbolic step towards his self-affirmation was his name change from Edward Alexander to Aleister. Here's an excerpt from his autobiography describing the reasons behind his name change:

> "For many years I had loathed being called Alick, partly because of the unpleasant sound and sight of the word, partly because it was the name by which my mother called me. Edward did not seem to suit me and the diminutives Ted or Ned were even less appropriate. Alexander was too long and Sandy suggested tow hair and freckles. I had read in some book or other that the most favourable name for becoming famous was one consisting of a dactyl followed by a spondee, as at the end of a hexameter: like Jeremy Taylor. Aleister Crowley fulfilled these conditions and Aleister is the Gaelic form of Alexander. To adopt it would satisfy my romantic ideals. The atrocious spelling A-L-E-I-S-T-E-R was suggested as the correct form by Cousin Gregor, who ought to have known better. In any case, A-L-A-I-S-D-A-I-R makes a very bad dactyl. For these reasons I saddled myself with my present nom-de-guerre—I can't say that I feel sure that I facilitated the process of becoming famous. I should doubtless have done so, whatever name I had chosen." [2]

Perhaps Crowley's most significant experiences of his youth were his homosexual relations which, according to his later biographer Lawrence Sutin, led him to an "encounter with an immanent deity". This triggered in him a great interest in occultism, secret societies and, more specifically, what he will later call Sex Magick.

Secret Societies

In his late twenties, Crowley joined many esoteric groups where he was either admired and rose high in the ranks or despised and expelled. Inspired by Arthur E. Waite's book, The Book of Black Magic and of Pacts, Crowley joined the Hermetic Order of the Golden Dawn–known as the "Great White Brotherhood" –in 1898. This secret society held within its membership elite and highly influential members of society. There he was introduced to ceremonial magic and the ritualistic usage of drugs.

In 1899, he reportedly became a member of the Old George Pickingil witch coven. However, he was not welcomed for long as a result of his irresponsible attitude and his inclinations toward homosexuality (which was shocking at that time, even to witches). The priestess of his coven later described him as "a dirty minded, evilly-disposed and vicious little monster!" ³.

Crowley in magician regalia

Crowley also became a high-ranking Freemason, joining several lodges and acquiring several Masonic degrees. In his autobiography, Crowley described his attainment of the 33rd (and last) degree of the Scottish Rite in Mexico:

> "Don Jesus Medina, a descendant of the great duke of Armada fame, and one of the highest chiefs of Scottish Rite free-masonry. My cabbalistic knowledge being already profound by current standards, he thought me worthy of the highest initiation in his power to confer; special powers were obtained in view of my limited sojourn, and I was pushed rapidly through and admitted to the thirty-third and last degree before I left the country." ⁴

With the help of prominent author and Freemason John Yarker, Crowley obtained other Masonic degrees including the 3° In France by the Anglo-Saxon Lodge No. 343, 33° of the irregular 'Cerneau' Scottish Rite and 90°/95° of the Rite of Memphis/Misraim ⁵. According to the United Grand Lodge of England however, whose recognition is generally considered the standard for Masonic validity, none of these Masonic bodies were considered regular and he was never considered an official Freemason.

"The Book of the Law", the Thelema and the Aeon of Horus

In 1904, Crowley and his new wife Rose visited Egypt for their honeymoon. It is during this trip that he wrote his most famous book Liber Legis, The Book of the Law, which would become the cornerstone of his life.

According to his own account, Crowley's wife led him into a museum in Cairo where she showed him a seventh century BCE mortuary stele known as the Stele of Ankh-ef-en-Khonsu (which will be later revered as the Stele of Revealing). Crowley was astounded by the exhibit's number: 666, the number of the Beast in the Book of Revelation.

Later during their stay in Egypt, Crowley and Rose took part in a magical ritual during which he alleges to have received a message from an entity named Aiwass. As a result of this communication, Crowley wrote the first three chapters of the Book of the Law – a mystical text which, he believed, would revolutionize the future of mankind.

The Stele of Revealing, exhibit number 666.

"It announced the advent of a new eon in which Crowley has become the priest-prince of a new religion, the Age of Horus. He was to formulate a link between humanity and the "solar-spiritual force, during which the god Horus would preside for the next two thousand years over the evolution of consciousness on this planet. (...)

The message from Aiwaz, whom Crowley understood to be his own guardian angel, convinced him that his mission in life was to give the coup de grace to the Age of Osiris with its moribund appendage, the Christian faith, and build on the ruins a new religion based on the law of the Thelema – Greek for 'will'." [6]

"Had! The manifestation of Nuit.
The unveiling of the company of heaven.
Every man and woman is a star.
Every number is infinite; there is no difference.
Help me, o warrior lord of Thebes, in my unveiling before the Children of men!"
- The opening lines of the Book of the Law

"By his adepts, the Book of the Law was described as containing occult formulae of cosmic scope, "some openly expressed, some veiled in the most complex web of qabalistic ciphers ever woven into a single text." Nor was it just a piece of "automatic writing," said Crowley, but a clear cut message from an intelligence of superhuman power and knowledge, some extraterrestrial transcendental source, "one of the real hidden masters who would thereafter manifest to him." [7]

Crowley's depiction of Aiwass

According to Crowley's protégé Kenneth Grant, anyone possessing the capacity for understanding the language of symbolism "will be staggered with the accuracy of the summary of the spirit of the eon" [8]. In other words, the same way the Bible ruled over Western Civilization during the past two millenniums, the Thelema would describe the spirit of the next two thousand years.

> "In the Aeon of Horus the dualistic approach to religion will be transcended through the abolition of the present notion of a God external to oneself. The two will be united. "Man will no longer worship God as an external factor, as in Paganism, or as an internal state of consciousness, as in Christianity, but will realize his identity with God." The new Aeon of Horus, based on the union of the male and female polarities, will involve the magical use of semen and ecstasy, culminating in an apotheosis of matter – "in the realization of the old Gnostic notion that matter is not dual but one with the Spirit" — symbolized by the androgynous Baphomet of the Templars and the Illuminati." [9]

The Book of the Law became the basis of Thelema, which revolved around three key philosophical ideas:

1- Do what thou wilt shall be the whole of the Law;
2- Love is the law, Love under will;
3- Every man and every woman is a star.

The unicursal hexagram, main symbol of the Thelema

It is widely believed that the saying "Do What Thou Wilt" means "do what you want", therefore describing an egoistic quest for instant gratification and pleasure. However, initiates of the philosophy disagree with this description of the axiom as they believe it is meant to be interpreted on a metaphysical level. Thelema is Greek for "The Will". The main aim of this philosophy is the realization of one's True Will, which is described as one's "higher calling" or purpose in life, regardless of ethical or moral barriers.

> "There are no "standards of Right". Ethics is balderdash. Each Star must go on its own orbit. To hell with "moral principle"; there is no such thing." [10]

Crowley incorporated these teachings into his newly-founded A∴ A∴ (Argenteum Astrum or the Silver Star), a magical order meant to be a successor of the defunct Hermetic Order of the Golden Dawn. To generate interest in his order, Crowley also published The Equinox – A Journal of Scientific Illuminism (a term borrowed from Adam Weishaupt's Order of the Illuminati) where he divulged esoteric rituals and techniques. His later work entitled Book of Lies captured the attention of the head of the Ordo Templi Orienti (O.T.O) Theodor Reuss, who soon made him an initiate and Grand Master of the O.T.O. The reason given for such a recognition: his knowledge of sexual magic.

The O.T.O. and Sex Magick

The O.T.O's magical and initiatory system has among its innermost reaches a set of teachings on sex magick. One might even observe that the acronym of this order is rather phallic. Sex magick is the use of the sex act, or the energies, passions or arousals it evokes, as a point of which to focus the will or magical desire in the non-sexual world. It has been equated with the "life force" and the "kundalini". Through the ritualistic use of sexual techniques, inspired by Tantric schools of the East, the initiate can use the immense potency of sexual energy to reach higher realms of spirituality.

> "The order had rediscovered the great secret of the Knights Templar, the magic of sex, not only the key to ancient Egyptian and hermetic tradition, but to all the secrets of nature, all the symbolism of Freemasonry, and all systems of Religion. [11]"

Crowley, known as the "Great Baphomet" of the O.T.O.

To set in motion the "occult forces which would result in the illumination of all by 2000 A.D.," Crowley became convinced that his mission was to "cure the world from sexual repression". To achieve his goal, he determined to study every detail of sexual behavior and bring every sexual impulse up to the region of rational consciousness. To this end he experimented with altered states of consciousness, including hashish, cocaine and opium.

Crowley would eventually introduce (not without protest) the practice of homosexual sex magick into the O.T.O. as one of the highest degrees of the Order for he believed it to be the most powerful formula [12]. It was clear that Crowley felt the accusations against the original Templars of practising sodomy and orgies with women had been based in fact, but not understood by their detractors.

Crowley also kept with him a series of "Scarlet Women": the best known of these was Leah Hirsig, the so-called "Ape of Thoth". Together they would indulge in drinking sessions, drugs and sexual magic. It is believed that Crowley made multiple attempts with several of these women to begat a "Magickal child" (see Roman Polanski's Rosemary's Baby), none of which reportedly worked. He instead fictionalized his attempts in a book called "Moonchild", published in 1929. In the Thelema, the Scarlet woman is equated with Babalon – The Great Mother, the Mother of Abominations of the book of Revelation. Crowley and his protégés would often dabble and experiment with this concept.

Secret Agent 666

As Crowley's antics were picked up by the press, he soon became infamous as a black magician, a satanist and drug addict and would be dubbed "The Wickedest Man in the World". However, unclassified documents revealed that this did not stop the British intelligence from hiring him as an agent. (It was not the first time that the British Crown hired the services of renown occultists; a famous example of such association can be found in the link between John Dee and Queen Elizabeth I.)

The most significant work on the subject of Crowley's spy career is Richard B. Spence's Agent 666. Using documents gleaned from British, American, French and Italian archives, Secret Agent 666 sensationally reveals that Crowley played a major role in the sinking of the Lusitania, a plot to overthrow the government of Spain, the thwarting of Irish and Indian nationalist conspiracies, and the 1941 flight of Rudolf Hess.

During his research Spence uncovered a document from the U.S. Army's old Military Intelligence Division supporting Crowley's own claim to having been a spy:

> "Aleister Crowley was an employee of the British Government … in this country on official business of which the British Consul, New York City has full cognizance" [13]

According to Spence:

> "Crowley was an adept amateur psychologist, had an uncanny ability to influence people and probably utilized hypnotic suggestion in his undercover work. The other thing he made good use of was drugs. In New York, he carried out very detailed studies on the effects of mescaline (peyote). He would invite various friends over for dinner, fix them curry and dose the food with mescaline. Then he observed and took notes on their behavior. Mescaline was later used by intelligence agencies for experiments in behavior modification and mind control.[14]"

During World War II, Crowley became editor of a pro-German magazine called The Fatherland, in which he published incendiary, anti-British articles. He later claimed that these writings were so absurd and outlandish that they ultimately helped the cause of the British. Crowley also proposed many ideas to help the allies, most of which were rejected. One of them, while initially dismissed, was later implemented. This involved dropping occult pamphlets on the German countryside that predicted dire outcome for the war and depicted Nazi leadership as Satanic. His expertise in communications, propaganda and the management of public opinion would be used to make his Thelema a major force in today's popular culture.

Important Protégés

As head of the O.T.O in California, Crowley tutored many individuals who had a great impact on American Society. One of them is Jack Parsons.

Jack Parsons

Jack Parsons, was an American rocket propulsion researcher at the California Institute of Technology. He was one of the principal founders of the Jet Propulsion Laboratory and the Aerojet Corp. His rocket research was some of the earliest in the United States, and his pioneering work in the development of solid fuel and the invention of JATO units for aircraft was of great importance to the start of humanity's space age. The noted engineer Theodore von Kármán, Parsons's friend and benefactor, declared that the work of Parsons and his peers helped usher in the age of space travel. In fact, the Parsons crater on the dark side of the moon is named after him.

> "He (Jack Parsons) has been described as 'the one single individual who contributed the most to rocket science' and as an individual 'who traveled under sealed orders from the US Government' [15]"

Behind closed doors, Parsons was deeply steeped in occultism and became a prominent member of the O.T.O., where he partook in rather extreme sex magick rituals:

> "Among Parsons' many sex partners was that of his own mother (their incestuous encounters were filmed). Both mother and son engaged in bestiality and both appear to have been among that species of psychotic who can function normally in public and achieve positions of authority over others. [16]"

In 1942, Parsons was appointed as head of the Agapé O.T.O. Lodge by Aleister Crowley. Like Crowley, Parsons was obsessed with the idea of creating a "magickal child" with Babalon or the Scarlet Woman.

> "The purpose of Parson's operation has been underemphasized. He sought to produce a magickal child who would be a product of her environment rather than of her heredity. Crowley himself describes the Moonchild in just these terms. The Babalon Working itself was preparation for what was to come: a Thelemic messiah. [17]"

Parsons with fellow members of Agape Lodge.

There was no clear separation between Parson's professional and occult lives. In fact, he was known to recite Crowley's poem Hymn to Pan before each rocket test.

Parson later associated with an individual who would become hugely influential: L. Ron Hubbard, the man who would establish the Church of Scientology.

Parsons took a great liking to Hubbard, who was then a U.S. Navy Captain, and initiated him to the secrets of the O.T.O.

> "In a 1946 communiqué to Crowley, Parsons wrote: 'About three months ago I met (US Navy) Capt. L. Ron. Hubbard...Although Ron has no formal training in Magick, he has an extraordinary amount

of experience and understanding in the field...He is the most thelemic person I have ever met and is in complete accord with our principles. He is also interested in establishing the New Aeon...We are pooling our resources in a partnership that will act as a limited company to control our business ventures. [18]"

Portion of a 1969 article on the link between Hubbard and Crowley.

Hubbard's Church of Scientology is today an extremely influential and well-funded sect that boasts within its ranks more than 8 million members, including high-profile celebrities like Tom Cruise, Will Smith, John Travolta and Lisa Marie Presley.

Popular Culture

Although Crowley died nearly penniless, fighting a heroin addiction, his legacy is nevertheless nothing less than colossal. Crowley's impact on today's popular culture is noticeable on many levels, whether it is through direct references to his persona or through Thelema-inspired works.

The most obvious examples of Crowley's influence on popular culture are the references made by the rock stars who were enamored with his persona and philosophy such as the Beatles and Jimmy Page.

Crowley on the Beatles' Sgt. Pepper's Lonely Hearts Club Band album cover

Crowley also inspired numerous movie characters including Le Chiffre – James Bond's arch-villain in Ian Fleming's Casino Royale and Satanist witch Adrian Marcato in Rosemary's Baby. Today, references to Crowley and his Thelema can be found in odd places such as the anime Yu-Gi-Oh! where one of the characters of the series is named Alister in honor of him. This character bears on his forehead "The Seal of Orichalcos", which is a carbon-copy of Crowley's unicursal hexagram.

Alister bearing the unicursal hexagram on his forehead.

Beyond these direct references, an astute analyst can detect the influence of Crowley's Thelemic philosophy and his vision of a New Aeon in countless mass media products. In fact, prominent members of the O.T.O. were (and still are) heavily involved in the production of Hollywood movies, embedding within their plots Thelemic tenets. Science fiction is a favored genre to expose viewers to predictive programming.

> "OTO initiates authored mass market stories, especially science fiction, with subliminal, occult themes published in popular books and magazines. Among the most influential of these were Robert Heinlein's Stranger in a Strange Land, A.H. White's Rocket to the Morgue and the aforementioned Arthur C. Clarke's "The Sentinel" and Childhood's End. (…)
>
> By means of the newly burgeoning genre of science fiction, the OTO was able to shape the vision of America through predictive programming, which forecasts an "inevitable future," thereby influencing everything from the architecture of our cities to the design of our automobiles and conception of what constitutes "progress and liberation" in the future. (…)
>
> The OTO's ability to transform America consisted in the linkage of this brazen lying with science and science fiction, molding media and medicine in their image and likeness and creating a new "Thelemic" religion for the masses. [19]"

In Conclusion

Today, Crowley is regarded as either a misunderstood mystical genius or a depraved charlatan, a prophet for an era of spiritual enlightenment or a Satanic harbinger of the Anti-Christ, an agent for the sexual liberation of mankind or drug-addicted pederast. Were his spiritual visions true or did he con thousands of followers? Answering this question today is practically irrelevant. As a youth, Crowley wished to become a celebrity and to change the course of history and, in his own way, he accomplished both objectives. Not only did his peculiar character make him something of a cult icon, his philosophic and esoteric works are today a major force influencing mainstream culture, values and spirituality.

Unlike most historical figures who lose their relevancy as the years go by, Crowley's influence is steadily increasing in the 21st century. This is not only a result of luck or natural evolution, however. Crowley and his O.T.O. maintained ties with high-level members of the British and American governments, as well as with influential figures in science, law and culture. The world's elite, predominated by Illuminist values, are in perfect accord with Crowley's Thelema. These connections facilitated the dissemination and acceptance of his works in popular culture. Crowley did not only predict society's abandonment of traditional religions and the embrace the Aeon of Horus, he was part of the motor that made these changes happen. His vision of a New Aeon also coincides with the Illuminati's age-old plan for a secular world order ruled by an "enlightened" elite. The wording might be different, but the hermetic philosophical background is the same. Let's say that Crowley and the Establishment see "eye to eye" on the subject … and this eye is the Eye of Horus.

[1] Lawrence Sutin, "Do What Thou Wilt: A Life of Aleister Crowley
[2] Aleister Crowley, The Confessions of Aleister Crowley: An Autohagiography
[3] Rosemary Ellen Guiley, The Encyclopedia of Witches and Witchcraft
[4] Op. Cit. Crowley
[5] Op. Cit Sutin
[6] Peter Tompkins, The Magic of Obelisks
[7] Ibid.
[8] Op Cit. Thompson
[9] Ibid.
[10] Aleister Crowley, The Old and New Commentaries to Liber AL
[11] Theodor Reuss, Oriflamme
[12] Jason Newcomb, Sexual Sorcery
[13] Richard A. Spence quoting a U.S. military document, Secret Agent 666
[14] Op. Cit. Spence
[15] Michael A. Hoffman II, Secret Societies and Psychological Warfare
[16] Ibid.
[17] Richard Metger, John Whiteside Parsons: Anti-Christ Superstar
[18] Ibid
[19] Ibid

The Mysterious Connection Between Sirius and Human History

Since ancient times and across multiple civilizations, Sirius, the dog star, has been surrounded with a mysterious lore. Esoteric teachings of all ages have invariably attributed to Sirius a special status and the star's importance in occult symbolism is an attestation of that fact. What makes Sirius so special? Is it simply due to the fact that it is the brightest star in the sky? Or is it also because humanity has an ancient, mysterious connection with it? This article looks at the importance of Sirius throughout History and secret societies and will describe the symbolism surrounding it.

Sirius is located in the constellation Canis Major – also known as the Big Dog – and is therefore known as the "dog star". It is over twenty times brighter than our sun and is twice as massive. At night time, Sirius is the brightest star in the sky and its blue-white glare never failed to amaze star gazers since the dawn of time. No wonder Sirius has been revered by practically all civilizations. But is there more to Sirius than meets the eye?

Artifacts of ancient civilizations have revealed that Sirius was of a great importance in astronomy, mythology and occultism. Mystery schools consider it to be "sun behind the sun" and, therefore, the true source of our sun's potency. If our sun's warmth keeps the physical world alive, Sirius is considered to keep the spiritual world alive. It is the "real light" shining in the East, the spiritual light, where as the sun illuminates the physical world, which is considered to be a grand illusion.

Associating Sirius with the divine and even considering it as the home of humanity's "great teachers" is not only embedded in the mythology of a few primitive civilizations: It is a widespread belief that has survived (and even intensified) to this day. We will look at the importance of Sirius in ancient times, analyze its prominence in secret societies and we will examine these esoteric concepts as they are translated in popular culture.

In Ancient Civilizations

In Ancient Egypt, Sirius was regarded as the most important star in the sky. In fact, it was astronomically the foundation of the Egyptians' entire religious system. It was revered as Sothis and was associated with Isis, the mother goddess of Egyptian mythology. Isis is the female aspect of the trinity formed by herself, Osiris and their son Horus. Ancient Egyptians held Sirius in such a high regard that most of their deities were associated, in some way or another, with the star. Anubis, the dog-headed god of death, had an obvious connection with the dog star and Toth-Hermes, the great teacher of humanity, was also esoterically connected with the star.

The Egyptian calendar system was based on the heliacal rising of Sirius that occurred just before the annual flooding of the Nile during summer. The star's celestial movement was also observed and revered by ancient Greeks, Sumerians, Babylonians and countless other civilizations. The star was therefore considered sacred and its apparition in the sky was accompanied with feasts and celebrations. The dog star heralded the coming of the hot and dry days of July and August, hence the popular term "the dog days of summer".

Several occult researchers have claimed that the Great Pyramid of Giza was built in perfect alignment with the stars, especially Sirius. The light from these stars were said to be used in ceremonies of Egyptian Mysteries.

> "This ancient people (Egyptians) knew that once every year the Parent Sun is in line with the Dog Star. Therefore, the Great Pyramid was so constructed that, at this sacred moment, the light of the Dog Star fell upon the square "Stone of God" at the upper end of the Great Gallery, descending upon the head of the high priest, who received the Super Solar Force and sought through his own perfected Solar Body to transmit to other Initiates this added stimulation for the evolution of their Godhood. This then was the purpose of the "'Stone of God,' whereon in the Ritual, Osiris sits to bestow upon him (the illuminate) the Atf crown or celestial light." "North and South of that crown is love," proclaims an Egyptian hymn. "And thus throughout the teaching of Egypt the visible light was but the shadow of the invisible Light; and in the wisdom of the ancient country the measures of Truth were the years of the Most High. [1]

Recent scientific discoveries relating to the Great Pyramid and its mysterious "air shafts" have lead researchers to further confirm the importance of Sirius within the pyramid.

A fascinating aspect of Sirius is the consistency of the symbolism and meanings attached to it. Several great civilizations have indeed associated Sirius with a dog-like figure and viewed the star as either the source or the destination of a mysterious force. In Chinese and Japanese astronomy, Sirius is known as the "star of the celestial wolf". Several aboriginal tribes of North America referred to the star in canine terms: the Seri and Tohono O'odham tribes of the southwest describe the Sirius as a "dog that follows mountain sheep", while the Blackfoot call it "Dogface". The Cherokee paired Sirius with Antares as a dog-star guardian of the "Path of Souls". The Wolf (Skidi) tribe of Nebraska knew it as the "Wolf Star", while other branches of knew it as the "Coyote Star". Further north, the Alaskan Inuit of the Bering Strait called it "Moon Dog". [2]

The Dogon Tribe and Atlantis

In 1971, the American author Robert Temple published a controversial book entitled The Sirius Mystery where he claimed that the Dogons (an ancient African tribe from Mali) knew details about Sirius that would be impossible to be know without the use of telescopes. According to him, the Dogon understood the binary nature of Sirius, which is, in fact, composed of two stars named Sirius A and Sirius B. This lead Robert Temple to believe that the Dogons had "direct" connections with beings from Sirius. While some might say "you can't be Sirius" (sorry), a great number of secret societies (who have historically held within their ranks some of the world's most influential people) and belief systems teach about a mystic connection between Sirius and humanity.

In Dogon mythology, humanity is said to be born from the Nommo, a race of amphibians who were inhabitants of a planet circling Sirius. They are said to have "descended from the sky in a vessel accompanied by fire and thunder" and imparted to humans profound knowledge. This lead Robert Temple to theorize that the Nommos were extraterrestrial inhabitants of Sirius who travelled to earth at some point in the distant past to teach ancient civilizations (such as the Egyptians and Dogons) about the Sirius star system as well as our own solar system. These civilizations would then record the Nommos' teachings in their religions and make them a central focus of their Mysteries.

The Dogon's mythology system is strikingly similar to the ones of other civilizations such as the Sumerians, Egyptians, Israelites and Babylonians as it includes the archetypal myth of a "great teacher from above". Depending on the civilization, this great teacher is known as eith Enoch, Thoth or Hermes Trismegistus and is said to have taught humanity theurgic sciences. In occult traditions, it is believed that Thoth-Hermes had taught the people of Atlantis, which, according to legend, became the world's most advanced civilization before the entire continent was submerged by the Great Deluge (accounts of a flood can be found in the mythologies of countless civilizations). Survivors from Atlantis travelled by boat to several countries, including Egypt, where they imparted their advanced knowledge. Occultists believe that the inexplicable resemblances between distant civilizations (such as the Mayas and the Egyptians) can be explained by their common contact with Atlanteans.

> "Was the religious, philosophic, and scientific knowledge possessed by the priestcrafts of antiquity secured from Atlantis, whose submergence obliterated every vestige of its part in the drama of world progress? Atlantean sun worship has been perpetuated in the ritualism and ceremonialism of both Christianity and pagandom. Both the cross and the serpent were Atlantean emblems of divine wisdom. The divine (Atlantean) progenitors of the Mayas and Quichés of Central America coexisted within the green and azure radiance of Gucumatz, the "plumed" serpent. The six sky-born sages came into manifestation as centers of light bound together or synthesized by the seventh – and chief – of their order, the "feathered" snake. The title of "winged" or "plumed" snake was applied to Quetzalcoatl, or Kukulcan, the Central American initiate. The center of the Atlantean Wisdom-Religion was presumably a great pyramidal temple standing on the brow of a plateau rising in the midst of the City of the Golden Gates. From here the Initiate-Priests of the Sacred Feather went forth, carrying the keys of Universal Wisdom to the uttermost parts of the earth.
>
> (...)
>
> From the Atlanteans the world has received not only the heritage of arts and crafts, philosophies and sciences, ethics and religions, but also the heritage of hate, strife, and perversion. The Atlanteans instigated the first war; and it has been said that all subsequent wars were fought in a fruitless effort to justify the first one and right the wrong which it caused. Before Atlantis sank, its spiritually illumined Initiates, who realized that their land was doomed because it had departed from the Path of Light, withdrew from the ill-fated continent. Carrying with them the sacred and secret doctrine,

these Atlanteans established themselves in Egypt, where they became its first "divine" rulers. Nearly all the great cosmologic myths forming the foundation of the various sacred books of the world are based upon the Atlantean Mystery rituals." [3]

Is Thoth-Hermes-Trismegistus the equivalent of the Dogon's Nommos, who are believed to originate from Sirius? Ancient texts concerning Hermes describe him as a teacher of mysteries who "came from the stars". Furthermore, Thoth-Hermes was directly connected with Sirius in Egyptian mythology.

"The dog-star: the star worshipped in Egypt and reverenced by the Occultists; by the former because its heliacal rising with the Sun was a sign of the beneficent inundation of the Nile, and by the latter because it is mysteriously associated with Toth-Hermes, god of wisdom, and Mercury, in another form. Thus Sothis-Sirius had, and still has, a mystic and direct influence over the whole living heaven, and is connected with almost every god and goddess. It was "Isis in the heaven" and called Isis-Sothis, for Isis was "in the constellation of the dog", as is declared on her monuments. Being connected with the Pyramid, Sirius was, therefore, connected with the initiations which took place in it." [4]

"The Trismegistic treatise 'The Virgin of the World' from Egypt refers to 'the Black Rite', connected with the 'black' Osiris, as the highest degree of secret initiation possible in the ancient Egyptian religion – it is the ultimate secret of the mysteries of Isis. This treatise says Hermes came to earth to teach men civilization and then again 'mounted to the stars', going back to his home and leaving behind the mystery religion of Egypt with its celestial secrets which were some day to be decoded." [5]

Interpreting the mythology of ancient cultures is not an exact science and connections are inherently difficult to prove. However, the symbolic link between Sirius and occult knowledge has constantly appeared throughout History and has seamlessly traveled through the ages. In fact, it is as revered today as it was millenniums ago. Modern secret societies such as the Freemasons, the Rosicrucians and the Golden Dawn (which are considered to be Hermetic Orders due to the fact their teachings are based on those of Hermes Trismegistus) all attribute to Sirius the utmost importance. An educated look at their symbolism provides a glimpse at the profound connection between Sirius and occult philosophy.

Sirius in Occult Symbolism and Secret Societies

To claim that Sirius is "important" to Hermetic Orders would be a gross understatement. The dog star is nothing less than the central focus of the teachings and symbolism of secret societies. The ultimate proof of this fact: many secret societies are actually named after the star.

In the Tarot

The seventeenth numbered major trump is called Les Étoiles, (French for The Star), and portrays a young girl kneeling with one foot in water and the other on and, her body somewhat suggesting the swastika. She has two urns, the contents of which she pours upon the land and sea. Above the girl's head are eight stars, one of which is exceptionally large and bright. Count de Gébelin considers the great star to be Sothis or Sirius; the other seven are the sacred planets of the ancients. He believes the female figure to be Isis in the act of causing the inundations of the Nile which accompanied the rising of the Dog Star. The unclothed figure of Isis may well signify that Nature does not receive her garment of verdure until the rising of the Nile waters releases the germinal life of plants and flowers. [6]

In Freemasonry

In Masonic lodges, Sirius is known as the "Blazing Star" and a simple look at its prominence in Masonic symbolism reveals its utmost importance. The Masonic author William Hutchinson wrote about Sirius: "It is the first and most exalted object that demands our attention in the Lodge." The same way the light of Sirius made its way into the Great Pyramid during initiations, it is symbolically present in Masonic lodges.

> "The Ancient Astronomers saw all the great Symbols of Masonry in the Stars. Sirius glitters in our lodges as the Blazing Star." [7]

Sirius, the Blazing Star, at the center of the Masonic mosaic pavement.

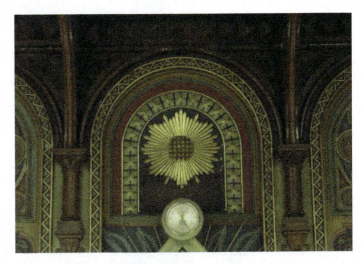

The Blazing Star shining upon members of a Masonic lodge

> "(The Blazing Star) originally represented SIRIUS, or the Dog-star, the forerunner of the inundation of the Nile; the God ANUBIS, companion of ISIS in her search for the body of OSIRIS, her brother and husband. Then it became the image of HORUS, the son of OSIRIS, himself symbolized also by the Sun, the author of the Seasons, and the God of Time; Son of ISIS, who was the universal nature, himself the primitive matter, inexhaustible source of Life, spark of uncreated fire, universal seed of all beings. It was HERMES, also, the Master of Learning, whose name in Greek is that of the God Mercury." [8]

In Freemasonry, it is taught that the Blazing Star is a symbol of deity, of omnipresence (the Creator is present everywhere) and of omniscience (the Creator sees and knows all). Sirius is therefore the "sacred place" all Masons must ascend to: It is the source of divine power and the destination of divine individuals. This concept is often represented in Masonic art.

To achieve perfection, the initiate must successfully understand and internalize the dual nature of the world (good and evil; masculine and feminine; black and white, etc.) through alchemical metamorphosis. This concept is symbolically represented by the union of Osiris and Isis (the male and female principles) to give birth to Horus, the star-child, the Christ-like figure, the perfected man of Freemasonry – who is equated with the Blazing Star.

> "The sun and moon ... represent the two grand principles ... the male and the female ... both shed their light upon their offspring, the blazing star, or Horus." [9]

Secret Arcana

Masonic art portraying Sirius, the Blazing Star, as the destination of the Mason's journey.

The Egyptian hieroglyph representing Sirius has been esoterically interpreted to be a representation of this cosmic trinity. This concept is so crucial for Freemasons, that it was embedded in some of the most important structures in the world.

The hieroglyph representing Sirius contains three elements: a "phallic" obelisk (representing Osiris), a "womb-like" dome (representing Isis) and a star (representing Horus).

The Washington Monument, an Egyptian obelisk representing the male principle, is directly connected with the dome of the Capitol, representing the female principle. Together they produce Horus an unseen energy represented by Sirius.

As stated by Albert Pike above, the Egyptian god Horus and the star Sirius are often associated. In Masonic symbolism, the eye of Horus (or the All-Seeing Eye) is often depicted surrounded by the glittering of light of Sirius.

A Masonic tracing board depicting the sun above the left pillar (representing the masculine), the moon above the right pillar (representing feminine) and Sirius above the middle pillar, representing the "perfected man" or Horus, the son of Isis and Osiris. Notice the "Eye of Horus" on Sirius.

The Eye of Horus inside a triangle (symbolizing deity) surrounded by the glow of Sirius, the Blazing Star

The All-Seeing Eye inside the Blazing Star in Masonic art.

Given the symbolic correlation between the All-Seeing Eye and Sirius, the next image becomes self-explanatory.

The light behind the All-Seeing Eye on the American dollar bill is not from the sun, but from Sirius. The Great Pyramid of Giza was built in alignment with Sirius and is therefore shown shining right above the Pyramid. A radiant tribute to Sirius is therefore in the pockets of millions of citizens.

Order of the Eastern Star

The symbol of the OES is an inverted star, similar to the Blazing Star of Freemasonry.

Considered to be the "female version" of Freemasonry (although men can join), the Order of the Eastern Star (OES) is directly named after Sirius, the "Star rising from the East". A "general public" explanation of the origins of the Order's name claims it originated from the "Star of the East" that lead the Three Magis to Jesus Christ. A look into the occult meaning of the Order's symbolism however makes it clear that the OES is a reference to Sirius, the most important star of Freemasonry, its parent organization.

Madame Blavatsky, Alice Bailey and Theosophy

Helena Blavatsky and Alice Bailey, the two main figures associated with Theosophy, have both considered Sirius to be a source esoteric power. Blavatsky stated that the star Sirius exerts a mystic and direct influence over the entire living heaven and is linked with every great religion of antiquity.

Alice Bailey sees the Dog Star as the true "Great White Lodge" and believes it to be the home of the "Spiritual Hierarchy". For this reason she considers Sirius as the "star of initiation".

> "This is the great star of initiation because our Hierarchy (an expression of the second aspect of divinity) is under the supervision or spiritual magnetic control of the Hierarchy of Sirius. These are the major controlling influences whereby the cosmic Christ works upon the Christ principle in the solar system, in the planet, in man and in the lower forms of life expression. It is esoterically called the brilliant star of sensitivity." [10]

Not unlike most many esoteric writers, Bailey considers Sirius to have a great impact on human life.

> "All that can be done here in dealing with this profound subject is to enumerate briefly some of the cosmic influences which definitely affect our earth, and produce results in the consciousness of men everywhere, and which, during the process of initiation, bring about certain specific phenomena.
>
> First and foremost is the energy or force emanating from the sun Sirius. If it might be so expressed, the energy of thought, or mind force, in its totality, reaches the solar system from a distant cosmic centre via Sirius. Sirius acts as the transmitter, or the focalising centre, whence emanate those influences which produce self-consciousness in man." [11]

Aleister Crowley, the A.A. and Kenneth Grant

In 1907, Crowley started his own occult order called the A.A. – short for Argentium Astrum, which can be translated to 'The Order of the Silver Star'. The 'Silver Star' was, of course, a reference to Sirius. Even if Crowley almost always referred to the dog star in veiled terms, the whole of his magickal philosophy, from his development as a young Freemason through to his final years as the Head of the O.T.O, is wholly in accordance with the Sirian influence, which was identified and expressed by other writers of his era. His alleged contact with his Holy Guardian Angel that later led to the channelling of 'Liber AL: The Book of the Law' is believed to have originated from Sirius.

If Crowley used code words to describe Sirius, his protégé Kenneth Grant has explicitly and extensively written about the dog star. Throughout his numerous books, he often described Sirius as being a powerful center of magickal magnetic power. His belief that the star holds the central key to unlocking the mysteries of the Egyptian and Typhonian traditions has strengthened over time and became a central focus of his research. One of Grant's most important and controversial thesis was his discovery of the "Sirius/Set current", which is an extra-terrestrial dimension connecting Sirius, the Earth and Set, the Eyptian god of Chaos – who was later associated with Satan.

> "Set is the initiator, the Opener of mans' consciousness to the rays of the Undying God typified by Sirius – the Sun in the South." [12]

> "Sirius, or Set, was the original "headless one" – the light of the lower region (the south) who was known (in Egypt) as An (the dog), hence Set-An (Satan), Lord of the infernal regions, the place of heat, later interpreted in a moral sense as 'hell'." [13]

Although each occult philosophy describes Sirius in a slightly different matter, it is still consistently regarded as the "sun behind the sun", the true source of occult power. It is perceived as the cradle of human knowledge and the belief of the existence of a strong connection between the star and planet Earth never seems to become outdated. Is there a true link between Sirius and Earth? Is the dog star an esoteric symbol representing something happening in the spiritual realm? It is both? One thing is for sure, the cult of Sirius is not a "thing of the past" and is very alive today. An in-depth look at our popular culture, which is heavily influenced by occult symbolism, reveals numerous references to Sirius.

Sirius in Popular Culture

Direct references to Sirius in popular culture are too many to enumerate (e.g. see the name and the logo of the most important satellite radio in the world). A more interesting aspect of popular culture to analyze are the coded references to Sirius. Important movies have indeed made veiled yet profound references to the dog star (apparently intended to those "in the know"), where the star plays the role it was always given by the Mysteries: as an initiator and a divine teacher. Here are some examples.

In Disney's Pinocchio, based on a story written by Freemason Carlo Collodi, Gepetto prays to the brightest star in the sky to have a "real boy". The Blue Fairy (her color is a reference to Sirius' light-blue glow) then descends from the heavens to give life to Pinocchio. Throughout the marionette's quest to become a boy (an allegory for esoteric initiation), the Blue Fairy guides Pinocchio towards the "right path". Sirius is therefore represented as a source of life, a guide and a teacher.

The theme song of the movie Pinocchio is also an ode to Sirius.

> *When you wish upon a star, makes no difference who you are*
> *Anything your heart desires will come to you*
> *If your heart is in your dreams, no request is too extreme*
> *When you wish upon a star as dreamers do*
>
> *(Fate is kind, she brings to those who love*
> *The sweet fulfillment of their secret longing)*
>
> *Like a bolt out of the blue, fate steps in and sees you thru*
> *When you wish upon a star, your dreams come true*

In the Truman Show, a spotlight – used to imitate the light of a star in Truman's fake world – falls from the sky and nearly hits him. The label on the spotlight identifies it as Sirius. Truman's encounter with Sirius gives him a glimpse of "true knowledge" and prompts his quest for truth. Sirius is therefore the "star of initiation". It caused Truman to realize the limitations of the his studio world (our material world) and lead him to freedom (spiritual emancipation).

In Harry Potter, the character named Sirius Black is most likely a reference to Sirius B. (the "darker" star of Sirius' binary system). He is Harry Potter's godfather, which makes Sirius, once again, a teacher and a guide. The wizard can turn into a big black dog, another link with the "dog star".

In Conclusion

From the dawn of civilization to modern times, from remote tribes of Africa to the great capitals of the modern world, Sirius was – and still is – seen as a life-giver. Despite the disparity between cultures and epochs, the same mysterious attributes are given to the dog star, which can lead us to ask: how can all theses definitions synchronize so perfectly? Is there a common source to these myths about Sirius? The dog star is invariably associated with divinity and is regarded as a source of knowledge and power. These connections are particularly evident when one examines the teachings and the symbolism of secret societies, who have always taught about a mystical link with this particular celestial body. Is there a secret link between human evolution and Sirius? Unlocking this secret would mean unlocking one of humanity's greatest mysteries.

[1] Marshall Adams, The Book of the Master
[2] J.B. Holberg, Sirius: Brightest Diamond in the Night Sky
[3] Manly P. Hall, The Secret Teachings of All Ages
[4] Helena Blavatsky, Theosophical Glossary
[5] Robert Temple, The Sirius Mystery
[6] Manly P. Hall, The Secret Teachings of All Ages
[7] Albert Pike, Morals and Dogma
[8] Ibid.
[9] Pike, op. cit.
[10] Alice Bailey, Esoteric Astrology
[11] Alice Bailey, Initiation, Human and Solar
[12] Kenneth Grant, The Magical Revival
[13] Ibid.

Origins and Techniques of Monarch Mind Control

Monarch Programming is a method of mind control used by numerous organizations for covert purposes. It is a continuation of project MK-ULTRA, a mind-control program developed by the CIA, and tested on the military and civilians. The methods are astonishingly sadistic (its entire purpose is to traumatize the victim) and the expected results are horrifying: The creation of a mind-controlled slave who can be triggered at anytime to perform any action required by the handler. While mass media ignores this issue, over 2 million Americans have gone through the horrors of this program. This article looks at the origins of Monarch programming and some of its methods and symbolism.
NOTE: This article contains disturbing elements and might trigger Monarch survivors.

Monarch programming is a mind-control technique comprising elements of Satanic Ritual Abuse (SRA) and Multiple Personality Disorder (MPD). It utilizes a combination of psychology, neuroscience and occult rituals to create within the slaves an alter persona that can be triggered and programmed by the handlers. Monarch slaves are used by several organizations connected with the world elite in fields such as the military, sex slavery and the entertainment industry. This article will look at the origins of Monarch programming, its techniques and its symbolism.

Origins

Throughout the course of history, several accounts have been recorded describing rituals and practices resembling mind control. One of the earliest writings giving reference to the use of occultism to manipulate the mind can be found in the Egyptian Book of the Dead. It is a compilation of rituals, heavily studied by today's secret societies, which describes methods of torture and intimidation (to create trauma), the use of potions (drugs) and the casting of spells (hypnotism), ultimately resulting in the total enslavement of the initiate. Other events ascribed to black magic, sorcery and demon possession (where the victim is animated by an outside force) are also ancestors of Monarch programming.

It is, however, during the 20th century that mind control became a science in the modern sense of the term, where thousands of subjects have been systematically observed, documented and experimented on.

One of the first methodical studies on trauma-based mind control were conducted by Josef Mengele, a physician working in Nazi concentration camps. He initially gained notoriety for being one of the SS physicians who supervised the selection of arriving prisoners, determining who was to be killed and who was to become a forced

laborer. However, he is mostly known for performing grisly human experiments on camp inmates, including children, for which Mengele was called the "Angel of Death".
Mengele is infamous for his sordid human experiments on concentration camps prisoners, especially on twins. A

Joseph Mengele, 1935

part of his work that is rarely mentioned however, is his research on mind control. Much of his research in this field was confiscated by the Allies and is still classified to this day.

> "DR. GREEN (Dr. Joseph Mengele): The most significant programmer, perhaps one could give him the title of the father of Monarch Programming was Joseph Mengele, an ex-Nazi Concentration Camp doctor. Thousands of Monarch mindcontrolled slaves in the U.S. had "Dr. Green" as their chief programmer."[1]

"Dr. Joseph Mengele of Auschwitz notoriety was the principle developer of the trauma-based Monarch Project and the CIA's MK Ultra mind control programs. Mengele and approximately 5, 000 other high ranking Nazis were secretly moved into the United States and South America in the aftermath of World War II in an Operation designated Paperclip. The Nazis continued their work in developing mind control and rocketry technologies in secret underground military bases. The only thing we were told about was the rocketry work with former Nazi star celebrities like Warner Von Braun. The killers, torturers, and mutilators of innocent human beings were kept discretely out of sight, but busy in U.S. underground military facilities which gradually became home to thousands upon thousands of kidnapped American children snatched off the streets (about one million per year) and placed into iron bar cages stacked from floor to ceiling as part of the 'training'. These children would be used to further refine and perfect Mengele's mind control technologies. Certain selected children (at least the ones who survived the 'training') would become future mind controlled slaves who could be used for thousands of different jobs ranging anywhere from sexual slavery to assassinations. A substantial portion of these children, who were considered expendable, were intentionally slaughtered in front of (and by) the other children in order to traumatize the selected trainee into total compliance and submission." [2]

Mengele's research served as a basis for the covert, illegal CIA human research program named MK-ULTRA.

MK-ULTRA

Project MK-ULTRA ran from the early 1950s to at least the late 1960s, using American and Canadian citizens as its test subjects. The published evidence indicates that Project MK-ULTRA involved the use of many methodolo-

gies to manipulate individual mental states and alter brain functions, including the surreptitious administration of drugs and other chemicals, sensory deprivation, isolation, and verbal and sexual abuse.
The most publicized experiments conducted by MK-ULTRA involved the administration of LSD on unwitting hu-

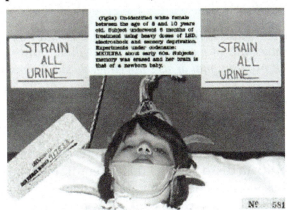

Declassified picture of a young MK-ULTRA subject, 1961.

man subjects, including CIA employees, military personnel, doctors, other government agents, prostitutes, mentally ill patients, and members of the general public, in order to study their reactions.

However, the scope of MK-ULTRA does not however stop. Experiments involving violent electroshocks, physical and mental torture and sex abuse were used in a systematic matter on many subjects, including children.
Although the admitted goals of the projects were to develop torture and interrogation methods to use on the country's enemies, some historians asserted that the project aimed to create "Manchurian Candidates", programmed to perform various acts such as assassinations and other covert missions.

MK-ULTRA was brought to light by various commissions in the 1970s, including the Rockefeller Commission of 1975. Although it is claimed that the CIA stopped such experiments after these commissions, some whistle-blowers have come forth stating that the project simply went "underground" and Monarch Programming has become the classified successor of MK-ULTRA.

The most incriminating statement to date made by a government official as to the possible existence of Project MONARCH was extracted by Anton Chaitkin, a writer for the publication The New Federalist. When former CIA Director William Colby was asked directly, "What about monarch?" he replied angrily and ambiguously, "We stopped that between the late 1960s and the early 1970s." [3]

Monarch Programming

Although there has never been any official admittance of the existence of Monarch programming, prominent researchers have documented the systematic use of trauma on subjects for mind-control purposes. Some survivors, with the help of dedicated therapists, were able to "deprogram" themselves to then go on record and disclose the horrifying details of their ordeals.

Monarch slaves are mainly used by organizations to carry out operations using patsies trained to perform specific tasks, who do not question orders, who do not remember their actions and, if discovered, who automatically commit suicide. They are the perfect scapegoats for high-profile assassinations (see Sirhan Sirhan), the ideal candidates for prostitution, sex slavery and snuff pornography. They are also the perfect puppet performers for the entertainment industry.

> "What I can say is I now believe that ritual-abuse programming is widespread, is systematic, is very organized from highly esoteric information which is published no-where, has not been on any book or talk show, that we have found it all around this country and at least one foreign country.
>
> People say, "What's the purpose of it?" My best guess is that the purpose of it is that they want an army of Manchurian Candidates, ten of thousands of mental robots who will do prostitution, do child pornography, smuggle drugs, engage in international arms smuggling, do snuff films, all sorts of very lucrative things, and do their bidding and eventually the megalomaniacs at the top believe they'll create a Satanic Order that will rule the world". [4]

Monarch programmers cause intense trauma to subjects through the use of electroshock, torture, sexual abuse and mind games in order to force them to dissociate from reality – a natural response in some people when they are faced with unbearable pain. The subject's ability to dissociate is a major requirement and it is, apparently, most readily found in children that come from families with multiple generations of abuse. Mental dissociation enables the handlers to create walled-off personas in the subject's psyche, which can then be programmed and triggered at will.

> "Trauma-based mind control programming can be defined as systematic torture that blocks the victim's capacity for conscious processing (through pain, terror, drugs, illusion, sensory deprivation, sensory over-stimulation, oxygen deprivation, cold, heat, spinning, brain stimulation, and often, near-death), and then employs suggestion and/or classical and operant conditioning (consistent with well-established behavioral modification principles) to implant thoughts, directives, and perceptions in the unconscious mind, often in newly-formed trauma-induced dissociated identities, that force the victim to do, feel, think, or perceive things for the purposes of the programmer. The objective is for the victim to follow directives with no conscious awareness, including execution of acts in clear violation of the victim's moral principles, spiritual convictions, and volition.
>
> Installation of mind control programming relies on the victim's capacity to dissociate, which permits the creation of new walled-off personalities to "hold" and "hide" programming. Already dissociative children are prime "candidates" for programming". [5]

Monarch mind control is covertly used by various groups and organizations for various purposes. According to Fritz Springmeier, these groups are known as "The Network" and form the backbone of the New World Order.

Origins of the Name

Monarch mind control is named after the Monarch butterfly – an insect who begins its life as a worm (representing undeveloped potential) and, after a period of cocooning (programming) is reborn as a beautiful butterflies (the Monarch slave). Some characteristics specific to the Monarch butterfly are also applicable to mind control.

> "One of the primary reasons that the Monarch mind-control programming was named Monarch programming was because of the Monarch butterfly. The Monarch butterfly learns where it was born (its roots) and it passes this knowledge via genetics on to its offspring (from generation to generation). This was one of the key animals that tipped scientists off, that knowledge can be passed genetically. The Monarch program is based upon Illuminati and Nazi goals to create a Master race in part through genetics. If knowledge can be passed genetically (which it is), then it is important that parents be found that can pass the correct knowledge onto those victims selected for the Monarch mind control." [6]
>
> "When a person is undergoing trauma induced by electroshock, a feeling of light-headedness is evi-

denced; as if one is floating or fluttering like a butterfly. There is also a symbolic representation pertaining to the transformation or metamorphosis of this beautiful insect: from a caterpillar to a cocoon (dormancy, inactivity), to a butterfly (new creation) which will return to its point of origin. Such is the migratory pattern that makes this species unique." [7]

Method

The victim/survivor is called a "slave" by the programmer/handler, who in turn is perceived as "master" or "god." About 75% are female, since they possess a higher tolerance for pain and tend to dissociate more easily than males. Monarch handlers seek the compartmentalization of their subject's psyche in multiple and separate alter personas using trauma to cause dissociation.

The following is a partial list of these forms of torture:

1. Sexual abuse and torture
2. Confinement in boxes, cages, coffins, etc, or burial (often with an opening or air-tube for oxygen)
3. Restraint with ropes, chains, cuffs, etc.
4. Near-drowning
5. Extremes of heat and cold, including submersion in ice water and burning chemicals
6. Skinning (only top layers of the skin are removed in victims intended to survive)
7. Spinning
8. Blinding light
9. Electric shock
10. Forced ingestion of offensive body fluids and matter, such as blood, urine, feces, flesh, etc.
11. Hung in painful positions or upside down
12. Hunger and thirst
13. Sleep deprivation
14 Compression with weights and devices
15. Sensory deprivation
16. Drugs to create illusion, confusion, and amnesia, often given by injection or intravenously
17. Ingestion or intravenous toxic chemicals to create pain or illness, including chemotherapy agents
18. Limbs pulled or dislocated
19. Application of snakes, spiders, maggots, rats, and other animals to induce fear and disgust
20. Near-death experiences, commonly asphyxiation by choking or drowning, with immediate resuscitation
22. Forced to perform or witness abuse, torture and sacrifice of people and animals, usually with knives
23. Forced participation in child pornography and prostitution
24. Raped to become pregnant; the fetus is then aborted for ritual use, or the baby taken for sacrifice/enslavement
25. Spiritual abuse to cause victim to feel possessed, harassed, and controlled internally by spirits or demons
26. Desecration of Judeo-Christian beliefs and forms of worship; dedication to Satan or other deities
27. Abuse and illusion to convince victims that God is evil, such as convincing a child that God has raped her
28. Surgery to torture, experiment, or cause the perception of physical or spiritual bombs or implants
29. Harm or threats of harm to family, friends, loved ones, pets, and other victims, to force compliance
30. Use of illusion and virtual reality to confuse and create non-credible disclosure [8].

> *"The basis for the success of the Monarch mind-control programming is that different personalities or personality parts called alters can be created who do not know each other, but who can take the body at different times. The amnesia walls that are built by traumas, form a protective shield of secrecy that protects the abusers from being found out, and prevents the front personalities who hold*

the body much of the time to know how their System of alters is being used. The shield of secrecy allows cult members to live and work around other people and remain totally undetected. The front alters can be wonderful Christians, and the deeper alters can be the worst type of Satanic monster imaginable–a Dr. Jekyll/Mr. Hyde effect. A great deal is at stake in maintaining the secrecy of the intelligence agency or the occult group which is controlling the slave. The success rate of this type of programming is high but when it fails, the failures are discarded through death. Each trauma and torture serves a purpose. A great deal of experimentation and research went into finding out what can and can't be done. Charts were made showing how much torture a given body weight at a given age can handle without death." [9]

"Due to the severe trauma induced through ECT, sexual abuse and other methods, the mind splits off into alternate personalities from the core. Formerly referred to as Multiple Personality Disorder, it is presently recognized as Dissociative Identity Disorder and is the basis for MONARCH programming. Further conditioning of the victim's mind is enhanced through hypnotism, double-bind coercion, pleasure-pain reversals, food, water, sleep and sensory deprivation, along with various drugs which alter certain cerebral functions". [10]

Dissociation is thus achieved by traumatizing the subject, using systematic abuse and using terrifying occult rituals. Once a split in the core personality occurs, an "internal world" can be created and alter personas can be programmed using tools such as music, movies (especially Disney productions) and fairy tales. These visual and audio aids enhance the programming process using images, symbols, meanings and concepts. Created alters can then be accessed using trigger words or symbols programmed into the subject's psyche by the handler. Some of the most common internal images seen by mind control slaves are trees, Cabalistic Tree of life, infinity loops, ancient symbols and letters, spider webs, mirrors, glass shattering, masks, castles, mazes, demons, butterflies, hour glasses, clocks and robots. These symbols are commonly inserted in popular culture movies and videos for two reasons: to desensitize the majority of the population, using subliminals and neuro-linguistic programming and to deliberately construct specific triggers and keys for base programming of highly-impressionable MONARCH children. 11 Some of the movies used in Monarch programming include The Wizard of Oz, Alice in Wonderland, Pinocchio and Sleeping Beauty .

The movie The Wizard of Oz is used by Monarch handlers to program their slaves. Symbols and meanings in the movie become triggers in the slave's mind enabling easy access to the slave's mind by the handler. In popular culture, veiled references to Monarch programming often use analogies to The Wizard of Oz and Alice in Wonderland.

In each case, the slave is given a particular interpretation of the movie's storyline in order to enhance programming. For example, a slave watching The Wizard of Oz is taught that "somewhere over the rainbow" is the "happy place" dissociative trauma slaves must go to in order to escape the unbearable pain being inflicted upon them. Using the movie, programmers encourage slaves to go "over the rainbow" and dissociate, effectively separating their minds from their bodies.

"As mentioned before, the hypnotist will find children easier to hypnotize if they know how to do it with small children. One method that is effective is to say to the small children, "Imagine you are watching a favorite television show." This is why the Disney movies and the other shows are so important to the programmers. They are the perfect hypnotic tool to get the child's mind to dissociate in the right direction. The programmers have been using movies since almost day one to help children learn the hypnotic scripts. For children they need to be part of the hypnotic process. If the hypnotist allows the child to make up his own imagery, the hypnotic suggestions will be stronger. Rather than telling the child the color of a dog, the programmer can ask the child. This is where the books and films shown the child assist in steering its mind in the right direction. If the hypnotist talks to a child, he must take extra precaution not to change the tone of his voice and to have smooth transitions. Most of the Disney films are used for programming purposes. Some of them are specifically designed for mind-control." [12]

Levels of Monarch Programming

The levels of Monarch Programming identify the slave's "functions" and are named after the Electroencephalography (EEG) brainwaves associated with them.

Regarded as "general" or regular programming, ALPHA is within the base control personality. It characterized by extremely pronounced memory retention, along with substantially increased physical strength and visual acuity. Alpha programming is accomplished through deliberately subdividing the victims personality which, in essence, causes a left brain-right brain division, allowing for a programmed union of Left and Right through neuron pathway stimulation.

BETA is referred to as "sexual" programming (sex slaves). This programming eliminates all learned moral convictions and stimulates the primitive sexual instinct, devoid of inhibitions. "Cat" alters may come out at this level. Known as Sex-Kitten programming, it is the most visible kind of programming as some female celebrities, models, actresses and singers have been subjected to this kind of programming. In popular culture, clothing with feline prints often denote sex-kitten programming.

DELTA is known as "killer" programming and was originally developed for training special agents or elite soldiers (i.e. Delta Force, First Earth Battalion, Mossad, etc.) in covert operations. Optimal adrenal output and controlled aggression is evident. Subjects are devoid of fear and very systematic in carrying out their assignment. Self-destruct or suicide instructions are layered in at this level.

THETA – Considered to the "psychic" programming. Bloodliners (those coming from multi-generational Satanic families) were determined to exhibit a greater propensity for having telepathic abilities than did non-bloodliners. Due to its evident limitations, however, various forms of electronic mind control systems were developed and introduced, namely, bio-medical human telemetry devices (brain implants), directed-energy lasers using microwaves and/or electromagnetics. It is reported these are used in conjunction with highly-advanced computers and sophisticated satellite tracking systems. [13]

In Conclusion

It is difficult to remain objective when describing the horrors endured by Monarch slaves. The extreme violence, the sexual abuse, the mental torture and sadistic games inflicted on victims by "notable scientists" and high-level officials prove the existence of a true "dark side" in the powers that be. Despite the revelations, the documents and the whistle-blowers, a great majority of the population ignores, dismisses or avoids the issue altogether. Over two million Americans have been programmed by trauma mind-control since 1947 and the CIA publicly admitted its mind control projects in 1970. Movies such as The Manchurian Candidate have directly referred to the subject, even depicting actual techniques, such as electroshock, the use of trigger words and microchip implementation. Several public figures we see on our TV and movie screens are mind control slaves. Famous people such as Candy Jones, Celia Imrie and Sirhan Sirhan have gone on record and disclosed their mind control experiences…and yet the general public claims that it "cannot exist".

The research and funds invested in project Monarch do not however only apply to mind control slaves. Many of the programming techniques perfected in these experiments are applied on a mass scale through mass media. Mainstream news, movies, music videos, advertisements and television shows are conceived using the most advanced data on human behavior ever compiled. A lot of this comes from Monarch programming.

[1] Fritz Springmeier, The Illuminati Formula to Create a Mind Control Slave
[2] Ken Adachi, Mind Control the Ultimate Terror
[3] Anton Chaitkin, "Franklin Witnesses Implicate FBI and U.S. Elites in Torture and Murder of Children", The New Federalist
[4] D. Corydon Hammond, Ph.D. Ellen P. Lacter, Ph.D., The Relationship Between Mind Control Programming and Ritual Abuse
[5] Ibid.
[6] Ron Patton, Project Monarch
[7] Ellen P. Lacter, Ph.D., Kinds of Torture Endured in Ritual Abuse and Trauma-Based Mind Control
[8] Springmeier, op. cit.
[9] Patton, op. cit.
[10] Ibid.
[11] Springmeier, op. cit.
[12] Patton, op. cit.

Who is Baphomet?

Baphomet is an enigmatic, goat-headed figure found in several instance in the history of occultism. From the Knights Templar of the Middle-Ages and the Freemasons of the 19th century to modern currents of occultism, Baphomet never fails to create controversy. But where does Baphomet originate from and, most importantly, what is the true meaning of this symbolic figure? This article looks at the origins of Baphomet, the esoteric meaning of Baphomet and its occurrence in popular culture.

Throughout the history of Western occultism, the name of the mysterious Baphomet is often invoked. Although it became commonly know name in the twentieth century, mentions of Baphomet can be found in documents dating from as early as the 11th century. Today, the symbol is associated with anything relating to occultism, ritual magic, witchcraft, Satanism and esoterica. Baphomet often pops up in popular culture to identify anything occult.

The most famous depiction of Baphomet is found in Eliphas Levi's "Dogme et Rituel de la Haute Magie", a 1897 book that became a standard reference for modern occultism. What does this creature represent? What is the meaning of the symbols around it? Why is it so important in occultism? To answer some of these questions, we must first look at its origins. We'll first look at the history of Baphomet and several examples of references to Baphomet in popular culture.

Origins of the Name

There are several theories concerning the origins of the name of Baphomet. The most common explanation claims that it is an Old French corruption of the name of Mohammed (which was Latin-ized to "Mahomet") – the Prophet of Islam. During the Crusades, the Knights Templar stayed for during extended periods of time in Middle-Eastern countries where they became acquainted with the teachings of Arabian mysticism. This contact with Eastern civilizations allowed them to bring back to Europe the basics of what would become western occultism, including Gnosticism, alchemy, Kabbalah and Hermetism. The Templars' affinity with the Muslims led the Church to accuse them of the worship of an idol named Baphomet, so there are some plausible links between Baphomet and Mahomet. However, there are other theories concerning the origins of the name.

Eliphas Levi, the French occultist who drew the famous depiction of Baphomet argued that the name had been derived from Kabbalistic coding:

> "The name of the Templar Baphomet, which should be spelt kabalistically backwards, is composed of three abbreviations: Tem. ohp. AB., Templi omnium hominum pacts abbas, "the father of the temple of peace of all men". [1]

Arkon Daraul, an author and teacher of Sufi tradition and magic argued that Baphomet came from the Arabic word Abu fihama(t), meaning "The Father of Understanding". [2]

Dr. Hugh Schonfield, whose work on the Dead Sea Scrolls is well-known, developed one of the more interesting theories. Schonfield, who had studied a Jewish cipher called the Atbash cipher, which was used in translating some of the Dead Sea Scrolls, claimed that when one applied the cipher to the word Baphomet, it transposed into the Greek word "Sophia", which means " knowledge" and is also synonymous with "goddess".

Possible Origins of the Figure

The modern depiction of Baphomet appears to take its roots from several ancient sources, but primarily from pagan gods. Baphomet bears resemblances to gods all over the globe, including Egypt, Northern Europe and India. In fact, the mythologies of a great number of ancient civilizations include some kind of horned deity. In Jungian theory, Baphomet is a continuation of the horned-god archetype, as the concept of a deity bearing horns is universally present in individual psyches. Do Cernunnos, Pan, Hathor, the Devil (as depicted by Christianity) and Baphomet have a common origin? Some of their attributes are strikingly similar.

The ancient Celtic god Cernunnos is traditionally depicted with antler horns on his head, sitting in "lotus position", similar to Levi's depiction of Baphomet. Although the history of Cernunnos is shrouded in mystery, he is usually said to be the god of fertility and nature.

In Britain, an aspect Cerennunos was named Herne. The horned god has the Satyr-like features of Baphomet along with its emphasis on the phallus.

Pan was a prominent deity in Greece. The nature god was often depicted with horns on its head and the lower body of a goat. Not unlike Cerenunnos, Pan is a phallic deity. Its animalistic features are an embodiment of the carnal and procreative impulses of men.

Pope Sylvester II and the Devil (1460). In Christianity, the devil has similar features to the pagan gods described above as they are the main inspiration for these depictions. The attributes embodied by these gods became the representation of what is considered evil by the Church.

The Devil Card from the Tarot of Marseilles (15th century). This card's depiction of the devil, with its wings, horns, breasts and hand sign is undoubtedly a major influence in Levi's depiction of Baphomet.

Goya's 1821 painting "Great He-Goat" or "Witches Sabbath". The painting depicts a coven of witches gathered around Satan, portrayed as a half-man, half-goat figure.

Eliphas Levi's Baphomet

In 1861, the French occultist Eliphas Levi included in his book Dogmes et Rituels de la Haute Magie (Dogmas and Rituals of High Magic) a drawing that would become the most famous depiction of Baphomet: a winged humanoid goat with a pair of breasts and a torch on its head between its horns. The figure bears numerous similarities to the deities described above. It also includes several other esoteric symbols relating to the esoteric concepts embodied by the Baphomet. In the preface of his book, Levi stated:

> "The goat on the frontispiece carries the sign of the pentagram on the forehead, with one point at the top, a symbol of light, his two hands forming the sign of Hermeticism, the one pointing up to the white moon of Chesed, the other pointing down to the black one of Geburah. This sign expresses the perfect harmony of mercy with justice. His one arm is female, the other male like the ones of the androgyn of Khunrath, the attributes of which we had to unite with those of our goat because he is one and the same symbol. The flame of intelligence shining between his horns is the magic light of

the universal balance, the image of the soul elevated above matter, as the flame, whilst being tied to matter, shines above it. The ugly beast's head expresses the horror of the sinner, whose materially acting, solely responsible part has to bear the punishment exclusively; because the soul is insensitive according to its nature and can only suffer when it materializes. The rod standing instead of genitals symbolizes eternal life, the body covered with scales the water, the semi-circle above it the atmosphere, the feathers following above the volatile. Humanity is represented by the two breasts and the androgyn arms of this sphinx of the occult sciences." [3]

This depiction of Baphomet by Eliphas Levi's from his book Dogmes et Rituels de la Haute Magie (Dogmas and Rituals of High Magic) became the "official" visual representation of Baphomet.

In Levi's depiction, Baphomet embodies the culmination of the alchemical process – the union of opposing forces to create Astral Light – the basis of magic and, ultimately, enlightenment.

A close look at the details of the image reveals that each symbol is inevitably balanced with its opposite. Baphomet himself is an androgynous character as it is bearing the characteristics of both sexes: female breasts and a rod representing the erect phallus. The concept of androgeniety is of a great importance in occult philosophy as it is representative the highest level of initiation in the quest of becoming "one with God".

Baphomet's phallus is actually Hermes' Caduceus – a rod intertwined with two serpents. This ancient symbol is has been representing Hermetism for centuries. The Caduceus esoterically represents the activation of chakras, from the base of the spine to the pineal gland, using serpentine power (hence, the serpents) or Astral Light.

> *"The Science is a real one only for those who admit and understand the philosophy and the religion; and its process will succeed only for the Adept who has attained the sovereignty of will, and so become the King of the elementary world: for the grand agent of the operation of the Sun, is that force described in the Symbol of Hermes, of the table of emerald; it is the universal magical power; the spiritual, fiery, motive power; it is the Od, according to the Hebrews, and the Astral light, according to others.*
>
> *Therein is the secret fire, living and philosophical, of which all the Hermetic philosophers speak with the most mysterious reserve: the Universal Seed, the secret whereof they kept, and which they represented only under the figure of the Caduceus of Hermes."* [4]

Baphomet is therefore symbolic of the alchemical Great Work where separate and opposing forces are united in perfect equilibrium to generate Astral Light. This alchemical process is represented on Levi's image by the terms Solve and Coagula on Baphomet's arms. While they accomplish opposite results, Solving (turning solid into liquid) and Coagulation (turning liquid into solid) are two necessary steps of the alchemical process – which aims to turn stone into gold or, in esoteric terms, a profane man into an illuminated man. The two steps are on arms pointing in opposite directions, further emphasizing their opposite nature.

Baphomet's hands form the "sign of Hermetism" – which is a visual representation of the Hermetic axiom "As Above, So Below". This dictum sums up the whole of the teachings and the aims of Hermetism, where the microcosm (man) is as the macrocosm (the universe). Therefore, understanding one equals understanding the other. This Law of Correspondence originates from the Emerald Tablets of Hermes Trismegistus where it was stated:

> "That which is Below corresponds to that which is Above, and that which is Above, corresponds to that which is Below, to accomplish the miracles of the One Thing". [5]

The mastery of this life force, the Astral Life, is what is called by modern occultists "magick".

The Magician tarot card displaying the Hermetic axiom "As Above, So Below"

> "The practice of magic – either white or black – depends upon the ability of the adept to control the universal life force – that which Eliphas Levi calls the great magical agent or the astral light. By the manipulation of this fluidic essence the phenomena of transcendentalism are produced. The famous hermaphroditic Goat of Mendes was a composite creature formulated to symbolize this astral light. It is identical with Baphomet the mystic pantheos of those disciples of ceremonial magic, the Templars, who probably obtained it from the Arabians." [6]

Each of Baphomet's hands point towards opposing moons, which Levi calls the Chesed and the Geburah – two opposing concepts taken from the Jewish Kabbalah. In the Kabalistic Tree of Life, the Sefirot, Chesed is associated with "kindness given to others" while Geburah refers to the "restraint of one's urge to bestow goodness upon others, when the recipient of that good is judged to be unworthy and liable to misuse it". These two concepts are opposed and, as everything else in life, an equilibrium must be found between the two.

The most recognizable feature of Baphomet is, of course, its goat head. This monstrous head represents man's animal and sinful nature, its egoistic tendencies and its basest instincts. Opposed to man's spiritual nature (symbolized by the "divine light" on its head), this animal side is regardless viewed as a necessary part of man's dualistic nature, where the animal and the spiritual must unite in harmony. It can also be argued that Baphomet's grotesque overall appearance might serve to ward off and repel the profane who are uninitiated to the esoteric meaning of the symbol.

In Secret Societies

Although Levi's 1861 depiction of Baphomet is the most famous one, the name of this idol has been circulating for over a thousand years, through secret societies and occult circles. The first recorded mention of Baphomet as a part of an occult ritual appeared during the era of the Knights Templar.

THE KNIGHTS TEMPLAR

It is widely accepted by occult researchers that the figure of Baphomet was of a great importance in the rituals of the Knights Templar. The first occurrence of the name Baphomet appeared in a 1098 letter by crusader Anselm of Ribemont stating:

> "As the next day dawned they called loudly upon Baphometh while we prayed silently in our hearts to God; then we attacked and forced all of them outside the city walls." [7]

During the Templar trials of 1307, where Knight Templars were tortured and interrogated by request of King Philip IV of France, the name of Baphomet was mentioned several times. While some Templars denied the existence of Baphomet, others described it as being either a severed head, a cat, or a head with three faces.

While books aimed for mass consumption often deny any link between the Knights Templar and Baphomet, claiming it to be an invention of the Church to demonize them, almost all reputed authors on occultism (who wrote books intended for initiates) acknowledge that the link. In fact, the idol is often referred to as "the Baphomet of the Templars".

> "Did the Templars really adore Baphomet? Did they offer a shameful salutation to the buttocks of the goat of Mendes? What was actually this secret and potent association which imperilled Church and State, and was thus destroyed unheard? Judge nothing lightly; they are guilty of a great crime; they have exposed to profane eyes the sanctuary of antique initiation. They have gathered again and have shared the fruits of the tree of knowledge, so that they might become masters of the world. The judgement pronounced against them is higher and far older than the tribunal of pope or king: "On the day that thou eatest thereof, thou shalt surely die," said God Himself, as we read in the Book of Genesis. (...)
>
> Yes, in our profound conviction, the Grand Masters of the Order of the Templars worshipped the Baphomet, and caused it to be worshipped by their initiates; yes, there existed in the past, and there may be still in the present, assemblies which are presided over by this figure, seated on a throne and having a flaming torch between the horns. But the adorers of this sign do not consider, as do we, that it is a representation of the devil: on the contrary, for them it is that of the god Pan, the god of our modern schools of philosophy, the god of the Alexandrian theurgic school and of our own mystical Neo-platonists, the god of Lamartine and Victor Cousin, the god of Spinoza and Plato, the god of the primitive Gnostic schools; the Christ also of the dissident priesthood. This last qualification, ascribed to the goat of Black Magic, will not astonish students of religious antiquities who are acquainted with the phases of symbolism and doctrine in their various transformations, whether in India, Egypt or Judea." [8]

FREEMASONRY

Shortly after the release of Levi's illustration, the french writer and journalist Léo Taxil released a series of pamphlets and books denouncing Freemasonry, charging lodges with worshipping the devil. At the center of his accusations was Baphomet, which was described as the Mason's object of worship.

"Les mystères de la franc-maçonnerie" (Mysteries of Freemasonry) accused Freemasons of satanism and worshipping Baphomet. Taxil's works raised the ire of Catholics.

In 1897, after causing quite a stir due to his revelations on French Freemasonry, Léo Taxil called a press conference where he announced that many of his revelations were fabrications 9. Since then, this series of events has been dubbed the "Léo Taxil Hoax". However, some would argue the probability that Taxil's confession may have been coerced in order to quell the controversy involving Freemasonry.

Whatever the case may be, the most likely connection between Freemasonry and Baphomet is through symbolism, where the idol becomes an allegory for profound esoteric concepts. The Masonic author Albert Pike argues that, in Freemasonry, Baphomet is not an object of worship, but a symbol, the true meaning of which is only revealed to high-level initiates.

> "It is absurd to suppose that men of intellect adored a monstrous idol called Baphomet, or recognized Mahomet as an inspired prophet. Their symbolism, invented ages before, to conceal what it was dangerous to avow, was of course misunderstood by those who were not adepts, and to their enemies seemed to be pantheistic. The calf of gold, made by Aaron for the Israelites, was but one of the oxen under the layer of bronze, and the Karobim on the Propitiatory, misunderstood. The symbols of the wise always become the idols of the ignorant multitude. What the Chiefs of the Order really believed and taught, is indicated to the Adepts by the hints contained in the high Degrees of Free-Masonry, and by the symbols which only the Adepts understand." [10]

Aleister Crowley

The British occultist Aleister Crowley was born about six months after the death of Eliphas Levi, causing him to believe that he was Levi's reincarnation. Partly for this reason, Crowley was known within the O.T.O., the secret society he popularized, as "Baphomet".

The British occultist Aleister Crowley was born about six months after the death of Eliphas Levi, causing him to believe that he was Levi's reincarnation. Partly for this reason, Crowley was known within the O.T.O., the secret society he popularized, as "Baphomet".

Here's Crowley's explanation of the etymology of the name Baphomet, taken from his 1929 book The Confessions of Aleister Crowley:

> *"I had taken the name Baphomet as my motto in the O.T.O. For six years and more I had tried to discover the proper way to spell this name. I knew that it must have eight letters, and also that the numerical and literal correspondences must be such as to express the meaning of the name in such a ways as to confirm what scholarship had found out about it, and also to clear up those problems which archaeologists had so far failed to solve.... One theory of the name is that it represents the words ???? ??????, the baptism of wisdom; another, that it is a corruption of a title meaning "Father Mithras". Needless to say, the suffix R supported the latter theory. I added up the word as spelt by the Wizard. It totalled 729. This number had never appeared in my Cabbalistic working and therefore meant nothing to me. It however justified itself as being the cube of nine. The word ?????, the mystic title given by Christ to Peter as the cornerstone of the Church, has this same value. So far, the Wizard had shown great qualities! He had cleared up the etymological problem and shown why the Templars should have given the name Baphomet to their so-called idol. Baphomet was Father Mithras, the cubical stone which was the corner of the Temple."* [11]

Baphomet is an important figure in the Thelema, the mystical system he established at the beginning of the 20th century. In one of his most important works, Magick, Liber ABA, Book 4, Crowley describes Baphomet as a divine androgyne:

> *"The Devil does not exist. It is a false name invented by the Black Brothers to imply a Unity in their ignorant muddle of dispersions. A devil who had unity would be a God ... 'The Devil' is, historically, the God of any people that one personally dislikes ... This serpent, SATAN, is not the enemy of Man, but He who made Gods of our race, knowing Good and Evil; He bade 'Know Thyself!' and taught Initiation. He is 'The Devil' of the Book of Thoth, and His emblem is Baphomet, the Androgyne who is the hieroglyph of arcane perfection ... He is therefore Life, and Love. But moreover his letter is ayin, the Eye, so that he is Light; and his Zodiacal image is Capricornus, that leaping goat whose attribute is Liberty."* [12]

The Ecclesia Gnostica Catholica, the ecclesiastical arm of Ordo Templi Orientis (O.T.O.), recites during its Gnostic Mass "And I believe in the Serpent and the Lion, Mystery of Mystery, in His name BAPHOMET." [13] Baphomet is considered to be the union of Chaos and Babalon, masculine and feminine energy, the phallus and the womb.

The Church of Satan

Although not technically a secret society, Anton Lavey's Church of Satan remains an influential occult order. Founded in 1966, the organization adopted the "Sigil of Baphomet" as its official insignium.

The Sigil of Baphomet was probably heavily inspired by this illustration from Stanislas de Guaita's La Clef de la Magie Noire (The Key to Black Magic).

According to Anton Lavey, the Templars worshipped Baphomet as a symbol of Satan. Baphomet is prominently present during in Church of Satan rituals as the symbol is placed above the ritualistic altar.

The Sigil of Baphomet, the official symbol of the Church of Satan features the Goat of Mendes inside an inverted pentagram.

In The Satanic Bible, Lavey describes the symbol of Baphomet:

> "The symbol of Baphomet was used by the Knights Templar to represent Satan. Through the ages this symbol has been called by many different names. Among these are: The Goat of Mendes, The Goat of a Thousand Young, The Black Goat, The Judas Goat, and perhaps the most appropriately, The Scapegoat.
>
> Baphomet represents the Powers of Darkness combined with the generative fertility of the goat. In its "pure" form the pentagram is shown encompassing the figure of a man in the five points of the star – three points up, two pointing down – symbolizing man's spiritual nature. In Satanism the pentagram is also used, but since Satanism represents the carnal instincts of man, or the opposite of spiritual nature, the pentagram is inverted to perfectly accommodate the head of the goat – its horns, representing duality, thrust upwards in defiance; the other three points inverted, or the trinity denied. The Hebraic figures around the outer circle of the symbol which stem from the magical teachings of the Kabala, spell out "Leviathan", the serpent of the watery abyss, and identified with Satan. These figures correspond to the five points of the inverted star." [14]

In Conclusion

Baphomet is a composite creation symbolic of alchemical realization through the union of opposite forces. Occultists believe that, through the mastery of life force, one is able to produce magick and spiritual enlightenment. Eliphas Levi's depiction of Baphomet included several symbols alluding to the raising of the kundalini – serpentine power – which ultimately leads to the activation of the pineal gland, also known as the "third eye". So, from an esoteric point of view, Baphomet represents this occult process.

However, over time the symbol has come to signify much more than its esoteric meaning. Through controversies, Baphomet became, depending of the point of view, a representation of everything that is good in occultism or everything that is evil in occultism. It is, in fact, the ultimate "scapegoat", the face of witchcraft, black magick and Satanism. The fact that the symbol is rather monstrous and grotesque has probably helped propel the symbol to its level of infamy as it never fails to shock organized religions while attracting those who rebel against them.

Since gaining widespread recognition in popular culture, the image of Baphomet is now used as a symbol of anything regarding occultism and ritualism. In corporate-owned mass media, which has ties with secret societies, the figure of Baphomet appears in the oddest places, often to audiences too young to understand the occult reference (Secret Arcana's sister site Vigilant Citizen documents the occurrences of Baphomet and other occult symbols in music videos, movies and fashion). Is Baphomet used in pop culture as a symbol of the power of the occult elite over the ignorant masses?

After centuries of myths, hoaxes, propaganda and disinformation on both sides of the spectrum, can we truly answer the the original question posed by this article: "Who is Baphomet?". Is it a symbol of Satan or of spiritual enlightenment? Is it a symbol of good or evil? The answer lies within the symbol itself: It is both. In Egyptian mythology, Toth Hermes was a mediating power between good and evil, making sure neither had a decisive victory over the other. Baphomet represents the accomplishment on this cosmic task on a very small scale, within oneself. Once perfect equilibrium is attained on a personal level, the occult initiate can point one hand towards the heavens and one hand towards the earth and pronounce this hermetic axiom which reverberated through millenniums: "As Above, So Below".

[1] Eliphas Levi, Dogmes et Rituels de la Haute Magie
[2] Arkon Daraul, A History of Secret Societies
[3] Eliphas Levi, Dogme et Rituel de la Haute Magie
[4] Albert Pike, Morals and Dogma
[5] English translation of the Emerald Tablet
[6] Manly P. Hall, The Secret Teachings of All Ages
[7] Malcom Barber and Keith Bate, Letters from the East: Crusaders, Pilgrims and Settlers in the 12th-13th Centuries
[8] Op. Cit. Levi
[9] The Confessions of Léo Taxil, April 25 1897
[10] Albert Pike, Morals and Dogma
[11] Aleister Crowley, The Confessions of Aleister Crowley
[12] Aleister Crowley, Magick, Liber ABA, Book 4
[13] Helena and Tau Apiron, "The Invisible Basilica: The Creed of the Gnostic Catholic Church: An Examination"
[14] Anton Lavey, The Satanic Bible

The Order of the Illuminati: Its Origins, Its Methods and Its Influence on the World Events

The Order of the Illuminati is often at the center of debates about the impact of secret societies on human history. Is the Illuminati a myth or does it truly secretly rule the world? As the number of people asking that question has grown, facts about the Order have become diluted with misconceptions and disinformation, making objective research on the subject difficult. This article attempts to shed some factual light on the Order of the Illuminati by reviewing some of the most important documents on the subject.

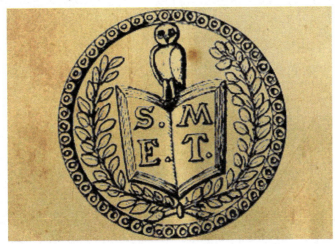

The world "Illuminati" is thrown around rather freely to describe the elite group that is secretly running the world. Most have a general idea of the meaning of the term, but are confused about the concepts and the ideas relating to it. Is the Illuminati the same thing as Freemasonry? What are their goals? What are their beliefs? Why do they act in secret? Do they practice occultism? Attempting to objectively research the subject can become an arduous task as most sources end up being either dismissive disinformation pieces that deny (and even ridicule) anything related to the Illuminati or, at the other end of the spectrum, espouse ill-informed fear mongering based on rumors and misconceptions. In both cases, the researcher ends up with the same result: a distorted version of the truth.

Considering that Secret Societies are supposed to be, by definition, secret, and that history is often rewritten by those in power, obtaining the unbiased truth about the Illuminati is a challenge. This article does not claim to "reveal" or "expose" everything that is to be known about the Illuminati; it rather attempts draw a more precise picture of the Order by citing authors who have extensively studied the subject. Whether they are, at the end of the day, critics or apologists of the Illuminati, these authors base their thoughts on credible facts. Some of the most interesting documents on the Illuminati were written by initiates of Secret Societies as they understood the philosophical and spiritual undercurrent driving the movement forward. Using these works, we will look at the origins, the methods and the impacts of the Illuminati on world history.

Types of Secret Societies

Although several groups called themselves "Illuminati" in the past, the most influential and memorable of them was the Bavarian Illuminati. Founded on May 1, 1776, the organization created by Adam Weishaupt blurred the line between "spiritual" and "political" Secret Societies. By mixing the occult sciences of Freemasonry and

Rosicrucianism while conspiring to achieve precise political goals, the Illuminati became an actor on the world stage. While most Secret Societies of the time catered to rich people and their fascination with occultism, the Bavarian Illuminati actively sought to profoundly change the world.

Secret Societies have existed throughout the course of history, each of them with different aims and with different roles in society. While the Egyptian mystery schools were part of the Egyptian institution, other groups were secret due to their subversive and conspiratorial aims. These two next quotes, written by two famous political figures, describe these opposing views on Secret Societies:

> *"Did Zanoni belong to this mystical Fraternity, who, in an earlier age, boasted of secrets of which the Philosopher's Stone was but the least; who considered themselves the heirs of all that the Chaldeans, the Magi, the Gymnosophists, and the Platonists had taught; and who differed from all the darker Sons of Magic in the virtue of their lives, the purity of their doctrines, and their insisting, as the foundation of all wisdom, on the subjugation of the sense, and the intensity of Religious Faith?"*
> - Sir Edward Bulwer Lytton, 1884 [1]

> *"The governments of the present day have to deal not merely with other governments, with emperors, kings and ministers, but also with the secret societies which have everywhere their unscrupulous agents, and can at the last moment upset all the governments' plans."*
> - British Prime Minister Benjamin Disraeli, 1876

These quotes describe different realms of influence of Secret Societies. The first one refers to the spiritual side while the second describes the political side. Not all Secret Societies dwell in the spiritual and not all of them get involved in political machinations. The Bavarian Illuminati operated in both realms.

> *"Spiritual brotherhoods are pledged to Wisdom and guiding humanity towards the realm of the Infinite; Political brotherhoods [are comprised] of power-seekers who cloak their manipulative agenda in darkness. (...)*
>
> *All secret societies share certain fundamental themes. Membership is restricted to those who have an abiding interest in the subject. Thus, a spiritual group will attract people seeking more knowledge of a particular teacher or type of practice. The student is aware of the subject matter in advance and will approach the group for further instruction. More rarely, an individual may be "tapped" by the group because of a perceived affinity to its purpose.*
>
> *In a political secret society, membership is restricted to those who share an ideological affinity with the goals the group represents. At the furthest end of the political spectrum, the mission will be revolution. Such a society will go to great lengths to defend itself. (...)*
>
> *The Illuminati are perceived by many as spanning the chasm between the spiritual and the political secret society. Often credited (or blamed) for influencing the French Revolution in 1787, the Illuminati taught a doctrine of social and political liberation that hinged on the equality of man, the embrace of rationalism, and the denial of crown and church as the legitimate institutions for the regulation of social and moral values. (...) While the views of the Illuminati may sound quite advanced for the time, the European revolutions they are believed to have encouraged degenerated into brutal bloodbaths whose singular lack of moral compass was appalling."* [2]

While some believe that Adam Weishaupt was the sole mastermind of the Illuminati and that his organization rose to glory and died in less than twelve years, most researchers initiated in occultism believe that the Bavarian Illuminati was the rare appearance of an ancient Brotherhood that could be traced back to the Knight Templars of the Middle-Ages.

Manly P. Hall, a 33rd Degree Freemason and prolific author, described in his pamphlet "Masonic Orders of Fraternity" an "Invisible Empire" that has been silently working for centuries towards social change. It periodically became visible throughout History, through different organizations who bore different names. According to him, these groups have a great yet silent impact on society, even transforming the educational system to form future generations.

> "The direct descent of the essential program of the Esoteric Schools was entrusted to groups already well-conditioned for the work. The guilds, trade unions, and similar protective and benevolent Societies had been internally strengthened by the introduction of a new learning. The advancement of the plan required the enlargement of the boundaries of the philosophic overstate. A World Fraternity was needed, sustained by a deep and broad program of education according to the "method". Such a Fraternity could not immediately include all men, but it could unite the activities of certain kinds of men, regardless of their racial or religious beliefs or the nations in which they dwelt. These were the men of "towardness", those sons of tomorrow, whose symbol was a blazing sun rising over the mountains of the east. (...)
>
> It was inevitable that the Orders of Fraternity should sponsor world education. (...) The program included a systematic expansion of existing institutions and the enlargement of their spheres of influence.
>
> Slowly, the Orders of Universal Reformation faded from public attention, and in their places appeared the Orders of World Brotherhood. Everything possible was done to prevent the transitions from being obvious. Even history was falsified to make certain sequences of activity unrecognizable. The shift of emphasis never gave the impression of abruptness, and the motion appeared as a dawning of social consciousness. The most obvious clues to the secret activity have been the prevailing silence about the origin and the impossibility of filing the lacunae in the records of seventeenth- and eighteenth- century fraternal Orders. (...)
>
> The Orders of Fraternity were attached by slender and almost invisible threads to the parent project. Like earlier Schools of the Mysteries, these Fraternities were not in themselves actual embodiments of the esoteric associations, but rather instruments to advance certain objectives of the divine plan." [3]

Here, Hall mentions a "silence" and lack of information regarding the workings of Secret Societies during the 17th and 18th century, the epoch during which the Bavarian Illuminati was active. It is during this time period that Secret Societies took action, causing revolutions, overthrowing Monarchical and Papal powers and taking hold of the banking system. Was the Bavarian Illuminati part of the Invisible Empire described by Hall? Is it still active today? Let's first look at Adam Weishaupt and his infamous Secret Society.

Adam Weishaupt, Trained by the Jesuits

Adam Weishaupt was born in Ingolstadt, Bavaria on February 6, 1748. His father died when he was seven and his godfather, Baron Ickstatt, entrusted his early education to the most powerful group of the time: the Jesuits. Known for its subversive methods and conspiratorial tendencies, the Society of Jesus had a stronghold on Bavaria's politics and educational system.

> "The degree of power to which the representatives of the Society of Jesus had been able to attain in Bavaria was all but absolute. Members of the order were the confessors and preceptors of the electors;

hence they had a direct influence upon the policies of government. The censorship of religion had fallen into their eager hands, to the extent that some of the parishes even were compelled to recognize their authority and power. To exterminate all Protestant influence and to render the Catholic establishment complete, they had taken possession of the instruments of public education. It was by Jesuits that the majority of the Bavarian colleges were founded, and by them they were controlled. By them also the secondary schools of the country were conducted." [4]

The inner-workings of the Society of Jesus was quite similar to the occult Brotherhoods it was apparently working against. It functioned with degrees, initiation rites, elaborate rituals and esoteric symbols and had been suppressed countless times in several countries due to its subversive tendencies.

In 1773, Weishaupt's godfather used his great influence at the University of Ingolstadt to place his godson as chair of canon law. At that time, the institution was under heavy Jesuitical dominance and that particular position was traditionally held by influential Jesuits. Weishaupt's growing embrace of Age of Enlightenment philosophies placed him at odds with the Jesuits and all kinds of political drama ensued. Despite this fact, Weishaupt learned a lot from the Jesuit's organization and their subversive methods to obtain power. It is during this time that the idea of a Secret Soceity began to enter Weishaupt's thoughts.

> *"Brilliant, and well trained in the conspiratorial methods of access to power, young Weishaupt decided to organize a body of conspirators, determined to free the world from the Jesuitical rule of Rome."* [5]

While some authors believe that the Jesuits (who were suppressed by papal bull in 1773) used Weishaupt to perpetuate their rule, others state that he was seeking to overthrow their powerful hold on Bavarian. On a wider scale, he was convinced that the world would profit from the overthrow of all governmental and religious institutions in the world to replace them by a world-wide, yet secretive, committee of "initiates". To acheive his aims, he would use Jesuit methods against the Jesuits.

As Weishaupt pursued his studies, he also became knowledgeable in occult mysteries and Hermetism. He recognized the attractive power of this mysterious knowledge and understood that Masonic lodges would be the ideal venue to propagate his views. He therefore sought to become a Freemason, but was quickly disenchanted with the idea.

> *"His imagination having taken heat from his reflections upon the attractive power of the Eleusinian mysteries and the influence exerted by the secret cult of the Pythagoreans, it was first in Weishaupt's thought to seek in the Masonic institutions of the day the opportunity he coveted for the propagation of his views. From this, original intention, however, he was soon diverted, in part because of the*

difficulty he experienced in commanding sufficient funds to gain admission to a lodge of Masons, in part because his study of such Masonic books as came into his hands persuaded him that the "mysteries" of Freemasonry were too puerile and too readily accessible to the general public to make them worthwhile". [6]

Weishaupt soon realized that, to achieve his aims, it would be necessary for him to create his own secretive group, composed of powerful individuals who would embrace his views and help him propagate them.

> *"He deemed it necessary, therefore, to launch out on independent lines. He would form a model secret organization, comprising "schools of wisdom," concealed from the gaze of the world behind walls of seclusion and mystery, wherein those truths which the folly and egotism of the priests banned from the public chairs of education might be taught with perfect freedom to susceptible youths."* [7]

The goal of Weishaupt's organization was simple yet monumental: to overthrow all political and religious institutions in order to replace it with a group of Illuminati initiates. According to him "universal happiness complete and rapid could be achieved by disposing of hierarchy, rank and riches. Princes and nations will disappear without violence from the earth; the human race will become one family; the world will be the abode of reasonable men". On May 1, 1776, the Order of the Illuminati was founded.

The Bavarian Illuminati

Weishaupt's Illuminati began humbly with only five members, but after a few years and with powerful connections, the Order became a major political force across the world. Influential deciders, rich industrials, powerful noblemen and mysterious occultists joined the Order and participated in its conspiratorial objectives. Some historians claim that the Order's quick rise to success was due to a secret meeting between Weishaupt and a mysterious figure named Cagliostro, the most powerful occultist of the time.

> *"In Ingolsstadt, Cagliostro is believed to have met Adam Weishaupt, professor of philosophy and canon law at the university, who in 1776, had founded the sect of Illuminati. Calling themselves heirs to the Knights Templar, they declared their interest in using celestial intervention as achieved by Cagliostro for the furtherance of a program of worldwide religious reform, but one more radical than Cagliostro's, "committed to avenging the death of the Templar's Grand Master Molay by reducing to dust the triple crown of the popes and disposing of the last of the Capet Kings."*
>
> *Cagliostro obliged, and described in prophetic detail the decapitation of Louis XVI, an event hardly to be envisaged at that time as anything but improbable."* [8]

The Bavarian Illuminati was originally comprised of three primary grades: Novice, Minerval and Illuminated Minerval. Each grade was designed to achieve particular objectives while assuring complete control and dominance to the apex of the pyramid. Here's a brief look at each grade.

Novice

Entry-level members of the Bavarian Illuminati were attracted and introduced to the Order using attractive vocabulary (the quest for wisdom and betterment) and occult lore. They were however introduced to a highly monitored and controlling hierarchy, one that resembles the system of the Jesuits. There was no mention of the Order's political aims.

> *"Once enrolled, the instruction of each Novice was to be in the hands of his enroller, who kept well*

hidden from his pupil the identity of the rest of his superiors. Such statutes of the order as he was permitted to read impressed upon the mind of the Novice that the particular ends sought in his novitiate were to ameliorate and perfect his moral character, expand his principles of humanity and sociability, and solicit his interest in the laudable objects of thwarting the schemes of evil men, assisting oppressed virtue, and helping men of merit to find suitable places in the world. Having had impressed upon him the necessity of maintaining inviolable secrecy respecting the affairs of the order, the further duties of subordinating his egoistic views and interests and of according respectful and complete obedience to his superiors were next enjoined. An important part of the responsibility of the Novice consisted in the drawing-up of a detailed report (for the archives of the order), containing complete, information concerning his family and his personal career, covering such remote items as the titles of the books he possessed, the names of his personal enemies and the occasion of their enmity, his own strong and weak points of character, the dominant passions of his parents, the names of their parents and intimates, etc. Monthly reports were also required, covering the benefits the recruit had received from and the services he had rendered to the order. For the building-up of the order the Novice must undertake his share in the work of recruitment, his personal advancement to the higher grades being conditioned upon the success of such efforts. To those whom he enrolled he became in turn a superior; and thus after a novitiate presumably two years in length, the way was open for his promotion to the next higher grade." [9]

When a Novice proved to his superiors to be worthy of advancement, he was initiated to the grade of Minerval.

Minerval

Minerval seals of the Bavarian Illuminati. These pendants, worn around the necks of Minerval initiates, featured the Owl of Minerva Also known as the Owl of Wisdom, this symbol is still found today in powerful places: around the White House, hidden on the dollar bill or on the insignia of the Bohemian Club.

The term Minerval is derived from Minerva who was the Roman goddess of poetry, medicine, wisdom, commerce, weaving, crafts, magic, and the music. She is often depicted with her sacred creature, an owl, which symbolizes her ties to wisdom. An ancient symbol of the mysteries, Minerva is prominently featured in places such as the Library of Congress and the Great Seal of California.

The second grade of the Illuminati was one of indoctrination. The initiates were lectured on the spiritual principles of the Order but had little information regarding the true aims of Weishaupt and his close circle of administrators.

"The ceremony of initiation through which the Novice passed into the grade Minerval was expected to disabuse the mind of the candidate of any lingering suspicion that the order had as its supreme object the subjugation of the rich and powerful, or the, overthrow of civil and ecclesiastical government. It also pledged the candidate to be useful to humanity; to maintain a silence eternal, a fidelity inviolable, and an obedience implicit with respect to all the superiors and rules of the order; and to

sacrifice all personal interests to those of the society." 10

Minervals were permitted to meet some of their superiors (Illuminated Minervals) and to engage in discussions with them. This privilege alone was a great source of motivation for the new initiates.

Illuminated Minerval

Selected from among the Minerval, the Illuminated Minerval were given specific tasks to accomplish in order to prepare them to take action in the "real world". Most of their work consisted in the study of mankind and the perfection of methods to direct it. Each Illuminated Minerval was entrusted with a small group of Minervals who were scrutinized, analyzed and lead towards specific directions. Lower-grade members of the Order therefore became test subjects for techniques that might be applied to the masses in general.

> *"To the grade Illuminated Minerval were admitted those Minervals who in the judgment of their superiors were worthy of advancement. Elaborate initiatory ceremonies fixed in the candidate's mind the notions that the progressive purification of his life was to be expected as he worked his way upward in the order, and that the mastery of the art of directing men was to be his special pursuit as long as he remained in the new grade. To accomplish the latter, i.e., to become an expert psychologist and director of men's consciences, he must observe and study constantly the actions, purposes, desires, faults, and virtues of the little group of Minervals who were placed under his personal direction and care. For his guidance in this difficult task a complicated mass of instructions was furnished him.*
>
> *In addition to their continued presence in the assemblies of the Minervals, the members of this grade came together once a month by themselves, to hear reports concerning their disciples, to discuss methods of accomplishing the best results in their work of direction and to solicit each other's counsel in difficult and embarrassing cases. In these meetings the records of the assemblies of the Minervals were reviewed and rectified and afterwards transmitted to the superior officers of the order."* 11

From this basic structure, the Illuminati began its expansion. Everything was in place for Weishaupt to achieve an important goal: the infiltration of Freemasonry.

Infiltration of Freemasonry

In 1777, the year following the creation of the Illuminati, Weishaupt joined the Masonic lodge of Theodore of Good Counsel in Munich. Not only did he successfully propagate his views into the lodge, he also managed to get the lodge to be "virtually absorbed into the Illuminist order almost immediately". 12

A definite alliance between the Illuminati and Freemasonry became possible in 1780 when a prominent figure by the name of Baron Adolf Franz Friederich Knigge was initiated into Weishaupt's Order. The German diplomat's Masonic connections and organizational skills were promptly put to use by the Order. Knigge would go on to accomplish two important tasks for the Illuminati: He revised the hierarchy of the Order, created new higher grades and allowed the full integration of Masonic lodges into the system.

> *"Two weighty consequences promptly followed as the result of Kinigge's advent into the order. The long-sought higher grades were worked out, and an alliance between the Illuminati and Freemasonry was effected."* 13

Knigge's influence upon the Order was profound and immediate. The new system he devised attracted Freemasons and other powerful figures, which gave the movement great momentum. Here's the system devised by Knigge:

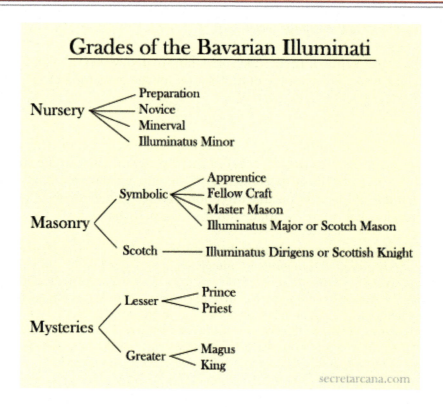

Knigge's kept the Order's original grades untouched but added new grades above them. The second level of the Illuminati incorporated the grades of Freemasonry making therefore the Brotherhood simply a part of the wider Illuminist superstructure.

> "The grade Novice (a part of the system only in a preparatory sense) was left unchanged by Knigge, save for the addition of a printed communication to be put into the hands of all new recruits, advising them that the Order of the Illuminati stands over against all other forms of contemporary Freemasonry as the one type not degenerate, and as such alone able to restore the craft to its ancient splendor. (...)
>
> The three symbolic grades of the second class seem to have been devised solely for the purpose of supplying an avenue whereby members of the various branches of the great Masonic family could pass to the higher grades of the new order." [14]

Knigge, an influential North German diplomat and occultist joined the Illuminati in 1780. He is here shown displaying the sign of the Hidden Hand

The highest grades of the Order were restricted to a select few and included powerful individuals and influential figures. The grade of Prince held within its ranks National Inspectors, Provincials, Prefects and Deans of the Priests. At the top of the pyramid were the Magus (also known as Areopagites), which comprised the supreme heads of the Order. Their identities were safely guarded and are still difficult to confirm today.

Knigge's strategy gave impressive results and allowed the Illuminati to become an extremely powerful movement.

> *"The new method of spreading Illuminism by means of its affiliation with Masonic lodges promptly demonstrated its worth. Largely because of the fine strategy of seeking its recruits among the officers and other influential personages in the lodges of Freemasonry, one after another of the latter in quick succession went over to the new system. New prefectures were established, new provinces organized, and Provincials began to report a steady and copious stream of new recruits. (...) Students, merchants, doctors, pharmacists, lawyers, judges, professors in gymnasia and universities, preceptors, civil officers, pastors, priests — all were generously represented among the new recruits. Distinguished names soon appeared upon the rosters of the lodges of the new system. Duke Ferdinand of Brunswick, Duke Ernst of Gotha, Duke Karl August of Saxe-Weimar, Prince August of Saxe-Gotha, Prince Carl of Hesse, Baron Dalberg, the philosopher Herder, the poet Goethe, the educationist Pestalozzi, were among the number enrolled, By the end of 1784 the leaders boasted of a total enrollment of between two and three thousand members 106. and the establishment of the order upon a solid foundation seemed to be fully assured."* [15]

Weishaup, however, did not enjoy his Order's success for long. Suspicions of Illuminati conspiracy against governments and religious arose across Europe. Seeing a credible threat against its power, the Bavarian government launched an edict outlawing all communities, societies and brotherhoods that existed without due authorization of the law. Furthermore, internal disagreements between Weishaupt and the higher ups of his Order lead to disputes and dissension. In the midst of it all, some members went directly to the authorities and testified against the Order, an opportunity that was not missed by the Bavarian government.

> *"Out of the mouths of its friends, the accusations which its enemies made against the order were to be substantiated. By the admissions of its leaders, the system of the Illuminati had the appearance of an organization devoted to the overthrow of religion and the state, a band of poisoners and forgers, an association of men of disgusting morals and depraved tastes."* [16]

By 1788, through the use of aggressive legislation and criminal charges, the Bavarian Illuminati was apparently dissipated and destroyed by the government. While some see here the conclusion of the story of the Illuminati, one must not forget that the tentacles of Illuminism had the time to spread way beyond to confines of Bavaria to reach Masonic lodges across Europe. In other words, the Illuminati was never destroyed, it simply went underground. A year later, an important event would prove that Illuminism was more alive and potent then ever: the French Revolution.

The French Revolution

The violent overthrow of the French Monarchy in 1789 symbolizes to many the victory of Jacobinism and Illuminism over the traditional institutions of the time. The adoption of the Declaration of Human Rights officially recorded Masonic and Illuminist values into the core of the French government. The country's new motto "Liberté, Égalité et Fraternité" (Freedom, Equality and Brotherhood) was said to be a famous Masonic saying that was used in French lodges for centuries.

The official document of the Declaration of Human Rights contains several occult symbols referring to Secret Societies. First, the symbol of the All Seeing Eye within a triangle, surrounded by the light of the blazing star Sirius, is found above everything else (this symbol is also found on the Great Seal of the United States). Underneath the title is depicted an Ouroboros (a serpent eating its own tail), an esoteric symbol associated with Alchemy, Gnosticism and Hermetism, the core teachings of Masonry. Right underneath the Ouroboros is a red phrygian cap, a symbol representing Illuminist revolutions across the world. The entire Declaration is guarded by Masonic pillars.

Backlash Against Illuminism

If though Bavarian Illuminati was said to be dead, the ideas it promoted still became a reality. The Freemasons and Rosicrucians were still thriving, and the Illuminati appeared to be living through them. Europe was undergoing profound turmoil as a new class of people took the helms of power. Critics began to emerge, revealing to the masses the secret forces behind the changes they were witnessing.

Leopold Hoffman, a Freemason who was convinced that the Illuminati corrupted his Brotherhood, published a series of articles in his journal entitled Wiener Zeitschrift. He claimed that the lower grades of the Illuminati had been dissolved, but the highest degrees were still active. He also added that Freemasonry was being "subjugated by Illuminism" and transformed to serve its ends. He also stated that the French Revolution was the result of years of Illuminist propaganda.

In 1797, John Robinson, a Scottish physician, mathematician and inventor (he invented the siren) published a book entitled "Proofs of a Conspiracy against All the Religions and Governments of Europe, carried on in the Secret Meetings of the Free Masons, Illuminati, and Reading Societies". This devout Freemason became disenchanted when he realized that his brotherhood had been infiltrated by the Illuminati. Here's an excerpt of his book:

> "I have found that the covert of a Mason Lodge had been employed in every country for venting and propagating sentiments in religion and politics, that could not have circulated in public without exposing the author to great danger. I found, that this impunity had gradually encouraged men of licentious principles to become more bold, and to teach doctrines subversive of all our notions of morality—of all our confidence in the moral government of the universe—of all our hopes of improvement in a future state of existence—and of all satisfaction and contentment with our present life, so long as we live in a state of civil subordination. I have been able to trace these attempts, made, through a course of fifty years, under the specious pretext of enlightening the world by the torch of philosophy, and of dispelling the clouds of civil and religious superstition which keep the nations of Europe in

darkness and slavery.

I have observed these doctrines gradually diffusing and mixing with all the different systems of Free Masonry; till, at last, AN ASSOCIATION HAS BEEN FORMED for the express purpose of ROOTING OUT ALL THE RELIGIOUS ESTABLISHMENTS, AND OVERTURNING ALL THE EXISTING GOVERNMENTS OF EUROPE. I have seen this Association exerting itself zealously and systematically, till it has become almost irresistible: And I have seen that the most active leaders in the French Revolution were members of this Association, and conducted their first movements according to its principles, and by means of its instructions and assistance, formally requested and obtained: And, lastly, I have seen that this Association still exists, still works in secret, and that not only several appearances among ourselves show that its emissaries are endeavouring to propagate their detestable doctrines, but that the Association has Lodges in Britain corresponding with the mother Lodge at Munich ever since 1784. . . The Association of which I have been- speaking is the order of ILLUMINATI, founded, in 1775 [sic], by Dr. Adam Weishaupt, professor of Canon-law in the University of Ingolstadt, and abolished in 1786 by the Elector of Bavaria, but revived immediately after, under another name, and in a different form, all over Germany. It was again detected, and seemingly broken up; but it had by this time taken so deep root that it still subsists without being detected, and has spread into all the countries of Europe" [17]

Augustin Barrel, a French Jesuit priest also published in 1797 a book linking the French Revolution to the Bavarian Illuminati. In "Mémoires pour servir à l'histoire du Jacobisime", he traced back the slogan "Liberty and Equality" back to the early Templars and claimed that, in the higher degrees of the order, liberty and equality is explained not only by "war against kings and thrones" but by "war against Christ and his altars". He also provided details pertaining to the Illuminist take-over of Freemasonry.

"Barruel charged that not only the lower order of Masonry were duped by Weishaupt, but also those of Weishaupt's own Illuminati, for whom he had provided another top-secret level of direction known as the Aeopagus, a withdrawn circle of directors of the whole order, who alone knew its secret aims. To Barruel, such revolutionary leaders as La Rochefoucauld, Lafayette, and the duc d'Orléans, had become Illuminati agents and dupes of more extreme radicals such as Danton, provocateurs who sparked the Illuminati-directed rebellion. Barruel further charged that the entire French Masonic establishment had been converted to Weishaupt's revolutionary ideas, its lodges turned into secret committees which planned bloodshed." [18]

Propagation in America

Most of America's Founding Fathers were part of Secret Societies, whether the Freemasons, the Rosicrucians or others. Some of them travelled to Europe and were well versed in the doctrines of the Illuminati.

From 1776 to 1785 – when the Bavarian Illuminati was openly active – Benjamin Franklin was in Paris serving as the ambassador of the United States to France. During his stay, he became Grand Master of the lodge Les Neufs Soeurs which was attached with the Grand Orient of France. This Masonic organization was said to have become the French headquarters of the Bavarian Illuminati. It was particularly influential in organizing of the French support for the American Revolution and was later part of the process towards the French Revolution.

In 1799, when German minister G.W. Snyder warned George Washington of the Illuminati plan "to overthrow all governments and religion", Washington replied that he had heard "much of the nefarious and dangerous plan and doctrines of the Illuminati". He however concluded his letter by stating: "I believe notwithstanding, that none of the Lodges in this country are contaminated with the principles ascribed to the society of Illuminati".

In another letter to Snyder, written a month later, Washington continued on the topic:

> "It was not my intention to doubt that, the Doctrines of the Illuminati, and principles of Jacobinism had not spread in the United States. On the contrary, no one is more truly satisfied of this fact than I am.
>
> The idea that I meant to convey, was, that I did not believe that the Lodges of Free Masons in this Country had, as Societies, endeavoured to propagate the diabolical tenets of the first, or pernicious principles of the latter (if they are susceptible of separation). That Individuals of them may have done it, or that the founder, or instrument employed to found, the Democratic Societies in the United States, may have had these objects; and actually had a separation of the People from their Government in view, is too evident to be questioned."

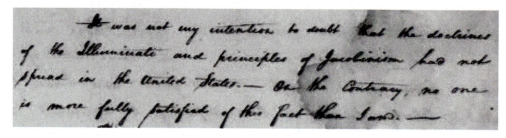

Part of the original letter written by George Washington regarding the Illuminati

Judging by this letter, George Washington was obviously well aware of the doctrines of the Illuminati And even if he did not believe that the Masonic institutions of the United States propagated its doctrines, he concedes that individuals might have undertaken that endeavour.

After the Bavarian Illuminati

Today, the term Illuminati is used to loosely describe the small group of powerful individuals who are working towards the creation of a World Government, with the issue of a single world currency and a single world religion. Although it is difficult to determine if this group descends directly from the original Bavarian Illuminati or that it even uses the term Illuminati, its tenets and methods are in perfect continuation of it. As stated above, the name that is used to describe the occult elite can change. And, ultimately, the name is irrelevant; what needs to be recognized is the underlying current that has existed for centuries.

According the Manly. P Hall, the Bavarian Illuminati was part of what he calls the "Universal Brotherhood", an invisible Order at the "source" of most Hermetic Secret Societies of the past. It has worked for centuries towards the transformation of mankind, guiding it through a worldwide alchemical process. The same way the alchemical Great Work seeks to turn crude metals into gold, it claims to work towards a similar metamorphosis of the world. According to Hall, the Universal Brotherhood sometimes makes itself visible, but under the guise of different names and symbols. This would mean that the Knights Templars, Freemasons, Rosicrucians, and Illuminati are temporary visible manifestations of an underlying force that is infinitely more profound and more powerful. However, human beings being what they are – weak toward greed and power-lust – these movements often become corrupted and end up conspiring against the masses for more power and material gain.

> "Certainly there was an undercurrent of things esoteric, in the most mystical sense of the word, beneath the surface of Illuminism. In this respect, the Order followed exactly in the footsteps of the Knights Templars. The Templars returned to Europe after the Crusades, bringing with them a num-

ber of choice fragments of Oriental occult lore, some of which they had gathered from the Druses of Lebanon, and some from the disciples of Hasan Ibn-al-Sabbah, the old wizard of Mount Alamut.

If there was a deep mystical current flowing beneath the surface of Illuminism, it is certain that Weishaupt was not the Castalian Spring. Perhaps the lilies of the Illuminati and the roses of the Rosicrucians were, by a miracle of Nature, flowing from the same stem. The old symbolism would suggest this, and it is not always wise to ignore ancient landmarks. There is only one explanation that meets the obvious and natural requirements of the known facts. The Illuminati were part of an esoteric tradition which had descended from remote antiquity and had revealed itself for a short time among the Humanists of Ingolstadt. One of the blossoms of the "sky plant" was there, but the roots were afar in better ground". [19]

Hall concludes that the Illuminati existed long before the advent of Weishaupt's Order and that it still exists today. It was under the guise of defeat and destruction that the Illuminati realized its greatest victories.

"Weishaupt emerged as a faithful servant of a higher cause. Behind him moved the intricate machinery of the Secret School. As usual, they did not trust their full weight to any perishable institution. The physical history of the Bavarian Illuminati extended over a period of only twelve years. It is difficult to understand, therefore, the profound stir which this movement caused in the political life of Europe. We are forced to the realization that this Bavarian group was only one fragment of a large and composite design.

All efforts to discover the members of the higher grades of the Illuminist Order have been unsuccessful. It has been customary, therefore, to assume that these higher grades did not exist except in the minds of Weishaupt and von Knigge. Is it not equally possible that a powerful group of men, resolved to remain entirely unknown, moved behind Weishaupt and pushed him forward as a screen for its own activities?

The ideals of Illuminism, as they are found in the pagan Mysteries of antiquity, were old when Weishaupt was born, and it is unlikely that these long-cherished convictions perished with his Bavarian experiment. The work that was unfinished in 1785 remains unfinished in 1950. Esoteric Orders will not become extinct until the purpose which brought them into being has been fulfilled. Organizations may perish, but the Great School is indestructible". [20]

The Great Seal of the United States features the unfinished Great Pyramid of Giza, a symbol of the unfinished work of the Esoteric Orders: a New World Order. The Seal was adopted on the American dollar by Franklin Delano Roosevelt, a 32nd Degree Freemason and a Knight of Pythias with ties Manly P. Hall.

The Illuminati Today

If the Illuminist Agenda is still alive today, what form does it take? From the esoteric and spiritual point of view, some modern Secret Societies such as the O.T.O. (Ordo Templi Orientis) have claimed to be the heirs of Illuminism. Other researchers stated that there exists hidden Orders above the 33 "visible" degrees of Freemasonry that form the Illuminati. As they are, by definition, secret, obtaining details about these Orders is quite difficult.

The political side of modern Illluminism is a lot more visible and its plans are obvious. An increasingly restrictive and concentrated group is being entrusted with the creation of important decisions and policies. International committees and organizations, acting above elected officials are today creating social and economic policies that are applied on a global level. This phenomenon is rather new in world history as a rather than kingdoms or nation-states, a non-elected shadow government, composed of the world's elite, is gradually becoming the center of world power.

> "On another political plane are ideological groups such as the Council on Foreign Relations, or participants in the World Economic Forum. Here we find leaders in politics, business, finance, education, and the media who share a belief in the value of global solutions; are in position of high authority and influence; and represent different levels of involvement with the inner circle of the group. Most members simply welcome the opportunity to associate with other well-known luminaries and are honored by being offered membership or attendance privileges. Yet, the ideology at the highest levels of such groups supports a world government – to be administered by a class of experts and planners, entrusted with running centrally organized social and political institutions. Although members may be persuaded to add their considerable voices to certain transnational political and economic policies, they may bot be as supportive (or even aware) of the long-range ambitions of the inner circle. While these groups quite often hold their meetings in secret, their membership lists are a matter of public record. It is the central agenda that is disguised." [21]

The main elite groups and councils are: the International Crisis Group, the Council on Foreign Relations, the World Economic Forum, the Brookings Institution, Chatham House, the Trilateral Commission and the Bilderberg Group. The Bohemian Club is known to hold informal gatherings of the world elite punctuated with strange ceremonies and rituals. The Club's insignia is an Owl similar to the one found on the Bavarian Illuminati's Minerval seal.

Insignia of the Bohemian Club

If one would carefully study the members and attendees of these exclusive clubs, one would notice that they combine the most powerful politicians, CEOs and intellectuals of the time with lesser known individuals with famous names. They are descendants of powerful dynasties that rose to power by taking over vital aspects of modern economies, such as the banking system, the oil industry or mass media. They have been associated with game changing events, such as the creation of the Federal Reserve in 1913. This act completely modified the banking system of the United States, placing it in the hands of a few elite corporations. A proof of this is the court decision of 1982 stating that "The Reserve Banks are not federal instrumentalities for purposes of the FTCA [the Federal Tort Claims Act], but are independent, privately owned and locally controlled corporations".

In his book "Bloodlines of the Illuminati", controversial author Fritz Springmeier claims that today's Illuminati is formed from the descendants of thirteen powerful families whose ancestors had close or distant ties to the original Bavarian Illuminati. According to Springmeier, the 13 bloodlines are: the Astors, the Bundys, the Collins, the DuPonts, the Freemans, the Kennedys, the Li, the Onassis, the Reynolds, the Rockefellers, the Rothschilds, the Russells and the Van Duyns. [22]

There is no doubt that by virtue of the material and political resources they own, some of these families have a great deal of power in today's world. They appear to form the core of what we call today the Illuminati. However, are they conspiring to create a New World Order? Here's a quote from David Rockefeller's memoirs that might answer some questions:

> "For more than a century, ideological extremists at either end of the political spectrum have seized upon well-publicized incidents such as my encounter with Castro to attack the Rockefeller family for the inordinate influence they claim we wield over American political and economic institutions. Some even believe we are part of a secret cabal working against the best interests of the United States, characterizing my family and me as 'internationalists' and of conspiring with others around the world to build a more integrated global political and economic structure – one world, if you will. If that is the charge, I stand guilty, and I am proud of it." [23]

In Conclusion

The story of the Illuminati has been repressed or revealed, debunked or exposed, ridiculed or exaggerated countless times – all depending on the point of the authors and whether they are "apologists" or "critics". To obtain the absolute truth about a group that was always meant to be secret is quite a challenge and one must use a great deal of judgment and discernment to differentiate the facts from the fabrications. As it is not possible to answer all of the questions relating to the Illuminati, this article simply attempted to draw a more precise picture of the Order and to present important facts relating to it.

Today's political atmosphere is quite different from the time of Weishaupt and the American Founding Fathers, yet there are still many similarities. While the Bavarian Illuminists purportedly denounced the political and religious oppression of the Vatican, as democracies merge into a single world government, as privacy and freedoms become replaced by "security" and high tech surveillance, as schools crack down on critical thinking, as mass media dumbs-down and disinforms the masses, as secret operations carry out crimes against humanity and as all major protests get violently repressed by a growing police state, it is easy to draw the conclusion that a similarly repressive system is currently being instated. Did the Illuminati truly "liberate" the Western World from the oppression of the Vatican or did it simply continue in its footsteps?

> "The minority, the ruling class at present, has the schools and press, usually the Church as well, under its thumb. This enables it to organize and sway the emotions of the masses, and make its tool of them."
> - Albert Einstein

[1] Sir Edward Bulwer Lytton, Zanoni
[2] James Wasserman, The Mystery Traditions
[3] Manly P. Hall, Masonic Orders of Fraternity
[4] Vernon L. Stauffer, The European Illuminati
[5] Peter Tomkins, The Magic of Obelisks
[6] Stauffer, Op. Cit.
[7] Ibid
[8] Tompkins, op. cit.
[9] Stauffer, op. cit.
[10] Ibid
[11] Ibid
[12] Hall, op. cit.
[13] Ibid
[14] Ibid
[15] Ibid
[16] Ibid
[17] John Robinson, Proofs of a Conspiracy
[18] Tompkins, op. cit.
[19] Hall, op. cit.
[20] Ibid
[21] Wasserman, op. cit.
[22] Fritz Springmeier, The Bloodlines of the Illuminati
[23] David Rockefeller, Memoirs